APPLIED MANAGEMENT SCIENCE

A Computer-Integrated Approach for Decision Making

JOHN A. LAWRENCE, JR.
California State University—Fullerton

BARRY ALAN PASTERNACK
California State University—Fullerton

JOHN WILEY & SONS, INC.
New York • Chichester • Weinheim • Brisbane • Singapore • Toronto

To our wives Shari and Kathleen
and our children:
Jami and Jonelle Lawrence
and
Jeffrey, Laura, Julia, and Alyssa Pasternack

Acquisitions Editor	Beth Lang Golub
Developmental Editor	Rachel Nelson
Marketing Manager	Carlise Paulson
Designer	Laura Boucher
Photo Editor	Hilary Newman
Illustration Coordinator	Anna Melhorn
Cover Illustration	Ralph Butler

This book was set in 10/12 Novarese by University Graphics, Inc. and printed and bound by Courier/Westford. The cover was printed by Lehigh Press.

Recognizing the importance of preserving what has been written, it is a policy of John Wiley & Sons, Inc. to have books of enduring value published in the United States printed on acid-free paper, and we exert our best efforts to that end.

Library of Congress Cataloging in Publication Data:
Lawrence, John A.
    Applied management science : a computer-integrated
  managerial approach / John A. Lawrence, Jr., Barry A. Pasternack.
        p.   cm.
  Includes index.
  ISBN 0-471-13776-6 (cloth/CD-ROM : alk. paper)
    1. Management—Mathematical models.   2. Decision support
systems.   3. Communication in management.   4. Management
science. I. Pasternack, Barry A.
HD30.25.L39   1998
658.4'033—dc21   97-24497
                                                              CIP

Printed in the United States of America

10 9 8 7 6 5 4 3 2

JOHN A. LAWRENCE, JR.

John Lawrence is a professor and a past department chairman of the Department of Management Science and Information Systems at California State University, Fullerton, where he has received several awards for his teaching, professional, and service contributions. He has spent over 25 years developing and teaching introductory and advanced upper division and graduate courses in management science and statistics for students majoring in business and economics at the university. He has presented and published several papers on the role and structure of management science courses in business curricula.

Dr. Lawrence received his B.S. in Operations Research from Cornell University and worked at IBM in Endicott, New York, and with NASA at the Kennedy Space Center at Cape Canaveral, Florida. After serving as a communications officer with the U.S. Navy, he received his M.S. and Ph.D. in Industrial Engineering and Operations Research from the University of California, Berkeley, with a research emphasis in linear programming.

Dr. Lawrence has served as a consultant to several companies in the areas of linear programming, inventory, and quality control and has published papers in these areas in professional journals. For over 15 years, he and coauthor Barry Pasternack wrote study guides for the management science texts published by Anderson, Sweeney, and Williams for West Publishing Company.

BARRY A. PASTERNACK

Barry Alan Pasternack is a professor and chair of the Management Science/Information Systems Department at California State University, Fullerton. During his 20 years on the faculty, he has been the recipient of several awards for teaching, research, and service. For five years he served as the Executive Director of the University's Center for Professional Development. Currently he is a member of the California State University State-wide Academic Senate and is past President of the campus chapter of the California Faculty Association, as well as a former member of the Association's Statewide Board of Directors. He has served as a University Educational Policy Fellow and a Bautzer Faculty Fellow.

Dr. Pasternack received his B.A. in mathematics from Antioch College, having spent his junior year studying statistics and operations research at the University of Birmingham in England. He earned his M.S. and Ph.D. degrees in Operations Research from the University of California, Berkeley, with a research emphasis in stochastic processes. Upon graduation from Berkeley, Dr. Pasternack worked for three years in the Network Planning Department of Bell Laboratories.

In addition to his teaching experience at Fullerton, Dr. Pasternack has also been a faculty member at Stevens Institute of Technology, Boston University, and California Polytechnic University, Pomona, and an invited guest lecturer at the Czechoslovak Management Center. He has served as a consultant to numerous corporations and governments, including the nations of Thailand, Zambia, and Ghana. He has also done work for NASA in the area of avionics and for the Department of Health and Human Services in the area of mental health care utilization.

Dr. Pasternack's research interests include inventory systems, channel coordination, gambling theory, and optimal option strategies. He is the author of some two dozen publications, and his work has appeared in such journals as *Naval Research Logistics*, *Marketing Science*, *Interfaces*, *SIAM Journal on Applied Mathematics*, and *Journal of the Operational Research Society*. Dr. Pasternack helped develop the Educational Testing Service assessment examination in business and is one of the contributors to the latest edition.

You may be wondering why, as a business major, you are taking this management science course. When I started taking the course at Cal State Fullerton, I was wondering the same thing. After a while, though, my professor, John Lawrence, one of the authors of this text, showed me the importance of management science in my education. In today's information-based, fast-paced society, this course will play a key role in your future, whatever path you may choose. The ideas presented in this course provide reliable solutions to everyday problems that occur in business, whether you work in Marketing, Accounting, Finance, Management, or Economics. At times you may find the information overwhelming and challenging, but it is actually quite applicable. This text was written to help you gain an understanding of how to apply the ideas presented in the many areas of business.

For as many hours as you have spent in the classroom, at some point, you probably have wondered how you would apply what you have learned to your life. As a full-time employee for a swimsuit manufacturer, that was the first question that came to my mind. I wondered, "How can I apply these general ideas to specific day-to-day problems in my career?" As a purchasing manager, using techniques discussed in this text, I have been able to solve quality problems concerning our fabrics. I have used forecasting to aid in my future fabric and trim purchases. And I have benefited from inventory modeling because it guides me in the total quantities I need to order and a time frame in which to re-order. In the near future I will be getting more involved in the production process, where I already see the immediate application of linear programming to assist in determining our product mix.

Management science is applicable to all segments of business. The following are a few more examples:

- Decision analysis is used to evaluate various production scenarios given the likelihood of sales, production shutdowns, etc.

- Forecasting is useful in making long-term and short-term business decisions. A controller could use forecasting to make predictions on the future of his/her company.

- Quality control is extremely important to a company because its reputation, costs and market shares, and legal responsibilities are at risk. In manufacturing, it is important that a company designs and produces a product that conforms to the specification that satisfies the needs of the end user.

- In making any business decision, linear programming, PERT/CPM, inventory modeling, queuing, and simulation assist the individual in making the best decisions with a limited amount of resources available.

The best approach is to keep an open mind while using this text and listening to your instructor. You may not believe it now, but many of the concepts presented here will most likely cross your path in the future as you use them to help you make decisions in your chosen careers.

Dana Linderman
California State University Fullerton
School of Business

Management scientists are faced with dynamic, challenging situations that require fore-thought, analysis, and solutions on a daily basis. How does American Airlines management know how to schedule its flight crews for maximum efficiency? How were the individual tasks necessary to rebuild the Santa Monica Freeway after the 1994 Los Angeles earthquake coordinated to complete the project? How does Citibank management know how many tellers should be working at a particular time during the day? Management science is an intriguing field that combines quantitative procedures, hypothesis formulation, and reasoning to analyze such complex problems with the goal of improving operations. It can be viewed as a process of:

- Developing mathematical models of complex situations
- Using or deriving solution techniques for analyzing these models
- Using spreadsheets or other specialized computer programs to perform the necessary mathematical operations to solve the models
- Analyzing the results of the computer output in order to recommend appropriate courses of action
- Communicating these recommendations to management

We decided to write a textbook in management science after finding existing texts lacking in areas that we feel are crucial to the understanding and appreciation of the field. In our experience, we have found that many traditional management science texts place some emphasis on mathematical modeling but concentrate primarily on solution techniques and reading, rather than *analyzing*, computer outputs. A more recent trend in management science texts is to place a heavy emphasis on solving models by "programming" spreadsheets to perform the operations that have traditionally been done by specialized or integrated management science software packages. Virtually none of these texts adequately explores the problems analysts face in gathering data to build mathematical models, in analyzing the results from a model, and in preparing comprehensive reports. These glaring deficiencies were our motivation for writing this text, *Applied Management Science: A Computer-Integrated Approach For Decision Making*.

GOALS

Our primary objective in writing this text is to provide a balanced approach reflective of our teaching pedagogy and professional and consulting experiences. In meeting this overarching objective, we have identified three goals that exemplify the message of our book. First, we feel that it is important for students of management science to *be aware of the pitfalls encountered in building mathematical models and to be able to build the most appropriate model possible from the available data*. Second, students should also *be cognizant of the solution techniques and the software available to solve the models*. Finally, students should *be able to analyze and effectively present results to the appropriate decision maker*. These issues are the primary focus of our text.

FEATURES

The goals we set out to meet are intended to take mathematical modeling a couple of steps further by emphasizing the decision-making process and the communication of results. We approach each topic via a narrative of a business situation and illustrate the model-building process, taking great care to emphasize the model's assumptions and limitations. Each chapter is then organized around a clearly defined set of pedagogical features designed to guide the student through the management science process.

RELEVANCE

Every chapter opens with a brief *vignette* describing a scenario reflective of those managers face every day. Throughout the chapter a number of similar scenarios are introduced in highlighted *applications*, many of which are revisited throughout the chapter as new concepts and variables are introduced.

STUDENT PEDAGOGY

Within the textual narrative, important terminology is introduced that is critical to understanding the concepts applied to solving the problem at hand. These *key concepts* are boldfaced throughout the text and defined in a highlighted box so that the student can easily find the explanation when first learning the concept and when reviewing for exams. *Key equations and calculations* are treated similarly, boxed and highlighted for easy recognition. The steps involved in calculating many of these equations are also accentuated, helping the student grasp and recall the procedures. The last section of each chapter is a *summary* of the concepts and main points of the chapter material. The summary is written in an approachable, narrative style, providing a review of the key concepts of the chapter. Where appropriate, a *notational summary* of the mathematical symbols introduced in the chapter is also presented.

ANALYSIS
OF THE MODELS

Each model introduced in the chapter is solved using appropriate management science software (Excel, WINQSB, or Lindo) and analyzed from a manager's perspective. The actual algorithms and other solution approaches for solving each model are included on the accompanying CD-ROM (packaged with this text), not because we feel they are any less important, but because including them within the text disrupts the flow of the discussion of the model formulations and analyses.

COMMUNICATION
OF RESULTS

The management scientist's job does not end when a solution is found. In fact, the most important responsibility of the management scientist is to communicate the results of the analysis to the organization's management. Therefore, we have devoted an entire section of Chapter 2, *"The Management Science Process,"* to instructing the student in how to communicate the results of a management science study to an organization's management. The student is asked to take the perspective of a member of a consulting group called the Student Consulting Group. All subsequent chapters include additional business *memorandums* developed by the Student Consulting Group to various organizations. These memorandums analyze the situation at hand, evaluate various decision alternatives, and recommend an appropriate course of action.

PROBLEM SOLVING

Consistent with our philosophy of problem solving as an integral component of the management science process, the text is replete with numerous *problems and cases*, many based on actual real-world situations (with modified data for illustrative purposes). We have selected a wide variety of problems from all the functional areas of business as well as many government and public sectors. The cases represent more elaborate models that frequently require the use of more than one management science technique. Each can be used as a project requiring a comprehensive written report. In addition to an average of 25 problems and two cases per chapter in the text, approximately ten additional problems and one or two additional cases per chapter are included on the CD-ROM. Solutions to selected problems are included in the back of the text.

UNIQUE CONTENT
FEATURES

The 13 chapters of the parent text include the topics typically covered in an introductory management science course. As noted above, one additional chapter unique to this text is Chapter 2, *"The Management Science Process,"* which focuses on how a management science study is actually performed and gives tips on how to write an effective business report. In addition to these 13 chapters, auxiliary topics that are frequently omitted in the introductory course due to the degree of complexity or lack of time are included on the CD-ROM:

◇   In our experience, many management science studies involve issues of quality. Therefore, we have devoted an entire chapter, *Chapter 14, "Quality Management,"* to this topic, which bridges the gap between management science, operations management, and statistics.

◇   *Chapter* 15 provides a comprehensive overview of *"Markov Processes."*

◇   Non-linear models are grouped together in *Chapter 16, "Non-Linear Models: Dynamic, Goal, and Non-Linear Programming."*

◇   Four supplementary units on the CD-ROM provides coverage of more complicated mathematical concepts and derivations: *Duality, The Simplex Method, Branch and Bound Algorithms for Integer Programming Problems,* and *Algorithms for Network Models.*

◇   An additional supplementary unit, *Review of Probability and Statistics,* provides a brief review of material covered in a first course in statistics (up through regression). While many topics in the text can be taught without the use of statistics, many cannot, and a course in probability and statistics is assumed to be a prerequisite. This brief statistical review can be used as the basis for a first lecture or review assignment in the course so that all students are "up to speed" with statistics. In some cases, more advanced statistical topics are necessary to solve some problems; these are discussed in the appropriate chapter rather than in the review supplement.

◇   Beginning with Chapter 3, additional chapter appendices, included on the CD-ROM, provide more extensive mathematical and theoretical coverage of additional algorithms, mathematical derivations, heuristics, and calculations.

◇   As we noted above, additional problems and cases for Chapters 3–13 are included on the CD-ROM, providing an extensive problem set of examples and scenarios to analyze and solve.

◇   The complete WINQSB software package developed by Yih-Long Chang is included on the CD-ROM, along with WINQSB and/or Excel files for the problems and applications presented in Chapters 2–16.

COMPUTER INTEGRATION

Finally, a note about our approach to the computer solution of mathematical models. As we mentioned above, we use Excel and the integrated management science software package WINQSB (and, in a few cases, the linear programming package LINDO for Windows) to solve models developed in the text. Data files for all the problems introduced in the chapters are included on the CD-ROM; many have both an Excel and a WINQSB (and even a LINDO) data file. Although this is not a text on programming mathematical models into spreadsheets or a manual on how to use WINQSB, appendices have been included to provide sufficient instructions for solving the models in the chapter. We have elected to include Excel because there are literally millions of copies of Excel in use worldwide and many problems can be solved fairly easily using a spreadsheet approach. At the same time, WINQSB is specifically designed to solve management science models without programming cells. It is, for the most part, spreadsheet based, and we have found that it requires just a few minutes of start-up time for students to master its basic features.

SUPPLEMENTS

In addition to the CD-ROM packaged with the text, *Applied Management Science: A Computer-Integrated Approach for Decision Making* is supplemented by a comprehensive ancillary package, which includes the following:

◇ *PowerPoint Presentations* Written by Zvi Goldstein of California State University—Fullerton, these interactive slide presentations parallel the material presented in the text and enhance the exposition by including animated graphical examples.

◇ *Instructor's Manual with Complete Solutions* This manual contains suggestions for first-time instructors and extensive outlines and objectives for each chapter of the text and CD-ROM. In addition, complete solutions for all end-of-chapter problems and cases are provided in this valuable teaching tool.

◇ *Test Bank* Developed by Kenneth Lawrence of New Jersey Institute of Technology, this comprehensive test package includes more than 1200 multiple-choice, computer-based, short answer, true-false, and critical thinking questions. An IBM computerized version of the entire test bank is also available with editing features to help instructors customize exams.

◇ *Wiley/Nightly Business Report Video Series* This video collection contains segments from the highly respected *Nightly Business Report* program. Selected for their applicability to management science topics, each of the segments is approximately 3 to 5 minutes long and can be used to introduce topics to the student, enhance lecture material, and provide dynamic real-world business examples directly related to the concepts introduced in the text.

◇ *Internet Web Site* You can access the Wiley home page at www.wiley.com/college. The Lawrence/Pasternack web site supports and extends the text presentation with links to companies, internet exercises, and other material.

◇ *Quantitative Business Custom Publishing Program* This custom publishing program allows you to choose a subset of chapters from *Applied Management Science: A Computer-Integrated Approach for Decision Making*, and supplement it with selected chapters from other Wiley texts in Operations Management and Business Statistics to create your own custom textbook. Contact your local Wiley sales representative for more details.

FLEXIBLE STRUCTURING OF A COURSE AROUND THIS TEXT

Applied Management Science: A Computer-Integrated Approach for Decision Making is part of a comprehensive learning program that can be adapted to virtually any emphasis one wishes to place on the course. We envision using this text in either a one- or two-semester course to meet any or all of the following objectives:

- **Teach modeling and analysis of output:** Utilize the examples in the main text and its extensive problem set, which can be supplemented by additional problems from the CD-ROM.

- **Include a focus on communication/presentation:** Accentuate the study of Chapter 2 and include one or more of the numerous cases included in the parent text and the CD-ROM.

- **Focus on spreadsheet/software solutions:** Assign the appendices at the end of each chapter, which give ample instructions for using Excel, WINQSB, and LINDO; the software package, WINQSB, and data files for all text examples are available on the CD-ROM.

- **Provide more mathematical/theoretical coverage:** Refer to the supplements on the CD-ROM that discuss and illustrate:
  - the simplex model
  - the dual simplex method
  - the branch and bound approach for mixed integer models
  - the branch and bound approach for binary models
  - the transportation simplex algorithm
  - the out of kilter algorithm
  - the Hungarian method for assignment problems
  - the branch and bound approach for traveling salesman problems
  - the Dijkstra shortest path algorithm
  - the Greedy minimal spanning tree algorithm
  - the Ford-Fulkerson maximum flow algorithm
  - the golden search technique for unimodel optimization
  - tests for concavity and convexity
  - the method of steepest ascent
  - the modified simplex approach for quadratic programming
  - Daniel's test for trend
  - tests for autocorrelation
  - forecasting by taking first differences
  - the interpolation method for generating random variable inputs in simulation
  - variance reduction techniques
  - tests for normality of data
  - the Silver-Meal heuristic
  - the Wagner-Whitten algorithm
  - development of formulas for inventory models
  - transition diagrams, balance equations for finding steady state queuing results

- **Expand beyond the "basic" topics in management science:** Cover additional and/or more advanced topics that are included on the CD-ROM, such as duality, quality management, Markov processes, dynamic programming, goal programming, and nonlinear programming.

Given the organization and variety of materials included in the parent text, the CD-ROM, and the ancillary package, we hope this text can more than fulfill your needs.

$\mathcal{A}$CKNOWLEDGMENTS

No book such as this could have been written without the help of many individuals. Among the many people who have assisted us in this endeavor, we would like to thank Zvi Goldstein, Robert Miller, Prem Gupta, Marla Robinson, Nat Sankahavasi, Glen Dorin, and Steven Conroy, for providing us with assistance in the development of problems and cases. We would also like to thank Yih-Long Chang for providing the WINQSB software package for use with this text and Ken Lawrence for his work as technical proofreader (checking all the mathematical material) and supplements author of the Test Bank.

Development of this text was assisted by the invaluable insights provided by the following colleagues who served as reviewers:

Yi-Long Chang
Georgia Institute of
Technology

Gary Meek
The University of Akron

James Rice
University of Wisconsin,
Oshkosh

John Farr
U.S. Military Academy

Robert Meier
Fort Hays State University

Syed Shah
Central Michigan University

David Larson
University of New Orleans

Barin Nag
Towson State University

Martin Young
University of Michigan

Kenneth Lawrence
New Jersey Institute of
Technology

Leonard Presby
William Paterson State
College

Jack Yurkiewicz
Pace University

Jack Leu
California State University,
San Marcos

Ramaswamy Ramesh
State University of New York,
Buffalo

Glenn Zabowski
McGill University

We also gratefully acknowledge the wonderful staff at John Wiley & Sons who helped transform our manuscript into a finished text. Of particular importance to making this endeavor a success was our developmental editor, Rachel Nelson, who helped shepherd this project from beginning to end; our acquisitions editor, Beth Lang Golub; Elisa Adams, whose guidance at the inception of this project prevented us from generating a 1600-page text; the editorial assistance provided by Pui Szeto, Amy Hegarty, and Evy Farakis; the excellent production staff made up of Ed Winkleman, Hilary Newman, Anna Melhorn, and Laura Boucher; coordination of the supplements package by Joan Kalkut; and the marketing staff, led by Leslie Hines. We would also like to thank Joanna Koperski and the staff of JAL Graphics for their creative renderings of the illustrations in the text.

We also thank our secretarial staff Suzanne Tappe, Sonia Robles, and Grace McCormick and the computer support team including Glen Shiery and Kay Sullivan at Cal State Fullerton.

Finally, we would like to thank our families, without whose love and support this book could not have been written.

John A. Lawrence, Jr.
Barry A. Paternack
California State University, Fullerton

BRIEF CONTENTS

CD-ROM CONTENTS

CONTENTS

CHAPTER 11

INVENTORY MODELS BASED ON NONSTATIONARY DEMAND   485

CHAPTER 12

QUEUING THEORY   531

CHAPTER 13

SIMULATION   582

COMPANY APPLICATIONS

Chapter	Application	Topic (& section)
1 INTRODUCTION	• producing hamburgers at Burger King • scheduling crews at American Airlines • planning the Sony advanced traveler information system • rebuilding the Interstate 10 Freeway • planning environmental policy in Finland • cooking at Mrs. Fields • transporting trash in New York City • quality management at Ford Motor Company	• linear programming (1.4) • integer linear programming (1.4) • shortest path algorithms (1.4) • critical path method (1.4) • decision analysis (1.4) • forecasting (1.4) • simulation model (1.4) • quality management (1.4)
2 THE MANAGEMENT SCIENCE PROCESS	• United Airlines • Delta Hardware Stores **Memorandum** *Shipment plan for paint from the Phoenix plant*	• use of management science models to increase profits and customers satisfaction in a constrained environment (chapter opener) • problem definition (2.2); building a mathematical model (2.3); solving a mathematical model (2.4); comunication/monitoring of results (2.5)
3 LINEAR PROGRAMMING	• Steelcase, Inc. • Galaxy Industries **Memorandum** *Optimal production quantities for Space Rays and Zappers* • Navy Sea Rations	• establishing periodic production schedules (using LP models) (chapter opener) • procedure used to construct LP models (3.2) • diet problem (minimization problems) (3.11)
4 LINEAR PROGRAMMING APPLICATIONS	• San Miguel Corporation • Galaxy Industries—An Expansion Plan • Jones Investment Service • St. Joseph Public Utility Commission • Euromerica Liquors • Vertex Software, Inc. • United Oil Company • The Powers Group • Mobile Cabinet Company **Memorandum** *Cabinet production schedule for the third quarter* • Aircraft fleet assignments • Air pollution control	• refining & developing integrative strategies to enhance growth & strength (chapter opener) • maximization; sensitivity analysis; objective function; unit coversion; definitional variables; percentage constraints (4.3) • minimization; sensitivity analysis (4.4) • ignoring integer restrictions; definitional variable; infeasibility; multiple optimal solutions (4.5) • choosing an objective; lower bound constraints; unboundedness; "slightly" violated constraints (4.6) • choosing an objective function; rounding non-integer values (4.7) • variable definitions for blending models; calculation of objective coefficients; ratio constraints; definitional variables (4.8) • determining appropriate decision variables; multi-period cash flow-linking constraints; spreadsheet presentation (4.9) • selecting proper decision variables; minimization objective; determining proper objective coefficients; inventory/production linking constraints (4.10) • LP in business & government (4.11) • LP in business & government (4.11)

CHAPTER	APPLICATION	TOPIC (& SECTION)
	• Allocating blood to hospitals (health care)	• LP in business & government (4.11)
	• Bank portfolios	• LP in business & government (4.11)
	• Agriculture	• LP in business & government (4.11)
	• Fire protection (emergency services)	• LP in business & government (4.11)
	• Defense/aerospace contractors	• LP in business & government (4.11)
	• Land-use planning	• LP in business & government (4.11)
	• Dairy industry	• LP in business & government (4.11)
	• Solid waste management	• LP in business & government (4.11)
	• Deployment of aircraft & sea lift forces (military)	• LP in business & government (4.11)
5 INTEGER LINEAR PROGRAMMING	• Glen Dorin	• using ILP to determine an optimal overall expansion, manufacturing, & distribution strategy (chapter opener)
	• Boxcar Burger Restaurants	• complexities of ILPs (5.2)
	• Shelley Mednick (investment problem)	• mixed integer linear programming model (5.4)
	• Sunset Beach lifeguard assignments	• personnel scheduling (5.6)
	• Salem City Council	• binary integer linear programming (5.7)
	• Globe Electronics, Inc. **Memorandum** *Recommendation for monthly operations*	• facility location problem (5.8)
6 NETWORK MODELS	• Nature's Way	• use of network models to find optimal solutions (chapter opener)
	• Carlton Pharmaceuticals	• a transportation problem (6.2)
	• Depot Max	• a general network model (6.2)
	• Montpelier Ski Company **Memorandum** *Third quarter production planning for Glide-Rite skis*	• using a transportation model for production scheduling (6.2)
	• Ballston Electronics	• an assignment problem (6.3)
	• The Federal Emergency Management Agency (FEMA)	• a traveling salesman problem (6.3)
	• Fairway Van Lines	• a shortest path problem (6.5)
	• The Metropolitan Transit District	• a minimal spanning tree problem (6.6)
	• United Chemical Company	• a maximal flow problem (6.7)
7 PROJECT SCHEDULING	• 1992 riots in South Central L.A. (Taco Bell) and 1994 L.A. earthquake (Santa Monica Freeway)	• coordination & management of individual tasks to complete a project (chapter opener)
	• Klone Computers, Inc. **Memorandum** *Project scheduling for the development of the Klonepalm 2000 Palmbook computer*	• project scheduling (7.2); PERT/CPM approach (7.5); resource leveling (7.6); use of probabilities in a PERT analysis (7.7); cost analysis using probabilities (7.9)
	• Tom Larkin's Political Campaign	• critical path method (7.10); operating optimally within a fixed budget (7.10); PERT/cost technique (7.11)
8 DECISION ANALYSIS	• Kern Corporation	• Decision analysis approach to determining the optimal course of action (chapter opener)
	• Publisher's Clearing House	• constructing a payoff table (8.2)
	• Tom Brown (investment decision)	• payoff tables, decision-making criteria (8.3), EVPI (8.4), EVSI (8.5), Utility (8.7)

Chapter	Application	Topic (& section)
	• Bill Galen Development Company **Memorandum** *5th & Main Street property* • IGA Supermarket	• decision trees (8.6) • game theory (8.8)
9 FORECASTING	• Franklin Quest • YoHo Brand Yo-Yos • American Family Products Corporation • Canadian Faculty Association (CFA) **Memorandum** *Forecasted membership for the fiscal year* • Troy's Mobil Station	• systems for forecasting retail demand (chapter opener) • stationary forecasting model (9.2); moving averages (9.2); exponential smoothing (9.2); performance measures (9.3) • Holt's method (9.4), linear regression method (9.4) • classical decompositon method for multiplicative models (9.5) • multiple regression approach for additive models with trend & seasonal effects (9.5)
10 INVENTORY MODELS BASED ON STATIONARY DEMAND	• Dicom Appliances • Allen Appliance Company **Memorandum** *Inventory policy for Citron juicers* • Farah Cosmetics Company • Scanlon Plumbing Company	• determining optimal production policy (chapter opener) • economic order quantity model (10.2); determining optimal order quantity under an all units discount schedule (10.3), determining safety stock (10.6), review systems (T,M) policies (10.7) • production lot size model (10.4) • planned shortage model (10.5)
11 INVENTORY MODELS BASED ON NONSTATIONARY DEMAND	• Lucifer Technologies • The *Sentinel* Newspaper • Wendel's Bakery **Memorandum** *Inventory policy for glazed donuts at State University* • Little Trykes Toys, Inc. • Golden West Homes	• use of single-period inventory model (chapter opener) • single-period inventory model (demand modeled by a discrete distribution) (11.1) • single-period inventory model (demand modeled by a continuous probability distribution) (11.1) • material requirements planning (11.2) • Wagner-Whitin algorithm (11.3); Silver Meal heuristic (11.3)
12 QUEUING THEORY	• Carl's Jr. • Hank's Hardware • Mary's Shoes **Memorandum** *Operations at the New Market Mall store* • Littletown Post Office • Ted's TV Repair Shop • Ryan Roofing Company • Pacesetter Homes • Wilson Foods Talking Turkey Hot Line • Hargrove Hospital Maternity Ward • Big Boys Sound, Inc. • McMurray Machine Company	• queuing analysis of drive-thru waiting lines (chapter opener) • Poisson arrival distribution (12.2); exponential services distribution (12.2) • M/M/1 queuing systems (12.4) • M/M/k queuing systems (12.5) • M/G/1 queuing systems (12.6) • M/M/k/F queuing systems (12.7) • M/M/1//m queuing systems (12.8) • economic analysis of queuing systems (12.9) • economic analysist of queuing system (12.9) • tandem queuing systems (12.10) • assembly line balancing (12.11)
13 SIMULATION	• Hunt Wesson	• using simulation analysis to redesign bottling process to meet production requirements (chapter opener)

CHAPTER	APPLICATION	TOPIC (& SECTION)
	• Jewel Vending Company (JVC) • Lanford Sub Shop • Allen Appliance Company **Memorandum** *Inventory policy for Doughboy bread makers*	• Monte Carlo simulatin (13.2) • next event simulation of an M/M/1 system (13.4) • fixed-time simulation approach of an inventory system (13.5)
14 QUALITY MANAGEMENT	• Ropak Corporation • Little Trykes Toys, Inc. • Troy's Service Station • Duralife Batteries • McMurray Lawn Mower Manufacturing Company • Motel 8 • Bartucci Food Products • Panasony Appliance Company **Memorandum** *Ensuring proper tuning dial resistance for the Model 6210S clock radio*	• quality control, testing, & engineering procedures (chapter opener) • fishbone diagram for a manufacturing operation (14.2); testing for process control using p charts (14.5); standardization p charts (14.5) • fishbone diagram for a service operation (14.2) • control limits for $\overline{X}$ and R charts (14.3) • process control chart approach (14.3); meeting design specifications (14.3) • constructing ranges for the R_m chart (14.4) • use of X and R_m charts (14.4) • economic analysis to determine product design specifications and whether full inspection is worthwhile (14.6)
15 MARKOV PROCESSES	• Southern California Edison • Fast-food restaurant selection **Memorandum** *Increasing profitability of Sandpoint Caesar's* • Rolley's Rentals • Freeway travel in southern California • Craftmade Comfort Beds • Dr. Dale Bandon, DDS • Stacy's Department stores • Gambling in Los Vegas	• using Markoc process models to plan proper release of water to generate hydroelectric power (chapter opener) • transition matrices for processes with no absorbing states (15.2); determining state probabilities (15.4); market share analysis (15.7) • transition matrices for processes with no absorbing states (15.2); determining profitability of a business venture (15.7); determing the value of a business (15.7) • transition matrices for processes with no absorbing states (15.2) • transition matrices for processes with no absorbing states (15.2); estimating long-term expected income (15.7) • transition matrices for processes with absorbing states (15.3); determining state probabilities (15.4); estimating an allowance for doubtful accounts (15.7) • transition matrices for processes with absorbing states (15.3); determining actuarial costs (15.7) • transition matrices for processes with absorbing states (15.3); determining the effect of initial stake size and gambling strategy on probability of reching a goal (15.8)
16 NONLINEAR MODELS: DYNAMIC, GOAL, AND NONLINEAR PROGRAMMING	• Cal Worthington—used car commercials • U.S. Department of Labor • Northwestern Computer • Playco Toys, Inc.	• use of a non-linear programming model to determine the optimal number of commercials to air while staying within a budget (chapter operner) • using dynamic programming to solve a resource allocation problem (16.2) • using dynamic programming to solve a knapsack problem (16.4) • using dynamic programming to solve reliability problem (16.4)

Chapter	Application	Topic (& section)
	• CJM Industries **Memorandum** *Production scheduling for the 1957 Chrysler convertible project*	• using dynamic programming to solve a production and inventory problem (16.4)
	• New England Cycle Company	• preemptive goal programming (16.5)
	• Toshi Camera	• one-variable unconstrained nonlinear programming problems (16.7); one-variable constrained nonlinear programming problems (16.8)
	• PBI Industries	• Kuhn-tucker optimality conditions (16.8)
		• quadratic programming (16.8)

INTRODUCTION

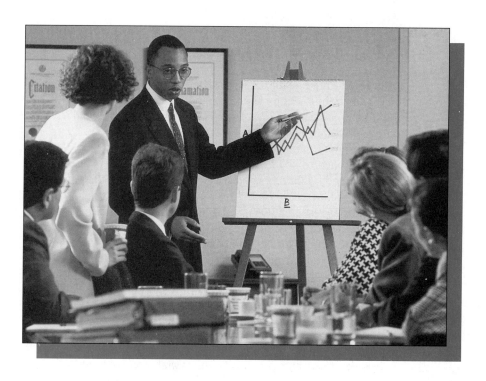

1.1 BUSINESS AND MANAGEMENT SCIENCE

Every enterprise has an objective it wishes to accomplish. Companies that operate for profit want to provide products or services to customers in order to make money for their owners or stockholders. A nonprofit organization such as a hospital may want to provide services to patients at minimum cost. The stated objective of government entities is to serve their citizens well.

No matter what the enterprise, certain responsibilities and restrictions affect the organization's ability to meet its objectives. For example, a manufacturing company's suppliers demand payment in a reasonable time period; their employees demand a fair wage and good working conditions; their distributors expect good products at reasonable prices so they can make a profit; and their customers expect both quality and prompt efficient service. There are also various government agencies (local, state, and federal) that expect the company to obey laws and regulations, pay taxes, function safely, and operate so as not to endanger the community or national security. The scarcity of needed resources, including capital, personnel, equipment, space, and technology, further limits a company's ability to succeed.

Nonprofit organizations, such as charities, municipal hospitals, public television stations, public universities, and the military, also operate in a restrictive environment. While turning a profit is not the goal of such enterprises, they are responsible to their overseers (donors, subscribers, voters, taxpayers) to provide the best possible service.

In general, the goal of both for-profit and not-for-profit organizations is to optimize the use of available resources, given all the internal and external constraints placed on them. Success is usually measured by how well they do so. Thus, an organization is always looking for ways to run more efficiently, more effectively, and, in the case of profit-motivated businesses, more profitably; in other words, organizations want "to do the best they can with what they've got." This is the realm in which management science operates.

1.2 WHAT IS MANAGEMENT SCIENCE?

If you were to read 50 different texts and papers in the field, you would most likely find 50 different definitions for the term "management science." All, however, sound a common theme. *Management science is a discipline that adapts the scientific approach for problem solving to decision making.*

Modern-day management science grew out of successful applications of the scientific approach to solving military operational problems during World War II. Hence, it was originally dubbed "operational research." After the war, as this approach found its way into all areas of the military, government, and industry, the term was shortened to "operations research (OR)." As *managers* in business began using operations research approaches to aid in decision making, the term "management science (MS)" was coined. Today, there is little distinction between the terms, and they are used interchangeably in the literature.

So what exactly is the MS/OR approach? Philip McCord Morse, who established the pioneer operations research group within the Navy during World War II, and George Kimball, who was head of the Washington research section of this group, defined it in the first book ever published in the field in 1951 as:

> A scientific method of providing *executive* departments with a quantitative basis for decisions regarding operations under their control.[1]

They note that, from the beginning, the field supported the executive function but was distinct from it.

Gene Woolsey, a leader in MS/OR consulting, defines MS/OR as:

> The use of logic and mathematics in such a way as to not interfere with common sense.[2]

In his definition, Woolsey introduces two important concepts: logic and common sense. Both play a key role in any MS/OR analysis. As we will discuss in Chapter 2, much of management science deals with mathematical modeling and developing or applying quantitative solution techniques. Some of the models can be quite complex, and some of the solution techniques can be quite sophisticated. But when management science is actually used, it should, as Woolsey bluntly puts it, "look, feel, and taste like common sense."

Since MS/OR had its roots in military applications during World War II, it might be useful to examine the military's official definition of MS/OR. According to U.S. Army Pamphlet 600-3, MS/OR involves:

> The use of techniques such as statistical inference and decision theory, mathematical programming, probabilistic models, network and computer science [to solve complex operational and strategic issues].

Although this definition is more specific about the approaches used in MS/OR, it again emphasizes the decision-making purpose of the field.

---

[1]Little, John D. C., "Operations Research in Industry: New Opportunities in a Changing World," *Operations Research*, Vol. 39, No. 4, July–Aug., 1991, pp. 531–542.

[2]Hesse, Rick and Gene Woolsey, *Applied Management Science: A Quick and Dirty Approach*, Science Research Associates, 1980.

Even the best results from the best models are relatively useless, however, if they are not communicated in a clear, coherent way to the decision maker. Thus, we offer our own definition of **management science**:

Management Science

Management science is the scientific approach to executive decision making, which consists of

1. The art of *mathematical modeling* of complex situations
2. The science of the development of *solution techniques* used to solve these models
3. The ability to effectively *communicate* the results to the decision maker

---

1.3 A BRIEF HISTORY OF MANAGEMENT SCIENCE

Doing the best you can with the resources at your disposal is an age-old problem. It was not until the late nineteenth and early twentieth centuries, however, that the rudiments of the modern-day quantitative approach for decision making took shape. Figure 1.1 shows a time line denoting some of the significant developments in management science during the twentieth century. Disciplines specific to management science are included in parentheses.

Whereas much of the early research done in management science was concerned with developing the tools necessary to solve complex decision problems, today the principal focus of the field is on developing models and systems for such areas as health care services, environmental impact studies, neural networks, global warming, international economics, transportation systems, total quality management, flexible manufacturing, telecommunications, banking, and robotics.

As a result of the proliferation of microcomputers, together with the development of optimization software for such systems, increasingly more problems are being solved using management science techniques. Today all major spreadsheet packages (Lotus 1-2-3, Excel, Quatro Pro) include many management science tools as either standard or easy-to-add features. In many cases, for less than $50 or $100, individuals can buy integrated management science software packages in which each module is sufficient to perform many tasks that just a few years ago would have required large mainframe computers with expensive dedicated software. The WINQSB software included in this text is an example of one such integrated package.

Many individuals and organizations who may not have even heard of management science now use such models routinely in their businesses. Furthermore, management science continues to be a mainstay in large organizations. From General Motors to Bell Laboratories, American Airlines to Federal Express, Weyerhauser to Whirlpool, management science has proven successful in improving corporate operations. Municipal, state, and federal government agencies routinely undertake many projects using a management science approach. And, though the Cold War may be over, the United States Department of Defense still requires and utilizes management science models in both its daily operations and emergency or wartime situations, such as Operation Desert Storm in 1991.

As we move into the twenty-first century, there is overwhelming evidence that major organizations are looking for individuals in all disciplines who have strong quantitative, computer, and communications skills. Management science, with its emphasis on all these areas, as well as its direct application to problems of optimization and efficiency, will continue to be an important element in a well-rounded business education.

Management Science Time Line

-1890s
- Frederick Taylor develops the field of "scientific management" applying the scientific approach to improving operations in a production setting. (*Industrial Engineering*)

-1900s
- Henry Gantt develops a control chart approach for minimizing machine job completion times. (*Project Scheduling*)
- Andrey A. Markov studies how systems change over time. (*Markov Processes*)
- The general assignment approach is developed. (Networks)

-1910s
- F.W. Harris develops approaches to determine the optimal inventory quantity to order. (*Inventory Theory*)
- E.K. Erlang develops a formula for determining the average waiting time for telephone callers. (*Queuing Theory*)

-1920s
- William Shewart introduces the concept of control charts.
- H. Dodge and H. Romig develop the technique of acceptance sampling. (*Quality Control*)

-1930s
- Jon von Neuman and Oscar Morgenstern develop strategies for evaluating competitive situations. (*Game Theory*)

-1940s
- World War II provides the impetus for the application of mathematical modeling for solving military problems.
- George Dantzig develops the simplex method for solving problems with a linear objective and linear constraints. (Linear Programming)
- The first electronic computer is developed.

-1950s
- H. Kuhn and A.W. Tucker determine required conditions for optimality for problems with a non-linear structure. (*Non-linear Programming*)
- Ralph Gomory develops a solution procedure for problems in which some variables are required to be integer valued. (*Integer Programming*)
- PERT and CPM are developed. (*Project Scheduling*)
- The Operations Research Society of America (ORSA) and The Institute of Management Science (TIMS), two professional societies dealing with management science issues, are established.
- Richard Bellman develops a methodology for solving multistage decision problems. (*Dynamic Programming*)

-1960s
- John D.C. Little proves a theoretical relationship between the average length of a waiting line and the average time a customer spends in line. (*Queuing Theory*)
- Specialized simulation languages such as SIMSCRIPT and GPSS are developed. (*Simulation*)

-1970s
- The microcomputer is developed.

-1980s
- N. Karmarkar develops a new procedure for solving large-scale linear programming problems. (Linear Programming)
- The personal computer is developed.
- Specialized management science software packages that can run on microcomputers are developed.

-1990s
- Spreadsheet packages begin including optimization modules.
- TIMS and ORSA merge to form the Institute of Operations Research and Management Science (INFORMS).

FIGURE 1.1   Management Science Time Line

1.4 MANAGEMENT SCIENCE APPLICATIONS

Management science applications affect us every day. A Chicago nurse cut overtime expenses at her hospital by thousands of dollars through better scheduling of nurses; a Texas rancher saved money by using a lower cost mixture of feed grains; a New York coal wholesaler reduced his customers' energy expenses by determining the least expensive blend of coal that meets a customer's specifications regarding sulphur and ash content and heating values.

Management science analyses can be used in a wide variety of situations and can have a dramatic impact on the effectiveness of an organization's operations, as the following examples show.

PRODUCING HAMBURGERS AT BURGER KING

Burger King, a division of Grand Metropolitan Corporation, uses *linear programming* to determine how different cuts of meat should be blended together to produce hamburger patties for its restaurants. The objective of this analysis is to produce the patties at minimum cost while still meeting certain specifications such as fat content, texture, freshness, and shrinkage. As the cost of different cuts of meat changes, the company reevaluates its model to determine whether its recipe should be modified.

SCHEDULING CREWS AT AMERICAN AIRLINES

Scheduling aircraft crews is a complex problem involving such factors as the type of aircraft to be flown, the cities of origination and termination for the flight, the intermediary cities visited by the aircraft, and the length of the flight. Federal and union rules govern the placement of personnel on the aircraft. To address these issues, American Airlines has developed an *integer linear programming* model that allows the company to quickly determine an optimal flight schedule for its personnel.

PLANNING THE SONY ADVANCED TRAVELER INFORMATION SYSTEM

The marriage of the microprocessor with the Global Positioning Satellite System has enabled Sony Corporation to develop an onboard navigation system capable of giving directions to a car's driver. This information is especially valuable during traffic conditions such as rush hour congestion. The software is based on a management science technique known as the *shortest path algorithm*.

REBUILDING THE INTERSTATE 10 FREEWAY

Following the disastrous California earthquake in January 1994, Interstate 10, a main freeway serving the Los Angeles area, needed to be rebuilt quickly. The project's prime contractor was given a fairly short five-month deadline to reopen the roadway. To encourage the work to be done as quickly as possible, the contractor was offered a bonus of $500,000 for each day by which it was able to beat the deadline. Using a project scheduling technique known as the *critical path method*, the contractor was able to schedule work crews so as to be able to complete the repair work a month earlier than the project deadline. As a result, the contractor collected a $15 million bonus.

PLANNING ENVIRONMENTAL POLICY IN FINLAND

Political decisions about environmental issues are often complex. To assist in the development of a comprehensive framework for future water policy issues in Finland, that country's National Board of Waters and the Environment used a *decision analysis* approach to analyze a wide range of issues. Among the items studied were standards for allowable water level changes in lakes resulting from energy production and measures to fight acid rain.

COOKING AT
MRS. FIELDS

Mrs. Fields operates a nationwide chain of cookie shops specializing in fresh-baked chocolate chip cookies. The chain has equipped each shop with a PC-based information system to aid personnel in deciding when additional cookies should be baked and the amounts that should be produced. This system relies on management science techniques such as *inventory modeling* and demand *forecasting*.

TRANSPORTING TRASH
IN NEW YORK CITY

The New York City Department of Sanitation handles over 20,000 tons of garbage per day. To dispose of this trash, the department operates three incinerators. Refuse is also sent by barge from marine transfer stations to the Fresh Kills Landfill. To determine future operational plans for this landfill, the Department of Sanitation undertook a management science analysis. The result of this analysis was the development of the BOSS (barge operation systems simulation) model. This *simulation model* enabled the Department of Sanitation to determine the number of additional barges that should be purchased to handle future demands. It also helped plan the dispatching of these barges.

ESTABLISHING
QUALITY
MANAGEMENT AT
FORD MOTOR
COMPANY

During the 1970s U.S. automobile manufacturers saw a steady decline in their market share due to competition from Japanese and European manufacturers. In response, the Ford Motor Company embarked on a "Quality Is Job One" campaign. Suppliers were held to tighter standards, and new quality control procedures were developed. As a result of these *quality management* activities, Ford Motor Company was able to reverse its decline in market share and profitability.

As these examples illustrate, management science techniques been applied in numerous settings. They have been used to increase profitability and improve performance. In some cases, they have meant the difference between an enterprise's success and failure.

1.5 WHAT THIS TEXT IS ALL ABOUT

Management science techniques are useful in a wide variety of business situations. Perhaps this is why the demand for individuals with training in management science is expected to increase dramatically over the next decade. Surveys printed in such periodicals as *Money* magazine and the *Los Angeles Times* have consistently ranked "management scientist" as one of today's fastest growing occupations.

Management science can be a rewarding profession, but we realize that many of you may select some other career path. Why then, you may ask, should I study management science? The answer lies in the objectives of this text:

1. **To gain a familiarity with management science approaches**

    Although you may never actually conduct a management science study, you should be skilled enough to know when such a study is warranted. The tools of management science can substantially improve an enterprise's performance. Recognizing when such opportunities arise and knowing how to take advantage of them are key traits of a successful manager.

    Of critical importance in this regard is the ability to communicate with the individual or group who is carrying out the management science study. Unfortunately, all too often consultants tend to speak in technical terms and appear to be communicating in a foreign language. By understanding management science concepts, managers can be more effective in their dealings with the individuals performing the analyses. Equally important, managers well schooled in management science are better able to determine whether the consultant carrying out the project is on the right track.

2.   *To gain skills in quantitative decision making*

Throughout your career you will constantly be faced with decision-making situations. The training you attain mastering the concepts of this text can serve as a valuable aid in improving these decision-making skills. In particular, identifying the objective you wish to accomplish and knowing the constraints that limit your options are fundamental management science skills.

Management science includes the development of mathematical models and approaches for solving such problems. However, a solution to a model is no more than that. If the model has been misformulated or does not include all the critical elements of the underlying real-world problem, it may have limited applicability. One of our goals in this text is to make you aware that solutions to quantitative models are rarely the solutions to real-world problems. Rather, the model solutions provide insights useful in determining the ultimate recommendation.

3.   *To improve your overall knowledge of business*

The examples used to illustrate the management science principles in this text are drawn from all aspects of business. It is our hope that through this approach you will gain not only an appreciation of how management science can be used in your particular discipline of interest, but also a greater insight into the other business disciplines as well.

4.   *To improve your communication skills*

One of the most important elements in the success of an individual's career is his or her ability to communicate. You can prepare the best analysis in the world, but if you cannot communicate your results so that your recommendations are adopted, your efforts will be in vain.

In this text we stress the communication of the results of a management science analysis. To that end, each of the subsequent chapters includes a business report to guide you in identifying the types of issues that can be raised in reporting the results of an analytical study.

5.   *To gain greater familiarity with the computer*

One reason why the field of management science is expected to show tremendous growth is the continuing increase in computer power that organizations will enjoy. Enterprises that in the past could not afford to undertake a management science study because they lacked computer resources now find that the tools for undertaking such analyses are readily available at affordable prices.

A little more than a decade ago, few management science students had ready access to computer software that could be used to solve the problems dealt with in this text. By necessity, the emphasis of the management science course was on understanding the mathematical algorithms underlying the techniques. Problems had to be simple enough to be solved using pencil and paper, and key management issues could not be considered. With the decline in price of microcomputers and the availability of inexpensive management science software, however, emphasis has shifted away from the mathematics to an understanding of the assumptions that underlie each technique and the identification of the data necessary to obtain an answer.

Specific topic areas in this text can be analyzed using commercial software packages such as LINDO for linear programming models, GINO for non-linear programming models, Primavera for project management, and Simscript for simulation models. There are also general purpose management science software packages such as WINQSB (included on the accompanying CD-ROM) and STORM, which can be used to solve nearly all the models we discuss in this text. Additionally, many of the models considered lend themselves to easy and natural spreadsheet formulations.

In this text we use both WINQSB and Excel to solve our models. You may wonder why we do not concentrate on using just one of these packages. The reason is because both have their advantages and disadvantages, and both add value to the discussion in this text.

WINQSB is easy to use, is formatted to look and feel like a spreadsheet (in fact, in most cases you can import Excel files into WINQSB), and is set up so that the user need only concentrate on inputting the relevant data. The output for the modules is easy to read and gives precisely the information the management scientist desires to make business decisions. Since the focus of this text is not on programming but on building models and using results from these models to make management decisions, this makes the use of WINQSB highly attractive.

On the other hand, Excel is a very popular, well-proven package that is accessible and readily understood by most users. There are millions of copies of Excel in use worldwide, and support and literature for Excel are abundant. Many of the models in this text fit easily into a spreadsheet format. Thus, in this text, where appropriate, we have included Excel printouts along with many appendices giving Excel instructions for solving these models.

However, when using a spreadsheet, even for the most basic models, cells must be "programmed," thus creating the opportunity for logic and input errors. Additionally, for some models, add-in modules are required or the user must program a macro using VISUAL BASIC. Since this is not a text on "how to program management science models in Excel" (such texts do exist), we have presented instructions only for models that do not require add-ins or macros.

1.6 ORGANIZATION OF THE TEXT

Each of the subsequent chapters of this text begins with a story. We hope it will intrigue you while it demonstrates how management science techniques can improve operations. The introductory section of each chapter serves to introduce the topics covered in the chapter. These topics are elucidated through the use of easy-to-understand examples. Emphasis is placed on the assumptions underlying the models presented and the use of the model output in decision making. Extensive use is made of computer output in detailing these concepts. Communication of the results of a management science analysis is illustrated through the use of a business memorandum in each chapter. Because our focus is on the information provided by the model rather than on the technique used to solve the model discussions of the technical steps underlying the techniques are left for appendices. At the conclusion of each chapter you will find an extensive problem set as well as a number of business cases that integrate the concepts covered in the chapter.

THE CD-ROM On the accompanying CD-ROM are modules that complement and expand the topics in the text including:

- The WINQSB software package
- A review of the statistical concepts used in the text
- Appendices describing the algorithms and formula derivations used in the chapters
- Additional problems and cases for Chapters 3 through 13

- Supplements describing duality and the simplex method of linear programming
- Additional chapters on Quality Management, Markov Processes, and Non-linear Models
- WINQSB and Excel files for the models presented in the chapters

Using the CD-ROM in conjunction with the text allows the reader to select a level of mathematical treatment for each topic commensurate with his or her needs. References to material contained on the CD-ROM are designated by the ⊙ symbol in the margin.

THE MANAGEMENT SCIENCE PROCESS

United Airlines operates a fleet of hundreds of different types of aircraft and employs thousands of people as pilots, flight attendants, ticket agents, ground crews, and service personnel in its operations throughout the United States, Canada, Central and South America, Europe, Asia, and Australia. The complexity of its operations requires United to be highly mechanized and to utilize the latest mathematical tools, information, and computer technology so that it can:

- Develop master flight schedules
- Forecast demand for its routes
- Determine which planes to purchase and which to lease
- Assign planes and crews to the routes
- Set fares
- Accept reservations in various fare categories
- Purchase fuel
- Schedule airport ticket agents and service personnel
- Schedule maintenance crews

- Maintain service facilities
- Lease airport gates
- Design and monitor its frequent flyer program

Factors impacting these decisions include:

- Budget, equipment, and personnel restrictions
- Union agreements regarding the scheduling of personnel
- Federal Aviation Administration maintenance guidelines
- Safe distance and aircraft turnaround time requirements
- The flexibility to react in real time to complications due to weather, congestion, and other causes.

These are but a few of the complicated and interrelated problems and constraints affecting United's bottom-line profitability. Proper planning and operations require more sophisticated analyses than merely making educated guesses. Accordingly, United Airlines makes liberal use of management science models to increase profits and customer satisfaction in a constrained environment.

2.1 $\mathscr{M}$ATHEMATICAL MODELING AND THE MANAGEMENT SCIENCE PROCESS

Many problems requiring managerial decisions lend themselves to quantitative or management science analyses. Throughout this text numerous decision problems, each with specific objectives and restrictions, are presented and analyzed from a management science perspective. In this chapter, however, we examine the *general* management science process by detailing the steps required for a successful analysis. It is important for the analyst and the decision maker alike to be cognizant of the particulars of this process so that management science can be applied correctly and assume its proper role in managerial decision making.

MATHEMATICAL
MODELING

Management science relies on *mathematical modeling*, a process that translates observed or desired phenomena into mathematical expressions. For example, suppose, NewOffice Furniture produces three products—desks, chairs, and molded steel (which it sells to other manufacturers)—and is trying to decide on the number of desks (D), chairs (C), and pounds of molded steel (M) to produce during a particular production run. If NewOffice nets a $50 profit on each desk produced, $30 on each chair produced, and $6 per pound of molded steel produced, the total profit for a production run can be modeled by the expression:

$$50D + 30C + 6M$$

Similarly, if 7 pounds of raw steel are needed to manufacture a desk, 3 pounds to manufacture a chair, and 1.5 pounds to produce a pound of molded steel, the amount of raw steel used during the production run is modeled by the expression:

$$7D + 3C + 1.5M$$

A **constrained mathematical model** is a model with an objective and one or more constraints. *Functional constraints* are "$\leq$", "$\geq$", or "$=$" restrictions that involve expressions with one or more variables. For example, if NewOffice has only 2000 pounds of raw steel available for the production run, the functional constraint that expresses the fact that it cannot use more than 2000 pounds of raw steel is modeled by the inequality:

$$7D + 3C + 1.5M \leq 2000$$

Variable constraints are constraints involving only one of the variables. Examples of variable constraints that will be discussed in this text include the following:

Variable Constraint	Mathematical Expression
Nonnegativity constraint	$X \geq 0$
Lower bound constraint	$X \geq L$ (a number other than 0)
Upper bound constraint	$X \leq U$
Integer constraint	$X =$ integer
Binary constraint	$X = 0$ or 1

In the NewOffice example, no production can be negative; thus, we require the nonnegativity constraints $D \geq 0$, $C \geq 0$, and $M \geq 0$. If at least 100 desks must be produced to satisfy contract commitments, and due to the availability of seat cushions, no more than 500 chairs can be produced, these can be expressed by the variable constraints $D \geq 100$ and $C \leq 500$, respectively. Finally, if the quantities of desks and chairs produced during the production run must be integer valued (the amount of molded steel need not be integer valued), we have the following constrained mathematical model for this problem:

$$
\begin{array}{lllll}
\text{MAXIMIZE} & 50D + 30C + & 6M & & \text{(Total profit)} \\
\text{SUBJECT TO:} & 7D + 3C + 1.5M & \le & 2000 & \text{(Raw steel)} \\
& D & \ge & 100 & \text{(Contract)} \\
& C & \le & 500 & \text{(Cushions)} \\
& D, C, M & \ge & 0 & \text{(Nonnegativity)} \\
& D, C \text{ are integers} & & &
\end{array}
$$

Constrained mathematical models can usually be solved to determine a good solution, and, in many cases, a "best" or *optimal* solution, for the model. Using an appropriate solution technique for the above constrained mathematical model, for example, we can show that producing 100 desks, 433 chairs, and two-thirds of a pound of molded steel yields a maximum total profit of $17,994. Any other combination of desks, chairs, and molded steel that satisfies all of the constraints will yield a profit less than $17,994. Solving constrained mathematical models is a primary focus of much of this text.

CLASSIFICATION OF
MATHEMATICAL
MODELS

There are various ways to classify mathematical models; one way is by the purpose of the model. **Optimization models** seek to maximize a quantity (profit, efficiency, etc.) or minimize a quantity (cost, time, etc.) that may be restricted by a set of constraints (limitations on the availability of capital, personnel, and supplies; requirements to meet contract deadlines; etc.). At times, however, the function of a model is not to maximize or minimize any particular quantity, but to describe or predict events (sales forecasts, project completion dates, etc.) given certain conditions. These models are known as **prediction models**.

Prediction models are almost always part of larger optimization models, however. For example, the manager of a fast-food restaurant could use a prediction model to determine the reduction in average customer waiting time and the corresponding increase in sales resulting from hiring an additional clerk. The information gained from the results of this prediction model could then be used as input for an optimization model to determine whether the benefits from the predicted increase in sales and reduction in customer waiting time more than offsets the costs of hiring the additional clerk.

Another way to classify mathematical models is by the degree of certainty of the data in the model. **Deterministic models** are those in which the profit, cost, and resource data are assumed to be known with certainty, whereas in **probabilistic** or **stochastic models**, one or more of the input parameters' values are determined by probability distributions. For example, in a manufacturing process in which the speed of an assembly line can be controlled by operators, the number of parts per hour arriving at one station on the assembly line from another could be modeled using a deterministic arrival rate. By contrast, the number of customer arrivals per hour at a major supermarket would not be known with certainty; accordingly, a stochastic model would be more appropriate in this case.

The ability to solve mathematical models and obtain meaningful results is of primary importance to the decision maker. Methods for solving stochastic models can be more time consuming and complex than those for deterministic models. In such cases, the "accuracy" achieved by using a stochastic model is somewhat sacrificed for the expediency of having a deterministic model that can readily be solved. This approach is discussed in more detail in Section 2.4.

THE MANAGEMENT
SCIENCE PROCESS

Management science is a discipline that adapts the scientific method to provide management with key information for executive decision making. In its simplest form, management science can be thought of as a four-step procedure, as shown in Figure 2.1.

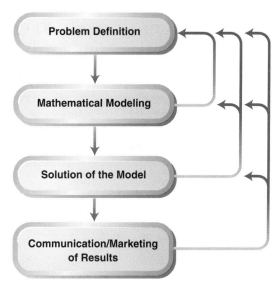

FIGURE 2.1   The Management Science Process

Projects rarely proceed smoothly through this sequential process, however. Usually, models have to be revised, solution approaches altered, or reports rewritten, as historical, simulated, or current data are used to verify and fine tune the original sets of assumptions and data. Hence, parts of the process may need to be repeated until the analyst is comfortable with the results. In the next four sections of this chapter, the complexities and thought processes involved in each of the four phases of the management science process are discussed in detail.

THE TEAM CONCEPT

Building good mathematical models is an art that is at the heart of the management science process. The greater the knowledge of the project under study, the more reliable the model is in assessing the true situation. While relatively small projects requiring a management science approach are sometimes assigned to a single consultant or specialist, most larger projects utilize a *team approach* that capitalizes on the talents of the management science analyst as well as those from other relevant business or scientific disciplines germane to the project.

   The petroleum industry is one that has made liberal use of management science models. One such model involves the purchase of crude oil and the manufacture and distribution of various grades of gasoline. In addition to the management science analyst, the "team" responsible for constructing the model and evaluating its results might consist of some or all of the following:

Team Member	*Expertise*
Chemical engineer	Petroleum blending requirements
Economist	Forecasts of oil prices
Marketing analyst	Forecast of market demand for gasoline
Financial officer	Analysis of cash flow
Accountant	Cash flow/tax requirements
Production manager	Analysis of production capabilities
Transportation specialist	Distribution of refined oil products

Each individual member of this team brings to the project his or her own perspective and can make contributions that might otherwise be lost with a more narrow focus.

2.2   THE MANAGEMENT SCIENCE PROCESS—STEP 1: DEFINING THE PROBLEM

The most important part of the modeling process is identifying the problem under consideration. As noted management consultant Peter Drucker has stressed, the wrong answer to the right question is not fatal, for revisions can be made and different alternatives may be explored; however, the right answer to the wrong question can be disastrous. It is critical that the problem be properly defined before enormous amounts of time and energy are expended on perhaps a worthless (or worse) model and solution.

"PROBLEMS" IN MANAGEMENT SCIENCE

Management science is generally applied in three situations:

1. Designing and implementing new operations or procedures
2. Evaluating an ongoing set of operations or procedures
3. Determining and recommending corrective action for operations and procedures that are producing unsatisfactory results

When contemplating new operations or procedures, the "problem" facing the management scientist is to recommend approaches that will yield profitable and efficient results within a reasonable time period, given limited or no previous historical data. A company contemplating the introduction of a new product, for example, will need to determine the exact production process, the materials and labor required, and the production quantities based on forecasted demand for its product and the availability of required resources. In this case the management science analysis revolves around the question, "*How do we get started?*"

When analyzing an ongoing business venture, a "problem" does not necessarily refer to a department or an operation that is experiencing substandard or unacceptably low results. For example, a small grocery store generating $500,000 a year in gross profits may not seem to have a problem. But could a change in operations yield another $100,000? The management science analysis here is attempting to answer the question, "*Can we do better?*"

Management science is also applied when a company has experienced significant or repetitive failures or shortfalls. Russell Ackoff, a pioneer in the field, refused to characterize such situations as "problems" but rather as "messes." He referred to such cases in management science as "mess management." In this case, the management science analysis is a response to a cry for "*Help!*"

In each of these situations, an analyst is typically faced with some or all of the following factors:

1. "Fuzzy," incomplete, or conflicting data
2. "Soft" constraints (i.e., goals rather than restrictions)
3. Differing opinions among and between workers and management
4. Very limited budgets for analyses
5. Narrow time frames for solutions and recommendations
6. Political "turf wars"
7. No firm idea by management of exactly what is wanted (managers sometimes look to the consultant to tell *them* what *they* want)

PROBLEM DEFINITION

The analyst's success will be determined in large part by how well these factors are dealt with in the problem definition phase of the project. Table 2.1 suggests steps to be taken in this process.

TABLE 2.1   PROBLEM DEFINITION

1. Observe operations
2. Ease into complexity
3. Recognize political realities
4. Decide what is *really* wanted
5. Identify constraints
6. Seek continuous feedback

Observe Operations

Those performing a management science analysis should make every effort to observe the problem from various points of view within the organization, with the goal of understanding the problem *at least as well as, if not better than,* those individuals directly involved. In a manufacturing process, the perspectives of managers, foremen, and workers might be solicited. In a service operation, input might come from supervisors, clerks, and support personnel. Frequently, accounting personnel can also provide valuable insights into the true nature of the problem.

In an effort to get a feel for what's really going on, it is important that the management science team "speak the same language" as those supplying input data and those responsible for making the ultimate decisions. Since recommendations will often be based on what many in the firm consider "voodoo mathematics," it is important to establish *credibility* early with these personnel and to reinforce it throughout the entire process. The analysts must realize that decision makers, in particular, take a critical look at recommendations stemming from a management science study since the success of any implemented policy will directly affect the evaluation of their performance.

Ease into Complexity

At the beginning of the study, the team should strive to ask simple, basic questions of individuals, which do not go beyond the realm of each person's expertise. This avoids putting those questioned on the defensive and aids in establishing the trust and respect that are crucial to the success of the analysis.

By initially asking similar questions of workers at all levels on the organization chart, the analysts may find that there are differences in opinion as to the exact nature of the problem. Once the individuals or units who have expertise in each of several key areas have been identified, the team can then probe more deeply into complex issues in a significantly less intimidating manner.

Recognize Political Realities

Analysts should always be cognizant of the politics present in any organization. Natural conflicts may exist between labor and management and between various managers. Operating in this kind of environment, the management science team can expect to receive distorted or incomplete information from each group. A manager is naturally reluctant to provide negative information that would show her division to be inefficient; a foreman most likely will not provide information that might result in significant reductions of his resources or personnel; and a worker will not offer suggestions that might result in the elimination of her job! Thus, all information gathered by the management science team must be scrutinized with these limitations in mind.

Decide What Is Really Wanted

Two situations typify the environment that exists before a management science analysis begins:

1. Management has a *fuzzy* idea of what the problem is.
2. Management has a *definite* idea of what (it thinks) the problem is.

There is rarely an in-between. In either case, the management science team should try to decide for itself what is needed.

An example of the first case involves a store that carries a product that has not been selling well. Management might simply indicate that "something is wrong here" and may actually be looking for help in identifying the root causes of the problem. The "problem" could be defined quite differently, and the possible recommendations vary greatly depending on such factors as the age of the items, the amount of advertising done by both the manufacturer and the store, the relationship between the store and the manufacturer, the "seasonality" of the product, and so on. Gathering relevant facts is crucial to accurate problem definition.

The following situation represents the second case. A health products distribution company, which orders products from various manufacturers and distributes them to local stores, was not able to fill over 10% of its orders because of inventory stockouts. The company was convinced that, in order to reduce lost revenues due to excessive stockouts, it should reduce stockouts to less than 4%. To meet this objective, however, the company was concerned that it might have to carry an excessive amount of inventory. Management science consultants were called in to develop an effective ordering policy.

Upon further investigation of the situation, it was determined that while reducing stockouts on high-volume, high-profit items was indeed crucial to company profits, less stringent inventory policies were necessary for lower-volume, lower-profit items. In fact, the resulting model, which was credited with saving the company hundreds of thousands of dollars annually, actually recommended an increase in the probability of stockouts for these items! The moral is simple: *the management science team should make certain that the company is sure of its objective before developing and solving a model.*

Identify Constraints

Businesses operate in a restrictive environment. It is important to seek input from various operational levels to identify these restrictions or constraints. Advertising budgets for a beer company, warehouse space limitations for a department store, the order of task completion in a construction project, and the maximum size of a waiting line at a supermarket checkout stand are all examples of constraints that might be included in mathematical models. Only those restrictions that could possibly affect operations should be included. Those that will obviously be satisfied by any reasonable solution should be omitted.

Seek Continuous Feedback

In order for the management science team to solve the "right" problem, the analysts need to seek *ongoing* feedback from management, both orally and by written communication (or e-mail), in the problem formulation stage. This allows both parties to continuously modify their initial perceptions and remain "in sync" about the problem.

Communications should be concise, articulate, and precise so that there is no misunderstanding on either side of what will be modeled and solved. This consensus allows the modeling phase to proceed more smoothly and gives more credence to the recommendations based on the solution of the model.

PROBLEM IDENTIFICATION FOR DELTA HARDWARE

To help motivate the development and solution of a mathematical model, throughout the remainder of this chapter, we will analyze a situation faced by Delta Hardware Stores. After soliciting input and analyzing the situation, the management at Delta Hardware and the management science team mutually agreed on the following problem statement.

DELTA HARDWARE STORES—PROBLEM STATEMENT

Delta Hardware Stores is a regional retailer with warehouses in three cities in California: San Jose in northern California, Fresno in central California, and Azusa in southern California. Each month, Delta restocks its warehouses with its own brand of paint (among other products). Delta has its own paint manufacturing plant in Phoenix, Arizona. Although the plant's production capacity is sometimes insufficient to meet monthly demand, a recent feasibility study commissioned by Delta found that it was not cost effective to expand production capacity at this time. To meet demand, Delta subcontracts with a national paint manufacturer to produce paint under the Delta label and deliver it (at a higher cost) to any of its three California warehouses.

Given that there is to be no expansion of plant capacity, the problem is to determine a least cost distribution scheme of paint produced at its manufacturing plant and shipments from the subcontractor to meet the demands of its California warehouses.

2.3 THE MANAGEMENT SCIENCE PROCESS—STEP 2: BUILDING A MATHEMATICAL MODEL

According to David Gray, a senior consultant with American Airlines Decision Technologies, the solution to an applied management science problem may be "the organization of scattered thoughts, ideas, and conflicting objectives and constraints into a more logical coherent decision framework for a client who is too close to the problem to solve it objectively." While simple, common-sense, nonquantitative approaches may solve some problems, in most cases large amounts of quantitative data need to be organized into this "more logical coherent decision framework."

Mathematical modeling is a procedure that recognizes and verbalizes a problem and then quantifies it by turning the words into mathematical expressions. While modeling requires a number of basic skills, in some sense, mathematical modeling is an art that improves with experience. Some of the steps involved in the modeling process include:

Mathematical Modeling

1. Identify decision variables
2. Quantify the objective and constraints
3. Construct a model shell
4. Data gathering—Consider time/cost issues

IDENTIFY DECISION VARIABLES

A crucial step in building a mathematical model is determining those factors in the decision-making process over which the decision maker has control. These items are known as the *controllable inputs* or *decision variables* for the problem. For example, in a manufacturing process, the quantity of goods produced and the amount of overtime assigned during the week are controllable inputs, or decision variables, for the model. The shift foremen or plant managers (the decision makers) make these determinations. Decision variables usually include a *time frame*. In this case, it is important that the decision variables reflect the production and overtime schedules as *"per week."*

The number of machines in the plant, the amount of resources needed to make one unit of the product, and the overall plant capacity are factors over which the manager has no direct influence. They are the *uncontrollable inputs*, or *parameters*.

In many cases, determining the appropriate decision variables is the hardest part of building a mathematical model. Frequently, the rest of the modeling process follows quite naturally once the decision variables have been properly defined. The following is a quick rule of thumb for determining the decision variables of a mathematical model.

Defining Decision Variables

1. Ask, "What does the decision maker want to learn by solving this problem?" In other words, "Does the decision maker have the authority to decide the numerical value (amount) of the item?" If the answer is "yes," it is a decision variable.

2. Be very precise in the units (and if appropriate, the time frame) of each decision variable.

Variable Definition for Delta Hardware

Let us apply this approach to the Delta Hardware problem.

DELTA HARDWARE STORE PROBLEM—VARIABLE DEFINITION

After analyzing the problem as presented, it is clear that the decision maker has no control over demand, production capacities, or unit costs. The decision maker is simply being asked, "How much paint should be shipped *this month* (note the time frame) from the plant in Phoenix to San Jose, Fresno, and Azusa, and how much extra should be purchased from the subcontractor and sent to each of the three cities to satisfy their orders?"

There are six decisions to be made, hence six decision variables. These can be expressed as

$X1$ = amount of paint shipped this month from Phoenix to San Jose
$X2$ = amount of paint shipped this month from Phoenix to Fresno
$X3$ = amount of paint shipped this month from Phoenix to Azusa
$X4$ = amount of paint subcontracted this month for San Jose
$X5$ = amount of paint subcontracted this month for Fresno
$X6$ = amount of paint subcontracted this month for Azusa

The choice of the variable names is arbitrary.

QUANTIFY THE OBJECTIVE FUNCTION AND CONSTRAINTS

The objective of most management science studies, and of *all* optimization models, is to figure out how to do the best you can with what you've got. "The best you can" implies maximizing something (such as profit or efficiency) or minimizing something (such as costs or time).

Although a company may be satisfied with a substantial improvement over a current situation, the goal usually is to seek an optimal value for some *objective function*. *Total profit maximization* (Total Profit = Total Revenues − Total Costs) is perhaps the most common objective for mathematical models. Note that if costs are constant, maximizing profit is equivalent to maximizing revenue; if revenues are constant, it is equivalent to minimizing cost.

Most management science models are formulated to maximize or minimize a single objective function. Cases in which two or more conflicting objectives exist are called *multicriteria decision problems*. (Multicriteria problems are discussed briefly in Chapter 16 on the accompanying CD-ROM.)

As discussed in Section 2.2, when seeking the optimal value for an objective function, one is usually operating under restrictive conditions, or *constraints*. Examples of typical constraints include limits on the amount of resources available (workers, machines, budgets, etc.) and contractual requirements for monthly production.

Constraints can also be definitional in nature. A constraint expressing that the inventory at the end of a month is equal to the inventory at the beginning of the month plus production minus sales during the month is an example of one such definitional constraint. The following is a useful aid for writing constraints.

Writing Constraints

1. Create a limiting condition *in words* in the following manner:

   (The amount of a resource required)
   ⟨Has some relation to⟩
   (The availability of the resource)

2. Make sure the units on the left side of the relation are the same as those on the right side.

3. Translate the words into mathematical notation using known or estimated values for the parameters and the previously defined symbols for the decision variables.

4. Rewrite the constraint, if necessary, so that all terms involving the decision variables are on the left side of the relationship, with only a constant value on the right side.

CONSTRUCT MODEL SHELLS

In the formative stages of model building, generic symbols can be used for the parameters until the actual data are determined. In the NewOffice Furniture example described in Section 2.1, the symbols A1, A2, and A3 might have been used to represent the amount of steel required to make one desk, one chair, and one pound of molded steel, respectively, and the symbol B could have been used to represent the amount of steel available during the production run. Thus, the functional constraint could be written as the following *shell*:

$$A1*D + A2*C + A3*M \le B$$

When it was determined that it takes 7 pounds of raw steel to make a desk, 3 pounds of raw steel to make a chair, and 1.5 pounds of raw steel to make a pound of molded steel, and that there were 2000 pounds of steel available weekly, the appropriate substitutions for A1, A2, A3, and B would be made to the shell, giving the constraint: $7D + 3C + 1.5M \le 2000$.

Model Shell for Delta Hardware

By having a model shell, the modeler can focus directly on the exact data required to complete the model. Let us illustrate this procedure for the Delta Hardware problem.

DELTA HARDWARE STORE PROBLEM—FORMULATING THE MODEL SHELL

Although the actual data have not yet been collected, it is certain that there is a finite production capacity at the paint plant in Phoenix as well as an upper bound on the amount of paint available from the subcontractor. There are also different requirements for paint at each of the three Delta warehouses.

Further investigation by the management science team indicates that the delivery trucks that transport the paint from Phoenix to the warehouses carry 1000 gallons of paint at a time. Since Delta requires the warehouses to order in units of 1000, this is equivalent to ordering a certain number of truckloads. The cost of shipping each truck load can then be determined based on the time and distance between Phoenix and each of the warehouse cities.

It has also been determined that the cost of purchasing the paint from the subcontractor is higher than manufacturing the paint in Phoenix, and to obtain the best prices from the subcontractor, orders must be in 1000-gallon increments. The subcontractor charges a fixed fee for each 1000 gallons ordered and a delivery charge to each of the three warehouse cities. This delivery charge varies depending on the city.

The objective is to minimize the total overall monthly costs of manufacturing, transporting, and subcontracting paint, subject to

1. The Phoenix plant cannot operate beyond its capacity.
2. The amount ordered from the subcontractor cannot exceed a maximum limit.
3. The orders for paint at each warehouse will be fulfilled.

Since truckloads and purchases from the subcontractor are based on *thousands* of gallons of paint, let us assume that the decision variables X1, X2, . . . , X6 are defined in these units. For example, X1 will represent the number of thousands of gallons of paint (i.e., truckloads) shipped from Phoenix to San Jose, X6 will represent the number of thousands of gallons of paint subcontracted this month for Azusa, and so on.

To determine the overall costs, one must determine: (1) the manufacturing cost per 1000 gallons of paint at the plant in Phoenix (M); (2) the respective truckload shipping costs from Phoenix to San Jose, Fresno, and Azusa (T1, T2, T3); (3) the fixed purchase cost per 1000 gallons from the subcontractor (C); and (4) the respective shipping charges per 1000 gallons from the subcontractor to San Jose, Fresno, and Azusa (S1, S2, S3). Minimizing total monthly costs can then be written as:

MINIMIZE (M+T1)X1 + (M+T2)X2 + (M+T3)X3 + (C+S1)X4 + (C+S2)X5 + (C+S3)X6

To write the constraints, we need to know (in thousands of gallons): (1) the capacity of the Phoenix plant (Q1); (2) the maximum number of gallons available from the subcontractor (Q2); and (3) the respective orders for paint at the warehouses in San Jose, Fresno, and Azusa (R1, R2, R3). The constraints can then be written as:

1. The number of truckloads shipped out from Phoenix cannot exceed the plant capacity:

$$X1 + X2 + X3 \leq Q1$$

2. The number of thousands of gallons ordered from the subcontractor cannot exceed the order limit:

$$X4 + X5 + X6 \leq Q2$$

3. The number of thousands of gallons received at each warehouse equals the total orders of the warehouse:

$$
\begin{array}{rrrrr}
X1 & & + X4 & & = R1 \\
& X2 & & + X5 & = R2 \\
& & X3 & + X6 & = R3
\end{array}
$$

4. All shipments must be nonnegative and integer:

$$X1 \geq 0, X2 \geq 0, X3 \geq 0, X4 \geq 0, X5 \geq 0, X6 \geq 0$$

X1, X2, X3, X4, X5, X6 integer

Given this model shell, the modeler can now begin gathering data to determine or approximate values for the parameters M, C, T1, T2, T3, S1, S2, S3, Q1, Q2, R1, R2, and R3.

DATA GATHERING—
CONSIDER TIME/COST
ISSUES

All mathematical models are simply that—models of reality. There are usually numerous ways to model most situations, some quite simplistic, and others very complex. The modeler usually must ask the question, "Is a very sophisticated model that will give relatively accurate results needed, or will a simpler model which will likely yield less accurate, but hopefully, 'ball park' results suffice?" The answer depends on three time/cost considerations:

1. *The time and cost of collecting, organizing, and sorting relevant data*

   Data collection can be very time consuming and expensive. Key data may turn out to be unavailable or subject to error for a variety of reasons, including poor recordkeeping, company or union policies, ignorance, or evasiveness of potentially affected personnel. Substantial costs may be incurred to obtain *hard data* (precise values, good forecasts, or exact estimates) to analyze even one factor in the model.

   For example, months of continuous recordkeeping may be required to determine an arrival pattern of customers to a grocery store; estimating the typical production time for a single product might require lengthy and involved time and motion studies; sales projections can require hundreds of man-hours to analyze numerous voluminous reports. Even when raw data are readily available, organizing and sorting the data to obtain relevant information can itself be quite costly and time consuming.

   As an alternative to hard data, models can use *soft data*, such as short-term studies or even best guesses from experts. In general, the "harder" the data, the more costly and time consuming it is to obtain. Consequently, mathematical models often contain varying amounts of both hard and soft data.

2. *The time and cost of generating a solution approach*

   Conventional solution techniques exist for many "traditional" management science models including all those developed in this text. In "real life," however, mathematical models formulated by a management science team frequently fail to meet the required conditions of these models. In this case, we have two choices:

   1. Make some simplifying assumptions so that a standard solution technique may be used.

   or

   2. Develop a new solution technique, or modify an existing one, to handle this special problem.

   Using simplifying assumptions saves the time and cost of developing, testing, programming, and debugging a new technique; at the same time, it may result in an oversimplified, unrealistic model of the true situation. Thus, care must be taken not to make assumptions that will jeopardize the integrity of the results from the model.

3. *The time and cost of using the model*

   Managers and executives must respond rapidly to dynamically changing sets of conditions. For example, changing weather conditions could force an airline to reroute its entire fleet of planes and reassign flight personnel. New arrival and departure schedules, gate requirements, and crew and maintenance schedules must be generated quickly. Optimal solutions that could be generated "overnight," after the solution is required, are worthless.

   When selecting an appropriate model, the user of the model must also be considered. The sophistication of the model might be quite different, for example, if it is to be used by executives at General Motors, where a 1% improvement in efficiency would result in savings of tens of millions of dollars, as opposed to a small store where such a small percentage improvement may not even cover the cost of the study. The model could certainly be more complex (and costly) if it were monitored by a management science department within a large organization rather than a single employee with limited training in the field.

Judgments about these time/cost factors play a key role in determining the amount and methods of data collection and selecting the models to utilize. An informal "rule of thumb," known as the 80/20 *rule*, is often used as a guide when selecting an appropriate model. It states that, in general, a business client settles for 80% of the optimal solution at 20% of the cost to obtain it. Thus, simpler, easier to use, less costly (though admittedly less accurate) models are often selected to generate "good" results rather than "optimal" ones.

Determining the Model for Delta Hardware

Let us now consider the data collection and model selection for Delta Hardware.

DELTA HARDWARE STORE PROBLEM—DATA COLLECTION AND MODEL SELECTION

Initial data received by the management science analyst indicate that the warehouses in San Jose, Fresno, and Azusa are to be restocked with 4000, 2000, and 5000 gallons of paint, respectively. The subcontractor has agreed tó sell Delta paint for $5 per gallon ($5000 per 1000 gallons) plus shipping fees of $1200 per 1000 gallons to San Jose, $1400 per 1000 gallons to Fresno, and $1100 per 1000 gallons to Azusa.

Delta management has informed the analyst that no more than 50% of the total paint supplied to the warehouses (in this case 5500 gallons) is to be supplied by the subcontractor. Since shipments from the subcontractor are to be in 1000-gallon units, this implies that, at most, 5000 gallons will be supplied by the subcontractor.

The modeler must now decide which model to use and the appropriate data to analyze in order to determine the values of the other parameters in the model.

The structure of the model shell developed in this case is a standard management science model known as the *transportation problem*. But in this model, all factors other than manufacturing, ordering, and transportation costs have been ignored. Many other simplifying assumptions have been made, such as requiring that all trucks carry a full load of 1000 gallons of paint. In reality, partial truckloads or larger trucks might be used. It is also assumed that the cost of sending two trucks is exactly twice the cost of sending one truck, that this cost does not change, and that the cost of driving from Phoenix to a warehouse city is always the same. Also ignored are the facts that production rates and costs vary from month to month; external costs can change at a moment's notice; and additional subcontractor suppliers of paint might be solicited.

Although the model developed for Delta lacks a certain degree of reality, solution modules for transportation models are readily available in management science and spreadsheet packages. Thus, by using this simplified model, at least as a first pass to determine "ballpark" results, Delta can avoid the time and expense of deriving and testing more complex models. If the results from this approach prove suspect, a more sophisticated model can then be developed.

Having elected to use the transportation model, the next step is to determine the value of the parameters of the model shell. Certain hard data have already been ascertained:

- The number of orders (in thousands of gallons) at the San Jose, Fresno, and Azusa warehouses are, respectively, $R1 = 4$, $R2 = 2$, and $R3 = 5$.

- The maximum order limit from the subcontractor (in thousands of gallons) is $Q2 = 5$.

- The fixed purchase cost per 1000 gallons of paint from the subcontractor is $C = \$5000$.

- The shipping charges per 1000 gallons of paint from the subcontractor to San Jose, Fresno, and Azusa are, respectively, S1 = $1200, S2 = $1400, and S3 = $1100.

Data that are more difficult to obtain and prone to more uncertainty include the production limits at the Phoenix plant and the manufacturing and transportation costs.

Production Limit   Most likely, a theoretical plant production limit exists, which assumes that the plant runs continuously at full capacity with no machine failures, full staffing, and ample resources. Because such ideal conditions rarely exist, monthly production levels vary. One way for the model to account for such unpredictable problems might be to multiply the theoretical production limit by some reduction factor. Another alternative could be simply to ask the plant manager, "What's your best estimate for production capability this month?"

In this case, the modeler decided to forecast plant capacity based on past data. Accordingly, the monthly production data listed in Table 2.2 for the number of gallons produced over the past 24 months were obtained from company records (month 24 being the most recent month).

TABLE 2.2   DELTA'S MONTHLY PRODUCTION

Month	Production	Month	Production	Month	Production
1	7500	9	8000	17	7900
2	7000	10	7200	18	8000
3	6500	11	7700	19	7600
4	7000	12	7500	20	8000
5	7000	13	8100	21	3900
6	6500	14	8000	22	8100
7	7200	15	7600	23	7900
8	5000	16	8000	24	8100

These data show that, with the exception of month 21, production was relatively constant over the past 12 months. Upon further investigation, it was found that during month 21, one of the production machines was experiencing intermittent breakdowns and management shut down the plant for a week and a half to perform a major overhaul of all machines. It was therefore decided that data for month 21 was an *outlier*—data not representative of normal production levels—and should be discarded.

It was also discovered that 12 months ago the plant went from a $37\frac{1}{2}$-hour to a 40-hour work week. As a consequence, although data from months 1 to 12 were available, these data would not be used in the forecast. Thus, it was decided that monthly production would be forecasted based on the average of production for the past year, excluding month 21:

$$(8100 + 8000 + 7600 + \ldots + 8100)/11 = 7936 \text{ gallons}$$

Since, for model simplicity, full truckloads of 1000 gallons are assumed, a rounded amount of Q1 = 8 (thousand) gallons will be used for the production capacity.

Plant Production and Transportation Costs   To determine unit production costs, we must consider all direct and indirect costs that go into production, including warehouse and machine leasing, employee wages and benefits, utilities, insurance, and so on. Transportation costs might include loading in Phoenix and unloading in each of the warehouse cities, mileage, and per diem expenses, among others. The management science team relied on the data supplied by the accounting department in Table 2.3 detailing the manufacturing and shipping costs of paint manufactured at the Phoenix plant.

Using this information, and the assumption that the Phoenix plant expects a production capacity of 8000 gallons per month, we can calculate the per gallon production cost as: (Direct per Gallon Manufacturing Cost) + (Apportioned per Gallon Indirect Cost) = \$2.25 + (\$6000/8000) = \$3.00 per gallon. Thus, the production cost per 1000 gallons is M = \$3000.

TABLE 2.3   COSTS ASSOCIATED WITH PRODUCTION OF PAINT

Direct manufacturing costs	\$2.25/gallon
Indirect costs	\$6,000/month
Loading costs in Phoenix	\$100/truckload
Unloading costs in San Jose	\$150/truckload
Unloading costs in Fresno	\$100/truckload
Unloading costs in Azusa	\$120/truckload
Mileage/other costs to San Jose	\$800/truckload
Mileage/other costs to Fresno	\$550/truckload
Mileage/other costs to Azusa	\$430/truckload

Given the fact that each truckload will carry 1000 gallons of paint, the transportation costs to each warehouse can now be determined by (Load Cost in Phoenix) + (Unload Cost at the Warehouse) + (Mileage Cost to the Warehouse):

$$\text{San Jose:} \quad T1 = \$100 + \$150 + \$800 = \$1050$$
$$\text{Fresno:} \quad T2 = \$100 + \$100 + \$550 = \$\ 750$$
$$\text{Azusa:} \quad T3 = \$100 + \$120 + \$430 = \$\ 650$$

The complete mathematical model for Delta Hardware derived by substituting the parameter values into the model shell is:[1]

MINIMIZE: $4050X1 + 3750X2 + 3650X3 + 6200X4 + 6400X5 + 6100X6$
SUBJECT TO:

$$
\begin{array}{cccccccl}
X1 + & X2 + & X3 & & & & & \leq 8 \\
& & & X4 + & X5 + & X6 & \leq 5 \\
X1 & & & + & X4 & & = 4 \\
& X2 & & & + & X5 & = 2 \\
& & X3 & & & + & X6 = 5
\end{array}
$$

$X1 \geq 0, X2 \geq 0, X3 \geq 0, X4 \geq 0, X5 \geq 0, X6 \geq 0$ $X1, X2, X3, X4, X5, X6$ integer

2.4   THE MANAGEMENT SCIENCE PROCESS—STEP 3: SOLVING A MATHEMATICAL MODEL

Mathematical models are formulated so that they can be solved to provide input to a decision maker. Steps in the **model solution** process include:

Model Solution
1. Choose an appropriate solution technique.
2. Generate model solutions.
3. Test/validate model results.
4. Return to modeling step if results are unacceptable.
5. Perform "what-if" analyses.

---

[1]The development of this relatively simple model illustrates the fact that, when we use phrases in this text such as "The cost of shipping 1000 gallons of paint from Phoenix to San Jose is \$4050," much background work has been done to generate even this single "given" value.

CHOOSE AN
APPROPRIATE
SOLUTION TECHNIQUE

We've seen that the choice of the model to be used is linked to the considerations of the time, cost, and accuracy of using models for which solution techniques are known versus those for which solution techniques must be developed. Fortunately, there are large classes of problems for which efficient solution techniques have already been developed, many of which are discussed in this text.

Although some simplifying assumptions may be made so that a standard solution technique may be used, care must be taken to assure that the "meat" of the true problem has not been "assumed away." Oversimplifying models and misapplying management science tools have been primary impediments to the success and acceptance of management science approaches on a more global scale.

Management science teams often use algorithms to solve mathematical models. An **algorithm** is a structured series of steps that must be performed to solve the model. Usually, the individual steps involve simple, but repetitious, mathematical operations, such as adding, subtracting, multiplying, dividing, and comparing numbers.

Most algorithms are intended to provide an optimal solution for a model. Sometimes, however, problems can prove to be too complex, cumbersome, or time consuming to employ optimization algorithms. In such cases, a **heuristic**—a "rule of thumb" or common-sense procedure—may be employed to yield what the analyst feels may be a good, though not necessarily optimal, solution. Heuristic methods may range from simplistic procedures (such as "produce as much of the most profitable item as possible") to far more complex ones. They are sometimes used to generate a good *starting solution* for a model that is then improved upon by using an optimization algorithm.

Practitioners have emphasized time and time again that the most intuitive and simplest solution techniques are those that have the greatest likelihood of being understood and accepted by the client; hence, they have a higher probability of being implemented and used correctly. As Captain Richard Staats observed during the successful implementation of management science during the Persian Gulf War, "[Complex techniques] have a tendency to break down under the worst possible conditions."[2] Furthermore, complex techniques are usually far more costly.

Based on his vast experience as a management science consultant, Gene Woolsey has made three observations (which he calls *Woolsey's Laws*) that have served as a useful guide to the selection of a solution technique:

1. Managers would rather live with a problem they can't solve than use a technique they don't trust.

2. Managers don't want the best solution; they simply want a better one.

3. If the solution technique will cost you more than you will save, don't use it.

GENERATE MODEL
SOLUTIONS

Once a solution procedure has been selected, the model can finally be solved. Since most models involve manipulations of large amounts of data, the sheer volume and sequencing of these operations require the use of computers. Fortunately, all of the standard management science solution procedures have been programmed either as stand-alone products or as parts of comprehensive integrated management science packages. Current versions of most common spreadsheet programs include built-in optimizers that perform many optimization analyses.

TEST/VALIDATE
MODEL RESULTS

Because mathematical models are nothing more than simplifications of reality, optimal or heuristically generated solutions to a model may not be optimal or even good solutions for the true real-life situation. In fact, they may not even be possible. Thus, testing the model to validate its results is a key component of the solution phase. This

---

[2]Staats, Richard, "Desert Storm! A Re-examination of the Ground War in the Persian Gulf and the Key Role Played by OR," OR/MS *Today*, Vol. 18, No. 6, December, 1991, pp. 42–56.

can be a very time-consuming process. A few questions to ask in evaluating the validity of a model are:

1. Do the results make sense, or are they counterintuitive?
2. Can the solution be integrated successfully under current conditions, or will radical changes be necessary for implementation?
3. Does the solution provide a degree of continuity with present and future plans of the organization?

Both *historical and simulated (hypothetical) data* can be used to test the validity of the model. Each has its benefits and drawbacks.

Historical data can be used to judge directly how the results generated from the model would have performed under actual past conditions. Because the same data may have been used to generate many of the model's parameters, however, caution must be used when validating the model with historical data. Using historical data may tend to overstate the accuracy of the model, yielding biased results. In addition, such data may not reflect current conditions.

Using hypothetical data will yield hypothetical results, which may be hard to verify. If the results generated using hypothetical data defy common sense, however, this is a clear indication that the model needs to be modified. Using hypothetical data also allows for the input of extreme values of the parameters, which may not yet have occurred but for which the true solution may be obvious. Counterintuitive results for these extreme cases can provide another indication that the model may need modification.

Another approach used to validate a model is for the organization to do a pilot program using the model. This is perhaps the best way to get legitimate feedback of how well the model performs in real (and current) situations. There are drawbacks to this approach, however, including the cost of setting up and operating in real time, the learning curve of workers using and interpreting the model results (skewing initial performance results), and the length of time required for the pilot project to begin generating credible results. In many cases, the time period needed to validate the model's reliability may be so long that using a pilot program would not be feasible.

RETURN TO MODELING STEP IF RESULTS ARE UNACCEPTABLE

No model is 100% accurate, and no validation procedure is foolproof. If results of the validation tests prove unsatisfactory, the model should be reexamined. Assumptions should be reevaluated, data rechecked for accuracy, approximations loosened or tightened, and/or new constraints added. In the extreme, the entire model may have to be scrapped and a new one developed.

After any modifications are made, the new model must then be tested. This process of "model–solve–verify" continues until both the analysts and management feel comfortable about the model's ability to yield relatively valid results.

If, after numerous attempts to model the problem, management still lacks confidence in the results, it may conclude that this group should abandon its modeling attempts. Another group of analysts, taking a fresh approach to modeling the problem, may be able to develop a model that is more acceptable to management. Alternatively, management may conclude that a qualitative rather than a quantitative approach will have to suffice.

PERFORM "WHAT-IF" ANALYSES

The computer solution to a model is usually "an answer" for the model. Typically, however, a manager will want a *range* of options from which to choose. A good management science analyst should anticipate management concerns, potential new opportunities, and possible changes and be ready to discuss their impact. Managers are always impressed when many of their "what-if" questions have been anticipated and answered before they are asked.

All spreadsheet users are familiar with playing the what-if game. Similarly, most management science computer packages allow problems to be easily resolved in light of changes to the input data. In addition, many of these packages provide *sensitivity analysis* reports, which give the user valuable information about the effect of changes to the solution as certain parameters change. Based on such information, the management science team may often recommend additional courses of action that may not have occurred to the decision maker.

Solution to the Delta Hardware Model

delta.xls

Let us now consider the solution of the model developed for Delta Hardware Stores.

DELTA HARDWARE STORES PROBLEM—MODEL SOLUTION

Simplifying assumptions and approximations were made in the modeling phase so that the model would have deterministic unit shipping costs, known availabilities of paint at the production plant and from the subcontractor, and known demands by the warehouses. This was done because solution modules for this type of problem are readily available on spreadsheets and comprehensive management science software packages.

The model was solved using the SOLVER module from Excel, and yielded the screen shown in Figure 2.2. The screen shows the number of truckloads to be shipped from Phoenix and the number of thousands of gallons to be sent by the subcontractor to each of the three cities.

FIGURE 2.2   Excel Solution to Delta Hardware Problem

In addition Excel generates an Answer Report and a Sensitivity Report that give pertinent "what-if" information for the problem. Figure 2.3 is the Sensitivity Report. Although this report is discussed in detail in Chapter 3, we point out here that entries in the column labeled "Reduced Cost" indicate the amount that the shipping costs would have to be reduced before it would be cost effective to make a shipment between the corresponding "From-To" pairs. For example, the subcontractor would have to reduce its cost by more than $500 per 1000 gallons ($0.50 per gallon) to an amount less than $5900 per 1000 gallons before it would be economically feasible to ship paint from the subcontractor to Fresno. Similarly, it would have to reduce its cost by more than

Microsoft Excel 5.0c Sensitivity Report
Worksheet:[DELTA.XLS]Sheet1
Report Created: 12/22/98 14:37

Changing Cells

Cell	Name	Final Value	Reduced Cost	Objective Coefficient	Allowable increase	Allowable Decrease
$B$14	PHOENIX PLANT SAN JOSE	1	0	4050	2150	300
$C$14	PHOENIX PLANT FRESNO	2	0	3750	500	1E+30
$D$14	PHOENIX PLANT AZUSA	5	0	3650	300	1E+30
$B$15	SUBCONTRACTOR SAN JOSE	3	0	6200	300	2150
$C$15	SUBCONTRACTOR FRESNO	0	500	6400	1E+30	500
$D$15	SUBCONTRACTOR AZUSA	0	300	6100	1E+30	300

Constraints

Cell	Name	Final Value	Shadow Price	Constraint R.H. Side	Allowable increase	Allowable Decrease
$E$14	PHOENIX PLANT SHIPPED	8	-2150	8	3	1
$E$15	SUBCONTRACTOR SHIPPED	3	0	5	1E+30	2
$B$16	TOTAL SAN JOSE	4	6200	4	2	3
$C$16	TOTAL FRESNO	2	5900	2	1	2
$D$16	TOTAL AZUSA	5	5800	5	1	3

FIGURE 2.3   Sensitivity Report I

$300 per 1000 gallons ($0.30 per gallon) to an amount less than $5800 before it is cost effective to ship paint from the subcontractor to Azusa.

Other what-if information is also provided. The "Allowable Increase" and "Allowable Decrease" columns next to the column labeled "Objective Coefficient" indicate how much the corresponding objective function can change without changing the optimal solution. The column labeled "Shadow Price" shows how much the optimal total cost will change per 1 (thousand gallon) change in the corresponding supplies and demands, respectively. The columns labeled "Allowable Increase" and "Allowable Decrease" next to the "Constraint R. H. Side" column give the maximum change to the right-hand side for which these shadow prices remain valid.

To determine the impact of other cost changes on the optimal solution, we can simply modify the original problem to reflect the new price structure (an easy change in Excel and most other packages) and re-solve the problem.

Various questions should be addressed that are not reflected in the output to the above model. Of particular interest is the effect of Delta's production plant inability to meet the production quantity of 8000 gallons. For instance, suppose that only 7700 rather than 8000 gallons were produced at the Phoenix plant. Would Delta (1) send eight trucks with one only partially loaded? (2) store 700 gallons until the next month, incurring a storage expense? (3) use a common carrier delivery service to ship the 700 gallons in lieu of shipping a partial truckload? or (4) allow warehouse cities to order or receive less than 1000-gallon units? Each of these options leads to a more complicated analysis.

If it is assumed, however, that Delta rigidly adheres to its company policy of shipping only full truckloads of paint from Phoenix and ordering only in units of 1000 from the subcontractor, then, if production at the manufacturing plant is indeed 7700 gallons, only seven full truckloads can be sent from Phoenix. The input to the transportation model can then easily be modified to reflect a change to seven truckloads and re-solved to determine a new optimal solution. Any charges for producing the 700 gallons not shipped, including storage charges, would have to be added to the output from the transportation model to reflect the true overall cost.

The model for Delta Hardware was based on past data. With all of its assumptions and approximations, there is no way to verify the validity of the model results without actually putting them into practice. Thus, the "solution" transmitted to the decision maker, including any what-if analyses of costs and factory production, has to be evaluated for viability by company experts.

2.5 $\mathcal{T}$HE MANAGEMENT SCIENCE PROCESS—STEP 4: COMMUNICATING/MONITORING THE RESULTS

The final step in the management science process is the *post-solution phase*. This phase involves two functions:

The Post-Solution Phase

1. Prepare a business report or presentation
2. Monitor the progress of the implementation

PREPARE A BUSINESS REPORT OR PRESENTATION

Effective communication of the results of a management science study is essential to its success. An analysis is of little use if those who will be making the decisions and implementing the policies do not fully appreciate its value. The decision maker should completely understand the team's approach to the problem, the assumptions and approximations made, and the logic of any recommendations.

Oral presentations (using slides, videos, or presentation software such as PowerPoint) and business memos or reports are the traditional forms of communication. In Section 2.6, we present guidelines for writing effective business reports.

MONITOR THE PROGRESS OF THE IMPLEMENTATION

After a business presentation or report has been submitted, management will be responsible for implementation of the recommendations. These policies may result in changes that might be resisted by members of the firm. The management science team should be ready to stand side by side with management to share responsibility for the procedures required for implementation.

Once the new policies have been implemented, they should be constantly scrutinized. Given the dynamic nature of most business environments, it is almost inevitable that changes to the model will be required over time. The management science team should be prepared to determine when changes to the model are necessary and make such changes swiftly when called upon.

2.6 $\mathcal{W}$RITING BUSINESS REPORTS/MEMOS

GUIDELINES FOR PREPARING BUSINESS REPORTS/ PRESENTATIONS

Whether one is writing a report or preparing a presentation, it is important that the communication be well organized and presented in a clear manner that emphasizes the main recommendations of the study. The following are general guidelines for such presentations.

Be Concise

While not leaving out important details, get to the point. Managers do not like to read lengthy reports or attend lengthy presentations. In general the fewer words needed to make a point the better, and the more the report is appreciated. Do not fill the report with extraneous material. When choosing which what-if analyses to include, make sure the scenarios are plausible and have a reasonable likelihood of occurring.

Use Common, Everyday Language

The terminology and symbols used to represent decision variables and parameters in management science models may be familiar to the analyst, but avoid the use of technical terms and symbols in a report. For example, while the Delta Hardware problem included both the symbol "X1," which was used to represent the number of truckloads of paint shipped from Phoenix to San Jose, and the term "reduced cost," neither should appear in a business report. Know your audience and express the information in terms they can understand.

Whenever possible, let someone else proofread the report carefully for clarity and style. The proofreader should also check the report to ensure that it contains no misspellings and that paragraphs are well constructed and written in complete sentences.

Make Liberal Use of Graphics

The use of properly labeled charts, graphs, and pictures, and the minimization of text, make a report much more readable and appealing to the eye. A business report or presentation is one place where the saying "a picture is worth a thousand words" is actually an underestimation of a picture's worth. Managers prefer visualizing results that allow them to make comparisons easily. No one wants to find results or recommendations buried in lengthy, hard-to-find paragraphs.

The actual presentation of figures is also important. All charts and graphs should be large, and easy to read, and properly labeled, including the conditions under which the graph applies. Common sense should always guide a chart's preparation. For example, tables and graphs should not be split over two or more pages, if at all possible.

STRUCTURE OF A BUSINESS REPORT

Although there is no rigid structure for business reports, the following format has served the authors well in their industrial and consulting experiences.

Components of a Business Presentation

1. Introduction—problem statement
2. Assumptions/approximations made
3. Solution approach/computer program used
4. Results—presentation/analysis
5. What-if analyses
6. Overall recommendation
7. Appendices

Introduction—Problem Statement

The introduction should outline the problem that management and the management science team mutually agreed upon, so that there are no misunderstandings of the results discussed in the presentation. The actual length and style of the introduction will vary, depending on the audience for which the report is intended. Since the recipient is primarily interested in the recommendations, however, the introduction should be just long enough to explain the problem fully.

Assumptions/ Approximations Made

This section could be included either as part of the introduction or as a separate section. Because the recommendations are based on a mathematical model that is an idealization of real life, the decision maker should be aware of any simplifying assumptions or approximations that are made. This allows the decision maker to make an independent judgment as to the model's usefulness.

Solution Approach/ Computer Program Used

This section should be very brief (a sentence or two) and could also be part of a general introduction. In a slide presentation, it would most likely appear on one overhead outlining the procedure used. No details should be presented. A statement indicating that the problem was modeled as a linear program, a transportation model, or a periodic review inventory model may be all that is needed. For an audience not familiar with these terms, a brief one- or two-sentence description of the approach will suffice. Finally, a sentence detailing the computer program used (WINQSB, Excel, etc.) lends credence to the validity of the results.

Results—Presentation/ Analysis

This is the "meat" of the report and should be written concisely and clearly and include graphics. Charts and graphs should not only present the solution, but should also show *how the solution meets the restrictions of the problem*. Try to analyze the implications of the solution as they affect the business and note any unusual or striking conclusions that can be drawn from the results.

What-If Analyses

In this section the management science team demonstrates to the decision makers that they have considered contingencies that might result from changes in the assumptions and parameters of the model. Some information can be obtained from sensitivity reports contained in standard computer output; other results may be generated by resolving the model to account for these changes. Although several possibilities may be analyzed, this section may lose some of its appeal if too many contingencies are considered.

Overall Recommendation

This section differs from the Results section in that it gives the best overall recommendations after considering the what-if contingencies. These recommendations may indeed differ from those of the basic model. These recommendations can be prominently displayed through the use of boxes, color, or some other highlighting device. Again, using charts, tables, and pictures where possible is preferable to presenting results in paragraph form.

Appendices

Material in appendices can be much more technical. An appendix is the place to put supporting computer output or hand calculations, or to detail any approaches used. Depending on the recipients of the report, an appendix may include a complete mathematical model formulation, replete with mathematical symbols and notation.

BUSINESS MEMO FOR DELTA HARDWARE

We can now prepare a business memo for Delta management based on the results from the model developed and solved in Sections 2.3 and 2.4. As with all memos presented in this text, it will be assumed to be prepared by a team of management science consultants known as the Student Consulting Group.

In the following memo, using a few short paragraphs, the problem is clearly laid out, the assumptions are stated, and the approach is given. The results are then presented and the major findings highlighted.

What-if analyses include a statement of the effect of changes in subcontractor pricing (which can be determined directly from the computer output) and a graph showing how the total cost is affected by the production levels of 6000, 7000, 8000, 9000, and 10,000 gallons at the Phoenix plant. An overall recommendation is then presented in an easy-to-read table. Finally, other factors that could substantially affect costs are recommended for future study.

For space reasons, no appendices are given. In addition to the computer printout of the solution and total cost values for the various possible production levels at the Phoenix plant, such appendices might include (1) the complete mathematical model; (2) an analysis of the forecasted production level at Phoenix for the next month; and (3) calculations of the per gallon costs at the Phoenix plant. These appendices would be based on discussions of these topics developed earlier in this chapter.

MEMORANDUM

To: Patricia Winters
Delta Hardware Stores

From: Student Consulting Group

Subj: Shipment Plan for Paint from the Phoenix Plant

Delta Hardware Stores is seeking a shipping policy for paint from its Phoenix plant and an ordering policy of paint from its subcontractor to meet demand at its warehouses in San Jose, Fresno, and Azusa. The objective is to minimize the overall total cost of next month's operations.

The current company policy is to ship only trucks fully loaded with 1000 gallons of paint from the Phoenix plant to the warehouse cities. To obtain the lowest shipping fees and a $5 per gallon price for paint from your subcontractor, Delta's policy requires that shipments from its subcontractor must also be in 1000-gallon batches. You have directed that no more than 5000 gallons of paint be purchased next month from the subcontractor.

Since monthly production at the Phoenix plant has not been constant, production for the upcoming month was forecasted using production data of the past 12 months, excluding the period in which the plant was shut down for machine overhaul. Direct and indirect production and shipping costs attributed to the manufacture and distribution of the paint from the Phoenix plant were supplied by the accounting department.

Using these data, your problem was formulated as a transportation problem and solved using an Excel spreadsheet.

RESULTS

Based on a forecast of an 8000-gallon production level at the Phoenix plant for the coming month and the orders from the warehouse cities, we recommend the shipping pattern shown in Table I.

TABLE I Recommended Shipping Pattern For A Projected Production Capacity of 8000 Gallons

From	To	Gallons	Cost
Phoenix	San Jose	1000	$ 4,050
	Fresno	2000	$ 7,500
	Azusa	5000	$18,250
Subcontractor	San Jose	3000	$18,600
		Total Cost	$48,400

Shipments should be at these levels, unless the subcontractor lowers its ordering/shipping costs by more than $0.50 per gallon to Fresno or by more than $0.30 per gallon to Azusa. Below these values, it would be more cost effective for the subcontractor to send paint to Fresno or Azusa, respectively. As a result, Delta would decrease its shipment of paint from the Phoenix plant to those cities and increase its shipment of paint from Phoenix to San Jose by a similar amount.

Because monthly production levels at the Phoenix plant have varied, we have examined the effects of production levels between 6000 and 10,000 gallons. Figure I depicts the reduction in the total cost with increasing production levels from 6000 to 10,000 gallons at the Phoenix plant. These cost levels are attained as follows:

Achieving Minimum Total Cost

1. Fill the Fresno order from the Phoenix plant.
2. Fill as much of the Azusa order as possible from the Phoenix plant.
3. Use any remaining paint at the Phoenix plant to fill as much of the San Jose order as possible.
4. Meet the outstanding demand at any warehouse through shipments from the subcontractor.

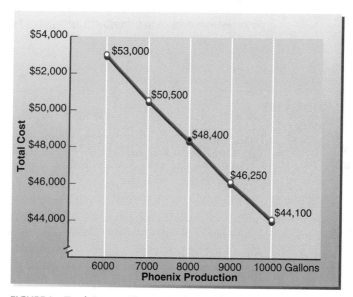

FIGURE I   Total Cost vs. Phoenix Production

RECOMMENDATION

Table II summarizes the recommended shipping patterns for the month based on production levels at the Phoenix plant varying between 6000 and 10,000 gallons.

TABLE II   Recommended Shipping Patterns

Plant Production	Shipments From	San Jose	To Fresno	Azusa
6000	Phoenix plant		2000	4000
	Subcontractor	4000		1000
7000	Phoenix plant		2000	5000
	Subcontractor	4000		
8000	Phoenix plant	1000	2000	5000
	Subcontractor	3000		
9000	Phoenix plant	2000	2000	5000
	Subcontractor	2000		
10,000	Phoenix plant	3000	2000	5000
	Subcontractor	1000		

PROPOSAL FOR ADDITIONAL STUDY

Production levels at the Phoenix plant may not be in 1000-gallon units. If production falls between 1000-gallon units, it may well be more cost effective to ship a large partial shipment and pay increased per gallon fees to the subcontractor than to pay the storage costs necessary to carry an inventory of a few hundred gallons of paint from this month to the next at the Phoenix plant. An analysis of these storage costs, partial truckload shipment costs from the Phoenix plant, and increased per gallon fees by the subcontractor should be conducted.

The Student Consulting Group is available to assist Delta Hardware in obtaining these data and determining optimal policies under these modified conditions.

2.7 Summary

This chapter discussed the management science approach to problem solving for decision making. This approach consists of four steps: (1) problem definition, (2) mathematical modeling, (3) solution of the model, and (4) communication and monitoring of results.

It is essential that both the decision maker and the management science analysts agree on the exact problem to be solved. Once that is done, time, cost, and complexity issues are considered when choosing an appropriate mathematical model. Solutions to management science models should include examinations of appropriate "what-if" analyses. A report or presentation of results should be carefully prepared in a clear and concise format utilizing tables, charts, and graphs to convey model results effectively.

Management science modeling offers the manager the opportunity to develop good solutions to complex problems based on supporting quantitative data. There are both advantages and disadvantages to using the management science approach, some of which are listed in Table 2.4.

TABLE 2.4   ADVANTAGES AND DISADVANTAGES OF USING THE MANAGEMENT SCIENCE APPROACH

Advantages	Disadvantages
1. Helps the decision maker focus on the true goals of the problem	1. Uses idealized models that may be oversimplified
2. Helps deal with a problem in its entirety	2. May not be cost effective
3. Helps sort out data that are relevant to the problem	3. Can be misused by untrained personnel
4. Describes the problem in concise mathematical relationships	4. Requires quantification of all model input
5. Helps reveal cause-and-effect relations in the problem	5. May create models requiring excessive computer resources
6. Can be used to solve complex problems with large amounts of data	6. May create models that are difficult to explain to users
7. Yields an optimal (or at least a good) solution	7. Can yield suspect or unsatisfactory results due to a rapidly changing environment

$\mathscr{P}$ROBLEMS

1. List the four steps in the management science process and give a brief statement about the importance of each step.

2. What is the difference between a parameter and a decision variable in a mathematical model?

3. United Airlines faces not only the situations described in the opening vignette to this chapter, but many other problems as well. Give five examples of optimization models and five examples of prediction models that you feel would be relevant to United Airlines.

4. *Management information systems* (MIS) are used in most industries to evaluate and transform raw data into useful, relevant, and organized information. Such systems make use of large computerized databases. Information provided by an MIS can be used in management science models to help determine optimal strategies and perform what-if analyses.

   Valley Foods is a wholesale food distributor that purchases over 5000 different products from 200 different suppliers. Approximately 100 local retail stores buy their products from Valley Foods. Demand for every item in Valley's inventory varies from month to month, depending on the needs of the customer and the prices Valley is charging for the items.

   Valley's costs include purchase costs from the manufacturer (on large orders it receives a discount), the cost of keeping goods in inventory, and "goodwill" costs should Valley be out of stock when a retail customer demands a product. At times, Valley itself encounters delays in filling its orders due to manufacturer's stockouts.

   a. What are some factors that Valley Foods might wish to consider in achieving its goal of company profit maximization?

   b. What databases and other information systems might be useful in building a profit maximization model for Valley Foods?

5. Ford Motor Company requires thousands of parts to build and assemble cars at its plants. The Villa Park Ford dealership requires parts to service its customers' Ford products. Both are concerned with finding optimal inventory policies.

   Ford Motor Company employs a large staff of personnel who use mathematical models to develop optimal inventory policies, whereas Villa Park Ford relies on the input of one service manager, who uses, at best, crude "mathematical models." Discuss why it is important for Ford Motor Company to employ sophisticated mathematical models to determine its inventory policies (with the associated expense of many high-paying analytical jobs), whereas it would probably not be worthwhile for Villa Park Ford to employ a full-time inventory analyst.

6. Turnercize, Inc. is considering introducing a new line of exercise equipment that you feel may be marketed successfully in a 30-minute infomercial. List some problems that could be evaluated using a management science analysis, which would help Turnercize evaluate the feasibility (and profitability) of such a marketing effort.

7. Crestline Bank would like to minimize its labor costs by hiring as few tellers as possible while still maintaining a stated service level. In particular, it desires the average waiting time for a customer from the time he or she enters a line until the transaction is completed to be at most three minutes. Define:

   T = the number of tellers employed by Crestline Bank
   W(T) = a function giving the average customer waiting time when there are T tellers

   Write a mathematical model for this problem. Is it an optimization or a prediction model?

8. The Dixie Champions tennis tournament will be held in Charlotte, North Carolina, on August 15, and it must be decided whether the event should be scheduled indoors or outdoors. Weather is a factor. For simplicity, assume that on August 15 Charlotte will either (a) be exceedingly hot and muggy, (b) be very pleasant, (c) have mild showers, or (d) have severe rain. Weather will certainly affect attendance (and profits), but much more so if the tournament is held outdoors. The following table relates predicted weather conditions to expected profit:

	Muggy	Pleasant	Showers	Rain
Outdoors	$25,000	$100,000	$30,000	−$25,000
Indoors	$45,000	$ 50,000	$45,000	$35,000

Define:

$$X1 = \text{the number of outdoor tournaments held}$$
$$X2 = \text{the number of indoor tournaments held}$$

a. Write the functional and variable constraints that express the fact that exactly one tournament will be held.

b. Write the objective function and (easily) solve for the optimal solution if the objective is to maximize the minimum expected profit.

9. The Baylor Medical Group is considering hiring an aggressive collection agency to assist in collecting on past due accounts. Its decision will depend on the number of accounts it anticipates will be past due by more than 90 days. The group has forecasted that if it does not hire the agency, 60% of the accounts will be paid within 30 days. It projects that 50% of those accounts more than 30 days past due will be paid off within 60 days; 70% of accounts more than 60 days past due will be paid off within 90 days; and only 20% of those accounts more than 90 days past due will be paid off in the next 30 days. Baylor anticipates that, on the average, it will have about 1000 outstanding accounts. Define:

$$A = \text{average number of accounts with less than 30-day balances}$$
$$B = \text{average number of accounts with balances between 30 and 60 days}$$
$$C = \text{average number of accounts with balances between 60 and 90 days}$$
$$D = \text{average number of delinquent accounts (over 90 days)}$$

Baylor would like to know the average number of delinquent accounts (those past due by more than 90 days) if it does not hire the collection agency.

a. Is this an optimization or a prediction model?

b. What is the objective?

c. Briefly describe what the constraints represent.

10. Flores File Company makes inexpensive, grey two-drawer, three-drawer, and four-drawer filing cabinets. It estimates that it makes a net profit of $4 for each two-drawer model, $6 for each three-drawer model, and $10 for each four-drawer model produced.

a. Write a mathematical expression for the objective of maximizing total net profit.

b. The filing cabinets are made from ⅜"-thick sheet metal. Each two-drawer cabinet requires 40 square feet of sheet metal; each three-drawer cabinet requires 55 square feet; and each four-drawer requires 70 square feet. For the current production run, Flores has 25,000 square feet of ⅜" sheet metal available. Write a constraint that states the following: "The number of square feet of sheet metal used cannot exceed the amount of sheet metal available."

11. The Institute for Operations Research and Management Science (INFORMS) has contracted with Sentinel Security to provide security service for its upcoming three-day, four-night national meeting in New York at a cost of $B.

During the meeting hours from 8:00 A.M. to 6:00 P.M., Sentinel will pay its security guards $D per hour. In the evening and night, security guards will be paid a lesser amount of $E per hour. INFORMS requires that at least N guards be on duty during the evening. During the day there should be at least two guards as well as one additional guard for every 1000 people attending the meeting. In addition to paying for its guards, Sentinel Security expects to have fixed expenses of $F (for equipment, communications, etc.) during the meeting.

Net profit to the firm is attained by subtracting its payments to its guards plus the fixed expenses from the contracted amount negotiated with INFORMS.

a. Formulate a model shell for this simplified problem whose objective is to maximize the net profit to Sentinel Security for supplying security service for T attendees to the national meeting in New York using the following decision variables:

$$X1 = \text{number of guards needed each day}$$
$$X2 = \text{number of guards needed each night}$$

b. Explain why this problem of maximizing net profit is equivalent to minimizing the variable cost of payments to its security guards.

c. INFORMS expects 2000 attendees, and it wishes to have at least two guards on duty each night. If the contracted price from INFORMS is $10,000, fixed costs are expected to be $1000, and Sentinal pays its guards $15 per hour for day security and $12 per hour for night security, develop a complete mathematical model for security at the INFORMS meeting.

d. Suppose attendance is expected to be 2200. Now what would be the model? (Did you forget to include in your constraints that the number of guards must be an integer?)

12. There are many ways to define decision variables in a mathematical model. For a model formulated with one set of decision variables to be equivalent to another model of the same problem formulated using a different set of decision variables, some or all of the coefficients of the model will have to be different. Consider the problem faced by Shari Winslow.

Shari has $4000 which she wants to put into a Keogh account before April 15. Doing so will save Shari over $1600 in federal and state taxes.

Shari is not an experienced investor, but she knows that she wants to invest in stocks rather than bonds or mutual funds. She has heard that financial expert, Craig Jaynes, has predicted large increases in the following stocks during the coming year:

- Shares of Topeka Electronics should rise to $50.
- Crosswind should experience a 20% rise in the value of its stock.
- Genserve should match the peak price of $75 it achieved during the past year.

The current share prices for Topeka Electronics, Crosswind, and Genserve are $42, $30, and $64, respectively. Shari has decided to invest in one or more of these companies for a year and then reevaluate her Keough investments. While her goal is to maximize the projected return over the coming year, she has decided to be somewhat conservative and invest at least $800 in Crosswind and at least $1000 in a one-year savings certificate of deposit paying 5%. She wants to invest no more than $2000 in either Topeka Electronics or Genserve.

a. Formulate this problem as a mathematical model using decision variables $X1$, $X2$, and $X3$ to represent the dollar investment in Topeka Electronics, Crosswind, and Genserve, respectively, and $X4$ to represent the amount invested in the savings certificate.

b. Formulate this problem as a mathematical model using decision variables $Y1$, $Y2$, and $Y3$, representing the number of shares of stock purchased in Topeka Electronics, Crosswind, and Genserve, respectively, with $X4$ still representing the amount invested in the savings certificate.

c. Suppose both the models in (a) and (b) were solved. How should the results compare?

13. Sometimes different managers or executives approach the same data with different objectives. Circuit Guys is a retail computer store that displays the latest computers from COMPAQ and IBM. The store averages a profit of $200 on every COMPAQ system sold and $300 on every IBM system sold. For each COMPAQ system displayed, the estimated probability that Circuit Guys will sell the system on a particular day is .02. Each IBM system displayed has an estimated probability of .01 of sale on that day.

a. One manager at Circuit Guys suggests that, since this is a new store, it should maximize the total number of units on display. Write the expression that models this objective.

b. Another manager feels that the way to impress corporate headquarters is to show a large number of sales at the new store. Write the expression that models this objective.

c. Still another manager maintains that the bottom line is what is important. He feels that, in the long run, maximizing expected profit is what the stockholders want. Write the expression that models this objective.

14. The following is a partial printout from WINQSB, the software accompanying this text on the CD-ROM. It was generated by making certain assumptions about the probability

System Performance Summary for Burger Haven

10-01-1995 11:08:56	Performance Measure	Result
1	System:M/M/5	From Formula
2	Customer arrival rate (lambda) per hour=	120.0000
3	Service rate per server (mu) per hour=	30.0000
4	Overall system effective arrival rate per hour=	120.0000
5	Overall system effective service rate per hour=	120.0000
6	Overall system utilization=	80.0000%
7	Average number of customers in the system (L)=	6.2165
8	Average number of customers in the queue (Lq)=	2.2165
9	Average number of customers in the queue for a busy system (Lb)=	4.0000
10	Average time customer spends in the system (W)=	0.0518 hours
11	Average time customer spends in the queue (Wq)=	0.0185 hours
12	Average time customer spends in the queue for a busy system (Lb)=	0.0333 hours
13	The probability that all servers are idle (Po)=	1.2987%
14	The probability an arriving customer waits (Pw or Pb)=	55.4113%
15	Average number of customers being balked per hour=	0
16	Total cost of busy server per hour=	$0
17	Total cost of idle server per hour=	$0
18	Total cost of customer waiting per hour=	$0
19	Total cost of customer being served per hour=	$0
20	Total cost of customer being balked per hour=	$0
21	Total queue space cost per hour=	$0
22	Total system cost per hour=	$0

System Performance Summary for Burger Haven

distribution of the time between customer arrivals and the service time distribution at Burger Haven Restaurant during lunch hours. The results are based on an estimated average arrival rate of customers during those hours of two per minute and an average service time of two minutes at each of five checkout stands. Management at Burger Haven is interested in the average number of customers in the system (L), the average number of customers in the queue (Lq), the average time each customer spends in the system (W), and the average time each customer spends in the queue (Wq). The difference between "system" and "queue" results is that "queue" results do not include the service operation.

a. Consider a fast-food establishment you have visited. Do these results seem acceptable?

b. List some what-if analyses a management scientist might perform to better inform management of its options.

15. The law of supply and demand states that if supply is limited and demand for a product is high, one should be able to charge a higher price for the product. Such was the case when the Mazda Miata sports car first was introduced. The base price (the sticker price) was about $13,000. Mazda shipped the first few to the United States to build up interest in the car while larger quantities were being produced.

Because Mazda initially shipped so few Miatas to the dealers and customer demand was high, many dealers added a surcharge of up to $7000 to the sticker price. Many considered this action "gouging," while others simply called it "sound business practice."

Suppose a management scientist has been able to forecast that if Springfield Motors charged $X (where X is in thousands of dollars) it could sell 54 − 2X Miatas in a month. Since each Miata costs Springfield Motors $11 (thousand), it will certainly not sell Miatas for less than $11,000. Mazda has informed Springfield Motors that if it sells Miatas for more than $21 (thousand), it will not ship it any Miatas.

a. Write a model for Springfield Motors' monthly revenue if it sells Miatas for $X (thousand). Remember: revenue equals selling price times the number of Miatas sold in a month. Note that this is a nonlinear function (i.e., it has a term with X raised to a power other than 1).

b. Write an optimization model for Springfield Motors monthly profit from selling Miatas subject to the limitations on price. Recall that Profit = Revenue − Cost.

c. Using differential calculus, find the price X that maximizes the objective function in (b). Show that this price falls within the limits of the constraints. How many Miatas should Springfield Motors expect to sell each month at this price? What would be the monthly profit of this policy to Springfield Motors?

16. Lawn fertilizer is rated according to three levels: nitrogen, phosphorus, and potassium. The nitrogen content affects the greening; the phosphorus affects the sturdiness of the root structure; and the potassium affects the disease-fighting capabilities of the fertilizer. For example, the rating of one Scotts Turf Builder product is 27–3–4 meaning that it consists of 27% nitrogen, 3% phosphorus, and 4% potassium.

Beauty Grow plans to market two lawn-fertilizing products, which it will call Beauty Green and Beauty Turf. It plans to sell a 20-pound bag of Beauty Green for $G and a 20-pound bag of Beauty Turf for $T. Lawn fertilizer is a mixture of many different compounds, but, for simplicity, let us suppose that it is a mixture of three, each of which has various amounts of nitrogen, phosphorus, and potassium. They sell for $C1, $C2, and $C3 *per pound*, respectively.

During a production run, limited amounts of each of the three compounds are available (L1, L2, and L3, respectively), and demand for bags of each of the two lawn fertilizers (D1 and D2) is limited.

a. What are the uncontrollable inputs (i.e., the parameters) for this problem?

b. The controllable inputs (i.e., the decision variables) for this problem are the total amount (pounds) of each of the three compounds that are to be mixed into bags of Beauty Green and the total number of pounds of each of the three compounds that are to be mixed into bags of Beauty Turf. Develop a notation and define the six decision variables for this problem. Be sure to include the units for your decision variables. (This is very important!)

17. Consider the Beauty Grow Fertilizer production problem above.

a. Use an appropriate sum of the decision variables to write model shells for the total number of: (i) pounds of Compound 1 used; (ii) pounds of Compound 2 used, and (iii) pounds of Compound 3 used.

b. Write model shells for: (i) bags of Beauty Green produced; and (ii) bags of Beauty Turf produced.

c. Using your answers to parts (a) and (b), write a model shell expressing the constraints on the amount of each compound used and the number of bags of each fertilizer produced.

d. Write a model shell for the profit function.

18. For the Beauty Grow Fertilizer production problem (Problem 16), the following table represents the percentage of nitrogen, phosphorus, and potassium in each of the three compounds:

	Nitrogen	Phosphorus	Potassium
Compound 1	N1%	P1%	K1%
Compound 2	N2%	P2%	K2%
Compound 3	N3%	P3%	K3%

Beauty Green is to be labeled 25–5–5 while Beauty Turf is to be labeled 10–18–5. These values are the minimum percentages of nitrogen, phosphorus, and potassium, respectively, that must be in each bag.

a. Write a model shell that states that the minimum percentage of nitrogen in Beauty Green is 25%. Do this by expressing the actual percentage of nitrogen as a weighted average of the percentage of nitrogen in each compound. It will take the following form:

(Proportion of Compound 1 in Beauty Green) (N1)
+ (Proportion of Compound 2 in Beauty Green) (N2)
+ (Proportion of Compound 3 in Beauty Green) (N3)
$$\geq 25$$

b. Write a model shell stating that the minimum percentage of nitrogen in Beauty Turf is 10%. Do this by expressing the actual percentage of nitrogen as a weighted average of the percentage of nitrogen in each compound. It will take the following form:

(Proportion of Compound 1 in Beauty Turf) (N1)
+ (Proportion of Compound 2 in Beauty Turf) (N2)
+ (Proportion of Compound 3 in Beauty Turf) (N3)
$$\geq 10$$

c. Constraints for the percentages of phosphorus and potassium in Beauty Green and Beauty Turf have the same form as those in (a) and (b). Develop a complete mathematical model for Beauty Grow Fertilizer using the following values of the parameters:

Selling price of a bag of Beauty Green:	$4.00
Selling price of a bag of Beauty Turf:	$3.50
Cost per pound of Compound 1:	$0.15
Cost per pound of Compound 2:	$0.12
Cost per pound of Compound 3:	$0.10
Demand (bags) of Beauty Green:	1000
Demand (bags) of Beauty Turf:	800
Availability (pounds) of Compound 1:	15,000
Availability (pounds) of Compound 2:	20,000
Availability (pounds) of Compound 3:	30,000

	Nitrogen	Phosphorus	Potassium
Compound 1	30%	20%	10%
Compound 2	10%	30%	10%
Compound 3	40%	10%	0%

CASE STUDY

CASE 1: *Gunther's Appliance Corporation*

Gunther's Appliance Corporation is a small manufacturer that produces toasters, microwave ovens, mixers, blenders, food processors, and steamers. A mathematical model was developed to determine the optimal production quantities for the month of July in order to maximize the company's total daily profit. Twenty constraints were included in the model, as outlined below:

Constraints	Relation
1	≤ 48 hours of production time are available.
2–6	Limits must be placed on five materials used in production.
7–8	Between 5% and 25% of production must be toasters.
9–10	Between 5% and 25% of production must be microwaves.
11–12	Between 5% and 25% of production must be mixers.
13–14	Between 5% and 25% of production must be blenders.
15–16	Between 5% and 25% of production must be food processors.
17–18	Between 5% and 25% of production must be steamers.
19	At least 50% of production must be toasters, mixers, and blenders.
20	At most 150 total items are to be produced daily.

The accompanying table shows the output generated by a management science package. The section labeled "Variables" provides the recommended production quantities

GUNTHER'S APPLIANCE CORPORATION

OBJECTIVE FUNCTION VALUE (MAXIMIZED): 1134.421

VARIABLES

NAME	VALUE	REDUCED COST	OBJ. COEF.	MIN VALUE	MAX VALUE
TOASTERS	35.579	0.000	3.000	2.650	4.000
OVENS	16.872	0.000	20.000	3.462	21.391
MIXERS	7.500	0.000	2.000	−5.256	3.220
BLENDERS	37.500	0.000	4.000	3.220	INFINITY
FOOD PROCESSORS	37.500	0.000	12.000	10.549	INFINITY
STEAMERS	15.049	0.000	5.000	4.063	6.111

CONSTRAINTS

NUMBER	SHADOW PRICE	SLACK	SIGN	RHS	MIN VALUE	MAX VALUE
1	20.976	0.000	<	48.000	46.031	53.719
2	0.000	2310.531	<	2800.000	489.469	INFINITY
3	0.037	0.000	<	2100.000	1947.500	2152.500
4	0.000	608.104	<	1000.000	391.896	INFINITY
5	0.000	1570.470	<	2000.000	429.531	INFINITY
6	0.000	1392.015	<	1600.000	207.985	INFINITY
7	0.000	28.079	>	0.000	−INFINITY	28.079
8	0.000	1.921	<	0.000	−1.921	INFINITY
9	0.000	9.372	>	0.000	−INFINITY	9.372
10	0.000	20.628	<	0.000	−20.628	INFINITY
11	1.220	0.000	>	0.000	−2.461	30.000
12	0.000	30.000	<	0.000	−30.000	INFINITY
13	0.000	30.000	>	0.000	−INFINITY	30.000
14	0.780	0.000	<	0.000	−2.461	32.240
15	0.000	30.000	>	0.000	−INFINITY	30.000
16	6.573	0.000	<	0.000	−3.351	9.734
17	0.000	7.549	>	0.000	−INFINITY	7.549
18	0.000	22.451	<	0.000	−22.451	INFINITY
19	0.000	11.159	>	0.000	−INFINITY	11.159
20	0.363	0.000	<	150.000	143.336	152.440

(and their objective function coefficients), whereas the section labeled "Constraints" provides information about how the constraints were satisfied. While a complete discussion of all the columns is presented in Chapter 3, the following is a brief explanation.

1. The optimal solution will remain the same if an objective function coefficient is changed to a value within the limits given in the columns labeled "MIN VALUE" and "MAX VALUE" in the VARIABLES section.

2. The column labeled "SLACK" in the CONSTRAINTS section shows how much of the right-hand side of a "≤" constraint is unused and how much of the right-hand side of a "≥" is exceeded by the proposed solution.

3. The column labeled "SHADOW PRICE" gives the net change to the profit per unit increase in the right-hand side coefficient of a constraint within the limits given in the columns labeled "MIN VALUE" and "MAX VALUE" in the CONSTRAINTS section.

Based on the output, write a brief memorandum to communicate relevant information that would be of interest to a potential decision maker at Gunther's. In your report, use appropriate charts, graphs, or tables to convey:

1. Your recommendation for daily production during July
2. How the constraints would be satisfied

LINEAR PROGRAMMING

Carol Haines is a manager at Steelcase, Inc., a leading manufacturer of office furniture, such as desks, tables, file cabinets, and credenzas. She and her staff are responsible for establishing periodic production schedules. To determine these schedules, they must take into account actual current and future projected orders, current inventory of finished goods and raw materials, availability of labor and machine time, storage capacities of its distributions system, and other factors. They must also consider the amount of money the company can borrow from its primary lending institution, the number of additional workers or layoffs that will be necessary, and the additional units of raw materials that must be purchased.

The production schedules are designed to meet some predetermined company objective. Usually, Steelcase's objective is to maximize projected long-term profit, but, occasionally, under various economic climates, its objective shifts to maximizing shorter-term (monthly or quarterly) profits, minimizing the time required to meet its largest order, minimizing the number of layoffs necessary to meet an acceptable profit (or loss) level, or some other criterion.

Carol's group is instrumental to Steelcase's profitability. The company's success depends on the group's ability to develop *programs* (or courses of action) that best meet the company's current stated objective. To do this the staff continuously monitors: (1) the factors that can be controlled in the production process; (2) Steelcase's current primary objective; and (3) the restrictions or constraints that may make it difficult to meet this objective.

Carol Haines and her staff use *linear programming* to model and solve such constrained optimization problems. Linear programming allows them to develop optimal production schedules and assess the effects of changing objectives, costs, revenues, and resource availabilities in a dynamic environment.

3.1 *I*NTRODUCTION TO LINEAR PROGRAMMING

Mathematical programming is the branch of management science that deals with solving optimization problems, in which we want to maximize a function (such as profit, expected return, or efficiency) or minimize a function (such as cost, time, or distance), usually in a constrained environment. The recommended course of action is known as a *program*; hence, the term *mathematical programming* is used to describe such problems.

As discussed in Chapter 2, a constrained mathematical programming model consists of three components: (1) a set of *decision variables* that can be controlled or determined by the decision maker; (2) an *objective function* that is to be maximized or minimized; and (3) a set of *constraints* that describe the restrictive set of conditions that must be satisfied by any solution to the model. The most widely used mathematical programming models are **linear programming models**:

Linear Programming Models

A **linear programming model** is a model that seeks to maximize or minimize a *linear* objective function subject to a set of *linear* constraints.

That's a mouthful! But all this means is that the objective function and constraints contain only mathematical terms involving variables that are raised to the first power (e.g., $5X_1$, $-2X_2$, or $0X_3$). Models with terms such as X_1^2, $(X_1)*(X_2)$, X_1/X_2, e^{X_2}, and $\sqrt{X_1}$ are classified as *nonlinear programming models*.

Linear programming models are important for three reasons.

Why Linear Programs Are Important

1. Many problems naturally lend themselves to a linear programming formulation, and many others can be closely approximated by models with this structure.

2. Efficient solution techniques exist for solving problems of this type.

3. The output generated by linear programming packages provides useful "what-if" information concerning the sensitivity of the solution to changes in the model's coefficients.

As a result, linear programming techniques have been applied successfully to many resource allocation problems in such diverse areas as manufacturing, finance, advertising, worker training, construction, oil refining, transportation, agriculture, military operations, and waste control, to name just a few. Several of these applications are illustrated through examples and end-of-chapter exercises in this and the ensuing chapters.

3.2 *A* LINEAR PROGRAMMING MODEL—A PROTOTYPE EXAMPLE

In this section we illustrate the procedure used to construct linear programming models by considering the situation faced by Galaxy Industries. Although this prototype model requires only two decision variables, it will be used to develop the concepts that hold true for linear programming models with any number of decision variables.

GALAXY INDUSTRIES

Galaxy.lpp
Galaxy.xls
Galaxy.ltx (Lindo)

Galaxy Industries is an emerging toy manufacturing company that produces two "space age" water guns that are marketed nationwide, primarily to discount toy stores. Although many parents object to the potentially violent implications of these products, the products have proven very popular and are in such demand that Galaxy has had no problem selling all the items it manufactures.

The two models, the Space Ray and the Zapper, are produced in lots of one-dozen each and are made exclusively from a special plastic compound. Two of the limiting resources are the 1200 pounds of the special plastic compound and the 40 hours of production time that are available each week.

Galaxy's marketing department is more concerned with building a strong customer demand base for the fledgling company's products than with meeting high production quotas. Two of its recommendations, which Galaxy's management has already accepted, are to limit total weekly production to at most 800 dozen units and to prevent weekly production of Space Rays from exceeding that of Zappers by more then 450 dozen. Table 3.1 summarizes the per dozen resource requirements and profit values (calculated by subtracting variable production costs from their wholesale selling prices).

Galaxy has reasoned that since the $8 profit per dozen Space Rays exceeds the $5 profit per dozen Zappers by 60%, the company could maximize its profit by producing as many Space Rays as possible, while remaining within the marketing guidelines, and using any remaining resources to produce Zappers. As a result, Galaxy has been producing 550 dozen Space Rays and 100 dozen Zappers weekly, earning a weekly profit of $4900. Management is interested in determining whether a different production schedule could improve company profits.

TABLE 3.1   GALAXY'S RESOURCE REQUIREMENTS AND PROFIT VALUES

Product	Profit per Dozen	Plastic (lb.) per Dozen	Production Time (min.) per Dozen
Space Ray	$8	2	3
Zapper	$5	1	4

SOLUTION

FORMULATION OF THE GALAXY INDUSTRIES MODEL

Recall that a mathematical model consists of three parts:

1. A well-defined set of decision variables
2. An overall objective to be maximized or minimized
3. A set of constraints

A helpful starting point for determining each of these components is to briefly summarize the details of the problem statement.

From the problem statement for Galaxy Industries we can make a number of observations:

- Production is to be in terms of dozens and scheduled on a weekly basis.
- The overall objective is to maximize weekly profit.
- Production must be scheduled so that the weekly supply of plastic and the availability of production time are not exceeded.

- The two marketing department guidelines concerning maximum total production and the product mix must be met.

Using this brief overview, we can now construct a mathematical model which management at Galaxy Industries can use to determine the most profitable product mix.

Decision Variables

The decision maker can control the production levels of Space Rays and Zappers. Noting that the production units are in terms of *dozens* and production is done on a *weekly* basis, we observe that the appropriate decision variables are:

$$X1 = \text{number of dozen Space Rays produced weekly}$$
$$X2 = \text{number of dozen Zappers produced weekly}$$

Objective Function

The objective of maximizing total weekly profit is obtained by summing the weekly profits of each of the two types of items produced. For each product the weekly profit is:

(Profit per Dozen Units Produced) $\times$ (Number of Dozen Units Produced Weekly)

Thus, the objective is to:

$$\text{MAXIMIZE } 8X1 + 5X2$$

Constraints

In addition to the nonnegativity constraints for the decision variables, there are four functional constraints:

1. The use of plastic
2. The weekly limit for production time
3. The maximum production limit of total units
4. The mix of Space Rays and Zappers

Our approach to formulating these constraints is first to express, in words, a restriction of the form:

(Some quantity) ⟨has some relation to⟩ (Another quantity)

We can then substitute mathematical functions or constants for the appropriate "quantities." Finally, if necessary, we can rewrite the expression so that all terms involving the decision variables are on the left side of the constraint and any constant term is on the right side.

Plastic

(The total amount of plastic used weekly) cannot exceed
(The amount of plastic available weekly)

Since each dozen Space Rays requires two pounds of plastic and each dozen Zappers requires one pound, the total amount of plastic used in a week is $2X1 + 1X2$. Because this amount cannot exceed the limit of 1200 pounds weekly, the constraint is:

$$2X1 + 1X2 \leq 1200$$

Production Time

(The amount of production minutes used weekly) cannot exceed
(The total number of production minutes available weekly)

Because each dozen Space Rays requires three minutes of labor and each dozen Zappers requires four minutes of labor, the total number of labor minutes used weekly is

$3X1 + 4X2$. This number cannot exceed the number of labor *minutes* available weekly. Since 40 *hours* are available, the number of available minutes is $(40)(60) = 2400$. Thus, the production time constraint is:

$$3X1 + 4X2 \le 2400$$

Total Production Limit

(The total number of dozen units produced weekly) cannot exceed
(The marketing limit)

The total number of dozens of units produced is simply the sum of the number of dozen Space Rays produced and the number of dozen Zappers produced. Since this is not to exceed 800 dozen, the constraint is:

$$X1 + X2 \le 800$$

Balanced Product Mix

(The number of dozen Space Rays produced weekly) cannot exceed
(The number of dozen Zappers) plus 450

The number of dozen Space Rays produced weekly is X1, and the number of dozen Zappers produced weekly is X2. So the appropriate constraint is:

$$X1 \le X2 + 450$$

Rewriting the equation so that X2 is on the left side yields:

$$X1 - X2 \le 450$$

Nonnegativity of Decision Variables
Negative production of Space Rays and Zappers is impossible. Thus,

$$X1, X2 \ge 0$$

The Mathematical Model   The complete mathematical model for Galaxy Industries is:

$$
\begin{array}{llll}
\text{MAX} & 8X1 + 5X2 & & \text{(Weekly profit)} \\
\text{ST} & & & \\
& 2X1 + 1X2 \le 1200 & & \text{(Plastic)} \\
& 3X1 + 4X2 \le 2400 & & \text{(Production time)} \\
& X1 + X2 \le 800 & & \text{(Total production)} \\
& X1 - X2 \le 450 & & \text{(Mix)} \\
& Xj \ge 0, j = 1,2 & & \text{(Nonnegativity)}
\end{array}
$$

This model is expressed using the standard mathematical programming abbreviations "MAX" for "Maximize" and "ST" for "subject to" or "such that" and grouping together all the nonnegativity constraints at the end of the model.

3.3   LIMITING ASSUMPTIONS OF LINEAR PROGRAMMING MODELS

Because linear models are solved so efficiently, linear programming formulations have proven quite valuable for solving numerous problems in business and government. As with all mathematical models, however, certain inherent assumptions must be made in order to use the linear programming approach. The modeler must be keenly aware of the impact of these assumptions on the real-life situation being modeled; if the assumptions are deemed unacceptable, the model must be modified or another model developed. Linear programming models are based on four assumptions.

Linear Programming Assumptions
1. The decision variables are *continuous*.
2. The parameters are known with *certainty*.
3. The objective function and constraints exhibit *constant returns to scale*.
4. There are *no interactions* between the decision variables.

CONTINUITY

FIGURE 3.1 Continuity

The **continuity assumption** (Figure 3.1) implies that decision variables can take on *any* value within the limits of the functional constraints. For example, in the linear programming model developed for Galaxy Industries, 14, 6.7, $\sqrt{20}$, π, and so on, are all permissible values.

In particular, X1 is *not* restricted to integer values or to any other subset of values in that range (such as 8, 16, 24, and 32). If any decision variable is restricted to integers, the model is an *integer programming model* rather than a linear programming model. For most production problems, an integer solution is not required, as any fractional values can simply be considered work in progress that will be completed during the next production period.

CERTAINTY

FIGURE 3.2 Certainty

The **certainty assumption** (Figure 3.2) asserts that all parameters of the problem are fixed, known constants. For example, the profit per dozen Space Rays is assumed to be *exactly* $8. This does *not* mean that this value follows a probability distribution with an average value of $8 and a standard deviation of $2 or that the profit is usually $8, but it may sometimes be a little more or a little less.

Although the certainty assumption is crucial for solving a linear model, the "optimal solution" to a linear program may be valid within a certain range of parameter values. Hence, in some cases, a parameter whose value may indeed follow a probability distribution or whose exact value is not known precisely can still be approximated successfully by assuming it is constant.

CONSTANT RETURNS
TO SCALE
(PROPORTIONALITY)

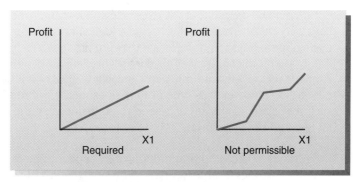

FIGURE 3.3   Constant Returns to Scale

In the Galaxy Industries example, each dozen Space Rays contributes $8 to profit. The *proportionality assumption* implies that if *two* dozen are produced, the profit will be $16, and if 100 dozen are produced, the profit will be $800. Similarly, since each dozen Space Rays requires two pounds of specially treated plastic, if *two* dozen are produced, four pounds of plastic will be used, and if 100 dozen are produced, 200 pounds will be used. There is no "learning curve" or different unit values for larger quantities.

The **constant returns to scale assumption** (Figure 3.3) is frequently violated in practice. For example, a good deal of time and expense might go into setting up a production run of Space Rays. Thus, if only one dozen Space Rays are produced, the unit production cost could be quite high. As more and more are made, however, production costs per unit tend to stabilize, yielding a relatively higher fixed unit profit. Conversely, if too many Space Rays are produced, from a supply and demand perspective, the selling price of Space Rays may have to be reduced, resulting in a decrease in its unit profit. When using a linear model, we must assume that the constant returns to scale assumption is reasonable within the range of possible values for the decision variables.

NO INTERACTIONS
(ADDITIVITY)

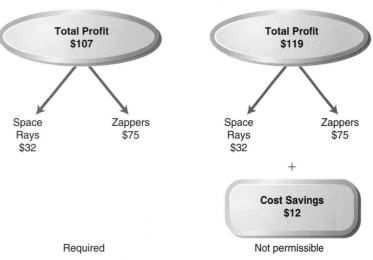

FIGURE 3.4   Additivity (No Interactions)

The **additivity assumption** (Figure 3.4) implies that the total value of some function can be found by simply adding the linear terms. In the model for Galaxy Industries, if the company produces X1 dozen Space Rays and X2 dozen Zappers, the total profit is the sum of the terms $8X1 + $5X2.

It could be argued that the expertise and materials required to produce both Space Rays and Zappers are similar. Thus, a logical conclusion is that the unit cost of producing Space Rays might be less if they are produced in conjunction with Zappers than if they are produced alone. This cost savings would depend on the production level of Zappers; that is, an "intermix term" involving X1X2 might be introduced. As we pointed out earlier, however, this type of term is expressly forbidden in linear programming. If such terms are significant and need to be included in the model, then linear programming is not the appropriate solution procedure.

Although these four assumptions may appear to be restrictive, they frequently provide "close enough" approximations for many practical situations.

3.4 THE SET OF FEASIBLE SOLUTIONS FOR LINEAR PROGRAMS

Exactly what production combinations of Space Rays and Zappers are possible for Galaxy Industries? And, of these possible production values, which one maximizes the objective function? A graphical representation of the model will help answer both questions.

To determine the set of possible production combinations, we graph one constraint and determine all the points that satisfy that constraint. Then we add a second constraint. Some points that satisfy this second constraint also satisfy the first; others do not, and we eliminate them from consideration. We repeat this process until all the constraints, including the nonnegativity constraints, have been considered.

Let us, in fact, begin with the nonnegativity constraints. Because both variables must be nonnegative, we consider points in the first quadrant. This is illustrated in Figure 3.5a. Next, we graph the plastic constraint: $2X1 + 1X2 \leq 1200$[1]. The shaded region in Figure 3.5b shows all the points satisfying the nonnegativity constraints and the plastic constraint.

Repeating this process for the production time constraint, $3X1 + 4X2 \leq 2400$, yields Figure 3.5c. The shaded region now contains all the points satisfying the nonnegativity constraints, the plastic constraint, and the production time constraint. Note that some of the points that satisfied only the plastic constraint and the nonnegativity constraints have been eliminated.

Figure 3.5d illustrates what happens when we add the constraint on total production, $X1 + X2 \leq 800$. As you can see, adding this constraint does not eliminate any additional points from consideration. Constraints with this characteristic are called redundant constraints.

Figure 3.6 shows the completed graph for this problem, which is formed by adding the mix constraint, $X1 - X2 \leq 450$, to the previously graphed constraints.[2] The shaded region of Figure 3.6, which consists of all the "possible" or "feasible" points satisfying all of the model's functional and variable constraints, is known as the **feasible region**.

---

[1] In cases in which both the coefficients of X1 and X2 are positive, first set X1 = 0 and solve for X2 (in this case X2 = 1200), yielding one point on the line. Then set X2 = 0 and solve for X1 (in this case X1 = 600). We can now draw 2X1 + X2 = 1200 by connecting these two points. The "<" part consists of all points below the line.

[2] The line X1 − X2 = 450 is generated differently since the coefficient of X2 is negative. One point (450,0) is determined as usual by setting X2 to zero and solving for X1. To find a second point on the line that is in the first quadrant, we set X1 to any number greater than 450 (say 850) and solve for X2. This yields X2 = 400. Connecting the point (450,0) with the point (850,400) gives the required line segment. Note that the point (0,0) is on the "<" side of the line. Hence, values to the left of the line represent the points giving X1 − X2 < 450.

FIGURE 3.5*a*   Nonnegativity Constraint

FIGURE 3.5*b*   Plastic Constraint

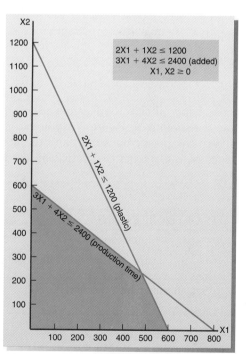

FIGURE 3.5*c*   Production Time Constraint

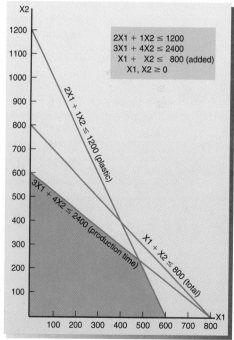

FIGURE 3.5*d*   Total Production Constraint

FIGURE 3.6 Mix Constraint

FIGURE 3.7 Interior, Boundary, Extreme. and Infeasible Points

---

Feasible Region

The set of all points that satisfy all the constraints of the model is called the **feasible region**.

INFEASIBLE AND FEASIBLE POINTS

Infeasible points—those lying outside the feasible region—violate one or more of the function or variable constraints. In Figure 3.7, you can see that the infeasible point (650,100) violates both the plastic constraint and the mix constraint. Figure 3.7 also illustrates three types of *feasible points* that satisfy all the constraints of the model, as defined in Table 3.2.

TABLE 3.2   TYPES OF FEASIBLE POINTS

Point	Characteristic	Example(s)
Interior point	Satisfies all constraints, but none with equality	(200,200)
Boundary point	Satisfies all constraints, at least one with equality	(100,525), (200,0)
Extreme point	Satisfies all constraints, two with equality	(0,0), (450,0), (480,240), (550,100) (0,600)

The characterization of these points is quite important. As we will show in the next section, an optimal solution to a linear programming model *must* occur at an extreme point, *may* occur at a boundary point, but can *never* occur at an interior point.

EXTREME POINTS

Because extreme points play a crucial role in determining the optimal solution to linear programming models, we should discuss them in a little more detail. Extreme points are the "corner points" of the feasible region, occurring at the intersection of two of the boundary constraints. The X1 and X2 values for extreme points can be found by solving the two equations in two unknowns that determine the point.

For example, to find the point at the intersection of boundaries of the plastic and the mix constraint, in Figure 3.7 we solve the following two equations in two unknowns:

$$2X1 + X2 = 1200$$
$$X1 - X2 = 450$$

Adding these two equations gives us $3X1 = 1650$, or $X1 = 550$. Substituting $X1 = 550$ into the second equation gives us $550 - X2 = 450$, or $X2 = 100$. Thus, this extreme point is $X1 = 550$, $X2 = 100$. Similarly, the extreme point at the intersection of the production time constraint and the X2 axis is $(0,600)$, which is found by solving the equations $3X1 + 4X2 = 2400$ and $X1 = 0$ (the equation of the X2 axis).

For models requiring three dimensions, an extreme point is a feasible point that lies at the intersection of three boundary constraints. Thus, we would have to solve *three* equations in *three* unknowns to determine these extreme points. This notion extends naturally to problems with any number of dimensions.

DEGENERACY

In some cases, in two dimensions, three or more boundary lines intersect at the same extreme point. This condition is called degeneracy. Any two of these boundary equations can be selected and solved simultaneously to determine the point. Degeneracy occurs in three-dimensional problems, when four or more boundary constraints intersect at the point; here any three can be selected. This concept also extends naturally to problems with any number of dimensions.

SLACK AND SURPLUS

Associated with each feasible point, there is *slack* on the "≤" constraints, which is found by subtracting the value of the left side of the constraint from the constant on the right-hand side.[3] Slack can be thought of as the amount of a resource that is left over at this point. If the point satisfies the "≤" constraint with equality, the slack is zero (the resource is used up); otherwise, it is positive.

Similarly, for each feasible point, *surplus* is associated with "≥" constraints, which is found by subtracting the constant on the right side from the value of the left side. The surplus indicates the extent to which some minimum restriction is exceeded at a given point. If the point satisfies the "≥" constraint with equality, the surplus is zero; otherwise, it is positive.

In general, no feasible point satisfies *all* the constraints with equality; that is, there is slack or surplus on at least some of the functional or variable constraints. Consider, for example, the boundary point $(100,525)$. The amount of slack or surplus of this point for each constraint is summarized in Table 3.3.

TABLE 3.3   SLACK AND SURPLUS

Constraint	Value of Left Side	Slack	Surplus
$2X1 + X2 \le 1200$	$2(100) + (525) = 725$	475	
$3X1 + 4X2 \le 2400$	$3(100) + 4(525) = 2400$	0	
$X1 + X2 \le 800$	$(100) + (525) = 625$	175	
$X1 - X2 \le 450$	$(100) - (525) = -425$	875	
$X1 \ge 0$	$(100) = 100$		100
$X2 \ge 0$	$(525) = 525$		525

[3]Although grammatically speaking, the constant appears on the "right side" not the "right-hand side," early developers of the field used this terminology and the term and its abbreviation "RHS" are today a common part of the lexicon of linear programming.

3.5 SOLVING GRAPHICALLY FOR AN OPTIMAL SOLUTION

All but the simplest linear programming models (those with only a few variables and constraints) make use of computer software to perform the voluminous (though straightforward) mathematical operations required in the solution process. Three such software packages—WINQSB, Excel, and LINDO—are discussed in Section 3.12. Here we present a graphical solution approach that can be used to solve problems with two variables, such as the Galaxy Industries model.

In Figure 3.7, we see that there are an *infinite number of points* in the feasible region. The question is, "Which one gives the maximum profit?" That is, "Which one maximizes the objective function 8X1 + 5X2?" If there were only five or ten feasible points, we could substitute simply the X1 and X2 values for each of these points into the objective function, and the point with the largest value would be the optimal solution. However, since the feasible region consists of an infinite number of points, we must take a different approach.

Suppose we ask, "Are there any solutions that would yield a $6000 weekly profit?" This is equivalent to saying, "Are there any feasible points that satisfy the following equation 8X1 + 5X2 = 6000?" When this line is graphed, as illustrated in Figure 3.8*a*, we see that it lies entirely above the feasible region. Thus, to our dismay, we find that no point in the feasible region gives a value of the objective function as large as 6000.

So let's set our sights lower. Let's see whether any solutions yield a $4000 weekly profit. Figure 3.8*b* shows us that when we draw the line, 8X1 + 5X2 = 4000, many solutions (the points on the line, 8X1 + 5X2 = 4000, that are in the feasible region) give us a $4000 weekly profit. Thus, Galaxy can do no worse than a $4000 weekly profit.

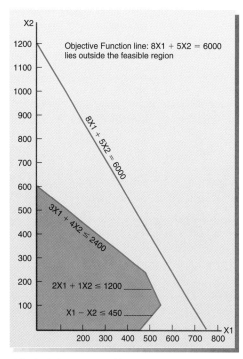

FIGURE 3.8*a* No Feasible Points Corresponding to an Objective Function Value of 6000

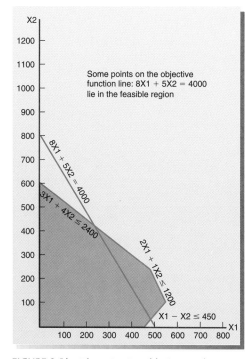

FIGURE 3.8*b* There Are Feasible Points That Have an Objective Function Value of 4000

If a $4000 profit can be made, perhaps even larger profits are possible. Are there any combinations of the decision variables that could yield, say, a $4400 profit or even a \$4800 profit? To determine whether Galaxy could attain such profits, we add the lines $8X1 + 5X2 = 4400$ and $8X1 + 5X2 = 4800$ to the graph. As shown in Figure 3.9, both lines intersect the feasible region.

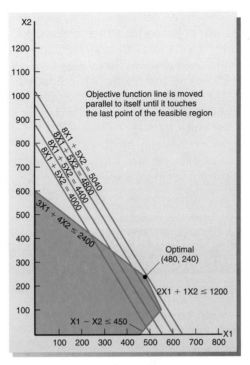

FIGURE 3.9   Determining the Optimal Point

Because the profit lines have the same slope, they are parallel; the lines yielding higher profits lie above those with lower profits. Therefore, if the objective function line is moved parallel to itself upward through the feasible region, the optimal feasible point is found when the objective function line touches the last point of the feasible region.

The last point of the feasible region that is touched by the objective function is the *extreme point* at the intersection of the limit for the availability of plastic ($2X1 + 1X2 = 1200$) and the limit on production time ($3X1 + 4X2 = 2400$). These constraints, which are satisfied with equality, are the *binding constraints* of the problem. The two other functional constraints and the nonnegativity constraints are the *nonbinding constraints*, which are not satisfied with equality at the optimal point.

To determine the values for X1 and X2 at the optimal point, the two *equations* of the binding constraints that must be solved are:

$$2X1 + 1X2 = 1200$$
$$3X1 + 4X2 = 2400$$

Multiplying the first equation by 4 gives us:

$$8X1 + 4X2 = 4800$$
$$3X1 + 4X2 = 2400$$

Subtracting the bottom equation from the top equation gives us $5X1 = 2400$, or $X1 = 480$. Substituting $X1 = 480$ into the original first equation gives us $2(480) + 1X2 = 1200$, or $X2 = 240$. Thus, the optimal solution is:

$$X1 = 480, X2 = 240$$

To determine the optimal profit, we substitute these values into the objective function:

$$8X1 + 5X2 = 8(480) + 5(240) = \$5040$$

Thus, we would recommend a weekly production of 480 dozen Space Rays and 240 dozen Zappers to management at Galaxy Industries, giving the company a $5040 weekly profit. Note that this is $140 (= $5040–$4900) more profitable than Galaxy's current "intuitive" weekly policy of producing 550 dozen Space Rays and 100 dozen Zappers.

This solution utilizes all the plastic and production hours (there is no slack for these constraints). There is slack on both of the other functional constraints, however. Since X1 + X2 = 480 + 240 = 720, there is a slack of 800 − 720 = 80 for the total production limit, and since X1 − X2 = 480 − 240 = 240, there is a slack of 450 − 240 = 210 for the product mix constraint.

To summarize, the following steps are used to find the optimal solution to a two-variable linear programming model graphically.

Graphical Solution Procedure for Two-Variable Linear Programs

1. Graph the constraints to find the feasible region.
2. Set the objective function equal to an arbitrary value so that the line passes through the feasible region.
3. Move the objective function line parallel to itself until it touches the last point of the feasible region.
4. Solve for X1 and X2 by solving the two equations that intersect to determine this point.
5. Substitute these values into the objective function to determine its optimal value.

EXTREME POINTS AND OPTIMAL SOLUTIONS

It is useful to recognize where the optimal solution for a linear program can occur. Consider problems that have the same feasible region as Galaxy Industries but different objective functions, as shown in Figure 3.10. Table 3.4 presents the optimal solution for various objective functions,[4] including the original objective function for Galaxy Industries (MAXIMIZE 8X1 + 5X2).

It is not coincidental that, in each case, the optimal solution occurs at an extreme point; rather, it is a fundamental property of linear programming.

Extreme Point Property of Optimality

If a linear programming problem has an optimal solution, an extreme point is optimal.

---

[4]For minimization problems, the objective function line is moved in the direction opposite to that for a maximization problem.

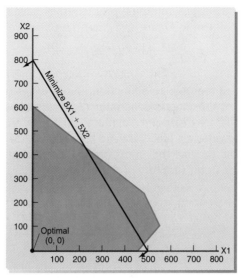

FIGURE 3.10a   Objective Function:
MINIMIZE 8X1 + 5X2

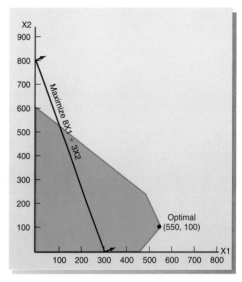

FIGURE 3.10b   Objective Function:
MAXIMIZE 8X1 + 3X2

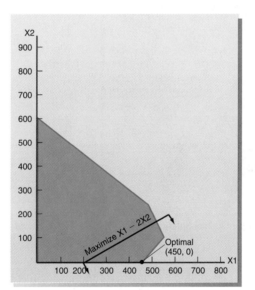

FIGURE 3.10c   Objective Function:
MAXIMIZE X1 − 2X2

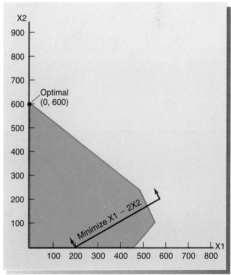

FIGURE 3.10d   Objective Function:
MINIMIZE X1 − 2X2

TABLE 3.4   OPTIMAL SOLUTIONS

Case	Objective Function	Optimal Extreme Point
Original	MAXIMIZE 8X1 + 5X2	(480,240)
(a)	MINIMIZE 8X1 + 5X2	(0,0)
(b)	MAXIMIZE 8X1 + 3X2	(550,100)
(c)	MAXIMIZE X1 − 2X2	(450,0)
(d)	MINIMIZE X1 − 2X2	(0,600)

ALTERNATE OPTIMAL
SOLUTIONS

In some cases, a linear programming problem may have more than one optimal solution. Suppose, as shown in Figure 3.11, that the objective function is:

$$\text{MAXIMIZE } 8X1 + 4X2$$

In this case, when we move the objective function line parallel through the feasible region, the slope of the objective function line ($-8/4 = -2$) is the same as the slope of the boundary of the plastic constraint ($-2/1 = -2$), and the last "point" that is touched is actually a *set* of points, namely, all those on the line $2X1 + X2 = 1200$ between the extreme points (480,240) and (550,100). Since at least one optimal solution is an extreme point, the fact that some optimal points are not extreme points does not violate the extreme point property of optimality.

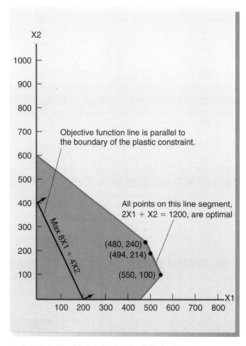

FIGURE 3.11   Multiple Optimal Solutions

Note, however, that if the objective function would have been MINIMIZE $8X1 + 4X2$, even though the slope is still parallel to the boundary of the plastic constraint, there is now a unique optimal solution, $X1 = 0$, $X2 = 0$. Thus, the slope of the objective function line being parallel to a boundary constraint is a *necessary* but not a *sufficient* condition for a model to have multiple optimal solutions.

As Figure 3.11 illustrates, there will never be just two optimal solutions. Any point on the line connecting two optimal points, which can be found by taking a weighted average of these two points, is also optimal. For example, since $X1 = 480$, $X2 = 240$ is one optimal solution, and $X1 = 550$, $X2 = 100$ is another, then a solution that puts a weight of .8 on the first point and a weight of .2 on the second yields another point on the line $2X1 + X2 = 1200$. This point will have coordinates of $X1 = .8(480) + .2(550) = 494$, and $X2 = .8(240) + .2(100) = 214$. Note that $2(494) + 1(214) = 1200$ and, thus, (494,214) is on the boundary line and is also an optimal solution. Similarly we can show that using weights of .9 and .1, .7 and .3, .5 and .5, or any other combination of weights of the form w and (1-w) will also give optimal solutions.

Alternate Optimal Solutions

1. For alternate optimal solutions to exist, the objective function must be parallel to a part of the boundary of the feasible region.
2. Any weighted average of optimal solutions is also an optimal solution.

Having more than one optimal solution allows the decision maker to consider secondary criteria in selecting an optimal strategy. For example, one optimal solution may have more of the decision variables equal to 0. In some cases, management might consider this a plus—fewer product types may mean more attention and better quality for the products that are produced. In other cases, this may be a minus—the greater the variety of products produced, perhaps the greater the likelihood of attracting more customers. Another optimal solution may have a more equal product mix than another, which, under some conditions, might be more appealing. In any event, having multiple optimal solutions affords management the luxury of being able to select that solution most to its liking from the set of optimal solutions.

WHY
"< CONSTRAINTS"
AND
"> CONSTRAINTS"
CANNOT BE PART
OF A LINEAR
PROGRAMMING
MODEL

The constraints of a linear programming model must consist of "$\leq$" constraints, "$\geq$" constraints, and "$=$" constraints. The "$<$" and "$>$" constraints are not allowed because, using them, there would be no "last" point touched by moving the objective function line parallel to itself through the feasible region.

For example, if both the plastic and production time constraints were the strict inequalities $2X1 + X2 < 1200$ and $3X1 + 4X2 < 2400$, respectively, the point (480,240) would not be feasible. The point (479.99,239.99) would be feasible, but the feasible point (479.999, 239.999) gives a higher objective function value and the point (479.9999,239.9999) an even higher value. Thus, there would be no "best value" because, no matter what solution was proposed, adding a "9" in the next decimal place would yield another feasible solution with an even better objective function value.

If a strict inequality is part of a formulation, the constraint should be approximated using a nonstrict inequality. For example, if Galaxy Industries required that less than 1200 pounds of plastic be used weekly ($2X1 + X2 < 1200$), in order to use linear programming solution methods, the mathematical modeler might approximate the constraint by $2X1 + X2 \leq 1199.99999$.

3.6 𝒯HE ROLE OF SENSITIVITY ANALYSIS OF THE OPTIMAL SOLUTION

Inevitably, once an optimal solution has been determined, questions arise about how sensitive the optimal solution is to changes in one or more of the input parameters or to other changes, such as the addition or elimination of constraints or variables. The effect of these changes is known as **sensitivity** or **post-optimality analysis**. Decision makers at Galaxy Industries might be interested in sensitivity analyses for the following reasons.

1. *Some of the input parameters may not have been known with certainty but are approximations or best estimates.*
    *   The profit coefficients might have been based solely on estimates of the production costs for Space Rays and Zappers.

- The 40 production hours might have assumed no vacations, illnesses, power failures, etc.
- The labor times to produce Space Rays and Zappers may have been approximations or averages.

2. *The model may have been formulated in a dynamic environment in which some of the parameters are subject to change.*

- The availability of specially treated plastic might be disrupted by weather, manufacturer stockouts, among other factors.
- The price of labor and materials could change.
- Higher or lower interest rates could change the profitability of each product.

3. *The manager may simply wish to perform a "what-if" analysis resulting from changes to some of the input parameters.*

- "What if" overtime is scheduled?
- "What-if" the marketing department modifies its recommendations?
- "What-if" another item is added to the product line?

Of course, if a change is made to a linear programming model, the problem can simply be re-solved. This can be a time-consuming process, however, that in many cases may not even be necessary. Rather, sensitivity reports generated by linear programming software packages can tell us at a glance the ramifications of certain changes to the objective function and the right-hand side coefficients of the model.

3.7   SENSITIVITY ANALYSIS OF OBJECTIVE FUNCTION COEFFICIENTS

Once the optimal solution to a linear programming model has been found, the decision maker may be concerned about how changes to any one of the objective function coefficients affect the optimal solution. As we discussed in Section 3.5, the optimal solution may change depending on the values of the objective function coefficients.

RANGE OF OPTIMALITY   Sensitivity analysis of an objective function coefficient focuses on answering the following question: "Keeping *all* other factors the same, how much can an objective function coefficient change without changing the optimal solution?"

Let us see what happens when the objective function coefficient per dozen Space Rays (which we designate as C1) changes from its current value of $8. Figure 3.12 illustrates what happens when this coefficient is decreased from $8 to $6, $4, $3.75, and $2, respectively. As you can see in Figure 3.12a and 3.12b, as C1 is *decreased* from $8 to $4, the optimal solution remains the extreme point (480,240). When C1 = 3.75, however, as shown in Figure 3.12c, the objective function line is parallel to (i.e., has the same slope as) the boundary line of the production time constraint,[5] and, although the extreme point (480,240) is still optimal, alternate optimal solutions now exist on the boundary line connecting the points (480,240) and (0,600). When C1 is decreased to $2, as shown in Figure 3.12d, the slope of the objective function line is now greater than that of the production time constraint, and the extreme point (0,600) is the new optimal solution.

---

[5]Recall the slope of a line of the form $aX1 + bX2 = c$ is $-a/b$. Thus, the slope of the production time constraint $3X1 + 4X2 = 2400$ is $-3/4$, or $-.75$, and the slope of the objective function $3.75X1 + 5X2$ is $-3.75/5$, or $-.75$.

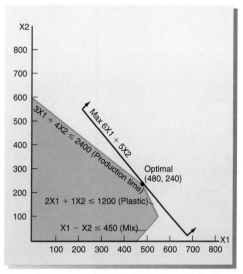

FIGURE 3.12a   Objective Function: MAX 6X1 + 5X2
Optimal Point: (480,240)

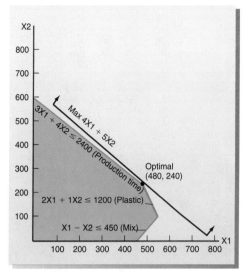

FIGURE 3.12b   Objective Function: MAX 4X1 + 5X2
Optimal Point: (480,240)

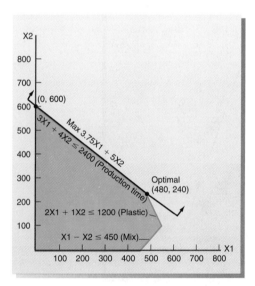

FIGURE 3.12c   Objective Function:
MAX 3.75X1 + 5X2 Optimal Points: Line Segment
Between (480,240) and (0,600)

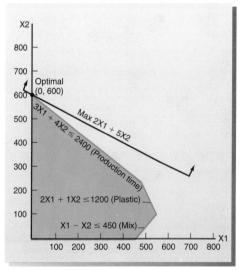

FIGURE 3.12d   Objective Function: MAX 2X1 + 5X2
Optimal Point: (0,600)

Similarly, as illustrated in Figure 3.13a, as C1 is *increased* from $8 to $9, the optimal solution remains the original one (480,240). But, as Figure 3.13b indicates, when C1 = 10, the objective function line is parallel to the boundary of the plastic constraint and multiple optimal solutions exist on this line between the extreme points (480,240) and (550,100). In Figure 3.13c we see that when C1 is increased to $11 the slope of the objective function line is less than that of the plastic constraint; in this case, (550,100) is the new optimal solution.

Thus, a range of values exists for C1, between $3.75 and $10, within which the current optimal solution (480,240) remains unchanged. This range is known as the **range**

FIGURE 3.13a   Objective Function: MAX 9X1 + 5X2 Optimal Point: (480,240)

FIGURE 3.13b   Objective Function: MAX 10X1 + 5X2 Optimal Points: Line Segment Between (480,240) and (550,100)

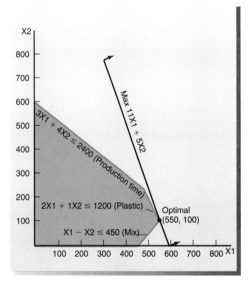

FIGURE 3.13c   Objective Function: MAX 11X1 + 5X2 Optimal Point: (550,100)

of optimality for C1. Note, however, that in this range, as C1 changes, although the optimal solution does not change, the optimal *objective function value* does. For example, when C1 = $4, since $4 is in the range of optimality, X1 = 480, X2 = 240 is still the optimal solution, but the optimal profit is now $4(480) + $5(240) = $3120.

Range of Optimality

The optimal solution will remain unchanged as long as an objective function coefficient lies within its **range of optimality** and there are no changes in any other input parameters. The value of the objective function *will* change if the coefficient multiplies a variable whose value is nonzero.

For problems involving two variables, we can find the range of optimality for an objective function coefficient by determining the range of values that gives a slope of the objective function line between the slopes of the binding constraints. In the Galaxy Industries problem, the binding constraints are $2X_1 + X_2 = 1200$ and $3X_1 + 4X_2 = 2400$, which have slopes of -2 and $-3/4$, respectively. The objective function coefficient per dozen Zappers is $C_2 = 5$; thus, the slope of the objective function line can be expressed as $-C_1/5$, and the range of optimality for C_1 is found by solving the following for C_1:

$$\frac{-2}{1} \leq \frac{-C_1}{5} \leq \frac{-3}{4}$$

Multiplying the expression by -5 gives us $10 \geq C_1 \geq 3.75$, or

$$3.75 \leq C_1 \leq 10$$

Similarly, to calculate the range of optimality for C_2, the slope of the objective function line, given that C_1 is its original value ($\$8$), can be expressed as

$$\frac{-2}{1} \leq \frac{-8}{C_2} \leq \frac{-3}{4}$$

Inverting this expression gives us $-1/2 \geq -C_2/8 \geq 4/3$. Multiplying by -8 gives us the range of optimality for C_2:

$$4 \leq C_2 \leq 10.667$$

MULTIPLE CHANGES—100% RULE

The ranges of optimality are valid only when a change is made to a single objective function coefficient. When *multiple* changes are made, it may be necessary to re-solve the problem to determine the new optimal solution. There is, however, one case in which we can be sure that the optimal solution does not change. It is expressed by the **100% rule**.

100% Rule

1. For each increase in an objective function coefficient, calculate (and express as a percentage) the ratio of the change in the coefficient to the maximum possible increase as determined by the limits of the range of optimality.

2. For each decrease in an objective function coefficient, calculate (and express as a percentage) the ratio of the change in the coefficient to the maximum possible decrease as determined by the limits of the range of optimality.

3. Sum all these percent changes. If the total is *less than* 100%, the optimal solution *will not change*. If the total is *greater than or equal to* 100%, the optimal solution *may* change.

To illustrate, suppose the profit per dozen Space Rays is changed from $\$8$ to $\$8.50$, a $\$0.50$ increase. Since the upper limit for its range of feasibility is $\$10$, a $\$2$ increase from $\$8$ is possible; the percentage change is $\$0.50/\$2 = 0.25$, or 25%. If, at the same time, the profit per dozen Zappers is decreased from $\$5$ to $\$4.50$, since the lower limit for its range of feasibility is $\$4$, a $\$1$ decrease from $\$5$ is possible; the percentage change is $\$0.50/\$1 = 0.50$, or 50%. Because the sum of these percentage changes is only 25% + 50% = 75%, the optimal solution will not change.

REDUCED COSTS

The optimal solution to the Galaxy Industries model has positive values for both of the decision variables, X1 and X2. Suppose the objective function had been MAX 2X1 + 5X2, however. As we saw in Figure 3.12d, the optimal solution with this objective function is X1 = 0, X2 = 600, which gives us an objective function value of $2(0) + $5(600) = $3000.

The reason why X1 = 0 (no Space Rays are to be produced) is because the $2 profit coefficient of X1 is not large enough to justify the production of Space Rays. It is then reasonable to ask, "How much will the profit coefficient of X1 have to increase before X1 can be positive (i.e., to justify the production of some Space Rays) in the optimal solution?" The answer is expressed by the **reduced cost** for this profit coefficient.

In Figures 3.12c and 3.12d, we saw that (0,600) is the optimal solution, until the profit coefficient for Space Rays increases to more than C1 = $3.75. At this point, the optimal solution changes to (480,240). Thus, C1 must increase by $1.75 from $2 to $3.75 before it would be economically feasible to produce Space Rays. Increasing the profit by $1.75 is equivalent to reducing the cost component of the coefficient by $1.75; hence, the reduced cost is −1.75.[6]

Another question that might arise is, "If X1 were made positive (i.e., if Space Rays were produced), how much would the profit change per dozen produced?" Again, the answer is expressed by the reduced cost. If X1 were required to be at least one unit (dozen), we would add the constraint X1 ≥ 1, as shown in Figure 3.14. The optimal solution is now X1 = 1, X2 = 599.25. This gives us an objective function value of $2(1) + $5(599.25) = $2998.25, which represents a $3000 − $2998.25 = $1.75 reduction to the optimal value of the objective function.

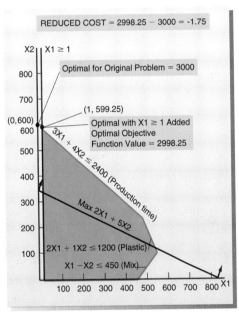

FIGURE 3.14 Reduced Cost Change in the Objective Function Value When a Variable at Zero Value Is Increased by 1

Reduced costs apply only to variables at zero value in the optimal solution. The reduced cost corresponding to a variable with a positive value is 0. This observation is part of an important property in linear programming known as **complementary slack-**

[6]The output of some computer programs uses the term "opportunity cost" rather than "reduced cost" and expresses its value without using the negative sign. For minimization problems, reduced costs would be positive and opportunity costs would be negative.

ness, which states that, at the optimal solution, either the variable is 0 or the reduced cost for the variable is 0. A second characteristic of the complementary slackness property is discussed in Section 3.8.

The above discussion is based on the assumption that the decision variable is restricted to "≥ 0". For models in which a variable is restricted to values greater than or equal to a lower bound other than 0, the lower bound would replace "0" both in interpretations of the reduced cost and in the complementary slackness property.[7]

Reduced Cost

The **reduced cost** for a variable at its lower bound (usually 0) yields:

1. The amount the profit coefficient must change before the variable can take on a value above its lower bound

2. The amount the optimal profit will change per unit increase in the variable from its lower bound

Complementary slackness: At the optimal solution, either a variable is at its lower bound or the reduced cost is 0.

3.8 SENSITIVITY ANALYSIS OF RIGHT-HAND SIDE VALUES

Any change in a right-hand side value of a binding constraint will change the optimal solution. For example, as shown in Figure 3.15, if the amount of available plastic is increased from 1200 to 1201 pounds, the new optimal solution is found by solving:

$$2X1 + X2 = 1201$$
$$3X1 + 4X2 = 2400$$

You can verify that this solution is $X1 = 480.4$, $X2 = 239.4$, giving an optimal objective function value of $\$8(480.4) + \$5(239.4) = \$5043.40$.

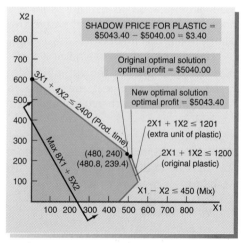

FIGURE 3.15   Shadow Price for Plastic 1201 Pounds of Plastic Available

---

[7]Some software programs allow the input of an upper bound for a variable. In these programs, if, at optimality, the variable is at its upper bound, the reduced cost associated with the variable will have the opposite sign as that for a variable at its lower bound.

The optimal solution is *not* affected by a change in a right-hand side value of a *non*binding constraint that is less than the slack or surplus for the constraint. Figures 3.16a and 3.16b show that if the right-hand side of the total production constraint is reduced from 800 to 750, while the slack for this constraint is reduced (from 80 to 30), the optimal solution remains the same (480,240); if this value is reduced from 800 to 700, however, the new optimal point is (500,200), giving us a new optimal objective function value of $8(500) + $5(200) = $5000.

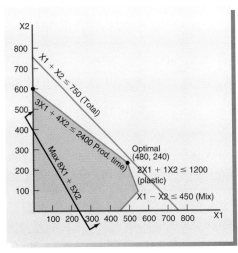

FIGURE 3.16a   Optimal Solution not Affected by Changing the Total Production Constraint to X1 + X2 ≤ 750

FIGURE 3.16b   Optimal Solution Changes When the Total Production Constraint Is Changed to X1 + X2 ≤ 700

Sensitivity analysis of right-hand side values focuses on two questions:

1.   Keeping *all* other factors the same, how much would the optimal profit change if the right-hand side of a constraint changed by one unit?

2.   For how many additional or fewer units will this per unit change be valid?

SHADOW PRICES

If the right-hand side value of a "≤" constraint is increased, the constraint becomes less restrictive; hence, the optimal value of the objective function can only improve (increase for a maximization problem, decrease for a minimization problem) or stay the same. Conversely, if the right-hand side value of a "≥" constraint is increased, the constraint becomes more restrictive and the optimal value of the objective function can only worsen or stay the same. The change in the optimal value of the objective function resulting from a one-unit increase in the right-hand side of a constraint is called its **shadow price**.[8]

We have seen that a one-unit increase in the amount of plastic to 1201 yields a new objective function value of $5043.40. Thus, the increase in the value of the objective function attained by this one additional unit of plastic is $5043.40 − $5040 = $3.40; that is, $3.40 is the shadow price for plastic.

To determine the shadow price for an extra minute of production time, we solve:

$$2X1 + X2 = 1200$$
$$3X1 + 4X2 = 2401$$

---

[8]Some software packages express this change as a *dual price*. There is no universal definition for a shadow or dual price. Depending on the software, it can represent the "improvement," "increase," "decrease," or simply that "change" in the optimal objective function value if a right-hand side constant is increased by one unit. Although shadow or dual prices may be expressed differently among software packages, the absolute values will be the same, and the meaning of the sign should be obvious.

Solving for X1 and X2, X1 = 479.8, X2 = 240.8, and the optimal objective function value is 8(479.8) + 5(240.4) = $5040.40. Hence, the shadow price for an extra *minute* of production time is $5040.40 − $5040.00 = $0.40. On an hourly basis, this is a $24 (= 60(.40)) per *hour* shadow price.

The optimal solution does not change from (480,240) if the right-hand side of either of the last two functional constraints (X1 + X2 ≤ 800 and X1 − X2 ≤ 450) is changed slightly since they are both nonbinding constraints. Accordingly, because the optimal solution remains the same, the optimal objective function value does not change. Hence, we conclude that *the shadow price for nonbinding constraints is* 0. This observation is the second characteristic of the *complementary slackness* principle for optimal solutions: either the constraint is satisfied with equality (the slack or surplus is 0) or the shadow price is 0.

Shadow Prices

The **shadow price** for a constraint measures the amount the optimal objective function value changes per unit increase in the right-hand side value of the constraint.

Complementary slackness: At the optimal solution, either a constraint is satisfied with equality or the corresponding shadow price is 0.

THE CORRECT
INTERPRETATION OF
SHADOW PRICES

Returning to the Galaxy Industries model, we find that the shadow price for plastic is $3.40 per pound. It would seem, then, that management should be willing to pay up to, but no more than, $3.40 for each additional pound of plastic. However, this would be true *only if the cost of plastic were not included in the calculation of the profit coefficients of the decision variables*. Let us now consider two cases.

Case I: Sunk Costs

Suppose the 1200 pounds of plastic were automatically delivered to Galaxy each week at a cost of $3 per pound or $3600 per week, and that production time is scheduled for 40 hours per week at $20 per hour ($0.33 per minute), for a total cost of $800. Because the $3600 for plastic and the $800 for production time must be paid regardless of the amount of plastic and production time actually used during the week, they are **sunk costs**. Thus, we would not include the cost of plastic or production time in determining the objective function coefficients for Space Rays and Zappers.

The net profit for the problem can be obtained by subtracting the total sunk costs of $4400 from the optimal objective function value of the model. Because additional pounds of plastic add $3.40, and additional minutes of production time add $0.40 to the optimal objective function value, these shadow prices do, in fact, represent an upper limit that management would be willing to pay for additional pounds of plastic and additional minutes of production time, respectively.

Case 2: Included Costs

Suppose, instead, that management could order any amount of plastic it wanted to, up to 1200 pounds per week at $3 per pound, and it could schedule any amount of production time, up to 2400 minutes. Management would then order only enough plastic and schedule only enough production time needed for the optimal solution.

In this case, the costs of the required plastic and production time (and perhaps other resources) should be *included* in the derivation of the profit coefficients of Space Rays and Zappers. For instance, suppose that the selling price was $17 per dozen Space Rays and $11 per dozen Zappers and that other production costs amounted to $2 per dozen Space Rays and $1.67 per dozen Zappers. Table 3.5 gives us the calculations required to determine the respective $8 and $5 objective function coefficients per dozen Space Rays and Zappers.

TABLE 3.5   OBJECTIVE FUNCTION COEFFICIENTS

	Space Rays (per dozen)	Zappers (per dozen)
Revenue		
Selling price	$17.00	$11.00
Costs		
Plastic (@ $3/lb.)	$ 6.00 (2 lbs.)	$ 3.00 (1 lb.)
Production time (@ $20/hr.)	$ 1.00 (3 min.)	$ 1.33 (4 min.)
Other	$ 2.00	$ 1.67
Total Costs	$ 9.00	$ 6.00
Unit Profit	$ 8.00	$ 5.00

The optimal solution (480,240) uses all 1200 pounds of plastic and all 2400 minutes of production time. The objective function value of $5040 is the net profit, which includes $3600 (= $3/lb. × (1200 lbs.)) spent for plastic and $800 (=$0.033/minute × (2400 minutes)) spent for production time.

Recall that when 1201 pounds of plastic are available, the optimal objective function value is $5043.40; this includes the $3603 (=$3/lb. × (1201 lbs.)) spent for plastic. Thus, the shadow price of $3.40 represents a *premium* above $3.00 which management should be willing to pay for an extra pound of plastic; that is, Galaxy should be willing to pay up to $6.40 (= $3.40 + $3.00) for an extra pound of plastic. Similarly, Galaxy would be willing to pay up to $0.73 (= $0.40 + $0.33) for an extra minute of production.

Sunk and Included Costs

Sunk costs—the cost of the resource is not included in the calculation of objective function coefficients—the shadow price is the value of an extra unit of the resource.
Included costs—the cost of the resource is included in the calculation of objective function coefficients—the shadow price is the premium value above the existing unit value for the resource.

RANGE OF FEASIBILITY   If 1202 pounds (two additional pounds) of plastic are available, the optimal solution found by solving the equations for the plastic and production time constraints, 2X1 + X2 = 1202 and 3X1 + 4X2 = 2400, is X1 = 481.6, X2 = 238.8. The optimal objective function value of $8(481.6) + $5(238.8) = $5046.80 represents an increase of $6.80, or $3.40 per pound, above the original optimal objective function value.

Similarly, if only 1199 pounds (one less pound) of plastic are available, the optimal solution found by solving the equations 2X1 + X2 = 1199 and 3X1 + 4X2 = 2400 is X1 = 479.2, X2 = 240.6, and the optimal objective function value is $5036.60, a decrease of $3.40 from the original optimal value.

In fact, as long as the plastic constraint and the production time constraint determine the optimal extreme point, each unit change in the availability of plastic contributes the shadow price of $3.40 to the optimal profit. The **range of feasibility** for plastic gives the limits on the right-hand value for plastic, such that these two constraints continue to determine the optimal point. It is given this name because, over this range of values, the solution to the current set of binding constraint equations is a *feasible* solution.

Figures 3.17a and 13.17b illustrate how the range of feasibility for plastic can be determined. Notice that by changing the right-hand side of the plastic constraint from 1200 to another number, the X2-intercept of the line changes but *the slope does not change.* Thus, by changing the right-hand side from 1200, the boundary of the plastic constraint

FIGURE 3.17*a*   Changes to Feasible Region When Availability of Plastic Increases

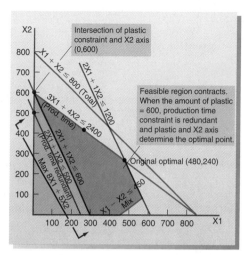

FIGURE 3.17*b*   Changes to Feasible Region When Availability of Plastic Decreases

moves *parallel to* the original constraint, and the optimal solution continues to be determined by the intersection of these two boundary lines until they generate an infeasible point.

In Figure 3.17*a*, as the availability of plastic increases, the plastic and production time constraints determine the optimal point until the line passes through the intersection of the production time and the mix constraint. This point (600,150) is determined by solving $3X1 + 4X2 = 2400$ and $X1 - X2 = 450$. At (600,150), the right-hand side of the plastic constraint is $2(600) + (150) = 1350$. For values above 1350, the intersection of the plastic and production time equations yields a point outside of the new feasible region shown in Figure 3.17*a*. Thus, 1350 is the upper limit of the range of feasibility for plastic.

Similarly, in Figure 3.17*b*, as the availability of plastic decreases, the plastic and production time constraints determine the optimal point until the line passes through the intersection of the production time boundary and the X2 axis at (0,600). As the line passes below this point, again, the intersection of the plastic and production time equations will produce infeasible points for the new feasible region. At (0,600), the right-hand side value of the plastic constraint is $(0) + (600) = 600$; that is, 600 is the lower value of the range of feasibility for plastic.

Thus, the range of feasibility of plastic—that is, the range of values for which the shadow price of $3.40 is valid—is between an availability of 600 and 1350 pounds. The ranges of feasibility for the right-hand side values of production minutes, total production, and difference in production mix can similarly be determined. Table 3.6 summarizes the results.

TABLE 3.6   RANGES OF FEASIBILITY

Constraint	Shadow Price	Range of Feasibility
Plastic	$3.40	600–1350
Production time	$0.40	2050–2800
Total production	$0	720–no limit
Product mix	$0	240–no limit

Note that in the range of feasibility, *the values of the variables in the optimal solution and the objective function value* DO CHANGE; it is *the shadow prices* that DO NOT *change.*

Range of Feasibility

The **range of feasibility** for the availability of a resource is the set of right-hand side values over which the same set of constraints determines the optimal point.

Within the range of feasibility, *the shadow prices remain constant*; however, the optimal solution will change.

MULTIPLE CHANGES

A 100% rule, analogous to the 100% rule for objective function coefficients, provides a sufficient condition for multiple changes that *will not affect the shadow prices*. Suppose, in the Galaxy Industries model, there are 100 additional pounds of plastic and one less production hour (60 production minutes) and that the limit on total production is to be increased by 100 dozen to 900 dozen.

Given that the upper limit for plastic (1350) is 150 units above its current value of 1200, the lower limit for production minutes (2050) is 350 below its current value of 2400, and there is no upper limit (i.e., the limit is ∞) for the total production, the sum of the percent changes is $100/150 + 60/350 + 100/\infty = 66.67\% + 17.14\% + 0\% = 83.81\%$. Since this sum is less than 100%, *the current shadow prices are still valid.*

3.9 OTHER POST-OPTIMALITY CHANGES

The addition or deletion of constraints, the addition or deletion of variables, and changes to the left-hand side coefficients of a linear programming model are additional post-optimality analyses that may be of interest to the decision maker. Typically, such changes are made directly to the model formulation and the problem is simply re-solved. However, there are some observations worth considering in these cases.

ADDITION OF
A CONSTRAINT

When a constraint is added to a linear programming model, the first step is to determine whether this constraint is satisfied by the current optimal solution. If it does, it is not necessary to re-solve the problem; the current solution will remain optimal.

If the new constraint is violated, however, sophisticated linear programming solution packages include routines that make use of the current optimal solution to arrive at the new optimal solution in a small fraction of the time it would take to solve the entire problem from scratch. Of course, the optimal objective function value will be worse than the original optimal value (smaller for maximization problems; larger for minimization problems) because the problem is now more constrained.

DELETION OF
A CONSTRAINT

If the constraint to be deleted from the model is nonbinding, the current optimal solution will not change. If it is binding, however, and it is a "≤" constraint, we can change its right-hand side value to $+\infty$; if it is a "≥" constraint, we change the right-hand side to $-\infty$. This change to a single right-hand side value allows sophisticated linear programming solution packages to use the current optimal solution to generate the new optimal solution much more rapidly than is possible by completely re-solving the problem from scratch. Since the problem is less restrictive, the new optimal solution will give a better optimal objective function than the original model.

DELETION OF
A VARIABLE

If the variable to be deleted is zero in the optimal solution, the change will not affect the optimal solution. If the value of the variable is not zero in the optimal solution, we can simply add a new constraint to the model which sets the variable to zero (e.g., $X1 = 0$) and use the efficient procedure for adding a new constraint to solve for the new optimal solution. Deleting a variable that was nonzero in the original optimal solution will result in a worse objective function value.

ADDITION OF A VARIABLE

When a variable is added, most packages dedicated to linear programming can again use the current optimal solution to generate a new optimal solution quickly. There is, however, a *net marginal profit* procedure that can determine whether the addition of the new variable will have any effect on the optimal solution. Net marginal profit is the difference between the objective function coefficient and the total marginal cost of the resources using the current values of the shadow prices.

To illustrate, suppose that a new product, Big Squirts, requiring three pounds of plastic and five minutes of production time, can be produced, yielding a profit of $10 per dozen. The new model is:

$$
\begin{array}{lllll}
\text{MAXIMIZE} & 8X1 + 5X2 + 10X3 & & \\
\text{ST} & 2X1 + \ X2 + \ 3X3 \le 1200 & \text{(Plastic)} \\
& 3X1 + 4X2 + \ 5X3 \le 2400 & \text{(Production time)} \\
& \ X1 + \ X2 + \ \ X3 \le \ \ 800 & \text{(Total units)} \\
& \ X1 - \ X2 \qquad\quad \le \ \ 450 & \text{(Space Ray/Zapper mix)} \\
& X1, X2, X3 \ge 0 &
\end{array}
$$

Recall that we determined the shadow prices for the constraints to be $3.40, $0.40, $0, and $0, respectively. Thus, the net marginal profit for the production of a dozen Big Squirts is:

$$\$10 - ((\$3.40)(3) + (\$0.40)(5) + (\$0)(1) + (\$0)(0)) = -\$2.20$$

Hence, it would be unprofitable to produce Big Squirts, and the current solution of producing 480 dozen Space Rays and 240 dozen Zappers remains optimal. If the profit per dozen Big Squirts had been $15, however, the net marginal profit would have been $2.80. This would indicate that there is a new optimal solution, which includes the production of Big Squirts, yielding a higher optimal profit.

CHANGES IN THE LEFT-HAND SIDE COEFFICIENTS

When a left-hand side coefficient is changed, the entire feasible region is reshaped. If the change is made in a coefficient in a nonbinding constraint, the first step is to ascertain whether the current optimal solution satisfies the modified constraint. If it does, it remains the optimal solution to the revised model; if it does not, or if the change is made in a coefficient of a binding constraint, both the optimal solution and the shadow prices change in ways that are more complex to calculate than changes resulting from modifications to objective function coefficients or right-hand side values. In this case, the model must be re-solved. Unlike the other post-optimality changes discussed in this section, most linear programming software packages do not provide sensitivity analysis for this case, and the model must be re-solved from scratch.

3.10 $\mathcal{M}$ODELS WITHOUT OPTIMAL SOLUTIONS—INFEASIBILITY AND UNBOUNDEDNESS

Not every solution to a linear programming model results in an optimal solution. Under certain conditions, linear programming models may have no feasible solutions at all, or they may have unbounded feasible regions with the possibility of theoretically generating infinite profits or negatively infinite total costs for the objective function value.

INFEASIBILITY

In some cases, a linear program possesses no feasible solutions whatsoever. For example, suppose that, in addition to the other constraints, management at Galaxy Industries wishes to produce at least 700 dozen Space Rays per week. This constraint is expressed as $X1 \geq 700$ and is illustrated in Figure 3.18. As you can see, there are no feasible points satisfying all the constraints.

On the one hand, **infeasibility** can occur because the problem has been misformulated at either the modeling or the data input stage. On the other hand, as was the case above, the problem may be modeled correctly but is overconstrained; management has simply given the modeler a situation to which there is no solution. If infeasibility is detected, some of the constraints must be relaxed in order to obtain a feasible solution. Note that changing the objective function will never make an infeasible problem feasible.

Infeasibility

A model that has no feasible points is an *infeasible* model.

UNBOUNDEDNESS

Consider the model for Galaxy Industries depicted in Figure 3.19. The model is constrained only by the nonnegativity constraints and the marketing constraint that Space Ray production should not exceed Zapper production by more than 450 dozen per week ($X1 - X2 \leq 450$). In this situation, the feasible region extends indefinitely, bounded only by the X1 axis, the X2 axis, and the functional constraint $X1 - X2 \leq 450$. Such a feasible region, which extends "forever" in a particular direction, is called an **unbounded feasible region**.

FIGURE 3.18   An Infeasible Problem

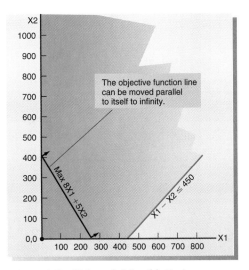

FIGURE 3.19   Unbounded Feasible Region
Unbounded Linear Program

Problems with unbounded feasible regions may or may not possess optimal solutions. In Figure 3.19, the objective function is the original objective function: MAXIMIZE $8X1 + 5X2$. Here the objective function line can be moved parallel through the feasible region, giving ever-increasing objective function values. This is an example of a linear program with an **unbounded solution**.

Unbounded Solutions

A linear program with an **unbounded solution** is one in which feasible solutions exist but there is no bound for the value of the objective function.

For a linear program to have an unbounded solution, the feasible region must be unbounded. But the fact that the feasible region is unbounded does not necessarily imply that the linear program has an unbounded solution. If the objective had been to MINIMIZE 8X1 + 5X2, although the feasible region is unbounded, (0,0) would have been the optimal point.

Linear programs with unbounded solutions are theoretically possible, but they do not occur in business situations. A business cannot make an infinite profit, or, in the case of a minimization problem, have an infinitely negative cost. If a computer program determines that a linear programming formulation of a "real" business problem has an unbounded solution, a data entry error must have occurred or some constraint has been omitted from the formulation.

3.11 $\mathcal{A}$ MINIMIZATION PROBLEM

The Galaxy Industries problem is a typical example of a common linear programming model known as a *product mix problem*. In its simplest form, this type of problem has a maximization objective function and all "≤" functional constraints; that is, management is trying to maximize something, but limited amounts of resources are restricting it or holding it back.

The inverse of this type of problem is one in which the objective function is to be *minimized* and the constraints are of the "≥" variety. Problems with this structure have come to be known as *diet problems*. This is because finding a least cost diet that meets minimum nutritional standards was one of the earliest applications of linear programming, dating back to the World War II era. The following Navy sea ration problem is a simplified version of a diet problem.

NAVY SEA RATIONS

The Department of the Navy has been downsizing and is looking for cost savings opportunities to meet mandated congressional budget cuts. One suggestion under consideration is to change the makeup of the content of Navy sea rations, the canned food supplies containing certain minimum quantities of Vitamin A, Vitamin D, iron, and other nutrients, which combat troops carry into battle.

According to Texfoods, the current supplier of sea rations for the Navy, each two-ounce portion of its product supplies 20% of the required amount of Vitamin A, 25% of the required amount of Vitamin D, and 50% of the required amount of iron. Each portion costs the Navy $0.60. Because all minimum standards must be met in each serving, the current sea ration container must contain 10 ounces of the Texfoods product (to meet the minimum amount of Vitamin A). This costs the Navy $3.00 (= 5 × $0.60) per serving.

The Navy is considering switching to another product from a different supplier, Calration. A two-ounce portion of Calration costs $0.50 and provides 50% of the minimum requirement of Vitamin A and 25% of the requirement of Vitamin D, but only 10% of the requirement for iron. Substituting the Calration product, the sea ration container would have to contain 20 ounces in order to meet the minimum iron requirement, costing the Navy $5.00 (= 10 × $0.50) per serving.

Navysea.lpp
Navysea.xls

One bright Navy lieutenant has suggested that a mixture of the two products might meet the overall standards at a lower cost than the current $3 per serving. The Navy has never worried about the taste of sea rations; hence, mixing them, either by combining them or by packing a portion of each, is an acceptable alternative. The lieutenant has been given permission to evaluate the idea.

SOLUTION

The following is a brief synopsis of the problem posed by the lieutenant:

- Determine the amount of two-ounce portions of each sea ration product in the mix.
- Minimize the total cost of the sea rations.
- Meet the minimum requirements for Vitamin A, Vitamin D, and iron.

Decision Variables

The following decision variables must be included in the problem:

$$X1 = \text{number of two-ounce portions of Texfoods product}$$
$$\text{used in a serving of sea rations}$$
$$X2 = \text{number of two-ounce portions of Calration product}$$
$$\text{used in a serving of sea rations}$$

Objective Function

The objective is to minimize the total cost of a serving of sea rations. Since each two-ounce serving of Texfoods costs $0.60 and each two-ounce serving of Calration costs $0.50, the objective function is:

$$\text{MINIMIZE } .60X1 + .50X2$$

Constraints

Each two-ounce portion of the Texfoods product provides 20% of the Vitamin A requirement; each two-ounce portion of the Calration product provides 50%. If X1 two-ounce portions of Texfoods and X2 two-ounce portions of Calration are included in the sea rations, this would give us $20X1 + 50X2$ percent of the requirement for Vitamin A. The constraint that at least 100% of the requirement of Vitamin A must be met can then be written as

$$(\text{The total percent of Vitamin A}) \geq (100 \text{ percent})$$

$$20X1 + 50X2 \geq 100$$

Similar constraints for Vitamin D and iron, respectively, are:

$$25X1 + 25X2 \geq 100$$

and

$$50X1 + 10X2 \geq 100$$

Together with the nonnegativity constraints, this gives us the following linear programming model:

$$\text{MINIMIZE} \quad .60X1 + .50X2$$
$$\text{ST}$$
$$20X1 + 50X2 \geq 100$$
$$25X1 + 25X2 \geq 100$$
$$50X1 + 10X2 \geq 100$$
$$X1, X2 \geq 0$$

This problem is illustrated in Figure 3.20. Note that the feasible region is unbounded. Since the objective is to minimize the objective function, however, the objective function line is moved downward toward the origin, and the optimal point is (1.5, 2.5).

FIGURE 3.20   Navy Sea Rations—Graphical Solution

Thus, the optimal solution is to mix 1.5 portions (= three ounces) of Texfoods product with 2.5 portions (= five ounces) of Calration product. This eight-ounce mixture meets the minimum requirements for Vitamin D and iron (the binding constraints). The percentage of Vitamin A in the mixture is 20(1.5) + 50(2.5) = 155%, a *surplus* of 155% − 100% = 55% above the minimum requirement for Vitamin A. The total cost per serving is $0.60(1.5) + $0.50(2.5) = $2.15, an $0.85, or 28.33% (= $0.85/$3.00), reduction in the cost of sea rations from the current $3 level.

An additional benefit of this solution is the reduced quantity of sea rations a sailor must carry—from 10 ounces to 8 ounces per serving. This reduction in weight means a significant reduction in the fuel consumption required to transport the sea rations to the sailors. Given the large supply of sea rations purchased by the Navy, this adds up to a considerable cost savings.

Reduced Costs

Because both decision variables are positive in the optimal solution, the reduced costs are zero. If one of the variables had been zero, then, for a minimization problem, increasing its value by one unit would increase the minimized value of the objective function; that is, the reduced cost for a minimization problem would be positive.

Ranges of Optimality

The optimal solution is at the intersection of the boundaries of the Vitamin D constraint: $25X_1 + 25X_2 \geq 100$ (slope = $-25/25 = -1$) and the iron constraint: $50X_1 + 10X_2 \geq 100$ (slope = $-50/10 = -5$). Thus, we can determine the range of optimality for the cost of the Texfoods portion by solving the following expression for C_1:

$$\frac{-50}{10} \leq \frac{-C_1}{.50} \leq \frac{-25}{25}$$

which gives us

$$.50 \leq C_1 \leq 2.50$$

For C2, we solve:

$$\frac{-50}{10} \leq \frac{-.60}{C2} \leq \frac{-25}{25}$$

which gives us

$$.12 \leq C2 \leq .60$$

Shadow Prices

The shadow prices for vitamins A and D and iron can be calculated as follows:

Vitamin A: Because there is surplus for the Vitamin A constraint, the shadow price for an extra percent of Vitamin A is 0.

Vitamin D: To determine the shadow price for Vitamin D, we need to solve

$$25X1 + 25X2 = 101$$
$$50X1 + 10X2 = 100$$

The solution to this pair of equations is $X1 = 1.49$, $X2 = 2.55$, giving an optimal objective function value of $2.169. Since the current optimal objective function value is $2.15, the shadow price is $2.169 − $2.15 = $0.019. Thus, if the Navy wants its sailors to have more than 100% of the *minimum* daily requirement of Vitamin D, each percent above the 100% minimum (but within its range of feasibility) will cost an additional $0.019.

Iron: The shadow price for iron is found by solving

$$25X1 + 25X2 = 101$$
$$50X1 + 10X2 = 100$$

The solution to this pair of equations is $X1 = 1.525$, $X2 = 2.475$, giving an optimal objective function value of $2.1525. The shadow price for an additional percent requirement of iron in the mixture within its range of feasibility is $2.1525 − $2.15 = $0.0025. Note that positive shadow prices for a minimization problem mean that the optimal solution will "worsen" (increase) as the right-hand side values increase.

Ranges of Feasibility

The ranges of feasibility for the three dietary components are as follows.

Vitamin A: In Figure 3.20, we can see that, as the Vitamin A constraint is moved downward (decreasing the right-hand side value from 100) by any amount, the Vitamin D and iron constraints will continue to determine the optimal point. While increasing the right-hand side for the Vitamin A constraint moves the Vitamin A upward, the Vitamin D and iron constraints will continue to determine the optimal point until the Vitamin A constraint passes through the optimal point (1.5, 2.5). At this point, the right-hand side of the Vitamin A constraint will be $20(1.5) + 50(2.5) = 155$. Feasibility therefore ranges from $-\infty$ to 155.

Vitamin D: The impact of changing the right-hand side value of the Vitamin D constraint is illustrated in Figure 3.21. As you can see, when the right-hand side of the Vitamin D constraint decreases, the Vitamin D and the iron constraints continue to give a feasible (and therefore optimal) solution, until the Vitamin D line moves downward through the intersection of the boundaries of the Vitamin A constraint $(20X1 + 50X2 = 100)$ and the iron constraint $(50X1 + 10X2 = 100)$. Solving these two equations for coordinates of this point gives us $X1 = 40/23$, $X2 = 30/23$. The vitamin D and iron constraints also determine the optimal point as the right-hand side increases, until the vitamin D con-

FIGURE 3.21   Navy Sea Rations Range of Feasibility for Vitamin D

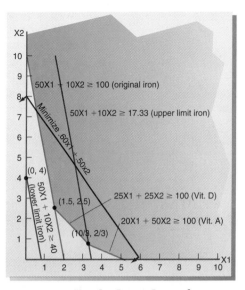

FIGURE 3.22   Navy Sea Rations Range of Feasibility for Iron

straint moves upward through the intersection of the boundary of the iron constraint and the X2 axis at the point X1 = 0, X2 = 10.

Substituting these values into the left side of the Vitamin D constraint, we find that the lower limit for the range of feasibility is 25(40/23) + 25(30/23) = 1750/23 = 78.087, and the upper limit is 25(0) = 25(10) = 250.

Iron: A similar approach is illustrated in Figure 3.22 for the iron constraint. The Vitamin D and the iron constraints continue to give a feasible solution, until the boundary for the iron constraint moves to the left through the boundary of the Vitamin D constraint and the X2 axis at X1 = 0, X2 = 4, or to the right through the intersection of the Vitamin A constraint (20X1 + 50X2 = 100) and the Vitamin D constraint (25X1 + 25X2 = 100) at X1 = 10/3, X2 = 2/3.

Substituting these values into the left side of the iron constraint, we find that the lower limit for the range of feasibility is 50(0) + 10(4) = 40, and the upper limit is 50(10/3) + 10(2/3) = 520/3 = 173.33.

3.12   COMPUTER SOLUTION OF LINEAR PROGRAMS WITH ANY NUMBER OF DECISION VARIABLES

All of the problems and exercises discussed in this chapter can be expressed using only two decision variables, allowing for a graphical analysis. However, practical models requiring more than two decision variables, like those presented in Chapter 4, can be reasonably solved only by using a linear programming computer software package. The major purpose of this chapter has been to familiarize you with the linear programming terminology and concepts that will allow you to correctly interpret and make use of the output from standard linear programming packages.

The algebraic technique commonly used in most software packages to solve linear programs is the *simplex algorithm*. Although the calculations required and the steps performed in the simplex algorithm are relatively simple, the algorithm gets its name from a mathematical term for the figure created in *n* dimensions by an extreme point and the n other extreme points that are *adjacent* to it.[9] The resulting figure is known as a *simplex*. A brief geometric interpretation of this algebraic approach is that the algorithm begins at one extreme point and evaluates the value of the objective function at adjacent extreme points in its quest to find the optimal solution. Supplement CD3 on the accompanying CD-ROM provides a complete discussion of the simplex algorithm.

Another solution approach, known as an *interior point method*, ultimately approaches the optimal extreme point by starting from an interior point. This method has been found to solve certain large linear programming models more rapidly than the simplex algorithm. It is the simplex algorithm, however, that is currently programmed in most software packages.

COMPUTER SOLUTION OF LINEAR PROGRAMS

Linear programming software can be used to solve models with two or more variables. The input to any package includes:

1. The objective function criterion (MAX or MIN)
2. The type of each constraint ($\leq$, $=$, $\geq$)
3. The actual coefficients for the problem

It might seem that for real-life problems, inputting all the coefficients would be a monumental task. After all, a problem with 500 decision variables and 300 constraints would require the entry of 150,000 coefficients. Fortunately, *matrix generators* and modeling languages exist that can generate most, if not all, of the coefficients for moderate to large linear programs. The typical output generated from linear programming software includes:

1. The optimal values of the objective function
2. The optimal values of the decision variables
3. Reduced costs for objective function coefficients
4. Ranges of optimality for objective function coefficients
5. The amount of slack or surplus on each constraint
6. Shadow (or dual) prices for the constraints
7. Ranges of feasibility for right-hand side values

Three such packages are WINQSB, Excel, and LINDO. WINQSB is an easy-to-use integrated management science package that is provided on the accompanying CD-ROM. Its linear programming module gives a complete, concise summary report and offers many graphic capabilities that can be used in preparing reports and presentations.

Linear programming models can also be solved on Excel using the "Solver" option from the "Tools" pull-down menu. Excel is a spreadsheet package with worldwide acceptance. Thus, the fact that millions of users can now solve linear programming models without the need for additional software makes Excel a popular solution choice.

LINDO is a dedicated linear programming package that is available in both a PC version and large commercial versions. Since most universities have site licenses for LINDO software, many instructors prefer using this proven package as their linear programming software.

Input instructions for each of these packages appear in the appendices at the end of this chapter. Figures 3.23 through 3.26 show the various output reports for the Galaxy Industries model.

---

[9]Two extreme points are adjacent if the set of equations that determine the points differ by only one equation.

WINQSB OUTPUT

As you can see from the top portion of WINQSB's combined report in Figure 3.23, the optimal solution is to produce 480 dozen Space Rays at a profit of $8 per dozen, contributing $3040 to the total profit, and 240 dozen Zappers at $5 per dozen, contributing $1200 to the total profit. Thus the optimal total profit |Objective Function (Max.)| is $5040. The reduced costs and the ranges of optimality are also shown. For our purposes, the column labeled "Basis Status" can be ignored.[10]

In the bottom half of the report, the column labeled "Left-Hand Side" indicates that this solution utilizes all 1200 pounds of plastic and all 2400 minutes of production time, which results in zero slack for both of these constraints (as indicated in the column labeled "Slack or Surplus"). A total of 720 dozen items is produced, which yields a slack of 80 dozen from the limit of 800 dozen; production of Space Rays exceeds that of Zappers by 240 dozen, a slack of 210 dozen from the limit of 450 dozen. The shadow prices and the ranges of feasibility for the constraints are also provided.

	Linear and Integer Programming							
File Format Results Utilities Window Help								
Combined Report for GALAXY INDUSTRIES								
17:50:21		Friday	August	09	1996			
Decision Variable	**Solution Value**	**Unit Cost or Profit c(j)**	**Total Contribution**	**Reduced Cost**	**Basis Status**	**Allowable Min. c(j)**	**Allowable Max. c(j)**
1	SPACERAY	480.00	8.00	3,840.00	0	basic	3.75	10.00
2	ZAPPER	240.00	5.00	1,200.00	0	basic	4.00	10.67
	Objective	Function	(Max.) =	5,040.00				
	Constraint	**Left Hand Side**	**Direction**	**Right Hand Side**	**Slack or Surplus**	**Shadow Price**	**Allowable Min. RHS**	**Allowable Max. RHS**
1	PLASTIC	1,200.00	<=	1,200.00	0	3.40	600.00	1,350.00
2	PRODTIME	2,400.00	<=	2,400.00	0	0.40	2,050.00	2,800.00
3	TOTAL	720.00	<=	800.00	80.00	0	720.00	M
4	MIX	240.00	<=	450.00	210.00	0	240.00	M

FIGURE 3.23   WINQSB Output—Galaxy Industries

EXCEL OUTPUT

Excel offers the user the possibility of generating three different reports: (1) an *answer report*; (2) a *sensitivity report*; and (3) a *limits report*. (This last report is of little value and will not be discussed here.)

Answer Report

In an answer report, like the one shown in Figure 3.24, the optimal value of the objective function and the optimal solution can be found in the columns labeled "Final Value." The amount of each resource used (left-hand side) is found in the column labeled "Cell Value," and the slack or surplus for each constraint is shown in the column labeled "Slack." The first row in each section, labeled "Cell," gives the cell reference in which the corresponding information is located on the spreadsheet.

---

[10]In general, if a variable is not at its lower bound (usually 0) or its upper bound (usually $+\infty$), the variable is *basic*. If the variable is *nonbasic*, its value is either its upper or lower bound.

FIGURE 3.24   Excel—Answer Report

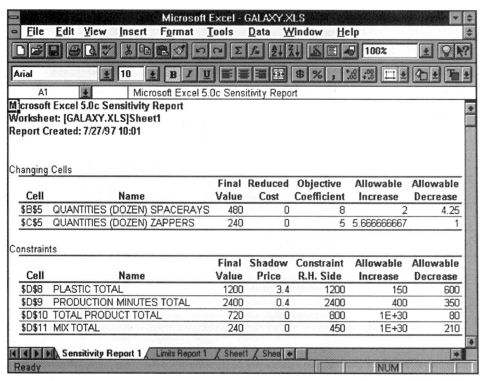

FIGURE 3.25   Excel—Sensitivity Report

Sensitivity Report

The sensitivity report (Figure 3.25) contains the remainder of the information found in the WINQSB combined report. Note, however, that rather than giving the exact limits of the ranges of optimality and feasibility, these ranges are expressed in terms of maximum increases and decreases in the current coefficients. Again, the first column of each section gives the location on the spreadsheet of the corresponding final values of the item under "Name."

LINDO OUTPUT

LINDO (Figure 3.26) uses the term "dual prices" rather than "shadow prices" and returns values with signs opposite those used in WINQSB and Excel. In addition, LINDO always returns nonnegative "reduced cost" values, whereas WINQSB and Excel return nonpositive values for maximization problems and nonnegative values for minimization problems.

OBJECTIVE FUNCTION VALUE

1)	5040.00000	

VARIABLE	VALUE	REDUCED COST
X1	480.000000	.000000
X2	240.000000	.000000

ROW	SLACK OR SURPLUS	DUAL PRICES
2	.000000	3.400000
3	.000000	.400000
4	80.000000	.000000
5	210.000000	.000000

RANGES IN WHICH THE BASIS IS UNCHANGED:

OBJ COEFFICIENT RANGES

VARIABLE	CURRENT COEFFICIENT	ALLOWABLE INCREASE	ALLOWABLE DECREASE
X1	8.000000	2.000000	4.250000
X2	5.000000	5.666667	1.000000

RIGHT-HAND SIDE RANGES

ROW	CURRENT RHS	ALLOWABLE INCREASE	ALLOWABLE DECREASE
2	1200.000000	150.000000	600.000000
3	2400.000000	400.000000	350.000000
4	800.000000	INFINITY	80.000000
5	450.000000	INFINITY	210.000000

FIGURE 3.26   LINDO Output

USING COMPUTER OUTPUT TO GENERATE A MANAGEMENT REPORT

Given the computer solution to the problem faced by Galaxy Industries, the following report can be prepared for Hal Barnes, Galaxy's production manager. This report compares the results of the recommended policy to those of the current policy at Galaxy Industries. It not only summarizes the results but also details the distribution of the resources as well as sensitivity issues that might be of interest to management. The statements made about the shadow price for plastic and production hours outside their ranges of feasibility are based on completely re-solving the problem.

MEMORANDUM

To: Hal Barnes, Production Manager
Galaxy Industries

From: Student Consulting Group

Subj: Optimal Production Quantities for Space Rays and Zappers

Galaxy Industries wishes to determine production levels for its Space Ray and Zapper water guns, which will maximize the company's weekly profit. It is our understanding that production of these products occurs in batches of one dozen each; however, any batch not completed in a given week is considered "work in progress" and will be finished at the beginning of the following week.

Physical production limitations include the amount of plastic (1200 pounds) and available production time (40 hours) to the company on a weekly basis. In addition, the company wishes to adhere to marketing recommendations that limit total production to 800 dozen units weekly and restrict weekly production of Space Rays to a maximum of 450 dozen more than the number of Zappers produced. Current weekly production levels of 550 dozen Space Rays and 100 dozen Zappers result in a $4900 weekly profit for Galaxy.

We have had the opportunity to determine the plastic and production time requirements for these products and to analyze Galaxy's situation. By assuming profit and production requirements are fixed and constant, we were able to solve this as a linear programming model using Excel.

ANALYSIS AND RECOMMENDATION

Based on the results of our model, we recommend that Galaxy change its production levels to the following:

Space Rays	480 dozen
Zappers	240 dozen
Weekly profit	$5040

The current and proposed policies are compared in Table I.

TABLE I. Current vs. proposed policies—Galaxy Industries

	Current Policy (Weekly basis)			
	Production (doz.)	Plastic (lb.)	Production Time (hr.)	Profit ($)
Space Rays	550	1100	27.50	$4,400
Zappers	100	100	6.67	$ 500
Total	650	1200	34.17	$4,900
Unused		0	5.83	

	Proposed Policy (Weekly basis)			
	Production (doz.)	Plastic (lb.)	Production Time (hr.)	Profit ($)
Space Rays	480	960	24.00	$3,840
Zappers	240	240	16.00	$1,200
Total	720	1200	40.00	$5,040
Unused		0	0	

As this table indicates, both policies produce less than the limit of 800 dozen suggested by the marketing department. The proposed policy has a more balanced production of Space Rays and Zappers than the present production policy. Under the current policy, weekly production of Space Rays exceeds that of Zappers by the maximum limit of 450 dozen. Under the proposed plan, this difference would be reduced to 240 dozen.

The $5040 weekly profit corresponding to the recommended production schedule represents a 2.9% (or $140) increase in weekly profit, or a $7280 annual increase in company profits. This amount could be used to increase marketing of the current products, fund production of the new Big Squirt model under development, or lease more efficient machines to improve product profit contributions.

Although this model is based on profit projections of $8 per dozen Space Ray units and $5 per dozen Zapper units, our analysis reveals that our recommendation would remain unchanged unless the Space Ray profit is higher than $10.00 or lower than $3.75 (a 25% underestimation or a 59% overestimation), or the Zapper profit is higher than $10.67 or lower than $4.00 (a 113% underestimation or a 20% overestimation). We are confident that our profit projections fall well within this margin of error.

If Galaxy has the opportunity to purchase additional plastic from its vendor, our analysis shows that it would prove profitable to purchase up to 150 pounds of plastic, as long as the cost does not exceed $3.40 per pound. If an additional 150 pounds of plastic are purchased, our recommendation is to produce 600 dozen Space Rays and 250 dozen Zappers. There is insufficient production time to make use of more than 150 additional pounds of plastic while still adhering to the marketing department restriction that Space Ray production not exceed Zapper production by more than 450 dozen.

If, in lieu of purchasing additional plastic, Galaxy considers scheduling overtime, we have concluded that scheduling up to 6⅔ hours of overtime will be profitable only if total overtime costs do not exceed $24 per hour. At this point, the limit on the maximum production of 800 dozen total units will be met by producing 400 dozen units each of Space Rays and Zappers.

Production Recommendations With Additional Resources			
Additional Resource	Space Rays (doz.)	Zappers (doz.)	Profit ($)
150 pounds of plastic	600	150	$5,550
6⅔ hours overtime	400	400	$5,200

These recommendations are based on changes in only one resource—plastic or overtime. The Student Consulting Group is available to analyze any combination of changes in plastic availability and overtime, changes in the marketing department's restrictions, or any other changes in the company's position. Please do not hesitate to call on us again for such analyses.

3.13 SUMMARY

We have presented the basic modeling approach for linear programming in this chapter. The decision variables in linear programming models are assumed to be continuous (not integer) and to have known, fixed coefficients in the objective function and constraints. The objective and the use of resources must exhibit constant returns to scale, and no interaction between the decision variables can take place.

A linear programming model will have either a unique solution or multiple optimal solutions and be either unbounded or infeasible. The key property of linear programs is that an optimal solution for a linear program will always occur at an extreme point.

We have also demonstrated a graphical solution to linear programming. While this procedure is appropriate for problems with only two variables, other solution methods, such as the simplex method, must be used to solve problems with more decision variables.

Software programs, such as WINQSB, Excel, or LINDO, can be used to solve linear programming problems. These programs produce the following important sensitivity analysis information:

Reduced cost   The amount an objective function coefficient must change in order for a variable to become positive in the optimal solution

Range of optimality   The range of values for an objective function coefficient such that the optimal solution does not change

Shadow (dual) price   The per unit change to the optimal objective function value when a right-hand side constant changes within its range of feasibility; if the resource cost is included in the calculation of the objective function coefficients, the shadow price will represent a "premium" value beyond the current price of the resource.

Range of feasibility   The range of values for a right-hand side constant in which the shadow price is valid

The following table gives the signs of the reduced costs and shadow (dual) prices at the optimal solution for each of these three packages, assuming that the problem is expressed in nonnegative variables with no upper bounds.

Signs At Optimality

	WINQSB and Excel		LINDO
Objective Function	Maximize	Minimize	Maximize or Minimize
Reduced Costs			
Variable = 0	≤ 0	≥ 0	≥ 0
Variable > 0	0	0	0
Shadow (Dual) Prices			
Nonbinding constraint	0	0	0
Binding "$\leq$" constraint	≥ 0	≤ 0	≥ 0
Binding "$\geq$" constraint	≤ 0	≥ 0	≤ 0
Binding "=" constraint	Either	Either	Either

Ranges of optimality and feasibility apply to making changes to a single coefficient only. A 100% rule gives a sufficient condition for these ranges to be valid when multiple changes to coefficients are made.

An important concept in linear programming is that of complementary slackness. For objective function coefficients, this principle states that, at optimality, either a variable is at its bound (usually 0) or its reduced cost is 0. For right-hand side coefficients, the complementary slackness principle states that, at optimality, either there is no slack (or surplus) on a given constraint or the value of its shadow price is 0.

WINQSB Input for the Galaxy Industries Model

- From the main menu, click on LP-ILP.
- From the pull-down File menu, select New Problem or click the first icon on the toolbar.
- The screen in Exhibit 3.1 appears in which we input the specifications for the model.

EXHIBIT 3.1

The input is the problem title (GALAXY INDUSTRIES), the number of variables (2), and the number of constraints (4). We will use the default value of a maximization objective function, nonnegative continuous (not integer) variable types, and the spreadsheet matrix format.

- Click on OK.

This gives us the screen in which to input the data (Exhibit 3.2).

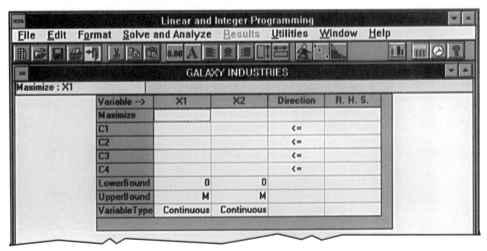

EXHIBIT 3.2

- Input the coefficients and the direction of constraints. (The default values can be changed by double clicking in the cell.)
- Pull down the Edit menu and select Variable Names and Constraint Names to change the variable and constraint names (if desired) from the default values of X1, X2, and so on, and C1, C2, and so on.

The Lower Bound of "0" notes that the variables are restricted to "≥ 0"; the Upper Bound of "M" implies that there is no upper bound ("M" implies that the bound is a number close to $+\infty$). Exhibit 3.3 shows the data entry for Galaxy Industries. The solution is obtained as follows:

- Pull down the Solve and Analyze menu and click on Solve the Problem."

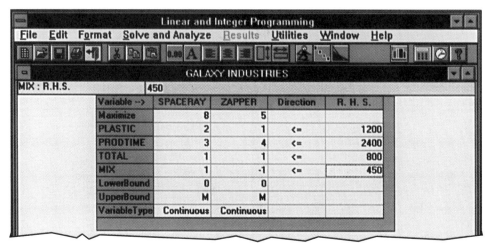

EXHIBIT 3.3

Once the problem has been solved, the Combined Report presented in Section 3.12 is displayed.[11] At this point, the user may wish either to save or to print the problem. These are options that are accessed in the File menu. We suggest that the file name for a saved linear programming file have the suffix .LPP. Saved files can be accessed from the File menu or by clicking on the second icon on the tool bar.

Many graphical analyses, which are excellent for making charts, are available by using the graph icon on the toolbar. WINQSB also includes an extensive Help menu.

---

[11]If the problem is unbounded or infeasible, this will be printed instead of a combined report.

APPENDIX 3.2

Excel Input for the Galaxy Industries Model

We assume the reader of this appendix is familiar with standard Excel functions, such as how to input formulas and the difference between absolute (denoted with $) and relative addresses.

When the Excel spreadsheet is first entered, you should begin by setting up the problem heading and the row and column labels as conveniently as possible, leaving one extra column that will indicate the value of the left-hand side of each constraint once variable values have been determined. "SUMPRODUCT" formulas will be put into these cells as well as into a cell that will calculate the objective function value.

The Excel spreadsheet reproduced here represents the input for the Galaxy Industries problem. In this presentation, row 5 is set aside for the value of the decision variables, row 6 for the profit generated by each decision variable, and column D for the total of the left-hand side of both the profit function and the constraints, but these could be placed anywhere on the spreadsheet.

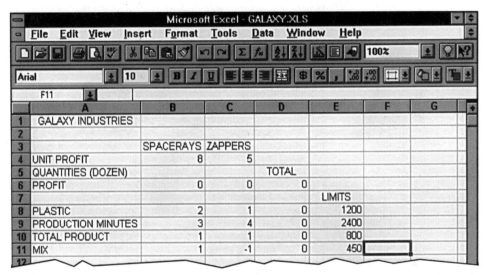

EXHIBIT 3.4

This spreadsheet (Exhibit 3.4) is generated as follows:

Enter Formulas for Profit Contributions

- In cell B6 enter =B4*B5.
- Copy B6 to all other product profit cells. (Here, B6 is only copied to C6; C6 is now =C4*C5.)
- In cell D6 enter =SUM(B6:C6)—*this is the objective function value.*

Enter Formulas for Left-Hand Side Values

- In cell D8 enter =SUMPRODUCT($B$5:$C$5,B8:C8) to generate the total left-hand side for the first constraint.
- Drag D8 to D11 to generate the left-hand side values for the other constraints.

> In cell D9 will be   =SUMPRODUCT($B$5:$C$5,B9:C9);
> In cell D10 will be =SUMPRODUCT($B$5:$C$5,B10:C10);
> In cell D11 will be =SUMPRODUCT($B$5:$C$5,B11:C11).

Now select the pull-down menu under Tools and click on Solver. . . . This gives us the dialog box in Exhibit 3.5.

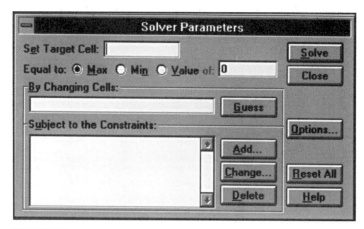

EXHIBIT 3.5

Denote the cells that hold the objective function value and the values of the variables and denote the objective function criterion

- Click on Options . . . and make sure that the Assume Linear Model box has an "X."
- Denote the cell that contains the objective function value by clicking on Target Cell and then clicking (or entering) the objective function cell (D6).
- Select the Objective Function Criterion in the row labeled Equal to: (Default is Max).
- Denote the location of the decision variables by clicking on By Changing Cells and then highlighting the cells that hold the values of the variables (B5 and C5).

Enter Nonnegativity Constraints

- Click on Add to get the Add Constraint dialog box.
- Enter the negativity constraints by clicking on the Cell Reference: side, then clicking (and dragging) the cells that hold the values of the variables (B5 and C5); change the sign to "≥" and enter a "0" in the Constraint:

The result is shown in Exhibit 3.6.

EXHIBIT 3.6

- Click on Add to return to add additional constraints.

Enter Functional Constraints

- Click on the Cell Reference: side, then click (and drag) the cells that hold the values of the left-hand side (D8 through D11).
- Leave the sign as "≤."
- Click on the Constraint side and click and drag the cells that have the right-hand side limits for the constraints (E8 through E11).

(You can see that grouping the "≤," "≥," and "=" constraints together makes the Excel input easier.)
The result is shown in Exhibit 3.7.

EXHIBIT 3.7

- Click on OK to return to the Solver Parameters dialog box, shown in Exhibit 3.8.

EXHIBIT 3.8

- Click on Solve.

The screens in Exhibits 3.9 and 3.10 appear. (The Solver Results dialog box will actually appear on the spreadsheet.)

	A	B	C	D	E	F	G
1	GALAXY INDUSTRIES						
2							
3		SPACERAYS	ZAPPERS				
4	UNIT PROFIT	8	5				
5	QUANTITIES (DOZEN)	480	240	TOTAL			
6	PROFIT	3840	1200	5040			
7					LIMITS		
8	PLASTIC	2	1	1200	1200		
9	PRODUCTION MINUTES	3	4	2400	2400		
10	TOTAL PRODUCT	1	1	720	800		
11	MIX	1	-1	240	450		

EXHIBIT 3.9

The screen in Exhibit 3.9 is the Excel spreadsheet after the optimal solution has been determined. The screen in Exhibit 3.10, labeled Solver Results, allows you to generate the reports based on the optimal solution. None, one, two, or all three reports can be selected; then click on OK. At this point you can save, edit, or exit from the problem or review the generated reports.

EXHIBIT 3.10

APPENDIX 3.3

LINDO Input for the Galaxy Industries Model

LINDO for Windows is a popular commercial program for solving linear and integer programming models that is available in many business and university settings. Rather than entering coefficients into cells of a spreadsheet, LINDO for Windows uses a "word processing" approach for data entry, utilizing the abreviations MAX for "Maximize," MIN for "Minimize," ST for "subject to," < for "≤," and > for "≥."

When you first enter LINDO you are presented with a blank screen with the work ⟨untitled⟩ on the window bar. In the window below this bar, begin by typing the objective function on the first line, the letters ST on the second line, and the functional constraints on the third and succeeding lines. You must make sure the variable names are spelled the same each time they are used; LINDO assumes, for example, that "x1" and "X1" are two different variables. LINDO also assumes that all variables are nonnegative; if one or more variables is unrestricted (say X7), it can be entered after the functional constraints by typing FREE X7. You signify that your data entry is complete by typing the word END.

Exhibit 3.11 shows the data input window for the Galaxy Industries problem.

EXHIBIT 3.11

Problems are solved in LINDO by selecting Solve from the Solve menu. If you answer "YES" at the DO RANGE (SENSITIVITY) ANALYSIS? prompt, you obtain the output shown in Figure 3.26 in Section 3.12

𝒫ROBLEMS

Problems in this chapter require only two decision variables and may be solved either graphically or by computer software, such as WINQSB, Excel, or LINDO.

1. PRODUCTION. Wilson Manufacturing produces both baseballs and softballs, which it wholesales to vendors around the country. Its facilities permit the manufacture of a maximum of 500 dozen baseballs and a maximum of 500 dozen softballs each day. The cowhide covers for each ball are cut from the same processed cowhide sheets. Each dozen baseballs require five square feet of cowhide, including waste, whereas each dozen softballs require six square feet. Wilson has 3600 square feet of cowhide sheets available each day.

   Production of baseballs and softballs includes making the inside core, cutting and sewing the cover, and packaging. It takes about one minute to manufacture a dozen baseballs and two minutes to manufacture a dozen softballs. A total of 960 minutes is available for production daily.

   a. Formulate a set of linear constraints that characterize the production process at Wilson Manufacturing.
   b. Graph the feasible region for this problem.
   c. Wilson is considering manufacturing either 300 dozen baseballs and 300 dozen softballs or 350 dozen baseballs and 350 dozen softballs. Characterize each of these solutions as an interior point, extreme point, or infeasible point and explain why, regardless of Wilson Manufacturing's objective, neither could be an optimal solution.
   d. If Wilson estimates that its profit is $7 per dozen baseballs and $10 per dozen softballs, determine a production schedule that maximizes Wilson's daily profit.
   e. Characterize each of the constraints as binding, nonbinding, or redundant.

2. MANUFACTURING. Golden Electronics manufactures several products, including 45-inch GE45 and 60-inch GE60 televisions. It makes a profit of $50 on each GE45 and $75 on each GE60 television produced. During each shift, Golden allocates up to 300 man-hours in its production area and 240 man-hours in its assembly area to manufacture the televisions. Each GE45 requires two man-hours in the production area and one man-hour in the assembly area, whereas each GE60 requires two man-hours in the production area and three man-hours in the assembly area.

   a. What production levels of GE45 and GE60 television sets optimize the expected profit per shift?
   b. What is the optimal expected profit per shift?
   c. Are limits on both the availability of production hours and assembly hours binding on the optimal solution? Explain.

3. MANUFACTURING. Consider each of the following changes to the Golden Electronics problem (problem 2) separately:

   a. Determine the range of optimality for the unit profit for GE60 televisions.
   b. What is the shadow price for extra assembly hours?
   c. Determine the range of feasibility for the shadow price of assembly hours.
   d. Determine the optimal solution if the unit profit for GE60 televisions were $300.
   e. If the unit profit for GE60 televisions were $300, what would be the reduced cost for the profit coefficient of GE45 televisions? Interpret.
   f. Suppose the unit profit for GE45 televisions were increased to $90. Would the optimal solution change?
   g. Suppose the unit profit for GE60 televisions were increased to $135. Would the optimal solution change?
   h. What conclusion can be drawn from the 100% rule if the unit profit for GE45 and GE60 televisions were simultaneously increased to $60 and $135, respectively? Solve for the new optimal solution. Is the 100% rule violated? Explain.

4. MANUFACTURING. Suppose that management at Golden Electronics (see problem 2) has decided to do extensive testing on every television manufactured to ensure its

quality standards. Each GE45 television will require inspection time of 30 minutes and each GE60 television 45 minutes.

  a. Reformulate the linear program for television production for Golden Electronics if management made available 80 hours for quality control inspections during each production run.

  b. Give an optimal solution that manufactures as many GE45 television sets as possible.

  c. Give an optimal solution that manufactures as many GE60 television sets as possible.

  d. Give an optimal solution that manufactures exactly three times as many GE45 television sets as GE60 television sets during a shift.

  e. What would be the optimal solution if the profit for GE45 television sets were (i) $49? (ii) $51?

  f. Suppose management made available 120 hours for quality control inspections during each shift. Characterize this constraint for the quality control inspections.

5. DIET PROBLEM. Charley Judd is a salesman for Futura Farm Foods, which is currently marketing a feed for dairy cattle called Moo Town Buffet. On a recent visit to Norfolk, Nebraska, Charley called on Dan Preston, a successful dairy farmer with a herd of 100 dairy cattle.

  Dan's success is due in part to a rigid diet he feeds his cattle. In particular, each cow receives a daily minimum of 100 units of calcium, 20,000 calories, and 1500 units of protein. To accomplish this, Dan has been giving his cattle Cow Chow Feed. Each ounce costs $0.015 and supplies 1 unit of calcium, 400 calories, and 20 units of protein. In contrast, each ounce of the Moo Town Buffet Feed would cost Dan $0.020 and supply 2 units of calcium, 250 calories, and 20 units of protein.

  a. How much is Dan Preston currently spending to feed a dairy cow each day using Cow Chow?

  b. Why would Charley Judd not be successful in persuading Dan Preston to abandon his use of Cow Chow and switch exclusively to Moo Town Buffet?

  c. Charley is a resourceful salesman, and he has offered Dan a plan to mix Cow Chow and Moo Town Buffet. The result would be a lower overall cost to Dan for a feed mixture that meets the minimum calcium, calorie, and protein requirements, and a sale for Charley. What overall mix should Charley recommend to minimize Dan's overall feeding cost per cow?

  d. How much would Dan Preston save daily by feeding his 100 cattle the mixture recommended by Charley Judd?

6. LABOR PLANNING. The Harris Company, a steel fabrication company, has negotiated a contract to supply Breuner Industries with steel trusses on a monthly basis. It employs both skilled workers and apprentices. The average output of a skilled worker is three trusses per hour; apprentices average two trusses per hour. Including benefits, each skilled worker costs the Harris Company $3840 per month, and each apprentice costs Harris $2400 per month.

  The Harris Company is a "union shop" and has negotiated the following agreements with the union which restrict the workforce to be used for the contract with Breuner Industries:

  • At least 25 skilled workers will be used.

  • At least 15 more skilled workers than apprentices will be used.

  • The maximum budget for labor costs is $200,000.

  How many skilled workers and apprentices should be assigned to the project to maximize the total monthly production of trusses? Assume each worker works 160 hours per month and both skilled workers and apprentices can be assigned "part-time" so that fractional values are permitted.

7. LABOR PLANNING. Consider the situation faced by the Harris Company in problem 6.

  a. Determine the shadow prices for each of the constraints. (i) Why is the shadow price for the first restriction zero? (ii) Explain the difference in sign between the shadow prices for second and third restrictions.

b. Suppose the first restriction is eliminated. What effect will this have on the optimal solution?

c. Using the concept of shadow prices, how much will the optimal profit change if the right-hand side of the second restriction were changed to (i) 17? to (ii) 13?

d. Using only the concept of shadow prices, give a bound on the change to the optimal profit if the right-hand side of the third restriction were changed (i) to $150,000; (ii) to $100,000.

e. Suppose the second restriction is eliminated. What effect will this have on the optimal solution?

f. Suppose that the monthly contract with Breuner Industries called for production of 30,000 trusses. How much over the $200,000 budget for labor costs will Harris be required to spend on the project to meet this objective? How many skilled workers and apprentices would now be assigned to the project?

8. MANUFACTURING. Klone Computers manufactures two models of its current line of personal computers: the KCU and the KCP. The KCU, which is purchased primarily by universities and other businesses that network their computers, is equipped with two floppy drives and no hard disk drive. The KCP is designed for home and personal use and is equipped with one floppy drive and one hard disk drive. Each model is housed in a tower case. During the current production run, Klone must manufacture at least 300 KCU computers to satisfy a contract to Texas State University. The following table summarizes the resource requirements and unit profits for each computer model and the resources available for the current production run.

Model	Floppy Drives	Hard Drives	Tower Cases	Production Hours	Unit Profit
KCU	2	0	1	0.4	$100
KCP	1	1	1	0.6	$250
Available	1800	700	1000	480	

Formulate and solve a linear program for Klone to determine its optimal production schedule for this production cycle. How many of the current inventory of floppy drives, hard disk drives, and tower cases will be used in the production cycle? How many are unused? Is all the available production time utilized?

9. MANUFACTURING. For the Klone Computer problem (problem 8):

a. Determine and interpret the range of optimality for each unit profit coefficient.

b. Suppose the unit profit for the KCU model were increased to $150 per unit. Does the optimal solution change? Does the total profit change? Suppose the profit for the KCU model could be increased to $200 per unit. Does the optimal solution change? Does the total profit change?

c. The unit profit coefficients took into account the $50 per unit cost to Klone of the floppy disk drives. Klone has negotiated a deal with another company to purchase floppy disk drives at $35 each. Will the optimal solution change? If so, what will be the new optimal profit?

d. Determine and interpret the shadow prices and range of feasibility for each of the four resources.

e. Determine and interpret the shadow price and the range of feasibility for the minimum production of 300 KCUs.

f. Suppose the constraint requiring the production of at least 300 KCU models were eliminated. Determine the new optimal solution. Interpret this result in light of the shadow price and the lower limit on the range of feasibility found in part (e).

10. ADVERTISING. Print Media Advertising (PMA) has been given a contract to market Buzz Cola via newspaper ads in a major Southern newspaper. Full-page ads in the weekday editions (Monday through Saturday) cost $2000, whereas on Sunday a full-page ad costs $8000. Daily circulation of the newspaper is 30,000 on weekdays and 80,000 on Sunday.

PMA has been given a $40,000 advertising budget for the month of August. The experienced advertising executives at PMA feel that both weekday and Sunday newspaper ads are important; hence, they wish to run the equivalent of at least eight week-day and at least two Sunday ads during August. (Assume that a fractional ad would simply mean that a smaller ad is placed on one of the days; that is, 3.5 ads would mean three full-page ads and one one-half page ad. Also assume that smaller ads reduce exposure and costs proportionately.) This August has 26 weekdays and 5 Sundays.

a. If the objective is to maximize cumulative total exposure (as measured by circulation) for the month of August, formulate a linear program to determine the optimal placement of ads by PMA in the newspaper during August.

b. Explain why the constraints on the maximum number of weekday ads and the maximum number of Sunday ads are both redundant.

c. Comment on the validity of the "no interaction" assumption of linear programming for this model.

d. Solve for the optimal solution.

11. ADVERTISING. For the Print Media Advertising problem (problem 10):

a. Determine and interpret the range of optimality for the exposure (circulation) of weekday and Sunday newspapers.

b. Determine and interpret the shadow prices for each constraint.

c. Suppose the minimum restriction for Sunday ads were eliminated. What would be the new optimal solution? What would be the reduced cost for Sunday ads?

12. MERCHANDISE DISPLAYS. The upscale toy store August Kids has a picture window with 100 linear feet of display space. The theme this month is bicycles and tricycles. At least ten tricycles and eight bicycles are to be displayed. Each tricycle needs three linear feet of space in the window display, and each bicycle requires five linear feet. August Kids makes a profit of $40 on each tricycle and $80 on each bicycle it sells. The probability that, on a given day, a displayed tricycle will be sold is .10 and that a displayed bicycle will be sold is .12. Solve for the optimal number of tricycles and bicycles August Kids should display in its picture window daily under each of the following objectives:

a. Maximize total expected daily profit.

b. Maximize the total expected number of daily sales of tricycles and bicycles.

c. Minimize the total number of tricycles and bicycles displayed.

13. PERSONAL INVESTMENTS. George Rifkin is considering investing some or all of a $60,000 inheritance in a one-year certificate of deposit paying a fixed 6% or a venture capital group project with a guaranteed 3% return but the potential of earning 10%. George would like to invest the minimum amount of money necessary to achieve a potential return of at least $4000 and a guaranteed return of at least $2000.

Formulate a mathematical model and recommend an investment strategy for George. How much of his $60,000 can he keep for his personal use during the year and still meet his investment criteria?

14. PERSONAL INVESTMENTS. Consider the situation faced by George Rifkin in problem 13. He has decided to invest the entire $60,000 inheritance. Besides the certificate of deposit paying 6% and the venture capital group paying a minimum of 3% (but with a potential maximum return of 10%), he is considering investing in an oil exploration company. Although this investment could yield a 100% one-year return, George could also lose his entire investment in the company. (Note: This is not a 0% return but a loss of 100%.)

a. Formulate a three-variable mathematical model for George that will maximize the potential value of his inheritance after one year, given the following investment criteria:

- At most $30,000 is to be invested in the oil exploration company.
- At least $20,000 is to be invested in the certificate of deposit.
- The value of the portfolio must be at least $40,000 at the start of next year.
- All $60,000 is to be invested.

b. Since the constraint modeling that all $60,000 is to be invested is an equality constraint, express the amount invested in the oil exploration company in terms of the two other variables (i.e., X3 = 60,000 − X1 − X2) and reformulate the problem as a two-variable model.

c. Solve for George's optimal investment strategy. What is the maximum potential return? Thus, what is the maximum potential value of the portfolio at the beginning of next year? What is the minimum value of the portfolio at the beginning of next year?

15. LEASE/BUY. Schick Industries needs to replace some of its aging equipment that produces molded frames for its best-selling Schick racing cycle. Schick can lease machines with a rated capacity of 2000 frames per month for $3000 monthly. Alternatively, it can purchase smaller machines with a rated capacity of 800 frames per month for $10,000 down and $1000 monthly.

Schick only has $50,000 available to purchase machines now, which limits the number of machines that it could purchase to five. Schick must produce at least 10,000 frames per month to keep up with customer demand.

a. Formulate a linear program for Schick to minimize its total monthly payments for machines.

b. Characterize the feasible region as bounded, unbounded, or infeasible.

c. Solve for the optimal solution.

d. Suppose that instead of minimizing total monthly payments, Schick wished to maximize total production capacity. Solve the problem with this objective and comment.

e. Comment on the validity of the linear programming assumptions for this model.

16. INTERNATIONAL SHIPPING. The Takahashi Transport Company (TTC) leases excess space on commercial vessels to the United States at a reduced rate of $10 per square foot. The only condition is that goods must be packaged in standard 30-inch-high crates.

TTC ships items in two standard 30-inch-high crates, one eight-square-foot crate (two feet by four feet) and one four-square-foot (two feet by two feet) specially insulated crate. It charges customers $160 to ship an eight-square-foot crate and $100 to ship the insulated four-square-foot crate. Thus, allowing for the $10 per square foot cost, TTC makes a profit of $80 per standard eight-foot crate and $60 on the four-foot crate.

TTC stores the crates until space becomes available on a cargo ship, at which time TTC receives payment from its customers.

TTC has been able to lease 1200 square feet of cargo space on the *Formosa Frigate* cargo ship, which leaves for the United States in two days. As of this date, TTC has 140 eight-square-foot crates and 100 insulated four-square-foot crates awaiting shipment to the United States. It has 48 hours to finish loading the crates, and it estimates the average loading time to be 12 minutes (.2 hour) per eight-square-foot crate and 24 minutes (.4 hour) per four-square-foot crate (owing to the special handling of the insulated crates).

Formulate and solve a linear program for TTC to optimize its profit on the upcoming sailing of the *Formosa Frigate*. What are the optimal values of the slack on each constraint in the optimal solution? Express this result in words.

17. INTERNATIONAL SHIPPING. Consider the situation faced by Takahashi Transport Company (TTC) in problem 16.

a. Determine the range of optimality for each profit coefficient.

b. Determine the range of feasibility for the number of square feet available, the loading time, the number of standard containers available, and the number of insulated containers available.

c. Determine the shadow price for each resource for which a range of feasibility was calculated in part (b). Do you think that any of these should be treated as a sunk cost? Given your answer, explain the meaning of each shadow price.

d. What problem would you have interpreting the shadow prices and the range of feasibility? (Hint: *Consider what would happen if there were one more square foot of space available. What would be the new optimal solution? Would this make sense?*)

e. Suppose that, at the last second, the *Formosa Frigate* decided to raise its charge per square foot from $10 to $12. Note how this change would affect the objective function coefficients. Using the 100% rule, show that the optimal solution would not change.

f. How does this $2 per square foot increase in leasing charges to TTC affect the shadow price for a square foot of space? Does this make sense?

18. POLITICAL CAMPAIGNING. Bob Gray is running for a seat in the House of Representatives from a very competitive district in Atlanta, Georgia. With six days to go in the campaign, he has 250 volunteers who can be assigned to either phone banks or door-to-door canvassing. The average time he expects a volunteer to spend on the campaign is 25 hours.

The campaign manager can staff 20 telephones from 8:00 A.M. to 10:00 P.M. each day. On the average, 30 voters can be reached by phone contact each hour, whereas only 18 voters can be reached each hour by door-to-door canvassing. However, Bob wants at least one-third of the remaining volunteer hours to be used for personal door-to-door contacts and at least 15 phones to be used on a continuous basis during the remaining days of the campaign.

a. How many volunteer hours should be allocated to phone contacts and how many to door-to-door canvassing if Bob wishes the maximum number of voters to be contacted during the final six days of the campaign?

b. Suppose Bob's campaign manager feels that door-to-door contacts are twice as valuable in terms of swaying voter opinion as phone contacts. How many volunteer hours should be allocated to phone contacts and how many to door-to-door canvassing if Bob wishes to maximize the "value" of the contacts during the final six days of the campaign?

19. STOCK INVESTMENTS. Idaho Investments is a small, newly formed investment group that will invest exclusively in local stocks. The group is planning its initial investment of $100,000, which it will allocate between two stocks—Tater, Inc. and Lakeside Resorts. If the group is successful with these investments, it plans to expand its portfolio further into other Idaho-based stocks. For each of the stocks, the group has estimated three numbers:

- The projected annual return per share with reinvested dividends

- A "potential" index—a number between 0 and 1 that measures the likelihood of high returns in a one-year period

- A "risk" index—a number between 0 and 1 that measures the likelihood of a substantial loss in a one-year period.

The portfolio potential factor is obtained by summing the products of the potential factor for an investment times the fraction of the total investment *dollars* in that investment. For example, if X1 is the amount invested in Tater and X2 is the amount invested in Lakeside Resorts, the portfolio potential would be:

(X1/100000)(potential index for Tater) + (X2/100000)(potential index for Lakeside)

The portfolio risk factor is obtained in a similar manner. The current share price and the group estimates for these factors are summarized in the following table.

Stock	Share Price	Estimated Annual Return	Potential Index	Risk Index
Tater, Inc.	$40	10%	.20	.30
Lakeside Resorts	$50	12%	.40	.80

Formulate and solve for the optimal investment strategy in order to maximize overall expected annual return for Idaho Investments if it wishes to:

- Invest all $100,000.

- Keep the portfolio potential at .25 or higher.

- Restrict the portfolio risk to .5 or lower.

20. BAKERY. Mary Custard's is a pie shop that specializes in custard and fruit pies. It makes delicious pies and sells them at reasonable prices so that it can sell all the pies it makes in a day. Every *dozen* custard pies nets Mary Custard's $15 and requires 12 pounds of flour, 50 eggs, and 5 pounds of sugar (and no fruit mixture). Every dozen fruit pies nets a $25 profit and uses 10 pounds of flour, 40 eggs, 10 pounds of sugar, and 15 pounds of fruit mixture.

On a given day, the bakers at Mary Custard's found that they had 150 pounds of flour, 500 eggs, 90 pounds of sugar, and 120 pounds of fruit mixture with which to make pies.

  a. Formulate a linear program that will give the optimal production schedule of pies for the day.

  b. Solve for the optimal production schedule.

  c. If Mary Custard's could double its profit on custard pies, should more custard pies be produced? Explain.

  d. If Mary Custard's raised the price (and hence the profit) on all pies by $0.25 ($3.00 per dozen), would the optimal production schedule for the day change? Would the profit change?

  e. Suppose Mary Custard's found that 10% of its fruit mixture had been stored in containers that were not air-tight. For quality and health reasons, it decided that it would be unwise to use any of this portion of the fruit mixture. How would this affect the optimal production schedule? Explain.

  f. Mary Custard's currently pays $2.50 for a five-pound bag of sugar from its bakery supply vendor. (The $0.50 per pound price of sugar is included in the unit profits given earlier.) Its vendor has already made its deliveries for the day. If Mary Custard's wishes to purchase additional sugar, it must buy it from Donatelli's Market, a small, local independent grocery store that sells sugar in one-pound boxes for $2.25 a box. Should Mary Custard's purchase any boxes of sugar from Donatelli's Market? Explain.

21. BAKERY. For the problem faced by Mary Custard's in problem 20:

  a. Each pie is baked and sold in an aluminum pie tin. Suppose at the start of the day Mary Custard's had 200 pie tins available. Would the production schedule change from that determined in part (b) of problem 20?

  b. Answer part (a) assuming that there were only 100 pie tins.

  c. Mary Custard's has, in the past, made a third type of pie—a chocolate pie. Given the current prices of ingredients, Mary Custard's estimates that it would net a profit of $27 per dozen chocolate pies. Each dozen chocolate pies requires 15 pounds of flour, 30 eggs, and 12 pounds of sugar (and no fruit mixture). Using the marginal cost analysis discussed in Section 3.9, show that it would not be profitable to bake any chocolate pies this day even if Mary Custard's had an abundant supply of chocolate.

  d. What is the minimum profit for a dozen chocolate pies which would justify their production?

22. MATERIAL BLENDING. Missouri Mineral Products (MMP) purchases two unprocessed ores from Bolivia Mining, which it uses in the production of various compounds. Its current needs are for 800 pounds of copper, 600 pounds of zinc, and 500 pounds of iron. The amount of each mineral found in *each* 100 *pounds* of the unprocessed ores and MMP's cost *per* 100 *pounds* are given in the following table.

Ore	Copper	Zinc	Iron	Waste	Cost
La Paz ore	20	20	20	40	$100
Sucre ore	40	25	10	25	$140

  a. Formulate and solve a linear program to determine the amount of each ore that should be purchased in order to minimize total purchasing costs.

  b. Calculate and interpret the range of optimality for the cost of 100 pounds of each unprocessed ore.

c. Suppose the cost of Sucre ore was $250 per 100 pounds. Why would the solution in part (a) not be optimal? What is the reduced cost for Sucre ore in this case? Explain.

d. Calculate and interpret the shadow prices and the range of feasibility for the requirements for copper, zinc, and iron.

e. Suppose a constraint were added that required that waste be limited to a maximum of 1000 pounds. Characterize this revised problem.

23. ADMINISTRATIVE SUPPORT. The federal government has asked Boeing Aircraft to resubmit its bid to be the prime contractor for a modified version of the space station. Boeing's design division is expected to need temporary additional secretarial support to handle a substantial increase in paperwork that will be generated until the bid is completed. Boeing can hire temporary personnel from Techhelp, a local temporary help firm specializing in technical secretarial support, or it can temporarily transfer secretarial staff from other divisions within the company.

Given the results of qualifications tests, it appears that an in-house secretary who is transferred can produce about 40 pages of usable work daily. Such work will require approximately two hours a day in technical assistance from supervisory personnel. Because he or she is less familiar with the Boeing environment than Boeing employees, it is estimated that a Techhelp employee can produce only 30 pages of work per day. Because of the Techhelp employee's higher degree of technical secretarial training, however, each employee only requires approximately one hour of technical assistance from supervisory personnel.

Boeing has allocated up to 10 workstations to the design division for additional secretarial support, so that the division can utilize at most 10 workers. It has further allocated one full-time employee for technical assistance providing eight hours of technical support time available daily.

a. Formulate a linear program to determine the optimal number of temporary Techhelp employees to hire and in-house transfers needed to maximize the total potential number of pages produced per day. Assume that fractional values represent workers assigned part-time to the division.

b. Why is there a non-zero reduced cost associated with the output of in-house transfers but not with the output of Techhelp employees? What is the reduced cost for the output of in-house transfers?

c. Calculate the range of optimality for each objective function coefficient. Explain in simple terms why the lower limit for the range of optimality for the output of in-house transfers is $-\infty$.

24. ADMINISTRATIVE SUPPORT. Consider the situation faced by Boeing in problem 23.

a. Determine and interpret the range of feasibility for the availability of the number of workstations and the number of hours of technical assistance available. Explain in simple terms why the upper limit of the range of feasibility for the number of workstations is $+\infty$.

b. Suppose, in monetary terms, Boeing feels that each additional potential page is worth $1 and the cost of a supervisor's time for technical assistance is $25 per hour. Using shadow prices, show why having up to two additional hours of supervisory assistance is profitable to the company.

c. Show (by re-solving the problem) why hiring a second full-time employee (increasing the hours of available technical support to 16) would not be in Boeing's best interest.

25. MANUFACTURING. Compaids, Inc. manufactures two types of slide-out keyboard trays for use with personal computers. Model CI5 is designed for desktop use. It can stand alone, or it can fit under a desktop CPU or monitor. Model UN8 is designed to be mounted underneath a desk with screws. Both units are manufactured from laminated particle board supplied by SSS Industries and use two slide assemblies purchased from Corrigation, Inc. The following table summarizes the wholesale selling price and requirements for each keyboard tray.

Model	Selling Price	Cost of Screws	Particle Board	Production Time
CI5	$11.10	$0.40	8 sq.ft.	4 min.
UN8	$12.40	$0.90	5 sq.ft.	6 min.

Each week, SSS can sell Compaids up to 15,000 square feet of laminated particle at $0.40 per square foot, and Compaids can purchase up to 4500 slide assemblies from Corrigation at $0.75 each. Screws are in abundant supply and do not restrict production. Up to five Compaids workers, working eight hours a day, five days a week, can be assigned to the production of the keyboard trays; however, their labor costs are considered sunk costs.

a. Show that the net unit profit for the model CI5 and UN8, excluding the sunk labor costs, are $6 and $8, respectively.

b. Solve for the optimal weekly production quantities, given the limits on laminated particle board, slide assemblies, and production time.

c. If 200 additional slide assemblies were made available each week, what is the most Compaids should consider paying for the 200 slide assemblies?

d. If one additional worker were made available, explain why the shadow prices would change.

e. What is the maximum selling price for the model CI5 units for which the optimal weekly production schedule, found in part (b), remains unchanged?

CASE STUDIES

CASE 1: *Kootenay Straw Broom Company*

The Kootenay Straw Broom Company, located in British Columbia, Canada, is a small, family-run business that hand-makes two models of straw brooms, the Pioneer and the Heritage models, which are sold in "country stores" throughout Canada and the northwestern United States. Given its current production capacity and selling price, Kootenay is able to sell all the brooms it produces.

The Pioneer model is the company's basic model. It consists of a plain wooden handle, utilizes one pound of straw, and takes an average of 15 minutes (.25 hours) to make. Kootenay sells them for $12.75 each. The Heritage model is the company's deluxe model. Although the same wooden handles are used, they are run through a decorative lathe and attached to a larger base consisting of 1.5 pounds of straw. These two factors increase the production time of the Heritage broom to 24 minutes (.40 hours), and Kootenay sells them for $18 each.

Kootenay receives daily deliveries of straw that is specially treated for their brooms from Tyler Farms. Tyler can supply Kootenay with up to 350 pounds daily of the specially treated straw. This straw costs Kootenay $1.50 per pound.

Kootenay purchases its handles from Adhor Mills, which manufactures the handles according to Kootenay's specifications. Adhor Mills is a two-hour drive from Kootenay. It currently makes only one daily delivery to Kootenay in a truck capable of hauling 30 boxes of 10 handles each (or 300 handles). Adhor charges Kootenay $7.50 per box of 10 for manufacture and delivery of the handles.

Adhor also makes a major delivery of products to a town 45 miles from Kootenay and has offered to swing by Kootenay with one additional box of 10 handles. However, the added expense for making this detour means that Kootenay would have to pay Adhor $25 for this extra box of 10 handles.

Kootenay averages 80 production hours per day. Since

Kootenay is a family-run business, it considers the daily cost of $2800 for its overhead and "family labor" of its 10 members as sunk costs required for the business. Kootenay is ready to consider several options that could increase the daily profit:

1. Seeking additional sources for treated straw
2. Taking Adhor Mills up on its offer to deliver an extra box of handles (for $25)
3. Adding a half-time worker (four hours per day) for $50 per day

Prepare a report for the Kootenay Straw Broom Company that evaluates the option or set of options it should implement. The report should:

1. Recommend an optimal production under current conditions.
2. Include a summary of the determination of unit profits of $10.50 and $15.00, respectively, for the Pioneer and Broom models, showing that the cost of both treated straw and broom handles are included in these calculations.
3. Show that after subtracting fixed costs, the business nets $500 per day.
4. Give a brief analysis of the sensitivity of the objective function coefficients.
5. Analyze the options using the correct interpretation of the shadow prices considering which costs are included and which costs are sunk. (*Remember*: Do not call them shadow prices in the report.)
6. Use the 100% rule to evaluate whether more than one option should be implemented. (Calculations, if shown, should be placed in an appendix.)

CASE 2: *Bay City Movers*

Bay City Movers is a local company that specializes in intercity moves. In the business plan submitted to its backers, Bay City has committed itself to a total trucking capacity of at least 36 tons.

The company is in the process of replacing its entire fleet of trucks with 1-ton pickup trucks and 2½-ton moving van-type trucks. The 1-ton pickup trucks will be manned by one worker, whereas the large vans will utilize a total of four personnel for larger moves.

Bay City Movers currently employs 48 workers and has facilities for 40 trucks. Pickup trucks cost the company $24,000; the moving vans cost $60,000. The company wishes to make a minimum investment in trucks that will provide a

trucking capacity of at least 36 tons while not requiring any new hires or trucking facilities.

Although the continuity assumption is violated (since the number of each truck purchased must be integer), use a linear programming model to determine the optimal purchase of pickup trucks and vans for Bay City Movers. You will find that alternative optimal solutions are possible. Prepare a report detailing several of these options and discuss the pros and cons of each. Among the alternatives you should present in your report are the following:

1. Purchasing only one type of truck—you can do this by adding the constraint X1 = 0 and solving, then elimi-

nating that constraint and adding the constraint X2 = 0. See which one gives the minimum objective function value.

2. Purchasing the same number of pickup trucks as moving vans—you can do this by adding the constraint X1 − X2 =0 and solving.

3. Purchasing the minimum total number of trucks—you can do this by adding a constraint that requires 24,000X1 + 60,000X2 to be the minimum investment amount and then adding a new objective function of MIN X1 + X2.

Note that in all three cases, the optimal solution turns out to have integer values. Also include in your report pertinent sensitivity information you feel would be of interest to management at Bay City Movers.

LINEAR PROGRAMMING APPLICATIONS

With assets totaling over $4.4 billion, San Miguel Corporation, the most diversified company in the Philippines, generates over 4% of that country's gross national product. Beverage production and distribution is a major component of the company's operations. San Miguel produces six brands of beer and bottles three wine and spirit brands at three different sites. It also bottles five brands of soft drinks for Coca-Cola Bottlers Philippines at 18 bottling plants.

Among its other endeavors are the manufacturing of packaging materials, such as glass containers, plastic crates, polybags, and cardboard boxes, and the development and manufacturing of animal feeds for its chicken, hog, and cattle interests. Other sources of profit are the manufacture and distribution of ice cream, butter, cheese, and other dairy and nondairy products, the raising of prawns for export, and the processing and trading of coconut oil.

Since 1971, management science, in general, and linear models, in particular, have had a significant impact on the company's bottom line. Projects in which linear models have played a major role include blending problems for determining animal feed mixes and ice cream base composition, distribution problems for determining allocations among its 68 production facilities and 230 sales offices, and marketing problems, such as minimizing the cost of television advertising. The output from some of these models has, in turn, been used as input for larger management science and expert systems projects.

Over the course of several years, use of these models has saved the company millions of dollars, allowing it to expand at a vigorous rate. By 1995, San Miguel had become the first non-Japanese and non-Australian firm to rank in the top 20 Asian food and beverage companies. As it looks to the future, San Miguel will continue to refine and develop integrative linear models in order to enhance its growth and financial strength.

4.1 $\mathscr{B}$UILDING GOOD LINEAR MODELS

Following World War II, the U.S. Air Force sponsored research for solving military planning and distribution models. In 1947, the simplex algorithm was developed for solving these types of linear models. Not long after, the first commercial uses of linear programming were reported in "large" businesses that had access to digital computers. Seemingly unrelated industries, such as agriculture, petroleum, iron and steel, transportation, and communications, saved millions of dollars by successfully developing and solving linear models for complex problems.

As computing power has become more accessible, the realm of businesses and government entities using linear models has expanded exponentially. Due to the widespread use of linear models today, it is important to recognize application areas that can benefit from the use of linear programming and to develop good, efficient models which aid the decision maker in making reliable business decisions. Three factors—familiarity, simplification, and clarity—are important considerations when developing such models.

The greater the modeler's *familiarity* with the relationships between competing activities, the limitations of the resources, and the overall objective, the greater the likelihood of generating a usable model. Viewing the problem from as many perspectives as possible (e.g., those of various management levels, front-line workers, and accounting) helps in this regard.

Linear models are always *simplifications* of real-life situations. Usually, some or all of the required linear programming assumptions discussed in Chapter 3 (continuity, constant returns to scale, additivity, and certainty) are violated by an actual situation. Because of the efficiency with which they are solved and the associated sensitivity analysis reports that are generated, however, linear models are generally preferable to more complicated forms of mathematical models.

When developing a model, it is important to address the following question: "Is a very sophisticated model needed, or will a less sophisticated model that gives fairly good results suffice?" The answer, of course, will guide the level of detail required in the model.

Although a model should reflect the real-life situation, we should not try to model every aspect or contingency of the situation. This could get us bogged down in minutiae, adding little, if any, real value to the model while unnecessarily complicating the solution procedure, delaying solution time, and compromising the usefulness of the model. As George Dantzig, the developer of the simplex algorithm for solving linear programming models, points out, however, "What constitutes the proper simplification, is subject to individual judgment and experience. People often disagree on the adequacy of a certain model to describe the situation."[1] In other words, although experience is the best teacher, you should be aware that even experienced management scientists may disagree as to what level of simplification is realistic or warranted in a model.

Finally, a linear programming model should be *clear;* that is, it should be easy to follow and as transparent as possible to the layperson. From a practitioner's point of view, the models should also be easy to input and yield accurate results in a timely manner.

Consider, for example, a model in which X1, X2, and X3 represent the production quantities of three television models to be produced during a production run. Suppose management wishes that no one model represents more than 40% of its total produc-

---

[1]Dantzig, George B., *Linear Programing and Extensions*, Princeton University Press, 1963.

tion. Although the total production is unknown, it can be represented by X1 + X2 + X3. Thus, the following three constraints can express the required conditions:

$$X1 \leq .4(X1 + X2 + X3)$$
$$X2 \leq .4(X1 + X2 + X3)$$
$$X3 \leq .4(X1 + X2 + X3)$$

or

$$.6X1 - .4X2 - .4X3 \leq 0$$
$$-.4X1 + .6X2 - .4X3 \leq 0$$
$$-.4X1 - .4X2 + .6X3 \leq 0$$

Written in this form, not only are the coefficients cumbersome to input into a linear programming computer module, but the constraints do not immediately convey to the layperson that each television model is not to exceed 40% of total production. To clarify the formulation, we could use a new decision variable, X4, known as a *definitional variable*, to represent the total production. Although X4 was not part of the original set of decision variables, we can now simply add it to the list.

The revised formulation must show that X4 = X1 + X2 + X3, but, as indicated in the following expressions, the percentage constraints written in terms of the definitional variable are now much easier to interpret:

$$X1 + X2 + X3 - X4 = 0$$
$$X1 \qquad\qquad - .4X4 \leq 0$$
$$X2 \qquad - .4X4 \leq 0$$
$$X3 - .4X4 \leq 0$$

While we have increased the number of constraints by adding the definitional constraint, the new set of constraints is easier to input and easier to read and interpret when checking the model.[2]

4.2 $\mathcal{L}$INEAR PROGRAMMING MODELS

Some of the tips we have offered for building mathematical models from this and the previous two chapters are summarized below in the form of a checklist. The issues of familiarity and simplification developed above and each of these modelling tips will be illustrated in the formulations of linear models from the private and public sectors presented in the succeeding sections.

In the next eight sections, we present several examples of how linear programming might be applied in business and government. Although each of these models has more than two decision variables and, thus, requires a computer solution, each one is still a scaled-down version of a real-life situation. In Section 4.11, we present a few of the thousands of documented cases of successful linear programming applications.

---

[2]The time needed to solve a linear programming problem typically depends on: (1) the number of constraints; and (2) the percentage of nonzeroes in the constraints. Although adding a definitional variable adds one more constraint to the formulation, the efficiency gained by having additional zeroes can more than offset this fact. A large number of definitional variables should not be added, however, unless they are going to be used to simplify other constraints.

A Checklist for Building Linear Models

1. Begin by listing the details of the problem in short expressions. (We have done this in Chapter 3 using "bullets.")

2. Determine the objective in general terms and then determine what is within the control of the decision maker to accomplish this goal. These controllable inputs are *decision variables*.

3. If, during the course of the formulation, you find that another decision variable is needed, add it to the list at that time and include it in the formulation.

4. Define the decision variables precisely using an appropriate time frame (i.e., cars per month, tons of steel per production run, etc.).

5. When writing a constraint or a function, first formulate it in words in the form: (some expression) ⟨has some relation to⟩ (another expression or constant); then convert the words to the appropriate mathematical symbols.

6. Keep the units in the expressions on both sides of the relation consistent (e.g., one side should not be in hours, the other in minutes).

7. If the right-hand side is an expression rather than a constant, do the appropriate algebra so that the end result is of the form:
   (mathematical function) ⟨has a relation to⟩ (a constant)

8. Use *definitional variables* when appropriate, particularly when many constraints involve percentages.

9. Indicate which variables are restricted to be nonnegative, which have upper or lower bounds, and which are restricted to be integer valued.

Sections 4.3 to 4.10 (1) show how linear programming models can be applied to different situations arising from the functional areas of business and government; (2) illustrate the modeling approach, including some of the problems that might arise in the modeling process; and (3) interpret, analyze, and extend the output from the three software packages discussed in Chapter 3 (WINQSB, Excel, and LINDO).

In the process, we illustrate a number of concepts. We discuss how to choose an appropriate objective function, define decision variables, and write accurate expressions to model the constraints. We present both maximization and minimization problems and discuss the correct interpretation of sensitivity output for both types of models. We also present problems that illustrate how to address unboundedness, infeasibility, and alternative optimal solutions, as well as how to round off variables with noninteger solution values in order to obtain integer values.

To simplify matters, we identify each problem by its applications area, the modeling and solutions concepts illustrated, and the software used to generate the computer output.

4.3 GALAXY INDUSTRIES—AN EXPANSION PLAN

Galaxy.lpp
Galaxy.xls
Galaxy.ltx

Applications Area:	Production, Overtime Scheduling
Concepts:	Maximization
	Sensitivity Analysis (All constraint types)
	Both Signs in Objective Function
	Unit Conversion
	Definitional Variables, Percentage Constraints
Software:	LINDO

Galaxy Industries has been very successful during its first six months of operation and is already looking toward product expansion and possible relocation within the year to a facility in Juarez, Mexico, where both labor and material costs are considerably lower. The availability of the cheaper labor and a contract with a local distributor to supply up to 3000 pounds of plastic at a substantially reduced cost will effectively double the profit for Space Rays to $16 per dozen and triple the profit for Zappers to $15 per dozen.

The new facility will be equipped with machinery and staffed with workers to facilitate a 40-hour regular time work schedule. In addition, up to 32 hours of overtime can be scheduled. Accounting for wages, benefits, and additional plant operating expenses, each scheduled overtime hour will cost the company $180 more than regular time hours.

Galaxy has been test marketing two additional products, tentatively named the Big Squirt and the Soaker, which appear to be as popular as the Space Ray and Zapper. Table 4.1 summarizes the profit and requirements for each product line.

TABLE 4.1   PROFIT AND REQUIREMENTS PER DOZEN

Product	Profit	Plastic (lb.)	Production Time (min.)
Space Rays	$16	2	3
Zappers	$15	1	4
Big Squirts	$20	3	5
Soakers	$22	4	6
Available		3000	40 hrs. (Reg.) 32 hrs. (O/T)

Galaxy has a signed contract with Jaycee Toys, Inc. to supply it with 200 dozen Zappers weekly once the relocation has taken place. The marketing department has revised its strategy for the post-relocation period. It has concluded that, to keep total demand at its peak, Galaxy's most popular model, the Space Ray, should account for exactly 50% of total production, while no other product line should account for more than 40%. But now, instead of limiting production to at most 800 dozen weekly, the department wishes to ensure that production will total at least 1000 dozen units weekly.

Management would like to determine the weekly production schedule (including any overtime hours, if necessary) that will maximize its net weekly profit.

SOLUTION

The following is a brief synopsis of the problem.

- Galaxy wants to maximize its Net Weekly Profit = (Weekly Profit from Sales)−(Extra Cost of Overtime).
- A weekly production schedule, including the amount of overtime to schedule, must be determined.
- The following restrictions exist:
  1. Plastic availability (3000 pounds)
  2. Regular time labor (2400 minutes)
  3. Overtime availability (32 hours)
  4. Minimum production of Zappers (200 dozen)
  5. Appropriate product mix

     (Space Rays = 50% of total production)
     (Zappers, Big Squirts, Soakers ≤ 40% of total production)
  6. Minimum total production (1000 dozen)

DECISION VARIABLES   Galaxy must not only decide on the weekly production rates but also determine the number of overtime hours to utilize each week. Thus, there are five decision variables:

$$X1 = \text{number of dozen Space Rays to be produced each week}$$
$$X2 = \text{number of dozen Zappers to be produced each week}$$
$$X3 = \text{number of dozen Big Squirts to be produced each week}$$
$$X4 = \text{number of dozen Soakers to be produced each week}$$
$$X5 = \text{number of } hours \text{ of overtime to be scheduled each week}$$

OBJECTIVE FUNCTION

The total net weekly profit will be the profit from the sale of each of the products less the cost of overtime. Since each overtime hour costs the company an extra $180, the objective function is:

$$\text{MAXIMIZE } 16X1 + 15X2 + 20X3 + 22X4 - 180X5$$

CONSTRAINTS

The following constraints exist in the Galaxy problem:

Plastic: (Amount of plastic used weekly) $\leq$ 3000 lbs.

$$2X1 + X2 + 3X3 + 4X4 \qquad \leq 3000$$

Production Time: (Number of production *minutes* used weekly) $\leq$
(Number of regular *minutes* available) + (Overtime *minutes* used)

Here,

Number of regular time *minutes* available = 60(40) = 2400
Number of overtime *minutes* used is 60(O/T hours used) = 60X4

Thus, the production time constraint is:

$$3X1 + 4X2 + 5X3 + 6X4 \leq 2400 + 60X5, \text{ or}$$
$$3X1 + 4X2 + 5X3 + 6X4 - 60X5 \leq 2400$$

Overtime Hours: (Number of overtime *hours* used) $\leq$ 32

$$X4 \qquad\qquad \leq 32$$

Zapper Contract: (Number of zappers produced weekly) $\geq$ 200 doz.

$$X2 \qquad\qquad \geq 200$$

Product Mix: Since each of the product mix restrictions is expressed as a percentage of the total production, to clarify the model we introduce the following definitional *variable*:

$$X6 = \text{Total weekly production (in dozens of units)}$$

Definitional Constraint: Before expressing the product mix constraints, we introduce the definitional *constraint* showing that the total weekly production, X6, is the sum of the weekly production of Space Rays, Zappers, Big Squirts, and Soakers: X6 = X1 + X2 + X3 + X4, or

$$X1 + X2 + X3 + X4 - X6 = 0$$

Now the product mix constraints can be written as

(Weekly production of Space Rays) = (50% of total production)

$$X1 \qquad = .5X6$$

(Weekly production of Zappers) $\leq$ (40% of total production)

$$X2 \qquad \leq .4X6$$

(Weekly production of Big Squirts) $\leq$ (40% of total production)

$$X3 \qquad \leq .4X6$$

(Weekly production of Soakers) $\leq$ (40% of total production)

$$X4 \qquad \leq .4X6$$

or

$$
\begin{aligned}
X1 && - .5X6 &= 0 \\
X2 && - .4X6 &\leq 0 \\
X3 && - .4X6 &\leq 0 \\
X4 && - .4X6 &\leq 0
\end{aligned}
$$

Total Production: (Total weekly production) $\geq$ 1000 dozen.

$$X6 \qquad \geq 1000$$

Nonnegativity: All decision variables ≥ 0

$$X1, X2, X3, X4, X5, X6 \geq 0$$

THE MATHEMATICAL MODEL

Thus, the complete mathematical model for the Galaxy Industries expansion problem is:

$$\text{MAXIMIZE} \quad 16X1 + 15X2 + 20X3 + 22X4 - 180X5 \qquad \text{(Weekly profit)}$$
ST:

$$
\begin{aligned}
2X1 + X2 + 3X3 + 4X4 && &\leq 3000 \text{ (Plastic)} \\
3X1 + 4X2 + 5X3 + 6X4 - 60X5 && &\leq 2400 \text{ (Production time)} \\
X5 && &\leq 32 \text{ (Overtime)} \\
X2 && &\geq 200 \text{ (Contract)} \\
X1 + X2 + X3 + X4 \qquad - X6 && &= 0 \text{ (Definition)} \\
X1 \qquad - .5X6 && &= 0 \text{ (Space Rays)} \\
X2 \qquad - .4X6 && &\leq 0 \text{ (Zappers)} \\
X3 \qquad - .4X6 && &\leq 0 \text{ (Big Squirts)} \\
X4 - .4X6 && &\leq 0 \text{ (Soakers)} \\
X6 && &\geq 1000 \text{ (Total)}
\end{aligned}
$$

$$X1, X2, X3, X4, X5, X6 \geq 0 \qquad \text{(Nonnegativity)}$$

LINDO OUTPUT

The problem was solved by LINDO, giving the output shown in Figure 4.1. Some observations are immediate from this output:

- The optimal weekly production schedule is for 1130 dozen units—565 dozen Space Rays (50%), 200 dozen Zappers (17.7%), and 365 dozen Big Squirts (32.3%).
- The optimal weekly profit is $13,580.
- The minimum total production is exceeded by 130 dozen (SURPLUS in row 11).
- No Soakers should be produced, unless the profit increases by $2.50 (REDUCED COST = $2.50) per dozen (to $24.50).
- All 32 hours of overtime (OVERT = 32) are used.

- An increase in the price of overtime will not change the optimal solution, unless the cost of overtime exceeds $270 per hour [$180 + (ALLOWABLE DECREASE OVERT of $90)].

Recognizing that rows (2) through (11) in the output correspond respectively to the functional constraints of the model, we also conclude the following:

- 2425 pounds of plastic (3000 − (SLACK in row 2 of 575)) will be used.
- Extra regular time *minutes* will add $4.50 to total profit (DUAL PRICE in row 3).
- Each overtime *hour* will add $90 to total profit (DUAL PRICE in row 4).

LP OPTIMUM FOUND AT STEP   9

OBJECTIVE FUNCTION VALUE

1)   13580.0000

VARIABLE	VALUE	REDUCED COST
SPACE	565.000000	.000000
ZAP	200.000000	.000000
BIGSQ	365.000000	.000000
SOAK	.000000	2.500000
OVERT	32.000000	.000000
TOTAL	1130.000000	.000000

ROW	SLACK OR SURPLUS	DUAL PRICES
2	575.000000	.000000
3	.000000	4.5.000000
4	.000000	90.000000
5	.000000	-.500000
6	.000000	-2.500000
7	.000000	5.000000
8	252.000000	.000000
9	87.000030	.000000
10	452.000000	.000000
11	130.000000	.000000

RANGES IN WHICH THE BASIS IS UNCHANGED:

OBJ COEFFICIENT RANGES

VARIABLE	CURRENT COEFFICIENT	ALLOWABLE INCREASE	ALLOWABLE DECREASE
SPACE	16.000000	4.000000	12.000000
ZAP	15.000000	.500000	INFINITY
BIGSQ	20.000000	INFINITY	.571429
SOAK	22.000000	2.500000	INFINITY
OVERT	-180.000000	INFINITY	90.000000
TOTAL	.000000	2.000000	6.000000

RIGHTHAND SIDE RANGES

ROW	CURRENT RHS	ALLOWABLE INCREASE	ALLOWABLE DECREASE
2	3000.000000	INFINITY	575.000000
3	2400.000000	920.000000	520.000000
4	32.000000	15.333330	8.666667
5	200.000000	280.000000	89.230800
6	.000000	99.428600	973.333300
7	.000000	486.666700	91.578970
8	.000000	INFINITY	252.000000
9	.000000	INFINITY	87.000030
10	.000000	INFINITY	452.000000
11	1000.000000	130.000000	INFINITY

FIGURE 4.1   LINDO Output for Galaxy Industries

Care must be taken when interpreting some of the information given in the output. For instance:

- Each increase in the number of dozen Zappers required to be produced *above* 200 to meet the contract will reduce the total profit by $0.50 (DUAL PRICE in row 5).

- Each dozen Space Rays *above* 50% that are allowed to be produced will add $5 to the total profit (DUAL PRICE in row 7).

The output also gives us the ranges of optimality and feasibility (expressed in terms of increases and decreases to the original values). Some of the output has no meaningful interpretation, however. For example, a dual price of −$2.50 for changes in the right-hand side of the definitional constraint in row 6: $X1 + X2 + X3 + X4 - X6 = 0$, and the range of optimality of (−$6 to $2) for the objective function coefficient of the total production are meaningless in the context of this problem.

4.4 JONES INVESTMENT SERVICE

Jones.lpp
Jones.xls

Applications Area:	Finance
Concepts:	Minimization
	Sensitivity Analysis (All constraint types)
Software:	Excel

Charles Jones is a financial advisor who specializes in making recommendations to investors who have recently come into unexpected sums of money from inheritances, lottery winnings, etc. He discusses investment goals with his clients, taking into account each client's attitude toward risk and liquidity.

After an initial consultation with a client, Charles selects a group of stocks, bonds, mutual funds, savings plans, and other investments that he feels may be appropriate for consideration in the portfolio. He then secures information on each investment and determines his own rating. With this information he develops a chart giving the risk factors (numbers between 0 and 100, based on his evaluation), expected returns based on current and projected company operations, and liquidity information. At the second meeting Charles defines the client's goals more specifically. The responses are entered into a linear programming computer model, and a recommendation is made to the client based on the results of the model.

Frank Baklarz has just inherited $100,000. Based on their initial meeting, Charles has found Frank to be quite risk-averse. Charles, therefore, suggests the following potential investments that can offer good returns with small risk.

Potential Investment	Expected Return	Jones's Rating	Liquidity Analysis	Risk Factor
Savings account	4.0%	A	Immediate	0
Certificate of deposit	5.2%	A	5-year	0
Atlantic Lighting	7.1%	B+	Immediate	25
Arkansas REIT	10.0%	B	Immediate	30
Bedrock Insurance annuity	8.2%	A	1-year	20
Nocal Mining bond	6.5%	B+	1-year	15
Minicomp Systems	20.0%	A	Immediate	65
Antony Hotels	12.5%	C	Immediate	40

Based on their second meeting, Charles has been able to help Frank develop the following portfolio goals.

1. An expected annual return of at least 7.5%

2. At least 50% of the inheritance in A-rated investments

3. At least 40% of the inheritance in immediately liquid investments

4. No more than $30,000 in savings accounts and certificates of deposit

Given that Frank is risk-averse, Charles would like to make a final recommendation that will minimize total risk while meeting these goals. As part of his service, Charles would also like to inform Frank of potential what-if scenarios associated with this recommendation.

SOLUTION

The following is a brief summary of the problem.

- Determine the amount to be placed in each investment.
- Minimize total overall risk.
- Invest all $100,000.
- Meet the goals developed with Frank Baklarz.

Defining the X's as the amount Frank should allot to each investment, the following linear model represents the situation:

$$
\begin{array}{lllllllllll}
\text{MINIMIZE} & & & 25X3 + & 30X4 + & 20X5 + & 15X6 + & 65X7 + & 40X8 & & \text{(Risk)} \\
\text{ST} & & & & & & & & & & \\
X1 + & X2 + & X3 + & X4 + & X5 + & X6 + & X7 + & X8 = & 100{,}000 & \text{(Total)} \\
.04X1 + .052X2 + & .071X3 + & .1X4 + & .082X5 + & .065X6 + & .2X7 + & .125X8 \geq & 7500 & \text{(Return)} \\
X1 + & X2 & & & X5 & & + X7 & \geq & 50{,}000 & \text{(A-Rated)} \\
X1 & & + X3 + & X4 & & & + X7 + & X8 \geq & 40{,}000 & \text{(Liquid)} \\
X1 + & X2 & & & & & & \leq & 30{,}000 & \text{(Savings/certificate} \\
& & & & & & & & & \text{of deposit)}
\end{array}
$$

$$XJ \geq 0 \; J = 1, \ldots, 8$$

The Excel answer and sensitivity reports appear in Figure 4.2.

RECOMMENDATION According to the answer report, Charles should recommend that Frank invest $17,333 in a savings account, $12,667 in a certificate of deposit, $22,667 in Arkansas REIT, and $47,333 in the Bedrock Insurance Annuity. This gives an overall risk value of 1,626,667 (an average risk factor of 16.27 per dollar invested). Any other combination of investments will give a higher risk value.

REDUCED COSTS According to the sensitivity report, for Atlantic Lighting to be included in the portfolio, its risk factor would have to be lowered by 4.67 to 20.33. Similarly, to include Nocal Mining, Minicomp Systems, or Antony Hotels requires a reduction in their risk factors of 0.67, 1.67, and 1.67, respectively.

RANGE OF OPTIMALITY For each investment, the "Allowable Increase" and "Allowable Decrease" columns in the sensitivity report give the minimum and maximum amounts that the risk factors can change without altering Charles's recommendation. For example, the range of optimality of the risk factor for the Bedrock Insurance annuity is between (20 − 0.5) and (20 + 0.43), or between 19.5 and 20.43. Recall that the range of optimality applies to changing one investment at a time. Since negative risk factors do not make sense, the minimum risk factors for the savings account and certificate of deposit would be 0.

SLACK OR SURPLUS According to the Answer Report, all the functional constraints are binding, with the exception of the constraint requiring that at least half of the portfolio ($50,000) be in

Microsoft Excel 5.0 Answer Report
Worksheet:[Book1]Sheet1
Report Created: 8/11/98 13:10

Target Cell (Min)

Cell	Name	Original Value	Final Value
$J$6	RISK TOTAL	0	1626666.667

Adjustable Cells

Cell	Name	Original Value	Final Value
$B$4	AMOUNT SAVINGS	0	17333.33333
$C$4	AMOUNT C/D	0	12666.66667
$D$4	AMOUNT ATL.LIGHT	0	0
$E$4	AMOUNT ARK.REIT	0	22666.66667
$F$4	AMOUNT BEDROCK	0	47333.33333
$G$4	AMOUNT NOCAL	0	0
$H$4	AMOUNT MINICOMP	0	0
$I$4	AMOUNT ANTONY	0	0

Constraints

Cell	Name	Cell Value	Formula	Status	Slack
$J$8	INVEST TOTAL	100000	$J$8=$K$8	Binding	0
$J$9	RETURN TOTAL	7500	$J$9>=$K$9	Binding	0
$J$10	A-RATED TOTAL	77333.33333	$J$10>=$K$10	Not Binding	27333.33333
$J$11	LIQUID TOTAL	40000	$J$11>=$K$11	Binding	0
$J$12	SAV/CD TOTAL	30000	$J$12<=$K$12	Binding	0
$B$4	AMOUNT SAVINGS	17333.33333	$B$4>=0	Not Binding	17333.33333
$C$4	AMOUNT C/D	12666.66667	$C$4>=0	Not Binding	12666.66667
$D$4	AMOUNT ATL.LIGHT	0	$D$4>=0	Binding	0
$E$4	AMOUNT ARK.REIT	22666.66667	$E$4>=0	Not Binding	22666.66667
$F$4	AMOUNT BEDROCK	47333.33333	$F$4>=0	Not Binding	47333.33333
$G$4	AMOUNT NOCAL	0	$G$4>=0	Binding	0
$H$4	AMOUNT MINICOMP	0	$H$4>=0	Binding	0
$I$4	AMOUNT ANTONY	0	$I$4>=0	Binding	0

FIGURE 4.2*a*   Excel Answer Report I—Jones Investment Service

Microsoft Excel 5.0 Sensivity Report
Worksheet:[Book1]Sheet1
Report Created: 8/11/98 13:10

Changing Cells

Cell	Name	Final Value	Reduced Cost	Objective Coefficient	Allowable Increase	Allowable Decrease
$B$4	AMOUNT SAVINGS	17333.33333	0	0	1.176470588	0.5
$C$4	AMOUNT C/D	12666.66667	0	0	0.5	1.176470588
$D$4	AMOUNT ATL.LIGHT	0	4.666666667	25	1E+30	4.666666667
$E$4	AMOUNT ARK.REIT	22666.66667	0	30	0.384615385	1.176470588
$F$4	AMOUNT BEDROCK	47333.33333	0	20	0.425531915	0.5
$G$4	AMOUNT NOCAL	0	0.666666667	15	1E+30	0.666666667
$H$4	AMOUNT MINICOMP	0	1.666666667	65	1E+30	1.666666667
$I$4	AMOUNT ANTONY	0	1.666666667	40	1E+30	1.666666667

Constraints

Cell	Name	Final Value	Shadow Price	Constraint R.H. Side	Allowable Increase	Allowable Decrease
$J$8	INVEST TOTAL	100000	-7.333333333	100000	4634.146341	6341.463415
$J$9	RETURN TOTAL	7500	333.3333333	7500	520	380
$J$10	A-RATED TOTAL	77333.33333	0	50000	27333.33333	1E+30
$J$11	LIQUID TOTAL	40000	4	40000	21111.11111	28888.88889
$J$12	SAV/CD TOTAL	30000	-10	30000	17333.33333	6333.333333

FIGURE 4.2*b*   Excel Sensitivity Report I—Jones Investment Service

A-rated investments. In fact, the amount in A-rated or better investments has a surplus of $27,333 above the $50,000 minimum. The total amount invested in A-rated investments is $77,333, or 77.333% of the portfolio.

SHADOW PRICES

The shadow prices in the sensitivity report give us the following information:

- If an extra dollar were invested above the $100,000, the risk would improve (decrease) by 7.33.
- For every extra dollar required in the expected annual return, the overall risk would increase by 333.33.
- For every extra dollar that must be made immediately liquid, the overall risk would increase by 4.
- For every extra dollar that is allowed to be invested in a savings account or a certificate of deposit, the risk would decrease by 10.
- No change in total risk would come from requiring that additional dollars be invested in A-rated investments.

RANGE OF FEASIBILITY

The Allowable Increase and Allowable Decrease to the original right-hand side coefficients give the range of feasibility of individual changes to the right-hand side within which the shadow prices remain constant. For example, the range of feasibility corresponding to the $7500 minimum return is ($7500 − $380) to ($7500 + $520) or from $7120 to $8020. An Allowable Decrease of 1E+30 is effectively infinity; thus, −∞ is the minimum right-hand side value in the range of feasibility for the amount invested in A-rated investments.

4.5   ST. JOSEPH PUBLIC UTILITY COMMISSION

stjo./lpp
stjo.xls
stjorev.lpp
stjorev.xls

Applications Area:	Public Sector
Concepts:	Ignoring Integer Restrictions
	Definitional Variable
	Infeasibility
	Multiple Optimal Solutions
Software:	WINQSB

The St. Joseph Public Utilities Commission has been charged with inspecting and reporting utility problems that have resulted from recent floods in the area. Concerns have been raised about the damage done to electrical wiring, gas lines, and insulation. The Commission has one week to carry out its inspections. It has been assigned three electrical inspectors and two gas inspectors, each available for 40 hours, to analyze structures in their respective areas of expertise. In addition, the Commission has allocated $10,000 for up to 100 hours (at $100 per hour) of consulting time from Weathertight Insulation, a local expert in home and industrial insulation.

These experts are assigned to inspect private homes, businesses (office complexes), and industrial plants in the area. The goal is to thoroughly inspect as many structures as possible during the allotted time in order to gather the requisite information. However, the minimum requirements are to inspect at least eight office buildings and eight industrial plants, and to make sure that at least 60% of the inspections are of private homes.

Once the total number of each type of structure to be inspected has been determined, the actual inspections will be done by choosing a random sample from those that are served by the St. Joseph Public Utility Commission. The Commission has mandated the following approximate inspection hours for each type of inspection:

	Electrical	Gas	Insulation
Homes	2	1	3
Offices	4	3	2
Plants	6	3	1

A team of management science consultants has been hired to suggest how many homes, office buildings, and plants should be inspected.

SOLUTION

The following is a brief summary of the problem faced by the St. Joseph Public Utilities Commission.

- St. Joseph must determine the number of homes, office complexes, and plants to be inspected.
- It wishes to maximize the total number of structures inspected.
- At least eight offices and eight plants are to be inspected.
- At least 60% of the inspections should involve private homes.
- At most, 120 hours (3×40) can be allocated for electrical inspections, 80 hours (2×40) for gas inspections, and 100 consulting hours for insulation inspection

The management science team has decided to formulate the problem as a linear program, although the results should be integer valued. If the linear program does not generate an integer solution, another method (such as integer or dynamic programming, which are discussed in later chapters) must be used, or St. Joseph could accept a feasible rounded solution.

DECISION VARIABLES

The team defined the following variables:

$X1$ = number of homes to be inspected
$X2$ = number of office complexes to be inspected
$X3$ = the number of industrial plants to be inspected

and they used the following definitional variable

$X4$ = total number of structures to be inspected

OBJECTIVE FUNCTION

The problem is to determine the maximum number of structures that can be inspected, subject to the constraints. Thus, the objective function of the model is simply:

MAXIMIZE X4

CONSTRAINTS

The definitional constraint for X4 is:

$$X1 + X2 + X3 - X4 = 0$$

The minimum number of office complexes and plants to be inspected are simply modeled as

$$X2 \geq 8$$
$$X3 \geq 8$$

The fact that at least 60% of the inspections must be of homes is modeled as

$$X1 \geq .6X4$$

or

$$X1 - .6X4 \geq 0$$

Finally, the constraints on the time limits for electrical, gas, and insulation inspections are:

$$2X1 + 4X2 + 6X3 \leq 120 \text{ (Electrical)}$$
$$1X1 + 3X2 + 3X3 \leq 80 \text{ (Gas)}$$
$$3X1 + 2X2 + 1X3 \leq 100 \text{ (Insulation)}$$

THE LINEAR PROGRAMMING MODEL

The complete linear programming model for the St. Joseph Public Utility Commission is:

$$
\begin{aligned}
\text{MAXIMIZE} \quad & X4 \quad \text{(Total structures)}\\
\text{ST} \quad & \\
X1 + X2 + X3 - X4 &= 0 \quad \text{(Definition)}\\
X2 &\geq 8 \quad \text{(Minimum offices)}\\
X3 &\geq 8 \quad \text{(Minimum plants)}\\
X1 \qquad\qquad - .6X4 &\geq 0 \quad (\geq 60\% \text{ Homes})\\
2X1 + 4X2 + 6X3 &\leq 120 \quad \text{(Electrical)}\\
X1 + 3X2 + 3X3 &\leq 80 \quad \text{(Gas)}\\
3X1 + 2X2 + 1X3 &\leq 100 \quad \text{(Insulation)}\\
X1, X2, X3, X4 &\geq 0
\end{aligned}
$$

WINQSB OUTPUT

WINQSB solved this problem using four variables and seven functional constraints.[3] Figure 4.3 shows the output that was generated. Needless to say, the Commission was not too pleased with this analysis. In fact, it was beginning to conclude that the management science consultants (and perhaps management science itself) could not be counted on to give it the results it wanted.

FIGURE 4.3   WINQSB Output—St. Joseph Public Utility Commission

The consultants pointed out the reason for infeasibility. Even if only the minimum eight offices and eight plants were inspected, 80 of the 120 electrical hours [4(8) + 6(8)] would be used, leaving only 40 hours to inspect homes. At two hours per home, a maximum of 20 homes could be inspected. Thus, a total of 36 structures would be inspected, only 20 of which would be homes. This represents only 55.56% of the total homes (= 20/36), not the minimum 60% the commission desired.

---

[3]An equivalent formulation would be to treat the constraints X2 ≥ 8, and X3 ≥ 8 as lower bounds and to enter them as such in the WINQSB spreadsheet.

In other words, the problem had been formulated correctly, but the Commission had simply given the consultants a set of constraints that were impossible to meet. Given this situation, after much debate the Commission decided that it could get by with inspecting a minimum of six office buildings and six plants. This would use up 60 electrical hours, leaving 60 electrical hours to inspect 30 homes, which far exceeds the 60% minimum limit on homes.

The Commission was about to initiate this action when it was pointed out that inspecting 30 homes, six office buildings, and six plants would use up 108 hours for insulation inspection [3(30) + 2(6) + 1(6)], exceeding the 100 available inspection hours. What to do?

The Commission finally agreed to call back the management science consultants for their recommendation. In the model formulation, the two constraints for the minimum number of office and plant inspections were changed to $X2 \geq 6$ and $X3 \geq 6$, respectively. WINQSB was then used to re-solve the problem giving the output shown in Figure 4.4.

Linear and Integer Programming

File   Format   Results   Utilities   Window   Help

Combined Report for ST. JOSEPH UTILITY

10:58:40		Tuesday	August	18	1998		
	Decision Variable	Solution Value	Unit Cost or Profit c[j]	Total Contribution	Reduced Cost	Basis Status	Allowable Min. c[j]	Allowable Max. c[j]
1	HOUSES	26.00	0	0	0	basic	-0.50	0
2	OFFICES	8.00	0	0	0	basic	0	1.00
3	PLANTS	6.00	0	0	0	basic	-M	0
4	TOTAL	40.00	1.00	40.00	0	basic	0	M
	Objective	Function	(Max.) =	40.00	(Note:	Alternate	Solution	Exists!!)
	Constraint	Left Hand Side	Direction	Right Hand Side	Slack or Surplus	Shadow Price	Allowable Min. RHS	Allowable Max. RHS
1	TOTAL	0	=	0	0	-1.00	-3.33	40.00
2	MIN OFF	8.00	>=	6.00	2.00	0	-M	8.00
3	MIN PLANT	6.00	>=	6.00	0	0	4.00	7.00
4	HOME PCT	2.00	>=	0	2.00	0	-M	2.00
5	ELECTRIC	120.00	<=	120.00	0	0.13	114.67	126.15
6	GAS	68.00	<=	80.00	12.00	0	68.00	M
7	INSULATE	100.00	<=	100.00	0	0.25	94.29	108.00

Results   Number Format

FIGURE 4.4   Re-solved WINQSB Output—St. Joseph Public Utility Commission

The optimal solution did turn out to have integer values, so the consultants could now report that a maximum of 40 structures (26 homes, eight office buildings, and six plants) could be inspected; 65% (= 26/40) of the structures inspected would be homes. All 120 electrical inspection hours and 100 insulation inspection hours would be used, and 12 hours of gas inspection time would remain unused.

However, the consultants noticed from the remark under line 4 of the WINQSB output that alternate optimal solutions exist. By selecting Obtain Alternate Optimal from the Results pull-down menu in WINQSB, the consultants were able to generate a second optimal combined report, shown in Figure 4.5. This report indicated that, by inspecting 27 homes, six office buildings, and seven plants, 40 structures could be inspected while satisfying all the constraints. In this case, 67.5% (= 27/40) would be homes, and 14 hours of gas inspection time would remain unused.

```
┌─ Linear and Integer Programming ─────────────────────── ▼ ▲ ┐
  File  Format  Results  Utilities  Window  Help
  [icons]   0.00 A ≡ ≡ ≡ [][] ⇄              [icons]
┌─ Combined Report for ST. JOSEPH UTILITY ──────────── ▼ ▲ ┐
```

11:02:46			Tuesday	August	18	1998		
	Decision Variable	Solution Value	Unit Cost or Profit c(j)	Total Contribution	Reduced Cost	Basis Status	Allowable Min. c(j)	Allowable Max. c(j)
1	HOUSES	27.00	0	0	0	basic	0	2.00
2	OFFICES	6.00	0	0	0	basic	-M	0
3	PLANTS	7.00	0	0	0	basic	0	2.00
4	TOTAL	40.00	1.00	40.00	0	basic	0	M
	Objective	Function	(Max.) =	40.00	(Note:	Alternate	Solution	Exists!!)
	Constraint	Left Hand Side	Direction	Right Hand Side	Slack or Surplus	Shadow Price	Allowable Min. RHS	Allowable Max. RHS
1	TOTAL	0	=	0	0	-1.00	-5.00	40.00
2	MIN OFF	6.00	>=	6.00	0	0	0	8.00
3	MIN PLANT	7.00	>=	6.00	1.00	0	-M	7.00
4	HOME PCT	3.00	>=	0	3.00	0	-M	3.00
5	ELECTRIC	120.00	<=	120.00	0	0.13	114.67	141.82
6	GAS	66.00	<=	80.00	14.00	0	66.00	M
7	INSULATE	100.00	<=	100.00	0	0.25	86.67	108.00

```
Results      Combined Report for ST. JOSEPH UTILITY
```

FIGURE 4.5   Combined Report—St. Joseph Public Utility Commission

Although any weighted average of these two solutions would also be optimal, since the first solution calls for inspecting 26 homes and the second 27 homes, any weighted average of the two solutions would yield a *fractional* solution of between 26 and 27 homes to be inspected. Thus, the consultants reported that these two solutions are the only optimal solutions that yield integers for the number of homes, office complexes, and plants to be inspected.

Faced with two feasible alternatives, the Commission had the opportunity to inject some political preferences into the decision process while still inspecting 40 structures.

4.6   EUROMERICA LIQUORS

Euro.lpp
Euro.xls
Eurorev.lp
Eurorev.xls

Applications Area: Purchasing

Concepts: Choosing an Objective
Lower Bound Constraints
Unboundedness
"Slightly" Violated Constraints

Software: Excel

Euromerica Liquors of Jersey City, New Jersey (Table 4.2), purchases and distributes a number of wines to retailers. Purchasing manager Maria Arias has been asked to order at least 800 bottles of each wine during the next purchase cycle. The only other direction Maria has been given is that, in accordance with a long-standing company policy, she is to order at least twice as many domestic (U.S.) bottles as imported bottles in any cycle. Management believes that this policy promotes a steady sales flow that keeps inventory costs at a minimum. Maria must decide exactly how many bottles of each type of wine the company is to purchase during this ordering cycle.

TABLE 4.2   EUROMERICA LIQUORS' WINE PURCHASES AND DISTRIBUTION

Wine	Country	Cost	Selling Price
Napa Gold	U.S.	$2.50	$4.25
Cayuga Lake	U.S.	$3.00	$4.50
Seine Soir	France	$5.00	$8.00
Bella Bella	Italy	$4.00	$6.00

SOLUTION

To summarize, Maria must:

- determine the number of bottles of each type of wine to purchase
- order at least 800 of each type
- order at least twice as many domestic bottles as imported bottles
- select an appropriate objective function

DECISION VARIABLES

The four decision variables are as follows.

$X1$ = bottles of Napa Gold purchased in this purchase cycle
$X2$ = bottles of Cayuga Lake purchased in this purchase cycle
$X3$ = bottles of Seine Soir purchased in this purchase cycle
$X4$ = bottles of Bella Bella purchased in this purchase cycle

OBJECTIVE FUNCTION

At first, Maria reasoned that since Euromerica Liquors' goal is to make good profits, her objective should be to maximize the profit from the purchases made during this purchase cycle. Because inventory costs are assumed to be small due to the company's ordering policy, she defined the profit coefficients in terms of the selling price minus the purchase cost per bottle. Thus, the unit profits for the respective decision variables are $1.75, $1.50, $3, and $2, and the objective function is:

$$\text{MAX } 1.75X1 + 1.50X2 + 3X3 + 2X4$$

CONSTRAINTS

The following constraints must be considered.

Minimum Production: At least 800 bottles of each of the wines are to be purchased:

$$X1 \geq 800$$
$$X2 \geq 800$$
$$X3 \geq 800$$
$$X4 \geq 800$$

These constraints could be entered in linear programming software either as functional constraints or as lower bound constraints that would replace the nonnegativity constraints for the variables.

Mix Constraint: (The number of bottles of domestic wine purchased) should be at least (twice the number of bottles of imported wine purchased):

$$X1 + X2 \geq 2(X3 + X4)$$

or

$$X1 + X2 - 2X3 - 2X4 \geq 0$$

THE MATHEMATICAL
MODEL

The complete model can now be formulated as

$$\text{MAXIMIZE} \quad 1.75X1 + 1.50X2 + 3X3 + 2X4$$

$$
\begin{array}{ll}
\text{ST} & X1 & \geq 800 \\
& X2 & \geq 800 \\
& X3 & \geq 800 \\
& X4 \geq 800 \\
X1 + & X2 - 2X3 - 2X4 \geq & 0
\end{array}
$$

Euromerica did not have any specialized linear programming packages, but it did have a copy of Excel, and Maria used the Solver function to solve the model. But when she did so the screen depicted in Figure 4.6 appeared. The message "The Set Target Cell values do not converge" is Excel's way of stating that the problem has an unbounded solution.

FIGURE 4.6   Excel Solver Results—Euromerica Liquors

But Euromerica cannot make an infinite profit! When Maria examined the model, she realized that she had ignored the following considerations when building the model:

• Euromerica has a finite budget for the procurement of bottles of wine during the purchase cycle.

• The suppliers have a finite amount of product available.

• There is a limit on demand from the wine-buying public.

Undaunted, Maria discussed the situation with management and discovered that they wished to commit no more than $28,000 to purchase wine during this cycle. She then contacted the wine producers and found out that there were ample supplies of Cayuga Lake and Bella Bella, but that only 300 cases of Napa Gold and 200 cases of Seine Soir were available (each case contains 12 bottles). Finally, she performed a market survey and, based on the results, concluded that no more than 10,000 total bottles should be purchased. Thus, the revised model is:

$$\text{MAXIMIZE} \quad 1.75X1 + 1.50X2 + 3X3 + 2X4$$

$$
\begin{array}{ll}
\text{ST} & X1 & \geq \quad 800 \\
& X2 & \geq \quad 800 \\
& X3 & \geq \quad 800 \\
& X4 \geq \quad 800 \\
X1 + & X2 - 2X3 - 2X4 \geq \quad 0 \\
2.50X1 + 3.00X2 + 5X3 + 4X4 \leq 28,000 \text{ (Budget)} \\
X1 & \leq \quad 3600 \text{ (Napa)} \\
& X3 & \leq \quad 2400 \text{ (Seine)} \\
X1 + & X2 + X3 + X4 \leq 10,000 \text{ (Total)}
\end{array}
$$

EXCEL OUTPUT

Solving by Excel gave the answer report shown in Figure 4.7. Maria rounded off the solution to full cases and placed them in the order shown in Table 4.3. Note that this

Microsoft Excel 5.0 Answer Report
Worksheet:[Book1]Sheet1
Report Created: 8/22/98 22:53

Target Cell (Max)

Cell	Name	Original Value	Final Value
$G$11	TOTAL PROFIT	16792	16790.90909

Adjustable Cells

Cell	Name	Original Value	Final Value
$B$5	BOTTLES NAPA	3600	3600
$C$5	BOTTLES CAYUGA	1964	1963.636364
$D$5	BOTTLES SEINE	1982	1981.818182
$E$5	BOTTLES BELLA	800	800

Constraints

Cell	Name	Cell Value	Formula	Status	Slack
$G$7	TOTAL DOMESTIC	5563.636364	$G$7>=2*$G$8	Binding	0
$G$9	TOTAL BOTTLES	8345.454545	$G$9<=10000	Not Binding	1654.545455
$G$10	TOTAL BUDGET	28000	$G$10<=28000	Binding	0
$B$5	BOTTLES NAPA	3600	$B$5>=800	Not Binding	2800
$C$5	BOTTLES CAYUGA	1963.636364	$C$5>=800	Not Binding	1163.636364
$D$5	BOTTLES SEINE	1981.818182	$D$5>=800	Not Binding	1181.818182
$E$5	BOTTLES BELLA	800	$E$5>=800	Binding	0
$B$5	BOTTLES NAPA	3600	$B$5<=3600	Binding	0
$D$5	BOTTLES SEINE	1981.818182	$D$5<=2400	Not Binding	418.1818181

FIGURE 4.7   Excel Answer Report I—Euromerica Liquors

TABLE 4.3   EUROMERICA LIQUORS' SOLUTION

Wine	Bottles	Cases	Cost	Profit
Napa Gold	3600	300	$ 9,000	$ 6,300
Cayuga Lake	1968	164	$ 5,904	$ 2,952
Seine Soir	1980	165	$ 9,900	$ 5,940
Bella Bella	804	67	$ 3,216	$ 1,608
Total	8352	696	$28,020	$16,800

proposal is $20 over the budget limit of $28,000. Although the $28,000 limit was a restriction, it was probably a strong guideline rather than a hard and fast value. Hence, Maria had no qualms about recommending this solution.

4.7 $\mathcal{V}$ERTEX SOFTWARE, INC.

Vertex.lpp
Vertex.xls
Vertex.ltx

Application Area:	Marketing Advertising Strategy
Concepts:	Choosing an Appropriate Objective Function
	Rounding Noninteger Values
Software:	LINDO

Vertex Software, Inc. has spent several man-years developing a new software product, LUMBER 2000, designed specifically for the building trade. The software keeps track of lumber supplies, needs, and cost accounting data.

Claire Greenwell, the marketing vice president at Vertex, and her staff have been given a budget of $125,000 to market the product over the next quarter. Claire has decided that $35,000 of the budget should be spent promoting the product at the national building trade show in New Orleans, which will be held during the quarter. This leaves her with $90,000 in funds for advertising in other media.

Because the product targets a specialized audience, Claire has ruled out television, radio, and mainstream magazine advertisements. Instead, she has decided to promote the product using black and white (B&W) and color ads in some or all of the following publications: *Building Today, Lumber Weekly,* and *Timber World. Building Today* is a weekday trade newspaper that accepts both full-page and half-page black and white advertising. *Lumber Weekly* and *Timber World* are glossy magazines that run both black and white and color ads. Claire and her staff have decided to run only full-page ads in these publications. The circulation and advertising cost data for each of these publications is summarized in Table 4.4.

TABLE 4.4 CIRCULATION AND ADVERTISING COSTS

Publication	Frequency	Circulation	Cost of Ad
Building Today	5 days/wk.	400,000	Full page $800 Half page $500 (B&W only)
Lumber Weekly	Weekly	250,000	B&W page $1500 Color page $4000
Timber World	Monthly	200,000	B&W page $2000 Color page $6000

Claire and the advertising staff at Vertex discussed the potential advertising and made the following subjective judgments:

1. A maximum of one ad should be placed in any one issue of any of the trade publications during the quarter.

2. At least 50 full-page ads should appear during the quarter.

3. At least eight color ads should appear during the quarter.

4. One ad should appear in each issue of *Timber World.*

5. At least four weeks of advertising should be placed in each of the *Building Today* and *Lumber Weekly* publications.

6. No more than $40,000 should be spent on advertising in any one of the trade publications.

Given all the marketing research and the subjective judgments of the staff, Claire needs to give management her marketing plan for the LUMBER 2000 software product.

SOLUTION

Claire's job is to:

- recommend the number of each type of ad to be placed during the quarter
- define a measure of "effectiveness" and maximize the "effectiveness" of the ad campaign
- stay within a $90,000 budget for print advertising
- place no more than 65 (= 5 × 13 weeks) and no less than 20 ads (= 5 × 4 weeks) in *Building Today*
- place no more than 13 and no less than four ads in *Lumber Weekly*
- place exactly three ads in *Timber World*
- place at least 50 full-page ads

- place at least eight color ads
- spend no more than $40,000 advertising in *Building Today*, no more than $40,000 advertising in *Lumber Weekly*, and no more than $40,000 advertising in *Timber World*

DECISION VARIABLES

Claire has identified the decision variables as the number of times each type of ad in each trade publication will be run during the quarter:

$X1$ = number of full-page B&W ads placed in *Building Today* during the quarter
$X2$ = number of half-page B&W ads placed in *Building Today* during the quarter
$X3$ = number of full-page B&W ads placed in *Lumber Weekly* during the quarter
$X4$ = number of full-page color ads placed in *Lumber Weekly* during the quarter
$X5$ = number of full-page B&W ads placed in *Timber World* during the quarter
$X6$ = number of full-page color ads placed in *Timber World* during the quarter

Since the restrictions seemed relatively straightforward, Claire has decided to model these first and then approach the issue of the proper objective.

CONSTRAINTS

Claire must consider the following constraints in her analysis:

Budget: The amount spent on print advertising cannot exceed $90,000:

$$800X1 + 500X2 + 1500X3 + 4000X4 + 2000X5 + 6000X6 \leq 90000$$

Total Ads Placed:

The number of *Building Today* ads placed cannot exceed 65: $X1 + X2 \leq 65$
The number of *Building Today* ads placed must be at least 20: $X1 + X2 \geq 20$
The number of *Lumber Weekly* ads placed cannot exceed 13: $X3 + X4 \leq 13$
The number of *Lumber Weekly* ads placed must be at least 4: $X3 + X4 \geq 4$
The number of *Timber World* ads placed must be 3: $X5 + X6 = 3$

Full-Page Ads: The number of full-page ads placed must be at least 50:

$$X1 + X3 + X4 + X5 + X6 \geq 50$$

Color Ads: The number of color ads placed must be at least eight: $X4 + X6 \geq 8$

Maximum Spending Limits:

No more than $40,000 can be spent on advertising in *Building Today*:

$$800X1 + 500X2 \leq 40000$$

No more than $40,000 can be spent on advertising in *Lumber Weekly*:

$$1500X3 + 4000X4 \leq 40000$$

No more than $40,000 can be spent on advertising in *Timber World*:

$$2000X5 + 6000X6 \leq 40000$$

OBJECTIVE FUNCTION

Finally, Claire's objective is to maximize the effectiveness of the media mix. But what constitutes "effectiveness"? At first, Claire and her marketing staff thought that circulation might be the appropriate measure. But they soon recognized the importance of other factors, including the type of ad placed and how well each publication matched the target profile of Vertex's market.

A *marketing exposure unit* is an overall performance measure for an ad, which can be defined to take into account these elements. After much discussion, Claire's marketing research group decided to define its exposure unit per ad as follows:

(Total Circulation) × (Publication Rating) × (Strength Rating)

The publication rating (between 0 and 1) is intended to measure how well the readership of each publication matches the marketing profile of potential customers. By contrast, the strength rating (between 0 and 1) measures the relative strength of the type of ad (full versus half page; color versus black and white).

Publication Rating

For each of the three publications, the marketing research group used a Delphi approach to rate the relative importance of key reader attributes that could affect sales. Table 4.5 summarizes the consensus of the group.

TABLE 4.5   KEY READER ATTRIBUTES

Attribute	Rating
Computer database user	.50
Large firm (>2M sales)	.25
Location (city or suburbs)	.15
Age of firm (>5 years)	.10

Next, the group surveyed the readership of the three publications. Table 4.6 summarizes the percentage of readers who answered "Yes" to the desired attributes.

TABLE 4.6   READERSHIP OF PUBLICATIONS

Attribute	Percentage of Readership		
	Building Today	*Lumber Weekly*	*Timber World*
Computer database user	60%	80%	90%
Large firm (>2M sales)	40	80	80
Location (city or suburbs)	60	60	80
Age of firm (>5 years)	20	40	50

The publication ratings for each of the three trade media were then found by weighting these percentages by the attribute rating:

$$Building\ Today: \quad .60(.50) + .40(.25) + .60(.15) + .20(.10) = .51$$
$$Lumber\ Weekly: \quad .80(.50) + .80(.25) + .60(.15) + .40(.10) = .73$$
$$Timber\ World: \quad .90(.50) + .80(.25) + .80(.15) + .50(.10) = .82$$

Strength Rating

A Delphi technique was also used to obtain a strength rating for each type of ad. The consensus of the group was as follows.

- Half-page ads are only 40% as effective as full-page ads.
- Color ads are twice as effective as black and white ads.

Based on a strength rating of "1" for the most effective ad (full-page color ads), the strength ratings for the three types of ads contemplated by Vertex were as follows.

Full page, color	1
Full page, B&W	.50
Half page, B&W (.40)(.50) =	.20

Objective Function Coefficients

Given the publication and strength ratings Claire's group used the following exposure units per ad (objective function coefficients).

Full page, B&W, *Building Today*:	$(400,000)(.51)(.50) = 102,000$
Half page, B&W, *Building Today*:	$(400,000)(.51)(.20) = 40,800$
Full page, B&W, *Lumber Weekly*:	$(250,000)(.73)(.50) = 91,250$
Full page, color, *Lumber Weekly*:	$(250,000)(.73)(1) = 182,500$
Full page, B&W, *Timber World*:	$(200,000)(.82)(.50) = 82,000$
Full page, color, *Timber World*:	$(200,000)(.82)(1) = 164,000$

THE LINEAR MODEL

The complete linear model for Vertex Software is as follows.

MAXIMIZE $102000X_1 + 40800X_2 + 91250X_3 + 182500X_4 + 82000X_5 + 164000X_6$

ST

$$
\begin{aligned}
800X_1 + 500X_2 + 1500X_3 + 4000X_4 + 2000X_5 + 6000X_6 &\leq 90{,}000 \\
X_1 + X_2 &\leq 65 \\
X_1 + X_2 &\geq 20 \\
X_3 + X_4 &\leq 13 \\
X_3 + X_4 &\geq 4 \\
X_5 + X_6 &= 3 \\
X_1 + X_3 + X_4 + X_5 + X_6 &\geq 50 \\
X_4 + X_6 &\geq 8 \\
800X_1 + 500X_2 &\leq 40{,}000 \\
1500X_3 + 4000X_4 &\leq 40{,}000 \\
2000X_5 + 6000X_6 &\leq 40{,}000
\end{aligned}
$$

All variables ≥ 0

LINDO OUTPUT

Claire solved the problem using the company's LINDO software obtaining the output shown in Figure 4.8. Although the result was not quite an integer solution, Claire decided to round off the number of ads in *Lumber Weekly* to five black and white ads and eight color ads, which gives the solution shown in Table 4.7.

TABLE 4.7   ROUNDED SOLUTION—VERTEX SOFTWARE

Publication	Type	Number	Cost
Building Today	Full page, B&W	50	$40,000
Lumber Weekly	Full page, B&W	5	$ 7,500
	Full page, color	8	$32,000
Timber World	Full page, B&W	2	$ 4,000
	Full page, color	1	$ 6,000
		66	$89,500

```
LP OPTIMUM FOUND AT STEP   9
            OBJECTIVE FUNCTION VALUE
  1)        7362500.00

   VARIABLE        VALUE        REDUCED COST
     BTFULL     50.000000          .000000
     BTHALF       .000000     22950.000000
       LWBW      4.799998          .000000
      LWCOL      8.200001          .000000
       TWBW      2.000000          .000000
      TWCOL      1.000000          .000000

       ROW  SLACK OR SURPLUS  DUAL PRICES
        2)         .000000     20.500000
        3)       15.000000        .000000
        4)       30.000000        .000000
        5)         .000000  36500.000000
        6)        8.999999        .000000
        7)         .000000  41000.000000
        8)       16.000000        .000000
        9)        1.200000        .000000
       10)         .000000    107.000000
       11)         .000000     16.000000
       12)    30000.000000        .000000


   RANGES IN WHICH THE BASIS IS UNCHANGED:
                OBJ COEFFICIENT RANGES
   VARIABLE     CURRENT       ALLOWABLE       ALLOWABLE
                  COEF        INCREASE        DECREASE
     BTFULL  102000.000000    INFINITY      36720.000000
     BTHALF   40800.000000  22950.000000      INFINITY
       LWBW   91250.000000  39999.990000   22812.500000
      LWCOL  182500.000000  60833.330000   40000.000000
       TWBW   82000.000000  82000.000000   64000.000000
      TWCOL  164000.000000  64000.000000   82000.000000
                RIGHTHAND SIDE RANGES
       ROW     CURRENT       ALLOWABLE       ALLOWABLE
                  RHS         INCREASE        DECREASE
        2    90000.000000   8000.000000    4000.000000
        3       65.000000      INFINITY      15.000000
        4       20.000000     30.000000       INFINITY
        5       13.000000      2.000000       2.999998
        6        4.000000      8.999999       INFINITY
        7        3.000000      2.000000       1.333333
        8       50.000000     16.000000       INFINITY
        9        8.000000      1.200000       INFINITY
       10    40000.000000   4000.000000    8000.000000
       11    40000.000000   4000.000000    8000.000000
       12    40000.000000      INFINITY   30000.000000
```

FIGURE 4.8   LINDO Output—Vertex Software

Before making this recommendation, Claire checked to determine if this rounded solution satisfied all the constraints. As you can see, this recommendation comes in $500 below the $90,000 budget. A check of the other constraints yields the output shown in Table 4.8.

TABLE 4.8   ROUNDED SOLUTION WITH CONSTRAINTS—VERTEX SOFTWARE

Restriction	Minimum Limit	Maximum Limit	Solution
Ads in *Building Today*	20	65	50
Ads in *Lumber Weekly*	4	13	13
Ads in *Timber World*	3	3	3
Full-page ads	50	—	66
Color ads	8	—	9
Maximum budget in *Building Today*	—	$40,000	$40,000
Maximum budget in *Lumber Weekly*	—	$40,000	$39,500
Maximum budget in *Timber World*	—	$40,000	$10,000

Thus, the rounded solution is feasible, and the overall effectiveness rating of this solution is 102,000(50) + 40,800(0) + 91,250(5) + 182,500(8) + 82,000(2) + 164,000(1) = 7,344,250, which is 99.752% of the optimal noninteger solution of 7,362,500. Claire knew she could not be sure that these rounded values would give the optimal integer solution.[4] But, in light of this excellent feasible result, she decided not to use a more complicated model that would restrict the variables to integers, and so she recommended the foregoing solution to management.

4.8 UNITED OIL COMPANY

United.lpp
United.xls

Applications Area:	Oil Production
Concepts:	Variable Definitions for Blending Models
	Calculation of Objective Coefficients
	Ratio Constraints
	Definitional Variables
	Alternate Optimal Solutions
Software:	WINQSB

United Oil blends two input streams of crude oil products—alkylate and catalytic cracked—to meet demand for weekly contracts for regular (12,000 barrels), mid-grade (7500 barrels), and premium (4500 barrels) gasolines. Each week United can purchase up to 15,000 barrels of alkylate and up to 15,000 barrels of catalytic cracked. Because of demand, it can sell all blended gasolines, including any production that exceeds its contracts.

To be classified as regular, mid-grade, or premium, gasolines must meet minimum octane and maximum vapor pressure requirements. The octane rating and vapor pressure of a blended gasoline is assumed to be the weighted average of the crude oil products in the blend. Relevant cost/pricing, octane, and vapor pressure data are given in Tables 4.9 and 4.10.

United must decide how to blend the crude oil products into commercial gasolines in order to maximize its weekly profit.

TABLE 4.9   COST/PRICING, OCTANE, AND VAPOR PRESSURE DATA—UNITED OIL

Crude Oil Product Data			
Product	Octane Rating	Vapor Pressure (lb./sq. in.)	Cost per Barrel
Alkylate	98	5	$19
Catalytic cracked	86	9	$16

TABLE 4.10   GASOLINE OCTANE RATING, VAPOR PRESSURE, AND BARREL PROFIT

Blended Gasoline Requirements			
Gasoline	Minimum Octane Rating	Maximum Vapor Pressure	Selling Price per Barrel
Regular	87	9	$18
Mid-grade	89	7	$20
Premium	92	6	$23

---

[4]In the next chapter, we discuss approaches to solving linear models with integer restrictions.

SOLUTION

The problem for United Oil is to:

- determine how many barrels of alkylate to blend into regular, mid-grade, and premium and how many barrels of catalytic cracked to blend into regular, mid-grade, and premium each week
- maximize total weekly profit
- remain within raw gas availabilities
- meet contract requirements
- produce gasoline blends that meet the octane and vapor pressure requirements

DECISION VARIABLES
(FIRST PASS)

The pending decision is to determine how much of each input stream (X, Y) to blend into each of the three grades (1, 2, 3) each week:

$X1$ = number of barrels of alkylate blended into regular weekly
$X2$ = number of barrels of alkylate blended into mid-grade weekly
$X3$ = number of barrels of alkylate blended into premium weekly
$Y1$ = number of barrels of catalytic cracked blended into regular weekly
$Y2$ = number of barrels of catalytic cracked blended into mid-grade weekly
$Y3$ = number of barrels of catalytic cracked blended into premium weekly

OBJECTIVE FUNCTION

The profit made on a barrel of crude product blended into a commercial gasoline is the difference between the selling price of the blended gasoline and the cost of the crude product. Table 4.11 gives the profit coefficients. The objective function is:

$$\text{MAX } -1X1 + 1X2 + 4X3 + 2Y1 + 4Y2 + 7Y3$$

TABLE 4.11   PROFIT COEFFICIENTS FOR OIL

Variable	Crude Product Cost	Gasoline Selling Price	Barrel Profit
X1	$19	$18	−$1
X2	$19	$20	$1
X3	$19	$23	$4
Y1	$16	$18	$2
Y2	$16	$20	$4
Y3	$16	$23	$7

CONSTRAINTS

United must consider the following constraints in its analysis:

Crude Availability: United cannot blend more than the product available from either input source. The total amount blended from a source is simply the sum of the amounts blended into regular, mid-grade, and premium gasoline:

$$X1 + X2 + X3 \leq 15{,}000$$
$$Y1 + Y2 + Y3 \leq 15{,}000$$

Contract Requirements: Although the contract requirements must be met, they may be exceeded; thus, although at least 12,000 barrels of regular must be produced, the actual amount produced will be the sum of the amounts of alkylate and catalytic cracked blended into regular: X1 + Y1. Similarly, the amount of mid-grade gas produced will be X2 + Y2, and the amount of premium gas produced will be X3 + Y3. Since these quantities are of interest to United Oil (and will figure into the remaining constraints), to simplify the formulation, definitional variables can be used.

DECISION VARIABLES (SECOND PASS)

Define

R = barrels of regular gasoline produced weekly
M = barrels of mid-grade gasoline produced weekly
P = barrels of premium gasoline produced weekly

Doing so requires adding the following definitional constraints:

$$X1 + Y1 - R = 0$$
$$X2 + Y2 - M = 0$$
$$X3 + Y3 - P = 0$$

The contract constraints can then be written as

$$R \geq 12000$$
$$M \geq 7500$$
$$P \geq 4500$$

Octane and Vapor Constraints: The octane rating for regular gasoline is the weighted average of the octane ratings for alkylate and catalytic cracked blended into regular. The appropriate weights are the ratios of the amount of alkylate to the amount of regular and the amount of catalytic cracked to the amount of regular, respectively:

98 (Amount of alkylate in regular/Total amount of regular) +
86 (Amount of catalytic cracked in regular/Total amount of regular) =
98(X1/R) + 86(Y1/R)

Since this must be at least 87, the constraint is:

$$98(X1/R) + 86(Y1/R) \geq 87$$

The terms (X1/R) and (Y1/R) make this a *nonlinear* constraint. Since R will be positive in the optimal solution, however, multiplying both sides by R gives the following linear constraint:

$$98X1 + 86Y1 \geq 87R$$

or

$$98X1 + 86Y1 - 87R \geq 0$$

The remaining octane and vapor pressure constraints are constructed similarly; thus, the complete set of octane and vapor pressure restrictions is:

$$98X1 + 86Y1 - 87R \geq 0$$
$$98X2 + 86Y2 - 89M \geq 0$$
$$98X3 + 86Y3 - 92P \geq 0$$
$$5X1 + 9Y1 - 9R \leq 0$$
$$5X2 + 9Y2 - 7M \leq 0$$
$$5X3 + 9Y3 - 6P \leq 0$$

THE MATHEMATICAL MODEL

The complete model is as follows.

$$
\begin{array}{llllllllll}
\text{MAXIMIZE} & -1X1 + & 1X2 + & 4X3 + & 2Y1 + & 4Y2 + & 7Y3 & & & \\
\text{ST} & X1 + & X2 + & X3 & & & & & & \leq 15{,}000 \\
& & & & Y1 + & Y2 + & Y3 & & & \leq 15{,}000 \\
& X1 & & & + Y1 & & & - R & & = 0 \\
& & X2 & & & + Y2 & & & - M & = 0 \\
& & & X3 & & & + Y3 & & & - P = 0 \\
& & & & & & & R & & \geq 12{,}000 \\
& & & & & & & & M & \geq 7500 \\
& & & & & & & & & P \geq 4500 \\
& 98X1 & & & + 86Y1 & & & - 87R & & \geq 0 \\
& & 98X2 & & & + 86Y2 & & & - 89M & \geq 0 \\
& & & 98X3 & & & + 86Y3 & & & - 92P \geq 0 \\
& 5X1 & & & + 9Y1 & & & - 9R & & \leq 0 \\
& & 5X2 & & & + 9Y2 & & & - 7M & \leq 0 \\
& & & 5X3 & & & + 9Y3 & & & - 6P \leq 0 \\
\end{array}
$$

All variables ≥ 0

WINQSB OUTPUT

According to the WINQSB combined report, shown in Figure 4.9, alternate optimal solutions exist for United Oil. In the one based on the output below, all 30,000 barrels will be used, making 12,000 barrels of regular (consisting of 1000 barrels of alkylate and 11,000 barrels of catalytic cracked), 7500 barrels of mid-grade (3750 barrels of alkylate and 3750 barrels of catalytic cracked), and 10,500 barrels of premium (10,250 barrels of alkylate, 250 barrels of catalytic cracked), netting a weekly profit of $82,500.

Combined Report for United Oil

	22:57:01		Tuesday	September	15	1998		
	Decision Variable	Solution Value	Unit Cost or Profit c(j)	Total Contribution	Reduced Cost	Basis Status	Allowable Min. c(j)	Allowable Max. c(j)
1	ALK/REG	1,000.00	-1.00	-1,000.00	0	basic	-M	-1.00
2	ALK/MID	3,750.00	1.00	3,750.00	0	basic	-M	1.00
3	ALK/PREM	10,250.00	4.00	41,000.00	0	basic	4.00	M
4	CAT/REG	11,000.00	2.00	22,000.00	0	basic	2.00	7.45
5	CAT/MID	3,750.00	4.00	15,000.00	0	basic	4.00	10.00
6	CAT/PREM	250.00	7.00	1,750.00	0	basic	1.55	7.00
7	REGULAR	12,000.00	0	0	0	basic	-M	5.00
8	MIDGRADE	7,500.00	0	0	0	basic	-M	3.00
9	PREMIUM	10,500.00	0	0	0	basic	-3.00	M
	Objective	Function	(Max.)=	82,500.00	(Note:	Alternate	Solution	Exists!!)

	Constraint	Left Hand Side	Direction	Right Hand Side	Slack or Surplus	Shadow Price	Allowable Min.RHS	Allowable Max.RHS
1	ALKYLATE	15,000.00	<=	15,000.00	0	4.00	9,000.00	M
2	CAT.CRACK	15,000.00	<=	15,000.00	0	7.00	14,750.00	18,166.67
3	REGULAR	0	=	0	0	-5.00	-300.00	30.61
4	MIDGRADE	0	=	0	0	-3.00	-199.12	1,583.33
5	PREMIUM	0	=	0	0	0	-652.17	1,583.33
6	REG CONT	12,000.00	>=	12,000.00	0	-5.00	8,437.50	12,272.73
7	MID CONT	7,500.00	>=	7,500.00	0	-3.00	0	8,000.00
8	PRE CONT	10,500.00	>=	4,500.00	6,000.00	0	-M	10,500.00
9	REG OCT	0	>=	0	0	0	-3,000.00	28,500.00
10	MID OCT	22,500.00	>=	0	22,500.00	0	-M	22,500.00
11	PRE OCT	60,000.00	>=	0	60,000.00	0	-M	60,000.00
12	REG VP	-4000.00	<=	0	4,000.00	0	-4,000.00	M
13	MID VP	0	<=	0	0	0	-9,500.00	1,000.00
14	PRE VP	-9,500.00	<=	0	9,500.00	0	-9,500.00	M

FIGURE 4.9   WINQSB—Combined Report for United Oil

It can be seen from the shadow prices that extra barrels of alkylate will add $4 to the weekly profit, whereas each extra barrel of catalytic cracked will add $7; if contract requirements for regular or mid-grade are increased, weekly profits will decrease by $5 and $3, respectively.

The octane ratings for the gasoline blends are:

$$\text{Regular:} \quad 98(1000/12,000) + 86(11,000/12,000) = 87.00$$
$$\text{Mid-grade:} \quad 98(3750/7500) + 86(3750/7500) \quad = 92.00$$
$$\text{Premium:} \quad 98(10,250/10,500) + 86(250/10,500) = 97.7$$

The vapor pressure ratings for the gasoline blends are:

$$\text{Regular:} \quad 5(1000/12,000) + 9(11,000/12,000) = 8.67$$
$$\text{Mid-grade:} \quad 5(3750/7500) + 9(3750/7500) \quad = 7.00$$
$$\text{Premium:} \quad 5(10,250/10,500) + 9(250/10,500) = 5.0$$

By using the Obtain Alternate Solution from the Results menu in WINQSB, two additional optimal solutions are generated. One produces 12,000 barrels of regular with 3375 barrels of alkylate and 8625 barrels of catalytic crack, 7500 barrels of mid-grade with 3750 barrels of alkylate and 3750 barrels of catalytic crack, and 10,250 barrels of premium with 7875 barrels of alkylate and 2625 barrels of catalytic crack; the other produces 12,000 barrels of regular with 11,000 barrels of alkylate and 1000 barrels of catalytic crack, 7500 barrels of mid-grade with 6125 barrels of alkylate and 1375 barrels of catalytic crack, and 10,250 barrels of premium with 7875 barrels of alkylate and 2625 barrels of catalytic crack. Any weighted average of these three optimal solutions is also optimal.

4.9 THE POWERS GROUP

Powersbk.lpp
Powersbk.xls

Applications Area: Cash-Flow Accounting

Concepts: Determining Appropriate Decision Variables
Multiperiod Cash-Flow Linking Constraints
Redundant Constraints
Spreadsheet Presentation

Software: Excel

The Powers Group has decided to invest at least $5 million in a venture capital project with Gramm Crackers Enterprises, a company started by Sid Gramm to develop and market interactive programs and games, taking advantage of the latest developments in computer technology.

Powers' commitment to invest the money is contingent on arriving at an acceptable financial structure and resolving all the legal details. It is now January 1, and Powers estimates that resolution should take until about April 1, at which time it must have at least $5 million in liquid assets to invest.

Powers currently has $9 million available for short-term investments. The partners have decided to invest these funds only in two-month term accounts paying 4.20% per annum (.7% over two months), three-month construction loans paying 6.00% per annum (1.5% over three months), and passbook savings accounts currently paying 2.4% per annum (.2% over a one-month period). On April 1, Powers will reevaluate its financial position and decide whether even more investment in Gramm Crackers is warranted.

Powers' investment strategy has always been one of diversity and caution. Accordingly, during this quarter, the directors have determined that the company should always have at least $2 million liquid in passbook savings and that, at no time during the three-month period, should the investment in either of the other two less liquid term options exceed $4 million. Interest on the passbook savings is earned monthly, whereas the interest earned on term accounts and construction loans is paid at maturity. Powers has decided to seek an investment strategy that will maximize the interest earned and accrued *during* the three-month interim period.

SOLUTION

A synopsis of the problem for the Powers Group indicates that the group should:

- decide how much is to be invested in each option during each month
- maximize the return on all investments made during the three-month quarter
- invest a total of $9 million during January
- keep at least $2 million liquid in passbook savings at all times
- have at least $5 million liquid for the venture capital investment with Gramm Crackers on April 1
- have a maximum of $4 million in either of the term investment options during any one month

DECISION VARIABLES

The amount invested in any option during any one month is a function of the amount already invested that has not matured, plus any new investment in the option. Thus, the decision variables can be defined as the amount of *new investment* in each option during each month. The variable names are summarized in Table 4.12.

TABLE 4.12   THE POWERS GROUP DECISION VARIABLES

	Amount of New Investment during		
	January	February	March
Term accounts	T1	T2	T3
Construction loans	C1	C2	C3
Passbook savings	P1	P2	P3

OBJECTIVE FUNCTION

The objective is to maximize the interest earned *during* the quarter. Investments that have not matured at the end of March are assumed to have earned interest proportional to the term rate. This means that new investment in two-month term accounts at the beginning of March will have earned one-half their term interest (.0035%), money invested in construction loans at the beginning of February will have earned two-thirds their term interest (.010%), and money invested in construction loans at the beginning of March have earned one-third their term interest (.005%). Thus, the objective function is:

MAX $.007T1 + .015C1 + .002P1 + .007T2 + .010C2 + .002P2 + .0035T3 + .005C3 + .002P3$

CONSTRAINTS

The Powers Group must consider the following constraints in its analysis.

Amount invested in January: The amount invested in January is $9 million (since all money can at least be put into a passbook savings account):

$$T1 + C1 + P1 = 9 \text{ (in millions)}$$

Amount available for investment in succeeding months: The amount available for investment on February 1 and March 1, and the amount available on April 1 for the venture capital project, is the amount of liquid cash available at each point in time. That amount is:

1.007 (Amount invested in term accounts two months ago) +

1.015 (Amount invested in construction loans three months ago) +

1.002 (Amount invested in passbook savings one month ago)

Thus, the amounts available for investment on February 1, March 1, and April 1, respectively, are:

$$\text{February 1:} \quad 1.002P1$$
$$\text{March 1:} \quad 1.007T1 + 1.002P2$$
$$\text{April 1:} \quad 1.015C1 + 1.007T2 + 1.002P3$$

The investment constraints for February 1 and March 1 are then:

$$T2 + C2 + P2 = 1.002P1$$
$$T3 + C3 + P3 = 1.007T1 + 1.002P2$$

On April 1, the amount that must be available is $5 (million):

$$1.015C1 + 1.007T2 + 1.002P3 \geq 5$$

Minimum investment in passbook account: For each month, the minimum invested in a passbook account is $2 million. This is expressed by the following three constraints:

$$P1 \geq 2$$
$$P2 \geq 2$$
$$P3 \geq 2$$

Maximum investment in term accounts and construction loans: The amount invested in term accounts during a month is the amount of new investment during that month plus the amount that was invested in a term account at the beginning of the previous month. Since these amounts cannot exceed $4 million (and since there was no investment prior to January 1), the appropriate constraints are:

$$T1 \qquad \leq 4$$
$$T1 + T2 \qquad \leq 4$$
$$T2 + T3 \leq 4$$

For construction loans, the total amount invested includes new amounts during the current month plus new amounts from the previous *two* months. Again, since there was no investment in construction loans prior to January 1, these conditions are modeled by:

$$C1 \qquad \leq 4$$
$$C1 + C2 \qquad \leq 4$$
$$C1 + C2 + C3 \leq 4$$

When formulating mathematical models, if any of the constraints are redundant, they can be eliminated to reduce the input data and speed the computation time. Here, since $T1 + T2 \leq 4$, then T1 itself must not exceed 4. Thus, $T1 \leq 4$ is a redundant constraint. Similarly, since $C1 + C2 + C3 \leq 4$, both the constraints $C1 \leq 4$ and $C2 + C3 \leq 4$ are redundant.

THE MATHEMATICAL
MODEL

Eliminating these redundant constraints gives us the following mathematical model for the Powers Group:

MAXIMIZE $.007T1 + .015C1 + .002P1 + .007T2 + .010C2 + .002P2 + .0035T3 + .005C3 + .002P3$

ST

$$
\begin{array}{l}
T1 + C1 + P1 = 9 \\
-1.002P1 + T2 + C2 + P2 = 0 \\
-1.007T1 \qquad\qquad -1.002P2 + T3 + C3 + P3 = 0 \\
1.015C1 \qquad +1.007T2 \qquad\qquad +1.002P3 \le 5 \\
P1 \ge 2 \\
P2 \ge 2 \\
P3 \ge 2 \\
T1 + T2 \le 4 \\
T2 + T3 \le 4 \\
C1 + C2 + C3 \le 4
\end{array}
$$

All variables ≥ 0

EXCEL OUTPUT

The company used Excel to solve for the optimal solution. One benefit of using a spreadsheet approach is that the model information can be expressed using various sections of the spreadsheet. This format, which disguises the fact that this is a linear programming model, is frequently more appealing to the layperson than are the mathematical formats used in other linear programming software. The Excel input for this model is given in Appendix 4.1. The spreadsheet output is shown in Figure 4.10.

FIGURE 4.10   Excel Output—The Powers Group

As you can see in the columns labeled "New Investment," in January, $3 million should be invested in term accounts, $4 million in construction loans, and the minimum $2 million in passbook accounts. In February, all the interest from the passbook savings should be invested in new term accounts. In March, all interest from passbook savings and the principal and interest from the January term accounts should be reinvested in term accounts. Although only $5 million was needed for the venture capital project with Gramm Crackers on April 1, $6,068,028 will be available. If the company follows this strategy, the total interest earned over the three-month period will be $103,615.50.

4.10 *M*OBILE CABINET COMPANY

Mobile.lpp
Mobile.xls

Applications Area:	Multiperiod/Overtime Planning
Concepts:	Selection of Proper Decision Variables
	Minimization Objective
	Determination of Proper Objective Function Coefficients
	Inventory/Production Linking Constraints
	Management Memo
Software:	WINQSB

The Mobile Cabinet Company produces cabinets used in mobile and motor homes. Cabinets produced for motor homes are smaller and made from less expensive materials than are those for mobile homes. The home office in Ames, Iowa, has just distributed to its individual manufacturing centers the production quotas required during the upcoming summer quarter. The scheduled production requirements for the Lexington, Kentucky, plant are given in Table 4.13.

TABLE 4.13   PRODUCTION REQUIREMENTS—MOBILE CABINET COMPANY

	July	August	September
Motor home	250	250	150
Mobile home	100	300	400

Each motor home cabinet requires three man-hours to produce, whereas each mobile home cabinet requires five man-hours. Labor rates normally average $18 per hour. During July and August, however, when Mobile employs many part-time workers, labor rates average only $14 and $16 per hour, respectively. A total of 2100 man-hours are available in July, 1500 in August, and 1200 in September. During any given month, management at the Lexington plant can schedule up to 50% additional man-hours, using overtime at the standard rate of time and a half. Material costs for motor home cabinets are $146; for mobile home cabinets they are are $210.

The Lexington plant expects to have 25 motor home and 20 mobile home assembled cabinets in stock at the beginning of July. The home office wants the Lexington plant to have at least 10 motor home and 25 mobile cabinet assemblies in stock at the beginning of October to cover possible shortages in production from other plants.

The Lexington plant has storage facilities capable of holding up to 300 cabinets in any one month. The costs for storing motor home and mobile home cabinets from one month to the next are estimated at $6 and $9 per cabinet, respectively. Management at the Lexington plant would like to devise a monthly production schedule that will minimize their costs over the quarter.

SOLUTION

Management at the Lexington plant should:

- determine the number of motor home and mobile home cabinets to produce in each of the next three months; how many are to be produced in regular time and how many in overtime?
- minimize the total costs over the quarter
- meet the minimum shipping requirements each month
- meet the minimum in-stock requirements for October
- schedule no more than the maximum number of regular hours and overtime hours
- store no more than 300 cabinets in any one month

DECISION VARIABLES
(FIRST PASS)

Management wishes to schedule production of motor home cabinets (X) and mobile home cabinets (Y) over the three months of July (J), August (A), and September (S), during regular time (R) and overtime (O). Thus, it wants to find the values for the variables in the following schedule.

QUARTERLY PRODUCTION SCHEDULE LEXINGTON PLANT

	July		August		September	
	Regular	Overtime	Regular	Overtime	Regular	Overtime
Motor home	XJR	XJO	XAR	XAO	XSR	XSO
Mobile home	YJR	YJO	YAR	YAO	YSR	YSO

OBJECTIVE FUNCTION

The objective is to minimize the total costs over the quarter. The total production cost for the quarter is the sum of the unit production costs (material and labor) times the production quantities for the quarter. Table 4.14 shows the calculations for the unit production costs for each decision variable.

TABLE 4.14   UNIT PRODUCTION COSTS—MOBILE CABINET COMPANY

Variable	Material Costs	Labor Costs	Total Unit Costs
XJR	$146	3($14) = $ 42	$188
XJO	$146	3($21) = $ 63	$209
XAR	$146	3($16) = $ 48	$194
XAO	$146	3($24) = $ 72	$218
XSR	$146	3($18) = $ 54	$200
XSO	$146	3($27) = $ 81	$227
YJR	$210	5($14) = $ 70	$280
YJO	$210	5($21) = $105	$315
YAR	$210	5($16) = $ 80	$290
YAO	$210	5($24) = $120	$330
YSR	$210	5($18) = $ 90	$300
YSO	$210	5($27) = $135	$345

But wait! In addition to these production costs, Mobile also faces storage costs of $6 for each motor home cabinet and $9 for each mobile home cabinet stored from one month to the next. Thus, we must determine the number of motor home and mobile home cabinets stored from July to August, August to September, and September to October. This requires the use of decision variables not yet defined. But no problem — we'll define them now.

DECISION VARIABLES
(SECOND PASS)

SXJ = number of motor home cabinets stored at the end of July
SYJ = number of mobile home cabinets stored at the end of July
SXA = number of motor home cabinets stored at the end of August
SYA = number of mobile home cabinets stored at the end of August
SXS = number of motor home cabinets stored at the end of September
SYS = number of mobile home cabinets stored at the end of September

The objective function can now be written as follows.

$$MIN\ 188XJR + 209XJO + 194XAR + 218XAO + 200XSR + 227XSO +$$
$$280YJR + 315YJO + 290YAR + 330YAO + 300YSR + 345YSO +$$
$$6SXJ +\ \ 9SYJ +\ \ 6SXA +\ \ 9SYA +\ \ 6SXS +\ \ 9SYS$$

CONSTRAINTS

Mobile must consider the following constraints in its analysis:

Monthly Production: Each month, the total production plus beginning of the month inventory must be at least as great as the shipping quotas scheduled by the home office in Ames, Iowa. Any extra production is the amount stored for the next month. Thus, for each month:

(Beginning Inventory) + (Monthly Production) = (Shipping Quota) + (Amount Stored)

This relationship yields the following production constraints:

$$25 + (XJR + XJO) = 250 + SXJ \quad \text{(July—Motor home)}$$
$$SXJ + (XAR + XAO) = 250 + SXA \quad \text{(August—Motor home)}$$
$$SXA + (XSR + XSO) = 150 + SXS \quad \text{(September—Motor home)}$$
$$20 + (YJR + YJO) = 100 + SYJ \quad \text{(July—Mobile home)}$$
$$SYJ + (YAR + YAO) = 300 + SYA \quad \text{(August—Mobile home)}$$
$$SYA + (YSR + YSO) = 400 + SYS \quad \text{(September—Mobile home)}$$

October In-Stock Requirements: The number of motor home and mobile home cabinets on hand at the beginning of October are simply those stored at the end of September. Thus, the required beginning inventories for October can be expressed as

$$SXS \geq 10 \quad \text{(Motor home cabinets)}$$
$$SYS \geq 25 \quad \text{(Mobile home cabinets)}$$

Production Hours: The limits on the number of regular time hours and overtime hours available can be expressed by the following relationships:

(Regular Time Hours Used) ≤ (Regular Time Hours Available)
(Overtime Hours Used) ≤ (Overtime Hours Available)

This yields[5]

$$3XJR + 5YJR \leq 2100 \quad \text{(July—Regular time)}$$
$$3XJO + 5YJO \leq 1050 \quad \text{(July—Overtime)}$$
$$3XAR + 5YAR \leq 1500 \quad \text{(August—Regular time)}$$
$$3XAO + 5YAO \leq 750 \quad \text{(August—Overtime)}$$
$$3XSR + 5YSR \leq 1200 \quad \text{(September—Regular time)}$$
$$3XSO + 5YSO \leq 600 \quad \text{(September—Overtime)}$$

Maximum Storage Limits: The plant is restricted to a maximum storage of 500 finished units in any one month. Thus, for each month:

(Motor Home Cabinets Stored) + (Mobile Home Cabinets Stored) ≤ 300

Thus,

$$SXJ + SYJ \leq 300 \quad \text{(July limit)}$$
$$SXA + SYA \leq 300 \quad \text{(August limit)}$$
$$SXS + SYS \leq 300 \quad \text{(September limit)}$$

THE MATHEMATICAL MODEL

Rearranging the terms of the monthly production constraints and adding the nonnegativity constraints, we obtain the following model.

---

[5]If these constraints were taken alone, overtime hours could be used before regular time hours. But, because of the larger objective coefficients associated with overtime products, the linear programming solution will necessarily use all regular hours for a month before using overtime hours.

MINIMIZE   188XJR + 209XJO + 194XAR + 218XAO + 200XSR + 227XSO + 280YJR + 315YJO + 290YAR + 330YAO + 300YSR +
345YSO + 6SXJ + 6SXA + 6SXS + 9SYJ + 9SYA + 9SYS

ST

XJR + XJO			−SXJ		= 225
XAR + XAO			+SXJ −SXA		= 250
XSR + XSO			+SXA −SXS		= 150
YJR + YJO			−SYJ		= 80
YAR + YAO			+SYJ −SYA		= 300
YSR + YSO			+SYA −SYS	= 400
			SXS		≥ 10
				SYS	≥ 25
3XJR +	5YJR				≤ 2100
3XJO +	5YJO				≤ 1050
3XAR +	5YAR				≤ 1500
3XAO +	5YAO				≤ 750
3XSR +	5YSR				≤ 1200
3XSO +	5YSO				≤ 600
		SXJ +	SYJ		≤ 300
		SXA +	SYA		≤ 300
		SXS +	SYS		≤ 300

All Variables ≥ 0

WINQSB ANALYSIS   Figure 4.11 shows the combined report from WINQSB. Although the output indicates that alternative optimal solutions exist, when these alternative solutions were investi-

Combined Report for Mobile Cabinet Company

22:55:44   Tuesday   September   22   1998

	Decision Variable	Solution Value	Unit Cost or Profit c(j)	Total Contribution	Reduced Cost	Basis Status	Allowable Min. c(j)	Allowable Max. c(j)
1	MOT-REG-J	225.00	188.00	42,300.00	0	basic	185.00	188.00
2	MOT-O/T-J	0	209.00	0	0	at bound	209.00	M
3	MOT-REG-A	250.00	194.00	48,500.00	0	basic	193.40	194.00
4	MOT-O/T-A	0	218.00	0	0	at bound	218.00	M
5	MOT-REG-S	160.00	200.00	32,000.00	0	basic	-29.40	200.60
6	MOT-O/T-S	0	227.00	0	3.60	at bound	223.40	M
7	MOB-REG-J	285.00	280.00	79,800.00	0	basic	280.00	285.00
8	MOB-O/T-J	95.00	315.00	29,925.00	0	basic	280.00	315.00
9	MOB-REG-A	150.00	290.00	43,500.00	0	basic	290.00	291.00
10	MOB-O/T-A	131.00	330.00	43,230.00	0	basic	324.00	330.00
11	MOB-REG-S	144.00	300.00	43,200.00	0	basic	299.00	339.00
12	MOB-O/T-S	0	345.00	0	6.00	at bound	339.00	M
13	MOT-INV-J	0	6.00	0	3.00	at bound	3.00	M
14	MOT-INV-A	0	6.00	0	0.60	at bound	5.40	M
15	MOT-INV-S	10.00	6.00	60.00	0	basic	-223.40	M
16	MOB-INV-J	300.00	9.00	2,700.00	0	basic	-M	12.00
17	MOB-INV-A	281.00	9.00	2,529.00	0	basic	-30.00	10.00
18	MOB-INV-S	25.00	9.00	225.00	0	basic	-339.00	M

Objective	Function	(Min.)=	367,969.00	(Note:	Alternate	Solution	Exists!!)

	Constraint	Left Hand Side	Direction	Right Hand Side	Slack or Surplus	Shadow Price	Allowable Min.RHS	Allowable Max.RHS
1	MOTOR-J	225.00	=	225.00	0	209.00	66.67	416.67
2	MOTOR-A	250.00	=	250.00	0	218.00	31.67	281.67
3	MOTOR-S	150.00	=	150.00	0	223.40	-10.00	181.67
4	MOBILE-J	80.00	=	80.00	0	315.00	-15.00	195.00
5	MOBILE-A	300.00	=	300.00	0	330.00	169.00	319.00
6	MOBILE-S	400.00	=	400.00	0	339.00	269.00	419.00
7	MOTOR-O	10.00	>=	10.00	0	229.40	0	41.67
8	MOBILE-O	25.00	>=	25.00	0	348.00	0	44.00
9	REG-J	2,100.00	<=	2,100.00	575.00	-7.00	1,525.00	2,575.00
10	O/T-J	475.00	<=	1,050.00	0	0	475.00	M
11	REG-A	1500.00	<=	1,500.00	95.00	-8.00	1,405.00	2,155.00
12	O/T-A	655.00	<=	750.00	0	0	655.00	M
13	REG-S	1,200.00	<=	1,200.00	600.00	-7.80	1,105.00	1,855.00
14	O/T-S	0	<=	600.00	0	0	0	M
15	INV-J	300.00	<=	300.00	0	-6.00	281.00	415.00
16	INV-A	281.00	<=	300.00	19.00	0	281.00	M
17	INV-S	35.00	<=	300.00	265.00	0	35.00	M

FIGURE 4.11   WINQSB—Combined Report for Mobile Cabinet Company

gated the total monthly production for each product was found to be the same in each solution; only the distribution about which cabinets were to be produced in regular time and which in overtime differed.

Based on the output, the following memo to Charles Lindstrom, vice president for production at the Mobile Cabinet Company Plant in Lexington, Kentucky, was prepared. Key points in the memo concern the value of extra labor hours and storage space.

M E M O R A N D U M

To: Charles Lindstrom
         Vice President for Production

From: Student Consulting Group

Subj: Cabinet Production Schedule for the Third Quarter

The following report details production recommendations for the third quarter at the Mobile Cabinet Company, Lexington, Kentucky. Based on the following input from your production manager, the results were generated using a linear programming model to minimize the total overall material, labor, and storage costs for the quarter.

- Production times average three hours for motor home cabinets and five hours for mobile home cabinets.
- There is an ample supply of production materials to support any production schedule.
- Normal labor time is restricted to 2100 man-hours at $14 per hour in July, 1500 hours at $16 per hour in August, and 1200 hours at $18 per hour in September.
- Up to 1050 hours of overtime, at a cost of time and a half of the regular time rate, can be scheduled in July, 750 in August, and 600 in September.
- The cost to store cabinets is approximately $6 per month for motor home cabinets and $9 per month for mobile home cabinets. Existing storage facilities, capable of storing up to 300 cabinets, will be utilized.
- The delivery schedule set by the home office will be met. Mobile will have 25 motor home and 20 mobile home cabinets available at the start of July. Ten motor home and 25 mobile home cabinets are to be in stock at the beginning of October.

RECOMMENDED PRODUCTION/STORAGE SCHEDULE

Schedule I is a recommended production schedule for manufacturing 635 motor home cabinets and 805 mobile home cabinets during the third quarter, which should meet the home office requirements at minimum total cost.

SCHEDULE I   MOBILE CABINET COMPANY
LEXINGTON PLANT
RECOMMENDED PRODUCTION/STORAGE SCHEDULE

	Beginning Inventory (a)	Production Regular (b)	Production Overtime (c)	Monthly Shipments (d)	Quantity Stored (e=a+b+c−d)
July					
Motor home	25	225	0	250	0
Mobile home	20	285	95	100	300

| | Beginning Inventory (a) | Production | | Monthly Shipments (d) | Quantity Stored (e=a+b+c−d) |
		Regular (b)	Overtime (c)		
August					
Motor home	0	250	0	250	0
Mobile home	300	150	131	300	281
September					
Motor home	0	160	0	150	10
Mobile home	281	144	0	400	25

LABOR UTILIZATION

The production schedule in Schedule I utilizes all the regular time available each month and requires the use of 475 overtime hours in July and 655 overtime hours in August; each of these is below the maximum amount of overtime that could be scheduled for the month. No overtime is required in September.

Additional hires to increase the amount of regular time will be economically beneficial to the plant *only if* workers can be found for less than $7.00 per hour in July, $8.00 in August, and $7.80 in September. Each of these amounts is well below current average monthly wage rates.

Since overtime hours cost the company less in July than in August, it may seem that more overtime should be scheduled during July. However, this would result in production that would exceed the storage limitation of 300 units for the month. Figure I details the recommended labor utilization over the quarter.

FIGURE I   Labor Utilization—Third Quarter

ADDITIONAL STORAGE

If additional storage space could be rented, the ability to store 115 additional units would reduce the total quarterly cost by $690. The savings would result from utilizing all the available overtime in July to produce mobile home cabinets. However, this cost savings must be measured against any additional costs that would be incurred, including transportation and rent fees. Since no additional storage is required for August and September, and outside storage facilities usually require more than one month's rental, renting additional space may not justify the minimal cost savings.

BUDGET/COSTS

Schedule II gives relevant quarterly cost information for budgeting purposes. Note that the larger and less costly overall workforce for July and August has material and storage cost ramifications.

SCHEDULE II   MOBILE CABINET COMPANY
LEXINGTON PLANT
THIRD-QUARTER COST REQUIREMENTS

| | Production | | Labor | | | | |
	Regular Quantity (a)	Overtime Quantity (b)	Regular Cost (c)	Overtime Cost (d)	Material Cost (e)	Inventory Cost (f)	Total Cost (g=c+d+e+f)
July							
Motor	225	0	$ 9450	$ 0	$ 32,850	$ 0	$ 42,300
Mobile	285	95	19,950	9975	79,800	2700	112,425
Total July	510	95	$29,400	$ 9975	$112,650	$2700	$154,725
August							
Motor	250	0	$12,000	$ 0	$ 32,500	$ 0	$ 48,500
Mobile	150	131	12,000	15,720	59,010	2529	89,259
Total August	400	131	$24,000	$15,720	$ 95,510	$2529	$137,759
September							
Motor	160	0	$ 8640	$ 0	$ 23,360	$ 60	$ 32,060
Mobile	144	0	12,960	0	30,240	225	43,425
Total September	304	0	$21,600	$ 0	$ 53,600	$ 285	$ 75,485
Quarter Totals	1214	226	$75,000	$25,695	$261,760	$5514	$367,969

According to this schedule, the need for capital to purchase materials sharply declines during each month over the quarter. Labor costs remain fairly level from July to August, and then tail off substantially in September, as shown in Figures II and III.

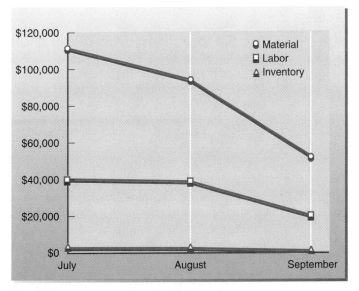

FIGURE II   Distribution of Costs—Third Quarter

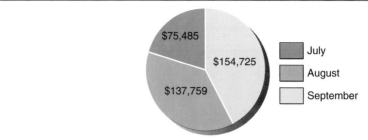

FIGURE III   Monthly Cost Requirements—Third Quarter

OVERALL RECOMMENDATION

Given the input from the production manager, we recommend the foregoing production and storage schedule (Schedule I) to minimize plant costs for the quarter. Significant changes in the material, labor, or storage costs or availabilities could affect this recommendation. Should any such changes occur, we welcome the opportunity to present a revised proposal.

4.11   APPLICATIONS OF LINEAR MODELS IN BUSINESS AND GOVERNMENT

From its roots in military planning operations, linear programming models quickly spread into numerous industries. Oil, food processing, iron and steel, and communications companies were some of the first to reap huge rewards from employing linear models.

Today, with the increased availability of computing power, more and more businesses have the opportunity to take advantage of linear programming models. Banking models, large economic/financial models, marketing strategy models, production scheduling and labor force planning models, computer design and networking models, and health care and medical models are but a few notable examples of successful linear programming applications. In this section, we briefly chronicle just a handful of the thousands of actual documented uses of linear programming models.[6]

AIRCRAFT FLEET ASSIGNMENTS

Typically, the marketing department of an airline delivers a schedule between pairs of cities based on its estimates of demand and the operating cost for each type of aircraft in those markets. Some flight segments entail "deadheading"—flying without passengers to get the appropriate aircraft to a particular city in time for a scheduled flight. Linear models have been utilized to schedule aircraft to accommodate an acceptable schedule while maximizing the total profit made from assigning the aircraft over a predetermined schedule.

TELE-COMMUNICATIONS NETWORK EXPANSION PLANNING

Telecommunications companies are expanding and modernizing their networks at a rapid rate in order to meet growing demand from customers, implement the most recent technological advances, and prepare for an onslaught of additional services. These companies must make tradeoffs between expanding cable capacities by either providing a dedicated cable for each required circuit or using concentrators (devices such as elec-

---

[6]In a number of these applications, some of the decision variables are restricted to integer values or take on values of only 0 or 1. Models with these restrictions are discussed more fully in Chapter 5.

tronic multiplexers, remote switches, and fiber optic terminals) to perform traffic compression operations that combine incoming signals on several lines to a single composite signal requiring only one outgoing line. Linear models have been used to minimize the total cost of the network expansion and installation.

AIR POLLUTION
CONTROL

Government regulatory agencies set limits on the amounts of various types of emissions—carbon monoxide, hydrocarbons, nitrogen oxides, and sulphur dioxide—by all polluting sources. Industries and individuals can reduce these emissions in various ways. Linear models have been developed to determine the extent to which each abatement approach for each polluting source can be utilized to meet government regulations at minimum cost.

HEALTH CARE
APPLICATIONS:
ALLOCATING BLOOD
TO HOSPITALS

Blood is collected at various blood bank sites and allocated to hospitals within the blood bank's distribution area. Over time, blood deteriorates and "expires"; however, some expired blood can be used for other purposes. One objective of nonprofit blood banks, such as those in Great Britain, is to allocate blood bank supplies to hospitals to minimize the expected value of the blood that will expire. Linear models have been used to meet this objective, while ensuring that hospitals meet their minimum requirements for different blood types.

BANK PORTFOLIOS

The profitability of a bank over any quarterly time period is a function of the distribution of its assets. Banks must comply with various regulations and policies, however, such as maintaining required capital ratios and adequate reserves. They also must stay within certain limits on risk asset ratios and real estate loans. Given a set of expected rates of returns for their various assets, banks have used linear models to assist them in maximizing the overall net rate of return of their portfolios.

AGRICULTURE

Farmers must allocate areas for planting various crops and raising livestock, subject to many internal and external restrictions, such as government subsidies, availability of capital and labor, land and irrigation usage limits, transportation, and equipment usage. Based on a set of reasonable price expectations and reliable estimates for input-output yields for all farm products, linear programming has been used to develop land-use and livestock production plans to maximize total yearly profit. The sensitivity results of linear programming analyses provide the farm planner with the important "what-if" information needed to make intelligent planning decisions.

EMERGENCY
SERVICES—FIRE
PROTECTION

Municipalities must decide which emergency service projects they can undertake. When it comes to fire protection, such projects include water supply allocations, fire department equipment and personnel, emergency communications systems, and fire safety control programs. Each of these projects affects the level of fire protection and, hence, the insurance rates charged to the community. Political and other factors determine a minimum level of such services. Linear models have been developed to minimize the total cost of providing emergency fire services while assuring at least adequate standards of service in all required fire support areas.

DEFENSE/AEROSPACE
CONTRACTORS

Defense/aerospace companies receive contracts to build particular components for the military and NASA. In each case, the components must be delivered to the prime contractor at various points in time throughout the term of the contract. Once the contract expires, however, little or no future funding will be left for the component. Thus, the company must "gear up" by hiring and training qualified personnel to meet the time demands for the product, with the full knowledge that many of the trained workers will be terminated by the time the contract expires.[7] Linear models have been successfully applied to determine production schedules and hiring and layoff policies that meet target demands while minimizing total project costs.

LAND-USE PLANNING

Periodically, large parcels of unincorporated county lands are developed to accommodate increasing demand for housing and services. Possible uses for some or all the land include residential housing, churches, centers of local and regional commerce, offices, manufacturing activities, and open or recreational space. Community concerns include the effects of newly generated trips on existing transportation corridors, inherent "conflict" among land uses, and the impact on the environment. Linear models have been used to minimize one or more of these measures while operating within the constraints of total acreage available for development, maximum and minimum limits on the acreage allotted to any one use, public service capacities, budget restrictions and bond or mortgage financing.

THE DAIRY INDUSTRY

At milk processing plants, numerous dairy products are produced directly from processed milk, including several varieties of milk, cheeses, butters, and powdered milks. Still other products, such as whey powder, whey cream, and lactose, are produced from a byproduct of the cheese-making process. Each day, managers at these plants must make scheduling decisions for product flow, equipment (evaporators and driers) utilization, personnel assignments, and transportation arrangements. Linear models have played a role in determining optimal production schedules that take into account equipment capacity limitations, demand requirements, supply restrictions, product flow, and process conversion ratios.

SOLID WASTE
MANAGEMENT

Since the middle of the twentieth century, two factors have contributed to the exponential growth in the generation of solid waste and the urgent need to confront the problem of its disposal: (1) the movement of population to urbanized areas of the country; and (2) the increasing use of throwaway products and disposable containers. Cash-strapped communities face the problem of finding inexpensive landfill sites, constructing new sites near areas with high-demand concentrations, and transporting solid waste to the facilities. Linear models have been developed to help communities determine the economic viability of constructing intermediate and ultimate disposal sites as well as the appropriate routing of solid waste to disposal sites.

THE MILITARY:
STRATEGIC
DEPLOYMENT OF
AIRCRAFT AND SEA
LIFT FORCES

The Defense Department, at times, must meet certain deployment obligations (measured in kilotons of materials) to various theaters of operation. Under increasing pressure from congressional and administrative sources to reduce costs, the military has used linear models designed to do so while still meeting mission objectives. Given the availability and capacities of existing ships and aircraft and their requirements at different deployment sites at different points in time, one such model minimizes the total expected procurement and operational costs needed to complete the mission.

---

[7]This is an example of a typical problem in linear programming known as the "on-the-job training problem." These problems can be quite large, with thousands of variables and constraints.

These are but a few of the numerous applications areas of linear optimization models. The list also encompasses such additional areas as traffic analysis, fast-food operations, transportation, assignment of medical personnel, coal, steel, gas, chemical, and paper production, recycling, educational assignments, worker evaluations, awarding of contracts, manufacturing, railroads, forestry, school desegregation, government planning, tourism, and sports scheduling. Each year hundreds of new applications appear in the professional literature. Add to that the numerous unreported models that are regularly utilized in business and government, and you can see that linear programming continues to play a significant role in today's world.

4.12 SUMMARY

Linear programming applications abound in business and government. In this chapter, we have presented useful hints for formulating linear models. We have shown how definitional variables can simplify the formulation of models that include a large number of constraints involving percentages. We have also modeled several illustrative examples from the functional areas of business using the approaches outlined in the first section. All the models were solved using WINQSB, Excel, or LINDO software. In addition to the illustrative business examples, we have outlined applications from various industries to illustrate the breadth of linear programming applications.

Excel Spreadsheet for the Powers Group Model

Data and constraints can be located in various places on a spreadsheet, giving the appearance that, in some cases, a spreadsheet is more user friendly than models presented using matrix input.

For the Powers Group model discussed in Section 4.9, a rectangular area is set aside for the month-by-month new investment in the three investments (B5:D7). The available limits for new investment are set down for each month. For January, the limit is a fixed $9 million; for February and March, it depends on the distribution of the previous month's investments. These are all shown in cells B9:D9.

The total amount invested in each investment in each month is shown to the right in cells F5:H7. This is important because of the minimum limits on passbook investments and the maximum limits for construction loans and term accounts.

Finally, a cell is set aside for the amount available for investment in Gramm Crackers (E11) and for the total interest earned over the three-month period (E13). Exhibit 4.1 is the spreadsheet that is used.

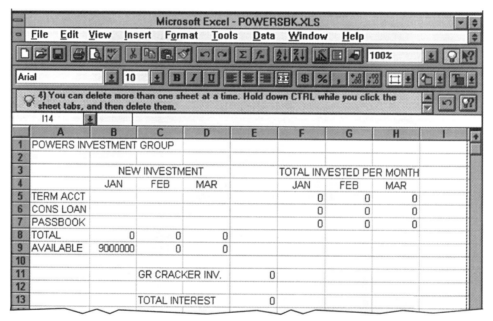

EXHIBIT 4.1

The formulas for the individual cells are as follows.

Cell	Formula
B8	=SUM(B5:B7)
C8	=SUM(C5:C7)
D8	=SUM(D5:D7)
B9	9000000
C9	=1.002*B7
D9	=1.002*C7+1.007*B5
F5	=B5
F6	=B6
F7	=B7
G5	=B5+C5
G6	=B6+C6
G7	=C7

```
H5     =C5+D5
H6     =B6+C6+D6
H7     =D7
E11    =1.015*B6+1.007*C5+1.002*D7
E13    =.007*B5+.015*B6+.002*B7+.007*C5+.01*C6 +.002*C7+.0035*D5+.005*D6+.002*D7
```

The spreadsheet in Exhibit 4.2 is the Solver dialog box, which shows the objective function cell and the constraint formulas. The spreadsheet output produced by Solver is given in Section 4.2.

EXHIBIT 4.2

PROBLEMS

1. MANUFACTURING. Kelly Industries manufactures two different structural support products used in the construction of large boats and ships. The two products, the Z345 and the W250, are produced from specially treated zinc and iron and are produced in both standard and industrial grades. Kelly nets a profit of $400 on each standard Z345 and $500 on each standard W250. Industrial models net a 40% premium.

   Each week, up to 2500 pounds of zinc and 2800 pounds of iron can be treated and made available for production. The following table gives the per unit requirements (in pounds) for each model.

   | | Z345 | | W250 | |
	Standard	Industrial	Standard	Industrial
Zinc	25	46	16	34
Iron	50	30	28	12

   Kelly has a contract to supply a combined total of at least 20 standard or industrial Z345 supports to Calton Shipbuilders each week. Company policy mandates that at least 50% of the production must be industrial models and that neither Z345 models nor W250 models can account for more than 75% of weekly production. By adhering to this policy, Kelly feels, it can sell all the product it manufactures.

   Determine a weekly production plan for Kelly Industries. What interpretation can you give to the fractional values that are part of the optimal production quantities?

2. MANUFACTURING. Consider the optimal solution obtained for the Kelly Industries problem (problem 1).
   a. What proportion of the production are W250 models? What does that tell you about how the profit will be affected if the 75% limit is loosened or eliminated?
   b. State whether you should buy *additional* shipments of zinc, should they become available at the following premiums above zinc's normal cost.
      i.   100 pounds for $1,500
      ii. 100 pounds for $2,600
      iii. 800 pounds for $10,000
      iv. 900 pounds for $12,000
      v.   900 pounds for $25,000
   c. The net unit profit coefficients were estimates (albeit scientific ones). By considering the ranges of optimality, comment on this statement: "The optimal solution is not sensitive to small errors in the estimation of the unit profit coefficients."

3. FINANCIAL INVESTMENT. The Investment Club at Bell Labs has solicited and obtained $50,000 from its members. Collectively, the members have selected the three stocks, two bond funds, and a tax-deferred annuity shown in the following table as possible investments.

Investment	Risk	Projected Annual Return
Stock—EAL	High	15%
Stock—BRU	Moderate	12%
Stock—TAT	Low	9%
Bonds—long term		11%
Bonds—short term		8%
Tax-deferred annuity		6%

   The club members have decided on the following strategies for investment:
   - All $50,000 is to be invested.
   - At least $10,000 is to be invested in the tax-deferred annuity.
   - At least 25% of the funds invested in stocks are to be in the low-risk stock (TAT).
   - At least as much is to be invested in bonds as stocks.
   - No more than $12,500 of the total investment is to be placed in investments with projected annual returns of less than 10%.

a. Formulate and solve a linear program that will maximize the total projected annual return subject to the conditions set forth by the Investment Club members.

b. What is the projected rate of return of this portfolio? What rate of return should investors expect on any additional funds received, given the restrictions of the club? Explain why this rate would hold for all additional investment dollars.

c. For which investment possibilities are the estimates for the projected annual return most sensitive in determining the optimal solution?

d. Give an interpretation of the shadow prices for the right-hand side of each constraint.

4. RETAILING. Bullox Department Store is ordering suits for its spring season. It orders four styles of suits. Three are "off-the-rack suits": (1) polyester blend suits, (2) pure wool suits, and (3) pure cotton suits. The fourth style is an imported line of fine suits of various fabrics. Studies have given Bullox a good estimate of the amount of hours required of its sales staff to sell each suit. In addition, the suits require differing amounts of advertising dollars and floor space during the season. The following table gives the unit profit per suit as well as the estimates for salesperson-hours, advertising dollars, and floor space required for their sale.

Suit	Unit Profit	Salesperson Hours	Advertising Dollars	Display Space (sq. ft.)
Polyester	$35	0.4	$2	1.00
Wool	$47	0.5	$4	1.50
Cotton	$30	0.3	$3	1.25
Import	$90	1.0	$9	3.00

Bullox expects its spring season to last 90 days. The store is open an average of 10 hours a day, 7 days a week; an average of two salespersons will be in the suit department. The floor space allocated to the suit department is a rectangular area of 300 feet by 60 feet. The total advertising budget for the suits is $15,000.

a. Formulate the problem to determine how many of each type of suit to purchase for the season in order to maximize profits and solve as a linear program.

b. From the solution to part (a) you will note that at least one of the suit lines will not be carried. Suppose management wishes to carry at least 200 suits from each line. Amend your formulation and re-solve for the optimal solution. What effect does this have on profitability?

5. RETAILING. Consider the problem faced by Bullox Department Store in problem 4(a).

a. Determine the range of optimality for the unit profit of polyester suits. For polyester suits, what would be the effect on the optimal solution of

   i. overestimating their unit profit by $1

   ii. underestimating their unit profit by $1

   iii. overestimating their unit profit by $2

   iv. underestimating their unit profit by $2

b. Show whether each of the following strategies, individually, would be profitable for Bullox:

   i. utilizing 400 adjacent square feet of space that had been used by women's sportswear. This space has been projected to net Bullox only $750 over the next 90 days.

   ii. spending an additional $400 on advertising.

   iii. hiring an additional salesperson for the 26 total Saturdays and Sundays of the season. This will cost Bullox $3600 in salaries, commissions, and benefits but will add 260 salesperson-hours to the suit department for the 90-day season.

c. Suppose we added a constraint restricting the total number of suits purchased to no more than 5000 for the season. How would the optimal solution be affected?

6. DIET PROBLEM. Grant Winfield is a 71-year-old grandfather who likes to mix breakfast cereals together for taste and as a means of getting at least 50% of the recommended daily allowances (RDA) of five different vitamins and minerals. Concerned about his

sugar intake, he wishes his mixture to yield the lowest possible amount of sugar. For taste, each of the cereals listed in the following table must make up at least 10% of the total mixture. The table shows the amounts of the vitamins, minerals, and sugar contained in one ounce together with $\frac{1}{2}$ cup of skim milk.

PERCENTAGE OF RDA PER OUNCE WITH $\frac{1}{2}$ CUP SKIM MILK

| | Vitamins | | | | | Sugars |
	A	C	D	B6	Iron	(Grams)
Multigrain Cheerios	30	25	25	25	45	12
Grape Nuts	30	2	25	25	45	9
Product 19	20	100	25	100	100	9
Frosted Bran	20	25	25	25	25	15

a. Formulate and solve for the number of ounces in each cereal that should be mixed together in order to minimize total sugar intake while providing at least 50% of the RDA for each of Vitamins A, C, D, B6, and iron. How much sugar would be consumed in the process?

b. How much total cereal does Grant need to eat to achieve the minimum 50% RDA in all five categories? How much milk does he consume in doing this?

c. Determine the shadow prices for this problem. Interpret the shadow prices and the corresponding ranges of feasibility.

d. If Grant eliminates the restriction that each cereal must account for at least 10% of the mixture, then, by inspection, why wouldn't any Frosted Bran be included in the mix? Verify this conclusion by deleting these constraints from the original formulation and re-solving.

7. MANUFACTURING. Darien Facade Company manufactures doors for sale to local construction companies. Its reputation for quality work within the building industry has enabled it to sell all the doors it manufactures. Each week 10 employees, each working eight-hour shifts, five days a week, are assigned to the two manufacturing processes—production and finishing. Of the 400 man-hours available weekly, 250 are assigned to manufacturing and 150 to finishing. The following table gives the production and finishing times per door and the unit profits.

Door	Manufacturing Time (min.)	Finishing Time (min.)	Unit Profit ($)
Standard	30	15	$ 45
High glazed	30	30	$ 90
Engraved	60	30	$120

a. Formulate and solve for the optimal weekly profit for Darien Facade.

b. How would the solution to part (a) change if management were to allocate the 400 man-hours between the two departments in an optimal manner? How many hours should be allocated to manufacturing and to finishing?

8. MAKE OR BUY. Consider the situation faced by the Darien Facade Company in problem 7a. For the upcoming week, Darien has committed itself to satisfying a contract for 280 standard, 120 high-glazed, and 100 engraved doors for the Sherwood Development Company. To satisfy the contract, Darien may have to purchase some premanufactured doors from an outside supplier.

Darien will only use premanufactured doors in the production of standard and high-glazed models but not engraved doors. Those sold as standard doors require only six minutes of finishing time to meet Darien's standards and will net Darien only a $15 profit. Those used for high-glazed doors require the full 30 minutes of finishing time and yield Darien a net $50 profit.

a. Assuming 250 hours of in-house manufacturing time and 150 hours of in-house finishing time, determine the number of each type of door Darien should manufacture in-house as well as how many premanufactured doors Darien should purchase and sell as standard and high-glazed doors in order to maximize its profit for the week.

b. How would the solution to part (a) change if Darien's management were to allocate the 400 man-hours between the two departments in an optimal manner? How many hours should be allocated to manufacturing and to finishing?

9. FOOD SERVICE. Jami Gourmen operates a food truck that primarily services workers at construction and industrial sites. Jami is particularly popular because she only uses fresh ingredients purchased each morning from a local distributer. These include:

3 8-pound Swift turkey breasts (@ $20 each)	$ 60
3 12-pound Butchers roast beefs (@ $42 each)	$126
3 10-pound Hormel honey cured hams (@ $30 each)	$ 90
3 8-pound Alpine Swiss cheeses (@ $18 each)	$ 54
300 sourdough rolls	$ 60
miscellaneous condiments	$ 30

In addition to this $420 in fixed daily food costs, Jami incurs $280 in other daily costs, including gas, truck payments, insurance, and wages for an assistant.

Jami slices each of the meats and cheeses into one-ounce portions first thing in the morning; then she makes sandwiches from these ingredients, wraps them in plastic wrap, and stores them on the truck. She has space to store up to 300 sandwiches and has no problem selling all the sandwiches she makes. The following table gives the ounces of each ingredient in each of the five sandwiches she sells as well as her current selling prices.

Sandwich	Price	Turkey	Beef	Ham	Cheese
Turkey De-Lite	$2.75	4	0	0	1
Beef Boy	$3.50	0	4	0	1
Hungry Ham	$3.25	0	0	4	2
Club	$4.00	2	2	2	2
All Meat	$4.25	3	3	3	0

Formulate and solve for the optimal number of each type of sandwich to make daily. Given that she operates 200 days per year, what does Jami *net* annually from making and selling sandwiches?

10. FOOD SERVICE. For the situation faced by Jami Gourmen in problem 9:

a. What is the range of optimality for the selling price of each sandwich?

b. What are the shadow prices and the ranges of feasibility for the different meats, cheese, and rolls? Give a precise interpretation of these shadow prices.

c. If the price on all sandwiches were raised by $0.10 each, would the optimal solution change? What assumption do you have to make about the demand for the sandwiches in this case?

d. Using only the ranges of optimality, what is the strongest statement you can make about the optimal solution if the prices on all the sandwiches were raised by $0.25 (and the assumption you made in part c still holds)? Modify the problem and determine the new optimal solution.

e. Jami is considering buying another bulk package of one of the meats or cheese. If only one additional bulk package is purchased, which would be the most profitable to Jami?

11. APPAREL INDUSTRY. Exclaim! Jeans is setting up a production schedule for the coming week. Exclaim! can make four jean products: men's and women's jackets and pants. Although it can make different sizes of each, the variation in material usage and labor between sizes is negligible. Each jacket and pair of pants goes through cutting and stitching operations before being boxed. The following table gives the profit, denim, cutting time, stitching time, and boxing time required *per* 100 *items*, as well as the total resource availabilities during the week.

Item	Profit	Denim (yd.)	Cutting (hr.)	Stitching (hr.)	Boxing (hr.)
Men's jackets	$2,000	150	3	4.0	.75
Women's jackets	$2,800	125	4	3.0	.75
Men's pants	$1,200	200	2	2.0	.50
Women's pants	$1,500	150	2	2.5	.50
Available this week		2500	36	36.0	8

Develop and solve a linear programming model for Exclaim! Jeans which will maximize its profit for the week.

12. APPAREL PRODUCTION. For the problem faced by Exclaim! Jeans (problem 11), suppose that, in addition to the existing restrictions, management wishes to produce at least 500 of each item. Add these constraints to your linear program and re-solve the problem.

 a. What is the result? To what do you attribute this result?

 b. Suppose the minimum production for each item is 300. What is the optimal solution?

 c. Interpret the reduced costs for the result in part (b) and discuss the complementary slackness conditions for the objective function coefficients.

13. APPAREL PRODUCTION. Consider the problem faced by Exclaim! Jeans in problem 11.

 a. Determine the reduced costs and the ranges of optimality for each of the profit coefficients.

 b. Determine the shadow prices and the ranges of feasibility for the number of hours available for each operation.

 c. Suppose we added a constraint that requires at least 50% of the items manufactured to be women's items. How would this affect the optimal solution? Suppose instead that the added constraint requires that at least 50% of the items manufactured are men's items. How would this affect the optimal solution?

14. PORTFOLIO ANALYSIS. Sarah Williams has $100,000 to allocate to the investments listed in the following table. Bill Wallace, her investment counselor, has prepared the following estimates for the potential annual return on each investment.

Investment	Expected Return	Minimum Return	Maximum Return
Bonanza Gold (high-risk stock)	15%	−50%	100%
Cascade Telephone (low-risk stock)	9%	3%	12%
Money market account	7%	6%	9%
Two-year Treasury bonds	8%	8%	8%

Sarah wishes to invest her money in such a way as to maximize her expected annual return based on Bill Wallace's projections, with the following restrictions:

• At most $50,000 of her investment should be in stocks.

• At least $60,000 of her investment should have the potential of earning a 9% or greater annual return.

• At least $70,000 should be liquid during the year; this implies that at most $30,000 can be in two-year Treasury bonds.

• The minimum overall annual return should be at least 4%.

• All $100,000 is to be invested.

Assume that the investments will perform independently of one another so that the returns on the investment opportunities are uncorrelated. Formulate and solve a linear program for Sarah.

15. BLENDING—OIL REFINING. California Oil Company (Caloco) produces two grades of unleaded gasoline (regular and premium) from three raw crudes (Pacific, Gulf, and Middle East). The current octane rating, the availability (in barrels), and the cost per barrel for a given production period are given in the following table.

Crude	Octane	Availability	Cost
Pacific	85	3000 barrels	$14.28/barrel
Gulf	87	2000 barrels	$15.12/barrel
Middle East	95	8000 barrels	$19.74/barrel

For this period, Caloco has contracts calling for a minimum of 200,000 gallons of regular and 100,000 gallons of premium gasoline, and it has a refining capacity of 400,000 total gallons. (A barrel is 42 gallons.) Caloco sells regular gasoline to retailers for $0.52 and premium gasoline for $0.60 per gallon.

To be called "regular," the refined gas must have an octane rating of 87 or more; premium must have an octane rating of 91 or more. Assume that the octane rating of any mixture is the weighted octane rating of its components.

a. Solve for the optimal amount of each crude to blend into each gasoline during this production period.

b. Suppose Caloco could obtain an additional 50,000 gallons in refining capacity for the period by putting other projects on hold. Putting these projects on hold is estimated to cost Caloco $5000 in contract penalties. Should the company absorb these fees and secure this extra 50,000-gallon refining capacity?

c. Given your answer to part (a), calculate the amount Caloco would spend purchasing Middle East oil for the period. Suppose Middle East distributors currently have a glut of crude and are in need of some hard currency. They are willing to enter into a contract with Caloco to sell it all 8000 barrels at $16.80 a barrel. Would the Middle East distributors receive more cash from Caloco under this arrangement? Would it be profitable to Caloco to accept this offer? Discuss the ramifications of this action for domestic oil producers.

16. AGRICULTURE. BP Farms is a 300-acre farm located near Lawrence, Kansas, owned and operated exclusively by Bill Pashley. For the upcoming growing season, Bill will grow wheat, corn, oats, and soybeans. The following table gives relevant data concerning expected crop yields, labor required, expected preharvested expenses, and water required (in addition to the forecasted rain). Also included is the price per bushel Bill expects to receive when the crops are harvested.

Crop	Yield (bu./acre)	Labor (hr./acre)	Expenses ($/acre)	Water (acre-ft./acre)	Price ($/bu.)
Wheat	210	4	$50	2	$3.20
Corn	300	5	$75	6	$2.55
Oats	180	3	$30	1	$1.45
Soybeans	240	10	$60	4	$3.10

Bill wishes to produce at least 30,000 bushels of wheat and 30,000 bushels of corn, but no more than 25,000 bushels of oats. He has $25,000 to invest in his crops, and he plans to work up to 12 hours per day during the 150-day season. He also does not wish to exceed the base water supply of 1200 acre-feet allocated to him by the Kansas Agricultural Authority.

Formulate the problem for BP Farms as a linear program and solve for the optimal number of acres of each crop Bill should plant in order to maximize his total expected return from the harvested crops.

17. AGRICULTURE. For the BP Farms problem (problem 16):

a. If the selling price of oats remains $1.45 a bushel, to what level must the yield increase before oats should be planted? If the yield for oats remains 180 bushels per acre, to what level would the price of oats have to rise before oats should be planted?

b. If there were no constraint on the minimum production of corn, would corn be planted? How much would the profit decrease if corn were not grown?

c. La Mancha Realty owns an adjacent 40-acre parcel, which it is willing to lease to Bill for the season for $2000. Should Bill lease this property? Why or why not?

18. PERSONNEL EVALUATION. At Nevada State University, the process for determining whether or not a professor receives tenure is based on a combination of qualitative evaluations and a quantitative formula derived by using linear programming. The process works as follows.

In an Annual Personnel File (APF), the professor submits evidence of his or her (1) teaching effectiveness, (2) research performance, (3) other professional activities, and (4) on-campus professional service. A personnel committee of three evaluators (who are full professors) independently evaluate the professor's file and assign a numerical rating between 0 and 100 to each of the four categories. For each category, the scores from the three evaluators are averaged together to give a single score for that category.

To determine the maximum overall score for the professor, a linear program is used for selecting the best weights (percentages) to assign to each category, satisfying the following university criteria.

- Teaching must be weighted at least as heavily as any other category.

- Research must be weighted at least 25%.

- Teaching plus research must be weighted at least 75%.

- Teaching plus research must be weighted no more than 90%.

- Service is to be weighted at least as heavily as professional activities.

- Professional activities must be weighted at least 5%.

- The total of the weights must be 100%.

Professor Anna Sung is up for tenure. To receive tenure, she must receive a weighted total score of at least 85. The three personnel committee members evaluated Anna as follows:

Committee	Teaching	Research	Professional	Service
Ron	90	60	90	80
Mabel	75	60	95	95
Nick	90	75	85	95

Will Professor Sung be awarded tenure?

19. BANK LOAN POLICIES. Montana State Savings Bank is currently scheduling $10 million in deposits. First trust deeds yield 9%, second trust deeds 10.5%, automobile loans 12.25%, and business loans 11.75%. In addition, Montana State Savings Bank can invest in risk-free securities yielding 6.75%. Regulatory commissions of the state and federal governments require the following:

- At most one-third of deposits must be in risk-free securities.

- Home loans (first and second trust deed) cannot exceed the amount in risk-free securities.

- Business loans may not account for more than 49% of the total loans and trust deed investments.

- Automobile loans may not exceed 50% of the home loans (first and second trust deeds).

How should Montana State Bank invest the $10 million in deposits?

20. MAIL ORDER. Top Mountain Inc. sells outdoor apparel and equipment through its mail order catalog. Among other items, it produces a traditional walking shoe and both a medium- and a high-grade hiking boot. For this year's catalog, Top Mountain expects to net $5 per pair of walking shoes, $6 per pair of medium-grade hiking boots, and $8 per pair of high-grade hiking boots.

A linear programming model was solved, taking into account demand, availability of materials, labor costs, etc. The combined report from WINQSB is as follows:

Combined Report for Top Mountain, Inc.							
22:52:27		Tuesday	September	29	1998		
Decision Variable	Solution Value	Unit Cost or Profit c(j)	Total Contribution	Reduced Cost	Basis Status	Allowable Min. c(j)	Allowable Max. c(j)
1 WALKING	1,000.00	5.00	5,000.00	0	basic	3.33	5.33
2 MEDIUM	0	6.00	0	-1.67	at bound	-M	7.67
3 HIGHGRADE	6,000.00	8.00	48,000.00	0	basic	7.50	M
Objective	Function	(Max.)=	53,000.00				
Constraint	Left Hand Side	Direction	Right Hand Side	Slack or Surplus	Shadow Price	Allowable Min.RHS	Allowable Max.RHS
1 C1	7,000.00	<=	10,000.00	3,000.00	0	7,000.00	M
2 C2	20,000.00	=	20,000.00	0	2.67	10,000.00	29,000.00
3 C3	1,000.00	>=	1,000.00	0	-0.33	0	6,785.71
4 C4	-22,000.00	<=	5,000.00	27,000.00	0	-22,000.00	M
5 C5	19,000.00	>=	9,000.00	10,000.00	0	-M	19,000.00

Combined Report for Top Mountain, Inc.

a. Based on this report, the production department has recommended that no medium-grade hiking boots be produced for the season. The $6 unit profit for medium-grade hiking boots is based on a current projected catalog price of $45 and unit production costs of $39. If production costs could be cut by 5%, why would the production department change its recommendation not to produce medium-grade hiking boots?

b. Suppose Top Mountain imported cheaper leather that reduced costs (and, therefore, increased profits) on walking shoes by $0.25 per pair. What is the potential effect of this change on the optimal production schedule and profit? What assumptions have you made?

c. Suppose Top Mountain is considering using a less costly water repellent that would reduce production costs for the medium-grade hiking boots by $0.50 per pair. What is the potential effect of implementing this policy on the current recommended production schedule?

d. Suppose Top Mountain implemented both actions—importing cheaper leather for walking shoes and using a less costly water repellent on medium-grade hiking boots. Without re-solving the problem, can you conclude that the optimal production schedule will change?

21. ADVERTISING. JL Foods is planning to increase its advertising campaign from $1.4 million to $2 million based, in part, on the introduction of a new product, JL Taco Sauce, to accompany its traditional products, JL Ketchup and JL Spaghetti Sauce. In the past, JL Foods promoted its two products individually, splitting its advertising budget equally between ketchup and spaghetti sauce.

From past experience, the marketing department estimates that each dollar spent *only* advertising ketchup increases ketchup sales by four bottles and each dollar spent *only* advertising spaghetti sauce increases its sales by 3.2 bottles. Since JL makes $0.30 per bottle of ketchup and $0.35 per bottle of spaghetti sauce sold (excluding the sunk cost of the given advertising budget), this amounts to a return of $1.20 (=4 × $0.30) per advertising dollar on ketchup and $1.12 (=3.2 × $0.35) per advertising dollar on spaghetti sauce. Because taco sauce is a new product, its initial return is projected to be only $0.10 per bottle, but each advertising dollar spent solely on taco sauce is estimated to increase sales by 11 bottles. The company also projects that sales of each product would increase by another 1.4 bottles for each dollar spent on joint advertising of the three products.

JL wishes to maximize its increase in profits this year from advertising while also "building for the future" by adhering to the following guidelines for this year's advertising spending:

- A maximum of $2 million total advertising
- At most $400,000 on joint advertising
- At least $100,000 on joint advertising
- At least $1 million promoting taco sauce, either individually or through joint advertising

- At least $250,000 promoting ketchup only
- At least $250,000 promoting spaghetti sauce only
- At least $750,000 promoting taco sauce only
- At least as much spent this year as last year promoting ketchup, either individually or by joint advertising
- At least as much spent this year as last year promoting spaghetti sauce, either individually or by joint advertising
- At least 7.5 million total bottles of product sold

Determine the optimal allocation of advertising dollars among the four advertising possibilities (advertising for each product individually and joint advertising). Give the total return per advertising dollar of this solution and express this as a percentage of the $2 million advertising budget.

22. ADVERTISING. Refer to the solution for the situation faced by JL Foods in problem 21.

a. What is the return on additional advertising dollars?

b. Since the return on advertising taco sauce only and on joint advertising would be the least certain, determine their ranges of optimality and comment.

c. What would be the effect of eliminating the minimum amount of joint advertising? What would be the effect of raising the maximum amount of joint advertising by $100,000?

d. Suppose the constraint requiring that at least $750,000 be spent promoting only taco sauce were lowered to $700,000. How much would the profit increase?

23. HEALTH FOODS. Health Valley Foods produces three types of health food bars in two-ounce sizes: the Go Bar, the Power Bar, and the Energy Bar. The Energy Bar also comes in an eight-ounce size. The three main ingredients in each bar are a protein concentrate, a sugar substitute, and carob. The recipes for each bar in terms of percentage of ingredients (by weight) and the daily availabilities of each of the ingredients are as follows.

Bar	% Protein Concentrate	% Sugar Substitute	% Carob
Go	20	60	20
Power	50	30	20
Energy	30	40	30
Daily availability	600 lbs.	1000 lbs.	800 lbs.

The following costs are incurred in the production of the health food bars:

Costs	
Labor and packaging (2-oz. bars)	$0.03/bar
Labor and packaging (8-oz. bars)	$0.05/bar
Protein concentrate	$3.20/lb.
Sugar substitute	$1.40/lb.
Carob	$2.60/lb.

Health Valley's wholesale selling prices to health food stores are $0.68, $0.84, and $0.76, respectively, for two-ounce sizes of the Go Bar, the Power Bar, and the Energy Bar, and $3.00 for the eight-ounce Energy Bar. The company has facilities for producing up to 25,000 two-ounce bars and 2000 eight-ounce bars daily. It manufactures at least 2500 of each of the two-ounce bars daily. No two-ounce bar is to account for more than 50% of the total production of two-ounce bars, and the total production (by weight) of Energy Bars is not to exceed more than 50% of the total production (by weight).

Determine an optimal daily production schedule of health food bars for Health Valley Foods.

24. BOAT BUILDERS/DISTRIBUTION. California Catamarans builds the Matey-20 catamaran boat in three locations: San Diego, Santa Ana, and San Jose. It ships the boats to its company-owned dealerships in Newport Beach (NB), Long Beach (LB), Ventura (VEN), San Luis Obispo (SLO), and San Francisco (SF). Production costs and capacities vary from plant to plant, as do shipping costs from the manufacturing plants to the dealerships. The following tables give costs, capacities, and demands for August.

COSTS

Plant	Production Cost	Shipping Cost to				
		NB	LB	VEN	SLO	SF
San Diego	$1,065	$200	$220	$280	$325	$500
Santa Ana	$1,005	$125	$125	$280	$350	$400
San Jose	$ 975	$390	$365	$300	$250	$100

PLANT CAPACITIES AND AUGUST DEMAND

Plant Capacity		August Demand	
San Diego	38	Newport Beach	42
Santa Ana	45	Long Beach	33
San Jose	58	Ventura	14
		San Luis Obispo	10
		San Francisco	22

Develop a production and shipping schedule for the Matey-20 catamaran for this period that minimizes the total production and shipping costs.

25. ACCOUNTING. Clyadetics is a firm that purchases raw propellant from Titan Industries and can produce three different solid fuel products. Named Fuel Alpha, Fuel Beta, and Fuel Gamma, these products are sold to NASA for use in a variety of programs. The following table details the tons of raw propellant, processing time, and quality control/ testing time required per ton of finished fuel product as well as the resource availability for the next period.

	Solid Fuel			
	Alpha	Beta	Gamma	Available
Raw propellant (tons/ton)	3	1	4	30
Processing time (hr./ton)	30	10	20	250
Quality control/testing time (hr./ton)	40	30	30	170

The following is the current balance sheet for Clyadetics.

Cash assets	$ 600,000	Bank loan	$ 800,000
Accounts receivable	$1,000,000	Long-term loan	$ 200,000
Inventory	$ 0	Equity	$1,000,000
Plant/equipment	$ 400,000		
	$2,000,000		$2,000,000

Financial data for the process are summarized as follows.

Raw Propellant Cost*	$10/pound	
	Direct Labor Cost per Ton	Selling Price** per Ton
Alpha fuel	$60,000	$200,000
Beta fuel	$40,000	$120,000
Gamma fuel	$50,000	$195,000
Period Expenses		
Cash expenses	$50,000	
Dividends paid	$20,000	
New plant purchases	$30,000	
Period Depreciation***	$30,000	

*Purchased from Titan Industries.

**Sold to NASA.

***Depreciation does not affect the cash position during the period.

Taxes will be paid from profits at the end of the period at the rate of 32% of profits. Assume that all accounts receivable ($1.6 million) will be available at the start of the next period for raw materials, direct labor, and period expenses. Using the financial data and balance sheets, determine the production strategy that Clyadetics should undertake for the next period. Analyze the sensitivity report.

CASE STUDIES

CASE 1: *Calgary Desk Company*

It is August and the Calgary Desk Company (CALDESCO) of Calgary, Alberta, is about to plan the production schedule for its entire line of desks for September. CALDESCO is a well-established manufacturer. Due to an internal policy of production quotas (which will be detailed later), it has been able to sell all desks manufactured in a particular month. This, in turn, has given the company reliable estimates of the unit profit contributed by each desk model and style.

The Desks

CALDESCO manufactures a student size desk (24 in. × 42 in.), a standard size desk (30 in. × 60 in.), and an executive size desk (42 in. × 72 in.) in each of the three lines: (1) economy, (2) basic pine, and (3) hand-crafted pine.

The economy line uses aluminum for the drawers and base and a simulated pine-laminated 1-inch particle board top. Although the basic pine desk use 1½-inch pine sheets instead of particle board, they are manufactured on the same production line as the tops of the economy line models. Because its drawers and base are made of wood, however, a different production line is required for this process.

Hand-crafted desks have solid pine tops that are constructed by craftsmen independent of any production line. This desk line uses the same drawers and base (and hence the same production line for this process) as the basic pine desk line. Hand-crafted desks are assembled and refinished by hand.

Production

Production Line 1 is used to manufacture the aluminum drawers and base for the economy models; production line 2 is used to manufacture the tops for the economy and basic models. There are two production lines 3, which are used to manufacture drawers and bases for the basic and hand-crafted lines. (Two lines are necessary to meet production targets.)

The production times available on the three production lines are summarized on the Excel spreadsheet below. The time requirements (in minutes) per desk for the three different types of production lines, the finishing and assembly times, and the time required to hand-craft certain models are also summarized on the spreadsheet.

Labor

CALDESCO currently employs a workforce of 30 craftsmen, but due to vacations, illnesses, etc., CALDESCO expects to have only an an average of 80% of its craftsmen available throughout the month. Each available craftsman works 160 hours per month. The expected total labor availability, which is also given on the spreadsheet is:

(.80) ∗ (30 craftsmen) ∗ (160 hours/craftsmen) ∗ (60 minutes/hour) = 230,400 worker-minutes.

Each craftsman in CALDESCO's shop is capable of doing all the tasks required to make any model desk; including running of the manufacturing lines, assembling the product, or performing the detailed operations necessary to produce the hand-crafted models.

Two craftsmen are required for each production line, but only a single craftsman is needed for hand crafting and for assembly and finishing. Thus the total amount of man-minutes required to produce a desk = 2 × (the total production line time) + (hand crafting time) + (assembly/finishing time).

Materials Requirements

As detailed earlier, the economy desks use aluminum and laminated particle board, whereas the basic and hand-crafted models use real pine. The amounts of aluminum, particle board, and 1½-inch thick pine sheets (in square feet) required to produce each style of desk are summarized on the spreadsheet along with the September availability of aluminum, particle board, and pine sheets.

Company Policy/Quotas

CALDESCO has been able to sell all the desks it produces and to maintain its profit margins in part by adhering to a set of in-house quotas. These maximum and minimum quotas for desk production are given on the spreadsheet.

CALDESCO will meet all outstanding orders for September. These are also summarized on the spreadsheet.

Profit Contribution

The unit profits, which have been determined for each style of desk, are also summarized on the spreadsheet.

The Report

Prepare a report recommending a production schedule to CALDESCO for September. In your report, analyze your results, detail the amount of each resource needed if your recommendation is implemented, and discuss any real-life factors that might be considered that have not been addressed in this problem summary nor listed on the spreadsheet. Include some appropriate "what-if" analyses. Your report should give a complete description/analysis of your final recommendation complete with tables, charts, graphs, etc. The complete model and the computer printouts are to be included in appendices.

(Note: The Excel file giving the spreadsheet is CALGDESK.XLS on the CD-ROM.)

	A	B	C	D	E	F	G	H	I	J	K	L
1	CALDESCO--SEPTEMBER											
2												
3	PROFIT, ORDERS, MATERIALS (SQ.FT.), PRODUCTION TIME (MIN) PER DESK											
4												
5	LINE	SIZE	PROFIT	SEPT. ORDERS	ALUMINUM	PARTICLE BOARD	PINE SHEETS	LINE 1 TIME	LINE 2 TIME	LINE 3 TIME	ASSEM./ FINISHING	HAND-CRAFTING
6	ECONOMY	STUDENT	20	750	14	8		1.5	1		10	
7		STANDARD	30	1500	24	15		2.0	1		11	
8		EXECUTIVE	40	100	30	24		2.5	1		12	
9	BASIC	STUDENT	50	400			22		1	3	15	
10		STANDARD	80	1500			40		1	4	18	
11		EXECUTIVE	125	100			55		1	5	20	
12	HAND-	STUDENT	100	25			25			3	20	50
13	CRAFTED	STANDARD	250	150			45			4	25	60
14		EXECUTIVE	325	50			60			5	30	70
15												
16												
17	RESOURCE AVAILABILITY FOR SEPTEMBER											
18												
19	LABOR(MAN-MINUTES)			230400								
20	ALUMINUM (SQ.FT.)			65000								
21	PARTICLE BOARD(SQ.FT.)			60000								
22	PINE SHEETS(SQ.FT.)			175000								
23	PRODUCTION LINE 1 (MIN.)			9600								
24	PRODUCTION LINE 2 (MIN.)			9600								
25	PRODUCTION LINE 3 (MIN.)			19200								
26												
27	PRODUCTION QUOTAS (OF TOTAL PRODUCTION)											
28												
29		MIN %	MAX %									
30	ECONOMY	20	50									
31	BASIC	40	60									
32	HAND-CR.	10	20									
33	STUDENT	20	35									
34	STANDARD	40	70									
35	EXECUTIVE	5	15									

Production Process

CASE 2: Todd & Taylor

Jerry Todd, a managing partner of the investment firm of Todd and Taylor, is designing a portfolio for Greg Edmonds. Greg has $500,000 cash to invest, and Jerry has identified 11 different investments, falling into four broad categories, that both Jerry and Greg feel would be potential candidates for the portfolio.

Table I lists the investments and their important characteristics. The expected annual after-tax returns account for all commissions and service charges. Note that Beekman Corporation stock and Beekman Corporation bonds are two separate investments, whereas Calton REIT is a single investment, a stock that is also a real estate investment.

Jerry's objective is to construct a portfolio for Greg that maximizes his total estimated after-tax return over the next year, subject to a number of concerns Greg has raised regarding his portfolio, including:

1. The average risk factor must be no greater than 55.

2. The average liquidity factor must be at least 85.

3. At least $10,000 is to be invested in the Beekman Corporation.

4. At least 20% but not more than 50% of the "nonmoney" portion of the portfolio should be from any one category of investment.

5. With the exception of the money category investments, no more than 20% of the portfolio ($100,000) should be in any one investment.

6. At least $25,000 should be invested in the money market fund.

7. A minimum investment of $125,000 should be in bonds.

8. At most 40% of the total portfolio in investments with

TABLE I   CHARACTERISTICS OF INVESTMENTS

Category	Investment	Estimated Annual After-Tax Return	Liquidity Factor	Risk Factor
Stocks	Beekman Corporation	8.5%	100	62
	Taco Grande	10.0%	100	71
	Calton REIT	10.5%	100	78
	Qube Electronics	12.0%	100	95
Bonds	LA Power	5.8%	95	19
	Beekman Corporation	6.3%	92	33
	Metropolitan Transit	7.2%	79	23
Real estate	Socal Apartment Partnership	9.0%	0	50
	Calton REIT		(See above)	
Money	T-Bill account	4.6%	80	0
	Money market fund	5.2%	100	10
	Certificate of deposit	7.8%	0	0

expected annual after-tax returns of less than 10% are to have risk factors exceeding 25.

9. At least one-half of the portfolio must be totally liquid (i.e., have a liquidity factor of 100).

Prepare a report to help Jerry develop a portfolio for Greg. Include in the report the following analyses:

- the expected after-tax return on the investment plan
- the amount by which each of Greg's restrictions was met, including the determination of the overall risk and liquidity factors
- the expected after-tax return for additional investment above $500,000
- the most sensitive after-tax return estimates that could affect the optimal solution
- the effect of a relaxation in the minimum dollar amount to be placed in the money market fund

CHAPTER 5

INTEGER LINEAR PROGRAMMING

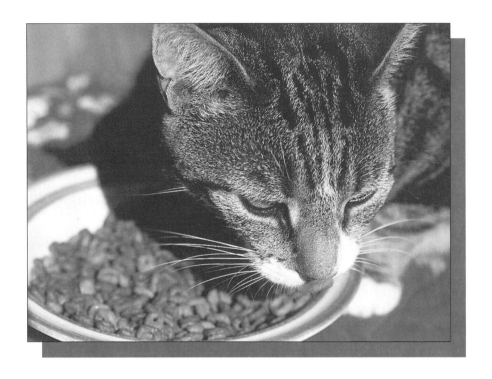

Glen Dorin is an entrepreneur who has successfully manufactured and marketed gourmet pet food to pet stores throughout California, Nevada, and Arizona. Glen has performed a market analysis for product demand outside this region and has found significant support for expanding operations nationwide as well as internationally. In fact, he has received commitments from several Japanese marketers to carry his products in Japan, providing they can be shipped in adequate supplies within the year. Negotiations with potential European distributors are ongoing, but Glen feels confident that deals similar to those reached with the Japanese will materialize.

Current production facilities in southern California do not have the capacity to produce the levels required to support Glen's expansion plans. Accordingly, Glen has been actively searching the country for additional manufacturing sites. The choice of sites is crucial to the success of his enterprise, since low labor and transportation costs are key to his profitability.

The mathematical model that Glen will use for controlling costs includes several *binary* (0 or 1) decision variables to indicate whether a particular plant location will be selected and whether a particular route is used to transport goods. Some of the *integer* decision variables in the model are the number of employees and the number of trucks required at each plant. Also incorporated are *continuous* decision variables, such as the percentage of different ingredients blended into the pet food, the number of pounds of raw materials shipped from various suppliers, and the amount of product shipped to various distributors from each plant.

Glen has been able to model his situation using linear constraints. Because some of the decision variables of the model are required to be integers, he will use an *integer linear programming* approach to determine an optimal overall expansion, manufacturing, and distribution strategy for his enterprise.

5.1 *I*NTRODUCTION TO INTEGER LINEAR PROGRAMMING (ILP)

The focus of Chapters 3 and 4 was on the formulation and analysis of linear programming problems that allow decision variables to take on a continuous range of values within the confines of the other constraints. For many models, however, some or all of the decision variables make sense only if they are restricted to integer values. These are known as **integer linear programming (ILP)** models. The number of aircraft United Airlines will purchase this year from McDonnell-Douglas; the number of machines needed for production at Galaxy Industries; the number of trips a company president will take to potential new markets in the Pacific Rim; the number of police personnel to be assigned to the night shift in Portland, Oregon—these are all examples of integer decision variables.

WHEN ARE INTEGER
VARIABLES REQUIRED?

It is easy to reason that decision variables expressed in pounds, inches, hours, acres, and the like, need not be restricted to integers. But even if a decision variable represents airplanes, televisions, or desks, depending on the context of the problem, it still may not be necessary to require that these variables take on integer values.

For example, an integer requirement would be essential for the number of MD-11 aircraft McDonnell-Douglas sells to United Airlines. However, the number of MD-11s McDonnell-Douglas produces in a year need not necessarily be an integer. If McDonnell-Douglas's optimal annual production of MD-11s were 24.37, the .37 of an aircraft would be considered work in progress to be completed at a later date. Thus, when determining whether or not a variable should be integer valued, we should ask, "Does the model represent a one-time decision or an ongoing operation?"

DIFFICULTIES WITH
MODELS REQUIRING
INTEGER VARIABLES

Why is it important to designate whether or not a variable is required to be integer valued? It might seem that restricting variables to integers would actually simplify the solution process, since a finite[1] number of integer points exist, compared to an infinite number for linear programming models.

But, alas, much is lost when integer requirements are imposed. Compared to linear programming solution methods, unless the problem has some special structure (such as the network problems we will discuss in the next two chapters), algorithms for solving models with integer-valued decision variables are more complex, require *much* more computation time, and do not yield valuable sensitivity analysis information. Thus, if an integer programming formulation is not essential, it is worthwhile to keep a linear programming structure.

Integer linear programming models (ILPs) can be classified as follows:

Model	Types of Decision Variables
All-integer (AILP)	All are integers.
Mixed-integer (MILP)	Some, but not all, are integers.
Binary (BILP)	All are either 0 or 1.

In this chapter, we examine the characteristics of each of these models and discuss complexities that can arise in the solution process, including the effects of rounding noninteger values of linear programming solutions. We also discuss the problem of obtaining meaningful sensitivity analyses to AILP and MILP problems. Although general solution approaches for integer models are briefly outlined in the chapter, we focus mainly on problem formulation and analysis of output from programs such as WINQSB

---

[1]If the feasible region is unbounded, at least the number of feasible solutions is countably infinite, as opposed to continuously infinite.

and Excel. Algorithms for solving AILPs and MILPs are included in Supplement CD4 on the accompanying CD-ROM.

5.2 COMPLEXITIES OF ILPS

We've noted that a number of complications arise when integer restrictions are placed on some or all the decision variables of a linear model. To illustrate, let us consider the problem faced by Boxcar Burger Restaurants.

BOXCAR BURGER RESTAURANTS

Boxcar.lpp
Boxcar.xls
Boxcar.ltx

Boxcar Burger is a new chain of fast-food establishments planning to expand to locations in and around the Washington, D.C., area. Although the food is of high quality and geared to today's health concerns, the main attraction is the boxcar motif. In downtown locations, the interiors of former office buildings are decorated to resemble the inside of a boxcar, while at suburban locations, fast-food sites are remodeled into Boxcar Burger restaurants by using actual boxcars.

The company has $2.7 million available for the expansion. Each suburban location requires a $200,000 investment, and each downtown location a $600,000 investment. It is projected that, after expenses, the net weekly profit generated by suburban locations open 24 hours per day will average $1200. The downtown locations will be open only 12 hours per day, but, because of the extremely high customer volume during the work week, projections indicate that net weekly profits will average $2000. The company wishes to open at least two restaurants downtown.

Boxcar Burger currently employs 19 managers to run the restaurants. Each suburban location will require three managers for its 24-hour per day operation, whereas the company feels it can get by with just one manager for each downtown location.

Boxcar Burger would like to determine how many restaurants it should open in suburban and downtown Washington, D.C., locations in order to maximize its total net weekly profit.

SOLUTION

The following is a brief synopsis of the problem facing Boxcar Burger:

- Boxcar Burger must decide how many suburban and downtown locations to open in the Washington, D.C., area.
- It wishes to maximize its total average net weekly profits.
- Boxcar Burger's total investment cannot exceed $2.7 million.
- At least two downtown restaurants are to be opened.
- No more than the current 19 managers can be assigned.

Decision Variables

Let,

$X1$ = number of suburban Boxcar Burger restaurants to be opened

$X2$ = number of downtown Boxcar Burger restaurants to be opened

Objective Function

The objective is to maximize total average net weekly profits:

$$MAX\ 1200X1 + 2000X2$$

Constraints

The following constraints apply:

1. The total investment cannot exceed $2.7 million. In $100,000s this can be written as

$$2X1 + 6X2 \leq 27$$

2. The number of downtown restaurants is at least 2:

$$X2 \geq 2$$

3. The number of managers needed cannot exceed 19:

$$3X1 + X2 \leq 19$$

The Mathematical Model

Clearly, the number of restaurants opened must be an integer. Thus, the complete mathematical programming formulation for the Boxcar Burger problem is:

$$
\begin{array}{ll}
\text{MAX} & 1200X1 + 2000X2 \\
\text{ST} & \\
& 2X1 + 6X2 \leq 27 \\
& X2 \geq 2 \\
& 3X1 + X2 \leq 19 \\
& X1, X2 \geq 0 \text{ and integer}
\end{array}
$$

Since both decision variables are required to be integers, this model is an example of an all-integer linear program (AILP). To solve the AILP, we could begin by solving the *relaxed problem*, the linear model that ignores the integer constraints. If the optimal solution to the relaxed problem turns out to consist of integer values for X1 and X2, then the optimal solution to the AILP has been found without expressly imposing the integer restrictions.

Figure 5.1 shows the linear programming solution to this problem. Unfortunately, the optimal solution to the relaxed problem is $X1 = 5\frac{7}{16}$, $X2 = 2\frac{11}{16}$. Because the values of the variables are not integers, additional steps must be taken.

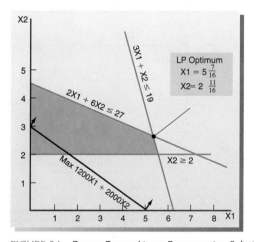

FIGURE 5.1   Boxcar Burger Linear Programming Solution

WHY NOT SIMPLY
ROUND THE VALUES?

We can round the fractional part of any mixed number in several ways: rounding up, rounding off, or rounding down. In this problem, if both fractions are *rounded up*, the solution obtained is X1 = 6, X2 = 3. From Figure 5.2, we observe that this point is not in the feasible region; that is, it violates at least one of the functional constraints. If both fractions are *rounded off* to the nearest whole number, the integer solution generated is X1 = 5, X2 = 3. Again, this is an infeasible point. Finally, if both fractions are *rounded down*, the solution generated is X1 = 5, X2 = 2, *is* a feasible point. But is this the optimal integer solution?

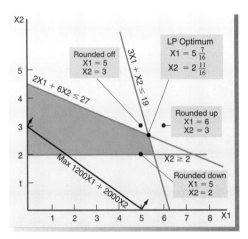

FIGURE 5.2   Boxcar Burger Rounded Solutions

FIGURE 5.3   Boxcar Burger Feasible Integer Points

To answer this question, let us determine the set of all feasible points for the AILP. A feasible point must be both (1) in the feasible region of the LP (i.e., it must satisfy the functional and nonnegativity constraints) and (2) integer valued. As Figure 5.3 shows, there are 13 feasible integer points for this problem.

Table 5.1 lists all 13 feasible integer points and gives the value of the objective function (1200X1 + 2000X2) for each.

TABLE 5.1   FEASIBLE INTEGER POINTS AND OBJECTIVE FUNCTION VALUES FOR BOXCAR BURGER

Feasible Point	X1	X2	Objective Function Value
1	0	2	$ 4,000
2	1	2	$ 5,200
3	2	2	$ 6,400
4	3	2	$ 7,600
5	4	2	$ 8,800
6	5	2	$10,000
7	0	3	$ 6,000
8	1	3	$ 7,200
9	2	3	$ 8,400
10	3	3	$ 9,600
11	4	3	$10,800 ⟵— AILP optimum
12	0	4	$ 8,000
13	1	4	$ 9,200

The "rounded down" solution, X1 = 5, X2 = 2, gives a very good value for the objective function of $10,000, but it does not give the *best* value of $10,800. Notice that the *optimal* AILP solution, X1 = 4, X2 = 3, is not obtained from any form of rounding.

It can be shown, however, that if the objective function is MAXIMIZE 2500X1 + 2000X2, while the optimal linear programming solution is still X1 = $5\frac{7}{16}$, X2 = $2\frac{11}{16}$, the rounded down solution, X1 = 5, X2 = 2, *would be* the optimal AILP solution. Accordingly, the following outcomes are possible from rounding the optimal linear programming solution:

Possible Outcomes from Rounding to Integer Values

1. The rounded point may be infeasible.
2. The rounded point may be feasible but not optimal.
3. The rounded point may be the optimal point.

Imposing integer restrictions adds two more constraints to this problem: (1) X1 is an integer, and (2) X2 is an integer. As we pointed out in Chapter 3, whenever constraints are added to a problem, *the value of the objective function cannot improve*. In a maximization problem, this means that the value of the objective function will decline (or stay the same) from its optimum LP value. For example, the optimal AILP solution for the Boxcar Burger model gives us an objective function value of $10,800, compared to the optimal LP objective function value of $1200(5\frac{7}{16}) + 2000 (2\frac{11}{16}) = $11,900$.

Two questions arise from this analysis.

1. ***For any integer problem, why not simply enumerate all feasible integer points and select the one with the best value for the objective function (as we did above)?***

The answer is that for most real-life problems, even if the feasible region is bounded, the number of feasible integer points can be in the thousands, millions, or even billions, and identifying all feasible integer points is itself quite a task. Hence, this approach is simply impractical, even using the highest speed computers and the best computer codes.

2. ***Is rounding ever done?***

The answer to this question is an emphatic, "*yes*," particularly if the values of the positive decision variables are relatively large and the values of the objective function coefficients are relatively small. For example, suppose a producer of multiple vitamins used linear programming to determine the production quantities of 50-tablet, 100-tablet, and 500-tablet bottles to be produced during a production run. If the unit profits for these items are $1.20, $1.75, and $4.80, respectively, and the linear program indicates that 12,253.43, 34,876.90, and 22,623.47 bottles, respectively, should be produced, then rounding these quantities will have little effect on either the value of the objective function or the viability of the constraints.

Of course, the feasibility of any rounded solution should be checked. If the rounded solution does, in fact, violate some constraints, we need to determine whether the violations are significant. For instance, in the vitamin example, suppose one constraint is a marketing restriction requiring that no product is to account for more than 50% of production. If the above solution were rounded to 12,253 50-tablet bottles, 34,877 100-tablet bottles, and 22,623 500-tablet bottles, the proportion of 100-tablet bottles would now be 50.001%—is this so terrible?

On the other hand, if rounding yields a solution that is simply not possible (there is just not enough of a particular resource to achieve this solution), the rounded solution would have to be altered. In this case, a trial and error approach might be used.

Although neither rounding nor rounding and using trial and error is guaranteed to produce the true optimal integer solution, they are usually "pretty good" solutions (as was the case in the Boxcar Burger example). It is important to check the difference between the objective function values of the optimal LP solution and the result of rounding using trial and error. If the difference is not very great, it may not be worthwhile to use an integer programming optimization procedure that could tie up computer resources for long periods with no guarantee that the optimal result would be better or even different.

5.3 $\mathcal{S}$ENSITIVITY IN ILP

In Chapter 3, we examined the value of linear programming sensitivity analyses. One of the biggest drawbacks of using ILP models is the lack of such analyses.

For example, consider the Boxcar Burger example discussed in Section 5.2. Suppose we wished to find the range of values for the profit of suburban restaurants (currently, C1 = 1200), which keeps the optimal AILP solution the same (X1 = 4, X2 = 3). If we connect the feasible AILP points that are "farthest out" in all possible directions,[2] we can then attempt to apply the techniques discussed in Chapter 3 to find ranges of optimality for the objective function coefficients.

As illustrated in Figure 5.4, the point (4,3) will remain the optimal point as long as the objective function coefficients yield a slope between $-\frac{1}{3}$ (the slope of the line between (1,4) and (4,3)) and -1 (the slope of the line between (4,3) and (5,2)). We can then verify the following ranges of optimality for C1 and C2:

$$6\tfrac{2}{3} \leq C1 \leq 20$$

$$12 \leq C2 \leq 36$$

The difficulty with this analysis is that we would have to know the "farthest-out" integer points, which itself is a computationally complex problem. Furthermore, the slope of the lines connecting these points usually has no relationship to the slopes of the lines formed by the functional constraints. In this model, for example, the slope of one of the lines restraining the objective function is -1. No functional constraint has this slope. The other restraining line has a slope of $-\frac{1}{3}$, which is only coincidentally the slope of the first functional constraint line.

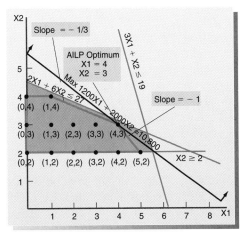

FIGURE 5.4   Boxcar Burger Connecting the "Furthest Out" Points

Integer linear programming offers no parallel to shadow price analysis. In *linear programming*, a shadow price of $10 for a resource implies that the marginal improvement for *each* extra unit of the resource is $10, as long as the change occurs within the resource's range of feasibility. Two extra units of the resource would improve the objective function $20, and half an extra unit would improve it by $5. This is not the case for integer models, however. For example, in the Boxcar Burger model, consider the constraint for investment:

$$2X1 + 6X2 \leq 27 \ (\$100,000s)$$

---

[2]This is called forming the "convex hull" of the feasible region. If the feasible region is unbounded, it cannot be done.

As you can see in Figure 5.5a, the current solution (4,3) remains optimal as the right-hand side *decreases*, until the amount available for investment (the right-hand side of this constraint) reaches 26 ($100,000). But if the investment slips even one penny below 26 ($100,000), the point (4,3) is no longer even feasible and the integer point (5,2) becomes the new optimal solution, with an optimal weekly profit of $1200(5) + $2000(2) = $10,000. Thus, decreasing the amount of investment will have no effect on the optimal weekly profit unless the amount of the decrease exceeds 1 ($100,000). If the decrease exceeds 1 ($100,000) even slightly, a decrease in total weekly profit of $10,800 − $10,000 = $800 occurs.

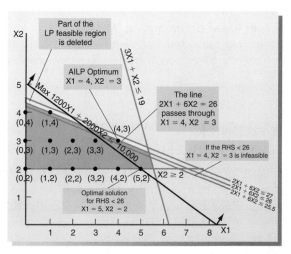

FIGURE 5.5a   Boxcar Burger Investment Constraint Changed to: 2X1 + 6X2 ≤ 26 and 2X1 + 6X2 ≤ 25.5

Similarly, Figure 5.5b shows that *increasing* the amount of investment will have no effect on the optimal solution until the amount equals 28 ($100,000), an increase of 1 ($100,000). If $99,999.99 extra is invested, the optimal solution is still (4,3). Then, with the next penny, the right-hand side is increased to 28 ($100,000), and two new integer points (2,4) and (5,3) are now feasible. The optimal AILP solution is now (5,3), giving an optimal weekly profit of $1200(5) + $2000(3) = $12,000. This is a $12,000 − $10,800 = $1200 increase in weekly profits. Thus, for the first $99,999.99, no additional profit is made; then, with the next penny, there is an increase of $1200!

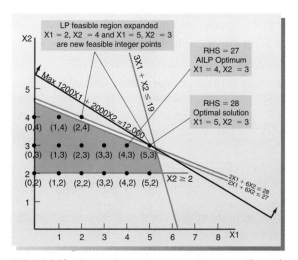

FIGURE 5.5b   Boxcar Burger Investment Constraint Changed to: 2X1 + 6X2 ≤ 28

This example points out that there is no pattern to the disjoint effects of changes to the objective function and right-hand side coefficients. When changes occur, they occur in big "steps," rather than the smooth, marginal changes experienced in linear programming. Thus, unfortunately, when we contemplate changes in either objective function coefficients or right-hand side values, re-solving the problem is usually the only viable means for determining the resulting effect.

5.4 $\mathcal{M}$IXED INTEGER LINEAR PROGRAMMING (MILP)

A **mixed integer linear programming (MILP)** model is one in which some, but not all, of the variables are restricted to integers. To illustrate the case of an MILP with a minimization objective function, consider the situation faced by a novice investor, Shelley Mednick.

Shelley.lpp
Shelley.xls

SHELLEY MEDNICK INVESTMENT PROBLEM

After many years of earning extremely low bank interest rates, Shelley Mednick has decided to give the stock market a try. This is her first time investing, and she wants to be extra cautious. She has heard that a new stock offering from TCS, a telecommunication company, is being sold at $55 per share (including commissions) and is projected to sell at $68 per share in a year. She is also considering a mutual fund, MFI, which one financial newsletter predicts will yield a 9% return over the next year.

For this first venture into the market, Shelley has set extremely modest goals. She wants to invest just enough so that the expected return on her investment will be $250. Furthermore, since she has more confidence in the performance of the mutual fund than the stock, she has set the restriction that the maximum amount invested in TCS is not to exceed 40% of her total investment, or $750, whichever is smaller.

She would like to know what combination of shares of TCS and investment in MFI is necessary to meet her goal of a projected $250 gain for the year.

SOLUTION

The problem facing Shelley Mednick can be summarized as follows:

- Determine the number of shares of TCS and the amount of money to invest in MFI
- Minimize the total dollar investment
- Earn a projected yearly return of at least $250
- Invest no more than 40% of her total investment and no more than $750 in TCS stock

Decision Variables

Let

$X1$ = number of shares of TCS Shelley should purchase
$X2$ = amount of money Shelley should invest in MFI

Since a fractional number of shares of stock cannot be purchased, $X1$ must be integer valued. At the same time, the amount invested in MFI need not be restricted to an integer amount; hence, $X2$ is a continuous variable.

Objective Function

Shelley's objective is to minimize her total dollar investment. Since X1 is expressed in shares of TCS, it must be converted to a dollar amount invested by multiplying the number of shares purchased by the $55 share price. Thus, the objective function is:

$$\text{MINIMIZE } 55X1 + X2$$

Constraints

The following constraints apply to Shelley's situation.

1. ***The projected yearly return must be at least $250.***   Since each share of TCS is expected to increase by $68 − $55 = $13 and each dollar invested in MFI is expected to earn 9%, this constraint becomes:

$$13X1 + .09X2 \geq 250$$

2. ***The amount invested in TCS must be no more than 40% of the total investment.***   The amount to be invested in TCS is 55X1. The total amount invested is (55X1 + X2). Thus, 55X1 ≤ .40(55X1 + X2), or 55X1 ≤ 22X1 + .40X2. Rearranging the terms gives us:

$$33X1 - .40X2 \leq \quad 0$$

3. ***The amount invested in TCS must be no more than $750:***

$$55X1 \qquad \leq 750$$

The Mathematical Model

The complete model can be written as

$$
\begin{aligned}
\text{MINIMIZE} \quad & 55X1 + \quad X2 \\
\text{ST} \quad & \\
& 13X1 + .09X2 \geq 250 \\
& 33X1 - .40X2 \leq \quad 0 \\
& 55X1 \qquad\quad \leq 750 \\
& X1, X2 \geq 0 \\
& X1 \text{ integer}
\end{aligned}
$$

This model is an MILP since X1 is required to be an integer while X2 is not.

Again, our first attempt to solve this problem is to ignore the integer restriction and solve it as a linear program. As Figure 5.6 illustrates, the optimal solution to the linear program is X1 = 12.24, X2 = 1009.79, yielding a total investment of 55(12.24) + 1009.79 = $1682.99. Since this result does not provide an integer value for X1, we need to take a different approach.

Because only one of the variables is required to be an integer, the set of feasible points for the MILP is not a set of disjoint points but, rather, the series of parallel line segments corresponding to the integer values for X1 within the feasible region for the relaxed model shown in Figure 5.7.

As we can see from this graph, the optimal MILP solution in which X1 is an integer is X1 = 12, X2 = 1044.44. Thus, Shelley should purchase 12 shares of TCS and invest $1044.44 in MFI, for a total investment of 55(12) + 1044.44 = $1704.44. Note that when the additional integer constraint is added, the objective function value is worse (higher) than the optimal linear programming solution by $1704.44 − $1682.99 = $21.45.

FIGURE 5.6   Shelley Mednick Investment Linear Programming Solution

FIGURE 5.7   Shelley Mednick Investment Mixed Integer Linear Programming Solution

5.5   SOLVING INTEGER PROGRAMMING MODELS

Numerous approaches other than rounding and total enumeration have been proposed to solve ILPs. Among the algorithms incorporated in computer software for solving general MILPs are cutting plane and branch and bound approaches.

In a **cutting plane** approach, the integer restrictions are initially ignored and the problem is solved as a linear program. Then, if the optimal solution fails to provide integer values for those variables restricted to be integers, a new constraint is added that will make this solution infeasible but will not eliminate any feasible point that provides integer values for these variables. The problem is then re-solved with the added constraint, and the process is continued until an optimal solution (if there is one) satisfying the integer constraints is attained.

Figure 5.8 illustrates the first iteration of a cutting plane approach for the Boxcar Burger problem. As you can see, the new constraint makes the linear programming solution ($X1 = 5\frac{7}{16}$, $X2 = 2\frac{11}{16}$) infeasible, but none of the feasible integer points has been eliminated from the feasible region.

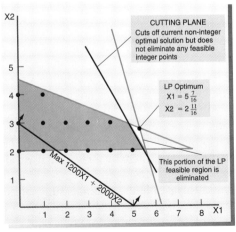

FIGURE 5.8   Example of a Cutting Plane

WINQSB, Excel, and LINDO, as well as many other software programs, use what is called a **branch and bound** approach for finding the optimal solution. As in the cutting plane approach, the problem is solved as a linear program first, ignoring the integer restrictions. If some of the variables restricted to be integers have noninteger values in the optimal solution, then one of these variables is selected and two new constraints are formed: one imposes an *upper bound* on the selected variable by restricting its value to be *at most* the integer part of its current value; the other imposes a *lower bound* on the selected variable by restricting its value to be *at least* the integer part of its current value plus one. Clearly, neither of these constraints is satisfied by the current optimal solution. Two new linear programs (called *branches*) are then created and solved: one adds the upper bound constraint to the current constraint set; the other adds the lower bound constraint to the current constraint set. This process is systematically repeated until an optimal integer solution is found (if there is one).[3]

To illustrate, consider the Boxcar Burger problem in which both X1 and X2 are required to be integers. If in the current LP optimal solution (X1 $= 5\frac{7}{16}$, X2 $= 2\frac{11}{16}$), we arbitrarily select X1 to branch on, the branch and bound approach then constructs two new linear programs. In one, the constraint X1 $\leq$ 5 is added to the current set of constraints (Figure 5.9a), and in the other, the constraint X1 $\geq$ 6 is added (Figure 5.9b). In neither case is the current optimal point (X1 $= 5\frac{7}{16}$, X2 $= 2\frac{11}{16}$) feasible. In fact, there are no feasible solutions in the second case. In the first case, the optimal solution occurs at the point X1 $= 5$, X2 $= 2\frac{5}{6}$. Since X2 still is not an integer, the process is repeated by branching to two new programs (one adds X2 $\leq$ 2; the other adds X2 $\geq$ 3). This approach continues until an optimal integer solution is attained.

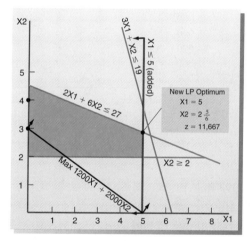

FIGURE 5.9a   Boxcar Burger X1 $\leq$ 5 added

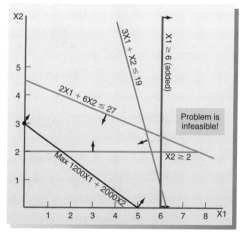

FIGURE 5.9b   Boxcar Burger X1 $\geq$ 6 added

When solving problems using computer software, the internally programmed solution procedure is transparent to the user, who must only make sure that the integer restrictions have been correctly entered. As shown in Appendix 5.1, this input procedure is very easy in WINQSB, Excel, and LINDO. However, because of the arguments given in Section 5.4, the output will not include any meaningful sensitivity analyses.

---

[3]The exact steps of the branch and bound approach are illustrated in Supplement CD4 on the accompanying CD-ROM.

5.6 $\mathcal{A}$ PERSONNEL SCHEDULING PROBLEM—AN EXAMPLE OF A COMPUTER SOLUTION

One problem that requires an integer solution is the assignment of personnel or machines to meet some minimum coverage requirements. The situation faced by the City of Sunset Beach is a classic example of one such problem.

SUNSET BEACH LIFEGUARD ASSIGNMENTS

Sunset.lpp
Sunset.xls

In the summer, the City of Sunset Beach staffs lifeguard stations seven days a week. Regulations require that city employees (including lifeguards) work five days a week and be given two consecutive days off. For most city employees, these days are Saturday and Sunday, but for lifeguards, these are the two busiest days of the week.

Insurance requirements mandate that Sunset Beach provide at least one lifeguard per 8000 average daily attendance on any given day. Table 5.2 gives the average daily attendance figures and the minimum number of lifeguards required during the summer months, at Sunset Beach.

TABLE 5.2   AVERAGE DAILY ATTENDANCE
AND LIFEGUARD REQUIREMENTS

Day	Average Attendance	Lifeguards Required
Sunday	58,000	8
Monday	42,000	6
Tuesday	35,000	5
Wednesday	25,000	4
Thursday	44,000	6
Friday	51,000	7
Saturday	68,000	9

Given the current budget situation, Sunset Beach would like to determine a schedule that will employ as few lifeguards as possible.

SOLUTION

Sunset Beach's problem is to:

- Schedule lifeguards over five consecutive days
- Minimize the total number of lifeguards required
- Meet the minimum daily lifeguard requirements

Decision Variables

Sunset Beach must decide how many lifeguards to schedule beginning Sunday and working for five consecutive days, the number to schedule beginning Monday and working for five consecutive days, and so on:

$X1$ = number of lifeguards scheduled to begin on Sunday
$X2$ = number of lifeguards scheduled to begin on Monday
$X3$ = number of lifeguards scheduled to begin on Tuesday
$X4$ = number of lifeguards scheduled to begin on Wednesday
$X5$ = number of lifeguards scheduled to begin on Thursday
$X6$ = number of lifeguards scheduled to begin on Friday
$X7$ = number of lifeguards scheduled to begin on Saturday

Objective Function

The goal is to minimize the total number of lifeguards scheduled:

$$\text{MIN } X1 + X2 + X3 + X4 + X5 + X6 + X7$$

Constraints

For each day, at least the minimum required number of lifeguards must be on duty. Those on duty on Sunday begin their shift either on Sunday, Wednesday, Thursday, Friday, or Saturday; those on duty on Monday begin their shift either on Monday, Thursday, Friday, Saturday, or Sunday; and so on. Thus,

$$(\text{The number of lifeguards on duty Sunday}) \geq 8$$

or

$$X1 \qquad + X4 + X5 + X6 + X7 \geq 8$$

For Monday the constraint would be:

$$X1 + X2 \qquad + X5 + X6 + X7 \geq 6$$

The Mathematical Model

The constraints for the other days are similarly derived, yielding the following model:

$$
\begin{aligned}
\text{MIN } \quad & X1 + X2 + X3 + X4 + X5 + X6 + X7 \\
\text{ST} \quad & \\
& X1 \qquad\qquad\quad + X4 + X5 + X6 + X7 \geq 8 \text{ (Sunday)} \\
& X1 + X2 \qquad\qquad + X5 + X6 + X7 \geq 6 \text{ (Monday)} \\
& X1 + X2 + X3 \qquad\qquad + X6 + X7 \geq 5 \text{ (Tuesday)} \\
& X1 + X2 + X3 + X4 \qquad\qquad + X7 \geq 4 \text{ (Wednesday)} \\
& X1 + X2 + X3 + X4 + X5 \qquad\qquad \geq 6 \text{ (Thursday)} \\
& \qquad X2 + X3 + X4 + X5 + X6 \qquad \geq 7 \text{ (Friday)} \\
& \qquad\qquad X3 + X4 + X5 + X6 + X7 \geq 9 \text{ (Saturday)} \\
& \qquad\qquad \text{All variables} \geq 0 \text{ AND Integer}
\end{aligned}
$$

If the integer restrictions are ignored, the optimal solution is to hire $9\frac{1}{3}$ lifeguards. Unless part-time lifeguards are employed, this is a meaningless solution.

We solved the integer problem using Excel, as shown in Figure 5.10.

	LIFEGUARDS		
DAY	PRESENT	REQUIRED	BEGIN SHIFT
SUNDAY	9	8	1
MONDAY	8	6	0
TUESDAY	6	5	1
WEDNESDAY	5	4	1
THURSDAY	6	6	3
FRIDAY	7	7	2
SATURDAY	9	9	2
TOTAL LIFEGUARDS		10	

FIGURE 5.10   Excel Output—Sunset Beach Lifeguard Assignments

As you can see in the cell labeled "TOTAL LIFEGUARDS," a minimum of 10 lifeguards are needed. From the column labeled "BEGIN SHIFT," we see that one lifeguard starts his or her shift on Sunday, one on Tuesday, one on Wednesday, three on Thursday, two on Friday, and two on Saturday. Nine lifeguards will be on duty on Sunday, and eight will be on duty on Monday, surpassing the minimum requirements on these two days by one and two, respectively. Six lifeguards will be on duty Tuesday and five on Wednesday, one more than the minimum requirements. For the remainder of the week, only the minimum number of required lifeguards will be on duty on any given day.

5.7 $\mathscr{B}$INARY INTEGER LINEAR PROGRAMMING (BILP)

One special case of ILP occurs when all the variables of the model can take on only one of two values: 0 or 1. Such variables are called *binary variables*, and the models are called 0–1 programs or **binary integer linear programs (BILPs)**. Any situation that can be modeled by "yes/no," "good/bad," "right/wrong," or "0/1" can be thought of as a binary variable.

The following are some of the many examples of binary variables that may be found in business modeling:

$X = 1$ if a new health care plan is adopted
$= 0$ if it is not
$X = 1$ if assembly line B is used to produce deluxe models
$= 0$ if it is not
$X = 1$ if a new police station is built downtown
$= 0$ if it is not
$X = 1$ if the items on a production run are accepted as "good"
$= 0$ if they are not
$X = 1$ if Highway 50 is used when traveling between two cities
$= 0$ if it is not
$X = 1$ if a particular constraint must hold
$= 0$ if it is not necessary
$X = 1$ if a new plant is to be located in Gary, Indiana
$= 0$ if it is not
$X = 1$ if a third shift is to be used
$= 0$ if it is not

As these examples illustrate, it is convenient to think of a binary variable as a project: $X = 1$ means that the project is undertaken; $X = 0$ means that it is not. Given this interpretation of a binary decision variable, we now examine several types of constraints that arise frequently in BILPs by considering the situation faced by the City Council in Salem, Oregon.

SALEM CITY COUNCIL

Salem.lpp
Salem.xls

At its final meeting of the fiscal year, the Salem City Council will be making plans to allocate funds remaining in this year's budget. Nine projects have been under consideration throughout the entire year.

To gauge community support for the various projects, questionnaires were randomly mailed to voters throughout the city asking them to rank the projects (9 = highest priority, 1 = lowest priority). The council tallied the scores from the 500 usable responses it received. Although the council has repeatedly maintained that it will not be bound by the results of the questionnaire, it plans to use this information while taking into account other concerns when making the budget allocations.

The estimated cost of each project, the estimated number of permanent new jobs each would create, and the questionnaire point tallies are summarized in Table 5.3.

TABLE 5.3   PROJECT COSTS, NEW JOBS, AND POINT TALLIES

	Project	Cost ($1000)	New Jobs	Points
X1	Hire seven new police officers	$400	7	4176
X2	Modernize police headquarters	$350	0	1774
X3	Buy two new police cars	$ 50	1	2513
X4	Give bonuses to foot patrol officers	$100	0	1928
X5	Buy new fire truck/support equipment	$500	2	3607
X6	Hire assistant fire chief	$ 90	1	962
X7	Restore cuts to sports programs	$220	8	2829
X8	Restore cuts to school music	$150	3	1708
X9	Buy new computers for high school	$140	2	3003

The council's goal is to maximize the total perceived voter support (as evidenced through the questionnaires), given other constraints and concerns of the council, including the following:

- $900,000 remains in the budget.
- The council wants to create at least 10 new jobs.
- Although crime deterrence is a high priority with the public, the council feels that it must also be fair to other sectors of public service (fire and education). Accordingly, it wishes to fund at most three of the police-related projects.
- The council would like to increase the number of city emergency vehicles but feels that, in the face of other pressing issues, only one of the two emergency vehicle projects should be funded at this time. Thus, *either* the two police cars *or* the fire truck should be purchased.
- The council believes that if it decides to restore funds cut from the sports programs at the schools, it should also restore funds cut from their music programs, and vice versa.
- By union contract, any additional school funding must go toward restoring previous cuts before any new school projects are undertaken. Consequently, both sports funds and music funds must be restored before new computer equipment can be purchased. Restoring sports and music funds, however, does not imply that new computers *will* be purchased, only that they *can* be.

The council would also like to convey to the public that it is fiscally responsible, concerned about safety, interested in job growth, and sensitive to Salem's educational needs.

To show fiscal responsibility:

- The council would like to carry over at least $250,000 to next year's budget. Consequently, year-end spending can be at most $900,000 − $250,000 = $650,000.

To show concern for public safety:

- The council would like to fund at least three of the police and fire projects
- They wish to add the seven new police officers.

To show interest in job growth:

- The council would like to create at least 15, not just 10, new full-time jobs.

To demonstrate sensitivity to educational issues:

- The council would like to fund all three educational projects.

The council members realize that there are not enough funds to meet all five of these objectives, but they feel that the voters will look favorably upon them if at least three of the five are met.

SOLUTION

The Salem City Council must choose which projects to fund. Its objective is to determine, within the constraints and concerns listed earlier, the set of projects that maximizes public support for its decisions as evidenced through the returned questionnaires.

Decision Variables
The variables, $X1, X2, \ldots X9$, are a set of binary decision variables: $Xj = 1$ if project j is funded, and $Xj = 0$ if project j is not funded.

Objective Function
The council's objective is to maximize the overall point score of the funded projects:

MAXIMIZE $4176X1 + 1774X2 + 2513X3 + 1928X4 + 3607X5 + 962X6 + 2829X7 + 1708X8 + 3003X9$

Constraints
Earlier, we listed the various concerns and constraints on the Salem City Council. Here we categorize them according to typical types of BILP constraint.

1. **Resource Allocation Constraints**
   Examples of resource allocation constraints include such considerations as capital budgeting (e.g., a maximum budget limit on project funding) or accomplishment of objectives (e.g., a minimum number of new jobs created).

1A. **Capital Budgeting Constraints**
   The maximum amount of funds to be allocated cannot exceed $900,000. If the coefficients represent the number of thousands of dollars, this constraint is:

$400X1 + 350X2 + 50X3 + 100X4 + 500X5 + 90X6 + 220X7 + 150X8 + 140X9 \leq 900$

1B. **Goal Accomplishment Constraints**
   The number of new jobs created must be at least 10:

$$7X1 + X3 + 2X5 + X6 + 8X7 + 3X8 + 2X9 \geq 10$$

2. **K out of N / Mutually Exclusive Constraints**
   Sometimes limits are placed on the number of projects to be performed (K) within a certain subset (N) of the projects. A set of N projects is said to be a mutually exclusive set if exactly (or at most) $K = 1$ of the N projects is to be performed.

2A. **Maximum of K Out of N Projects Constraints**
   The number of police-related activities to be funded is at most 3:

$$X1 + X2 + X3 + X4 \leq 3$$

2B. **Mutually Exclusive Projects Constraints**
   Either the two police cars should be purchased or the fire truck should be purchased. This is equivalent to saying that the number of police car purchase projects plus the number of fire truck purchase projects to be funded is exactly 1:

$$X3 + X5 = 1$$

3.   *Corequisite* or *Prerequisite* Projects *Constraints*

At times the choice of projects may be influenced by a required sequencing. In particular, sometimes projects require that certain other projects also be done. These are known as corequisite projects. Other times, one or more projects must be done before it is possible to do another. The first set is said to be prerequisite for the latter project. Note that if a prerequisite project is done, this does not imply that the latter project will be done, only that it can be done.

3A.   *Corequisite Projects Constraints*

If sports funds are restored music funds will be restored, and if sports funds are not restored music funds will not be restored. This constraint implies that the number of restored music fund projects funded must equal the number of sports fund projects funded; that is, $X7 = X8$, or:

$$X7 - X8 = 0$$

3B.   *Prerequisite Projects Constraints*

Sports funding and music funding must be restored before new computer equipment can be purchased. This relationship can be expressed as two prerequisite constraints: the number of sports funding projects funded must be at least as great as the number of computer equipment purchase projects funded ($X7 \geq X9$) AND the number of music funding projects funded must be at least as great as the number of computer equipment purchase projects funded ($X8 \geq X9$), or:

$$X7 - X9 \geq 0$$

and

$$X8 - X9 \geq 0$$

Note that, taken together, these constraints mean that if $X9 = 1$, then both $X7$ and $X8$ must be 1, but if either or both $X7$ and $X8 = 1$, $X9$ is not required to be 1.

4.   K *Out of* N CONSTRAINTS *Must Hold*

Sometimes when the functional constraints are formulated for a mathematical program (linear, integer, binary, nonlinear), only some (K) of a certain subset of (N) constraints must hold. (If $K = 1$, the constraints are sometimes referred to as EITHER/OR constraints.) We illustrate the situation facing the Salem City Council using only constraints that have binary variables, but the concept extends to any mathematical programming model.

The council would like to satisfy at least three of the following five constraints:

1.   Have at least a $250,000 reserve, or the total amount spent on projects this year cannot exceed $900,000 - $250,000 = $650,000$:

$$400X1 + 350X2 + 50X3 + 100X4 + 500X5 + 90X6 + 220X7 + 150X8 + 140X9 \leq 650$$

2.   At least three police and fire projects should be funded:

$$X1 + X2 + X3 + X4 + X5 + X6 \geq 3$$

3.   The project that involves adding the seven new police officers should be funded:

$$X1 = 1$$

4.   At least 15 new jobs should be created (not just 10):

$$7X1 + X3 + 2X5 + X6 + 8X7 + 3X8 + 2X9 \geq 15$$

5. Three education projects should be funded:

$$X7 + X8 + X9 = 3$$

The condition that at least three of the five objectives are to be met can be expressed by introducing binary variables Y1, Y2, Y3, Y4, and Y5. Here,

Yi = 1 if constraint i is ignored (the objective is NOT met)

= 0 if constraint i is not ignored (the objective IS met)

A two-step approach can then be used to modify the above functional constraints to meet the objective.

Step 1:   Multiply each Yi by a large value, denoted as M, and do the following:

1.   If the corresponding constraint is a "≤" constraint, add the term M*Yi to the right-hand side of the constraint. (Then if Yi = 1, the right-side of the constraint itself is very large; hence, the original condition need not hold.)

2.   If the corresponding constraint is a "≥" constraint, subtract the term M*Yi from the right-hand side of the constraint. (Here if Yi = 1, the right-side of the constraint itself is a very large negative number; thus, again, the original condition need not hold.)

3.   If the corresponding constraint is an "=" constraint, first convert the constraint into two constraints, one a "≤" constraint, the other a "≥" constraint.[4] Then apply conditions (1) and (2) using the *same* binary variable Yi in each of the new created inequalities.

Step 2:   Add the constraint: ΣYi ≤ N − K to the set of functional constraints.

Since at least K out of the N constraints must be satisfied, the total number of these constraints that will *not* be satisfied (ΣYi) is restricted to be at most N − K.

This two-step technique is applied to the Salem City Council situation as follows.

Step 1:   Modify the five conditional constraints as follows:

$$400X1 + 350X2 + 50X3 + 100X4 + 500X5 + 90X6 + 220X7 + 150X8 + 140X9 \le 650 + M*Y1$$

$$X1 + X2 + X3 + X4 + X5 + X6 \ge 3 - M*Y2$$

$$X1 \ge 1 - M*Y3$$
$$X1 \le 1 + M*Y3$$

$$7X1 + X3 + 2X5 + X6 + 8X7 + 3X8 + 2X9 \ge 15 - M*Y4$$

$$X7 + X8 + X9 \ge 3 - M*Y5$$
$$X7 + X8 + X9 \le 3 + M*Y5$$

Step 2:   Add the constraint that requires that at least three of the five conditional constraints hold (at most two do *not* hold):

$$Y1 + Y2 + Y3 + Y4 + Y5 \le 2$$

COMPLETE MODEL FOR THE SALEM CITY COUNCIL

The complete model for the Salem City Council, which includes the objective function, the functional and conditional constraints, and the binary restrictions, can now be stated as follows:

---

[4]For example, a constraint of the form 3X1 + 2X2 + 4X3 = 12 will hold if both of the following are satisfied: 3X1 + 2X2 + 4X3 ≤ 12, and 3X1 + 2X2 + 4X3 ≥ 12.

MAXIMIZE
4176X1 + 1774X2 + 2513X3 + 1928X4 + 3607X5 + 962X6 + 2829X7 + 1708X8 + 3003X9
ST

$$
\begin{array}{l}
400X1 + 350X2 + 50X3 + 100X4 + 500X5 + 90X6 + 220X7 + 150X8 + 140X9 \leq 900 \\
7X1 + \qquad\qquad X3 + \qquad\qquad 2X5 + X6 + 8X7 + 3X8 + 2X9 \geq 10 \\
X1 + X2 + X3 + X4 \qquad\qquad\qquad\qquad\qquad\qquad\qquad \leq 3 \\
\qquad\qquad\qquad X3 + \qquad\qquad X5 \qquad\qquad\qquad\qquad\qquad = 1 \\
\qquad\qquad\qquad\qquad\qquad\qquad\qquad\qquad\qquad X7 - X8 \qquad = 0 \\
\qquad\qquad\qquad\qquad\qquad\qquad\qquad\qquad\qquad X7 - \qquad X9 \geq 0 \\
\qquad\qquad\qquad\qquad\qquad\qquad\qquad\qquad\qquad\qquad X8 - X9 \geq 0
\end{array}
$$

$$
400X1 + 350X2 + 50X3 + 100X4 + 500X5 + 90X6 + 220X7 + 150X8 + 140X9
$$
$$
- M*Y1 \leq 650
$$
$$
X1 + X2 + X3 + X4 + X5 + X6 \quad + M*Y2 \geq 3
$$
$$
X1 + \qquad\qquad\qquad\qquad\qquad\qquad M*Y3 \geq 1
$$
$$
X1 - \qquad\qquad\qquad\qquad\qquad\qquad M*Y3 \leq 1
$$
$$
7X1 + \qquad X3 + \qquad 2X5 + X6 + 8X7 + 3X8 + 2X9
$$
$$
+ M*Y4 \geq 15
$$
$$
X7 + X8 + X9
$$
$$
+ M*Y5 \geq 3
$$
$$
X7 + X8 + X9
$$
$$
- M*Y5 \leq 3
$$
$$
Y1 + Y2 + Y3 + Y4 + Y5 \quad 2
$$

All Xj and Yi = 0 or 1

Since all the variables (both the Xjs and the Yis) are restricted to either 0 or 1, this problem is a BILP. The problem was solved using WINQSB, giving the output shown in Figure 5.11.

Combined Report for SALEM CITY COUNCIL

10:22:53		Friday	March	27	1998
Decision Variable	Solution Value	Unit Cost or Profit c(j)	Total Contribution	Reduced Cost	Basis Status
1 POLICE	0	4,176.0000	0	4,176.0000	at bound
2 HDQTRS	0	1,774.0000	0	1,774.0000	at bound
3 POLCAR	1.0000	2,513.0000	2,513.0000	2,513.0000	at bound
4 POLBONUS	1.0000	1,928.0000	1,928.0000	0	basic
5 FIREENG	0	3,607.0000	0	0	basic
6 ASSTCHF	1.0000	962.0000	962.0000	0	basic
7 SPORTS	1.0000	2,829.0000	2,829.0000	0	basic
8 MUSIC	1.0000	1,708.0000	1,708.0000	0	basic
9 COMPUTER	1.0000	3,003.0000	3,003.0000	0	basic
10 Y1	1.0000	0	0	0	at bound
11 Y2	0	0	0	0	basic
12 Y3	1.0000	0	0	0	at bound
13 Y4	0	0	0	0.0000	at bound
14 Y5	0	0	0	0	basic
Objective	Function	(Max.)=	12,943.0000		
Constraint	Left Hand Side	Direction	Right Hand Side	Slack or Surplus	Shadow Price
1 BUDGET	750.0000	<=	900.0000	150.0000	0
2 1ONEWJOBS	15.0000	>=	10.0000	5.0000	0
3 <=3POLPRJ	2.0000	<=	3.0000	1.0000	0
4 EMERGVEH	1.0000	=	1.0000	0	3,607.0000
5 SPTS=MUS	0	=	0	0	-1,708.0000
6 IFCMP-SPTS	0	>=	0	0	3,003.0000
7 IFCMP-MUS	0	>=	0	0	0
8 RESERVE	-9,250.0000	<=	650.0000	9,900.0000	0
9 >=3POL/FIR	3.0000	>=	3.0000	0	0
10 7POL>1	10,000.0000	>=	1.0000	9,999.0000	0
11 7POL<1	-10,000.00	<=	1.0000	10,001.0000	0
12 15NEWJOBS	15.0000	>=	15.0000	0	0
13 EDUC>=3	3.0000	>=	3.0000	0	0
14 EDUC<=3	3.0000	<=	3.0000	0	0
15 >=3GOALS	2.0000	<=	2.0000	0	0

FIGURE 5.11   WINQSB Combined Report for Salem City Council

Much to the council's surprise, the optimal solution does not include the two items people most wanted: hiring seven new police officers (X_1) and purchasing a new fire engine (X_5)! Nor does the solution call for any renovations to the police station. All other projects would be funded, however, and three of the five goal constraints are met: (1) at least three police/fire projects are funded; (2) at least 15 new jobs are created (there are exactly 15 with this solution); and (3) all three education projects are funded.

This problem assumed that each of the five items was equally important. If this were not the case, the council might have wished to prioritize its objectives. Problems that involve prioritized objectives are known as *goal programming problems*. These are discussed in the non-linear models Chapter 16 on the accompanying CD-ROM.

5.8 $\mathcal{F}$IXED CHARGE/FACILITY LOCATION PROBLEMS

One assumption frequently made for linear programming models is that fixed costs can be ignored, since there is nothing a decision maker can do to control them. Hence, fixed costs are typically excluded from such models, and the objective is either to minimize total variable cost or maximize total variable profit. This approach, however, relies on the assumption that the fixed cost will always occur. In some cases, this is an incorrect assumption.

For example, suppose that a car manufacturer will need to use a plant in Lexington, Kentucky, to produce a particular type of sports car. The unit cost to manufacture the sports car is $12,000, and the cost to lease the plant in Lexington is $9 million per year. If 8000 sports cars are manufactured during the year, the total cost will be 8000($12,000) + $9,000,000 = $105,000,000; if 800 are manufactured, the cost is 800($12,000) + $9,000,000 = $18,600,000, and so on. However, if no sports cars are manufactured, the company will not lease the Lexington plant, and the total cost will be $0, not $9 million. In other words, the fixed cost is valid only if the production quantity is positive. This is an example of a **fixed charge problem**.

The Fixed Charge Problem

If a product has a fixed cost F associated with any production, then the total cost of producing X units is:

$$CX + F \quad \text{if } X > 0$$
$$0 \quad \text{if } X = 0$$

THE FACILITY LOCATION PROBLEM

One class of problems that requires the use of a fixed charge model is the determination of which of several possible locations should be operated in order to maximize or minimize some objective function, such as profit, cost, or time. Common *facility location problems* include the location of plants, operations within a plant, emergency services (police stations, fire stations, MASH units, etc.), branch offices for banks, and supply centers for construction projects. Considerations in facility location problems include the following.

1. Fixed costs associated with the operation of each location
2. Variable costs or profits associated with operations at each location
3. Constraints that are valid only if a certain location is selected

To illustrate the concept of a facility location problem, consider the situation faced by Globe Electronics, Inc.

GLOBE ELECTRONICS, INC.

Globe.lpp
Globe.xls
Globefac.lpp
Globefac.xls

Globe Electronics, Inc. manufactures two styles of remote control cable boxes (the G50 and the G90) that various cable companies supply to their customers when cable service is established. Different companies require different models. During the late 1980s and early 1990s, due to an explosion in the demand for cable services, Globe expanded rapidly to four production facilities located in Philadelphia (the original plant), St. Louis, New Orleans, and Denver. The manufactured items are shipped from the plants to regional distribution centers located in Cincinnati, Kansas City, and San Francisco; from these locations they are distributed nationwide.

Because of a decrease in demand for cable services and technological changes in the cable industry, demand for Globe's products is currently far less than the total of the capacities at its four plants. As a result, management is contemplating closing one or more of its facilities.

Each plant has a fixed operating cost, and, because of the unique conditions at each facility, the production costs, production time per unit, and total monthly production time available vary from plant to plant, as summarized in Table 5.4.

TABLE 5.4   PRODUCTION COSTS, TIMES, AVAILABILITY

Plant	Fixed Cost/Month ($1000)	Production Cost (per 100) G50	G90	Production Time (Hr./100) G50	G90	Available Hours per Month
Philadelphia	40	1000	1400	6	6	640
St. Louis	35	1200	1200	7	8	960
New Orleans	20	800	1000	9	7	480
Denver	30	1300	1500	5	9	640

The cable boxes are sold nationwide at the same prices: $22 for the G50, and $28 for the G90.

Current monthly demand projections at each distribution center for both products are given in Table 5.5.

TABLE 5.5   MONTHLY DEMAND PROJECTIONS

	Demand		
	Cincinnati	Kansas City	San Francisco
G50	2000	3000	5000
G90	5000	6000	7000

To remain viable in each market, Globe must meet at least 70% of the demand for each product at each distribution center. The transportation costs between each plant and each distribution center, which are the same for either product, are shown in Table 5.6.

Globe management wants to develop an optimal distribution policy utilizing all four of its operational plants. It also wants to determine whether closing any of the production facilities will result in higher company profits.

TABLE 5.6   TRANSPORTATION COSTS PER 100 UNITS

	To		
	Cincinnati	Kansas City	San Francisco
From			
Philadelphia	$200	$300	$500
St. Louis	$100	$100	$400
New Orleans	$200	$200	$300
Denver	$300	$100	$100

SOLUTION

Globe's problem is to

- Determine the number of G50 and G90 cable boxes to be produced at each plant
- Determine a shipping pattern from the plants to the distribution centers
- Maximize net total monthly profit
- Not exceed the production capacities at any plant
- Ensure that each distribution center receives between 70% and 100% of its demand

The linear program Globe uses to solve for the optimal solution with all four plants operating is developed below. In this formulation, the following representation for the cities is used:

$$i = 1 \text{ (Philadelphia)} \qquad j = 1 \text{ (Cincinnati)}$$
$$i = 2 \text{ (St. Louis)} \qquad j = 2 \text{ (Kansas City)}$$
$$i = 3 \text{ (New Orleans)} \qquad j = 3 \text{ (San Francisco)}$$
$$i = 4 \text{ (Denver)}$$

Decision Variables
Management must decide how many G50 and G90 cable boxes it will produce at each plant (i):

$$X_i = \text{hundreds of G50 cable boxes produced at plant } i \text{ monthly}$$
$$Z_i = \text{hundreds of G90 cable boxes produced at plant } i \text{ monthly}$$

Given these production schedules, management must then decide how many units of each product will be shipped from each plant i to each production center j:

$$X_{ij} = \text{hundreds of G50 cable boxes shipped from plant } i$$
$$\text{to distribution center } j \text{ each month}$$
$$Z_{ij} = \text{hundreds of G90 cable boxes shipped from plant } i$$
$$\text{to distribution center } j \text{ each month}$$

Thus, there are 12 X_{ij} variables, $X11, X12, \ldots, X43$ representing the distribution of the G50 cable boxes, and 12 Z_{ij} variables, $Z11, Z12, \ldots, Z43$ representing the distribution of the G90 cable boxes.

Objective Function
The gross profit per 100 G50 cable boxes produced at plant i (X_i) is:

$$\text{(Revenue per 100)} - \text{(Production cost per 100)}$$

The revenue per hundred G50's, regardless of where they are manufactured, is $22(100) = $2200, and the production costs per hundred G50s are $1000, $1200, $800, and $1300 for plants 1, 2, 3, and 4, respectively. Subtracting these costs from the $2200 revenue, the total gross profit made by producing G50 cable boxes can be expressed as $1200X1 + 1000X2 + 1400X3 + 900X4$.

Similarly, the total gross profit made by producing G90 cable boxes can be shown to be: $1400Z1 + 1600Z2 + 1800Z3 + 1300Z4$.

The variable shipping costs given in Table 5.6 must also be accounted for in the objective function. These costs are multiplied by the variables X_{ij} and Z_{ij}, respectively. Thus, the objective is:

$$
\begin{aligned}
\text{MAXIMIZE} \quad & 1200X1 + 1000X2 + 1400X3 + 900X4 + 1400Z1 + 1600Z2 \\
& + 1800Z3 + 1300Z4 - 200X11 - 300X12 - 500X13 - 100X21 \\
& - 100X22 - 400X23 - 200X31 - 200X32 - 300X33 - 300X41 \\
& - 100X41 - 100X43 - 200Z11 - 300Z12 - 500Z13 - 100Z21 \\
& - 100Z22 - 400Z23 - 200Z31 - 200Z32 - 300Z33 - 300Z41 \\
& - 100Z41 - 100Z43
\end{aligned}
$$

Note: This expression gives the total monthly profit *before subtracting the fixed monthly operating costs (totaling $125,000)*.

Constraints

The following constraints exist.

1. The model must ensure that the total amount shipped from a plant equals the amount produced in the plant. For G50 cable boxes, this is expressed by the following constraints:

$$X11 + X12 + X13 = X1$$
$$X21 + X22 + X23 = X2$$
$$X31 + X32 + X33 = X3$$
$$X41 + X42 + X43 = X4$$

and for G90 cable boxes:

$$Z11 + Z12 + Z13 = Z1$$
$$Z21 + Z22 + Z23 = Z2$$
$$Z31 + Z32 + Z33 = Z3$$
$$Z41 + Z42 + Z43 = Z4$$

2. Production time used at each plant cannot exceed the time available:

$$6X1 + 6Z1 \le 640$$
$$7X2 + 8Z2 \le 960$$
$$9X3 + 7Z3 \le 480$$
$$5X4 + 9Z4 \le 640$$

3. The amount of each product received by a distribution center cannot exceed its total demand or be less than 70% of its demand:

$$X11 + X21 + X31 + X41 \leq 20$$
$$X11 + X21 + X31 + X41 \geq 14$$
$$X12 + X22 + X32 + X42 \leq 30$$
$$X12 + X22 + X32 + X42 \geq 21$$
$$X13 + X23 + X33 + X43 \leq 50$$
$$X13 + X23 + X33 + X43 \geq 35$$
$$Z11 + Z21 + Z31 + Z41 \leq 50$$
$$Z11 + Z21 + Z31 + Z41 \geq 35$$
$$Z12 + Z22 + Z32 + Z42 \leq 60$$
$$Z12 + Z22 + Z32 + Z42 \geq 42$$
$$Z13 + Z23 + Z33 + Z43 \leq 70$$
$$Z13 + Z23 + Z33 + Z43 \geq 49$$

4. All variables are nonnegative:

$$\text{All } Xi, Zi, Xij, Zij \geq 0$$

Solution To The Mathematical Model

Solving this model yields the WINQSB output shown in Figure 5.12 (units are in hundreds). The optimal value of the objective function is $356,571. Subtracting the $125,000 in fixed costs results in a net monthly profit of $231,571 reported to management.

THE FIXED CHARGE
COMPONENT

The preceding solution assumed that all plants are operational. However, because of the large fixed cost components at each plant, this may not be the best overall solution. Globe should consider which plants it wishes to keep operational. Whether or not each plant remains operational can be expressed using the following binary decision variables:

$Y1$ = number of operational Philadelphia plants
$Y2$ = number of operational St. Louis plants
$Y3$ = number of operational New Orleans plants
$Y4$ = number of operational Denver plants

The fixed operating costs can be accounted for in the objective function by subtracting from the previous objective function the expression $40000Y1 + 35000Y2 + 20000Y3 + 30000Y4$.

The production constraints are modified as follows:

$$6X1 + 6Z1 \leq 640Y1$$
$$7X2 + 8Z2 \leq 960Y2$$
$$9X3 + 7Z3 \leq 480Y3$$
$$5X4 + 9Z4 \leq 640Y4$$

If plant i is closed ($Yi = 0$), then these constraints will force the corresponding production (Xi and Zi) to be 0, which, in turn, implies that all shipments from plant i (Xij and Zij) will also be 0.

Combined Report for Globe Electronics

	13:50:25		Monday	February	07	1998		
	Decision Variable	Solution Value	Unit Cost or Profit c(j)	Total Contribution	Reduced Cost	Basis Status	Allowable Min. c(j)	Allowable Max. c(j)
1	X1	38.57	1,200.00	46285.71	0	basic	1,200.00	1,200.00
2	X2	11.43	1,000.00	11428.57	0	basic	1,000.00	1,000.00
3	X3	0	1,400.00	0	0	basic	-M	1,485.71
4	X4	50.00	900.00	45,000.00	0	basic	814.29	1,000.00
5	Z1	0	1,400.00	0	-300.00	at bound	-M	1,700.00
6	Z2	110.00	1,600.00	176000.00	0	basic	1,600.00	1,666.67
7	Z3	68.57	1,800.00	123,428.60	0	basic	1,733.33	M
8	Z4	1.43	1857.14	1857.14	0	basic	1,300.00	1,300.00
9	X11	20.00	-200.00	-4,000.00	0	basic	-300.00	M
10	X12	18.57	-300.00	-5571.43	0	basic	-300.00	-300.00
11	X13	0	-500.00	0	-100.00	at bound	-M	-400.00
12	X21	0	-100.00	0	-100.00	at bound	-M	0
13	X22	11.43	-100.00	-1142.86	0	basic	-100.00	-100.00
14	X23	0	-400.00	0	-200.00	at bound	-M	-200.00
15	X31	0	-200.00	0	-185.71	at bound	-M	-14.29
16	X32	0	-200.00	0	-85.71	at bound	-M	-114.29
17	X33	0	-300.00	0	-85.71	at bound	-M	-214.29
18	X41	0	-300.00	0	-400.00	at bound	-M	100.00
19	X42	0	-100.00	0	-100.00	at bound	-M	0
20	X43	50.00	-100.00	-5,000.00	0	basic	-185.71	M
21	Z11	0	-200.00	0	0	at bound	-M	-200.00
22	Z12	0	-300.00	0	-100.00	at bound	-M	-200.00
23	Z13	0	-500.00	0	0	basic	-500.00	-200.00
24	Z21	50.00	-100.00	-5,000.00	0	basic	-100.00	M
25	Z22	60.00	-100.00	-6,000.00	0	basic	-200.00	M
26	Z23	0	-400.00	0	0	at bound	-M	-400.00
27	Z31	0	-200.00	0	-200.00	at bound	-M	0
28	Z32	0	-200.00	0	-200.00	at bound	-M	0
29	Z33	68.57	-300.00	-20,571.43	0	basic	-366.67	M
30	Z41	0	-300.00	0	-500.00	at bound	-M	200.00
31	Z42	0	-100.00	0	-300.00	at bound	-M	200.00
32	Z43	1.43	-100.00	-142.86	0	basic	-100.00	-100.00
	Objective	Function	(Max.)=	356,571.40	(Note:	Alternate	Solution	Exists!!)

	Constraint	Left Hand Side	Direction	Right Hand Side	Slack or Surplus	Shadow Price	Allowable Min.RHS	Allowable Max.RHS
1	C1	0	=	0	0	-1,200.00	-68.10	18.57
2	C2	0	=	0	0	-1,000.00	-11.43	18.57
3	C3	0	=	0	0	-1,014.29	-32.59	0
4	C4	0	=	0	0	-900.00	-75.43	50.00
5	C5	0	=	0	0	-1,700.00	0	1.43
6	C6	0.00	=	0	0	-1,600.00	-10.00	16.25
7	C7	0	=	0	0	-1,500.00	-41.90	1.43
8	C8	0	=	0	0	-1,300.00	-41.90	1.43
9	C9	231.43	<=	40.00	408.57	0	231.43	M
10	C10	960.00	<=	960.00	0	0	880.00	1090.00
11	C11	480.00	<=	480.00	0	42.86	186.67	490.00
12	C12	262.86	<=	640.00	377.14	0	262.86	M
13	C13	20.00	<=	20.00	0	1,000.00	14.00	88.10
14	C14	20.00	>=	14.00	6.00	0	-M	20.00
15	C15	30.00	<=	30.00	0	900.00	21.00	98.10
16	C16	30.00	>=	21.00	9.00	0	-M	30.00
17	C17	50.00	<=	50.00	0	800.00	35.00	128.00
18	C18	50.00	>=	35.00	15.00	0	-M	50.00
19	C19	50.00	<=	50.00	0	1,500.00	35.00	58.57
20	C20	50.00	>=	35.00	15.00	0	-M	50.00
21	C21	60.00	<=	60.00	0	1,500.00	42.32	68.57
22	C22	60.00	>=	42.00	18.00	0	-M	60.00
23	C23	70.00	<=	70.00	0	1,200.00	68.57	78.57
24	C24	70.00	>=	49.00	21.00	0	-M	70.00

FIGURE 5.12   WINQSB Combined Report for Globe Electronics

THE MATHEMATICAL
MODEL FOR THE FIXED
CHARGE PROBLEM

Changing the original linear program by subtracting the fixed operating costs in the objective function and modifying any constraint that is dependent on a facility being operational, gives the following MILP for the facility location problem faced by Globe Electronics, Inc.:

$$
\begin{aligned}
\text{MAXIMIZE}\quad & 1200X1 + 1000X2 + 1400X3 + 900X4 + 1400Z1 + 1600Z2 \\
+\ & 1800Z3 + 1300Z4 - 200X11 - 300X12 - 500X13 - 100X21 \\
-\ & 100X22 - 400X23 - 200X31 - 200X32 - 300X33 - 300X41 \\
-\ & 100X41 - 100X43 - 200Z11 - 300Z12 - 500Z13 - 100Z21 \\
-\ & 100Z22 - 400Z23 - 200Z31 - 200Z32 - 300Z33 - 300Z41 \\
-\ & 100Z41 - 100Z43 - 40000Y1 - 35000Y2 - 20000Y3 - 30000Y4
\end{aligned}
$$

ST

$$
\begin{aligned}
X11 + X12 + X13 - X1 &= 0 \\
X21 + X22 + X23 - X2 &= 0 \\
X31 + X32 + X33 - X3 &= 0 \\
X41 + X42 + X43 - X4 &= 0 \\
Z11 + Z12 + Z13 - Z1 &= 0 \\
Z21 + Z22 + Z23 - Z2 &= 0 \\
Z31 + Z32 + Z33 - Z3 &= 0 \\
Z41 + Z42 + Z43 - Z4 &= 0 \\
6X1 + 6Z1 - 640Y1 &\leq 0 \\
7X2 + 8Z2 - 960Y2 &\leq 0 \\
9X3 + 7Z3 - 480Y3 &\leq 0 \\
5X4 + 9Z4 - 640Y4 &\leq 0 \\
X11 + X21 + X31 + X41 &\leq 20 \\
X11 + X21 + X31 + X41 &\geq 14 \\
X12 + X22 + X32 + X42 &\leq 30 \\
X12 + X22 + X32 + X42 &\geq 21 \\
X13 + X23 + X33 + X43 &\leq 50 \\
X13 + X23 + X33 + X43 &\geq 35 \\
Z11 + Z21 + Z31 + Z41 &\leq 50 \\
Z11 + Z21 + Z31 + Z41 &\geq 35 \\
Z12 + Z22 + Z32 + Z42 &\leq 60 \\
Z12 + Z22 + Z32 + Z42 &\geq 42 \\
Z13 + Z23 + Z33 + Z43 &\leq 70 \\
Z13 + Z23 + Z33 + Z43 &\geq 49
\end{aligned}
$$

All Xi, Zi, Xij, Zij ≥ 0
All Yi = 0 or 1

This facility location problem for Globe Electronics was solved using WINQSB, producing the output shown in Figure 5.13.

The optimal solution to Globe's fixed charge problem is to close the Philadelphia plant (Y1) and to schedule monthly production according to the quantities shown in the output. This gives a net monthly profit of $266,115, which is $34,544 per month greater than the optimal monthly profit of $231,571 obtained when all four plants are operational.

A MANAGEMENT
REPORT

The results from this MILP model and the linear programming model used to solve the problem with no plant closures can form the basis for a management report. One item of interest to management may be a breakdown of the distribution of costs and production time under each plan so that Globe can determine where the major costs lie. In addition, management may wish to explore further options. These issues are addressed in the following memorandum to Globe Electronics.

Combined Report for Globe Electronics

	14:40:36		Monday	February	07	1998		
	Decision Variable	Solution Value	Unit Cost or Profit c(j)	Total Contribution	Reduced Cost	Basis Status	Allowable Min. c(j)	Allowable Max. c(j)
1	X1	0	1,200.00	0	0	basic	989.13	1,575.00
2	X2	11.43	1,000.00	11,428.57	0	basic	906.25	1,081.25
3	X3	28.04	1,400.00	39,260.87	0	basic	1,385.71	1,614.29
4	X4	60.53	900.00	54,475.16	0	basic	755.56	914.29
5	Z1	0	1,400.00	0	-384.16	at bound	-M	1,784.16
6	Z2	110.00	1,600.00	176,000.00	0	basic	1,507.14	1,707.14
7	Z3	32.52	1,800.00	58,527.95	0	basic	1,633.33	1,811.11
8	Z4	37.48	1,300.00	48,729.81	0	basic	1,288.89	1,539.58
9	X11	0	-200.00	0	0	basic	-300.00	175.00
10	X12	0	-300.00	0	-100.00	at bound	-M	-200.00
11	X13	0	-500.00	0	-300.00	at bound	-M	-200.00
12	X21	0	-100.00	0	0	at bound	-M	-100.00
13	X22	11.43	-100.00	-1,142.86	0	basic	-100.00	-18.75
14	X23	0	-400.00	0	-300.00	at bound	-M	-100.00
15	X31	20.00	-200.00	-4,000.00	0	basic	-200.00	-100.00
16	X32	8.04	-200.00	-1,608.70	0	basic	-214.29	-200.00
17	X33	0	-300.00	0	-100.00	at bound	-M	-200.00
18	X41	0	-300.00	0	-200.00	at bound	-M	-100.00
19	X42	10.53	-100.00	-1,052.80	0	basic	-244.44	-85.71
20	X43	50.00	-100.00	-5,000.00	0	basic	-200.00	M
21	Z11	0	-200.00	0	0	basic	-300.00	184.16
22	Z12	0	-300.00	0	-100.00	at bound	-M	-200.00
23	Z13	0	-500.00	0	-107.14	at bound	-M	-392.86
24	Z21	50.00	-100.00	-5,000.00	0	basic	-192.86	0
25	Z22	60.00	-100.00	-6,000.00	0	basic	-192.86	M
26	Z23	0	-400.00	0	-107.14	at bound	-M	-292.86
27	Z31	0	-200.00	0	-92.86	at bound	-M	-107.14
28	Z32	0	-200.00	0	-92.86	at bound	-M	-107.14
29	Z33	32.52	-300.00	-9,754.66	0	basic	-466.67	-288.89
30	Z41	0	-300.00	0	-392.86	at bound	-M	92.86
31	Z42	0	-100.00	0	-192.96	at bound	-M	92.86
32	Z43	37.48	-100.00	-3,748.45	0	basic	-111.11	139.58
33	Y1	0	-40,000.00	0	-40,000.00	at bound	-M	M
34	Y2	1.00	-35,000.00	-35,000.00	-35,000.00	at bound	-M	M
35	Y3	1.00	-20,000.00	-20,000.00	0	basic	-21,913.04	M
36	Y4	1.00	-30,000.00	-30,000.00	-30,000.00	at bound	-M	M
	Objective	Function	(Max.)=	266,114.97				
	Constraint	Left Hand Side	Direction	Right Hand Side	Slack or Surplus	Shadow Price	Allowable Min.RHS	Allowable Max.RHS
1	C1	0	=	0	0	-989.13	0	5.98
2	C2	0	=	0	0	-889.13	-10.57	5.98
3	C3	0	=	0	0	-989.13	-4.57	5.98
4	C4	0	=	0	0	-889.13	-10.57	13.84
5	C5	0	=	0	0	-1,573.29	0	5.23
6	C6	0	=	0	0	-1,473.29	-9.25	5.23
7	C7	0	=	0	0	-1,480.43	-5.87	7.69
8	C8	0	=	0	0	-1,280.43	-5.87	7.69
9	C9	0	<=	0	0	35.14	0	35.87
10	C10	0	<=	0	0	15.84	-74.00	41.85
11	C11	0	<=	0	0	45.65	-41.11	53.81
12	C12	0	<=	0	0	2.17	-52.86	69.18
13	C13	20.00	<=	20.00	0	789.13	14.02	24.57
14	C14	20.00	>=	14.00	6.00	0	-M	20.00
15	C15	30.00	<=	30.00	0	789.13	24.02	40.57
16	C16	30.00	>=	21.00	9.00	0	-M	30.00
17	C17	50.00	<=	50.00	0	789.13	36.16	60.57
18	C18	50.00	>=	35.00	15.00	0	-M	50.00
19	C19	50.00	<=	50.00	0	1,373.29	44.77	59.25
20	C20	50.00	>=	35.00	15.00	0	-M	50.00
21	C21	60.00	<=	60.00	0	1,373.29	54.77	69.25
22	C22	60.00	>=	42.00	18.00	0	-M	60.00
23	C23	70.00	<=	70.00	0	1,180.43	62.31	75.87
24	C24	70.00	>=	49.00	21.00	0	-M	70.00

FIGURE 5.13   WINQSB Combined Report for Globe Electronics Facilities

M E M O R A N D U M

To: Carol Copley, Vice President
            Globe Electronics, Inc.

From: Student Consulting Group

Subj: Recommendation for Monthly Operations

We have been asked to evaluate plant production of the G50 and G90 cable boxes manufactured at the Philadelphia, St. Louis, New Orleans, and Denver plants. Recent product demand projections for the coming year from the Cincinnati, Kansas City, and San Francisco distribution centers have dropped to such a point that a substantial amount of unused production time is available at the plants. Given the large fixed plant operating costs, we have been asked to evaluate the feasibility and the potential cost savings of closing one or more of the plants.

In our analysis we assumed that the demand forecast for the upcoming year, as shown in Table I, is an accurate reflection of future sales.

TABLE I   Monthly Demand Forecasts for the Next Fiscal Year

	Cincinnati	Kansas City	San Francisco
G50	2000	3000	5000
G90	5000	6000	7000

Based on production time data and the information in Table I, we developed profit maximization models for your situation. These models assume a $22 and $28 selling price for G50 and G90 models, respectively, and take into account the following:

1. The fixed operating cost at each plant
2. The variable production costs associated with each product at each plant
3. The unit transportation costs of shipping cable boxes from the plants to the distribution centers
4. Production not exceeding demand

Management's imposed condition that at least 70% of the demand for each product be supplied to each distribution center did not turn out to be a limiting factor in the analysis.

OPTIMAL PRODUCTION SCHEDULES

Given the current situation at the four plants in operation, Table II gives a production schedule that should maximize Globe's total net monthly profit.

TABLE II   Production/Transportation Schedule: All Plants Operational

Plant	Product	Amount	Cincinnati	Kansas City	San Francisco
Philadelphia	G50	3857	2000	1857	
	G90	0			
St. Louis	G50	1143		1143	
	G90	11000	5000	6000	
New Orleans	G50	0			
	G90	6857			6857
Denver	G50	5000			5000
	G90	143			143
Total	G50	10000	2000	3000	5000
	G90	18000	5000	6000	7000

Notice that, although this production plan meets the full demand at the distribution centers, no G50 models are produced in New Orleans, no G90 models are produced in Philadelphia, and only 143 G90 models are produced monthly at the Denver plant. As a result, there is considerable excess capacity at both the Philadelphia and Denver plants.

Under this plan, as shown in Table III, Globe will be utilizing only 1934 production hours, or 71% of available production capacity. Observe from Table IV that the Philadelphia plant will be *un*profitable, while the Denver plant will be only marginally profitable.

TABLE III Distribution of Production Time (Hours) All Plants Operational

Plant	G50	G90	Total	Total Capacity	Excess Capacity
Philadelphia	231	0	231	640	409
St. Louis	80	880	960	960	0
New Orleans	0	480	480	480	0
Denver	250	13	263	640	377
Total	561	1373	1934	2720	786

TABLE IV Distribution of Monthly Revenues and Costs (All Plants Operational)

Plant	Revenue Sales	Costs Production	Costs Transportation	Costs Operations	Total Cost	Net Profit
Philadelphia	$ 84,854	$ 38,570	$ 9,571	$ 40,000	$ 88,141	($ 3,287)
St. Louis	$333,146	$145,716	$12,143	$ 35,000	$192,859	$140,287
New Orleans	$191,996	$ 68,570	$20,571	$ 20,000	$109,141	$ 82,855
Denver	$114,004	$ 67,145	$ 5,143	$ 30,000	$102,288	$ 11,716
Total	$724,000	$320,001	$47,428	$125,000	$492,429	$231,571

Plant Closings Tables V, VI, and VII give a production and distribution schedule that would result from closing the Philadelphia plant. We estimate that, by closing the Philadelphia plant, Globe can achieve an approximate 15% increase in profit, from $231,571 to $266,115 per month. This is an annual increase in profit of $414,528.

TABLE V Production/Transportation Schedule (Philadelphia Plant Closed)

Plant	Product	Amount	Cincinnati	Kansas City	San Francisco
St. Louis	G50	1143		1143	
	G90	11000	5000	6000	
New Orleans	G50	2804	2000	804	
	G90	3252			3252
Denver	G50	6053		1053	5000
	G90	3748			3748
Total	G50	10000	2000	3000	5000
	G90	18000	5000	6000	7000

TABLE VI Distribution of Production Time (Hours) (Philadelphia Plant Closed)

Plant	G50	G90	Total	Total Capacity	Excess Capacity
St. Louis	80	880	960	960	0
New Orleans	252	228	480	480	0
Denver	303	337	640	640	0
Total	635	1445	2080	2080	0

TABLE VII   Distribution of Monthly Revenues and Costs (Philadelphia Plant Closed)

Plant	Revenue Sales	Costs Production	Transportation	Operations	Total Cost	Net Profit
St. Louis	$333,146	$145,716	$12,143	$35,000	$192,859	$140,287
New Orleans	$152,744	$ 54,952	$15,364	$20,000	$ 90,316	$ 62,428
Denver	$238,110	$134,909	$ 9,801	$30,000	$174,710	$ 63,400
Total	$724,000	$335,577	$37,308	$85,000	$457,885	$266,115

Based on this analysis, it would seem prudent to close the Philadelphia plant. The remaining three plants will then be fully utilized, and all projected demand will be met.

Because Globe Electronics has its roots in the Philadelphia area, however, the company may wish to examine additional alternatives. We conducted another analysis to determine the most profitable production schedule while keeping the Philadelphia plant operational.

The best production plan in this case is to close the Denver plant and execute the manufacturing and distribution plan detailed in Table VIII. Net profit under this plan would be $256,667 per month, approximately 4% less than if the Philadelphia plant were closed. Although this amounts to annual profit that is approximately $113,000 less than if the firm closes the Philadelphia plant, it is still approximately an 11% (or about a $300,000) annual increase over the best schedule with all plants operational.

Note that under this plan:

- The Philadelphia plant produces only G50 models.
- The St. Louis plant produces only G90 models.
- The New Orleans plant ships only to San Francisco.

TABLE VIII   Production/Transportation Schedule (Denver Plant Closed)

Plant	Product	Amount	Cincinnati	Kansas City	San Francisco
Philadelphia	G50	9333	2000	3000	4333
	G90	0			
St. Louis	G50	0			
	G90	12000	5000	6000	1000
New Orleans	G50	667			667
	G90	6000			6000
Total	G50	10000	2000	3000	5000
	G90	18000	5000	6000	7000

Such a pattern may have additional benefits or detractions of which we are unaware and which were not considered in our analysis. Barring such additional costs or cost savings, Tables IX and X detail the production time and cost distribution for this schedule. Note that this schedule also has the benefit of the availability of some excess capacity (at the Philadelphia plant) to cover any unanticipated surges in demand.

TABLE IX   Distribution of Production Time (Hours) (Denver Plant Closed)

Plant	G50	G90	Total	Total Capacity	Excess Capacity
Philadelphia	560	0	560	640	80
St. Louis	0	960	960	960	0
New Orleans	60	420	480	480	0
Total	620	1380	2000	2080	80

TABLE X Distribution of Monthly Revenues and Costs (Denver Plant Closed)

Plant	Revenues Sales	Costs Production	Costs Transportation	Costs Operations	Total Cost	Net Profit
Philadelphia	$205,326	$ 93,330	$34,665	$40,000	$167,995	$ 37,331
St. Louis	$336,000	$144,000	$15,000	$35,000	$194,000	$142,000
New Orleans	$182,674	$ 65,336	$20,000	$20,000	$105,336	$ 77,338
Total	$724,000	$302,666	$69,665	$95,000	$467,331	$256,669

SUMMARY AND RECOMMENDATION   The results of our analysis are as follows:

Options for Globe Electronics, Inc.

Option	Annual Profit
Close the Philadelphia plant	$3,193,380
Close the Denver plant	$3,080,028
All plants operational	$2,778,852

Although we have detailed the cost and transportation distribution of each plan, management must decide whether extenuating circumstances would make one of the less profitable plans more acceptable. Factors such as the impact on the community of plant closings, the costs (not included in this report) of actually closing a facility, and the benefits of a structured distribution pattern or available excess capacity to meet demand fluctuations should all be considered before a final decision is made.

Should management require further study on any of these points, we would be happy to assist in the analysis.

5.9 SUMMARY

Integer programming can be applied to numerous business situations. However, integer programming problems are generally far more complex and time consuming to solve than linear programming problems, and the optimal solution does not necessarily occur at the intersection of functional or nonnegativity constraints.

Three classifications of integer linear programs are: (1) all-integer linear programs (AILP); (2) mixed integer linear programs (MILP); and (3) binary integer linear programs (BILP). Techniques for solving integer programs include: (1) total enumeration, (2) rounding, (3) cutting plane techniques, and (4) branch and bound techniques. Rounding a solution can lead to the optimal solution, but it can also yield a solution that is infeasible or one that is feasible but not optimal.

A major drawback to any of these four methods is the lack of sensitivity analysis. As a result, the output of an integer programming problem contains little more than an exposition of the optimal solution and how much of each resource will be used.

Binary integer programs play a special role in mathematical models. Binary variables can be used to model logical conditions placed on a problem, such as mutually exclusive, prerequisite, corequisite, and the satisfying of K out of N possibilities. Two important binary problems are the fixed charge and the facility location problem. These problems use binary variables to assess fixed costs only when warranted.

Computer Input for MILP's

WINQSB

In WINQSB, integer or binary variables are designated by clicking on the cell for the "Variable Type" until the word "Integer" or "Binary" appears in the cell, as shown in Exhibit 5.1.

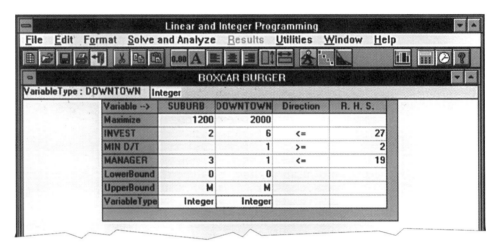

EXHIBIT 5.1   Designation of Integer Variables in WINQSB

Excel

In Excel, *integer* variables are denoted by using the Add screen in Solver, as shown in Exhibit 5.2. Here the Cell Reference includes the cells containing the values for the decision variables required to be integer. Then the Constraint bar is pulled down to "int."

EXHIBIT 5.2   Designation of Integer Variables in Excel

The same procedure is followed for *binary* variables, but, in addition, when using the Add screen, we would have to restrict the variables to "≤ 1", as shown in Exhibit 5.3.

EXHIBIT 5.3   Additional Constraints for Binary Variables

194

LINDO

In LINDO, the variables restricted to be integers are listed after the END statement on the data input screen by typing GIN (which stands for *general integer*) followed by a single variable name. Thus, if X1 and X5 were restricted to integers, the input would be.

END
GIN X1
GIN X5

If the first three variables listed in the program (say, X1, X2, X3) are restricted to integers, this conveyed by the following:

END
GIN 3

B*inary* variables are designated in LINDO by the INT command. Thus, if X3 and X6 are restricted to binary variables, the commands would be:

END
INT X3
INT X6

If the first five variables are restricted to be binary, this can be done using the following:

END
INT 5

PROBLEMS

Problems 1–8 can be solved graphically.

1. MANUFACTURING. Plant Equipment Corporation (PEC) manufactures two large industrial machines—a metal compactor and a drill press. Next month PEC will convert its production facilities to produce new machine designs and will cease producing the current models. PEC must determine its production schedule for this month, however.

   PEC could sell up to three compactors and two drill presses to customers who are not anxious to pay the increased price PEC will charge for the new models. Current models net PEC a $24,000 profit for metal compactors and $30,000 for drill presses. Each metal compactor requires 50 hours to produce, whereas each drill press requires 60 hours to produce; 160 production hours are available during the current month.

   a. Formulate this problem as an integer linear programming problem.

   b. Enumerate all feasible points to determine the optimal integer linear programming solution.

   c. Solve the problem as a linear program and note that when the optimal solution is rounded (up, down, or off), the result is *not* the optimal integer solution.

   d. Why would a linear programming model be a correct model if the production process were to continue indefinitely?

2. RESTAURANT OPERATION. Jackson's Sports Bar and Grill would like to minimize the cost of installing television sets throughout the restaurant so that it can accommodate a potential viewership of at least 750 patrons. It is considering purchasing two models of Sony televisions. The large-screen 60-inch model costs $3500 and, with proper placement, could be viewed by 150 customers. The 27-inch models cost $800 each and can be seen by 35 customers. Jackson's wishes to have at least one 60-inch television and no more than 20 27-inch models.

   a. Formulate the model for the problem faced by Jackson's.

   b. Solve for the optimal linear programming solution. Round the solution to integer values. What is the total cost of the rounded solution?

   c. Solve for the optimal solution for the integer programming model. Did you get the rounded solution of part (b)? What is the total cost of the optimal integer solution?

3. HAZARDOUS WASTE DISPOSAL. Environmental Waste Disposal, Inc. (EWD) of Chicago, Illinois, specializes in transporting hazardous waste to land fills. There are few such agencies in the area, and so a backlog of demand for these services has developed. The firm would like to purchase at least six new trucks and have the capability of transporting at least 9000 pounds of hazardous waste per day. Each truck will be used for only one trip per day from a client's location to the hazardous waste disposal site.

   Two companies manufacture the trucks required for this specialized operation. Safeco's model costs $60,000 and has a capacity of 3000 pounds of waste material. Kluge's model costs $40,000 and has a capacity of 1000 pounds of waste material.

   Each Safeco truck is equipped only with a front seat capable of transporting the driver and one other worker. The smaller Kluge model comes with both a front and back seat and is capable of transporting the driver and three other workers. EWD would like the capability of transporting a total of at least 18 workers on any given day.

   a. Formulate this problem as an integer linear programming model to minimize EWD's cost.

   b. Solve the problem using linear programming.

   c. Solve the problem as an integer linear program. Is the solution to the integer linear program a rounded solution of the linear programming model?

   d. What is the optimal total cost for the (i) linear programming solution and (ii) integer linear programming solution?

   e. Why should the total cost for the integer linear programming problem be larger than that of the linear programming problem?

4. PRODUCTION. Klone Computer (see Chapter 3, Problem 8) is making one last production run of its KCU and KCP computers before introducing its new line of models, which

includes CD-ROM drives, utilizes faster CPUs and floppy disk drives, and has larger hard disk drives. Because this is the last run of "old technology" machines, Klone's net profit per computer has been reduced from $100 and $250 to $75 and $105 for KCU and KCP models, respectively. The following table summarizes the resource requirements and unit profits for each computer model and the resources available for this *final* production run of these models.

Model	Floppy Drives	Hard Drives	Tower Cases	Production Hours	Unit Profit
KCU	2	0	1	.4	$ 75
KCP	1	1	1	.6	$105
Available	2800	1400	2000	960	

a. Formulate this problem and solve it as a *linear* program. Note that the optimal solution to the linear program gives integer values. Why is this also the optimal solution to the AILP model?

b. From the sensitivity analysis, determine the increase in profit Klone should experience from extra labor hours. What is the upper limit on labor hours in order for this extra profit per labor hour to be valid?

c. Suppose the number of labor hours increased from 960 to 970. According to the result in part (b), what should be the increase in profit for Klone Computer? Solve the *linear* programming model with 970 labor hours available. Show that this result is attained only with an optimal solution that has fractional values.

d. Round your solution to part (c) by (i) rounding off, (ii) rounding up, and (iii) rounding down. In each case determine whether the result is feasible or infeasible and determine the profit for the feasible results.

e. Solve for the optimal AILP solution for the model with 970 labor hours. Did you get any of the rounded answers of part (d)? Did you get the same increase in profit found in part (c)?

f. What is the difference in the optimal profit between the true optimal AILP solution and the best rounded LP solution? *Note:* This illustrates that when large quantities are involved, rounding the optimal linear programming solution usually gives a "good enough" answer.

5. HELICOPTER SERVICE. Wolfe Helicopters is to begin flying passengers from a helicopter pad in Berkeley, California, to the two large airports in the area, Oakland and San Francisco. Wolfe will operate two models—the HG30 and the WH10. The characteristics for each aircraft are given in the following table.

	Estimated Monthly Profit	Purchase Cost	Required Monthly Maintenance (Hours)	Capacity
HG30	$3,000	$600,000	20	20
WH10	$2,000	$200,000	60	8

Wolfe has $1,800,000 available to purchase helicopters, and it wishes to have a total fleet capacity of at least 25. It also has a service contract with HMC, a helicopter maintenance company, for up to 140 hours of maintenance per month. (Additional hours would require a complete renegotiation of the service contract at a much higher cost; thus, Wolfe wishes not to exceed the 140 hours of the contract.)

a. Formulate and solve for the mix of helicopters that would bring Wolfe its maximum monthly profit.

b. Show graphically that there are only five feasible integer solutions. Evaluate the profit of each and verify that the answer to part (a) is correct.

c. What would be Wolfe's optimal mix of helicopters if it had only $1,799,999 available to purchase helicopters? If Wolfe had only $1,799,999 for the purchase of helicopters, would you "invest" a dollar with Wolfe for a small percentage of the increased profits?

6. PHYSICAL FITNESS. Sarah Stone measures her performance in the gym as follows: 10 points for every Nautilus machine used, and 1 point for every minute on the treadmill. Including preparation time and transition time between machines, Sarah spends an average of 6.5 minutes on each Nautilus machine. Formulate an MILP for Sarah and determine the optimal number of Nautilus machines she should use and the number of minutes she should spend on the treadmill if:

- The total time of the workout is not to exceed 1 hour.

- At least 20 minutes must be spent on the treadmill.

- At least 5 different Nautilus machines should be used.

7. AIRCRAFT LEASING. Des Moines Airlines (DMA) is a small new commuter airline that will locate its hub in Des Moines, Iowa. DMA plans to have 11 mechanics, 15 pilots, and 21 flight attendants available daily.

DMA will be leasing two types of aircraft—the DM4 and the B77. The Federal Aviation Association's (FAA'S) mandatory requirements for these aircraft are summarized in the following table. DMA's objective is to maximize its total passenger capacity.

	Mechanics Required	Pilots Required	Flight Attendants Required
DM4	1	1	1
B77	1	2	3

a. Formulate and graph a feasible region for this problem. Without knowing the seat capacity on each aircraft, why can we say for certain that the optimal solution to the linear programming model would also be the optimal solution to the integer linear programming model? (Hint: *What are the possible optimal points for a linear programming model?*)

b. The seat capacity was 25 for the DM4 and 70 for the B77. What is the optimal leasing plan for DMA?

c. If DMA must make do with one less worker to operate its fleet, should it be a mechanic, a pilot, or a flight attendant?

d. Excluding certain fixed costs (including pilot costs), each seat of fleet capacity gives DMA a net yearly profit of $25,000. If DMA plans to pay its pilots $110,000 per year, including benefits, should it hire an additional pilot?

e. DMA is considering redesigning the interior of the B77 to increase its seat capacity beyond 70. What is the maximum seating capacity for which the leasing plan found in part (a) remains optimal?

f. Suppose DMA could squeeze one more row of three seats into each of the two types of aircraft, increasing the seating capacity of the DM4 to 28 and the B77 to 73. Given no other changes in the assumptions of the problem, would the optimal leasing decision change? What practical considerations might you consider before implementing such a change?

8. AIRCRAFT LEASING. Consider the problem faced by Des Moines Airlines (DMA) in problem 7. Now suppose that the B77 aircraft actually requires 4 flight attendants rather than three.

a. Solve for the optimal solution to the (i) linear programming model and (ii) integer programming model.

b. Explain why the optimal solution in (ii) gives a smaller total seat capacity than that in (i).

9. AIRCRAFT LEASING (*continued*). Consider the Des Moines Airlines (DMA) problem referred to in problem 7. Now suppose DMA is considering leasing a third aircraft, the L-200. The L-200, as currently configured, has a seating capacity of 110 and requires two mechanics, three pilots, and five flight attendants.

a. Solve the DMA problem as a *linear* program and show that the solution found in 7(b) remains optimal; that is, no L-200 aircraft should be leased.

   b. According to the sensitivity analysis for the linear program in part (a), what is the minimum seating capacity for the L-200 that would justify DMA leasing them?

   c. Suppose the seating arrangement of the L-200 could be reconfigured so that the capacity is increased to 120. Solve for the optimal leasing plan for DMA.

10. PRODUCTION. The R&D department of Little Trykes, Inc. has developed six new prototype tricycle models that can go into production in the coming year. The amount of plastic and the number of big and small wheels for each model, the monthly availabilities, the fixed cost of beginning production, and the unit profits excluding fixed costs are given in the following table.

	Unit Profit	Small Wheels	Big Wheels	Plastic (lb.)	Setup Costs
Liltryke	$1.50	3	0	.8	$16,500
Pinktryke	$2.00	1	2	1.2	$18,000
Herotryke	$2.25	2	1	1.5	$17,500
Robinhood	$2.75	2	1	2.1	$18,000
Jeeptryke	$3.00	2	1	1.8	$20,000
Monster	$3.50	0	3	3.0	$17,000
Available Monthly		10,000	8000	9000	

    Formulate a MILP model for this problem to determine how many units of each product should be produced if Little Trykes wishes to keep the amount of money spent on new setups to a maximum of $70,000. (Hint: *Convert all production data to yearly figures.*)

11. PRODUCTION (*continued*). For the problem faced by Little Trykes, Inc., (problem 10), assume that the maximum expenditure of $70,000 for new setups is just one part of five company goals. The other four are:

- If the Herotryke is produced, the Robinhood will not be produced.
- At least four new models are to be produced.
- If the Jeeptryke is produced, the Monster will also be produced.
- At least 1500 pounds of plastic should be left over each month for use in the company's other products.

    Management wishes to meet at least four of these five goals. Formulate a MILP model for this problem and solve for the optimal production schedule.

12. MERCHANDISING. Office Warehouse has been downsizing its operations. It is in the process of moving to a much smaller location and reducing the number of different computer products it carries. Coming under scrutiny are 10 products Office Warehouse has carried for the past year. For each of these products, Office Warehouse has estimated the floor space required for effective display, the capital required to restock if the product line is retained, and the short-term loss that Office Warehouse will incur if the corresponding product is eliminated (through liquidation sales, etc.).

Product Line	Manufacturer	Cost of Liquidation	Capital to Restock	Floor Space (ft²)
Notebook computer	Toshiba	$10,000	$15,000	50
Notebook computer	Compaq	$ 8,000	$12,000	60
PC	Compaq	$20,000	$25,000	200
PC	Packard Bell	$12,000	$22,000	200
MacIntosh computer	Apple	$25,000	$20,000	145
Monitor	Packard Bell	$ 4,000	$12,000	85
Monitor	Sony	$15,000	$13,000	50
Printer	Apple	$ 5,000	$14,000	100
Printer	HP	$18,000	$25,000	150
Printer	Epson	$ 6,000	$10,000	125

Office Warehouse wishes to minimize the loss due to liquidation of product lines subject to the following conditions:

- At least four of these product lines will be eliminated.

- The remaining products will occupy no more than 600 square feet of floor space.

- If one product line from a particular manufacturer is eliminated, all products from that manufacturer will be eliminated. (This affects Compaq, Packard Bell, and Apple.)

- At least two computer models (notebook, PC, or MacIntosh), at least one monitor model, and at least one printer model will continue to be carried by Office Warehouse.

- At most $75,000 is to be spent on restocking product lines.

- If the Toshiba notebook computer is retained, the Epson line of printers will also be retained.

a. Formulate this problem as a BILP, with $Y_i = 1$ representing the condition that product line i is to be liquidated.

b. Solve for the optimal policy for Office Warehouse.

13. SOFTWARE DEVELOPMENT. The Korvex Corporation is a company concerned with developing CD-ROM software applications that it sells to major computer manufacturers to include as "packaged items" when consumers purchase systems with CD-ROM drives. The company is currently evaluating the feasibility of developing six new applications. Specific information concerning each of these applications is summarized in the following table.

Application	Projected Development Cost	Programmers Required	Projected Present Worth Net Profit
1	$ 400,000	6	$2,000,000
2	$1,100,000	18	$3,600,000
3	$ 940,000	20	$4,000,000
4	$ 760,000	16	$3,000,000
5	$1,260,000	28	$4,400,000
6	$1,800,000	34	$6,200,000

Korvex has a staff of 60 programmers and has allocated $3.5 million for development of new applications.

a. Formulate a binary integer linear programming model for the situation faced by the Korvex Corporation.

b. Solve for the optimal choice of applications to be developed.

14. SOFTWARE DEVELOPMENT (*continued*). For the Korvex Corporation problem (problem 13), assume that the following additional conditions hold:

- It is anticipated that those interested in application 4 will also be interested in application 5, and vice versa. Thus, if either application 4 or application 5 is developed, the other must also be developed.

- The underlying concepts of application 2 make sense only if application 1 is included in the package. Thus, application 2 will be developed only if application 1 is developed.

- Applications 3 and 6 have similar themes; thus, if application 3 is developed, application 6 will not be developed, and vice versa.

- To ensure quality products, Korvex does not wish to expand its product line too rapidly. Accordingly, it wishes to develop at most three of the potential application products at this time.

a. Formulate constraints reflecting each of the above conditions.

b. Incorporate these constraints into the model developed for Problem 13 and determine the optimal choice of applications Korvex should develop.

15. RESTAURANT CREW ASSIGNMENT. Burger Boy Restaurant is open from 8:00 A.M. to 10:00 P.M. daily. In addition to the hours of business, a crew of workers must arrive one hour early to help set up the restaurant for the day's operations, and another crew of workers must stay one hour after 10:00 P.M. to clean up after closing.

Burger Boy operates with nine different shifts:

Shift		Type	Daily Salary
1.	7AM— 9AM	Part-time	$15
2.	7AM—11AM	Part-time	$25
3.	7AM— 3PM	Full-time	$52
4.	11AM— 3PM	Part-time	$22
5.	11AM— 7PM	Full-time	$54
6.	3PM— 7PM	Part-time	$24
7.	3PM—11PM	Full-time	$55
8.	7PM—11PM	Part-time	$23
9.	9PM—11PM	Part-time	$16

A needs assessment study has been completed, which divided the workday at Burger Boy into eight two-hour blocks. The number of employees needed for each block is as follows:

Time Block	Employees Needed
7AM— 9AM	8
9AM—11AM	10
11AM— 1PM	22
1PM— 3PM	15
3PM— 5PM	10
5PM— 7PM	20
7PM— 9PM	16
9PM—11PM	8

Burger Boy wants at least 40% of all employees at the peak time periods of 11:00 A.M. to 1:00 P.M. and 5:00 P.M. to 7:00 P.M. to be full-time employees. At least two full-time employees must be on duty when the restaurant opens at 7:00 A.M. and when it closes at 11:00 P.M..

a. Formulate a model Burger Boy can use to determine how many employees it should hire for each of its nine shifts to minimize its overall daily employee costs.

b. Solve for the optimal solution.

16. LAW ENFORCEMENT. The police department of the city of Flint, Michigan, has divided the city into 15 patrol sectors, such that the response time of a patrol unit (squad car) will be less than three minutes between any two points within the sector.

Until recently, 15 units, one located in each sector, patrolled the streets of Flint from 7:00 P.M. to 3:00 A.M.. However, severe budget cuts have forced the city to eliminate some patrols. The chief of police has mandated that each sector be covered by at least one unit located either within that sector or in an adjacent sector.

The accompanying figure depicts the 15 patrol sectors of Flint, Michigan. Formulate and solve a BILP that will determine the minimum number of units required to implement the chief's policy.

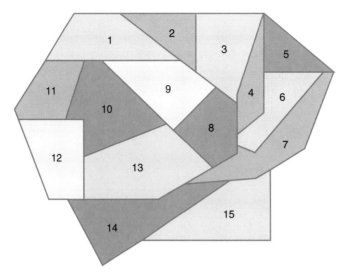

Police Patrol Sectors Flint, Michigan

17. VANPOOLING. Logitech, a rapidly growing high-tech company located in suburban Boston, Massachusetts, has been encouraging its employees to carpool. These efforts have met with only moderate success, and now the company is setting aside up to $250,000 to purchase small- and medium-size vans and minibuses to establish a vanpool program that will transport employees between various pickup points and company headquarters. Four models of vans and two models of minibuses are under consideration, as detailed in the following table.

	Maker	Cost	Passenger Capacity	Annual Maintenance
Vans				
Nissan	Japan	$26,000	7	$ 5,000
Toyota	Japan	$30,000	8	$ 3,500
Plymouth	U.S.	$24,000	9	$ 6,000
Ford (Stretch)	U.S.	$32,000	11	$ 8,000
Minibuses				
Mitsubishi	Japan	$50,000	20	$ 7,000
General Motors	U.S.	$60,000	24	$11,000

Formulate and solve a vehicle purchase model for Logitech that will maximize the total passenger capacity of the fleet given that:

- Up to $250,000 will be spent on vehicles.
- Annual maintenance cost should not exceed $50,000.
- Total number of vehicles purchased should not exceed eight.
- At least one minibus should be purchased.
- At least three vans should be purchased.
- At least half the vehicles should be made in the United States.

18. VANPOOLING (continued). It was pointed out that integer solutions are highly volatile with moderate changes to input coefficients. Consider the problem faced by Logitech (Problem 17).

a. Determine the optimal solution if the amount Logitech committed for vehicle purchase were: (i) $253,900*; (ii) $254,000; (iii) $249,900*; (iv) $259,900*; (v) $260,000. Comment.

b. Characterize the problem if the amount Logitech committed to the program were $100,000.

*You may have to change the integer tolerance of your computer program for these values. In WINQSB go to Change Integer Tolerance in the Solve and Analyze menu; in

Excel go to Tolerance in the Options dialogue box of Solver; in LINDO change the entry in IP Optimality Tol on the Options screen in the Edit menu.

19. MANUFACTURING. Floyd's Fabrication has just received an order from Gimbal Plumbing Fixtures for 100,000 specially designed three-inch-diameter casings to be delivered in one week. The contract price was negotiated up front; hence, Floyd's maximum profit will be obtained when its costs are minimized.

Floyd's has three production facilities capable of producing the casings. Production costs do not vary between locations, but the changeover (setup) costs do vary, as does the cost of transporting the finished items to Gimbal. The following table details these costs.

Location	Changeover Cost	Transportation Cost (per 1000)	Maximum Weekly Production
Springfield	$1,200	$224	65,000
Oak Ridge	$1,100	$280	50,000
Westchester	$1,000	$245	55,000

a. Formulate this problem as a fixed-charge MILP model.

b. Solve for the amount to be produced at each location.

20. PRODUCT DEVELOPMENT. The electric car division at Detroit Motor Company has promised that at least three new models will be developed and produced within the next four years. Accordingly, the company has committed up to 50 engineers this year, 60 next year, and 75 in the third year to this division. In addition, a support staff of up to 8 this year, 12 the next, and 20 the third year will be made available to the division.

Currently, six models are under consideration, code-named the Alpha, Beta, Delta, Gamma, Kappa, and Sigma, respectively. The projected number of engineering and support staff hours required each year for the development of each model and the expected net present worth profits of each potential electric car line are given in the following table.

	Year 1		Year 2		Year 3		Present Net Worth
	Engineer	Staff	Engineer	Staff	Engineer	Staff	($M's)
Alpha	15,000	5000	40,000	5000	40,000	8000	12
Beta	18,000	5000	25,000	4000	30,000	7000	11
Delta	19,000	3000	19,000	3000	19,000	3000	9
Gamma	20,000	4000	25,000	6000	30,000	7500	15
Kappa	8,000	2000	12,000	2000	18,000	3000	7
Sigma	22,000	5000	27,000	7000	32,000	8000	20

Detroit has decided that if the Alpha model is produced the Beta model should not be produced, and if the Sigma model is produced the Alpha model should be produced. If engineers work an average of 2500 hours a year, and support staff an average of 2000 hours per year, develop and solve a BILP model to determine which models the electric car division at Detroit should produce.

21. LABOR FORCE REDUCTIONS. Reductions in the defense budget are causing problems for Williams, Osborne, and Evans (WOE), a leading supplier of C^3I systems.[5] WOE is faced with the need to downsize its labor force, while, at the same time, reduce waste and improve its competitive position. Its problem is to develop a mix of labor skills and functions which will not only be adequate to perform ongoing work but also meet certain headcount or cost reduction goals.

The following table summarizes the levels and types of people currently at WOE, along with other relevant data.

---

[5] The authors wish to thank R. N. Miller of TRW for this problem.

Manpower Characteristic Summary

Grade	Title	Weekly Salary	Job Category	Time Charges		Current Headcount
				Direct	Overhead	
100	Operations manager	$1,600	Management	20%	80%	40
100	Department manager	$1,200	Management	30%	70%	200
100	Section head	$1,000	Management	80%	20%	900
100	Engineer	$ 800	Technical	100%	0%	6000
101	Technician	$ 600	Technical	100%	0%	3000
102	Business support	$ 500	Administration	30%	70%	150
103	Secretary	$ 350	Clerical	30%	70%	900

A number of goals have been established for the downsizing effort. These goals, which impact management's flexibility in achieving its objectives, are as follows:

- The combined total of operations managers and department managers should be reduced by 50%.
- The section head level of management should be eliminated.
- Operations managers are to number no more than 20% of the department managers.
- The ratio of technical personnel to management personnel must be at least 20:1.
- Between 5% and 10% of the total headcount must be clerical.
- Administration is to make up only 1% to 2% of the total headcount.
- Overhead charges must be between 5% and 10% of direct charges.
- Direct labor must equal $4.8 million weekly.
- At least six operations managers are needed to lead the diverse technical areas.
- Department manager direct labor charges should not make up more than 10% of the technical labor charges.
- The ratio of engineers to technicians should not exceed 4:1.
- To assure a balanced workforce, the percentage decrease or increase in headcount devoted to any grade level must not exceed 20%. (For example, there are currently 7140 grade-level 100s; this is 7140/11,190 = 63.8% of the total headcount. After downsizing, this percentage could increase or decrease by 0.2(63.8%) = 12.76%. Thus, the number of grade-level 100 personnel after downsizing must be between 51.04% and 76.56% of the new total headcount.)

What staff reduction plan minimizes WOE's total weekly payroll?

PROBLEMS 22–26 ARE EXAMPLES OF SPECIAL CASES OF INTEGER LINEAR PROGRAMS THAT WILL BE EXPLORED IN CHAPTER 6 AND IN CHAPTER 16 ON THE ACCOMPANYING CD-ROM. HERE WE FOCUS ON THE ILP APPROACH TO THESE PROBLEMS.

22. CONTRACT AWARDS. The City of Little Rock, Arkansas has four electrical projects that it has sent out for bids. Four different contractors have bid on each. Since all projects are to be performed simultaneously, only one project is to be awarded to each contractor. This table gives the respective bids (in $1,000's) for each of the projects.

Projects

Contractor	Repair Street Lighting (4th Street)	Install New Air Conditioners at High School	Modernize Courthouse Electrical Systems	Improve Lighting at Baseball Stadium
Green & Sons	55	12	33	22
Kalib Company	48	15	40	30
SSS Electric	50	14	37	35
Burke Electric	75	25	42	37

a. Formulate this problem as a BILP using binary decision variables Xij to denote whether or not Contractor i is to be awarded Project j.

b. Using a BILP approach, determine the optimal assignment of contractors to jobs.

(Note: This is an example of an "assignment problem," which will be discussed in Chapter 6.)

23. TRANSPORTATION. A Texas farm cooperative grows tomatoes in two different locations—Cleo Farms and Dixon Farms. These tomatoes are sent by truck to three different processing locations in Brownsville, Lubbock, and Denton. The current crop has produced 100,000 pounds of tomatoes at Cleo Farms and 160,000 pounds at Dixon Farms. Processing capacities at the three processing locations are 80,000 pounds at Brownsville, 64,000 pounds at Lubbock, and 132,000 at Denton.

   Transportation costs for shipping a truckload of tomatoes between each growing and processing location are given in the following table. [Each truckload consists of two tons (= 4000 pounds) of tomatoes.]

		To	
	Brownsville	Lubbock	Denton
From			
Cleo Farms	$375	$290	$315
Dixon Farms	$275	$325	$380

   The entire crop of tomatoes from the Cleo and Dixon farms is to be processed. Expressing all data in terms of truckloads, use AILP to determine the number of truckloads of tomatoes that should be sent from each farm to each processing location in order to minimize the total transportation costs to the farm cooperative.

(Note: This is an example of a "transportation problem," which will be discussed in Chapter 6.)

24. ROUTE SELECTION. Desert Trucking must deliver a piano from Palm Springs to Irvine, California. The accompanying figure gives the possible routes Desert Trucking can take.

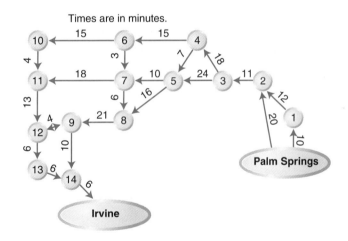

a. Define each route between two junctions as a binary variable. Write a BILP to minimize the time required to travel from Palm Springs to Irvine by including constraints with the following requirements: (i) one route must be taken out of Palm Springs; (ii) one route must be taken into Irvine; and (iii) for all other junctions "the number of routes taken that enter the junction" must equal "the number of routes taken that leave the junction."

b. Solve for the minimum transportation time for the delivery of the piano from Palm Springs to Irvine.

(Note: This is an example of a "shortest path problem," which will be discussed in Chapter 6.)

25. SPACE PROGRAM. Excess space on NASA space shuttle flights is used periodically to conduct experiments submitted by high school students. Suppose the value of each experiment is rated by a panel of judges and given a score between 0 and 100. The top

five projects will be considered for inclusion on the next flight of the *Endeavor* shuttle flight. Because the *Endeavor* does not have enough space to accommodate all five projects, NASA's goal is to maximize the total value of the experiments (as measured by the total score) that can be accommodated using the excess space available.

On the next flight, 98 cubic feet of space is available for student projects. The top five scores and their respective space requirements are summarized in the following table.

Place	Point Score	Volume (cubic feet)
1	100	99
2	95	75
3	80	51
4	55	50
5	40	49

a. Formulate this problem as a BILP model with one constraint. Solve for the optimal set of experiments.

b. Solve for the optimal set of experiments to take when there is: (i) 99 cubic feet available; (ii) 100 cubic feet available; and (iii) 101 cubic feet available. Note the discontinuity in the solution and the optimal value of the objective function as the space available increases from 98 to 101 cubic feet.

(*Note: This is an example of a "knapsack problem," which will be discussed in the* Nonlinear Models *chapter* (*Chapter 16*) *on the* CD-ROM).

26. NEWS COLLECTION. In 1996 CNN had to send a group of up to eight correspondents to cover an outburst of ethnic fighting in Sarajevo, Bosnia, in time for the 11:00 P.M. news report. There were no direct flights from their location in Italy to Sarajevo. CNN had the means to arrange "relatively safe" passage for a certain number of the correspondents along various routes utilizing a variety of means (two by car here, three by truck there, etc.). The accompanying figure shows these possible routes and the maximum number of correspondents that could be escorted along each route.

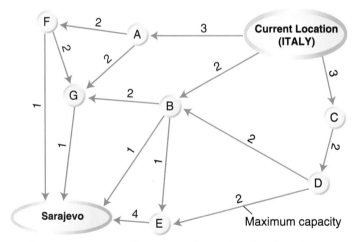

Numbers on arcs represent the maximum that can be taken along the route

a. Formulate an AILP model CNN could have used to maximize the number of correspondents that would have been able to find safe passage to Sarajevo. Use the decision variables, Xij, to represent the number of correspondents that travel from location i to location j.

b. Use AILP to solve for the maximum number of CNN correspondents that could have safely reached Sarajevo. What routes should they have taken?

(*Note: This is an example of a "maximal flow problem," which will be discussed in Chapter 6.*)

CASE 1: *Pentagonal Pictures, Inc.*

Pentagonal Pictures produces motion pictures in Hollywood and distributes them nationwide. Currently, it is considering 10 possible films; these include dramas, comedies, and action adventures. The success of each film depends somewhat on both the strength of the subject matter and the appeal of the cast. Estimating the cost of a film and its potential box office draw is inexact at best; still, the studio must rely on its experts' opinions to help it evaluate which projects to undertake.

The following table lists the films currently under consideration by Pentagonal Pictures, including the projected cost and box office gross receipts.

Film	Rating	Type	No-Name Cast		Big Star Cast	
			Cost	Box Office Gross	Cost	Box Office Gross
Two-Edged Sword	PG-13	Action	$ 5M	$ 8M	$10M	$15M
Lady in Waiting	R	Drama	$12M	$20M	$25M	$35M
Yesterday	PG	Drama	$ 8M	$10M	$12M	$26M
Golly Gee	PG	Comedy	$ 7M	$12M	$15M	$26M
Why I Cry	PG-13	Drama	$15M	$30M	$30M	$45M
Captain Kid	PG	Comedy	$10M	$20M	$17M	$28M
Oh Yes!	R	Comedy	$ 4M	$ 7M	$ 8M	$12M
Nitty Gritty	PG	Comedy	$11M	$15M	$14M	$20M
The Crash	R	Action	$20M	$28M	$40M	$65M
Bombs Away	R	Action	$25M	$37M	$50M	$80M

In addition to these production costs, each movie will have a $1 million advertising budget, which will increase to $3 million if the movie is to have a "big star" cast. Assume that the studio receives 80% of a film's gross receipts. The company would like to maximize its net profit (gross profit − production costs − advertising costs) for the year.

Pentagonal has a production budget of $100 million and an advertising budget of $15 million. In addition, it would like to adhere to the following restrictions:

1. At least half the films produced should have a rating of PG or PG-13.
2. At least two comedies are to be produced.
3. If *The Crash* is produced, *Bombs Away* will not be.
4. At least one drama is to be produced.
5. At least two films should have big name casts.
6. At least two PG films should be produced.
7. At least one action movie with a big name cast should be produced.

Prepare a report for Pentagonal Pictures that recommends which films should be produced and with which casts. Detail how the budgets will be spent. Include in your report a sensitivity analysis that considers how varying budgets for both production costs and advertising (while spending at most a total of $15 million) would affect your recommendation. Finally, discuss the effects of Pentagonal's seven restrictions and report the effect of requiring only six of the seven, five of the seven, and four of the seven to hold.

CASE 2: *Lake Saddleback Development Corporation*

Lake Saddleback Development Corporation (LSDC) is developing a planned community of homes and condominiums around a section of Lake Saddleback, Texas. The idea is to develop 300 acres of land it owns on and near the lake in such a way that it maximizes its profits from the development while offering an appropriate variety of different home plans in different products. In addition, the corporation wishes to analyze the feasibility of developing a 10-acre sports/recreational complex.

LSDC is building four products: (1) the Grand Estate Series; (2) the Glen Wood Collection; (3) the Lakeview Patio Homes; and (4) the Country Condominiums. Within each product are three to four floor plans of various styles, as described in the following list.

Plan	Selling Price	Size (sq. ft.)	Bedrooms	Bathrooms	Stories	Garage Size
Grand Estates						
The Trump*	$700,000	4000	5 + den	4	2	3 car
The Vanderbilt*	$680,000	3600	4 + den,	3	2	3 car
The Hughes*	$650,000	3000	4	3	1	3 car
The Jackson*	$590,000	2600	3	3	1	3 car
Glen Wood Collection						
Grand Cypress*	$420,000	2800	4 + den	3	2	3 car
Lazy Oak	$380,000	2400	4	3	2	2 car
Wind Row	$320,000	2200	3	3	2	2 car
Orangewood	$280,000	1800	3	$2\frac{1}{2}$	1	2 car
Lakeview Patio Homes						
Bayview*	$300,000	2000	4	$2\frac{1}{2}$	2	2 car
Shoreline	$270,000	1800	3 + den	$2\frac{1}{2}$	2	2 car
Docks Edge	$240,000	1500	3	$2\frac{1}{2}$	1	2 car
Golden Pier	$200,000	1200	2	2	1	2 car
Country Condominiums						
Country Stream	$220,000	1600	3	2	2	—
Weeping Willow	$160,000	1200	2	2	1	—
Picket Fence	$140,000	1000	2	$1\frac{1}{2}$	1	—

*Some of these models may occupy larger premium or lakeside lots with higher selling prices.

Lot Sizes

Lots for all models include the land on which the house resides, the garage (which is not considered part of the advertised square footage of the house), and yard space. It excludes outside parking and space for parks, roads, undeveloped landscape, and so on.

All models in the Grand Estate series are built on one-half acre lots, and 50 half-acre lots on the lake are to be used exclusively by the Grand Estate Series homes. The selling price of these exclusive homes will be an additional 30% plus $50,000 more than the models not on the lake. (For example, the $700,000 Trump model would sell for $960,000 if on the lake.) Each of the Grand Estate series plans must have at least eight units on the lake.

Some Grand Cypress models (in the Glen Wood Homes series) may be built on "premium" quarter-acre lots. These homes sell for $40,000 more than similar models on standard lots. In addition, some Bayview models (in the Lakeview Patio Homes series) may be built on "premium" one-sixth acre lots, which sell for $30,000 more than models built on standard lot sizes. No more than 25% of the total Grand Cypress models and 25% of the total Bayview models may be built on the premium lots.

Lot sizes for the Country Condominiums are fixed at 1500 square feet.

The minimum standard lot for homes in the Glen Wood and Lakeview series homes (except for the premium models) is $\frac{1}{10}$ of an acre. Lot sizes for certain models can be higher if the following calculation exceeds $\frac{1}{10}$ acre.

$$\text{Lot Size} = (\text{Ground Area of House})$$
$$+ (\text{Yard Size}) + (\text{Garage Size})$$

Ground Area The ground area of any single-story house is the advertised square footage of the house. The ground area for two-story homes is 75% of the advertised square footage.

Yard Size For homes in the Glen Wood series, yard sizes are 1200 square feet for single-story homes, and the same as the ground area of the house for two-story homes. For homes in the Lakeview Patio Home series, yard sizes are 900 square feet for single-story homes. For two-story homes in this series, the yard size is 600 square feet + 50% of the ground area of the house.

Garage Size Two-car garages occupy 500 square feet of ground space, and three-car garages occupy 750 square feet of ground space. Note that there are no garages for the Country Condominium models.

Parking

Current code requires one parking space per bedroom for each unit built. For example, outside parking space for two cars would be required for a four-bedroom house with a two-car garage. Each outside parking space will occupy 200 square feet of space. No more than 15 acres of the project may be used for *outside* parking. All parking for the Country Condominiums is outside.

Roads/Greenbelts, Etc.

A total of 1000 square feet per house is to be set aside for the building of roads, greenbelts, and small parks to add both to the aesthetics and necessities of the project.

Variety

Throughout the entire project, the following maximum and minimum percentages have been established by the marketing department (Note: Condominiums are included in the following figures.)

	Maximum	Minimum
Two-bedroom homes	25%	15%
Three-bedroom homes	40%	25%
Four-bedroom homes	40%	25%
Five-bedroom homes	15%	5%

In addition, none of the four products (Grand Estate, Glen Wood, Lakeview, and Country) is to make up more than 35% or less than 15% of the units built in the development. Furthermore, within each product, each plan must occupy between 20% and 35% of the total units of that product. For appearances' sake, no more than 70% of the single-family homes (all homes except the Country Condominiums) may be two-story homes.

Affordable Housing

In the affluent Lake Saddleback area, any house priced at $200,000 or below is considered "affordable" housing. The federal government requires at least 15% of the project to be designated affordable housing.

Profit

LSDC has determined the following percentages of the sales prices to be net profits:

Grand Estates	22%
Glen Wood	18%
Lakeview	20%
Country Condominiums	25%

Objectives

1. LSDC needs to determine the number of units of each plan of each product to build in order to maximize its profit.
2. If LSDC builds a 10-acre sports/recreation complex on the property, this would reduce the usable land by 10 acres and cost about $8 million to build. However, LSDC believes it can raise the cost of the homes as follows:

Grand Estates	5%
Glen Wood	3%
Lakeview*	2%
Country Condominiums	5%

All these increases can be considered additional profit to the net profit figures determined in the preceding. Naturally, LSDC will build this complex if this additional profit offsets its $8 million cost.

The Report

Prepare a detailed report analyzing this project and make suggestions for the number of each type of each unit to be built. Give and support your recommendations on whether or not to build the sports/recreation complex. Do appropriate "what-if" analyses and give a summary of your final recommendations.

Hint: You may wish to solve as a linear program and round.

---

*Except for the Golden Pier model, so that it may still qualify for affordable housing.

CHAPTER 6

NETWORK MODELS

Nature's Way is a regional distributor of health food products, whose primary customers live in southern California. Many manufacturers deliver their products directly to Nature's Way's warehouse, but for some products, Nature's Way must make the pickup itself. One of its weekly challenges is to schedule its big rig trucks for pickups from various manufacturers around the state. The locations of the pickups vary from week to week, but each truck must begin at the warehouse location in southern California, stop at several destinations to fill its trailer with products, and return.

Another situation the company faces involves the transportation of goods to its customers. In most instances, after Nature's Way receives a purchase order, the goods are taken from the company's inventory, loaded on small pickup trucks, and transported to the customer. In other cases, the company delivers the product directly from the manufacturer to the customer, leaving only a paper trail indicating that the item was in its inventory.

To determine how much product to order from manufacturers, Nature's Way employs several buyers, who review customer orders and the inventory position of the products within the company's warehouse. The buyers possess different skills and expertise, and Nature's Way must decide which buyers to assign to which group of manufacturers.

Each of these situations is typical of a problem that can be described using a *network model*. One network consists of the highways and cities the trucks must visit before returning to the warehouse. The company would like the trucks to make these trips at minimum cost. Another network is comprised of local streets that must be traversed in order to reach an ultimate destination in minimal time. Finally, there is a network of buyers and manufacturers that should be paired to maximize the efficiency of the purchasing operations.

The use of network models provides both a convenient way of expressing the situation pictorially and an efficient mechanism for finding optimal solutions with minimal input.

6.1   *I*NTRODUCTION TO NETWORKS

Our mental image of a network may be a series of wires that make up an electrical network, a system of roads that make up a transportation network, or perhaps a group of affiliated stations that make up a television network. Whatever the image, our concept involves some entities (microchips, cities, local television stations) that are somehow linked together (by wires, roads, satellite transmissions). The entity can have or use some resource (electrical current, delivery trucks, television programming) that is "delivered" over the links at some cost. This intuitive description does, in fact, provide the basis for what management scientists call **networks**.

In management science models, the "entities" are represented by *nodes* in the network, some of which are linked together by *arcs* connecting one node with another. At each of the nodes, there may be some quantity of a resource, such as current generated or required, trucks available or needed, or television shows sent or received. To "travel" on each of the arcs one must pay a cost in units, such as dollars, miles, or time, and the amount that can be "transported" over each of the arcs may be limited. These quantities are known as the *functions* defined on the nodes and arcs.

Network

A **network** problem is one that can be represented by

1. A set of nodes
2. A set of arcs
3. Functions defined on the nodes and/or arcs

Network models are important for three basic reasons:

1. Many business problems naturally lend themselves to a network formulation.
2. Network problems are integer mathematical programming problems, but, because of their special structure, under very unrestrictive conditions the integer constraints can be ignored and the optimal solution is guaranteed to be integer valued anyway.
3. Network problems can be solved by more compact and efficient algorithms than those used for general linear and integer programming problems.

While each of the network problems presented in this chapter can be modeled using linear programming, more efficient special-purpose algorithms have been developed for their solution. These algorithms are detailed on the accompanying CD-ROM. In this chapter, we analyze the output from such algorithms and examine how the information is used in decision making. Thus, our approach is to present for each model:

- a problem statement defining the model
- the network representation
- the assumptions required for a standard computer solution
- the linear programming formulation
- an analysis of the computer output for the problem

NETWORK
TERMINOLOGY

Most of the terms used in conjunction with network models have common-sense meanings, as described in the following.

Flow

When two nodes are connected by an arc, a *flow* of some kind (current, traffic, microwaves, time, etc.) can occur directly between them. The amount of flow the decision maker will choose to send between the two nodes is typically a decision variable. This flow can sometimes be restricted by a *maximum capacity* that is permitted along the arc. In other instances, a required lower bound may exist for the flow along an arc. In most, but not all, network problems, this lower bound is assumed to be 0 (there cannot be "negative flow"). Figure 6.1 indicates the notation used for the flow between nodes i and j.

FIGURE 6.1   Flow

For example, Xij could represent the amount of oil shipped from a port in Alaska (node i) to one in Los Angeles (node j) aboard a tanker. Uij would be the maximum amount of oil the ship could carry, and Lij the minimum amount of oil the company determines is economically feasible for the tanker to make the trip.

Directed/Undirected Arcs

Flow is sometimes allowed in only one direction. This can be indicated by putting an arrow at the end of the arc into the terminal node. In this case the arc is said to be a *directed arc*. In the absence of this restriction, no arrow is placed on the arc, and it is called an *undirected arc*. Directed and undirected arcs are depicted in Figure 6.2. Any undirected arc between two nodes can be replaced by two directed arcs, one in each direction. If the entire network is made up of directed arcs, the network is represented by a *directed graph*, or a *digraph*.

FIGURE 6.2   Directed/Undirected Arcs

A common example of an undirected arc is a pipe in which a liquid flows in either direction. A typical example of a directed arc is a one-way street.

Adjacent Nodes

A node (j) is *adjacent* to another node (i), if an arc joins node i to node j. Figure 6.3 illustrates this concept for both undirected and directed networks. Consider an undirected network, such as a network of power relay stations in which power can be transmitted either way between the stations. Power station i (node i) is adjacent to power station j (node j), and power station j is adjacent to station i, *if there is a power line (arc) between them*. In directed networks, such as a network of bases run by a batter in baseball,

In this undirected graph, node j is adjacent to node i, and node i is adjacent to node j, since there is an arc from node j to node i. Node j is also adjacent to node k, and node k is adjacent to node j. However, node i is not adjacent to node k, or vice versa.

In this directed graph, node j is adjacent to node i, but node i is not adjacent to node j, since there is no arc from node j to node i. However, node j is adjacent to node k, and node k is adjacent to node j.

FIGURE 6.3   Adjacent Nodes

third base (node j) is adjacent to second base (node i), but not vice versa. For node i to be adjacent to node j, there must be another directed arc from node j back to node i.

Paths/Connected Nodes

The collection of arcs formed by a series of adjacent nodes, such as nodes 1, 3, 4, 5 in Figure 6.4, is a *path* between node 1 and node 5. When a path exists between two nodes, these nodes are said to be *connected*. Since there is no path between nodes 1 and 7, these nodes are not connected.

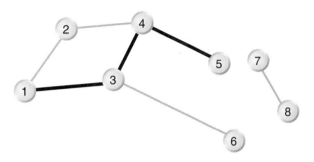

The selected arcs from node 1 to node 3, node 3 to node 4, and node 4 to node 5 form a **path** from node 1 to node 5; node 1 is **connected** to node 5.

There is **no path** between node 1 and node 7; node 1 is **not connected** to node 7.

FIGURE 6.4   Paths/Connected Nodes

Consider a system of highways connecting major cities in the United States and major cities in England. A series of highways connect Los Angeles and Chicago, and another series of highways connect London with Manchester. There is no series of highways between Chicago and London, however; thus, Chicago and London are not connected.

Cycles/Trees/Spanning Trees

Figures 6.5*a*, *b*, and *c* illustrate a set of arcs that form a cycle, a tree, and a spanning tree, respectively. In Figure 6.5*a*, a path can be traced from a node which returns to the same node without using any arc twice. This circuitous path is called a *cycle*. If the arcs of a series of connected nodes contain *no cycles*, as in Figure 6.5*b*, the resulting figure is a *tree*. A tree that connects *all* nodes in a network, as in Figure 6.5*c*, is a *spanning tree*.

A plane for a major shuttle service that travels from Washington, D.C., to New York to Boston forms a tree among the Washington, New York, and Boston destinations. If the plane then returns directly to Washington from Boston, however, it does not constitute a tree since it has made a cycle. By contrast, metropolitan subway systems are frequently constructed as a spanning tree where each station can be reached from any other station in the system, yet there are no cycles (owing to high construction costs).

It can be easily shown that a tree connecting n nodes consists of n-1 connected arcs. Thus, as shown in Figure 6.5*c*, a spanning tree:

1. connects all nodes of the network
2. contains no cycles
3. consists of n-1 arcs

Spanning trees play a significant role in many network analyses. For example, the optimal solution to many network optimization problems consists of flows along arcs that form a spanning tree for the network.[1]

_____
[1]For those who have studied the simplex method (in Supplement CD3 on the CD-ROM), a spanning tree is equivalent to the set of basic variables for a problem.

CYCLES

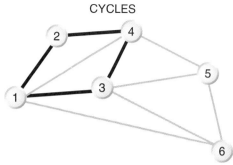

(a) The selected arcs form a **cycle**. A path can be traced from node 1 to node 1 via nodes 2,4, and 3, respectively.

TREES

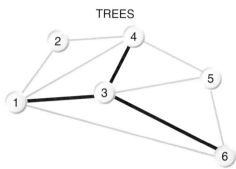

(b) The selected arcs shown form a **tree** connecting four nodes (nodes 1,3,4, and 6). They contain no cycles.

SPANNING TREES

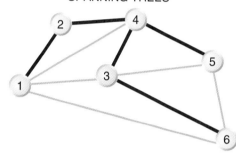

(c) The selected arcs from node 1 to node 2, node 2 to node 4, node 4 to node 5, node 3 to node 4, and node 3 to node 6 form a **spanning tree** for the network. All nodes are connected, and there are no cycles.

FIGURE 6.5   Cycles and Trees

6.2   THE TRANSPORTATION PROBLEM

Transportation problems arise when a cost-effective pattern is needed to ship items from origins that have limited supply to destinations that have demand for the goods. In its basic form, the transportation problem assumes that the cost of shipping items from a source to a destination is proportional to the number of units shipped between the two points. The basic transportation model can be summarized as follows.

Transportation Problem

1. There are m sources.
   The supply of a resource at source i is Si.

2. There are n destinations.
   The demand for the resource at destination j is Dj.

3. The unit shipping cost between nodes i and j is Cij.

Goal: Minimize the total shipping cost of supplying the destinations with the required demand from the available supplies at the sources.

To illustrate, consider the problem Carlton Pharmaceuticals is facing in "transporting" cases of vaccine from its production plants to its distribution warehouses.

Carlton.net
Carlton.xls

CARLTON PHARMACEUTICALS

Carlton Pharmaceuticals supplies drugs and other medical supplies to hospitals and pharmacies throughout the southern and midwestern United States. Carlton has three production plants (located in Cleveland, Ohio; Detroit, Michigan; and Greensboro, North Carolina) and four distribution warehouses (located in Boston, Massachusetts; Richmond, Virginia; Atlanta, Georgia; and St. Louis, Missouri).

Carlton routinely stocks its warehouses with drugs and medical supplies on an as-needed basis. Because the Hong Kong A flu virus has begun sweeping the nation, however, supplies of Carlton's flu vaccine are running short at its distribution warehouses, and there is a critical need to resupply all four warehouses within the week.

At full production, Carlton will be able to produce and make available for shipment 1200 cases of the vaccine in Cleveland, 1000 in Detroit, and 800 in Greensboro by the end of the week. Taking into account the population, the number of hospitals and doctors, and the likelihood of a flu epidemic in the service area of each warehouse, the company has decided to allocate the 3000 cases as follows: 1100 to Boston, 400 to Richmond, 750 to Atlanta, and 750 to St. Louis.

Because the shipping department will be unable to deliver the vaccine in time using its normal trucking/rail operations, the company has contacted a number of express freight delivery services in order to determine the lowest shipping price per case between each plant–warehouse pair of cities. These costs are given in Table 6.1.

TABLE 6.1 SHIPPING COST PER CASE OF VACCINE

	To			
	Boston	Richmond	Atlanta	St. Louis
From				
Cleveland	$35	$30	$40	$32
Detroit	$37	$40	$42	$25
Greensboro	$40	$15	$20	$28

Management at Carlton would like to ship the cases to the warehouses as economically as possible.

SOLUTION

The Carlton Pharmaceuticals problem is an example of a transportation problem, with the following characteristics: m = 3 sources, with supplies S1 = 1200, S2 = 1000, and S3 = 800, respectively; and n = 4 destinations, with demands D1 = 1100, D2 = 400, D3 = 750, and D4 = 750, respectively. The unit shipping costs (the Cij's) are the costs given in the problem statement (for example, C23 = 42). Carlton's goal is to minimize the total cost of shipping the cases from the production plants to the warehouse sites.

THE NETWORK

Figure 6.6 provides the network representation for the transportation problem faced by Carlton Pharmaceuticals. The nodes on the left side represent the sources; the function defined on these nodes is the supply of vaccine. The nodes on the right side represent the destinations; the function defined on these nodes is the demand for the vaccine. The arcs represent the transportation routes between each source and each destination; the function defined on the arcs is the unit shipping cost.

ASSUMPTIONS

In order to solve this problem, we make several simplifying assumptions so that it meets the criteria of a basic transportation model.

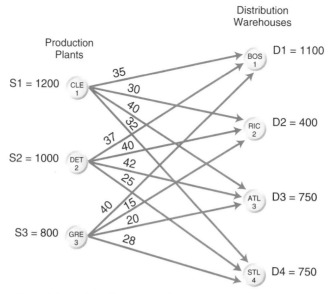

FIGURE 6.6   Carlton Pharmaceuticals Transportation Network Representation

1. **The per item shipping cost remains constant, regardless of the number of units shipped.** Although this assumption may be valid for the Carlton Pharmaceuticals problem, it would be violated if the express freight services offered discounts based on the quantities shipped or if there had been transportation expenses with a high fixed cost component. For example, suppose Carlton used its own trucks, each of which can hold up to 3000 cases, to transport the vaccine between the plants and the warehouses. If a truck transported only the vaccine, the cost of shipping 1000 cases would *not* be ten times the cost of shipping 100 cases because the fixed cost of operating the trucks (i.e., driver time, fuel, tolls, etc.) is independent of the quantities shipped. In such cases, using the basic transportation model would not be valid.

2. **All the shipping from the sources to the destinations occurs simultaneously (or within some fixed time frame).** If time is not a factor—that is, if Carlton does not have to resupply its warehouses within a week—Carlton could wait for more vaccine to be produced at plants with less expensive delivery charges.

3. **The vaccine can be shipped only between sources and destinations.** The vaccine is not shipped between one source and another source, or between one destination and another destination. There are also no shipments to intermediate destinations.

4. **The total supply equals the total demand.** The algorithm that solves the transportation problem is based on the assumption that the total supply equals the total demand. Although this may appear to be rather restrictive, any problem can easily be converted to this structure by using a *dummy destination* if total supply exceeds total demand, or a *dummy source* if total demand exceeds total supply. The unit shipping costs from each of the sources to a dummy destination or from a dummy source to each destination are all $0. The supply at a dummy source or the demand at a dummy destination is the difference between the actual total supply and total demand.

Figure 6.7 illustrates a scenario in which only 600 cases are required in St. Louis. Since total supply is 3000, and total demand is only 2850 now, a dummy warehouse is created with a demand of 150 cases. When a shipment is made from a plant to this dummy destination, this plant will have the corresponding number of cases left over (or not produced).

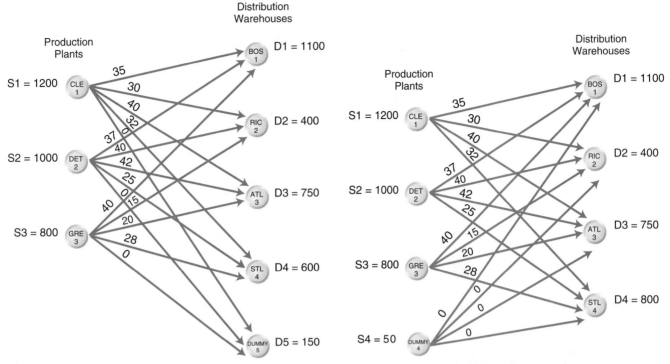

FIGURE 6.7   Carlton Pharmaceuticals Dummy Warehouse

FIGURE 6.8   Carlton Pharmaceuticals Dummy Plant

Similarly, Figure 6.8 illustrates a scenario in which demand at St. Louis is for 800 cases instead of 750. Although the total supply is still 3000, the total demand now is for 3050 cases. The problem that now arises is to determine an efficient way to ship the 3000 cases that are available. Here we add a dummy plant with a supply of 50 cases. When a shipment is made from this dummy plant to a warehouse, that warehouse will fall short of its desired demand by the corresponding amount.

In most computer packages with special-purpose transportation modules (including WINQSB), the creation of a dummy source or destination is done internally and is transparent to the user.

MATHEMATICAL PROGRAMMING FORMULATION

Given these assumptions, the Carlton Pharmaceuticals problem has the following structure:

MINIMIZE ⟨Total Shipping Cost⟩
ST
　　⟨Amount shipped from each source⟩ = ⟨Supply at that source⟩
　　⟨Amount received at each destination⟩ = ⟨Demand at that destination⟩
　　　　　　⟨No negative shipments⟩

It is not necessary to include the requirement that the number of cases shipped from each source to each destination be integer valued because of the special structure of the transportation problem. That is, as long as the supplies at each source and the demands at each destination are integers, the optimal solution will automatically be shipments of integer amounts.[2]

---

[2]This is so because the constraint matrix for a transportation problem can be written to be *totally unimodular*. A totally unimodular matrix consists of only 1's, 0's, or −1's arranged in a particular format. The optimal solution to problems with totally unimodular constraint matrices and integer right-hand sides will always be integer.

For the Carlton Pharmaceutical problem, we define:

$$X_{ij} = \text{amount shipped from source } i \text{ to destination } j$$

where i = 1 (Cleveland), 2 (Detroit), 3 (Greensboro), and

j = 1 (Boston), 2 (Richmond), 3 (Atlanta), 4 (St. Louis)

Thus, there are 12 decision variables: X_{11}, X_{12}, X_{13}, . . . , X_{34}. The amount shipped from a source, say, source 1, is the sum of the amount shipped from source 1 to destination 1 (X_{11}) plus the amount shipped from source 1 to destination 2 (X_{12}), and so on.

The amount shipped to a destination, say, destination 3, is the sum of the amounts shipped from source 1 to destination 3 (X_{13}) plus the amount shipped from source 2 to destination 3 (X_{23}), and so on. Thus, the mathematical programming problem for the Carlton Pharmaceutical problem is:

$$
\begin{array}{l}
\text{MINIMIZE} \quad 35X_{11} + 30X_{12} + 40X_{13} + 32X_{14} + 37X_{21} + 40X_{22} + 42X_{23} + 25X_{24} + 40X_{31} + 15X_{32} + 20X_{33} + 28X_{34} \\
\text{ST} \quad\quad X_{11} + X_{12} + X_{13} + X_{14} \quad\quad\quad\quad\quad\quad\quad\quad\quad\quad\quad\quad\quad\quad\quad\quad\quad\quad\quad = 1200 \\
\quad\quad\quad\quad\quad\quad\quad\quad\quad\quad X_{21} + X_{22} + X_{23} + X_{24} \quad\quad\quad\quad\quad\quad\quad\quad\quad\quad = 1000 \\
\quad\quad\quad\quad\quad\quad\quad\quad\quad\quad\quad\quad\quad\quad\quad\quad\quad\quad\quad\quad X_{31} + X_{32} + X_{33} + X_{34} = 800 \\
\quad X_{11} \quad\quad\quad\quad\quad\quad\quad\quad\quad + X_{21} \quad\quad\quad\quad\quad\quad + X_{31} \quad\quad\quad\quad\quad\quad\quad\quad = 1100 \\
\quad\quad\quad X_{12} \quad\quad\quad\quad\quad\quad\quad\quad\quad + X_{22} \quad\quad\quad\quad\quad\quad\quad\quad + X_{32} \quad\quad\quad\quad = 400 \\
\quad\quad\quad\quad\quad X_{13} \quad\quad\quad\quad\quad\quad\quad\quad\quad + X_{23} \quad\quad\quad\quad\quad\quad\quad\quad\quad + X_{33} \quad\quad = 750 \\
\quad\quad\quad\quad\quad\quad\quad X_{14} \quad\quad\quad\quad\quad\quad\quad\quad\quad + X_{24} \quad\quad\quad\quad\quad\quad\quad\quad\quad + X_{34} = 750 \\
\quad\quad\quad\quad\quad\quad\quad\quad\quad\quad\quad\quad X_{ij} \geq 0, \text{ for all } i \text{ and } j
\end{array}
$$

There is one constraint for each of the m = 3 sources and one constraint for each of the n = 4 destinations, or a total of m+n = 3 + 4 = 7 constraints.

COMPUTER SOLUTION

Because the model for a transportation problem is a linear program, we can use Excel to solve for the optimal solution, using Solver. Appendix 6.2 shows how to set up an Excel spreadsheet to solve for the optimal solution for transportation problems. The optimal spreadsheet resulting from using the Solver option to solve the problem is given in Figure 6.9.

Using a general linear programming package does not take advantage of the special structure of the transportation problem, however. A computer module designed specifically for the transportation problem, like the one in WINQSB, gives the output and sensitivity analysis in a format that is easy to read while requiring the user to input only:

1. The number of sources
2. The supplies at these sources
3. The number of destinations
4. The demands at these destinations
5. The unit shipping costs
6. The objective criterion (minimization or maximization)[3]

The WINQSB input screen for the Carlton Pharmaceuticals problem is given in Appendix 6.1 (see Exhibit 2). When we choose Solve the Problem from the Solve and Analyze menu, the output is as shown in Figure 6.10.

This screen gives the optimal number of cases to be transported from each plant to each warehouse, as well as the total cost of each individual shipment. Any other

---

[3]In computer packages other than WINQSB, which only solve transportation problems with minimization objective functions, the maximization objective function can be converted to a minimization problem by entering the "unit profits" as negative "unit costs."

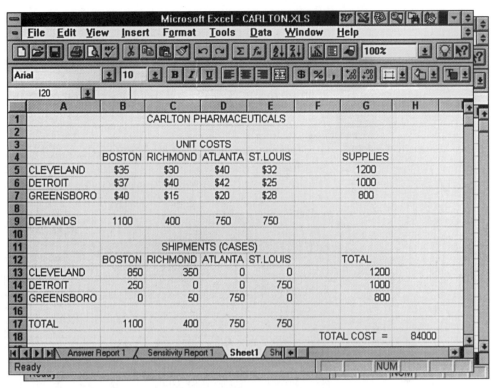

FIGURE 6.9   Excel Output—Carlton Pharmaceuticals

shipping pattern from the plants to the warehouses will result in a cost higher than $84,000. It is interesting to note that only 6 of the 12 possible transportation routes are used in the optimal solution. In general, as discussed in the appendices Supplement CD5 on the CD-ROM, unless alternative optimal solutions exist, the number of routes used will be at most k − 1, where k is the total number of all supply, demand, and dummy nodes.

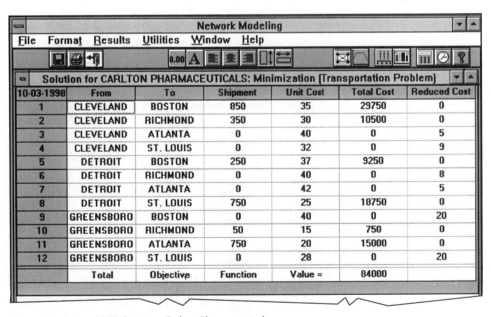

FIGURE 6.10   WINQSB Output—Carlton Pharmaceuticals

Interpreting the
Reduced Costs

Reduced cost information is given in both the WINQSB output and the sensitivity report of Excel. Recall from Chapter 3 that there are two interpretations for the reduced cost values. Because this is a minimization problem, the $5 reduced cost for shipments between Cleveland and Atlanta means that (1) the cost for shipments on this route must be *reduced* by at least $5 (to at most $35) before it becomes economically feasible to utilize this route; and (2) if this route is used under the current cost structure, then for each item that is shipped along this route, the total cost will *increase* by $5.

Other Sensitivity Analyses

Sensitivity analyses for the objective function coefficients can also be obtained from the sensitivity reports in Excel or WINQSB. Figure 6.11 shows the results generated by selecting Range of Optimality from the Results menu in WINQSB. The last two columns give the range of values for each unit shipping cost within which the optimal solution remains unchanged.

10-03-1998 13:02:24	From	To	Unit Cost	Reduced Cost	Basis Status	Allowable Min. Cost	Allowable Max. Cost
1	CLEVELAND	BOSTON	35	0	basic	30	44
2	CLEVELAND	RICHMOND	30	0	basic	10	35
3	CLEVELAND	ATLANTA	40	5	at bound	35	M
4	CLEVELAND	ST. LOUIS	32	9	at bound	23	M
5	DETROIT	BOSTON	37	0	basic	28	42
6	DETROIT	RICHMOND	40	8	at bound	32	M
7	DETROIT	ATLANTA	42	5	at bound	37	M
8	DETROIT	ST. LOUIS	25	0	basic	-M	34
9	GREENSBORO	BOSTON	40	20	at bound	20	M
10	GREENSBORO	RICHMOND	15	0	basic	10	35
11	GREENSBORO	ATLANTA	20	0	basic	-M	25
12	GREENSBORO	ST. LOUIS	28	20	at bound	8	M

FIGURE 6.11   Range of Optimality for Carlton Pharmaceuticals—WINQSB Output

Similarly, the sensitivity of the supplies and demands (right-hand sides of the constraints) can be analyzed using either Excel or WINQSB. In WINQSB, this is done by selecting Range of Feasibility from the Results menu, giving the output shown in Figure 6.12.

10-03-1998 13:07:32	Node	Supply	Demand	Shadow Price	Allowable Min. Value	Allowable Max. Value
1	CLEVELAND	1200	0	23	1200	1450
2	DETROIT	1000	0	25	1000	M
3	GREENSBORO	800	0	8	800	1050
4	BOSTON	0	1100	12	850	1100
5	RICHMOND	0	400	7	150	400
6	ATLANTA	0	750	12	500	750
7	ST. LOUIS	0	750	0	-M	750

FIGURE 6.12   Range of Feasibility for Carlton Pharmaceuticals—WINQSB Output

The shadow prices for the plants convey the cost savings realized for each extra case of vaccine available at the plant. For the warehouses, the shadow prices are the cost savings resulting from having an extra case demanded at the warehouse. Keep in mind, however, that extra demand at a warehouse means that total demand exceeds total supply. Thus, while there may be cost savings in the cases shipped, they come at the expense of some warehouse not obtaining its desired quantity of vaccine. The range of feasibility for both supply and demand (given in the last two columns of the WINQSB report) gives the range of values for the supplies and demands over which these shadow prices are valid.

SPECIAL CASES OF THE TRANSPORTATION PROBLEM

Cases may arise that *appear* to violate the assumptions necessary to solve a transportation problem using a standard transportation module. Here we consider just a few.

Blocked Routes

Sometimes one or more of the routes may be blocked or unusable for some reason. Entering an objective coefficient for the blocked route that is several magnitudes larger than the largest unit cost in the problem will ensure that this route will never be used in an optimal solution. In WINQSB, a coefficient of "+M" can be entered to accomplish this.

Minimum Shipments

Sometimes a minimum shipment for one or more of the routes is required. For example, suppose management at Carlton Pharmaceuticals required that at least 400 cases be shipped from Greensboro to Boston. Because the management scientist has no control over this constraint, he or she can simply set aside 400 cases for this route at the unit cost of $40 per case, or $16,000, reducing the supply at Greensboro to 400 and the demand at Boston to 700. The transportation problem is then solved using these modified quantities, and the $16,000 is simply added to the minimum cost of the revised problem.

Maximum Shipments/ Transhipment Nodes— The Capacitated Transhipment Model

Sometimes shipments take place by first transporting goods through one or more of several *transshipment* nodes before reaching their final destination. The transshipment nodes may be independent intermediate nodes (with no supply or demands of their own) or other supply or destination points. Such problems are known as **transshipment problems**. If, in addition, an upper limit is placed on the amount of flow along one or more arcs in the network, the problem is called a *capacitated transshipment* or a *general network* model.

When using a general linear programming module, such as the Solver routine in Excel, we can simply add upper bound constraints to the problem formulation. Other "tricks" can also be used to convert transshipment or general network problems into the format of a transportation problem.

Specialized software using more efficient solution approaches is often available for solving general network problems. WINQSB contains such a module. Input consists of identifying the supply or demand at each node and the unit cost and maximum (and minimum) capacity for using each arc. A dummy node is created (usually by the software) so that the total supply equals the total demand. The algorithm typically used by such modules, known as the *out-of-kilter algorithm*, is illustrated on the accompanying CD-ROM.

To illustrate the use of the general network model, consider the situation faced by Depot Max, an office supply superstore.

DEPOT MAX

Depotmax.het
Depotmax.xls

Depot Max has six stores located in the Dallas/Fort Worth area. It is Saturday night, and stores 5 and 6 have found themselves running low on the Model 65A Arcadia workstation that will be advertised in the Sunday *Dallas Morning News*. They request that 12 and 13 workstations, respectively, be shipped to them to cover the anticipated increase in demand from the ad.

Management has identified stores 1 and 2 as able to supply 10 and 15 workstations, respectively. However, the stores can only utilize the space available on delivery trucks currently scheduled to transport other supplies between the stores. The unit shipping costs and the maximum number of workstations that can be shipped between stores is shown in Figure 6.13. Depot Max wishes to transport the available workstations from stores 1 and 2 to stores 5 and 6, at minimum total cost.

Unit shipping costs are on top of the arcs.
Capacities are in **bold** on the bottom of the arcs.

FIGURE 6.13   Capacitated Transshipment Model Network Representation for Depot Max

SOLUTION

In this problem, some stores have supplies (supply nodes 1 and 2), other stores have demand for supplies (demand nodes 5 and 6), and still others can be used to send the supplies through but have no supply and demand of their own (transshipment nodes 3 and 4). There are also maximum limits that can be shipped on available trucks. These are the conditions required for using a general network model.

A general network model is somewhat more complex than a transportation problem because it has flows (Xij) that must satisfy the following conditions:

1. Supply nodes: The *net flow out* of the node [(flow out) − (flow in)] must equal the supply at the node.

$$X12 + X13 + X15 - X21 = 10 \text{ (Node 1)}$$
$$X21 + X24 \qquad - X12 = 15 \text{ (Node 2)}$$

2. Intermediate transshipment nodes: The total flow out of the node must equal the total flow into the node.

$$X34 + X35 = X13 \qquad \text{(Node 3)}$$
$$X46 \qquad = X24 + X34 \text{ (Node 4)}$$

3   Demand nodes: The *net flow into* the node [(flow in) − (flow out)] must equal the demand for the node.

$$X15 + X35 + X65 - X56 = 12 \text{ (Node 5)}$$
$$X46 + X56 \qquad - X65 = 13 \text{ (Node 6)}$$

4. Arcs: The flow along each arc must not exceed its upper bound capacity (Uij) or be less than its minimum flow requirements (Lij, which we assume here to be 0).

$$0 \le Xij \le Uij$$

By moving the variables from the right side to the left side in the equations for the intermediate transshipment nodes and multiplying the equations for the demand nodes by -1, we can write the mathematical programming formulation for the problem depicted in Figure 6.13 as follows.

$$
\begin{array}{lrrrrrrrrrr}
\text{MINIMIZE} & 5X12 & +10X13 & +20X15 & +6X21 & +15X24 & +12X34 & +7X35 & +15X46 & +11X56 & +7X65 \\
\text{ST} & X12 + & X13 + & X15 - & X21 & & & & & & = 10 \\
& -X12 & & & X21 + & X24 & & & & & = 15 \\
& & - X13 & & & & + X34 + & X35 & & & = 0 \\
& & & & & - X24 - & X34 & & + X46 & & = 0 \\
& & & - X15 & & & & - X35 & & + X56 - X65 & = -12 \\
& & & & & & & & - X46 - & X56 + X65 & = -13 \\
\end{array}
$$

$0 \le X12 \le 3; \; 0 \le X13 \le 12; \; 0 \le X15 \le 6; \; 0 \le X21 \le 7; \; 0 \le X24 \le 10;$
$0 \le X34 \le 8; \; 0 \le X35 \le 8; \; 0 \le X46 \le 17; \; 0 \le X56 \le 7; \; 0 \le X65 \le 5$

This is the structure required to solve the problem using the out-of-kilter algorithm.

The problem can be solved by WINQSB using the Network Flow option from the opening screen and inputting the cost, supply, and demand data. (The maximum capacities for the flows on each arc are entered by selecting Flow Bounds from the Edit menu.) The output shown in Figure 6.14 summarizes the optimal flow and the reduced costs, resulting in a minimum total shipping cost of $645; sensitivity analyses can also be generated.

Network Modeling						
File Format Results Utilities Window Help						
Solution for CAPACITATED TRANSSHIPMENT: Minimization (Network Flow Problem)						
10-03-1998	From	To	Flow	Unit Cost	Total Cost	Reduced Cost
1	Node1	Node3	9	10	90	0
2	Node1	Node5	6	20	120	-6
3	Node2	Node1	5	6	30	0
4	Node2	Node4	10	15	150	-13
5	Node3	Node4	1	12	12	0
6	Node3	Node5	8	7	56	-9
7	Node4	Node6	11	15	165	0
8	Node5	Node6	2	11	22	0
	Total	Objective	Function	Value =	645	

FIGURE 6.14   WINQSB Solution for Capacitated Transshipment Problem—Depot Max

USING A TRANSPORTATION MODEL FOR PRODUCTION SCHEDULING

Although transportation models are usually regarded as a way to optimize the transportation of goods, numerous other management science applications have been found to have the same model structure. The situation faced by the Montpelier Ski Company is an example of how a production planning situation can be expressed as a transportation model.

Montski.net
Montski.xls

MONTPELIER SKI COMPANY

The Montpelier Ski Company is planning its third-quarter production schedule of Glide-Rite snow skis. During the month of July, the company's plant employs a substantial number of college students. This number decreases in August as the students begin preparing to return to school; by September, the company employs no college students.

Because the company pays lower wages and benefits to college students than it does to its full-time staff, the number of college students it employs affects both the production capacity and the unit production costs during these months.

Montpelier is expected to have 200 pairs of Glide-Rite skis in inventory as it begins production in July. Forecasted demand and production capacities for the months of July, August, and September are given in Table 6.2.

TABLE 6.2   MONTPELIER SKI COMPANY: PAIRS OF SKIS

Month	Forecasted Demand	Production* Capacity
July	400	1000
August	600	800
September	1000	400

*These capacities can be increased up to 50% by scheduling overtime.

In addition to this demand from retail customers, Montpelier must have 1200 pairs of Glide-Rite skis available to ship to its company-owned Ski Chalet outlets around the country on September 30. It plans to start October with no inventory and to operate at full production capacity of 400 pairs of skis in regular time and 200 pairs of skis in overtime throughout the fourth quarter. The production costs of a pair of Glide-Rite skis based on normal wage rates are estimated at $25 for skis produced in July, $26 for those produced in August, and $29 for those produced in September. Although skis produced using overtime have the same material costs, extra labor and overhead costs add $5 to the production cost for a pair of skis produced in July, $6 in August, and $8 in September. The holding cost to store a pair of skis from one month to the next are figured at 3% of their production cost.

Montpelier's management would like to schedule production to minimize its costs for the quarter while meeting the monthly demand forecasts and the September 30 inventory requirement.

SOLUTION

Analysis of Demand

Since Montpelier already has 200 pairs of skis in inventory at the start of the quarter, the net demand to satisfy for the month of July is $400 - 200 = 200$ additional pairs. The demand for August is 600 pairs of skis. In September, Montpelier must have enough supply to meet its forecasted demand of 1000 pairs as well as the desired in-house inventory of 1200 pairs at the end of the month. Hence, the total requirement for September is for $1000 + 1200 = 2200$ pairs of skis.

Analysis of Supplies

For this problem, the production capacities can be thought of as the "supplies." There are two sets of production capacities for the quarter: the set of given capacities of 1000 (July), 800 (August), and 400 (September) for regular time production, and the set of capacities of 500 (July), 400 (August), and 200 (September) for overtime production. Thus, six "sources" of supply (July regular time, July overtime, August regular time, August overtime, September regular time, and September overtime) supply three "destinations" (end of July, end of August, and end of September.) Since total production capacity for the quarter is $1000 + 800 + 400 + 500 + 400 + 200 = 3300$, and total demand is $200 + 600 + 2200 = 3000$, Montpelier would want to create a dummy destination requiring 300 pairs of skis.

Analysis of Unit Costs

In addition to the unit production costs associated with manufacturing skis in regular time and overtime, Montpelier also incurs inventory storage costs. Skis manufactured in July incur no inventory costs if they are sold in July. If they are sold in August, however, a storage cost of 3% of the production cost will increase the cost of skis manufactured in regular time by $0.75 to $25.75 and for those manufactured overtime by $0.90 to $30.90. If they are sold in September, the total inventory costs are $1.50 and $1.80, respectively, bringing total unit costs to $26.50 per pair for skis produced during regular time and $31.80 per pair for skis produced during overtime.

Skis produced in August and sold in August incur no storage costs. Those sold in September, however, incur a storage cost of 3%, adding $0.78 to the $26 cost of skis produced in regular time and $0.96 to the $32 cost of skis produced in overtime. This brings the total unit costs to $26.78 and $32.96, respectively. Obviously, skis produced in August could not be sold in July, and skis manufactured in September could not be sold in either July or August. Because Montpelier must be "blocked" from doing this, we assign a cost of +M to these situations.

Figure 6.15 shows the transportation network for the Montpelier problem.

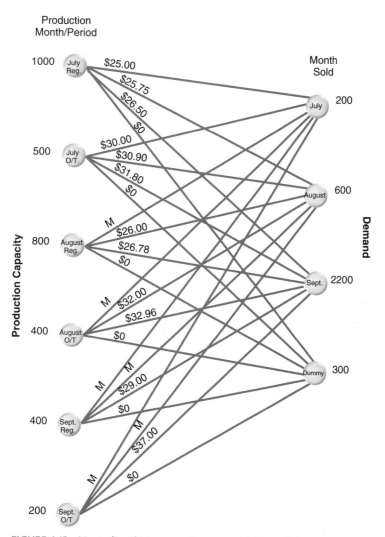

FIGURE 6.15   Montpelier Ski Company Transportation Network Representation: Production Schedule for July–September

COMPUTER SOLUTION

Solving the problem using WINQSB gives the output shown in Figure 6.16.

As you can see, the plant should run at capacity in July, producing 1000 pairs of skis in regular time and 500 pairs in overtime. This would necessitate storing 1500 − 200 = 1300 pairs of skis at the end of July.

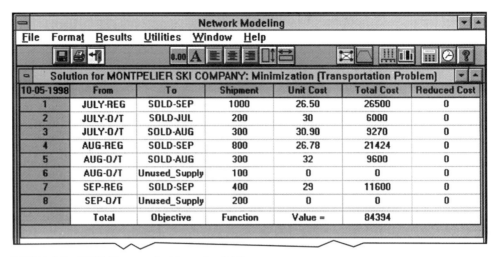

FIGURE 6.16   W/NQSB output for Montpelier Ski Company

In August, 800 pairs of skis should be produced in regular time and 300 in overtime. Because demand for August is only 600, this will add another $800 + 300 - 600 = 500$ skis to inventory. Hence, $1300 + 500 = 1800$ pairs of skis would be stored from August to September. In September only 400 skis should be produced. With retail demand for 1000 pairs in September, the desired 1200 pairs of skis will be available for shipment to the Ski Chalet stores at the end of the month.

The following memo to the production manager of the Montpelier Ski Company documents these results. The memo includes a sensitivity analysis for smoothing overtime production in the quarter motivated by an interpretation of the reduced costs.

M E M O R A N D U M

To: Gunter Klaus, Production Manager
Montpelier Ski Company

From: Student Consulting Group

Subj: Third-Quarter Production Planning for Glide-Rite Skis

We have prepared an analysis for Montpelier's production of Glide-Rite skis during the upcoming third quarter (July–September). This analysis considered:

1. The current inventory position of Glide Rite skis
2. The projected changing demand for skis during the third quarter
3. The company's desire to have an inventory position of 1200 pairs of skis at the end of September for shipment to its Ski Chalet stores
4. The anticipated regular time and overtime production capacities
5. The varying monthly production costs due to the mix of part-time college students and full-time experienced employees

Table I details the forecasts for monthly demand, production costs, and production capacity per pair of skis for the three-month period. The capacity and cost estimates are based, in part, on the level of college students employed by the company during the quarter. The monthly demand estimates are based on historical analysis, orders received to date, and a forecast of the trend in demand.

TABLE I   Third-Quarter Estimates per Pair of Glide-Rite Skis

Month	Forecasted Demand	Production Capacity		Production Costs	
		Regular	Overtime	Regular	Overtime
July	400*	1000	500	$25	$30
August	600	800	400	$26	$32
September	1000	400	200	$29	$37

*Montpelier's projected inventory position at the beginning of July is 200 pairs of Glide-Rite skis.

As per discussion with the Accounting Department, we used a 3% monthly holding cost rate in the analysis.

ANALYSIS

Using the information given, we developed a specially structured model in keeping with the objective of minimizing total third-quarter costs. The resulting production schedule is shown in Table II.

TABLE II   Third-Quarter Recommended Production Schedule, Glide-Rite Skis

Month	Beginning Inventory	Production Regular	Over-time	Ending Inventory	Monthly Costs Regular	Overtime	Inven-tory	Total
July	200	1000	500	1300	$25,000	$15,000	$1,020	$41,020
August	1300	800	300	1800	$20,800	$ 9,600	$1,374	$31,774
September	1800	400	0	0	$11,600	$ 0	$ 0	$11,600
							Total	$84,394

Figure I compares the regular time and overtime production on a monthly basis.

FIGURE I   Monthly Inventory Levels—Glide-Rite Skis

Following the assumption that demand and production rates will be relatively constant within each month of the third quarter, Figure II shows the company's inventory position for the quarter. Note that inventory should equal the desired level of 1200 pairs of skis at the end of September.

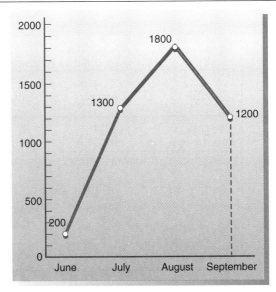

FIGURE II   Recommended Third-Quarter Production Schedule—Glide-Rite Skis

As you can see from Table II and Figures I and II, the production quantities and the company's inventory position vary substantially from month to month owing to differing monthly production costs.

September and Fourth-Quarter Production   The recommended schedule utilizes overtime heavily in July and August, and not at all in September. Because Montpelier will rely on full-time workers working overtime during the fourth quarter, it may wish to smooth the transition by scheduling some overtime production in September. A minimum cost schedule that meets the company's third-quarter objectives while operating at full overtime capacity during the month of September is presented in Table III.

TABLE III   Third-Quarter Recommended Production Schedule, Glide-Rite Skis
(Revised for full overtime production in September)

		Production				Monthly Costs		
Month	Beginning Inventory	Regular	Over-time	Ending Inventory	Regular	Overtime	Inven-tory	Total
July	200	1000	500	1300	$25,000	$15,000	$1,020	$41,020
August	1300	800	100	1600	$20,800	$ 3,200	$1,218	$25,218
September	1600	400	200	0	$11,600	$ 7,400	$ 0	$19,000
							Total	$85,238

If all full-time workers desire the opportunity to earn extra wages by working overtime, this revised policy, which shifts overtime production of 200 pairs of skis from August to September, would certainly increase goodwill between management and labor while increasing company costs in the third quarter by only $844 (approximately 1%). This relatively small increase might be more than offset by other factors not addressed in this study, such as start-up and shut-down costs for overtime production.

If not all workers wish to work overtime during September, the total cost for the quarter only increases by approximately $4.10 for each pair of skis produced during September overtime rather than in August. Any such shift will reduce the maximum inventory level during the third quarter as well as the variation in total monthly costs during the last two months of the quarter. We feel that such factors merit consideration when making final decisions for third-quarter production. Thus, unless there is some overriding rationale of which

we are unaware, we recommend that management solicit full-time worker input and honor all requests for overtime in September.

If there are any other modifications or scenarios that Montpelier Ski Company desires to investigate, please feel free to contact us.

6.3 THE ASSIGNMENT PROBLEM

In many business situations, management finds it necessary to assign personnel to
jobs, jobs to machines, machines to job locations within a plant, or salespersons to
territories within the distribution area of the business. In each of these cases, management would like to make the most effective or cost-efficient assignment of a set of
workers (or *objects*) to a set of *jobs* (or *assignments*). The criteria used to measure the effectiveness of a particular set of assignments may be total cost, total profit, or total time
to perform a set of operations. Such **assignment problems** are characterized as follows:

Assignment Problem

1. m workers are to be assigned to m jobs.

2. A unit cost (or profit) Cij is associated with worker i performing job j.

Goal: Minimize the total cost (or maximize the total profit) of assigning workers to jobs
so that each worker is assigned a job and each job is performed.

Which set is considered objects and which set assignments is irrelevant. For example,
assigning four machines to four projects is equivalent to assigning four projects to four
machines, as long as each project is completed and each machine is assigned.

The assignment problem has been studied extensively since the early part of the
twentieth century, and many solution algorithms have been proposed, including:
(1) total enumeration of all possibilities; (2) linear programming; (3) a transportation
approach (we will show that the problem is indeed a special case of the transportation
problem); (4) dynamic programming; (5) a binary branch and bound approach; and
(6) an efficient approach developed specifically for this problem, known as the Hungarian algorithm.[4]

The problem faced by Ballston Electronics is typical of problems for which the
assignment model is appropriate.

BALLSTON ELECTRONICS

Ballston.net
Ballston.xls

Ballston Electronics, a manufacturer of small electrical devices, has purchased an old
warehouse and converted it into a primary production facility. The physical dimensions
of the existing building left the architect little leeway for designing locations for the
company's five assembly lines and five inspection and storage areas, but these have
been constructed and now exist in fixed areas within the building.

The following is a simplified view of Ballston's manufacturing process. Products are
manufactured simultaneously on each assembly line. As items are taken off the assembly lines, they are temporarily stored in containers (moderately large bins) at the end
of each line. At approximately 30-minute intervals, the bins are physically transported

---

[4]Named for two Hungarian mathematicians who proved the underlying theorems on which the algorithm
is based.

from the temporary storage area near the end of the assembly line to one of the five inspection areas within the plant. Those products that pass inspection are stored in a space directly behind the inspection area, while those that do not pass are put into the inspection station's recycling bin.

Because different volumes of product are manufactured at each assembly line and different distances must be traversed from each assembly line to each inspection station, transporting items between each assembly line and inspection area location requires different times. The company must designate a separate inspection area for each assembly line.

An industrial engineer at Ballston has performed a study showing the times needed to transport finished products from each assembly line to each inspection area in minutes (see Table 6.3).

TABLE 6.3   MINUTES TO TRANSPORT FROM ASSEMBLY LINES
TO INSPECTION AREAS

		Inspection Area				
		A	B	C	D	E
	1	10	4	6	10	12
	2	11	7	7	9	14
Assembly Line	3	13	8	12	14	15
	4	14	16	13	17	17
	5	19	11	17	20	19

Under the current arrangement, which has been operational since Ballston moved into the building, work performed on assembly lines 1, 2, 3, 4, and 5 is transported to inspection areas A, B, C, D, and E, respectively. This arrangement of 1-A, 2-B, 3-C, 4-D, and 5-D requires 10 + 7 + 12 + 17 + 19 = 65 man-minutes of labor each half hour. Given that the average worker costs Ballston $12 per hour, Ballston incurs a labor cost of ($12)(65/60) = $13 during each half-hour period.

Since Ballston runs two eight-hour shifts a day, 250 days per year, it operates (250)(16) = 4000 hours a year, or (4000)(2) = 8000 half-hour periods annually. Thus, the total annual cost of moving items from the assembly lines to the inspection areas is ($13)(8000) = $104,000.

Ballston is under severe pressure to cut costs. One possible cost savings would result from a more efficient arrangement for this process. Accordingly, management would like to determine whether some other designation of production lines to inspection areas may require less total time, and, if so, what the annual savings would be.

SOLUTION

The problem Ballston Electronics faces is an example of the classic assignment problem consisting of m = 5 workers (the assembly lines) and m = 5 jobs (the inspection areas). Management can use the assignment model to determine how items will be transported from the assembly lines to the inspection areas in order to minimize the "total cost" (expressed in minutes). Each assembly line is assigned to *one* inspection area, and each inspection area services *one* line. Ballston can determine the actual dollar costs of a policy by multiplying the total time required to transport the products by the labor cost of $12 per hour.

Figure 6.17 shows the network representation for the Ballston assignment problem. As you can see, an assignment problem can be viewed as a transportation problem in which all the supplies and all the demands equal 1. Thus, techniques that solve the transportation problem can also be used to solve the assignment problem.

The complete mathematical programming formulation of the assignment problem parallels that of the transportation problem discussed in Section 6.2, except that the

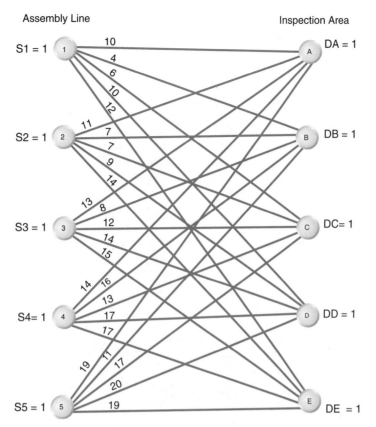

FIGURE 6.17   Ballston Electronics Assignment Network Representation

right-hand side for each constraint is 1. The Ballston problem contains 25 variables, X_{ij} (i and j both range from 1 to 5), defined as the number of assembly lines of type i assigned to inspection area j. Obviously, each X_{ij} can only be 1 (if assembly line i is assigned to inspection area j) or 0 (if it is not). But, again, because of the special structure of this problem, these restrictions can be ignored in the problem formulation.

ASSUMPTIONS AND RESTRICTIONS

The problem statement for the assignment model specified that the number of workers must equal the number of jobs. This is equivalent to the condition for the transportation problem, total supply must equal total demand. As in the transportation problem, this restriction can be met by adding "dummy" workers if the number of workers is less than the number of jobs, or dummy jobs if the number of jobs is less than the number of workers. The costs of making an assignment either from dummy workers or to dummy jobs are 0. A job given to a dummy worker will not be completed; similarly, a worker given a dummy job to perform will be unassigned.

Given that the number of workers equals the number of jobs (either naturally or by adding dummy workers or jobs), another restriction demands that each worker be assigned some job and that each job be performed. This implies that (1) no worker is left unassigned or is assigned to more than one job; and (2) no job is left undone or is assigned to more than one worker. Relaxation of these assumptions is discussed later in this section.

COMPUTER SOLUTION OF THE ASSIGNMENT PROBLEM

One approach to solving the assignment problem is to list all worker–job possibilities and choose the one with the lowest cost. For small problems that have only two or three workers and jobs, this may, in fact, be the most efficient method. We can easily show, however, that the number of such possibilities is m!. The problem faced by

Ballston Electronics involves m = 5 workers and jobs; thus, 5! = 120 such combinations exist. For problems requiring m = 8 assignments, over 40,000 assignment combinations are possible; for m = 11, almost 40,000,000; and for m = 20, almost 250,000,000,000,000,000.

Thus, we must employ a technique other than direct enumeration for problems of any practical size. Although the assignment problem can be formulated as a linear programming or a transportation model, an algorithm known as the *Hungarian method* has proven to be a quick and efficient way to solve such problems. This technique is programmed into many computer modules, such as the one in WINQSB, which are specifically designed to solve assignment problems. The only input needed for such modules is the matrix of assignment costs; any required dummy workers or jobs are automatically added.

Using WINQSB to solve the Ballston Electronics problem gives us the output shown in Figure 6.18. As you can see, only 55 man-minutes are required to transport products from the assembly lines to the inspection areas each half-hour. This is accomplished by reassigning line 1 to area C, line 2 to area D, line 3 to area E, line 4 to area A, and line 5 to area B. The labor savings is 10 man-minutes per half hour, or 32(10) = 320 man-minutes per day over the current arrangement, an average savings of 10/65 = 15.4%. The company will save (0.154)($104,000) = $16,000 annually.

Network Modeling						
File Format Results Utilities Window Help						
Solution for BALLSTON ELECTRONICS: Minimization (Assignment Problem)						
10-05-1998	From	To	Assignment	Unit Cost	Total Cost	Reduced Cost
1	LINE 1	AREA C	1	6	6	0
2	LINE 2	AREA D	1	9	9	0
3	LINE 3	AREA E	1	15	15	0
4	LINE 4	AREA A	1	14	14	0
5	LINE 5	AREA B	1	11	11	0
	Total	Objective	Function	Value =	55	

FIGURE 6.18   WINQSB Output—Ballston Electronics Assignment Problem

SPECIAL CASES IN ASSIGNMENT MODELS

The following "special cases" may arise in applying assignment models.

1. **A Worker Is Unable to Perform a Particular Job.**   This situation is similar to a blocked route in a transportation problem. Assigning a large value (+M in WINQSB) for the unit cost corresponding to this combination will prevent this assignment.

2. **A Worker Can Be Assigned to More Than One Job.**   If Worker 4 is allowed to perform up to two assignments, for example, we can insert a second Worker 4 row (designated as Worker 4') into the cost matrix with unit costs identical to the original Worker 4 row. Since this insertion results in an unbalanced problem, a dummy job must also be created. This is usually done internally by the software.

    This approach will work well if the number of workers able to be assigned more than one job is small. If several workers are allowed multiple assignments, however, it is better to model and solve the problem as a transportation problem; the "supplies" become the maximum number of jobs each worker is allowed to perform.

3. **The Problem Is a Maximization Problem.**   One way to solve a maximization assignment problem is to convert the problem from one of maximizing total profit to one of minimizing total "lost opportunity" or "regret" for not assigning the most profitable job to a given worker. This approach is outlined in the description of the

Hungarian algorithm in Supplement CD5 on the accompanying CD-ROM. A computer module specifically designed to solve assignment problems, such as that in WINQSB, does this automatically.

6.4 THE TRAVELING SALESMAN PROBLEM

The **traveling salesman problem** (which some designate the "traveling salesperson" problem) has been the subject of intense study for over half a century. In its simplest form, the traveling salesman problem can be expressed as follows:

The Traveling Salesman Problem

1. There are m nodes.

2. Unit costs Cij are associated with utilizing the arc from node i to node j.

Goal: Find the cycle that minimizes the total distance required to visit all nodes without visiting any node twice.

The problem gets its name from the situation faced by the traveling salesman who begins at his home city (City m) and visits each of m − 1 other cities (in no particular order) before returning to the home city. He wishes to make this *tour* at minimum total cost, without making a return visit to any city (even if returning to a city could yield a less expensive cost of returning home).

The traveling salesman problem, which can be expressed so easily in words, is cumbersome to express mathematically. A problem that involves 20 cities requires over 500,000 linear constraints; 50 cities requires over 500 trillion constraints; 120 cities,[5] well, ... Efficient algorithms, especially for large problems, have been elusive.

The traveling salesman problem has a variety of scheduling applications, including determining a salesperson's route, ordering drill positions on a drill press, school bus routings, and military bombing sorties. Such problems are also of theoretical importance to mathematicians because they represent a large class of difficult problems known as NP-*hard problems*. If an efficient solution scheme can be found for the traveling salesman problem, the same type of approach could be applied to solving any other NP-hard problem.[6]

A traveling salesman model can be used to solve the problem faced by officials at the Federal Emergency Management Agency (FEMA) after a recent earthquake in Southern California.

THE FEDERAL EMERGENCY MANAGEMENT AGENCY

Fema_ap.net
Fema.net

FEMA, the Federal Emergency Management Agency, has responded to a recent earthquake in southern California by setting up a home office in Northridge, near the quake's epicenter. The director in charge is responsible for visiting each of four local offices and returning to the home office in Northridge to file his reports and manage the operations.

---

[5]Around 6,000,000,000,000,000,000,000,000,000,000,000,000 linear constraints are required to express a traveling salesman problem of 120 cities.

[6]One example of an NP-hard problem is breaking a code used to encrypt a message.

Given the blockage of certain major transportation arteries, Table 6.4 gives the estimated travel time between each pair of offices.

TABLE 6.4   TRAVEL TIME (MINUTES) BETWEEN OFFICES

	To Office			
	1	2	3	4
Home office	30	45	65	80
Office 1		25	50	50
Office 2			40	40
Office 3				35

The director wishes to visit each local office and return to the home office in the shortest time possible.

SOLUTION

The FEMA situation is an example of a *symmetric* traveling salesman problem; that is, the travel time between a pair of offices is the same in each direction. For example, the travel time from office 1 to office 2 or from office 2 to office 1 is 25 minutes.[7] Figure 6.19 shows the network representation for this model.

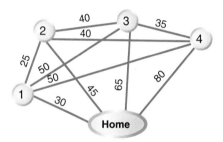

FIGURE 6.19   Federal Emergency Management Agency (FEMA) Traveling Salesman Network Representation

SOLUTION
APPROACHES FOR
THE TRAVELING
SALESMAN PROBLEM

One approach to solving a traveling salesman problem is to list every possible cycle, sum the values on the arcs for each cycle, and select the one yielding the lowest total. A problem with m nodes has (m-1)! possible cycles. For symmetric problems, since the total cost of a cycle is the same as the total cost of that cycle listing the nodes in reverse order, there are actually only (m-1)!/2 cycles. The (5-1)!/2 = 4!/2 = 12 different cycles for the FEMA problem are listed in Table 6.5.

Here, H stands for the home office, while O1, O2, O3, and O4 stand for offices 1, 2, 3, and 4, respectively. As this table indicates, the optimal cycle is H-O1-O2-O4-O3-H (or H-03-O4-O2-O1-H), with a minimum time of 195 minutes.

This method can only be used on the smallest of problems, however. The number of cycles for just 10 nodes is 181,440; for 15 nodes, the number swells to over 840 trillion. Obviously, for most practical problems, direct enumeration is unrealistic, even using the fastest computer and the best computer code.

You might think that this problem is akin to a typical assignment problem; here the workers are the "From" nodes, the jobs the "To" nodes, and the costs the times on

---

[7]In some traveling salesman models, the times are asymmetric. For example, if the northbound lanes between office 1 and office 2 were partially blocked, while the southbound lanes were clear, the time going north could be greater than the time going south.

TABLE 6.5   POSSIBLE CYCLES FOR FEMA

Cycle	Total Cost
1. H-O1-O2-O3-O4-H	210
2. H-O1-O2-O4-O3-H	195 ⟵ Minimum
3. H-O1-O3-O2-O4-H	240
4. H-O1-O3-O4-O2-H	200
5. H-O1-O4-O2-O3-H	225
6. H-O1-O4-O3-O2-H	200
7. H-O2-O3-O1-O4-H	265
8. H-O2-O1-O3-O4-H	235
9. H-O2-O4-O1-O3-H	250
10. H-O2-O1-O4-O3-H	220
11. H-O3-O1-O2-O4-H	260
12. H-O3-O2-O1-O4-H	260

the arcs between the nodes. This interpretation results in the symmetric matrix shown in the following table.

		To				
		H	O1	O2	O3	O4
	Home	—	30	45	65	80
F	Office 1	30	—	25	50	50
r	Office 2	45	25	—	40	40
o	Office 3	65	50	40	—	35
m	Office 4	80	50	40	35	—

When this approach is taken, however, WINQSB provides the output shown in Figure 6.20. As you can see, instead of one cycle over all the nodes, the result is two cycles: H-O2-O1-H and O3-O4-O3. These two cycles are called *subtours*.

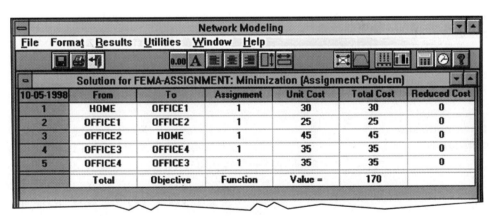

10-05-1998	From	To	Assignment	Unit Cost	Total Cost	Reduced Cost
1	HOME	OFFICE1	1	30	30	0
2	OFFICE1	OFFICE2	1	25	25	0
3	OFFICE2	HOME	1	45	45	0
4	OFFICE3	OFFICE4	1	35	35	0
5	OFFICE4	OFFICE3	1	35	35	0
	Total	Objective	Function	Value =	170	

FIGURE 6.20   WINQSB Output—FEMA Assignment Problem

Although using the assignment algorithm to solve a traveling salesman problem did not work in this case, another approach for solving relatively small problems with m = 20 or fewer nodes is based on a combination of the assignment problem (presented in Section 6.3) and the branch and bound technique used for solving integer linear programs (see Chapter 4). This method is illustrated in Supplement CD5 on the accompanying CD-ROM.

LINEAR PROGRAMMING
FORMULATION FOR
THE TRAVELING
SALESMAN PROBLEM

In order to build a mathematical model for the traveling salesman problem, we define the variables X_{ij} as the number of arcs used from i to j in the cycle. X_{ij} is 1 if the arc is on the tour, and 0 if it is not. Thus, two constraints are as follows.

1. The sum of the arcs used out of each node is 1.
2. The sum of the arcs used into each node is 1.

These are precisely the constraints of an assignment problem. As we showed above, however, using the assignment approach may result in a series of subtours. To prevent subtours from occurring, additional constraints, known as *subtour constraints*, must be added to the model. Unfortunately, there is no compact way to express mathematically the requirement, "No subtours." Instead, an inequality constraint must be created for each possible subtour.

For example, to state that the subtour H-O2-O1-H is not permissible, it must be true that all three arcs (H-O2, O2-O1, and O1-H) are *not* utilized at the same time. Referring to the home office as node 5, we find that this constraint is:

$$X52 + X21 + X15 \leq 2$$

To state that the subtour O1-O2-O3-O4-O1 is not permissible, the constraint is:

$$X12 + X23 + X34 + X41 \leq 3$$

Thus, to develop a linear programming formulation properly, all possible subtours must be identified and a constraint written forbidding each such subtour possibility. The FEMA problem has five 1-node subtour constraints, ten 2-node subtour constraints, ten 3-node subtour constraints, and five 4-node subtour constraints. These are as follows.

One-node subtour constraints

$X11 \leq 0, X22 \leq 0, X33 \leq 0, X44 \leq 0, X55 \leq 0$

Two-node subtour constraints

$X12 + X21 \leq 1, X13 + X31 \leq 1$
$X14 + X41 \leq 1, X15 + X51 \leq 1$
$X23 + X32 \leq 1, X24 + X42 \leq 1$
$X25 + X52 \leq 1, X34 + X43 \leq 1$
$X35 + X53 \leq 1, X45 + X54 \leq 1$

Three-node subtour constraints

$X12 + X23 + X31 \leq 2, X12 + X24 + X41 \leq 2$
$X12 + X25 + X51 \leq 2, X13 + X34 + X41 \leq 2$
$X13 + X35 + X51 \leq 2, X14 + X45 + X51 \leq 2$
$X23 + X34 + X42 \leq 2, X23 + X35 + X52 \leq 2$
$X24 + X45 + X52 \leq 2, X34 + X45 + X53 \leq 2$

Four-node subtour constraints

$X12 + X23 + X34 + X41 \leq 3$
$X12 + X23 + X35 + X51 \leq 3$
$X12 + X24 + X45 + X51 \leq 3$
$X13 + X34 + X45 + X51 \leq 3$
$X23 + X34 + X45 + X52 \leq 3$

Although certain of these constraints are redundant (an even greater number are redundant when the matrix is symmetric), the number of such constraints grows astronomically as the number of nodes in the problem increases. Solving a traveling salesman problem with even a modest number of nodes by linear programming can involve billions of constraints (or more). Even the fastest supercomputers cannot solve such problems in our lifetime.

COMPUTER SOLUTION OF THE TRAVELING SALESMAN PROBLEM

Computer modules, such as the one in WINQSB, can solve traveling salesman problems that have relatively few nodes, using a combination of the assignment and the branch and bound approaches. The output from the traveling salesman module of the network menu of WINQSB appears in Figure 6.21. Note that this is the same solution we obtained from complete enumeration.

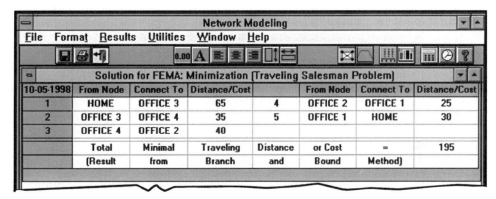

FIGURE 6.21   WINQSB Output—FEMA Traveling Salesman Problem

SPECIAL CASES

The following "special cases" may arise in applying the traveling salesman problem.

Revisiting Nodes

One special case of the traveling salesman problem occurs when the salesman *is* allowed to return to a city before returning home. For example, suppose a salesman is on the last leg of a trip, returning home to Boston from Los Angeles after already stopping in New York, Chicago, and Dallas. As frequent fliers know, airlines often give better fares to travelers who accept a change of plane rather than a nonstop flight. Thus, although the salesman may have already visited Chicago, it may be worthwhile to go there again on the return flight to obtain the cheaper air fare.

This situation can easily be converted to a traveling salesman problem by first finding the cheapest or shortest path from each city to each other city and substituting this value for the "direct distance" value. (Finding these "shortest paths" is the subject of the next section.) Although such prescreening requires additional work, algorithms for finding shortest distances are very efficient (see Section 6.5) and can be found quickly using a computer.

n-Person Traveling Salesman Problem

Consider a school bus routing problem in which n = 15 school buses must pick up students at 80 stops. Each school bus travels to several pickup points, but no two school buses visit the same point. The goal might be to minimize (1) the overall miles traveled, (2) the longest distance traveled by any bus, or (3) the total costs incurred. Such problems are known as *n-person traveling salesman problems*. Solutions to these problems are beyond the scope of this text.

6.5 𝒯HE SHORTEST PATH PROBLEM

We have all had occasion to look at a road map and try to plan the best route to our destination. This may mean finding the route of shortest distance or time, or, considering the costs of gasoline, maintenance, and tolls, the route of least cost. Our objective is to choose a path of minimum distance, time, or cost from a starting point, the *start node*, to a destination, the *terminal node*. Such problems are called **shortest path problems**.

Shortest path problems typically assume that the distance between any two nodes is nonnegative and that the arcs are bidirectional. For example, the distance from Cleveland to Chicago equals the distance from Chicago to Cleveland, and travel is permitted in either direction. The traditional shortest path problem is characterized as follows:

Shortest Path Problem

1. There are n nodes, beginning with start node 1 and ending with terminal node n.
2. Bidirectional arcs connect adjacent nodes i and j with nonnegative distances, dij.

Goal: Find the path of minimum total distance that connects node 1 to node n.

Again, linear programming models can be formulated and used to solve shortest path problems. However, certain specialized algorithms greatly reduce the computational time and effort required to determine an optimal solution. The *Dijkstra algorithm* (named for its Dutch developer, researcher E. W. Dijkstra) is particularly efficient for solving the traditional shortest path problem. The details of this algorithm are provided in Supplement CD5 on the accompanying CD-ROM.[8]

The shortest path problem differs from the traveling salesman problem in two ways: (1) not every node need be included on the path; and (2) we do not return to the start node. In a shortest path problem, if a round trip is required from node 1 to node n back to node 1, the minimum round trip distance is obtained by determining the shortest path from node 1 to node n and then retracing the same path to return to node 1 from node n.

The situation faced by Fairway Van Lines is a typical shortest path model.

FAIRWAY VAN LINES

Fairway.net

Fairway Van Lines is a nationwide household mover with franchisees located in every state of the continental United States. One of its current jobs is to move goods from a household in Seattle, Washington, to El Paso, Texas.

Fairway trucks travel interstate highways almost exclusively, since average driving speeds are reasonable and driving difficulty is minimal. The move will take place in the summer, so weather conditions should not be a factor.

Figure 6.22 shows the set of interstate highways (and a popular four-lane highway running from Las Vegas to Kingman, Arizona) Fairway trucks can travel to transport the goods. Management would like to determine the route of minimum distance from Seattle to El Paso.

---

[8]Although algorithms exist for problems for which either or both of these assumptions are invalid (most notably one attributed to R. W. Floyd), we will concentrate on problems with nonnegative bidirectional distances.

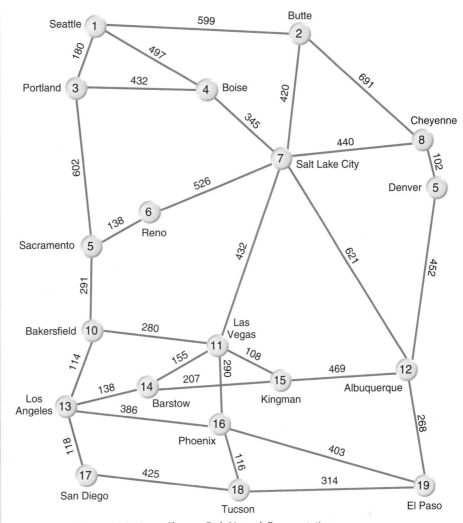

FIGURE 6.22   Fairway Van Lines Shortest Path Network Representation

SOLUTION

The Linear Programming Approach

This problem can be formulated and solved using a standard linear programming module. Binary decision variables Xij represent utilization of the highway *from* city i *to* city j. Xij is 1 if a truck travels on the highway from City i to City j; it is 0 if it does not. Thus, X12 = 1 implies that a truck uses the highway *from* Seattle *to* Butte, while X87 = 0 implies that the truck does not travel the highway *from* Cheyenne *to* Salt Lake City.

The objective is to minimize the total distance traveled from Seattle to El Paso, which is found by summing all the distances (dij) of the highways traveled. Since Xij = 1 for the highways traveled, and Xij = 0 for those not traveled, the objective can be expressed as: MINIMIZE Σ dij Xij.

The constraints for the shortest path model require that, for each city:

(The number of highways used to travel into the city) =
(The number of highways traveled leaving the city)

For example, the constraint for Boise (City 4) is:

X14 + X34 + X74 = X41 + X43 + X47

This implies that, if Boise were on the route, the number of highways traveled into Boise would be 1, and the number of highways traveled leaving Boise would also be 1. Similarly, if Boise were *not* used on the route, the number of highways traveled into Boise would be 0, as would the number of highways traveled leaving Boise.

In addition, we must ensure that the number of highways traveled out of Seattle is 1 and that the number of highways traveled into El Paso is 1. This is accomplished by adding the constraints

$$X12 + X13 + X14 = 1$$

and

$$X12,19 + X16,19 + X18,19 = 1$$

Together with the earlier constraints (the variables must be nonnegative and not exceed 1), these constraints make the problem a linear programming model. Because of its network structure, if the problem is solved using standard linear programming software, the optimal solution will be integer valued. That is, all the Xij's will be either 0 or 1.

The Network Approach

As an alternative to linear programming, Dijkstra's algorithm uses a network approach to solve the shortest path problem. In this technique, the shortest distances from the start node to each other node in the network are determined one at a time in the order of the closest nodes to the start node. Once the shortest distance has been found to the m closest nodes, the algorithm easily determines which node is the "(m+1)-st closest" and finds the shortest distance from Seattle (the start node) to that node. Thus, the Dijkstra algorithm not only finds the shortest distance from the start node to the terminal node in the network, but determines the shortest distance from the start node to all other nodes as well.

COMPUTER SOLUTION OF SHORTEST PATH PROBLEMS

In order to solve for the shortest distance using a computer module specifically written for this type of model (such as that found in WINQSB), we need only designate the start node and the terminal node and enter the distances of all arcs in the network. The WINQSB output for the Fairway Van Lines problem is shown in Figure 6.23.

Network Modeling
File   Format   Results   Utilities   Window   Help

Solution for Shortest Path Problem FAIRWAY VAN LINES			
10-05-1998	From	To	Distance/Cost	Cumulative Distance/Cost
1	SEA	BOI	497	497
2	BOI	SLC	345	842
3	SLC	ALB	621	1463
4	ALB	ELP	268	1731
	From SEA	To ELP	Distance/Cost	= 1731

FIGURE 6.23   WINQSB Output—Fairway Van Lines Shortest Path Problem

As you can see, the shortest distance from Seattle to El Paso is 1731 miles, which is obtained by traveling from Seattle to Boise to Salt Lake City to Albuquerque to El Paso. The screen also gives the minimum distance from Seattle to all the cities on this path. For example, the minimum distance from Seattle to Salt Lake City is 842 miles, obtained by traveling from Seattle to Boise to Salt Lake City. The shortest distance from Seattle to any other city can be obtained simply by changing the terminal node.

SPECIAL CASES

The following "special cases" may arise in shortest path problems.

Arcs With Different
Values Dependent
on the Direction

In some problems, the arc values between two nodes may be different, depending on the direction of the flow on the arc. For example, if the numbers on the arcs represent the travel times during the evening rush hour in the Washington, D.C., area, the time it takes to travel south from Washington to Woodbridge, Virginia, in the direction of the traffic, would be greater than the time it takes to travel north against the traffic. Such cases do not cause any computational problems, however; when using WINQSB, simply make sure that the box labeled "Symmetric Arc Coefficients" is not checked.

Unidirectional Arcs

It is also possible for an arc to be traversed in only one direction. This is the case, for example, if some of the routes are one-way streets. This is a special case of the one above; in this case, $+\infty$ (or $+M$) is assigned to the distance in the backwards direction of such a one-way arc.

6.6 THE MINIMAL SPANNING TREE PROBLEM

In Section 6.1, we defined a *tree* as a set of connected arcs that contains no cycles, and we showed that a *spanning tree* that connects all n nodes of a network consists of $n - 1$ arcs. Although there can be a large number of spanning trees in a network, the **minimal spanning tree** is the one that connects all the nodes in minimal total distance.

Minimal Spanning Tree Problem

1. There are n nodes.
2. There are distances dij between nodes i and j. The arcs are bidirectional.

Goal: Find the set of arcs that connects all the nodes in minimum total distance. (The result is a spanning tree.)

A minimal spanning tree approach typically is appropriate for problems for which redundancy is expensive (such as building trails between campsites in a national park) or the flow along the arcs is considered instantaneous (such as electrical current). To illustrate the concept of a minimal spanning tree, consider the simple three-node problem depicted in Figure 6.24.

FIGURE 6.24   A Minimal Spanning Tree

Suppose the arcs represent the cost (in $1000s) to connect three campsites. If the arcs between location 1 and location 2 and between location 2 and location 3 are selected, it will cost $3000 + $4000 = $7000 to connect all three locations. While the cost from location 1 to location 3 is $7000, compared to $5000 for a direct route between the two, the optimal strategy is to give up this convenience to minimize the overall total construction cost.

To further illustrate the use of a minimal spanning tree model, consider the situation faced by the Metropolitan Transit District.

THE METROPOLITAN TRANSIT DISTRICT

Metropol.net

The Metropolitan Transit District has held public hearings concerning the development of a new light rail transportation system for the city of Vancouver. As a result of these hearings, the district has decided to build a system linking eight residential and commercial centers at minimum cost to taxpayers.

The district's engineers have drafted a series of feasible lines, as illustrated in Figure 6.25. The district has solicited sealed bids from contractors interested in building some or all of the system, and determined the lowest feasible bid for each possible link. These costs may be further reduced on certain routes due to private funding pledges made by local businesses that have a stake in the design of the system.

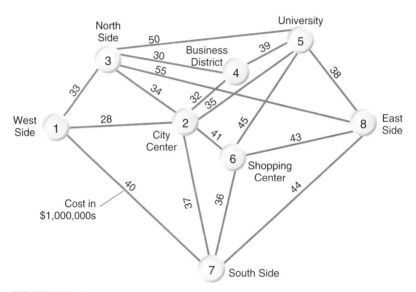

FIGURE 6.25   Metropolitan Transit District Spanning Tree Network Representation

The numbers on the arcs in Figure 6.25 represent the lowest bid less any amount pledged by local businesses (in $1 million). The district must decide which set of routes to select in order to minimize the total cost to taxpayers, while still providing a way to travel from any one of the centers to any of the other seven centers served by the system.

SOLUTION

The problem is to find the most cost-effective way to connect all eight centers. This is precisely the situation modeled by a minimal spanning tree problem.

A NETWORK
APPROACH

The minimal spanning tree problem does not lend itself to a convenient linear programming formulation. Fortunately, a very easy (some might even say trivial) algorithm can be applied to the network to solve the minimal spanning tree problem. This algorithm, which is illustrated in Supplement CD5 on the accompanying CD-ROM, is one of a class of techniques known as *Greedy algorithms*. The algorithm starts by being "greedy" and selecting the arc with the smallest arc length.[9] At each iteration, the

---

[9]Some versions of the Greedy algorithm, including the one used by WINQSB, start by choosing the arc of minimum distance from node 1 first rather than the arc with the minimum distance in the entire network. Either method will yield an optimal result.

algorithm is again greedy and adds the next smallest arc that connects to the set of arcs already selected, *while not forming a cycle*. This process is repeated until all nodes are connected; that is, n − 1 arcs have been selected.

COMPUTER SOLUTION OF MINIMAL SPANNING TREE PROBLEMS

Modules that use a greedy algorithm to solve minimal spanning tree models, such as the one found in WINQSB, simply require the user to input the number of nodes and the arc lengths. After doing so, the WINQSB output shown in Figure 6.26 was generated for the Metropolitan Transit District.

Network Modeling							
File Format Results Utilities Window Help							
Solution for Minimal Spanning Tree Problem METROPOLITAN TRANSIT DISTRICT							
10-05-1998	From Node	Connect To	Distance/Cost		From Node	Connect To	Distance/Cost
1	WEST SD	CITY CEN	28	5	SOUTH SD	SHOPPING	36
2	BUSINESS	NORTH SD	30	6	CITY CEN	SOUTH SD	37
3	CITY CEN	BUSINESS	32	7	UNIVERS	EAST SD	38
4	CITY CEN	UNIVERS	35				
	Total	Minimal	Connected	Distance	or Cost	=	236

FIGURE 6.26   WINQSB output for the Metropolitan Transit District

As you can see, the minimum taxpayer cost of building the light rail transit system is $236 million, using routes from the City Center to West Side, Business Center, University Center, and South Side, and routes from Business Center to North Side, from East Side to University Center, and from South Side to Shopping Center. The minimal spanning tree giving the recommended transit links is shown in Figure 6.27.

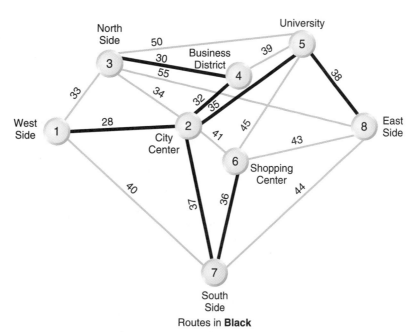

FIGURE 6.27   Metropolitan Transit District Minimum Cost Light Rail System

6.7   THE MAXIMAL FLOW PROBLEM

Have you ever been stuck in traffic and wondered why you weren't moving? Or have you ever attempted to call your mother on Mother's Day only to get the message, "We're sorry! All circuits are busy at this time. Please try again later." Both problems arise because the system is bottlenecked somewhere between you and your ultimate destination. Designing systems that eliminate or reduce such bottlenecks is a task that can be modeled as a maximal flow problem.

Maximal flow problems consist of a single start node, called the *source*, from which all flow emanates, and a terminal node, called the *sink*, into which the flow is deposited. Along the way, the flow travels on arcs connecting intermediate nodes. Each arc has a capacity that cannot be exceeded; the arc capacities need not be the same in each direction. For example, an arc corresponding to a "one-way street" may have a capacity of 400 cars per hour in one direction but a capacity of 0 cars per hour in the other.

The Maximal Flow Problem

1. There is a source node (labeled 1), from which the network flow emanates, and a terminal node (labeled n), into which all network flow is eventually deposited.

2. There are n − 2 intermediate nodes (labeled 2, 3, . . . , n − 1). At each of these nodes, the flow into the node must equal the flow out of the node.

3. There are capacities Cij for flow on the arc *from* node i to node j, and capacities Cji for flow *from* node j back to node i.

Goal: Find the maximum total flow possible out of node 1 that can flow into node n without exceeding the capacities on any arc.

The situation faced by United Chemical Company can be represented using a maximal flow model.

UNITED CHEMICAL COMPANY

The United Chemical Company is a small producer of pesticides and lawn care products. One production area contains a huge drum that holds up to 100,000 gallons of a poisonous chemical used in making various insecticides. The drum is routinely filled to a

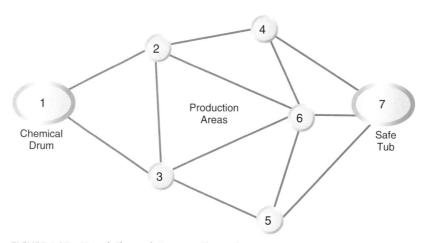

FIGURE 6.28   United Chemical Company Chemical Piping System

level somewhere between 80,000 and 90,000 gallons. The flow of the chemical is then regulated through a series of pipes to production areas, where the chemical is mixed with other ingredients and blended into finished products.

In Figure 6.28, the drum is denoted by node 1, and the production areas are labeled nodes 2, 3, 4, 5, and 6. Node 7 is the disposal area, where waste is deposited into a large "safe tub." It is then collected from the tub and disposed of in a manner consistent with federal regulations.

The flows during the production process occur at relatively low speeds that do not begin to approach the flow capacities of any of the pipes. But, as part of the company's Emergency Preparedness Plan, the Safety Division of the company must have a procedure to empty the tank completely into the safe tub in the event of an unforeseen emergency. In such an emergency, the company must shut the valves correctly at the production sites to regulate the flow so that the drum containing the poisonous chemicals can empty in the minimum amount of time.

Table 6.6 gives the volume that can flow through each pipe expressed in terms of thousands of gallons per minute.

TABLE 6.6   CAPACITY OF PIPES
(in 1000 gallons/minute)

		To					
		1	2	3	4	5	6	7
F	1		10	10				
r	2			1	8		6	
o	3		1			12	4	
m	4						3	7
	5						2	8
	6			4	3	2		2
	7							

The plan must determine which valves to open and shut, as well as provide an estimated time for total discharge of the poisonous chemicals into the secure waste area.

SOLUTION

Figure 6.29 gives a network representation for this problem. The numbers closest to each node indicate the capacity on the corresponding arc for flow *from* the node. Note

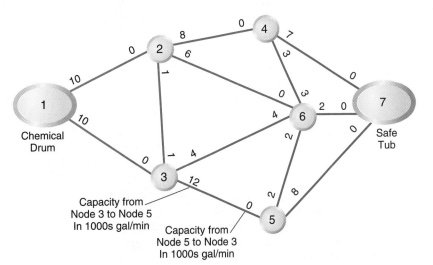

FIGURE 6.29   United Chemical Company Maximum Flow Network Representation

that flow is possible in either direction between nodes 2 and 3, 3 and 6, 4 and 6, and 5 and 6. Flow is restricted to one direction for all other arcs.

A LINEAR PROGRAMMING APPROACH

This problem can easily be formulated as a linear program and solved using a standard linear programming module. Again, because of the network structure, the solution will be integer valued. Using Xij to represent the flow (in thousands of gallons per hour from node i to node j), we can set out the linear programming formulation for the United Chemical problem as follows:

Objective
Maximize the flow out of source node 1:

$$\text{MAX } X12 + X13$$

Constraints
The total flow out of source node 1 must equal the flow into terminal node 7:

$$X12 + X13 = X47 + X57 + X67$$

For nodes 2, 3, 4, 5, and 6, the total flow into the node must equal the total flow out of the node:

$$
\begin{aligned}
\text{Node 2: } & X12 + X32 & = X23 + X24 + X26 \\
\text{Node 3: } & X13 + X23 + X63 & = X32 + X35 + X36 \\
\text{Node 4: } & X24 + X64 & = X46 + X47 \\
\text{Node 5: } & X35 + X65 & = X56 + X57 \\
\text{Node 6: } & X26 + X36 + X46 + X56 & = X63 + X64 + X65 + X67
\end{aligned}
$$

The flows cannot exceed the arc capacities:

$$X12 \leq 10;\ X13 \leq 10;\ X23 \leq 1;\ X24 \leq 8;\ X26 \leq 6;\ X32 \leq 1;$$
$$X35 \leq 12;\ X36 \leq 4;\ X46 \leq 3;\ X47 \leq 7;\ X56 \leq 2;\ X57 \leq 8;$$
$$X63 \leq 4;\ X64 \leq 3;\ X65 \leq 2;\ X67 \leq 2$$

The flows cannot be negative:

$$\text{All } Xij \geq 0$$

For this small problem, such data are relatively easy to input, and the linear programming solution can be obtained rather quickly. For larger problems, however, the network structure of the maximal flow problem can be exploited to give a more efficient solution procedure.

A NETWORK APPROACH

The network approach to the maximal flow problem is given in Supplement CD5 on the accompanying CD-ROM. The basic idea behind the algorithm is to find a path with capacity remaining on each of the arcs and to augment the flow on these arcs by the minimum remaining capacity of any arc on this path.

For example, consider the path from 1–2–4–7 in the original network. The capacity is 10 from 1–2, 8 from 2–4, and 7 from 4–7. Since flow along this path must flow through each arc, the maximal flow along this path is 7. (The arc from 4–7 could not handle a flow of 8 or 10.) If flow along this path is increased to 7, the arc from 4–7 is *saturated* and no additional flow can occur on the arc. The residual arc capacities are then modified to reflect the increased flow along this path. This procedure is repeated again and again until no path can be found from the source to the sink in which all arcs have positive residual capacity.

COMPUTER SOLUTION
OF THE MAXIMAL
FLOW PROBLEM

Modules that solve maximal flow problems by network methods, such as the module in WINQSB, require only a designation of a source node and a sink node and the flow capacities along each arc in the network. The flow capacities between two nodes can have different values, depending on the direction of the flow. In such cases, both a forward and a backwards capacity must be entered for the arc. The arc capacity data were entered into WINQSB, with node 1 designated as the source node and node 7 as the terminal node. The problem was solved generating the output shown in Figure 6.30.

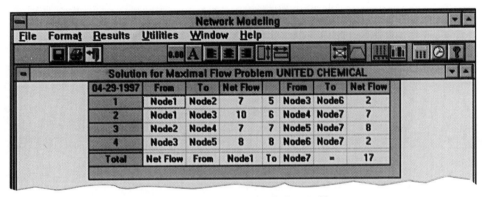

FIGURE 6.30   WINQSB Output—United Chemical Maximal Flow Problem

As you can see, the maximal flow is 17,000 gallons per minute, which can be obtained by sending the flows given in the output over the listed arcs. If the drum is full with 100,000 gallons, it will take about 100,000/17,000 = 5.88 minutes to empty the entire contents into the safe tub.

THE ROLE OF CUTS
IN MAXIMAL FLOW
NETWORKS

Consider drawing any straight line through the network which puts the source node 1 on one side of the line and the terminal node 7 on the other. In Figure 6.31a the line "cuts" the network in two, putting node 1 on one side of the cut and nodes 2, 3, 4, 5, 6, and 7 on the other. Since all flow that runs from node 1 to node 7 must cross this

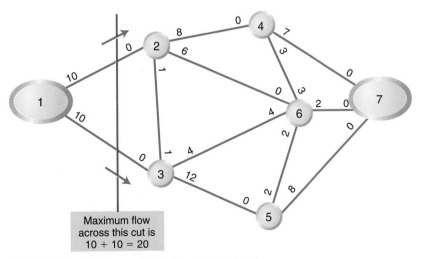

FIGURE 6.31a   Cut Between Nodes (1) and (2,3,4,5,6,7)

line, the sum of the arc capacities of 20 on the cut (10 from 1–2 and 10 from 1–3) provides one *upper bound* for the maximum flow from node 1 to node 7. The maximal flow would *equal* 20 if, in the optimal solution, the arcs from both 1–2 and 1–3 are saturated.

The sum of the arc capacities of *any* cut that puts node 1 on one side and node 7 on the other similarly provides an additional upper bound for the value of the maximum flow. Figures 6.31*b* and 6.31*c* illustrate two additional cuts. In Figure 6.31*b*, another upper bound is 27, found by summing the capacities on the arcs from 1–3, 2–3, 2–6, 4–6, and 4–7 (= 10 + 1 + 6 + 3 + 7). The upper bound of 20 from Figure 6.31*a* is a tighter upper bound, however.

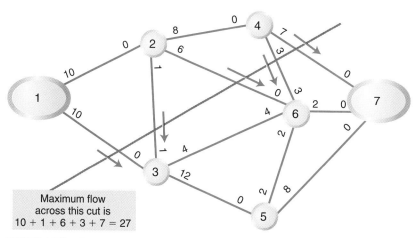

FIGURE 6.31*b*   Cut Between Nodes (1,2,4) and (3,5,6,7)

In Figure 6.31*c* we find still another upper bound by summing the capacities on the arcs from 4–7, 6–7, and 5–7. This gives us an upper bound of 7 + 2 + 8 = 17, which is less than our previously observed upper bound of 20. Because the capacities of any cut in the network place an upper bound on the maximum flow, the cut with the minimum capacity is the tightest upper bound for the total flow in the network. This lowest upper bound is actually met and is the value of the maximal flow. This condition is known as the **Max Flow/Min Cut** result.

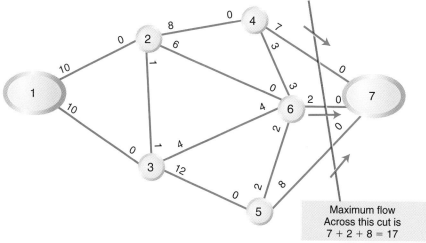

FIGURE 6.31*c*   Cut Between Nodes (1,2,3,4,5,6) and (7)

The Max Flow/Min Cut Theorem

1. The value of the maximum flow = the sum of the capacities of the minimum cut.

2. All arcs on the minimum cut are saturated by the maximum flow.

Returning to the WINQSB output, we saw that the maximum flow is indeed 17 and that all arcs on the cut of Figure 6.31*c* are saturated. That is, the flow on each of the arcs on the cut equals the capacity of the arc: the flow on the arc 4–7 is its capacity of 7; on the arc 6–7 is its capacity of 2; and on the arc 5–7 is its capacity of 8.

SPECIAL CASE—
MULTIPLE SOURCES
AND MULTIPLE SINKS

In some cases, there is more than one source node, more than one sink node, or both. Although, at first glance, this may not seem to fit the structure of a maximal flow model, a simple transformation of the problem is all that is required. Consider the case illustrated by Figure 6.32 in which nodes 2 and 3 are source nodes and nodes 6, 7, and 8 are sink nodes.

To convert this problem to the standard maximal flow problem, we can create a "supersource" and a "supersink," labeled node 1 and node 9, respectively, as in Figure 6.33. The capacities on the arcs leading out of the supersource are the sum of the

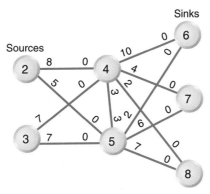

FIGURE 6.32   Maximum Flow Network with Multiple Sources and Sinks

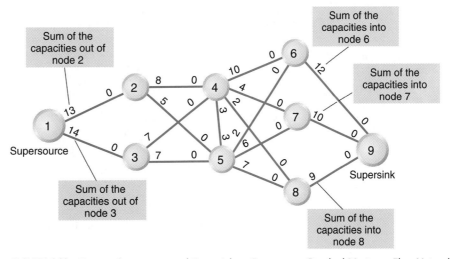

FIGURE 6.33   Using a Supersource and Supersink to Convert to a Standard Maximum Flow Network

capacities leading out of the corresponding source nodes, and the capacities of the arcs leading into the supersink are the sum of the capacities leading into the corresponding sink nodes. Thus, Figure 6.32 is a network that has the same structure as the standard maximal flow problem.

6.8 SUMMARY

Many typical managerial situations can best be expressed using network models. Network models—problems expressed in terms of nodes and arcs and functions defined on the nodes and/or arcs—are easy to work with. Because of their special structure, many network problems provide efficient solution techniques that are streamlined versions of linear programming algorithms or that do not rely on linear programming solution techniques at all to obtain an optimal solution.

We introduced several of the more typical network models in this chapter. The following table summarizes the characteristics of each of these models and lists some potential applications.

Network Model	Description	Applications
Transportation/Transshipment/ Capacitated Transshipment	Find the total minimum cost of shipping goods from supply points to destination points.	• Department store branch shipments • Monthly production scheduling • Marketing strategy approaches • Emergency supply allocation
Assignment	Find the minimum cost assignment of objects to tasks.	• Salesmen to territories • Pilots to aircraft • Programming tasks to programmers • Machines to locations
Traveling Salesman	Find the minimum cost of visiting *all* nodes of a network, returning to a starting node without repeating any node.	• Scheduling service crews • Designing robotics manufacturing equipment • Scheduling security patrols
Shortest Path	Find a path through *some* of the nodes of the network which minimizes the total distance from a source node to a destination node.	• Highway travel between cities • New road construction • Facility location • Equipment replacement
Minimal Spanning Tree	Find the minimum total distance that connects *all* nodes in the network.	• Sewer system design • Computer system layout • Cable television connections • Mass transit design
Maximal Flow	Find the maximum total flow possible from a source node to a sink node without violating arc capacities.	• Traffic flow systems • Production line flows • Shipping

WINQSB Input for Network Problems

All network problems discussed in this chapter can be solved using the NET module of WINQSB. When this module is selected, choices of network models are shown on the first screen (see Exhibit 6.1).

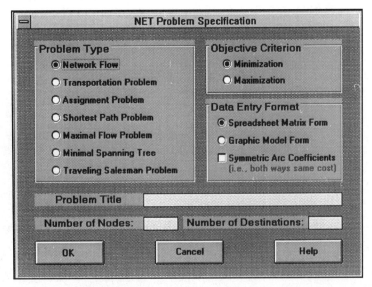

EXHIBIT 6.1   WINQSB Input Screen for Network Problems

At this stage, you select a model and choose whether your model has a minimization or a maximization objective (a default value for each model is initially chosen by the program) and decide how you wish to enter the data (we suggest the spreadsheet matrix form). You must also check the Symmetric Arc Coefficients box if the arcs are bidirectional with the same value in each direction. After giving the problem a title and giving the node information, click OK.

Input for all the models is straightforward. The nodes can be named in the Edit menu. In Exhibit 6.2, we show the input for the Carlton Pharmaceuticals problem discussed in Section 6.2.

Network Modeling

File   Edit   Format   Solve and Analyze   Results   Utilities   Window   Help

CARLTON PHARMACEUTICALS: Minimization (Transportation Problem)

Demand : Supply

From \ To	BOSTON	RICHMOND	ATLANTA	ST. LOUIS	Supply
CLEVELAND	35	30	40	32	1200
DETROIT	37	40	42	25	1000
GREENSBOF	40	15	20	28	800
Demand	1100	400	750	750	

EXHIBIT 6.2   WINQSB Input Screen for a Transportation Problem

From this screen you can select Solve the Problem from the Solve and Analyze menu to solve the problem and get the output screen we presented in this chapter. For some models, sensitivity analyses may be performed using the Results menu.

Excel Solution for Transportation Problems

Transportation models, assignment models, capacitated transshipment models, and maximal flow problems all have constraint structures that allow for easy setup and solution by Excel. In Exhibit 6.3, we show the Excel input for the transportation model given in Section 6.2. We begin by creating a matrix of unit cost coefficients (B5:E7), a column for the supplies, (G5:G7), and a row for the demands (B9:E9). A second matrix labeled the same way is set aside for the results in B13:E15. Cells G13:G15 are set aside for the total shipments from the supply nodes and cells B17:E17 for the total shipments to the demand nodes. A formula is placed in cell H18 that gives the total cost of the solution.

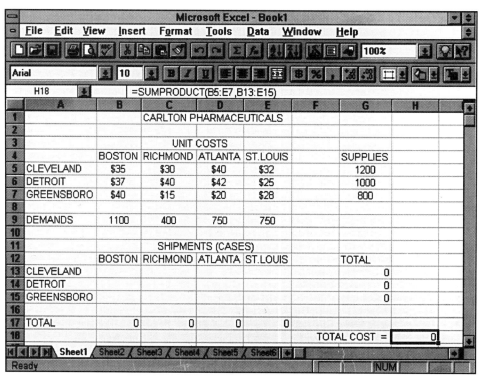

EXHIBIT 6.3   Excel Screen for a Transportation Problem

The following formulas have been entered:

> G13: =SUM(B13:E13)—pull this entry down to cells G14, G15
> C17: =SUM(B13:B15)—pull this entry across to cells D17, D18, D19
> H18: =SUMPRODUCT(B5:E7,B13:E15)

- Select Solver from the Tools menu and fill in the dialog box as shown in Exhibit 6.4

Note that the criterion has been changed to a minimization problem. The constraints restrict the variables to be nonnegative and require that the total units shipped equal the total supplies and the total units received equal the total demands, respectively. Clicking on Solve gives us the screen showing the optimal solution given in Section 6.2.

EXHIBIT 6.4   Solver Screen for a Transportation Problem

PROBLEMS

1. NW Lumber is a logging and lumber processor located in northern California, Oregon, and Washington. NW is currently logging in an area near Garberville, California, as well as Grant's Pass, Oregon, and Willard, Washington. It owns and operates processing plants in Eureka, California, Crescent City, California, and Coos Bay, Oregon. For the upcoming month, processing capacities are 2000 tons at Eureka, 1400 tons at Crescent City, and 1500 tons at Coos Bay. It is forecasted that NW could harvest 1600 tons of timber during the month at each of the three logging locations.

    The following table gives the transportation costs per ton. How should the 4800 tons of timber be shipped to the processing plants in the coming month in order to minimize total transportation costs for NW Lumber?

    TRANSPORTATION COST PER TON

	To		
	Eureka	Crescent City	Coos Bay
From			
Garberville	$175	$225	$250
Grant's Pass	$150	$100	$100
Willard	$300	$275	$200

2. Beckley, West Virginia, has solicited bids from interested construction firms for five projects it wishes to complete during this fiscal year. Six firms have submitted bids on the projects, as indicated in the following table. (An "X" means that the firm did not submit a bid for that project.)

	Refurbish Courthouse	Build New Library	Modernize Playground	Build Parking Structure	Improve City Park
Millard Associates	$800,000	$750,000	$300,000	$450,000	$200,000
QM Construction	$950,000	$725,000	X	$500,000	$275,000
Latham Brothers	X	X	$200,000	X	$225,000
Beckley Engineering	$650,000	$700,000	$250,000	$400,000	$225,000
WRT, Inc.	$700,000	$800,000	$175,000	$300,000	$300,000
B&P Enterprises	$850,000	$900,000	$270,000	$475,000	X

    Since the projects will be ongoing simultaneously, no firm will be able to complete more than one project.

    a. How should the contracts be awarded?

    b. If the total amount budgeted this year for these capital projects is $2 million, can all the projects be funded? If not, list some options the city of Beckley may wish to consider.

3. Calimex International is an agricultural company that has two primary regions for growing tomatoes, one in the Coachella Valley of California, the other in northern Mexico. During the peak season, tomatoes are picked daily and sent to one of three inspection stations in southern California. After the tomatoes have been inspected, they are transported to one of four packing houses.

    Each day 4500 pounds of tomatoes are picked in California, and 4000 pounds are picked in Mexico. Each inspection station can process over 10,000 pounds per day. The packaging plants can handle 1500, 2500, 2000, and 2500 pounds per day, respectively. Since total daily supplies amount to only 8500 pounds, capacity at the inspection stations imposes no constraints on the shipments. That is, all tomatoes that arrive at any of the three inspection stations can be processed and sent on to the packaging plants.

The following table gives the shipping cost per truck from each growing region to each inspection station and from each inspection station to each packaging plant; 500 pounds of tomatoes are shipped in each truck.

	Inspection Station				Packaging Plant			
	1	2	3		1	2	3	4
Region				Inspection Station				
California	$200	$400	$900	1	$1,000	$1,400	$1,800	$2,000
Mexico	$600	$200	$400	2	$1,800	$1,200	$1,400	$2,000
				3	$2,800	$1,600	$1,400	$ 800

a. Find the shipping pattern that minimizes transportation costs from the growing areas to the packaging plants.

b. Suppose a maximum of three trucks are available to travel each route. Which shipping pattern minimizes transportation costs from the growing areas to the packaging plants?

c. The situation modeled here consists of picking and loading tomatoes in the growing region, inspecting them at the inspection stations, and packing them at the packaging plants. Why might the assumption that the flow into the transshipment points (inspection stations) equals the flow out of the transshipment points be violated?

4. Jo Yu, vice president of Broadtech, Inc., a distributer of PC clone computers located in San Bernardino, California, must travel to the port of Los Angeles, located in San Pedro, California, to pick up a shipment of computers from Taiwan. The following is a freeway map of southern California with distances in miles shown on the arcs.

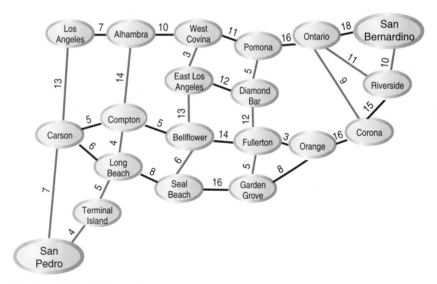

Southern California Freeway System

a. What route should Jo take to minimize the distance between his office and San Pedro?

b. Suppose Jo is traveling during the morning rush hour. Jo's average speed on east-west routes during rush hour is only 25 miles per hour, whereas he averages 40 miles per hour on north-south routes. (The routes considered east-west routes are in black; the north-south routes are in blue.) What route should Jo take to minimize the travel time between his office and San Pedro?

5. Clare Walker sells hospital supplies throughout the Midwest and Plains states. She depends on small, local commuter airlines for transport between cities. The following table gives the current air fares between the cities she must visit this week, as well as between these cities and her home in Kansas City. In which order should Clare visit the cities to minimize her total air fare cost for the week?

	To				
	Lincoln	Davenport	St. Louis	Tulsa	Wichita
From					
Kansas City	$200	$260	$ 75	$125	$125
Lincoln		$330	$145	$180	$100
Davenport			$100	$300	$275
St. Louis				$110	$165
Tulsa					$180

6. A recent tragic fire in Carbonville, Illinois, has prompted the City Council to draft a new ordinance requiring all buildings to have fully operational sprinkler systems installed by the end of the year. The Talcon Building is affected by this ordinance. From the original blueprints, engineers have designed positions for the location of eight powerful sprinkler heads that are to be connected to the sprinkler controller. The feasible connections between these eight sprinkler heads and the controller are depicted in the accompanying figure.

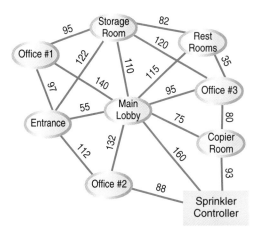

Talcon Building Sprinkler Location*
*Distances are in feet.

a. What design of the sprinkler system will minimize the total amount of pipe required (and hence give the maximal water pressure throughout the system)?

b. Suppose the engineers discovered that the connection between Office #1 and the Storage Room could not be made because of a recently installed air conditioning duct. What design of the sprinkler system would now minimize the total amount of pipe required?

7. Silverton is the latest planned community to be proposed for central Florida. The community will have two exits onto Interstate 4 and will consist of 11 small roads. The traffic capacities of each road (in terms of hundreds of vehicles per hour) are provided on the following map of the project. What is the maximal hourly flow of vehicles that can travel from the north exit of Interstate 4 through Silverton to the south exit of Interstate 4?

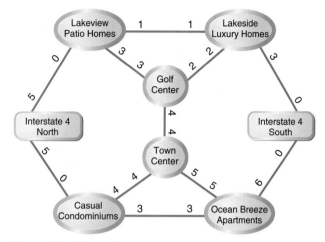

Silverton Road System*

*Capacities are in terms of 100's of vehicles per hour.

8. Pauline's, the Queen of Big Screen, is a chain of electronics stores specializing in big-screen televisions. In late January, the week before the Super Bowl, Pauline's always has a big sale. This January, two of its seven stores have excess supply of Mitsubishi 50-inch televisions, and the other five are requesting additional shipments. The word from Mitsubishi is that the orders will not arrive until after the Super Bowl. Hence, Pauline's has decided to redistribute some of its current inventory among its seven stores.

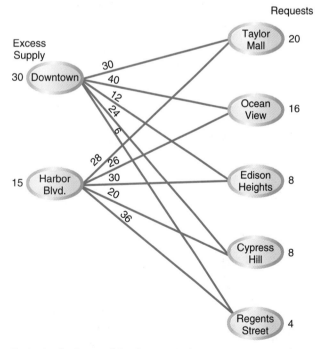

Pauline's: the Queen of Big Screen—Mileage Between Stores Shown on Arcs

a. What assumption about the individual transportation costs in the standard transportation model will most likely be violated in this situation?

b. The network shown in the accompanying figure shows the stores with excess demand (the Downtown store and Harbor Boulevard store) and the stores requesting additional televisions (stores at Taylor Mall, Ocean View Center, Edison Heights, Cypress Hill, and Regents Street). The network also shows the amount of excess supply, the demands, and the *distances* between those stores with supply and those with demand.

Transportation costs are figured at $0.50 per mile per television. This cost must be added to the fixed labor charges for loading and unloading, given in the following table.

Store	Labor Charges per Television
Downtown	$5.50
Harbor Boulevard	$4.50
Taylor Mall	$3.00
Ocean View Center	$3.25
Edison Heights	$3.75
Cypress Hill	$4.00
Regents Street	$5.00

How should the stock of 50-inch Mitsubishi televisions sets be redistributed prior to Super Bowl Sunday?

c. If each store requesting additional stock must receive at least 50% of its request, how should the stock of 50-inch Mitsubishi televisions sets be redistributed prior to Super Bowl Sunday?

d. What would happen if Pauline's insisted that every store requesting additional stock receive at least 75% of its request?

9. Lisa Alvarez has just been hired by Fox Television to help the station compete more successfully against the other commercial networks and cable television. Management has given her free reign to keep or bring in whomever she feels necessary to run the various operations: News, Sports, Features, Marketing, and Development. Lisa is considering seven people for the five positions. They have submitted resumes listing the following years of experience in each field.

YEARS OF EXPERIENCE

	News	Sports	Features	Marketing	Development
Tony Hernandez	8	7	0	0	2
Jim Lampsy	2	12	4	1	3
Monica Fish	7	2	7	2	4
Connie Chu	2	0	7	8	6
Scott Young	0	10	0	0	5
Linda Harlan	10	0	10	5	2
Ann Chambers	5	0	5	11	9

a. If years of experience is a measure of success, whom should Lisa choose to head each department?

b. Suppose Lisa is considering consolidating Features and Development into one unit. In this case, whom should she choose to head each department?

10. The Texas Education Association wishes to hold its annual meeting in one of three cities: Dallas, Austin, or Abilene. Representatives from 22 different school districts will attend, including representatives from the three possible host cities. The driving distances in miles are given in the following network. Assume that each attendee will drive the shortest route from his or her city to the meeting site.

a. Which site should be selected if the goal is to minimize the maximum driving distance of any attendee?

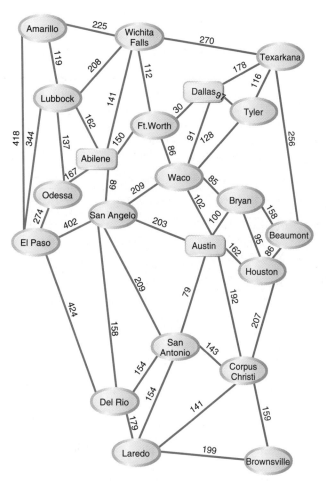

Texas Education Association

b. Which site should be selected if the goal is to minimize the average driving distance of all the attendees?

11. In designing a new digital circuit module for a component of the space shuttle, engineers must connect the six pins in the following figure with small strands of copper. In order to give maximum clarity to the signal, the total length of the wiring should be minimized.

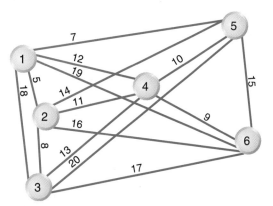

Digital Circuit Module*

*Distances are in millimeters.

a. If any number of wires can be attached to a single pin, find the minimum amount of wire required for the circuit design.

b. Suppose the pin size is so small that only two connections can be made at each pin. Show that, if a dummy node with distances of 0 from this node to every other node is included in the network, this problem can be formulated as a seven-node traveling salesman problem. Solve for the minimum amount of wire required for the circuit design under this condition.

12. Elders Tax Service employs tax specialists in four different regional offices who will be assigned to four separate accounts in various parts of the country. The costs (transportation, lodging, per diem, etc.) are given in the following table.

	Phoenix	Fresno	Austin	Miami
Ann Byers	$2,300	$3,210	$1,850	$4,000
Bill Cole	$2,850	$2,980	$3,320	$3,450
Ko Nguyen	$2,500	$2,500	$1,900	$3,200
Dave King	$3,000	$2,950	$2,875	$3,350

a. Determine the minimum cost assignment of tax specialists to cities.

b. Suppose Elders' client list has grown to 20 accounts in Phoenix, 15 in Fresno, 22 in Austin, and 36 in Miami and that Elders now employs 25 specialists in each of Ann's, Bill's, Ko's, and Dave's offices. If the assignment cost per specialist has not changed, determine the optimal number of specialists Elders should send from each office to each city.

13. Harris Rent-A-Truck operates exclusively in California and rents large-capacity vehicles designed primarily for household moves. One reason Harris fares well against its competitors in California is that it offers attractive one-way rates between the various cities it serves.

Although Harris has 250 trucks, at any point in time many of these trucks are rented and are not available for new customers. Every two weeks the company analyzes the location of the trucks it has available and attempts to balance its inventory by keeping at least 12 trucks at each of its seven locations. Thus, trucks are relocated to cities having fewer than 12 trucks from cities that have an excess. Transportation is to take no more than one day, however; hence, trucks in the northernmost areas of the state (Eureka and Redding) are unavailable to those in the southernmost areas (Los Angeles and Needles), and vice versa.

On March 15, Harris found that 160 of its trucks were out on rentals. The remaining 90 trucks were at the following locations:

> Eureka—11
> Redding—7
> San Francisco—6
> Fresno—25
> Bakersfield—18
> Los Angeles—7
> Needles—16

The following table gives the cost of relocating a truck between cities. These costs include driver time, gasoline, and driver return air/bus trip cost.

COST OF RELOCATING A TRUCK*

	To					
	Redding	San Francisco	Fresno	Bakersfield	Los Angeles	Needles
Eureka	$175	$250	$400	$480	N/A	N/A
Redding		$220	$380	$420	N/A	N/A
San Francisco			$300	$300	$350	$650
Fresno				$110	$200	$300
Bakersfield					$150	$275
Los Angeles						$350

(*Costs are the same in either direction.)

What should Harris's relocation strategy be on March 15?

14. Ponderosa Homes has just made a commitment to build the new gated community of Windstream. This community will consist of 110 homes in an undeveloped area off Hicks Canyon Boulevard. The gate for the community will be placed on a 150-foot-long street (tentatively called Venida Street) that will lead from Hicks Canyon Boulevard into the Windstream community. Venida Street as well as any other street constructed in the community, will be 35 feet wide.

Roads inside the community must be built so that every house has access to Venida and, hence, to all the other houses. Given the geography and other cost factors, the following figure shows the possible set of streets that can be built between the 10 clusters (of 11 homes each) and Venida Street. (Distances are in feet.)

Hicks Canyon Boulevard

The Windstream Community

Since Ponderosa Homes, and not the city, must pay for constructing the streets, and costs are proportional to the total area of streets built, what set of streets do you recommend Ponderosa build? Including Venida Street, what is the total square footage of streets required for the Windstream community?

15. The accounting firm of Barnes, Fernandez, and Chou has just hired six new junior accountants, who are to be placed into six specialty areas within the firm: auditing, corporate tax, personal tax, financial analysis, information systems, and general accounting. Each applicant has been given an overall skills test in the specialty areas; the results are presented in the following table.

BARNES, FERNANDEZ, AND CHOU TEST SCORES

	Auditing	Corporate Tax	Personal Tax	Financial Analysis	Information Systems	General Accounting
Amy Cheng	62	75	80	93	95	97
Bob Szary	75	80	82	85	71	97
Sue Crane	80	75	81	98	90	97
Maya Pena	78	82	84	80	50	98
Koo Thanh	90	85	85	80	85	99
Lyn Ortiz	65	75	80	75	68	96

a. If test scores are judged to be a measure of potential success, which junior accountant should be assigned to which specialty.

b. In addition to the primary specialty area, each new junior accountant will be trained in a second specialty so that the company has two junior accountants with training in each specialty area. Eliminating the original assignments found in part (a), what assignments now give the maximal potential for the second specialty?

16. Pisa Pizza makes home deliveries of pizzas. Pisa usually waits until six pizzas need to be delivered, but it will deliver any pizza that has been out of the oven for 12 minutes. During peak hours, the former condition usually applies.

    Vince Petralia is one of several college students working as a delivery person for Pisa Pizza. The following network depicts the time between the destinations of the six pizzas he is to deliver at 6:00 P.M.. Note that, because of traffic patterns, delivery times between points could depend on the direction traveled.

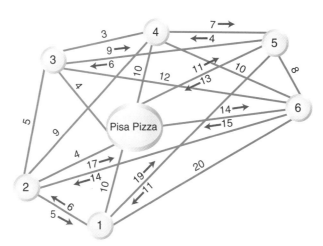

Pisa Pizza Delivery Times*

*Times are the same in each direction unless noted.

a. Suppose the time spent at each delivery point (walking to the door and collecting the money) is about one minute. What is the minimum time it will take Vince to deliver the six pizzas and return to Pisa Pizza?

b. Suppose the situation in part (a) is representative of a "typical" pizza run for Vince during his shift from 5:00 P.M. to 11:00 P.M.. Assume that, on the average, once Vince returns to Pisa Pizza he spends five minutes at the store (depositing the money collected from the previous run, waiting for and picking up the pizzas, and studying the map to determine the locations of the next set of deliveries). If he is paid $5 per hour by Pisa Pizza and averages a $1 tip from each pizza delivery, how much can Vince expect to earn in a typical night?

17. Build and Grow is a chain of five hardware stores serving southern Alabama and Mississippi. Each morning at 6:00, five large trucks are loaded at the warehouse with orders from each store. Given loading times at the warehouses and unloading time at the stores, the shipments are received at the stores by 1:00 P.M. and the trucks return to the warehouse by 5:00 P.M., where they are prepared for the next day's operations.

    Each truck usually goes out full, but, on occasion, there may be some excess capacity. Around 2:30 each afternoon, large vans travel between stores transferring goods that are needed by one and in excess supply at another.

    On April 23, the store at location 5 in the following network requested 500 50-pound bags of Topper Mulch from the warehouse after the delivery trucks from the warehouse to locations 4 and 5 had already left. No other store could spare any Topper Mulch for location 5. However, there was spare capacity in the trucks from the warehouse to stores 1, 2, and 3 of 200, 200, and 150 bags, respectively. This situation is depicted in the following network, along with the corresponding capacities left in the vans traveling between stores.

    Will location 5 be able to receive the 500 bags of Topper Mulch by the end of the day? If not, how many bags will it receive? How will the bags be transported?

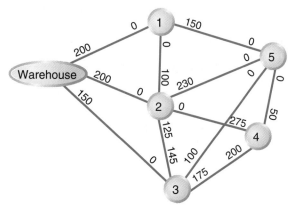

Build and Grow Distribution Network

18. Eastern Europe is interested in building a highway system similar to the Interstate Highway System of the United States. Currently, few such highways exist—none between Budapest, Hungary, and the Polish Baltic port of Gdansk. This route is of particular interest to Hungary, the Czech Republic, Slovakia, and Poland.

Funds for such construction in Eastern Europe are still scarce; thus, the governments have decided to build a superhighway between the two cities by expanding certain existing smaller highways and secondary roads, as shown in the following figure. What series of roads would minimize the highway distance between Budapest and Gdansk?

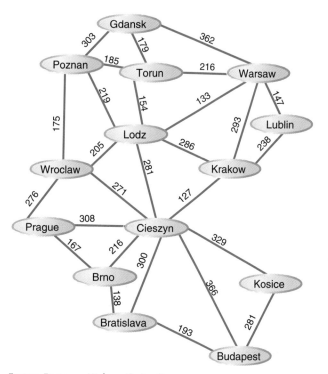

Eastern European Highway System*
*Distances are in kilometers.

19. The Police Department in Fargo, North Dakota, begins the morning shift by informing all first-shift patrol persons of the previous evening's activities and giving assignments to the various team members. On a particular day, the following three activities must be accomplished: (1) delivery of a DARE (Drug Abuse Resistance Education) lecture at a local elementary school; (2) instruction of the rookie police class in using the baton; and (3) preparation of a report for the evening's City Council meeting on drug activities over the past three months.

To help fulfill the mayor's promise of "keeping more police on the street," only three officers will be assigned to these activities. The goal is to minimize the total time these officers will be absent from street patrol. Given the expertise of each officer, the following are each officer's time estimates for each activity, including any preparation time that may be needed. Because the assignments will be occurring simultaneously, each officer will be assigned to only one of the activities.

	Expected Times (Hours)		
	DARE Lecture	Baton Training	Drug Analysis
Officer Borel	4	2	8
Officer Frank	4	3	7
Officer Klaus	3	1	6

a. Determine the minimal time assignment by direct enumeration of all possible combinations.

b. Draw the network representation of this problem.

c. Give the linear programming formulation for this problem and solve using a linear programming module.

d. Interpret this problem as a special case of the transportation problem and solve using the transportation approach.

e. Use the assignment approach to solve the problem.

20. Consider the police allocation problem for Fargo, North Dakota (Problem 19). Suppose that two additional officers are available for assignment to one of the three activities:

	Expected Times (hours)		
	Dare Lecture	Baton Training	Drug Analysis
Officer Muntz	5	4	5
Officer Clark	3	3	6

a. If you were to consider all possible assignments by direct enumeration, how many combinations would have to be considered? How many combinations would there be if there were *also* one additional activity? two additional activities?

b. Solve the five-officer, three-activity problem using the assignment approach to the model.

c. Suppose Officer Clark could perform two of the activities. Give the linear programming formulation for this problem and solve using a linear programming module.

d. Develop an assignment matrix for the problem in part (c) and solve.

21. Heavenly Flower Shop contracts with Floral Transportation Service (FTS) to deliver phone orders to the four cemeteries in town. FTS charges Heavenly a flat $2.50 per order plus $0.15 per mile for delivery per arrangement from one of Heavenly's two locations to the appropriate cemetery. The distances from Heavenly's two stores to the four cemeteries are given in the following table.

	Cemetery			
Heavenly Store Locations	Lilac Hills	Forest Glen	St. Mary's	Chelsea Pines
City Center	26	17	20	15
North Central	18	5	35	24

It is Memorial Day, and Heavenly has received telephone orders for 20 arrangements to be delivered to Lilac Hills, 16 to Forest Glen, 18 to St. Mary's, and 22 to

Chelsea Pines. Heavenly has enough flowers in its City Center location to make 45 arrangements, and enough in its North Central location to make 40 arrangements. Heavenly adds a flat $10 fee for delivery charges to all telephone orders.

How many of the orders for each cemetery should be filled at each location so that Heavenly maximizes its profit from delivery charges? What is the optimal profit?

22. Gerald Morris, president of Queen's County National Bank, makes periodic trips from the bank's home office to each of its seven branch offices in the Queen's County area. The following map shows the driving times (in minutes) between the home office and the branches. Since some of the routes are major highways, and others are surface streets with many stop lights, driving times are not directly proportional to the distance traveled.

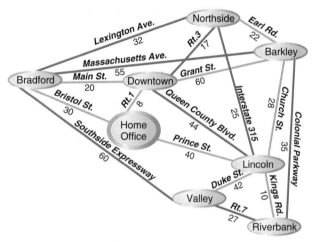

Queen's County National Bank Distances Between Branches

What are the minimum driving times and the routes that should be taken from the home office to each of the branches?

23. Next Tuesday, Gerald Morris, president of Queen's County National Bank (Problem 22), will make a surprise inspection of each branch office. He plans to leave the home office at 9:00 A.M., have a one-hour lunch break during the day, and return at 5:00 P.M..

a. In which order should Gerald Morris visit the branches to minimize his total driving time for the day if he wishes to visit or drive by any branch only once?

b. What is the minimum total driving time?

c. If Gerald is to spend the same amount of time inspecting each of the seven branch offices, how much time will he be able to spend at each branch?

24. For the Queen's County National Bank problem (Problems 22 and 23), Gerald Morris has decided that although he will not revisit any branch, he is willing to drive by a previously visited branch if doing so will decrease his overall driving time.

a. Find the minimum driving time between each branch pair.

b. Use your result for part (a) to determine the minimum driving time to visit each branch if Gerald can drive by a previously visited branch.

c. Assume that Gerald will spend the same amount of time at each branch. Give a minute-by-minute schedule that begins with his leaving the home office at 9:00 A.M. and ends with his return to the home office at 5:00 P.M.. Typical entries in the schedule might be:

10:14 Lv. Valley Branch—Drive Rt. 7 to Kings Rd.—to Lincoln Branch
10:51 Ar. Lincoln Branch—Meet with branch representatives
11:15 Lv. Lincoln Branch—Drive . . . .

Schedule Gerald's one-hour lunchbreak to be as close to 12:00 as possible.

25. Federal Electric produces compressors for air conditioning units. Labor and production costs average $60 per unit when units are produced during regular time and $66 per unit when they are produced in overtime. The average carrying (holding) cost for a unit from one quarter to the next is $15 per compressor. Thus, a unit produced in the first quarter during regular time but not sold until the third quarter would cost the company $60 to produce plus $30 in carrying costs ($15 for each of the two quarters stored). Each quarter, 750 hours of regular time and 500 hours of overtime are available for production. The average time it takes to produce a compressor is 30 minutes.

Given the following quarterly demand projections for compressors, what production plan minimizes total yearly costs for Federal Electric?

Quarter	Projected Demand
1	1250
2	625
3	3750
4	2500

CASE STUDIES

CASE 1: *Kaybee Amusements, Inc.*

Kaybee Amusements, Inc. is developing a theme park for the city of Baton Rouge, Louisiana. It is tentatively titled Heritageland; the concept is to build theme areas based on heritages common to six of the cultures that have influenced the Southern and Midwestern regions of the United States: (1) English; (2) French; (3) Spanish; (4) African; (5) German; and (6) Native American. Each of the six theme areas will have a theme restaurant, a cultural center with a 360° theater, a stage show pavilion, and amusement attractions. In addition, the park will include a main plaza area with a multicultural atmosphere and a parking lot.

The following map of the park includes all pedestrian corridors between the theme areas, the plaza, and the parking lot.

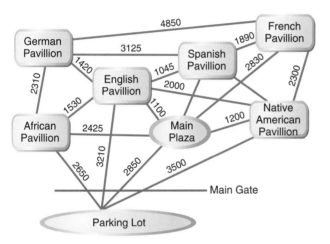

*Distances are in feet.

One of the proposed attractions is the Far West Streetcar Line, which, for a fee, will transport visitors in streetcars powered by underground cables. Because of costs, the park will only run seven streetcars, each starting in one theme area, traversing to a second area, and then returning to the original one through the same corridor. Each streetcar ride will move directly down the center of the pedestrian corridor running between the two theme areas. Kaybee would like to use the minimal distance of underground cable while enabling patrons to travel to any theme area, the plaza, and the parking lot via street cars.

For those who prefer a more modern form of transportation, a circuitous monorail system will be constructed to provide transportation among all areas. The links for the monorail system among areas will be constructed directly above pedestrian corridors. The monorail system will start at the parking lot and visit each theme area and the plaza once before returning to the parking lot for another run. To conserve costs, the minimum distance monorail line should be constructed.

Finally, for those who prefer walking (or do not wish to pay for the other modes of transportation within the park), the park will provide every visitor with a welcome brochure. One page in the brochure will be a map, including directions showing the visitor how to get "From Here to There" in the shortest walking distance.

Prepare a report for Kaybee Amusements suggesting the design of the most cost-effective streetcar and monorail routes. Also provide the copy for the page entitled "From Here to There" in the welcoming brochure that gives visitors the routes of shortest distance between any two theme areas, the plaza, and the parking lot.

CASE 2: *GSA Industries*

GSA Industries produces four models of prefabricated housing units in each of two locations: one in El Cajon, California, the other in Elkhart, Indiana. The manufactured houses are transported to regional distribution centers in Phoenix, Nashville, and Miami. Because of current economic conditions, GSA is able to sell all the units it manufactures during the year. The following table gives the outstanding orders for the year as well as the production plan GSA has approved for the Elkhart, Indiana plant.

ORDERS AND PRODUCTION QUANTITIES AT ELKHART, INDIANA

	Model			
	Picket Fence	Town House	Gentle Stream	El Presidente
Phoenix	50	60	60	90
Nashville	80	60	30	20
Miami	75	90	85	90
Production at Elkhart Plant	100	75	75	120

The El Cajon plant is being reconfigured for this year's models. The plant consists of four separate buildings, each of which will produce a different model. The number of prefabricated houses that can be produced in a building depends on many factors, including the size and shape of the building and the existing production facilities. The accompanying table gives the estimated production quantities of each model.

For example, if Building 1 is used to produce the Picket Fence Model, 30 such models can be produced; if it is used to produce the Town House model, 25 such models can be produced, and so on. Because of the design of Building 3, no El Presidente models can be produced in Building 3.

PRODUCTION LEVELS

	Model			
	Picket Fence	Town House	Gentle Stream	El Presidente
Building 1	30	22	20	10
Building 2	60	55	50	45
Building 3	40	35	30	N/A
Building 4	95	85	See text	65

These production quantities were determined by analyzing the rate at which various subassemblies can be manufactured and passed along to the next operation. The production

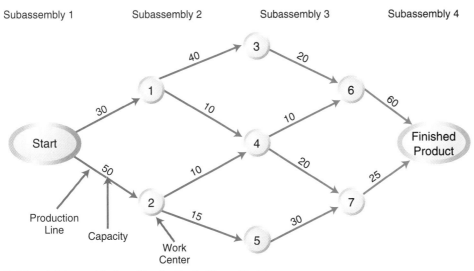

Building 4 Subassembly Capacities for Gentle Stream Model

of the subassemblies have constraining capacities. A network representation for the Gentle Stream model in Building 4 is shown above.

The gross profit per unit (excluding transportation costs and fixed labor and overhead cost) for GSA are given in the following table.

GROSS PROFIT PER UNIT

Model	Gross Profit
Picket Fence	$ 9,600
Town House	$11,520
Gentle Stream	$15,360
El Presidente	$19,200

Unit transportation charges from either the Elkhart, Indiana, plant or the El Cajon plant are independent of the model shipped. Thus, each model has exactly the same transportation cost between a particular pair of cities. The following unit transportation costs have been determined for the Elkhart, Indiana, plant.

UNIT TRANSPORTATION COSTS FROM ELKHART, INDIANA

To	Cost
Phoenix	$1,450
Nashville	$ 725
Miami	$2,500

The unit transportation costs from El Cajon depend on the mode and time of transportation. Various truck, rail, and boat routes are available under contract to GSA. These are summarized in the following table. The cost of changing modes of transportation at a city (rail to truck, truck to rail, or truck to ship) is $250 per vehicle.

SHIPPING ROUTES

From	To	No. of Days	Cost/day
Truck Routes			
El Cajon	Phoenix	1	$375
El Cajon	Dallas	3	$300
Phoenix	Rapid City	2	$250
Phoenix	Oklahoma City	2	$175
Dallas	New Orleans	1	$300
Rapid City	Chicago	3	$325
Rapid City	Oklahoma City	2	$250
Rapid City	Nashville	4	$200
Chicago	Nashville	2	$300
Chicago	Raleigh	3	$375
Oklahoma City	New Orleans	3	$225
Oklahoma City	Nashville	4	$300
Oklahoma City	Raleigh	5	$200
Nashville	Miami	3	$350
Raleigh	Miami	4	$250
Rail Routes			
El Cajon	Phoenix	2	$250
El Cajon	Dallas	4	$350
Phoenix	Rapid City	3	$175
Chicago	Nashville	3	$200
Chicago	Raleigh	4	$225
Oklahoma City	Raleigh	3	$250
Raleigh	Miami	3	$300
Boat Routes			
New Orleans	Miami	4	$400

Fixed labor costs at both plants combined are expected to be $3 million; other overhead is estimated to be $2 million.

Prepare a report for GSA that analyzes the El Cajon operation in light of previous commitments at the Elkhart, Indiana, plant. Analyze:

1. The maximum production capacity of the Gentle Stream model at Building 4 in El Cajon.

2. Which building should produce which model at the El Cajon plant in order to maximize gross profit. (Ignore transportation costs in this analysis and discuss why this is probably valid with this particular set of data. Discuss how the model would change if it were not valid.)

3. The minimal total transportation costs from El Cajon to each of the distribution cities. (Discuss any *time* implications of your recommendation.)

4. The allocation of each housing model from each production city to each distribution city.

5. The net profit for the company for the year.

CHAPTER 7

PROJECT SCHEDULING

During the last week of April 1992, the worst riots in recent U.S. history occurred in south central Los Angeles. Within a three-day period, hundreds of businesses were damaged or destroyed. Among them was a local Taco Bell restaurant.

To demonstrate its commitment to the people of the community, Taco Bell pledged to rebuild and reopen the restaurant in record time. On Tuesday, June 9, 1992, Taco Bell began a crash project to construct a new restaurant on the same site as the one devastated by the riots. At 10:00 A.M. on Thursday, June 11, just 48 hours later, construction of the new restaurant was completed, and the first taco was sold.

Less than two years later, in January 1994, another disaster struck the Los Angeles area. An earthquake measuring 6.7 on the Richter scale devastated homes, businesses, and property. Several freeways, including the Santa Monica Freeway, the most heavily traveled in the world, were severely damaged, as concrete cracked and bridges tumbled.

Roadways had to be repaired and bridges and overpasses retrofitted to meet earthquake standards. In only three months, more than two months ahead of what many had considered to be an overly optimistic schedule, the repair work was completed and the freeway was reopened. Because the project was completed well ahead of schedule, the federal government covered all costs, and contractors were awarded $15 million in bonuses for their efforts.

The positive outcomes in both of these cases were accomplished with considerable coordination and management of the numerous individual tasks that had to be performed. Response to a disaster, of course, is only one area in which project planning plays a crucial role. New product development, manufacture of existing products, conference planning, audit design, and development of marketing campaigns are just some of the many areas in which careful project planning is essential.

7.1 INTRODUCTION TO PROJECT SCHEDULING

We can think of a *project* as a collection of tasks a person or firm desires to complete in minimum time or at minimal cost. For example, in painting the outside of a house a contractor must: (1) select color(s); (2) purchase paint; (3) clean existing siding; (4) mask windows; (5) spray paint large areas; (6) hand paint trim; and (7) clean up. Factors affecting the completion time might include the number of painters the contractor employs, the availability of the individual paint colors, and the square footage and special details of the house. The painting contractor's primary objective might be to finish painting the outside of the house in minimal time so that he can move on to another project, or at minimal total cost so that he will earn the maximum profit from his work.

The tasks of a project are called *activities*. Estimated completion times (and sometimes costs) are associated with each activity of a project. Activities can be defined broadly or narrowly, depending on the situation. For example, an activity involved in bringing a new play to Broadway might be "Hire Cast." Although this description is appropriate for some models, in other cases it might be beneficial to subdivide this part of the project into much narrower sets of activities, such as:

"Hold Auditions for Principal Characters"

"Arrange for Call-Back Auditions of Principal Characters"

"Cast Principal Characters"

"Hold Auditions for Extras"

"Cast Extras"

"Hold Preliminary Run-Through"

"Make Final Cast Selections"

The degree of detail depends on both the application and the level of specificity in the available time and cost data.

In any project, certain activities must be completed before others are started, whereas others may be completed simultaneously. For a Broadway play, "Hire Cast" certainly must precede "Dress Rehearsal," but "Dress Rehearsal" need not precede "Advance Ticket Sales," or vice versa. Determining an accurate set of *precedence relations* among the activities—that is, detailing which activities must precede others—is crucial to developing an optimal schedule for the individual activities.

The completion time for each activity, and, thus, the overall project completion time, is generally related to the amount of resources committed to it. In the opening vignette, the completion time of the Taco Bell restaurant could not have been reduced from its *normal completion time* of almost two months to its *crash completion time* of two days without spending extra money (on overtime wages and talented crews willing to work at night). And, even though Taco Bell was committed to meeting a prepublicized deadline of 48 hours, it wished to do so at minimum total cost. Similarly, in the freeway repair problem, since contractors were offered a bonus of $15 million for completing the repairs before a specified date, additional resources were committed to critical activities in the successful effort to meet this deadline. In both cases, the positive results did not just happen. Rather, the successes were the results of careful and comprehensive project planning, scheduling, and monitoring.

OBJECTIVES OF PROJECT SCHEDULING

Project scheduling is used to plan and control a project efficiently and can determine:

1. The minimal expected completion time for a project.

2. Activities that are *critical*, in the sense that any delay to any of these activities will delay the entire project.

3. The earliest and latest time each activity can be started and completed.

4. The amount of slack time for each activity.

5. Which of two or more completion alternatives is the most cost effective.

6. The activities on which extra resources should be spent to meet a target project's completion date or to come in under budget.

7. Whether or not a current project is on schedule or is being completed within budget.

8. A schedule of activities that offers a relatively consistent level of resources (personnel, capital, equipment, etc.) while completing the project in minimal time.

9. A schedule of activities that completes the project in minimum time given limits on the availability of one or more of the resources.

These objectives can be accomplished using project scheduling approaches, such as PERT (Program Evaluation and Review Technique) and CPM (Critical Path Method). These methods, which were both developed in the mid 1950's, use project networks to help schedule a project's activities. Although the distinction between the two techniques has blurred in recent years, PERT is generally thought of as a method that treats the completion time of the activities as random variables with specific probability distributions, whereas CPM assumes that the completion time of an activity is solely dependent on the amount of money spent to complete the activity.

Both PERT and CPM require the modeler to identify the activities of the project and the *precedence relations* between them. This involves determining a set of *immediate predecessors* for each activity, consisting of those activities that must be completed just prior to its commencement. A *precedence relation chart* identifies the separate activities of the project and their precedence relations. From this chart a PERT/CPM network representation of the project can then be constructed.

7.2 ℐDENTIFYING THE ACTIVITIES OF A PROJECT

To illustrate the concepts of project scheduling, we consider the situation faced by Klone Computer, Inc.

Klone1.cpm

KLONE COMPUTERS, INC.

Klone Computers is a small manufacturer of personal computers which is about to design, manufacture, and market the Klonepalm 2000 palmbook computer. The company faces three major tasks in introducing a new computer: (1) manufacturing the new computer; (2) training staff and vendor representatives to operate the new computer; and (3) advertising the new computer.

When the proposed specifications for the new computer have been reviewed, the manufacturing phase begins with the design of a prototype computer. Once the design is determined, the required materials are purchased and prototypes manufactured. Prototype models are then tested and analyzed by staff personnel who have completed a staff training course. Based on their input, refinements are made to the prototype and an initial production run of computers is scheduled.

Staff training of company personnel begins once the computer is designed, allowing the staff to test the prototypes once they have been manufactured. After the computer design has been revised based on staff input, the sales force undergoes full-scale training.

Advertising is a two-phase procedure. First, a small group works closely with the design team so that once a product design has been chosen, the marketing team can begin an initial preproduction advertising campaign. Following this initial campaign and completion of the final design revisions, a larger advertising team is introduced to the special features of the computer, and a full-scale advertising program is launched.

The entire project is concluded when the initial production run is completed, the salespersons are trained, and the advertising campaign is underway. As a first step in generating a project schedule, Klone needs to develop a precedence relations chart that gives a concise set of individual tasks for the project and shows which other tasks must be completed prior to the commencement of each task.

SOLUTION

The entire project can be represented by the ten activities—five manufacturing, three training, and two advertising—given in Table 7.1. For easy reference, each activity is designated by a letter symbol.[1] After identifying the activities, we determine the immediate predecessors for each one using the reasoning in Table 7.2.

TABLE 7.1   KLONEPALM 2000 ACTIVITY DESCRIPTION

	Activity	Description
Manufacturing activities	A	Prototype model design
	B	Purchase of materials
	C	Manufacture of prototype models
	D	Revision of design
	E	Initial production run
Training activities	F	Staff training
	G	Staff input on prototype models
	H	Sales training
Advertising activities	I	Preproduction advertising campaign
	J	Postproduction advertising campaign

TABLE 7.2   IMMEDIATE PREDECESSORS FOR KLONEPALM 2000 ACTIVITIES

Activity	Requirements	Immediate Predecessors
A Prototype design	No requirements	—
B Purchase of materials	Materials can be purchased only after the prototypes have been designed (A).	A
C Manufacture of prototypes	Materials must be purchased (B) before the prototypes can be manufactured.	B
D Revision of design	Both prototype manufacturing (C) and staff input (G) must precede the design revision. However, since prototype manufacturing precedes staff input, it is not an *immediate* predecessor.	G
E Initial production run	The production run can begin after the design has been revised (D).	D
F Staff training	Staff training begins after the prototype is designed (A).	A
G Staff input on prototype	For staff input on prototypes, the prototype must be built (C) and the staff trained (F).	C,F

---

[1]Instead of letters, we could have used abbreviations or some other identifier. Which letter will designate which activity is a purely arbitrary decision and has no implications for which activity must be completed first.

TABLE 7.2 (continued)

Activity	Requirements	Immediate Predecessors
H Sales training	Salespersons can be trained immediately after the design revision (D).	D
I Preproduction advertising campaign	The initial preproduction advertising campaign can begin as soon as the prototypes have been designed (A).	A
J Postproduction advertising campaign	The large-scale postproduction advertising campaign begins when both the initial ad campaign has been completed (I) and the design has been revised (D).	D,I

These relations, along with Klone's estimates of the expected completion time for each activity (based on its past experiences manufacturing similar products), are summarized in the *precedence relations chart* shown in Table 7.3. In the next two sections, we will use this chart to construct graphical representations of the project.

TABLE 7.3 KLONEPALM 2000 PRECEDENCE RELATIONS CHART

Activity	Immediate Predecessors	Estimated Completion Time (days)
A	—	90
B	A	15
C	B	5
D	G	20
E	D	21
F	A	25
G	C,F	14
H	D	28
I	A	30
J	D,I	45

7.3 GANTT CHARTS

If each activity of the Klonepalm 2000 project were performed sequentially, ignoring the possibility that some of the activities of the project could be completed simultaneously, the estimated completion time of the project would be $90 + 15 + 5 + 20 + 21 + 25 + 14 + 28 + 30 + 45 = 293$ days. Since work on several of the activities *can* be underway at the same time, however, the time required to complete the project will be less than 293 days. The goal of the management science team is to schedule activities so that the entire project is completed in the minimal number of days.

A popular device used to display activities and monitor their progress is the **Gantt chart**.[2] In a Gantt chart, time is measured on the horizontal axis, each activity is listed on the vertical axis, and a bar is drawn corresponding to its expected completion time. In an *earliest time Gantt chart*, the bar begins at the earliest moment the activity can be started (which is when all the activity's immediate predecessors are expected to be completed). The end of the bar represents the earliest completion time for the activity.

Figure 7.1 is an earliest time Gantt chart constructed using the information in the precedence relations chart for the Klonepalm 2000 project (Table 7.3). The bars in this chart are constructed by scheduling the start time for an activity to begin immediately after the completion time of all its predecessors. For example, after activity A has been

---

[2]Named for Henry Gantt, who developed the first such chart in 1918.

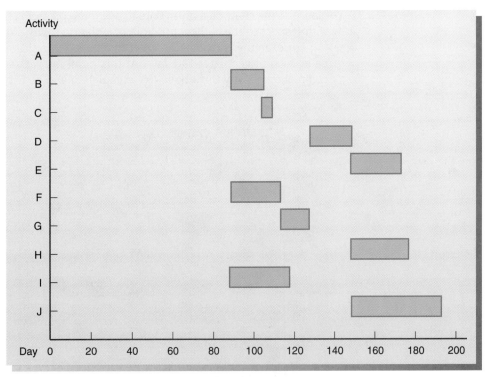

FIGURE 7.1   Klone Computers, Inc. Klonepalm 2000 Project

scheduled, activities B, F, and I (which require only that activity A be completed) are scheduled. After activity B is scheduled, activity C can then be scheduled. Once activities C and F have been scheduled, activity G is scheduled, and so on. Table 7.4 details the complete scheduling sequence of the activities. We can see from this Gantt chart, if things go as planned, and each activity is started at its earliest possible start date, the project can be completed in 194 days rather than 293 days.

TABLE 7.4   SCHEDULING SEQUENCE OF ACTIVITIES FOR THE KLONEPALM 2000 PROJECT

	Activities That Can Be Scheduled	Expected Completion Time	Predecessors (Finish Times)	Activity Schedule From	To
1	A	90	—	0	90
2	B	15	A (90)	90	105
	F	25		90	115
	I	30		90	120
3	C	5	B (105)	105	110
4	G	14	C (110), F (115)	115	129
5	D	20	G (129)	129	149
6	E	21	D (149)	149	170
	H	28		149	177
7	J	45	D (149), I (120)	149	194

MONITORING PROJECT PROGRESS ON A GANTT CHART

A crucial step in meeting a target completion date and containing costs is management's ability to monitor a project's progress. We can use a Gantt chart as a visual aid for tracking the progress of project activities by shading an appropriate percentage of the corresponding bar to document the completed work. A manager then need only glance at the chart on a given date to see if the project is being completed on schedule with respect to the earliest possible completion times of the activities.

For example, suppose the chart in Figure 7.2 indicates the progress of the Klonepalm 2000 project after 130 days. At this point, activities A, B, C, F, and G have been completed; activity D is about 40% completed; and activity I is about 50% completed.

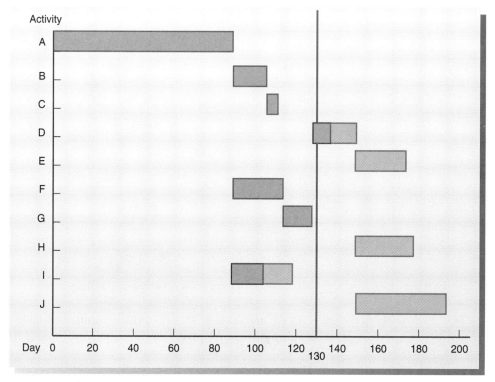

FIGURE 7.2   Klone Computers, Inc. Klonepalm 2000 Project: Monitoring Progress after 130 Days

It is important not to misinterpret the meaning of such a chart, however. We might be tempted to say that because activity I is only about one-half completed at day 130 (instead of being totally completed by day 120 as indicated by the bar on the Gantt chart), the project is running behind schedule. *This is not true.* In fact, the overall project might actually be running *ahead* of schedule! This is because activity I does *not* have to be completed by the earliest possible completion time indicated on the Gantt chart in order for the entire project to be completed within 194 days.

It turns out that as long as delays do not extend the completion time for activity I beyond day 149, the project will not be delayed. This potential misinterpretation points out one of the deficiencies of Gantt charts. Table 7.5 summarizes other pros and cons of the Gantt chart approach to project scheduling.

TABLE 7.5   ADVANTAGES AND DISADVANTAGES
OF THE EARLIEST TIME GANTT CHART APPROACH

Advantages	Disadvantages
1. The Gantt chart is easy to construct.	1. The Gantt chart gives only one possible schedule (the earliest) for the activities.
2. An earliest possible completion date can be determined.	2. It may not be possible to tell whether the project is behind schedule.
3. A schedule of earliest possible start and finish times for the activities is given that will meet the earliest possible project completion date.	3. Because precedence relations are not revealed on a Gantt chart, it is not obvious from the chart alone how a delay in one activity will affect the start date of another.

7.4   BUILDING PERT/CPM NETWORKS

Partly because of the limitations of Gantt charts, another approach to project scheduling, the PERT/CPM approach, is preferred for performing a more thorough analysis of possible project schedules.

The PERT/CPM approach to project scheduling is based on a network representation that reflects activity precedence relations. Management scientists have developed two possible designs for such networks. In an *activity on arc* (AOA) *network*, the nodes represent specific time points (events) denoting the completion of a set of activities; the activities themselves are represented by directed arcs between two nodes. In an *activity on node* (AON) *network*, the nodes designate activities and their completion times, and the arcs describe the precedence relations between activities.

AOA networks can be slightly more difficult to construct than AON networks and sometimes require the use of "dummy activities" to keep the precedence relations intact. Figure 7.3 gives an AOA network for the Klonepalm 2000 computer project. The gray lines labeled O1 and O2 are the dummy activities required to indicate that, while activities D and I are immediate predecessors of activity J, only activity D is an immediate predecessor of activities E and H.

In this chapter we will use AON networks, which are more easily understood and more often programmed into project scheduling software, including WINQSB. Figure 7.4

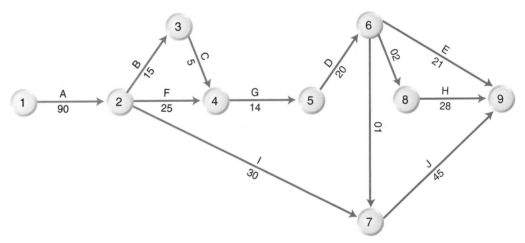

FIGURE 7.3   Activity on Arc (AOA) Representation of the Klonepalm 2000 Model

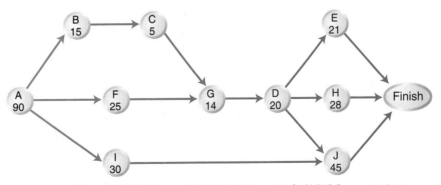

FIGURE 7.4   Klonepalm 2000 Computer Project Activity on Node (AON) Representation

shows the AON network for the Klonepalm 2000 project.[3] In this representation the nodes are labeled with the name of the activity and its completion time. When an activity immediately precedes one or more other activities, a directed arc is drawn from its node to each node representing one of these subsequent activities. This convenient network representation facilitates the PERT/CPM analyses of the project.

7.5   THE PERT/CPM APPROACH FOR PROJECT SCHEDULING

Two primary objectives of PERT/CPM analyses are (1) to determine the minimal possible completion time for the project; and (2) to determine a range of start and finish times for each activity so that the project can be completed in minimal time. To illustrate how the AON network can be used to achieve these objectives, let us return to the planning process faced by Klone Computers.

KLONE COMPUTERS, INC. (continued)

Klone1.cpm

Management at Klone Computers would like to schedule the activities of the Klonepalm 2000 project so that the project is completed in minimal time. In particular, management wishes to know:

1. The earliest completion date for the project
2. The earliest and latest start times for each activity which will not alter this date
3. The earliest and latest finish times for each activity which will not alter this date
4. The activities that must adhere to a rigid fixed schedule, and the activities that have slack in their schedule

SOLUTION

The PERT/CPM approach for the Klonepalm 2000 computer project is illustrated by referring to the AON network developed for this problem in Section 7.4.

EARLIEST START/FINISH TIMES—EARLIEST COMPLETION DATE

To determine the **earliest start time (ES)** and the **earliest finish time (EF)** for the activities, we make a *forward pass* through the network. We begin by evaluating all activities which have no immediate predecessor—in this case, only activity A. The ES for an activity with no predecessors is 0; its EF is simply the activity's completion time. Thus, for activity A, ES(A) = 0, EF(A) = 90.

We then proceed by selecting any node for which the EF of all its immediate predecessors has been determined—in this case B, F, and I. Since *all* of an activity's immediate predecessors must be completed before the activity can begin, the ES for this activity is the *maximum* of the EFs of its immediate predecessors. Its EF then equals its ES plus the time to complete the activity. Since activities B, F, and I require only the completion of activity A, and since the activity completion times for activities B, F, and I are 15, 25, and 30, respectively, we conclude:

$$ES(B) = 90 \qquad EF(B) = 90 + 15 = 105$$
$$ES(F) = 90 \qquad EF(F) = 90 + 25 = 115$$
$$ES(I) \, = 90 \qquad EF(I) \, = 90 + 30 = 120$$

---

[3]A finish node is not shown in WINQSB network representations.

Earliest Start/Finish Time for an Activity

ES = MAXIMUM EF of all its immediate predecessors
EF = ES + (Activity Completion Time)

We repeat this process until all nodes (including the finish node) have been evaluated, giving us a schedule of earliest start and finish times for each activity. The ES of the finish node is the earliest completion time for the project. The sequence of calculations that determine these times is given in Table 7.6.

TABLE 7.6   SEQUENCE OF ES AND EF CALCULATIONS

Activity	Immediate Predecessors (EF)	ES	EF
A	—	0	0 + 90 = 90
B	A (90)	90	90 + 15 = 105
F	A (90)	90	90 + 25 = 115
I	A (90)	90	90 + 30 = 120
C	B (105)	105	105 + 5 = 110
G	C (110), F (115)	115	115 + 14 = 129
D	G (129)	129	129 + 20 = 149
E	D (149)	149	149 + 21 = 170
H	D (149)	149	149 + 28 = 177
J	D (149), I (120)	149	149 + 45 = 194
Finish	E (170), H (177), J (194)	194	194

The ES and EF for each activity are represented on the PERT/CPM network by a pair of numbers above the node representing the activity, as shown in Figure 7.5.[4] Note that the earliest start and finish times of the activities are exactly those illustrated on the Gantt chart; we have verified that the earliest completion time for the project is 194 days. Unlike the Gantt chart, however, the network representation illustrates the precedence relations between the activities.

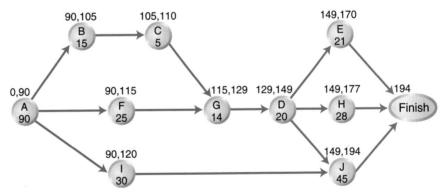

FIGURE 7.5   Earliest Start and Finish Times

LATEST START/FINISH TIMES

To determine the **latest start time (LS)** and **latest finish time (LF)** for each activity which allows the project to be completed by its minimal completion date, we make a *backwards pass* through the network. We begin by evaluating all activities that immediately

---

[4]WINQSB places the ES and EF in the upper part of the node above the node name.

precede the finish node. These are activities E, H, and J, which have completion times of 21, 28, and 45, respectively. The LF for each of these activities is the minimal project completion time (194 days); the LS for each is determined by subtracting the corresponding activity's completion time from this value. Thus,

$$LF(E) = 194 \quad LS(E) = 194 - 21 = 173$$
$$LF(H) = 194 \quad LS(H) = 194 - 28 = 166$$
$$LF(J) = 194 \quad LS(J) = 194 - 45 = 149$$

We continue the backwards pass by selecting a node for which the LS times for all its immediate successor nodes have been determined. This activity must be completed before *all* of the activities for which it is an immediate predecessor. Hence, its LF time is the *minimum* of the LS times of its immediate successor activities, and its LS is calculated by subtracting the activity completion time from its LF.

Latest Start/Finish Times for an Activity

LF = MINIMUM LS of all immediate successor activities
LS = LF − (Activity Completion Time)

We repeat this process until all nodes have been evaluated, as shown in Table 7.7.

TABLE 7.7   SEQUENCE OF LF AND LS CALCULATIONS

Activity	Immediate Successors (LS)	LF	LS
Finish	—	194	194
J	Finish (194)	194	194 − 45 = 149
H	Finish (194)	194	194 − 28 = 166
E	Finish (194)	194	194 − 21 = 173
I	J (149)	149	149 − 30 = 119
D	E (173), H (166), J (149)	149	149 − 20 = 129
G	D (129)	129	129 − 14 = 115
C	G (115)	115	115 − 5 = 110
F	G (115)	115	115 − 25 = 90
B	C (110)	110	110 − 15 = 95
A	B (95), F (90), I (119)	90	90 − 90 = 0

We denote the LS and LF for each activity on the PERT/CPM network by placing these numbers below the node representing it.[5] Figure 7.6 is a complete network representation showing both the earliest and latest start and finish times for the Klonepalm 2000 project.

THE CRITICAL PATH AND SLACK TIMES

In the course of completing a project, both planned and unforeseen delays can affect activity start or completion times. For example, revising the design of the computer (activity D), which is scheduled to take 20 days, may actually require 30 days. Or management may have to delay the start of sales training (activity H) by five days because the firm's training classroom might have been previously booked for another function. Some of these delays affect the overall completion date of the project; others may not.

---

[5]WINQSB places these numbers in the lower portion of the node.

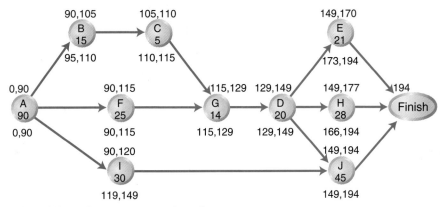

FIGURE 7.6   Earliest/Latest Start and Finish Times

To analyze the impact of such delays on the project, we determine the **slack time** for each activity. Slack time is the amount of time an activity can be delayed from its ES without delaying the project's estimated completion time. It is calculated by subtracting an activity's ES from its LS (or its EF from its LF). This value for an activity's slack time assumes that *only the completion time of this single activity has been changed* and that there are *no other delays to activities in the project*. Table 7.8 details the slack time calculations for each activity in the Klonepalm 2000 project.

TABLE 7.8   SLACK TIMES

Activity A: Slack (A) = LS(A) − ES(A) =	0 − 0 =	0
Activity B: Slack (B) = LS(B) − ES(B) =	95 − 90 =	5
Activity C: Slack (C) = LS(C) − ES(C) =	110 − 105 =	5
Activity D: Slack (D) = LS(D) − ES(D) =	119 − 119 =	0
Activity E: Slack (E) = LS(E) − ES(E) =	173 − 149 =	24
Activity F: Slack (F) = LS(F) − ES(F) =	90 − 90 =	0
Activity G: Slack (G) = LS(G) − ES(G) =	115 − 115 =	0
Activity H: Slack (H) = LS(H) − ES(H) =	166 − 149 =	17
Activity I: Slack (I) = LS(I) − ES(I) =	119 − 90 =	29
Activity J: Slack (J) = LS(J) − ES(J) =	149 − 149 =	0

When an activity has slack time, the manager has some flexibility in scheduling and may be able to distribute the workload more evenly throughout the project's duration without affecting its overall completion date. This is especially important in projects with limited staff or resources. This concept of *resource leveling* is discussed in more detail in the next section.

Activities that have *no* slack time (activities A, D, F, G, and J) are called **critical activities**. These activities must be rigidly scheduled to start and finish at their specific ES and EF times, respectively. Any delay in completing a critical activity will delay completion time of the entire project beyond 194 days by the corresponding amount.

Slack Time/Critical Activities

Slack time for an activity = LS − ES or LF − EF.
Critical activities are those with slack time = 0.

As Figure 7.7 illustrates, these critical activities form a path, called a **critical path**, from the start to finish nodes in the network. The sum of the completion times of the activities

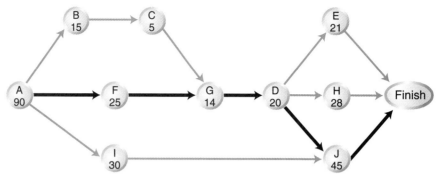

FIGURE 7.7   Critical Path

on the critical path is the minimal completion time for the project (90 + 25 + 14 + 20 + 45 = 194). Because it consists of the sequence of activities that cannot be delayed without affecting the earliest project completion date, the critical path is the *longest path in the directed network*.

It is possible to have more than one critical path in a PERT/CPM network. For example, if the completion time of activity E were 45 days rather than 21 days, both its earliest and latest start times would be 149, and its earliest and latest finish times would be 194. Thus, a second critical path giving a total completion time of 194 days consists of activities A, F, G, D, and E.

Critical Path

1. The critical activities (activities with 0 slack) form *at least one* critical path in the network.

2. A critical path is the longest path in the network.

3. The sum of the completion times for the activities on the critical path gives the minimal completion time of the project.

ANALYSIS OF POSSIBLE DELAYS

The ES, EF, LS, LF, and slack for each activity are frequently condensed into a single chart, known as an *activity schedule chart*, (see Table 7.9).

Using this chart and the PERT/CPM network, we can analyze the effect of possible delays in individual activities on the completion time of the entire project.

TABLE 7.9   ACTIVITY SCHEDULE CHART: KLONEPALM 2000 PROJECT

Activity	ES	EF	LS	LF	Slack
A	0	90	0	90	0
B	90	105	95	110	5
C	105	110	110	115	5
D	129	149	129	149	0
E	149	170	173	194	24
F	90	115	90	115	0
G	115	129	115	129	0
H	149	177	166	194	17
I	90	120	119	149	29
J	149	194	149	194	0

Single Delays

A delay in a single critical activity will result in an equivalent delay in the entire project. For example, if activity D, a critical activity with no slack, were delayed six days, the entire project would be delayed six days.

A delay in a noncritical activity will only delay the project by the amount the delay exceeds the activity's slack; a delay less than the slack time of the activity will not affect the project completion time. For example, since activity B has a slack of five days (as shown in the activity chart), delaying it by four days will not delay the entire project, while delaying it by seven will delay the project by $7 - 5 = 2$ days.

Multiple Delays

When there is a delay in starting or finishing more than one activity, the activity chart must be complemented by the PERT/CPM network representation to carry out the analysis. Let us consider three cases in which completion of two noncritical activities is delayed.

CASE 1: Activities E and I are each delayed 15 days.

From the activity chart we see that activity E has a slack time of 24 days and activity I has a slack time of 29 days. Thus, if either were delayed 15 days individually, the overall project completion date would be unaffected. But we must determine whether the delay in one of these activities will result in the added delay in the start of the other. From the PERT/CPM network (Figure 7.6) we see that there is no path from activity E to activity I. Hence, the completion time of activity E will have no effect on the completion time of activity I, and vice versa. PROJECT DELAY: 0 *days*

CASE 2: Activity B is delayed four days; activity E is delayed 15 days.

Again, if either of these delays occurred individually, the project would not be delayed. From the PERT/CPM network we see that since activity B has five days of slack, this delay does not affect the start and finish dates of activities G and D on the critical path. Thus, activities G and D can be completed on time, and, since activity E has 24 days of slack time, a delay of 15 days will not affect the minimum completion time of the project. PROJECT DELAY: 0 *days*

CASE 3: Activity B is delayed four days; activity C is delayed four days.

Once again, if only one of these delays occurs, the completion time of the entire project is not affected. However, as we see in Figure 7.8, if activity B is delayed four days, its EF is now 109 instead of 105. Thus, the ES for activity C is now 109. Adding the normal completion time of five days plus the four day delay for activity C, we see that its EF is now 118. Since the original LF for activity C is 115, there is a delay in the overall project completion time. PROJECT DELAY: $118 - 115 = 3$ days

FIGURE 7.8   Case 3: Delays Along the Same Path

In each of these three cases two noncritical activities are simultaneously delayed, but by less than their slack times. How do these cases differ? In Case 1, there is no path linking the two activities; hence, delaying one does not affect the other. In Case 2, the noncritical activities are on the same path but are separated by a critical activity. In both cases, the overall project completion date does not change.

In Case 3, however, the two noncritical activities are on the same path and are not separated by a critical activity. Here, a delay in one of the activities reduces the slack time available for the others on the path because activities along a noncritical path "share" the available slack time. In this case, further investigative analyses are required to accurately determine the total effect on the entire project.

7.6 RESOURCE LEVELING/RESOURCE ALLOCATION

During the course of a project, resources such as personnel, materials, and capital are expended on each activity. When preparing a project schedule, the limits of these resources must be considered because, while management may be committed to "doing what it takes" to complete a project in the minimal amount of time, it typically desires that resources be fairly evenly spread out during the life of the project.

For example, if the anticipated cost of a project is $1 million and the expected completion time of the project is 100 days, the firm will most likely prefer expenditures to be about $10,000 (=$1 million/100) per day, *if possible*, rather than $90,000 during each of the first 10 days of the project and $1111 per day for the remaining 90 days. However, financial resources may only become available or be required in unequal blocks. For example, a large certificate of deposit may mature on day 45, or a large lease payment may be due on day 74.

Allocation of other resources may also need attention. For example, in a production project in which workers can perform any activity of the project, management would most likely wish to minimize the number of workers required at any point in time. For a variety of reasons, including payroll and efficiency considerations, assigning, say, between 8 and 11 workers to a project at any point in time is generally preferable to a peak of 20 workers performing activities of the project on some days and only three or four on others.

Methods to control daily resource requirements and smooth out their use over the course of the project are known as **resource leveling** methods. Because of the mathematical complexities of the problem, true optimization methods for resource leveling are computationally difficult. By judiciously analyzing the results from the PERT/CPM approach, however, we can generally generate very good, if not truly optimal, solutions using heuristic methods. For example, if we can assume that once an activity has started it is worked on continuously until it is completed and that costs can be allocated equally throughout its duration, the following heuristic procedure can be used to "level" expenditures over the course of the project:[6]

A Heuristic for Resource Leveling

1. Consider the schedule that begins each activity at its ES.
2. Determine which activities have slack at periods of peak spending.
3. Attempt to reschedule the noncritical activities performed during these peak periods to periods of less spending, but within the time period between their ES and LF.

This procedure does not state how Step 3 is to be accomplished; that is part of the trial-and-error process. Some heuristic methods begin by analyzing the noncritical activities with the most slack during the period, whereas others begin by analyzing those that utilize the largest amount of resource during the period. To illustrate this latter approach, we revisit the situation at Klone Computer, Inc.

---

[6]These are typical assumptions made in resource leveling. Heuristic procedures also exist for problems in which either or both of these assumptions are violated.

KLONE COMPUTER INC. (revisited)

Management at Klone Computers wishes to design a schedule that will complete the Klonepalm 2000 project in minimal time (194 days), while keeping daily expenditures as constant as possible. Analysts have supplied management with the cost estimates for the activities shown in Table 7.10.

TABLE 7.10   COST ESTIMATES FOR KLONEPALM 2000 ACTIVITIES

Activity	Description	Total Cost ($1,000)	Total Time (Days)	Cost Per Day ($1,000)
A	Prototype model design	2,250	90	25
B	Purchase of materials	180	15	12
C	Manufacture of prototype models	90	5	18
D	Revision of design	300	20	15
E	Initial production run	231	21	11
F	Staff training	250	25	10
G	Staff input on prototype models	70	14	5
H	Sales training	392	28	14
I	Preproduction advertising campaign	510	30	17
J	Postproduction advertising campaign	1,350	45	30
	Total Cost =	5,623		

SOLUTION

As we saw in the last section, the Klonepalm 2000 project can be completed in 194 days as long as each activity is scheduled between its ES, EF, LS, and LF times. In Figure 7.9 we plot the cumulative daily expenditures using an earliest time assignment (the top solid line) and a latest time assignment (the bottom solid line) of the activities. For example, referring to Table 7.9, using an earliest time assignment, we estimate the total

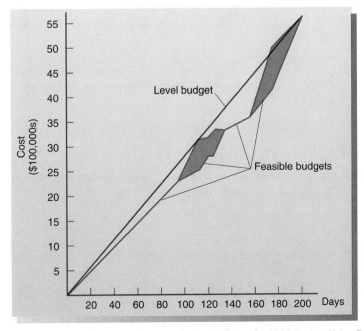

FIGURE 7.9   Cumulative Daily Expenditures—Klonepalm 2000 Project Using Earliest Time Assignments

cost at day 118 to be $3,261,000 since activities A, B, C, and F should be finished costing $2,770,000, three days of work on activity G should be complete costing 3($5000) = $15,000, and 28 days of activity I should be complete costing 28($17,000) = $476,000. The total cost using a latest time assignment of activities is estimated to be $2,785,000, since again, activities A, B, C, and F should be finished, three days of work on activity G should be complete, but activity I has not been started.

We see from Figure 7.9 that the two lines coincide between days 0 to 90 when, in both schedules, only activity A is being completed, and from days 129 to 149 when, again in both schedules, activities A, B, C, F, G, and I have been finished and only activity D is being completed. These two lines and the two shaded regions on either side of days 129 to 149 represent *feasible budgets*. The gray line represents a "level budget" of $28,985 (=$5,623,000/194) per day.

Although we cannot construct a feasible budget that is level throughout the duration of the project, our goal is to smooth the costs as evenly as possible while still completing the project within 194 days. Figure 7.10, which gives the daily expenditures of the ES schedule, can assist us in this task.

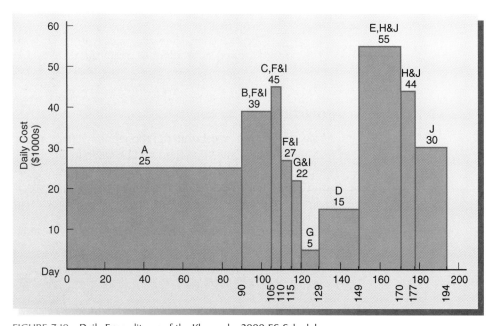

FIGURE 7.10   Daily Expenditures of the Klonepalm 2000 ES Schedule

As you can see, at day 91 activities B, F, and I are underway at a daily cost of $39,000 (12,000 + 10,000, + 17,000); at day 150 activities E, H, and J are underway at a daily cost of $55,000 (= 11,000 + 14,000 + 30,000); while at day 125, only activity G is in progress at a daily cost of only $5000. We can now use our resource leveling heuristic to smooth out these daily expenditures.

ITERATION I

The peak cost spike of $55,000 occurs between days 149 and 170 of the project. Both activities E and H have slack during this period. Since activity H has the higher daily cost, consider delaying its start. Activity H takes 28 days to complete and has a feasible schedule period from its ES (day 149) to its LF (day 194). The lowest daily cost during the feasible schedule period of activity H is $30,000 from day 177 to 194. *Action: Shift the scheduling of activity H to its latest start and finish time (166 and 194, respectively), yielding the resource scheduling chart shown in Figure 7.11.*

FIGURE 7.11   Resource Scheduling Chart: Iteration 1

ITERATION 2

There is still a spike of $55,000 from day 166 to 170, but shifting activity E to a later start time would simply shift or extend the spike. Thus, the maximum smoothing beyond day 149 has occurred. *Action: none.*

ITERATION 3

The next highest spike, $45,000, occurs between days 105 and 110 of the project. During this time, activities C, F, and I are currently scheduled. Of these, the noncritical activity with the highest daily cost is activity C ($18,000/day). The starting time for activity C could be delayed by up to five days, but since activities F and I are also currently scheduled during that time period, any delay in starting activity C would simply shift the peak period for days 105 to 110 to days 110 to 115. Thus, this delay would not result in any resource leveling. *Action: none.*

ITERATION 4

During the period from day 105 to 110, the noncritical activity with the next highest daily cost is activity I ($17,000/day), which can be shifted from its earliest start and finish times (days 90 to 120) to its latest start and finish time (days 119 to 149). *Action: Shift the scheduling of activity I to its latest start and finish time (119 and 149, respectively), yielding the resource scheduling chart shown in Figure 7.12.*

ITERATION 5

Rescheduling activity I to begin at its latest start time increases the expenditures between days 129 and 149 (during which time activities D and I are taking place) to a cost of $32,000 per day. However, there are two low-cost periods: between days 115 and 119 ($5000/day) and between days 110 and 115 ($10,000/day). Shifting activity I so that its start time coincides with the finish time of activity C (day 110) levels the resources even further. *Action: Shift the scheduling of activity I to days 100 to 140. This gives us the resource scheduling chart shown in Figure 7.13.*

In this iteration, there is still a peak of $32,000/day from days 129 to 140, but this represents a narrower time frame than before. It does not appear that any additional

FIGURE 7.12   Resource Scheduling Chart: Iteration 4

FIGURE 7.13   Resource Scheduling Chart: Iteration 5

shifting of noncritical activities will smooth the daily costs further. Thus, the schedule in Figure 7.13 appears to give the most consistent daily expenditures.

MANAGEMENT MEMO   Based on this analysis, the following memo to management summarizes the project and resource leveling results. Tables and graphs highlight the main points of the analysis.

M E M O R A N D U M

To: Stephen Chores
Klone Computers, Inc.

From: Student Consulting Group

Subj: Project Scheduling for the Development of the Klonepalm 2000
Palmbook Computer

We have conducted an analysis of the work assignments required to develop, produce, and market the Klonepalm 2000 computer. Based on interviews with management and staff, we have divided the project into ten broad tasks, consisting of five manufacturing, three training, and two advertising activities.

Manufacturing

1. Design the Klonepalm 2000 model
2. Purchase materials required to manufacture the product
3. Manufacture the first batch of prototype models
4. Design revision based on staff input
5. Produce initial production run for public distribution

Training

1. Staff training
2. Solicitation of staff input for product modifications
3. Training of sales personnel

Advertising

1. Preproduction advertising campaign to prepare the public (in general terms) for the introduction of the new model
2. Final advertising campaign

Proper scheduling of these tasks is crucial to ensure that the product will be ready for distribution at the earliest possible date. Accordingly, we have collected cost and time estimates from the departments involved in the project development. Although these data are only forecasts and best estimates, we feel that, because Klone has had experience developing other computer models in the past, these estimates should provide a reasonable foundation on which to base our recommendations.

RECOMMENDATIONS

Given a February 1 start date, we have developed a schedule for the individual tasks of the Klonepalm 2000 project using a standard project planning technique known as PERT (Programmed Evaluation and Review Technique). The schedule assumes a five-day work week and takes into account holidays such as Presidents Day, Memorial Day, Independence Day, and Labor Day. It also keeps daily expenditures as level as possible throughout the project while completing the project in a minimal time of 194 work days. The project should be completed by November 3, in time to meet the anticipated demand generated by the Christmas season.

THE SCHEDULE

The schedule we have developed using PERT is shown in Table I.

TABLE I   Klonepalm 2000 Schedule

Project Activity	Activity Cost	Work Days	Begin Date	Finish Date
Prototype design	$2,250,000	90	Feb. 1	June 8
Purchase of materials	$ 180,000	15	June 9	June 29
Manufacture of prototypes	$ 90,000	5	June 30	July 7
Revision of design	$ 300,000	20	Aug. 4	Aug. 31
Initial production run	$ 231,000	21	Sept. 1	Sept. 30
Staff training	$ 250,000	25	June 9	July 14
Staff recommendations	$ 70,000	14	July 15	Aug. 3
Sales training	$ 392,000	28	Sept. 26	Nov. 3
Preproduction advertising	$ 510,000	30	July 8	Aug. 18
Final advertising campaign	$1,350,000	45	Sept. 1	Nov. 3

We recommend using the time chart depicted in Figure I to schedule project tasks. Figure II shows the anticipated daily cost requirements of this schedule throughout the lifetime of the project.

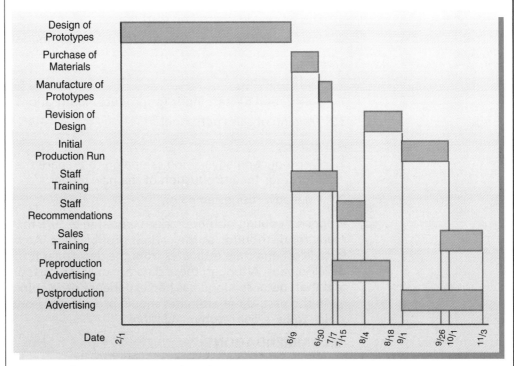

FIGURE I   Klone Computers, Inc.—Klonepalm 2000 Project

The average daily cost of the project is $28,985 and ranges from a low of $15,000 during the period from August 19 to August 31 to a high of $55,000 during the period from September 26 to September 30. Management should plan its financing accordingly.

In order to meet the target completion date of November 3, the following components must be completed on schedule:

1. Design of the prototype models

2. Staff training

3. Staff recommendations

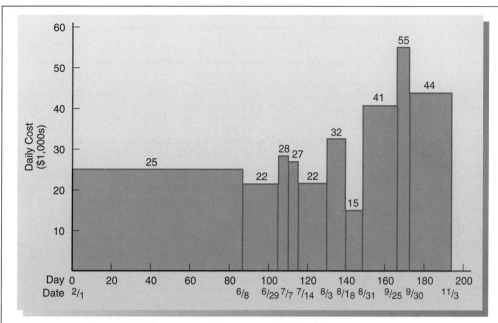

FIGURE II   Klonepalm 2000 Project: Daily Cost Requirements

4.   Revised product design

5.   Final adverting campaign

A delay in any one of these will extend the project beyond November 3. There is some flexibility in the scheduling of other activities which will still allow completion by the November 3 target date, as summarized in Table II.

TABLE II   Flexibility in Klonepalm 2000 Scheduling

Activity	May Start By	Must Finish By	Total Flexibility	Recommended Start Date
Purchase of materials	June 9	July 7	5 days*	June 9
Manufacture of prototypes	June 30	July 14	5 days*	June 30
Initial production run	Sept. 1	Nov. 3	24 days	Sept. 1
Sales training	Sept. 1	Nov. 3	17 days	Sept. 26
Preproduction advertising	June 9	Aug. 31	29 days	July 8

*The total flexibility in scheduling both the purchase of materials and the manufacturing of the prototypes is a *combined* total of five days.

Any change to the recommended start and finish times can result in additional project expenses, however, and will definitely affect the distribution of the daily expenditures required for the project. Should scheduling changes be required, we can supply you with revised time and expenditure distribution charts for the project.

RESOURCE ALLOCATION

In most projects one or more resources are in limited supply, and several activities may be competing for the same resources at the same time. The process of assigning these limited resources so as to minimize the total time required to complete a project is known as *resource allocation*. Typical resource allocation constraints might be:

- A maximum of 10 workers can be assigned each day.
- Payroll and expenses cannot exceed $44,000 on any day.
- Only two production machines are available.

The goal of a resource allocation problem is to minimize the overall project completion time while operating within a given set of constraints. The problem is complicated by the fact that, not only must the activities be scheduled according to the precedence relations given in the activity chart, but also the resources used at any one point in time cannot exceed their availability. Because activities can be scheduled in many different ways, even for relatively small projects, heuristic methods are generally used.

One such approach is to make a schedule one day at a time. On a day in which there is a higher demand for resources than there are resources available, those activities with the least amount of slack are scheduled first. Then previously assigned noncritical activities are examined and, *if possible*, rescheduled to free up resources for critical activities or other activities that now have no slack.

Following this approach it can be shown that if Klone Computer restricts maximum expenditures on any day to $44,000, using this heuristic approach, the project can be completed in 198 days with the cost schedule illustrated in Figure 7.14. This is a four-day delay from the original schedule, which had no such restriction.

FIGURE 7.14   Schedule of Activities with a Maximum Daily Expenditure of $44,000

 We emphasize again that heuristic methods do not guarantee optimal results. In general, however, such methods generate "good" solutions that at the very least, are feasible.

7.7 $\mathcal{P}$ERT—THE PROBABILISTIC APPROACH TO PROJECT SCHEDULING

Activity completion times are seldom known with 100% accuracy. When it comes to projects that have never been done before, subjective estimates for activity completion times must be made. Even in projects that are repeatedly performed, variability in the activity completion times occurs from one repetition to another. Given this uncertainty, PERT, a technique that treats activity completion times as random variables, can be used to determine the likelihood that a project will be completed within a certain time period.

One method used in PERT to convey activity variability without the undue burden of trying to make forecasts under a potentially limitless set of circumstances is the *three time estimate approach*. This approach, which is particularly useful for new projects, solicits three time estimates for each activity's completion time:

a = an optimistic time to perform the activity

m = the most likely time to perform the activity

b = a pessimistic time to perform the activity

Estimates a and b are reasonable "best case" and "worst case" scenarios that take into account normal fluctuations in performing the activity and any unforeseen events that may accelerate or deter its completion. The most likely time estimate, m, is an estimate of a usual or typical time to complete an activity; it corresponds to the statistical mode of the probability distribution for completion time.

In reality, we can never be certain that an activity will be completed even within the time period from a to b. There is always some (small) probability that the activity will require less time than the optimistic time, a, or more time than the pessimistic time, b. However, the time estimates selected for a and b should allow for only a relatively small chance, less than 1%, of this occurring.

With only these three points to work with (a, m, and b), it is difficult to give a true estimate of this underlying probability distribution. It is important, however, to have *some* estimate so that we can approximate the mean and standard deviation of the activity's completion time. Statisticians have found that a **Beta distribution** is useful in approximating distributions with limited data and fixed end points.

The Beta distribution (which many statisticians affectionately term the "chameleon" of the statistical world) can assume a wide variety of shapes, depending on the judicious choice of its defining parameters. Figures 7.15a, b, and c show a few forms of *unimodal Beta* distributions that can arise in a PERT analysis. In each case, all the probability lies within the extreme values a and b, and the highest probability density occurs at the modal value, m.

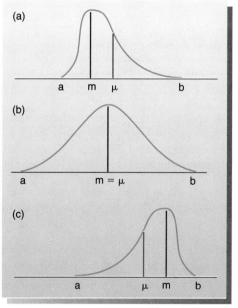

FIGURE 7.15   (a) Unimodal Beta Distribution Skewed Left; (b) Symmetric Unimodal Beta Distribution; (c) Unimodal Beta Distribution Skewed Right

In actuality, the assumption that activity times follow a Beta distribution has only a modest effect on the analysis of the completion time of the entire project. Of more concern are approximations for the average, or mean, activity completion time, μ, and its standard deviation, σ, which are based on the time estimates a, m, and b. These estimates are:

$$\mu = \frac{a + 4m + b}{6}$$

$$\sigma = \frac{b - a}{6}$$

The approximation for the mean, μ, is a weighted average of the three data points; $\frac{1}{6}$ of the weight is assigned to each of the extreme values a and b, and $\frac{4}{6}$ of the weight is assigned to the mode, m. The expression for the standard deviation, σ, is derived from the fact that, for many distributions (particularly smooth unimodal distributions), the range of values from the highest to the lowest ($b - a$) covers roughly six standard deviations.

It has been shown that if the mode is within roughly the middle 75% of the range between a and b, these approximations for μ and σ are very good estimates. For example, if a given activity has an optimistic completion time, $a = 10$ days, and a pessimistic completion time, $b = 30$ days, the range is $b - a = 20$ days. Thus, if the mode lies in the middle 15 days (=.75 × 20), from 12.5 to 27.5 days, the above formulas do indeed provide good approximations for the mean and standard deviation. For modal values *outside* this interval, correction factors have been derived for these approximations.

Assumptions for Distribution of Activity Times in PERT

For each activity in a PERT/CPM network:

1. The probability density function for the activity's completion time is a unimodal Beta distribution.

2. Average (Mean) Completion Time: $\mu = \dfrac{a + 4m + b}{6}$

3. Standard Deviation of Completion Time: $\sigma = \dfrac{b - a}{6}$

The probabilistic approach to project scheduling assumes that, for each activity, j, its mean, μ_j, and its standard deviation, σ_j, have been calculated. The procedure for determining the mean and standard deviation of the *project completion time* is then based on several simplifying assumptions.

ASSUMPTION 1: *A critical path can be determined by using the mean completion times for the activities as if they were fixed completion times. The expected time (average time) to complete the project is determined solely by the completion times of the activities on the critical path.*

This assumption implies that the critical path will not change even though the actual completion time of an activity on the critical path might be less than its average time, and/or the actual completion time of an activity off the critical path might be longer than its average time.

This assumption is, in fact, often questionable, as we see in Figure 7.16. Using the mean activity completion times, we find that the critical path is A–D, with an expected

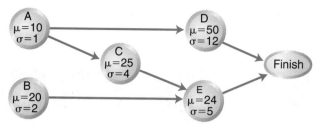

Mean and standard deviation of activity times for a project

FIGURE 7.16   Mean and Standard Deviation of Activity Times for a Project

completion time of 10 + 50 = 60 days. But the large standard deviations for activities C, D, and E make it likely that activity C could take 30 days instead of 25, activity E could take 28 days instead of 24, and activity D could take 40 days instead of 50. In this case, if the other activity times were equal to their mean time, the new critical path would be A–C–E, and the completion time would actually be 68 days rather than the 50 days of the revised A–D path. *Such a change in the critical path is expressly ruled out by assumption 1.*

ASSUMPTION 2: *The time to complete one activity is independent of the time to complete any other activity.*

This assumption implies that a hastening or a delay in the completion of one activity will have no effect on the completion time of the other activities in the project. This assumption should be checked for validity.

For example, in a project to build furnished apartments, one activity might be "install refrigerators in the apartments," and another might be "install washer/dryer units." If the same contractor were in charge of installing both the refrigerators and the washer/dryers, should labor problems with the contractor delay the installation of the refrigerators, installation of the washer/dryer units would also likely be delayed. If these installations were performed by different contractors, however, a delay by one subcontractor most likely would not affect the installation time of the other. *Assumption 2 reflects this latter situation.*

ASSUMPTION 3: *There are enough activities on the critical path so that the distribution of the project completion time can be approximated by a normal distribution.*

Recall that one form of the central limit theorem of statistics states that the sum of a large number of independently distributed random variables is approximately normally distributed, with a mean equal to the sum of the random variable means, and a variance equal to the sum of the random variable variances. In this case, the random variables are the activity completion times of the activities *on the critical path.*

Assumptions 1 and 2 state that the project completion time is determined by the activities on the critical path and that these variables are independent. As a general rule, we typically want to have 30 or more independent random variables in the sum to employ the central limit theorem. But, since we assume that each of these independent random variables has a distribution close to the shape of a normal distribution (as is the case for unimodal Beta distribution), far fewer than 30 independent random variables are necessary for the normal distribution to provide a good approximation. Since most real-life PERT problems have a significant number of activities on the critical path (each with a Beta distribution), assumption 3 usually does not present a problem.

Taken together, these three assumptions imply that the overall project completion time has an approximately normal distribution, with mean equal to the sum of the mean completion times along the critical path, and variance equal to the sum of the variances of the activities along the critical path. Note that we *sum variances, not standard deviations.* (Recall that a variance is simply the square of the standard deviation.)

To summarize, the following is the sequence of steps required to describe the overall completion time for a project:

Determining the Distribution of the Overall Project Completion Time

1. For each activity j, calculate:

$$\mu_j = \frac{a + 4m + b}{6}, \qquad \sigma_j = \frac{b - a}{6}$$

2. Determine the critical path using the μ_j's as fixed times.
3. The overall project completion time has a *normal distribution* with

$$Mean: \mu = \sum_{j \ on \ Critical \ Path} \mu_j$$

$$Variance: \sigma^2 = \sum_{j \ on \ Critical \ Path} \sigma_j^2$$

$$Standard \ deviation: \sigma = \sqrt{\sigma^2}$$

To illustrate the use of probabilities in PERT analyses, consider a revision of the model for the Klonepalm 2000 project.

Klone1.cpm

KLONE COMPUTERS, INC. (revised)

Rather than giving precise estimates for the activities of the Klonepalm 2000 project, the company has supplied the three time estimates for the completion of the activities shown in Table 7.11.

TABLE 7.11   TIME ESTIMATES FOR COMPLETION OF KLONEPALM 2000 ACTIVITIES

Activity	Optimistic	Most Likely	Pessimistic
A	76	86	120
B	12	15	18
C	4	5	6
D	15	18	33
E	18	21	24
F	16	26	30
G	10	13	22
H	24	28	32
I	22	27	50
J	38	43	60

Management at Klone is interested in the following:

1. The probability that the project will be completed within 194 days
2. A reasonable interval estimate of the number of days to complete the project
3. The probability that the project will be completed within 180 days
4. The probability that the project will take longer than 210 days
5. An upper limit for the number of days within which it can be virtually sure the project will be completed

SOLUTION

The mean, variance, and standard deviation for activity A can be found by:

$$\mu_A = \frac{76 + 4\,(86) + 120}{6} = 90$$

$$\sigma_A = \frac{120 - 76}{6} = 7.33$$

$$\sigma_A^2 = (7.32)^2 = 53.78$$

Similar calculations for the other activities give the results shown in Table 7.12.

TABLE 7.12   MEAN, VARIANCE, AND STANDARD DEVIATION OF KLONEPALM 2000 ACTIVITIES

Activity	μ	σ	σ^2
A	90	7.33	53.78
B	15	1.00	1.00
C	5	.33	.11
D	20	3.00	9.00
E	21	1.00	1.00
F	25	2.33	5.44
G	14	2.00	4.00
H	28	1.33	1.78
I	30	4.67	21.78
J	45	3.67	13.44

Note that the means for the activities are the same as those used in the previous PERT/CPM analysis. Thus, the critical path is A–F–G–D–J, and the expected completion time of the project, μ, is:

$$\mu = \mu_A + \mu_F + \mu_G + \mu_D + \mu_J$$
$$= 90 + 25 + 14 + 20 + 45 = 194$$

The project variance, σ^2, is:

$$\sigma^2 = \sigma_A^2 + \sigma_F^2 + \sigma_G^2 + \sigma_D^2 + \sigma_J^2$$
$$= 53.78 + 5.44 + 4.00 + 9.00 + 13.44$$
$$= 85.66$$

Thus the standard deviation for the project, σ, is:

$$\sigma = \sqrt{\sigma^2} = 9.255$$

If management is willing to accept the three assumptions underlying PERT, the completion time for the Klonepalm computer project can be modeled by a normal random variable with mean, $\mu = 194$ days and standard deviation, $\sigma = 9.255$ days. We can then use this model to answer the questions posed by management. In these analyses, we define the following random variable:

$$X = \text{completion time of the project}$$

We can then convert the normally distributed random variable, X, into the standard normal random variable, Z, by

$$Z = \frac{X - \mu}{\sigma}$$

Here, Z represents *the number of standard deviations X is from the mean*, μ. A table for the standard normal random variable (Appendix A) can then be used to determine the probability of completing the project within any given time period, including those of concern to management.

1. The first concern—the probability that the project will be completed within 194 days—can be expressed as P(X ≤ 194). Since 194 is the mean, μ, of the distribution,

$$P(X \le 194) = P(Z \le 0) = .5000$$

2. An interval in which we are reasonably sure the completion date lies depends on our interpretation of the words "reasonably sure." Here, we assume that "reasonably sure" means 95% sure. This includes the middle 95% of the probability from a normal distribution with $\mu = 194$ and $\sigma = 9.255$. This interval is:

$$\mu \pm z_{.025}\sigma$$

where $z_{.025}$ is the z-value that puts a probability of .025 in each tail of the normal distribution. $z_{.025} = 1.96$; hence, the interval is

$$194 \pm 1.96(9.255) = 194 \pm 18.14 \text{ days}$$

Because management would most likely prefer the interval in whole days, we round 18.14 up to 19 days, and the interval is one from 175 to 213 days.

3. The probability that the project will be completed within 180 days can be expressed as P(X ≤ 180). Referring to Figure 7.17, we see that when x = 180, z = (180 − 194)/9.255 = −1.51. Then, P(X ≤ 180) = P(Z ≤ −1.51) = .5000 − .4345 = .0655.

FIGURE 7.17   Probability of Completing the Klonepalm 2000 Project in 180 days

4. The probability that the project will take longer than 210 days can be expressed as P(X ≥ 210). Referring to Figure 7.18, when x = 210, z = (210 − 194)/9.255 = 1.73. Then, P(X ≥ 210) = P(Z ≥ 1.73) = .5000 − .4582 = .0418.

5. "Virtually sure" can mean different things to different people, so let us assume that management will accept a date by which it is 99% certain of completing the project. This situation is depicted in Figure 7.19.

FIGURE 7.18   Probability That the Klonepalm 2000 Project Will Take Longer Than 210 Days

FIGURE 7.19   (99%) Certainty of Completing the Klonepalm 2000 Project

The z-value such that $P(Z \leq z) = .9900$ is the value such that $P(0 \leq Z \leq z) = .4900$. From Appendix A, we see that this z-value is approximately 2.33. Since $z = (x - \mu)/\sigma$, then $x = \mu + z\sigma$. Thus,

$$x = \mu + z\sigma = 194 + 2.33(9.255) = 215.56 \text{ days}$$

As a result, we can report to management that we are virtually sure that the project will be completed within 216 days.

7.8 COMPUTER SOLUTION OF PERT/CPM NETWORKS

In Chapters 3 through 6, we illustrated how the Solver function in Excel can be used to solve models that can be expressed as linear programs. Here we present a linear programming approach that can be used within Excel to solve for the earliest completion time of a project and determine for each activity its ES, EF, LS, LF, and slack.

The mean completion times and standard deviations for each activity can easily be calculated within the spreadsheet. We then define the variables X_A, X_B, X_C, and so on, to represent the start time of the activities and X(FIN) as the finish time of the project. The objective is to MINIMIZE X(FIN). The constraint set includes one constraint for each immediate predecessor relationship in the project, stating that the start time for an activity must be at least as great as the finish time of the immediate predecessor.

In the Klonepalm 2000 model, the start time for activity G is constrained by the finish times of activities C and F. Since the finish times for activities C and F equal their start times plus their expected completion times, the two constraints are:

$$X_G \geq X_C + 5$$
$$X_G \geq X_F + 25$$

Using this approach, we can easily construct the complete linear program for the Klonepalm 2000 computer project as follows:

$$
\begin{aligned}
&\text{MIN X(FIN)} \\
\text{ST} \quad & \\
&X(FIN) \geq X_E + 21 \\
&X(FIN) \geq X_H + 28 \\
&X(FIN) \geq X_I + 45 \\
&X_E \geq X_D + 20 \\
&X_H \geq X_D + 20 \\
&X_I \geq X_D + 20 \\
&X_J \geq X_I + 30 \\
&X_D \geq X_G + 14 \\
&X_G \geq X_C + 5 \\
&X_G \geq X_F + 25 \\
&X_I \geq X_A + 90 \\
&X_F \geq X_A + 90 \\
&X_C \geq X_B + 15 \\
&X_B \geq X_A + 90 \\
&\text{All X's} \geq 0
\end{aligned}
$$

The Excel solution to this program provides a schedule of start times for the activities that will complete the project in minimal time. It may not return the ES times, however. It can be shown that if the objective function is changed to MINIMIZE $X_A + X_B + X_C + X_D + X_E + X_F + X_G + X_H + X_I + X_J + X(FIN)$, although the optimal value of this objective function is meaningless, the optimal solution will give a set of ES times for the activities. The EF times are then calculated by adding the activity completion times to their ES times.

After solving this linear program and determining that X(FIN) = 194, the LS times can be determined by (1) adding the constraint X(FIN) = 194 to the constraint set of the above program, and (2) changing the objective function criterion to MAXIMIZE $X_A + X_B + X_C + X_D + X_E + X_F + X_G + X_H + X_I + X_J + X(FIN)$. The LF times are calculated by adding the activity completion times to their LS times. Slack times are then calculated by subtracting the ES times from the LS times.

Cells in Excel can also be programmed to perform the forward and backwards pass through a given network. If rows correspond to the activities, and columns correspond to ES, EF, LS, LF and SLACK, a forward pass can be made using the following formulas:

$$\text{ES Cells:} = \text{MAX(EF } \textit{cells of the activity's immediate predecessors})$$
$$\text{EF Cells:} = \text{(ES Cell)} + \textit{Activity Completion Time}$$

The maximum of the EF cells gives the earliest completion time for the project. A backwards pass can be made using the following formulas:

$$\text{LF Cells:} = \text{MIN(LS } \textit{cells of the activity's immediate successors})$$
$$\text{LS Cells:} = \text{(LF Cell)} - \textit{Activity Completion Time}$$
$$\text{SLACK:} = \text{(LS Cell)} - \text{(ES Cell)}$$

Note that the entries in italics are different for each cell.

USING WINQSB

These approaches require substantial programming, which can require almost as much work as solving the problem by hand. Many spreadsheet-like programs, however, including the PERT/CPM module in WINQSB, are specifically designed for project scheduling networks and require no user programming.

Klone1.cpm

As we show in Appendix 7.1, we need only supply the immediate predecessors for each activity and the completion times (or a, m, and b in a three time approach) to the WINQSB module, and it will automatically return an activity schedule chart, give the mean and standard deviation of the critical path(s), and, if desired, generate an earliest and latest time Gantt chart. In addition, the module has the on-screen capability of determining the probability of completing the project within a specified time period. Figures 7.20a, b, and c are outputs from WINQSB for the Klonepalm 2000 problem using the three time estimate approach.

Activity Analysis for KLONEPALM 2000

10-25-1998 12:29:59	Activity Name	On Critical Path	Activity Mean Time	Earliest Start	Earliest Finish	Latest Start	Latest Finish	Slack (LS-ES)	Activity Time Distribution	Standard Deviation
1	A	Yes	90	0	90	0	90	0	3-Time estimate	7.3333
2	B	no	15	90	105	95	110	5	3-Time estimate	1
3	C	no	5	105	110	110	115	5	3-Time estimate	0.3333
4	D	Yes	20	129	149	129	149	0	3-Time estimate	3
5	E	no	21	149	170	173	194	24	3-Time estimate	1
6	F	Yes	25	90	115	90	115	0	3-Time estimate	2.3333
7	G	Yes	14	115	129	115	129	0	3-Time estimate	2
8	H	no	28	149	177	166	194	17	3-Time estimate	1.3333
9	I	no	30	90	120	119	149	29	3-Time estimate	4.6667
10	J	Yes	45	149	194	149	194	0	3-Time estimate	3.6667
	Project	Completion	Time	=	194	DAYS				
	Number of	Critical	Path(s)	=	1					

FIGURE 7.20a Activity Analysis for Klonepalm 2000

Critical Path(s) for KLONEPALM 2000	
10-25-1998	Critical Path 1
1	A
2	F
3	G
4	D
5	J
Completion Time	194
Std. Dev.	9.26

FIGURE 7.20*b*   Critical Path(s) for Klonepalm 2000

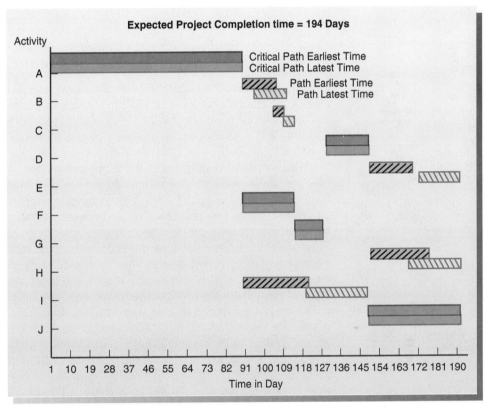

FIGURE 7.20*c*   The Gantt Chart for Klonepalm 2000

Other features in WINQSB allow it to adapt to different model structures, such as those for CPM and PERT/Cost, which we discuss in Sections 7.10 and 7.11. Because the WINQSB module is very flexible and is specifically designed for project scheduling, we will use it as needed in the remainder of this chapter.

7.9   COST ANALYSES USING THE EXPECTED VALUE APPROACH

We have seen that, under a certain set of assumptions, the completion time of a project can be approximated by a normally distributed random variable. This condition can be quite useful when evaluating whether or not to spend extra money in an attempt to shorten a project. In general, spending extra money should decrease the project completion time, but we must evaluate whether this potential decrease in project completion time is cost effective.

One analytical approach to this problem is to use the *expected value criterion* to evaluate possible alternatives. Although a more complete discussion of the expected value approach is detailed in Chapter 8, here we will give a brief example of how it can be applied to project scheduling.

The main idea behind the expected value approach is to compare the mean or expected profits (or costs) for each possible alternative. Recall that the expected value of any discrete random variable, Y, denoted $E(Y)$, is the weighted average of possible outcomes for Y, the weights being the probabilities for each possible outcome of Y; that is, $E(Y) = \Sigma P(y_i)y_i$.

The following example illustrates the use of the expected value approach in a situation faced by Klone Computers, Inc.

KLONE COMPUTERS: COST ANALYSIS USING PROBABILITIES

Klone1.cpm
Klone2.cpm

Klone has conducted an analysis of its two major competitors, which are known to be developing computers similar to its proposed Klonepalm 2000 models. According to this analysis, one competitor will have its model ready for market in 180 days, the other in about 200 days. Speedy completion of the Klonepalm 2000 project is therefore essential.

The analysis also indicated that if Klone can get the jump on both competitors and have its model ready for sale within 180 days, it should garner an additional profit of $1 million. If the Klonepalm 2000 is ready for sale after the first competitor's model is introduced, but before the second (i.e., between 180 and 200 days from now), Klone will gain an additional profit of $400,000.

In order to advance the anticipated completion date of the Klonepalm 2000 project, management is considering spending additional funds on training either the staff or the sales personnel. This training will involve extensive overtime and some travel, lodging, and meal expenses for both the trainers and the trainees.

Klone has estimated that by spending an additional $200,000 on sales training, it can reduce the optimistic, most likely, and pessimistic times for this training from 24, 28, and 32 days to 19, 21, and 23 days, respectively. It has also estimated that spending an additional $250,000 on training the technical staff can reduce the time estimates for staff training from 16, 26, and 30 days to 12, 14, and 16 days, respectively. Management would like to decide which, if either, of these options to pursue.

SOLUTION

EVALUATION OF SPENDING AN ADDITIONAL $200,000 FOR SALES TRAINING

The training of sales personnel, activity H, is not on the critical path for the project. Given the assumption that the overall completion time is determined solely by the activities on the critical path, a reduction in the expected completion time for activity H will not affect the overall completion time of the project. Thus, management should not spend the additional $200,000 for sales training.

EVALUATION OF SPENDING AN ADDITIONAL $250,000 FOR STAFF TRAINING

Staff training, activity F, *is* on the critical path. Hence, a reduction in its expected completion time will reduce the overall completion time of the project. But will the time savings justify the $250,000 expenditure? Using the expected value approach, we can evaluate both spending and not spending the additional $250,000. In this analysis, the gross additional profit earned by Klone is $1 million if the project is completed in less than 180 days, $400,000 if the project is completed within 180 to 200 days, and $0 if the project takes longer than 200 days to complete.

Case 1: The $250,000 *is not* spent on additional staff training.

This case represents our current situation, in which the project has an expected completion time of 194 days and a standard deviation of 9.255 days. As Figure 7.21 illustrates, when x = 180, z = (180-194)/9.255 = −1.51; and when x = 200, z = (200 − 194)/9.255 = .65. Thus the following probabilities exist:

$$P(X < 180) = P(Z < -1.51) = .5 - .4345 = .0655$$
$$P(180 < X < 200) = P(-1.51 < Z < .65) = .4345 + .2422 = .6767$$
$$P(X > 200) = P(Z > .65) = .5 - .2442 = .2578$$

Hence, if the $250,000 is *not* spent, the expected gross additional profit, E(Y), is:

$$E(Y) = .0655(\$1,000,000) + .6767(\$400,000) + .2578(\$0) = \$336,180$$

Because no additional funds were spent, this is also the net additional expected profit.

FIGURE 7.21   Project Completion Time Distribution If the $250,000 Is Not Spent

Case 2: The $250,000 *is* spent on additional staff training.

If the additional $250,000 is spent on activity F, its new time estimates are $a = 12$, $m = 14$, and $b = 16$. As a result,

$$\mu_F = (12 + 4(14) + 16)/6 = 14$$
$$\sigma_F = (16 - 12)/6 = .67$$
$$\sigma_F^2 = (.67)^2 = .44$$

From WINQSB (Figure 7.22a and b), we see that, with this change, the project has a new critical path (A–B–C–G–D–J) with a mean time of $\mu = 189$ days and a standard deviation of $\sigma = 9.0185$ days.

Activity Analysis for KLONEPALM 2000

10-25-1998 13:44:42	Activity Name	On Critical Path	Activity Mean Time	Earliest Start	Earliest Finish	Latest Start	Latest Finish	Slack (LS-ES)	Activity Time Distribution	Standard Deviation
1	A	Yes	90	0	90	0	90	0	3-Time estimate	7.3333
2	B	Yes	15	90	105	90	105	0	3-Time estimate	1
3	C	Yes	5	105	110	105	110	0	3-Time estimate	0.3333
4	D	Yes	20	124	144	124	144	0	3-Time estimate	3
5	E	no	21	144	165	168	189	24	3-Time estimate	1
6	F	no	14	90	104	96	110	6	3-Time estimate	0.6667
7	G	Yes	14	110	124	110	124	0	3-Time estimate	2
8	H	no	28	144	172	161	189	17	3-Time estimate	1.3333
9	I	no	30	90	120	114	144	24	3-Time estimate	4.6667
10	J	Yes	45	144	189	144	189	0	3-Time estimate	3.6667
	Project	Completion	Time	=	189	DAYS				
	Number of	Critical	Path(s)	=	1					

FIGURE 7.22*a*   WINQSB Activity Analysis for Klonepalm 2000

Critical Path(s) for KLONEPALM 2000	
10-25-1998	Critical Path 1
1	A
2	B
3	C
4	G
5	D
6	J
Completion Time	189
Std. Dev.	9.0185

FIGURE 7.22*b* WINQSB Critical Path(s) for Klonepalm 2000

FIGURE 7.23 Project Completion Time Distribution If the $250,000 Is Spent

As Figure 7.23 shows, now when x = 180, z = (180 − 189)/9.0185 = −0.99, and when x = 200, z = (200 − 189)/9.0185 = 1.22. The relevant probabilities are now:

$$P(X < 180) = P(Z < -0.99) = .5 - .3389 = .1611$$
$$P(180 < X < 200) = P(-0.99 < Z < 1.22) = .3389 + .3888 = .7277$$
$$P(X > 200) = P(Z > 1.22) = .5 - .3888 = .1112$$

Hence, if the $250,000 *is* spent, the expected gross additional profit, E(Y), is:

$$E(Y) = .1611(\$1,000,000) + .7277(\$400,000) + .1112(\$0) = \$452,180$$

Since $250,000 was spent to achieve this gross additional expected profit, however, the net additional expected profit derived from the additional staff training is $452,180 − $250,000 = $202,180. Because this is less than the net expected profit of $336,180 if the $250,000 is not spent, the additional staff training should not be undertaken. Thus, management should not pursue either of the two extra spending options for sales or staff training.

IS IT APPROPRIATE TO USE THE EXPECTED VALUE APPROACH?

A word of caution must be offered about using the expected value approach. An expected value is a "long-run average" value, which means that if the project were repeated over and over again, in the long run it would not pay to spend the additional $250,000 each time for staff training. However, many projects, including this one, are performed only once. Hence, while the results from an expected value analysis can be used as a guide, the decision maker should also consider other data, hunches, and judgments before making a final decision about whether or not to spend the $250,000 on additional staff training.

7.10 *T*HE CRITICAL PATH METHOD (CPM)

The **critical path method (CPM)** is a deterministic approach to project planning, based on the assumption that an activity's completion time can be determined with certainty. This time depends only on the amount of money allocated to the activity. The process of reducing an activity's completion time by committing additional monetary resources is known as *crashing*.

CPM assumes that there are two crucial time points for each activity: (1) its *normal completion time* (NT), achieved when the usual or *normal cost* (NC) is spent to complete the activity; and (2) its *crash completion time* (CT), the minimum possible completion time for the activity; the CT is attained when a maximum *crash cost* (CC) is spent. The assumption is that spending an amount greater than CC on an activity will not significantly reduce the completion time any further.

To illustrate this CPM assumption, think of a building project that includes the construction of a large brick wall. The wall will be completed in a normal time if the normal cost is paid to one bricklayer. If extra funds are available to hire two bricklayers, the completion time should be less; a third bricklayer could reduce the completion time even more. But there comes a point when the addition of another bricklayer will not significantly reduce the time further. Plaster between the bricks takes a certain time to dry, regardless of the number of bricklayers. Carried to the extreme, if there are more bricklayers than the number of bricks required for the wall, the completion time cannot be reduced further. Hence, an activity's crash cost is usually the cost at which most of its significant time reduction has been achieved. CPM analyses are based on the following **linearity assumption**:

CPM Linearity Assumption

If any amount between NC and CC is spent to complete an activity, the *percentage decrease* in the activity's completion time from its normal time to its crash time equals the *percentage increase* in cost from its normal cost to its crash cost.

Figure 7.24 illustrates the linearity concept of crashing. Here,

T = NT-CT = the maximum possible time reduction (crashing) of an activity

C = CC-NC = the maximum *additional* (crash) costs required to achieve the maximum time reduction

$M = \dfrac{C}{T}$ = the *marginal cost* of reducing an activity's completion time by one unit

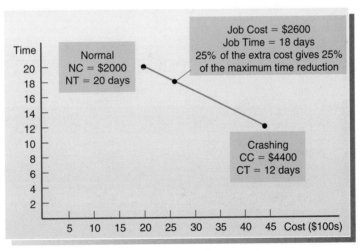

FIGURE 7.24   CPM Linearity Assumption

Figure 7.24 shows that as costs are increased from the normal cost, NC = $2000, to the maximum crash cost, CC = $4400, the activity's completion time is reduced proportionately from the normal time of NT = 20 days to the crash time of CT = 12 days. The maximum time reduction is T = 20 − 12 = 8 days, and the maximum additional cost is C = $4400 − $2000 = $2400. Thus, the cost per day reduction is M = C/T = $2400/8 = $300/day.

If management allocates $2600 to complete the activity ($600 more than its normal cost of $2000), the time reduction from this increase is $600/$300 = 2 days. That is, the activity is now expected to take 20 − 2 = 18 days to complete.

MEETING A DEADLINE AT MINIMUM COST

Suppose management is willing to commit additional monetary resources in an attempt to meet a deadline date, D. It would first check to see whether this can be accomplished by spending the normal costs for the activities. In other words, a deterministic PERT/CPM approach (discussed in Section 7.5) can be applied to a network using the normal activity times. If this analysis showed that the project could, indeed, be accomplished by time D, no additional funds would have to be spent on the project.

If, however, the completion time of the project using normal times exceeds the target completion date, management will need to spend additional resources to "crash" some of the activities to meet the target deadline. Its objective is to meet the target date at minimal additional cost. To illustrate this concept, consider the problem faced by Tom Larkin, who is considering running for mayor of Springfield, Missouri.

Tom.cpm
Tomcrash.cpm

TOM LARKIN'S POLITICAL CAMPAIGN

With six months (26 weeks) to go before the mayoral election, the incumbent mayor of Springfield, Missouri, has decided not to run for reelection. Tom Larkin, a supporter of the incumbent and a political activist in southern Missouri politics for almost 10 years, is now considering running for mayor himself.

Tom, his family, a few close friends, and political allies have met and decided on a set of campaign activities. Based on their years of political experience, they have been able to determine time and cost estimates for each of these activities. As shown in Table 7.13, under normal circumstances (i.e., if the campaign were not under a 26-week time constraint), a good mayoral campaign is estimated to cost $40,000.

TABLE 7.13   MAYORAL CAMPAIGN ACTIVITIES

Activity	Immediate Predecessors	Normal Schedule		Reduced Schedule	
		Time	Cost	Time	Cost
A. Hire campaign staff	—	4	2.0	2	5.0
B. Prepare position papers	—	6	3.0	3	9.0
C. Recruit volunteers	A	4	4.5	2	10.0
D. Raise funds	A,B	6	2.5	4	10.0
E. File candidacy papers	D	2	0.5	1	1.0
F. Prepare campaign material	E	13	13.0	8	25.0
G. Locate/staff headquarters	E	1	1.5	1	1.5
H. Run personal campaign	C,G	20	6.0	10	23.5
I. Run media campaign	F	9	7.0	5	16.0
Total Costs			40.0		101.0

Because of the short time until the election, the group has also estimated reduced time estimates (and increased cost estimates) for the campaign activities. Tom is interested in the most cost-efficient 26-week campaign.

Table 7.13 summarizes the activities, giving the immediate predecessors for the activities, the time estimates (in weeks), and the cost estimates (in $1000s) for both the normal and reduced schedules. As you can see, if all the activities are performed in their normal times, the campaign will cost Tom $40,000, while if each is done at its fastest rate, the campaign will cost $101,000.

SOLUTION

Using the techniques of Section 7.4, we can construct the PERT/CPM network shown in Figure 7.25 for Tom Larkin's political campaign. An analysis of this problem generated by WINQSB (Figure 7.26) using normal costs gives a minimal 36-week completion time for the campaign. The critical path consists of activities B, D, E, F, and I.

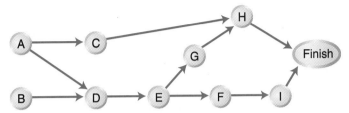

FIGURE 7.25   Tom Larkin Political Campaign PERT/CPM Network

	Activity Analysis for Tom Larkin Campaign (Normal Times)							
10-25-1998 13:40:09	Activity Name	On Critical Path	Activity Time	Earliest Start	Earliest Finish	Latest Start	Latest Finish	Slack (LS-ES)
1	A	no	4	0	4	2	6	2
2	B	Yes	6	0	6	0	6	0
3	C	no	4	4	8	12	16	8
4	D	Yes	6	6	12	6	12	0
5	E	Yes	2	12	14	12	14	0
6	F	Yes	13	14	27	14	27	0
7	G	no	1	14	15	15	16	1
8	H	no	20	15	35	16	36	1
9	I	Yes	9	27	36	27	36	0
	Project	Completion	Time	=	36	weeks		
	Number of	Critical	Path(s)	=	1			

FIGURE 7.26   WINQSB Activity Analysis for Tom Larkin Campaign (Normal Times)

Thus, to meet a 26-week deadline, some of the campaign activity times must be crashed. Table 7.14 details the normal and crash times and costs and the calculated values for the maximum time reduction (T) and marginal cost (M) for reducing each activity's completion time by one week.

TABLE 7.14   MAYORAL CAMPAIGN CRASH SCHEDULE

Activity	NT	NC	CT	CC	T	M
A	4	$ 2,000	2	$ 5,000	2	$1,500
B	6	$ 3,000	3	$ 9,000	3	$2,000
C	4	$ 4,500	2	$10,000	2	$2,750
D	6	$ 2,500	4	$10,000	2	$3,750
E	2	$ 500	1	$ 1,000	1	$ 500
F	13	$13,000	8	$25,000	5	$2,400
G*	1	$ 1,500	1	$ 1,500	—	—
H	20	$ 6,000	10	$23,500	10	$1,750
I	9	$ 7,000	5	$16,000	4	$2,250

*Note that no time reduction is possible for activity G.

In order to reduce the project time, the completion time of one or more of the critical activities must be crashed. When the completion time for a critical activity is reduced by a large enough amount, however, other paths will also become critical. To achieve further time reductions, activities on *all* critical paths must be crashed.

A heuristic approach to determine the amount of time each activity should be crashed can be developed by taking into account the following: (1) the project time is reduced only when activities on the critical path are reduced; (2) the maximum time reduction for each activity is limited; and (3) the amount of time an activity on the critical path can be reduced before another path also becomes a critical path is limited. For *very* small problems, an approach based on these observations can work rather well, but as the number of critical paths increases, the procedure becomes cumbersome rather rapidly.

LINEAR PROGRAMMING APPROACH TO CRASHING

Fortunately, the use of such a heuristic approach is unnecessary. A simple modification in the linear program given in Section 7.8 is all that is required. For this model, we now define two variables for each activity J:

$$X_J = \text{start time for activity J}$$
$$Y_J = \text{the amount by which activity J is to be crashed}$$

Since the normal cost must always be paid, the objective is to minimize the sum of the *additional* funds spent to reduce the completion times of activities. The cost per unit reduction for an activity is M_J, and the amount of time activity J is reduced is the decision variable, Y_J. Therefore, the total extra amount spent crashing activity J is $M_J Y_J$. Because we want to minimize the total additional funds spent to crash the project, the objective function is the sum of all such costs:

$$\text{MIN} \sum_J M_J Y_J$$

Constraints

There are three types of constraints in this approach:

1. **The project must be completed by its deadline date, D.** Since the project finish time is represented by the terminal node X(FIN), this constraint is expressed as

$$X(FIN) \leq D$$

2. **No activity can be reduced more than its maximum time reduction.** For each activity, J, there is a constraint of the form:

$$Y_J \leq T_J$$

3. **The start time for an activity must be at least as great as the finish time of all immediate predecessor activities.** This represents a series of constraints similar to those described in Section 7.8, of the form:

$$(\text{Start Time for Activity J}) \geq$$
$$(\text{Finish Time for an Immediate Predecessor for Activity J})$$

Now, however, the activity finish times are reduced by the amount of time each activity is crashed. Thus, if activity I is an immediate predecessor for activity J, there is a constraint of the form:

$$(\text{Start Time for Activity J}) \geq (\text{Start Time for Activity I}) +$$
$$(\text{Normal Time to Complete Activity I}) - (\text{Time Activity I Is Crashed})$$

For example, in the Tom Larkin political campaign problem, activity D has two immediate predecessors, activities A and B, with normal completion times of 4 and 6, respectively. Thus, two constraints in the linear program are:

$$X_D \geq X_B + (6 - Y_B)$$
$$X_D \geq X_A + (4 - Y_A)$$

Using this approach for all the precedence relations of the political campaign problem gives the following complete linear programming model for determining which activities to crash:

$$\text{MIN } 1500Y_A + 2000Y_B + 2750Y_C + 3750Y_D + 500Y_E + 2400Y_F + 1750Y_H + 2250Y_I$$

$$\text{ST}$$

$$X(FIN) \leq 26\} \qquad (1)$$

$$\left.\begin{array}{l} Y_A \leq 2 \\ Y_B \leq 3 \\ Y_C \leq 2 \\ Y_D \leq 2 \\ Y_E \leq 1 \\ Y_F \leq 5 \\ Y_H \leq 10 \end{array}\right\} \qquad (2)$$

$$\left.\begin{array}{l} X(FIN) \geq X_I + (9 - Y_I) \\ X(FIN) \geq X_H + (20 - Y_H) \\ X_I \geq X_F + (13 - Y_F) \\ X_H \geq X_G + 1 \\ X_H \geq X_C + (4 - Y_C) \\ X_G \geq X_E + (2 - Y_E) \\ X_F \geq X_E + (2 - Y_E) \\ X_E \geq X_D + (6 - Y_D) \\ X_D \geq X_B + (6 - Y_B) \\ X_D \geq X_A + (4 - Y_A) \\ X_C \geq X_A + (4 - Y_A) \\ \text{All } X_I \text{ and } Y_I \geq 0 \end{array}\right\} \qquad (3)$$

WINQSB Output

This linear programming problem can be solved using any standard linear programming package. Software packages that include project scheduling routines, such as WINQSB, require only input of the deadline, D, the normal completion times and costs (NT and NC), the crash completion times and costs (CT and CC), and the immediate predecessors for each activity. Using these data, the program calculates the constants M and T for each activity and internally sets up the appropriate linear program. It then calls the linear programming subroutine to solve for the optimal amount of time each activity should be crashed and generates an activity schedule chart.

The WINQSB results for this problem are given in Figure 7.27. As you can see, completing the project in 26 weeks requires $69,750 ($29,750 more than the total normal cost of $40,000) and, with the exception of activity C (recruiting volunteers), all activities must be rigidly scheduled.

Activity Analysis for Tom Larkin Campaign (After Crashing)

10-25-1998 14:36:50	Activity Name	Critical Path	Normal Time	Crash Time	Suggested Time	Additional Cost	Normal Cost	Suggested Cost
1	A	Yes	4	2	3	$1,500	$2,000	$3,500
2	B	Yes	6	3	3	$6,000	$3,000	$9,000
3	C	no	4	2	4	0	$4,500	$4,500
4	D	Yes	6	4	4	$7,500	$2,500	$10,000
5	E	Yes	2	1	1	$500	$500	$1,000
6	F	Yes	13	8	13	0	$13,000	$13,000
7	G	Yes	1	1	1	0	$1,500	$1,500
8	H	Yes	20	10	17	$5,250	$6,000	$11,250
9	I	Yes	9	5	5	$9,000	$7,000	$16,000
	Overall	Project:			26	$29,750	$40,000	$69,750

FIGURE 7.27a   WINQSB Crashing Analysis for Tom Larkin Campaign (After Crashing)

Activity Analysis for Tom Larkin Campaign (After Crashing)

10-25-1998 14:38:59	Activity Name	On Critical Path	Activity Time	Earliest Start	Earliest Finish	Latest Start	Latest Finish	Slack (LS-ES)
1	A	Yes	3	0	3	0	3	0
2	B	Yes	3	0	3	0	3	0
3	C	no	4	3	7	5	9	2
4	D	Yes	4	3	7	3	7	0
5	E	Yes	1	7	8	7	8	0
6	F	Yes	13	8	21	8	21	0
7	G	Yes	1	8	9	8	9	0
8	H	Yes	17	9	26	9	26	0
9	I	Yes	5	21	26	21	26	0
	Project	Completion	Time	=	26	weeks		
	Total	Cost of	Project	=	$69,750	(Cost on	CP=	$65,250)
	Number of	Critical	Path(s)	=	4			

FIGURE 7.27b   WINQSB Activity Analysis for Tom Larkin Campaign (After Crashing)

OPERATING OPTIMALLY WITHIN A FIXED BUDGET

The CPM approach presented for the Tom Larkin political campaign sought to find the minimum cost of conducting a campaign within 26 weeks. Many projects, however, including construction projects, marketing campaigns, and research and development studies, must operate within a given fixed budget. In such cases, the objective is to complete the project in minimum time, subject to the budget restrictions. The CPM approach can easily be modified for these models.

Tombudg.cpm

TOM LARKIN'S POLITICAL CAMPAIGN (Continued)

Tom Larkin has been assured by his closest political associates that he will be able to raise approximately $75,000 should he decide to run for mayor of Springfield, Missouri. Tom needs some time to think about his options but is aware that he must decide soon. He would like to know how soon he will have to make his decision in order to mount the kind of campaign outlined by his supporters.

SOLUTION

Tom is seeking the minimum time to mount the political campaign outlined earlier, while spending at most $75,000. Consider the linear program developed for Tom's original crashing problem. The time restriction of 26 weeks no longer applies; instead, Tom's objective is to minimize the total time to complete the campaign:

$$\text{MIN } X(\text{FIN})$$

Tom is now operating under a budgetary constraint that limits the amount spent on the campaign to $75,000, $35,000 more than the $40,000 minimum cost to perform all activities in their normal times. Thus, the constraint is:

(The total additional funds spent (above $40,000))

$\leq$

(The total extra funds available)

This can be expressed as $\Sigma M_j Y_j \leq 75,000 - 40,000$, or,

$$1500Y_A + 2000Y_B + 2750Y_C + 3750Y_D + 500Y_E + 2400Y_F + 1750Y_H + 2250Y_I \leq 35,000$$

Since the normal and crash times and the PERT/CPM network for the problem have not changed, constraint sets (2) and (3) remain the same. In effect, only the first constraint and the objective functions have switched positions between the two formulations.

The constrained budget model is another option in the PERT/CPM module of WINQSB. Keeping within a maximum budget of $75,000, the solution is summarized in Figure 7.28. As the output indicates, we can now achieve an additional time savings of 1.265 weeks and complete the project in 24.735 weeks by spending the additional $5250

Activity Analysis for Tom Larkin Campaign (After Crashing)

10-25-1998 14:52:55	Activity Name	Critical Path	Normal Time	Crash Time	Suggested Time	Additional Cost	Normal Cost	Suggested Cost
1	A	Yes	4	2	3	$1,500	$2,000	$3,500
2	B	Yes	6	3	3	$6,000	$3,000	$9,000
3	C	no	4	2	4	0	$4,500	$4,500
4	D	Yes	6	4	4	$7,500	$2,500	$10,000
5	E	Yes	2	1	1	$500	$500	$1,000
6	F	Yes	13	8	11.7349	$3,036.14	$13,000	$16,036.14
7	G	Yes	1	1	1	0	$1,500	$1,500
8	H	Yes	20	10	15.7349	$7,463.85	$6,000	$13,463.85
9	I	Yes	9	5	5	$9,000	$7,000	$16,000
	Overall	Project:			24.73	$34,999.98	$40,000	$74,999.98

FIGURE 7.28*a*   WINQSB Crashing Analysis for Tom Larkin Campaign (After Crashing)

Activity Analysis for Tom Larkin Campaign (After Crashing)

10-25-1998 14:53:55	Activity Name	On Critical Path	Activity Time	Earliest Start	Earliest Finish	Latest Start	Latest Finish	Slack (LS-ES)
1	A	Yes	3	0	3	0	3	0
2	B	Yes	3	0	3	0	3	0
3	C	no	4	3	7	5	9	2
4	D	Yes	4	3	7	3	7	0
5	E	Yes	1	7	8	7	8	0
6	F	Yes	11.7349	8	19.7349	8	19.7349	0
7	G	Yes	1	8	9	8	9	0
8	H	Yes	15.7349	9	24.7349	9	24.7349	0
9	I	Yes	5	19.7349	24.7349	19.7349	24.7349	0
	Project	Completion	Time	=	24.73	weeks		
	Total	Cost of	Project	=	$74,999.98	(Cost on	CP=	$70,499.98)
	Number of	Critical	Path(s)	=	4			

FIGURE 7.28*b*   WINQSB Activity Analysis for Tom Larkin Campaign (After Crashing)

to crash activity H (personal campaigning) further from 17 to 15.7349 weeks and to crash activity F (preparation of campaign material) from 13 weeks to 11.7349 weeks.

INCORPORATING TIME-DEPENDENT OVERHEAD COSTS INTO CPM FORMULATIONS

In addition to the costs of performing any individual activity, some projects have fixed daily, monthly, or yearly operational costs. Such costs might include telephone costs, repayment of debt, and consulting fees that are directly proportional to the length of the project. If the project carries a fixed weekly overhead cost of $K/week, then the total weekly overhead cost, $K[X(FIN)]$, must be figured into the mathematical model. Thus, for a model whose goal is to complete a project by some time D at minimum *total* cost, the term $K[X(FIN)]$ must be added to the minimization objective function, which now becomes:

$$\text{MIN} \sum_J M_J Y_J + K(X(FIN))$$

For example, if Tom Larkin estimated his administrative costs at $100 per week, and he wished to complete the campaign within 26 weeks at minimum total cost, the formulation would have the same maximum crash time and precedence constraints, but the objective function and first constraint of the new formulation would be:

$$\text{MIN } 1500Y_A + 2000Y_B + 2750Y_C + 3750Y_D + 500Y_E + 2400Y_F + 1750Y_H + 2250Y_I$$
$$+ 100X(FIN)$$
$$\text{ST} \qquad X(FIN) \leq 26$$

The optimal value for this objective function represents the minimal total variable costs for the problem. To determine the *total* cost of the project, the total sum of the normal activity costs would have to be added to this value.

On the other hand, if Tom's objective were to minimize the time to complete the project, subject to a certain budget, B, the term K|X(FIN)| must be added to the left side of the budget constraint:

$$\Sigma\ M_I Y_I\ +\ K(X(FIN))\ \leq\ B\ -\ \Sigma\ NC_I$$

Thus, if Tom wished to incorporate these weekly costs into the model to complete the project in minimum time given an overall budget of $75,000 ($35,000 above the normal activity costs), the objective function and first constraint of the formulation would be:

$$\text{MIN}\quad X(FIN)$$

ST

$$1500Y_A\ +2000Y_B\ +2750Y_C\ +3750Y_D\ +500Y_E\ +2400Y_F\ +1750Y_H\ +2250Y_I$$
$$+100X(FIN)\ \leq\ 35000$$

7.11 $\mathscr{P}$ERT/COST

Prior to the start of a project, management determines cost and time estimates and a set of precedence relations for the activities of the project. PERT/CPM analyses can then be used to calculate the expected project completion time and a set of earliest and latest start and finish times for each activity. Management can then use this information to set an appropriate schedule.

Once a schedule is in place, however, what *should* happen according to the schedule may differ greatly from what *actually* happens. Unexpected expenses can send a project way over budget, while unexpected delays in the completion of some activities can cause a project to fall behind schedule. Because management is interested in completing the project on time and within budget, it is important to be able to gauge a project's progress against scheduled time and cost estimates so that it can take corrective actions if necessary.

Accounting information systems can serve as a mechanism for monitoring the progress of a project, providing management with "snapshot" progress reports that summarize the allocation of total project expenses and activity completion status at any given instant. **PERT/Cost**,[7] is one such accounting information system that helps management determine whether the project is coming in under or over budget.

Unlike typical cost accounting systems, which are cost-center based (by location, function, or department), PERT/Cost is a project-oriented system that is based on analyzing a project that has been segmented into a collection of work packages. *Work packages* are sets of related activities within a project which share common costs or are under the control of one contractor, department, or individual. PERT/Cost utilizes work packages rather than individual activities because, for most projects, the large number and narrow detail of activities make it difficult, if not impossible, to determine how to allocate and measure costs (such as indirect and overhead costs).

Two assumptions are made concerning work packages in PERT/Cost systems:

Work Package Assumptions for a PERT/Cost System

1. Once a work package has begun, it is performed continuously until it has been completed.
2. The costs associated with a work package are spread evenly throughout its duration.

---

[7]Originally developed by the U.S. government as a way of controlling the costs of defense and NASA (National Aeronautics and Space Administration) projects.

The first assumption implies that once a work package has commenced, it will not be interrupted for a period of time, begun again, interrupted again, and so on. The second assumption implies that there are no huge costs at any single point of time during the duration of the work package; hence, costs are relatively constant from day to day and week to week. Given these assumptions, a forecasted (weekly)[8] cost for each work package can be calculated as follows:

$$\text{Work Package Forecasted Weekly Cost} = \frac{\text{Budgeted Total Cost for Work Package}}{\text{Expected Completion Time for Work Package}}$$

These estimates may be used to construct a range of feasible budgets using the approach outline in Section 7.6. Once a schedule is in place, a PERT/Cost system monitors the progress of a project as it is performed to see whether it is being completed on schedule and within budget. This is done by obtaining current completion and cost data for each work package, including the actual expenditures to date for the work package and an estimate of the percent of the work package completed, p. Using these data, we can calculate the value of the work done to date (expressed in terms of budgeted cost) and the expected time remaining to complete the work package as follows.

Current Status of a Work Package

Value of Work to date = p*(Budget for the Work Package)
Expected Remaining Completion Time = (l-p)*(Original Expected Completion Time)

COMPLETION TIME ANALYSIS

Using the estimates for the expected remaining completion times for each incomplete work package, we can use a standard PERT analysis to calculate a revised estimate for the project completion time. This estimate is compared to the project's original completion time estimate to discern whether the project is ahead or behind schedule.

COST OVERRUN/ UNDERRUN ANALYSIS

For each work package that is either completed or in progress, a *cost overrun* can be determined as follows.

Cost Overrun = (Actual Expenditures to Date) − (Value of Work to Date)

A negative cost overrun is a *cost underrun*. The cost overrun for a work package that has not yet been started is 0. The cost overruns and underruns for all work packages are then summed to determine a cost overrun or underrun for the entire project.

CORRECTIVE ACTION

What happens if a project is found to be behind schedule or experiencing a cost overrun? The obvious answer is for the manager to seek out the causes for the delay or cost overrun and determine whether corrective action needs to be taken. Perhaps an incorrect estimate was made of a project's completion time or cost. Unforeseen problems can

---

[8]Any time unit is acceptable.

also warrant a reassessment of work package completion times and costs. However, some delays or cost overruns may be the result of problems with one activity within the work package or with one department or contractor, which affect the costs and times of several activities.

In some cases, a moderate delay in the overall completion date of the project may be acceptable and no corrective action need be taken if the project is coming in as budgeted. In other cases, such as the Tom Larkin political campaign, meeting a target completion date is imperative.

Completed work packages that experienced cost overruns or delays are lost causes in terms of meeting project deadlines or budgets. Hence, attention must focus on work yet to be performed. If the project is behind schedule, the manager is interested in determining whether expediting some activities at additional cost is possible or desirable. For projects experiencing a cost underrun, additional resources may be channeled to problem activities. Even if there is no cost underrun, possible funding may be found within the budget by reducing allocations to some of the noncritical activities of the project.

If the project is coming in over budget, noncritical activities or work packages are evaluated first for cost savings. If reduced funding would cause a delay in a critical activity or work package, however, the estimated project completion date will have to be extended. This may be the price the manager has to pay to correct such cost overruns. Of course, the accumulated delay may be so great or the cost overrun so high that no amount of corrective action will facilitate either an "on-time" or "within budget" project.

The PERT/Cost technique is illustrated in the following revision to the Tom Larkin political campaign problem.

TOM LARKIN'S POLITICAL CAMPAIGN (revision)

Suppose that Tom Larkin were actually informed *nine* months (39 weeks) prior to election day that the incumbent mayor would not seek reelection, and that the meeting with his family and associates took place at that time. Tom's campaign treasurer, Chris Ngyuen, reported to Tom that an effective campaign should take 36 weeks and cost $40,000. (She based these projections on the normal cost and times of the project.) Given these estimates, Tom took three weeks to make his decision and, to no one's surprise, elected to enter the mayoral race.

Following Tom's directions, at the end of week 20, Chris prepared an assessment of the progress to date and the financial outlook for the campaign, as shown in Table 7.15. Tom wants to know if the campaign is on target for completion in 36 weeks and if it is progressing within budget. If it is not, he wants staff recommendations for corrective action.

TABLE 7.15   MAYORAL CAMPAIGN STATUS REPORT: END OF WEEK 20

Work Package	Expenditures	Status
A. Hire campaign staff	$ 2,600	Finished
B. Prepare position papers	$ 5,000	Finished
C. Recruit volunteers	$ 3,000	Finished
D. Raise funds	$ 5,000	Finished
E. File candidacy papers	$ 700	Finished
F. Prepare campaign material	$ 5,600	40% Complete
G. Locate/staff headquarters	$ 700	Finished
H. Run personal campaign	$ 2,000	25% Complete
I. Run Media campaign	$ 0	0% Complete
Expenditures to Date	$24,600	

SOLUTION

Because the number of activities in the campaign is so small and broadly defined, we will treat each as a work package. Using normal cost data for the campaign, given in Section 7.10, Table 7.16 summarizes the total budget, expected completion time, and forecasted weekly cost for each work package.

TABLE 7.16   BUDGET, COMPLETION TIME, AND COSTS
FOR MAYORAL CAMPAIGN WORK PACKAGES

Work Package	Budget	Expected Time	Forecasted Weekly Cost
A. Hire campaign staff	$ 2,000	4	$ 500
B. Prepare position papers	$ 3,000	6	$ 500
C. Recruit volunteers	$ 4,500	4	$1,125
D. Raise funds	$ 2,500	6	$ 417
E. File candidacy papers	$ 500	2	$ 250
F. Prepare campaign material	$13,000	13	$1,000
G. Locate/staff headquarters	$ 1,500	1	$1,500
H. Run personal campaign	$ 6,000	20	$ 300
I. Run media campaign	$ 7,000	9	$ 778

TIME ANALYSIS

Figure 7.29 shows the network remaining at the end of week 20. Only the darkened work packages (F, H, and I) remain to be completed. We use a start week of 20 (reflecting the current week) for completing "the rest of the work package." Since, at the end of week 20, work package F is only 40% complete and its anticipated completion time is 13 weeks, it is expected to take another $(.6)(13) = 7.8$ weeks to complete. Similarly, work package H is expected to require another $(1-.25)(20) = 15$ weeks to complete.

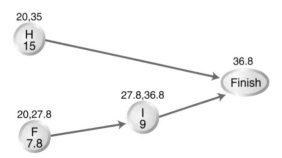

FIGURE 7.29   Status As of Week 20

Carrying out the remainder of the forward pass, we see that the current expected project completion date is now 36.8 weeks from inception. Thus, the staff must find a way of saving .8 weeks from the remaining schedule. This savings must come from work packages F or I.

COST ANALYSIS

Table 7.17 is one version of a *project cost control report*, which details the cost overruns and underruns for each work package by listing its total budgeted cost, the "to date" status of the percentage of completed work, the estimated value of its completed work to date, and its actual expenditures. The estimated value of the completed work is calculated by multiplying the percentage complete by its budgeted value. The cost overrun is the difference between this value and the actual cost to date.

TABLE 7.17   PROJECT COST CONTROL REPORT

Week = 20

Work Package	Budgeted Values		To Date Values			Cost Overrun
	Total Time	Total Cost	Percent Complete	Estimated Work Value	Actual Value	
A	4	$ 2,000	100%	$ 2,000	$ 2,600	$ 600
B	6	$ 3,000	100%	$ 3,000	$ 5,000	$2,000
C	4	$ 4,500	100%	$ 4,500	$ 3,000	($1,500)
D	6	$ 2,500	100%	$ 2,500	$ 5,000	$2,500
E	2	$ 500	100%	$ 500	$ 700	$ 200
F	13	$13,000	40%	$ 5,200	$ 5,600	$ 400
G	1	$ 1,500	100%	$ 1,500	$ 700	($ 800)
H	20	$ 6,000	25%	$ 1,500	$ 2,000	$ 500
I	9	$ 7,000	0%	$ 0	$ 0	$ 0
Total		$40,000		$20,700	$24,600	$3,900

For instance, the entries for work package F, which was budgeted for $13,000 and is currently 40% complete with expenditures of $5600, are calculated as follows.

$$\text{Estimated Work Value to Date} = .40(\$13,000) \qquad = \$5200$$
$$\text{Cost Overrun} \qquad\qquad = \$5600 - \$5200 = \$400$$

CORRECTIVE ACTION

The PERT/Cost analysis indicated that the campaign was experiencing both a cost overrun of $3900 and a project delay of .8 week. Tom may wish to divert funds from personal campaigning (work package H, which is not on the critical path) to preparing campaign material (F) and the media campaign (I). This diversion may involve less travel and personal appearances and save on security expenses.

A relatively minor shift in funds away from work package H could bring the campaign in within 36 weeks. Although the original target date of this work package is not met, the overall project deadline of 36 weeks is. Tom has only $6000 budgeted for work package H, however, and work package H itself is currently experiencing a $500 cost overrun. Although some of the resources might be shifted from H to meet the deadline, large shifts may increase the completion time of this work package so much that it would become a critical work package. In fact, there is not enough money left in the budget to both complete activity H in a reasonable amount of time and cover the current $3900 cost overrun.

Hence, an overall project cost overrun appears inevitable unless Tom can find ways to complete work packages F and I within their expected times at much lower projected costs. If the goal is not to come in too far above the targeted budget, Tom should try to make some cost savings in these work packages.

Another option might be for Tom to hold another fund raiser. This would be an added activity in the project, however, and could affect the completion time for the campaign.

COMPUTER SOLUTION TO PERT/COST

Many software packages for project scheduling include modules that perform PERT/Cost analyses that give work package time and cost overrun status for any time during the project. WINQSB, for instance, can generate a project cost control chart, a project time control chart, daily budgeted expenditures, and a graph of feasible budgets.

7.12 SUMMARY

Activity scheduling is an important factor in ensuring both the timeliness and cost effectiveness of a project. An activity is a separate component of a project, whose completion is generally key to the commencement of another activity or set of activities of the project. Two basic approaches to project scheduling, PERT and CPM, can help establish efficient scheduling of project activities.

PERT is the probabilistic approach to project scheduling, in which we assume that activity completion times are not known with certainty but vary according to a probability distribution with known mean and standard deviation. One method used to estimate an activity's mean time and standard deviation is the three-time estimate approach, which assumes a Beta distribution for an activity's completion time.

Given the time estimates for the mean and standard deviation for each activity, we assume that only the completion times for the activities on the critical path will determine the mean and standard deviation of the entire project. We also assume that there are enough activities on the critical path so that the normal distribution provides a reasonable approximation for the completion time of the project. Thus, a project's mean completion time is the sum of the mean completion times of the activities on the critical path, and its *variance* is the sum of the *variances* of the activity times on the critical path. The standard deviation of the project completion time is the square root of its variance.

The CPM approach assumes that activity completion times can be determined by the monetary amount spent to complete the activity. Computer programs can determine either the minimal amount of funding needed to complete a project within a specified time period or the minimal completion time of the project given a fixed budget.

Managers typically prefer a fairly consistent expenditure of resources. Resource leveling approaches can smooth the distribution of the necessary resources over the duration of a project. Projects may also be subject to resource constraints. In such cases, a resource allocation program can be used to make schedules that satisfy such restrictions. Heuristic methods are common in both resource leveling and resource allocation approaches.

PERT/Cost is an accounting system that can be used to determine the progress of a project during its completion. In particular, it can determine whether the project is on schedule and within budget. If the project is not, the system can indicate areas where corrective action may be taken to bring the project closer in line with targets.

WINQSB *Input for* PERT/CPM

WINQSB can be used to solve PERT/CPM problems. It can generate Gantt charts, activity schedules, and crash analyses for several different objectives, and it can perform PERT/Cost analyses. Here we show the initial input screen and the input for a three time estimate approach for the Klonepalm 2000 project. When the PERT CPM module is selected, the input screen shown in Exhibit 7.1 appears.

EXHIBIT 7.1

We have chosen Probabilistic PERT; hence, only normal times are checked in the CPM data field. The default activity time distribution is the three time estimate discussed in this chapter; however, this could be changed if the activities had some other known distribution.

If we were doing crash or PERT/Cost analyses, Deterministic CPM would be checked, and we would choose the appropriate data input from the CPM data field.

Once we click OK, we input the precedence relations, and provide the three time estimates in spreadsheet form, as shown in Exhibit 7.2.

Note that no entry is made in WINQSB for the FINISH mode.

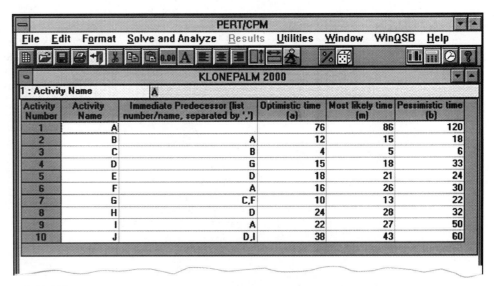

EXHIBIT 7.2

We then choose Solve the Critical Path from the Solve and Analyze menu, generating the activity schedule chart given in Section 7.8. The chart includes the mean, standard deviation, ES, EF, LS, LF, and slack times based on the mean activity times for each activity.

From the Results menu we can then generate screens showing the critical path(s) and Gantt charts. WINQSB can also perform an analysis of the probability that the project will be completed by a certain date.

PROBLEMS

1. Paul Nguyen is designing a new safety cap for medicine bottles to replace the cumbersome child safety caps used by manufacturers today. Construct an activity on node representation of the project, given the activities Paul has listed in the following table.

SAFETY CAP PROJECT

Activity	Immediate Predecessors
A. Complete design	—
B. Manufacture prototype	A
C. Test and redesign cap	B
D. Determine interest in product	B
E. Apply for patent	C
F. Manufacture limited quantities	C
G. Design packaging	C
H. Negotiate with manufacturers	D,E,F
I. Sign contract	H
J. Ship initial supplies	G,I

2. The library at Kaufman Products has just received authorization to spend up to $40,000 on new journal subscriptions and book purchases. Accordingly, the librarian has developed the following small project.

	Immediate Predecessors	Time (weeks)
A. Solicit input from employees	—	4
B. Identify obsolete material in library	—	3
C. Clear out space for new purchases	B	2
D. Hold sale/discard obsolete material	B	3
E. Review input from employees given budget and space requirements	A,C	2
F. Order/receive new materials	E	5

Draw an activity on node PERT/CPM network for the Kaufman Products librarian and use this representation to determine the expected number of weeks it will take before the new materials are in the library. What is the critical path? Explain its significance.

3. Francisco and Alana Roque are CPAs who have decided to open their own tax consulting service. They must first lease office space and secure the appropriate business insurance. They will then hire two senior tax experts who are up to date on the tax laws and are able to teach junior accountants.

   Once office space has been leased and the insurance obtained, the Roques can prepare their advertising brochures and hire 15 junior accountants. Training begins after all 15 junior accountants and the two senior tax experts have been hired.

   After the junior accountants have been trained and the advertising brochures printed, the Roques will begin soliciting clients.

   a. Prepare an activity chart for the seven different activities required for the Roques to begin their tax consulting service. Include a column denoting the immediate predecessors for each activity.

   b. From your activity chart in part (a) draw an activity on node PERT/CPM network for this project.

4. The Ohio Preservation Society (OPS) has discovered a house once occupied by Rutherford B. Hayes, the nineteenth President of the United States (1877–1881). OPS plans to restore the building to reflect the period during which the former president lived there and eventually open it for public tours. Contractors for the restoration project will have to do the following:

Wall/Ceiling Activities
A. Strip the existing wallpaper
B. Clean and repair the walls/ceilings
C. Paint the walls/ceilings
Flooring Activities
D. Remove old carpeting
E. Lay a floor foundation
F. Install, stain, and seal hardwood flooring
G. Install rugs and carpet runners (for tourists)
Exterior Activities
H. Sand and repair outside wood surfaces
I. Paint exterior to reflect the period

a. Construct an activity on node PERT/CPM network for the renovation project faced by OPS, assuming:

   i) The wall/ceiling activities, the flooring activities, and the exterior activities are listed in the order in which they are to be performed.

   ii) Cleaning and repairing the walls/ceilings, removing the old carpeting, and sanding and repairing the exterior must precede any painting activity (interior or exterior).

   iii) The walls/ceilings must be painted before hardwood flooring is installed, stained, and sealed.

   iv) All painting (interior and exterior) must be completed before new rugs and carpet runners are installed.

   v) Stripping the wallpaper, removing the old carpeting, and sanding and repairing the exterior may all commence at the same time.

b. If the estimated time of each wall/ceiling activity is two weeks, the estimated time of each flooring activity is one week, and the estimated time of each exterior activity is three weeks, draw a Gantt chart for the restoration project.

c. What is OPS's estimated completion time for the restoration project?

5. When buyers purchase new houses, they are frequently responsible for installing their own landscaping. The PERT/CPM network shown in the accompanying figure represents a landscaping project for a new home in Jackson, Mississippi. The times are in days.

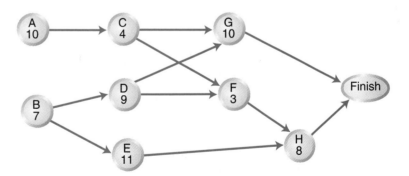

a. What are the expected completion time and the critical path for the landscaping project?

b. What are the earliest and latest start and finish times for activity C?

c. How long can activity A be delayed without delaying the minimum completion time of the project?

d. If activities A, C, and F are *each* delayed three days, how long will the landscaping project be delayed?

6. L&P Janitorial provides cleaning services to many clients, including the Johnson Tower complex. L&P personnel begin their operations at 10:00 P.M. and must leave before

6:00 A.M. the following morning. Certain cleaning operations must be completed before others are started, as illustrated by the following network. The times are in minutes.

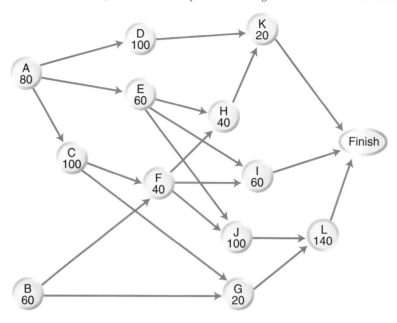

a. Prepare a chart giving the earliest and latest start and finish times and the slack times for each cleaning activity. Express the earliest and latest start and finish times as actual clock times (i.e., 10:00 P.M., etc.).

b. L&P Janitorial wants to conserve costs and will send the minimum number of workers required to complete a cleaning project. Employees work eight-hour shifts, and any worker can perform any of the cleaning operations. Show how the Johnson Tower complex project can be completed using only two workers. Give a schedule for each worker.

7. The following table is a plan for a major freeway renovation project at the intersection of Interstate Highway 5 and Highway 55, a major north-south freeway in Santa Ana, California.

Activity	Expected Time (months)	Immediate Predecessors
A. Obtain federal funding	16	—
B. Obtain state funding	28	—
C. Design/subcontract freeway lanes	14	A
D. Design/subcontract bridges/exits	22	A
E. Build new freeway sound walls	12	B,C
F. Rebuild southbound lanes	26	B,C
G. Rebuild transition roads/exits	18	D,E
H. Build new bridges/overpasses	50	D,E
I. Rebuild northbound lanes	44	F,G

a. Determine an overall estimated project completion time.

b. What is the effect of: (i) a delay in federal funding of five months? (ii) a delay in state funding of five months?

c. Suppose *each* activity has a standard deviation of four months. What is the probability that the freeway construction will be completed in: (i) six years; (ii) seven years; (iii) eight years; (iv) nine years?

8. The California Medical Association (CMA) is holding a meeting at the Anaheim Hilton Hotel on September 8. On that day, the CMA will host a theme party reception for the over 2000 members and spouses who are expected to attend. Stacey Geyer is the Hilton's convention services manager in charge of arranging the reception.
   Planning the meeting consists of the following activities:

TIME REQUIREMENTS FOR CMA RECEPTION

Task	Immediate Predecessors	Expected Days	Standard Deviation
A. Plan meeting with Howard Klein	—		
B. Secure an appropriate reception room	A	3	1
C. Plan theme	A	8	2
D. Plan menu (with Howard Klein)	C		
E. Hire musicians	C	7	2
F. Plan space layout of reception room	B,D	4	1
G. Review plans/charges with Howard Klein	E,F		

Stacey has been able to estimate the mean and standard deviation of activities B, C, E, and F, based on her past experience. Her estimates for activities A, D, and G, however, depend somewhat on Howard Klein, the arrangements chairperson for the CMA.

At this point, Stacey has estimated that the initial planning meeting with Howard Klein will take at least two days and as many as ten days, but most likely about three days. She feels that menu planning will take between one and three days, most likely two days. In order to review the plans and charges completely, Howard Klein must check with his arrangements committee. This will most likely take about 10 days but could take anywhere from 4 to 22 days.

a. Determine the critical path, the expected completion time, and the standard deviation of the completion time of the project.

b. Analyze the effect on the expected project completion time of each of the following.

   i)   Activity A is delayed five days

   ii)   Activity B is delayed five days

   iii)   Activity D is delayed five days

   iv)   Activity F is delayed five days

   v)   Activities B and D are each delayed five days

   vi)   Activities D and F are each delayed five days

c. Stacey would like to be relatively sure (99% sure) that the project is completed by September 1, a week before the actual reception. Here is a calendar for July and August for the current calendar year. To meet Stacey's goal, by what date should she begin her first meeting with Howard Klein? *Be sure to take into account the variability in completion times and do not count Saturdays and Sundays (or July 4, if relevant). Count August 31 as day 1; that is, if the project took only one day it would have to start on August 31. Round up any fraction of a day to a whole day.*

JULY								AUGUST						
S	**M**	**T**	**W**	**TH**	**F**	**S**		**S**	**M**	**T**	**W**	**TH**	**F**	**S**
1	2	3	4	5	6	7					1	2	3	4
8	9	10	11	12	13	14		5	6	7	8	9	10	11
15	16	17	18	19	20	21		12	13	14	15	16	17	18
22	23	24	25	26	27	28		19	20	21	22	23	24	25
29	30	31						26	27	28	29	30	31	

9. Consider the CMA scheduling problem (Problem 8). There is a possibility that another group may also be scheduling a meeting at the same time at the Anaheim Hilton, so that securing an appropriate reception room (activity B) *may* present more of a problem for Stacey Geyer. Accordingly, she has raised her pessimistic estimate of its completion time; the expected time is now 10 days (instead of three) and its standard deviation is 6 (instead of 1).

Show that, given the basic assumptions of PERT, the expected time of the project does not change from that derived in Problem 8. What basic PERT assumption *could* be violated under this scenario, however?

10. Consider the CMA scheduling problem (Problem 8). Howard Klein's schedule does not allow him to meet with Stacey for their initial planning session until 35 work days before the meeting on September 8; that is, the entire project must be completed in

35 days. If it is not completed within 35 days, the CMA will use an alternative backup site for the reception, and the Hilton will forego the $100,000 profit from the reception.

The agent for Billy and the Goats, the musicians the CMA wants to book for the reception (activity E), has indicated to the Hilton that, for an additional $3000, he can wrap up contract negotiations with the group in only two days (with no variance), instead of the projected seven days with a standard deviation of two days. Is it worth it for Stacey to spend the extra $3000? *Hint: Look carefully at the entire revised project.*

11. *Mustang and Me* is a new movie from Nickledime Studios about a 12-year-old boy and a talking 1965 Ford Mustang convertible. The film is due out in 16 weeks. Originally, the studio was simply going to promote this as a "feel good" movie. However, further research has shown that merchandising of the modified Mustang used in the movie could be quite lucrative if the products are available no later than the release date of the movie.

The following table details the activities of this project. Because of the studio's long experience with product design and distribution, it has been able to determine normal and crash times and costs for each of the activities. Times are in weeks, and costs are in $100,000s.

	Normal		Crash	
Activity	Time	Cost	Time	Cost
A. Design/test product	6	12	4	22
B. Hire workers	3	4	2	5
C. Train workers	3	5	3	5
D. Order/receive materials	2	10	1.5	12
E. Reconfigure machinery/setup	7	10	4	19
F. Advertise product	8	20	5	32
G. Production	8	12	4.5	26
H. Pay purchase orders	3	1	2	2

The following is the PERT/CPM network representation of the project.

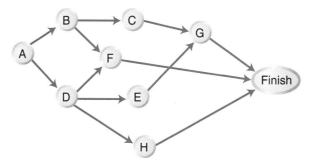

a. Write the linear program that models this situation.

b. Determine a minimum cost schedule to complete the project within 16 weeks.

12. Consider the merchandising problem faced by Nickledime Studios in problem 11. At present, the studio can only allocate $8 million to the merchandising project.

a. Write the linear program that models this situation.

b. What is the minimal completion time of the project, given this budgetary constraint?

13. Vertical software is software written using specific packages but designed especially for one company (or type of company). VSI (Vertical Software, Inc.) specializes in writing database programs for various industries. Recently, it signed a contract with the Rhode Island Basketball Officials Association to write an assigning and database system. The software takes the rankings of the officials (Levels 1, 2, 3, 4, and 5), each official's availability, and the level of official required for each game, and randomly assigns the appropriate officials to each game. The database of assignments must be accessible by date, level, school, and official.

Although the association is paying VSI for the program, VSI retains the right to market the product nationwide after development. The following is a simplified budget for the project.

Work Package	Immediate Predecessors	Expected Time (days)	Budget
A. Meet with association	—	2	$ 800
B. Write software	A	20	$9,000
C. Debug software	B	6	$1,500
D. Prepare brief manual	B	3	$1,000
E. Meet with RI assignors	D	2	$ 900
F. Test in RI for League season	C,E	40	$2,500
G. Make final changes	F	10	$4,000
H. Write complete manual	G	15	$5,000
I. Advertise	C,E	45	$9,500

After 50 days, VSI finds itself in the following position:

Work Package	Percent Complete	Expenditures to Date
A. Meet with association	100%	$1,000
B. Write software	100%	$8,000
C. Debug software	100%	$2,500
D. Prepare brief manual	100%	$1,000
E. Meet with RI assignors	100%	$1,000
F. Test in RI for League season	50%	$1,000
G. Make final changes	0%	$ 0
H. Write complete manual	0%	$ 0
I. Advertise	10%	$2,000

Is this project currently experiencing a cost overrun or underrun? Is it on target to be completed in its expected completion time? Should any corrective action be taken?

14. The Platters, a rock-and-roll group that had many hits in the late 1950s, has undergone many personnel changes since that era. However, a group performing under that name is still touring the country giving concerts. The group would like to stop in Detroit, Michigan, on its current tour. An "oldies" radio station, WDMI, is in charge of making the arrangements.

The station has listed the following activities that must be completed prior to the concert. Times are in weeks.

Activity	Immediate Predecessors	Optimistic	Most Likely	Pessimistic
A. Negotiate terms with Renaissance Center	—	3	4	5
B. Hire two local opening acts	A	2	4	12
C. Hire security	B	1	2	3
D. Hire all technicians	B	2	3	10
E. Line up ticket outlets	B	2	3	4
F. Complete initial radio/TV promotion	E	2	3	4
G. Arrange lodging/transportation	A	.5	1	1.5
H. Prepare final promotion/newspaper ads	F	4	5	12
I. Coordinate rehearsals	C,D,G	2	5	8
J. Arrange concession sales	A	5	13	15

a. Give an estimated completion time for this project.

b. Which activities have the most slack?

c. What is the probability that the project will be completed in 12 weeks?

d. Give a time within which the station can be 99% sure of completing the project.

15. The following is a PERT/CPM network for the construction of a new Senior Center in York, Pennsylvania. The times for the activities are in weeks.

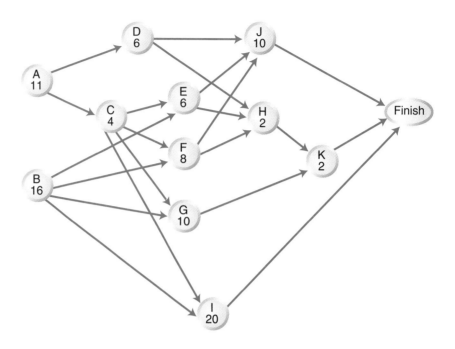

a. Determine the earliest and latest start and finish times and slack times for each activity in the project.

b. What is the critical path and the expected completion time for this project?

c. Activity H is the fencing activity. Because of other commitments, Kelly Fencing, the subcontractor in charge of building the fences for the project, will be delayed 10 weeks. Each week of delay in the construction of the Senior Center costs the investors in the project $5,000 due to lack of occupancy. Which of the following alternatives would you recommend to the investors in light of this information?

   i) Keep Kelly Fencing and its $6000 contract.

   ii) Hire Colonial Landscapers, even though Colonial will take four weeks to complete activity H (instead of two) and will charge $14,000.

   iii) Have its own landscaping crew (currently doing landscaping activity E) design and build the fencing. The design and purchase of the materials for the fencing will cost $6400 and will add four weeks to activity E. The actual construction of the fencing, activity H, will take six weeks and cost $9000.

16. QP Dolls, Inc. has developed a new doll it feels could turn into a "collector's item" through proper advertising on cable TV. The PERT/CPM network shown here models

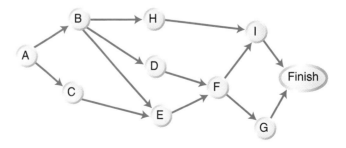

the activities (or work packages) of the project. Distribution of the total budgeted cost of $5,280,000 and expected completion times (in weeks) for each of the work packages are summarized in the following table.

Work Package	Expected Time	Budgeted Cost
A. Conduct market analysis	6	$ 240,000
B. Secure facilities/equipment	4	$ 300,000
C. Hire manufacturing supervisor/foremen	3	$ 150,000
D. Purchase manufacturing materials	3	$ 540,000
E. Hire/train workers	10	$ 900,000
F. Manufacture various prototypes	2	$ 300,000
G. Complete full-scale production	6	$1,350,000
H. Develop advertising campaign	6	$ 450,000
I. Prepare cable TV informercials	8	$1,050,000

a. Determine an earliest and latest schedule for each work package.

b. Develop a chart summarizing feasible budgets under both an earliest and a latest start time scenario, assuming that the budget for a work package will be distributed equally throughout its duration.

c. Construct a graph showing the range of feasible budgets over the life of the project.

17. Management at QP Dolls, Inc. (Problem 16) is concerned about controlling monthly costs.

a. Use a heuristic to determine a schedule of work packages to "level" the monthly expenditures as much as possible while still completing the project in the minimal amount of time.

b. Use a heuristic to determine a schedule of work packages so that the project can be completed in the minimal amount of time while spending no more than $250,000 in any month.

18. Consider the situation faced by QP Dolls, Inc. in problem 16. Management is giving some thought to putting extra resources into the project so that it can be completed within one-half year (26 weeks). Accordingly, each work package has been studied, and a set of crash times in weeks and costs has been developed:

Work Package	Crash Time	Crash Cost
A. Conduct market analysis	5	$ 300,000
B. Secure facilities/equipment	3	$ 400,000
C. Hire manufacturing supervisor/foremen	2	$ 240,000
D. Purchase manufacturing materials	2	$ 750,000
E. Hire/train workers	7	$1,440,000
F. Manufacture various prototypes	1	$ 390,000
G. Complete full-scale production	4	$3,200,000
H. Develop advertising campaign	3	$ 900,000
I. Prepare cable TV infomercials	4	$2,600,000

a. Determine a schedule for the work packages which minimizes the total cost of completing the project within 26 weeks. What is the minimum total cost?

b. Suppose QP will incur administrative and operational costs totaling $24,000 per week during this project. Modify your model to take into account these costs and solve for the optimal scheduling of the work packages. Did it change from the solution in part (a)?

c. Suppose QP only budgeted $6 million for this project. What is the minimum time to complete this project if: (i) the weekly fixed costs are ignored in the model; (ii) the weekly fixed costs are included in the model.

19. Consider the situation faced by QP Dolls, Inc. (problem 16). Assume QP decides to schedule the project according to the earliest time schedule for the activities [derived in part (a) of Problem 16], and bases its budget of $5,280,000 on the estimates given for the problem. At the end of week 15, only $2 million has been spent. The status of each work package is as follows.

Work Package	Percent Complete	Accumulated Cost
A. Conduct market analysis	100%	$250,000
B. Secure facilities/equipment	100%	$320,000
C. Hire manufacturing supervisor/foremen	100%	$140,000
D. Purchase manufacturing materials	50%	$300,000
E. Hire/train workers	60%	$590,000
F. Manufacture various prototypes	0%	$ 0
G. Complete full-scale production	0%	$ 0
H. Develop advertising campaign	50%	$400,000
I. Prepare cable TV infomercials	0%	$ 0

Using a PERT/Cost approach, determine the amount the project is ahead or behind schedule and the amount it is over or under budget. If the project is behind schedule or over budget, suggest some corrective actions that QP might attempt to rectify the situation.

20. It is June 1, and popular recording star Chocolate Cube is planning to add a separate recording studio to his palatial complex in rural Connecticut. The blueprints have been completed, and the following table lists the time estimates of the activities in the construction project.

CHOCOLATE CUBE RECORDING STUDIO

Activity	Immediate Predecessors	Optimistic Time (days)	Most Likely Time (days)	Pessimistic Time (days)
A. Order materials	—	1.0	2.0	9.0
B. Clear land	—	2.5	4.5	9.5
C. Obtain permits	—	2.0	5.0	14.0
D. Hire subcontractors	C	4.0	6.5	18.0
E. Unload/store materials	A	2.0	4.0	18.0
F. Primary structure	B,D,E	22.0	30.0	50.0
G. Install electrical work	F	15.0	20.0	37.0
H. Install plumbing	F	4.5	10.0	21.5
I. Finish/paint	G,H	12.0	15.0	24.0
J. Complete electrical studio	H	14.0	14.5	48.0
K. Clean-up	I,J	5.0	5.0	5.0

a. Determine the expected completion time and the critical path for this project. Also determine the expected earliest and latest start and finish dates for each of the separate activities. (Assume the workers work seven days per week, including July Fourth and Labor Day.)

b. Chocolate Cube has committed himself to a recording session beginning September 8 (99 days from now). What is the probability that he will be able to begin recording in his own personal studio on that date?

c. If his studio is not ready in 99 days, Chocolate Cube will be forced to lease his record company's studio, which will cost $120,000. For $3,500 extra, Eagle Electric, the company hired for the electrical installation (activity G), will work double time; each of the time estimates for this activity will therefore be reduced by 50%. Using an expected cost approach, determine if the $3,500 should be spent.

21. Golden West Homes is developing a new modular home model. The following table outlines the activities of the project. Times are expressed in days.

Activity	Immediate Predecessors	Optimistic Time	Most Likely Times	Pessimistic Time	Expected Cost
A. Conduct focus groups	—	14	20	32	$ 4,000
B. Determine key features/options	A	6	8	10	$ 3,000
C. Set out design specifications	B	2	4	12	$ 2,000
D. Draw up blueprints	C	5	6	7	$ 7,000
E. Determine heating requirements	D	2	2	2	$ 1,000
F. Select appointments	C	3	3	9	$ 800
G. Arrange for financing	D	4	11	12	$ 7,000
H. Plan marketing campaign	C	3	4	5	$ 4,000
I. Develop manufacturing specifications	E	2	5	14	$ 8,000
J. Obtain material for prototype	E,F	20	35	38	$ 600
K. Train workers	I	8	19	24	$ 7,200
L. Build prototype	J,K	10	12	14	$11,000
M. Determine selling prices	E,F	1	1	1	$ 900
N. Hold dealer meetings	L,M	3	5	7	$ 5,400
O. Prepare advertising literature	H,L,M	7	13	13	$ 6,200
P. Solicit initial orders	N	15	17	31	$ 800
Q. Determine order quantities	F	1	2	3	$ 400
R. Obtain materials	N,Q	14	26	32	$ 0
S. Schedule production	P	1	1	1	$ 150

a. Determine the expected completion time and the critical path for this project.

b. Because of production considerations, Golden West will lose $10,000 if this project is not completed within 114 days. What is the probability that the project will be completed within 114 days?

c. Suppose Golden West were to hire a meeting planning consultant to hold the dealer meetings (activity N). This would cost Golden West an additional $1000, but the activity is guaranteed to take exactly three days. Considering the $10,000 loss if the project is not completed in 114 days, should Golden West hire the consultant?

d. What is the most Golden West should be willing to pay for a meeting planning consultant who could hold dealer meetings in exactly three days?

22. Consider the Golden West Homes problem (problem 21). Suppose that after 63 days, Golden West has spent $34,000 on this project and the job status report is as follows.

Activity	Percent Complete
A. Conduct focus groups	100%
B. Determine key features/options	100%
C. Set out design specifications	100%
D. Draw up blueprints	100%
E. Determine heating requirements	100%
F. Select appointments	100%
G. Arrange for financing	40%
H. Plan marketing campaign	25%
I. Develop manufacturing specifications	100%
J. Obtain material for prototype	100%
K. Train workers	50%
L. Build prototype	0%
M. Determine selling prices	100%
N. Hold dealer meetings	0%
O. Prepare advertising literature	0%
P. Solicit initial orders	0%
Q. Determine order quantities	50%
R. Obtain materials	0%
S. Schedule production	0%

Assuming that Golden West developed its plans around the expected times to perform the activities, determine by how much the project is ahead or behind schedule. Is Golden West over or under budget? By how much?

23. The following is the PERT/CPM network for an audit of a large nationwide retailer conducted by Peat Marwick. The expected times are in days.

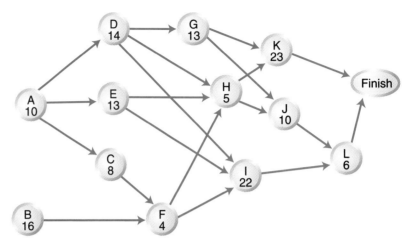

a. Determine the expected time to complete the auditing project.

b. The same personnel from Peat Marwick are assigned to perform activities K and L. Personnel can be reassigned so that activity K can be shortened by one day at the expense of an increase of one day in activity L (and vice versa). What distribution of time spent on activity K and activity L minimizes the overall expected time of the project? What is the minimal expected project completion time in this case?

c. Given your answer to (b), show how there is more than one critical path. If the standard deviation of each activity in the network is two days, determine the probability that the project will be completed within 60 days for each critical path.

Questions 24 and 25 are designed so that you can construct your own PERT/CPM network.

24. Suppose you are in charge of putting on a Broadway musical at your university. Develop an activity schedule for this project. Decide which activities have to be performed in sequence and which can be performed in parallel, and construct an appropriate PERT/CPM network. Your activities should include *but are not limited to* paying licensing fees; raising money; hiring a director; hiring principal actors; hiring extras; securing a rehearsal hall; rehearsing; building scenery; making costumes; holding dress rehearsal; advertising; and leasing a theater. See if you can place reasonable time estimates for each activity.

25. Strikes in Major League Baseball have some fans clamoring for a new professional baseball league. The success of the 1993 movie A *League of Their Own*, about a professional women's baseball league formed during World War II, has supported the popular contention that it may be quite feasible to form a new league in a minimal amount of time. Develop a PERT/CPM activity chart of no more than 15 work packages you feel would be relevant to the development of a new league. Try to make some reasonable time estimates for each work package.

CASE 1: *Oak Glen Country Club Villas*

Calico Construction is building the new Oak Glen Country Club Villas project, consisting of 18 buildings, each housing 12 condominiums. Each building will border the Oak Glen Golf Course designed by Jack Nicklaus. The minimum price for a condominium unit is $275,000, and buyers expect a high-quality project.

Response to the initial promotion was so great that Calico Construction presold all 216 units based solely on an artist's conception and schematic plans of the project. One

reason for the quick sellout may have been the "YOU CAN MOVE IN BY SUMMER" campaign. As part of this campaign, Calico promised rebates of $10,000 cash to all 216 buyers if all the facilities, buildings, and other amenities were not completed by June 15 of next year.

As of September 15, the project is well underway. The following PERT/CPM network details the precedence activities of the tasks remaining to be completed in the project.

All tasks except for activity R, the underground sewer

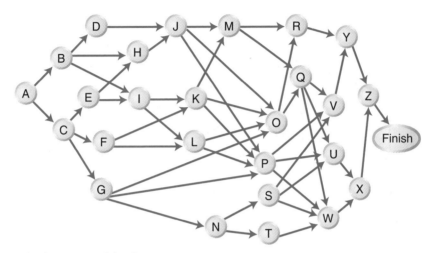

Oak Glen Country Club Villas

activity, and activity T, the stream building activity, have been assigned to the appropriate subcontractors. Three time estimates (in days) for each of the other activities have been determined and are given in the following table.

		Opti-mistic	Most Likely	Pessi-mistic
A.	Land measurements	5	8	15
B.	Layout of measurement stakes	7	12	20
C.	Analysis of surrounding environment	10	17	31
D.	Building of foundation	12	22	38
E.	Approval of construction papers	6	13	21
F.	Layout of building framework	11	15	27
G.	Gas line installment	9	18	22
H.	Electrical wiring	25	27	31
I.	Interior plumbing	18	20	35
J.	Wall construction	12	25	32
K.	Insulation	10	23	33
L.	Drywall	15	20	25
M.	Roofing	3	10	20
N.	Restaurant construction	25	40	55
O.	Swimming pool	9	20	40
P.	Fencing	6	10	21
Q.	Telephone lines	12	22	40
R.	Completion of underground sewers			

		Opti-mistic	Most Likely	Pessi-mistic
S.	Snack bar	10	20	30
T.	Stream building			
U.	Outside lighting	8	12	15
V.	Parking lots	3	5	7
W.	Drainage construction	5	10	18
X.	Safety inspection	9	15	25
Y.	Landscaping	6	24	40
Z.	Final permits/releases	10	15	25

Activity R, the underground sewer activity, consists of installing pipes and connections to join all 18 buildings to the main city sewer system. Calico Construction has two alternatives for this activity:

1. Reedy Brothers has submitted a bid of $300,000 for the design and construction of the required sewer project. It estimates a most likely completion time of 25 days, with a difference of plus or minus two days for the optimistic and pessimistic time estimates.

2. Calico can design the sewer project itself and hire another company, Paramount Construction, to build the system according to Calico's specifications. Paramount will charge Calico $20 per foot of sewer built. Paramount estimates that it can build between 200 and 360 feet of sewers per day; its most likely estimate is 300 feet per

day. To minimize disruption to the aesthetic beauty of the project, sewers will run underneath the paths between condominium buildings.

Activity T, the stream building activity, involves building a stream that runs throughout the project and connects the western and eastern boundaries. Again Calico has two alternatives:

1. Calico has received a bid of $400,000 from Lakepro, Inc. to design and build a meandering stream that will most likely be finished in 30 days, give or take five days.

2. Calico can design and direct the stream construction. The

actual work will be performed by the Oberlin Company, at a price of $50 per foot. Oberlin estimates that it will take a full day to complete 60 feet on the stream project. Since Calico would like to conserve costs, if it designs the stream, it will have the minimal distance and parallel paths between the condominium buildings. Calico estimates that overall completion time for this activity will be no more than 10 days longer or less than 10 days shorter than the Oberlin estimate.

The following is a map of the feasible pathways between the condominium buildings which may be used for sewer construction or stream construction.

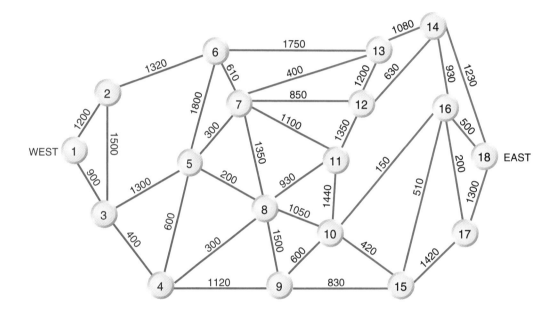

Assume that today is Monday, September 15, and that all work is to be done on a five-day-per-week basis includes holiday periods. Prepare a report for Calico Construction that will

1. Develop tentative target start and completion dates for each activity

2. Recommend which alternative to select for the sewer activity

3. Recommend which alternative to select for the stream activity

4. Estimate the total expected cost for the two contractors selected for the sewer and stream activities

5. Give a date by which you are 99% sure that the entire project will be completed

6. Recommend whether to spend $25,000 for additional legal assistance that would reduce the most likely time to attain the final permits and releases (activity Z) from 15 to 12 days and its pessimistic time from 25 to 18 days

To answer (6), compare the $25,000 expenditure to the expected savings from the increased probability of completing the project by June 15. Your report should also include any assumptions you made to apply your solution technique and some appropriate "what-if" analyses.

CASE 2: *Igloo Frozen Yogurt*

Fifty-eight days ago a nervous Board of Directors of Igloo Foods, owners of the Igloo Frozen Yogurt chain, watched as the company began a program to test market its product in London, England. The target opening date for the first store was four months (122 days) from the inception of the project. If the store proves successful, Igloo plans to open up at least

two dozen Igloo Frozen Yogurt stores across Great Britain and the European continent. This is the first such venture for Igloo Foods outside of the United States.

The project consists of the 18 work packages summarized in the following table, together with budget information and time estimates.

Work Package	Immediate Predecessor	Optimistic Time	Estimates Likely	Pessimistic (days)	Budget
A. Select vice president for Europe	—	5	9	13	$ 0
B. Select menu consultant	—	6	14	34	$ 2,000
C. Choose district for shop	A	8	13	30	$ 0
D. Make exact site selection	C	4	11	18	$ 15,000
E. Negotiate lease	D	9	10	11	$ 4,000
F. Design store layout	A	19	38	63	$ 40,000
G. Construct store	E,F	46	75	80	$260,000
H. Develop recipes	B	10	30	50	$ 15,000
I. Test recipes	H	9	16	17	$ 10,000
J. Purchase equipment	F,I	10	17	30	$150,000
K. Design accessories	F,I	16	22	28	$ 15,000
L. Purchase supplies	K	8	22	24	$100,000
M. Develop training program	J,K	15	23	43	$ 18,000
N. Train employees	M	8	10	18	$ 7,000
O. Select advertising agency	A	30	36	60	$ 12,000
P. Develop marketing program	D,O	41	47	77	$ 90,000
Q. Purchase advertising space	P	4	5	6	$ 80,000
R. Install signs	G,Q	3	6	21	$ 26,000

A timetable based on the three time estimate approach was used to generate a schedule of work packages for the project. Now, 58 days into the project, the Board of Directors has received the following project status report.

LONDON, ENGLAND PROJECT
Date: Day 58
Expenditures to Date: $195,000
Progress Report

Work Package	Percent Complete
A. Select vice president for Europe	100%
B. Select menu consultant	100%
C. Choose district for shop	100%
D. Make exact site selection	100%
E. Negotiate lease	50%
F. Design store layout	100%
G. Construct store	0%
H. Develop recipes	100%
I. Test recipes	100%
J. Purchase equipment	75%
K. Design accessories	25%
L. Purchase supplies	0%
M. Develop training program	0%
N. Train employees	0%
O. Select advertising agency	50%
P. Develop marketing program	0%
Q. Purchase advertising space	0%
R. Install signs	0%

Prepare a report for the Board of Directors of Igloo Foods which analyzes the progress of the project from both a budget and time point of view. Compare the initial probability of finishing the project in 122 days with the probability that the project will now be finished by the end of day 122. (Assume that the *standard deviation* for each unfinished work package is reduced by an amount proportional to the completion percentage of the work package.)

Igloo has planned a big gala "grand opening" for the morning of day 123 with visiting dignitaries and a popular rock band. If the project is not completed in time (by the end of day 122), the event will have to be canceled, and Igloo will suffer a $100,000 loss. Three suggestions have been proposed for reducing the times of certain of the remaining work packages:

Suggestion	Extra Expenditure	Projected Effect
1	$ 8000	Reduce the most likely and pessimistic times to purchase supplies (activity L) by 50%
2	$10,000	Reduce the expected training time of employees (activity N) by three days
3	$ 3000	Reduce the pessimistic time to install signs (activity R) to nine days

Include in your report a recommendation of which suggestion or combination of suggestions (if any) Igloo should consider adopting. Base your analysis on an expected value approach, and discuss the validity of such an approach in these circumstances.

CHAPTER 8

DECISION ANALYSIS

A division of Kern Corporation manufactures mason jars and lids used in canning fruits and vegetables. Although the division has generally been profitable, increased competition has recently eroded margins, and the firm is concerned about its long-term growth potential.

Management has identified several options: maintaining operations at existing levels, selling the division to a competitor, moving operations to a location where labor costs are lower, purchasing new machinery to increase productivity, identifying new product lines, or spinning off the operation to shareholders.

The outcomes of these different strategies will depend on the actions of competitors, the future of the canning industry, the firm's future cost of funds, and the resulting tax consequences, among other factors. To determine the best course of action, management must make projections regarding the growth of the industry, labor costs, anticipated actions of competitors, and the availability and cost of funds. Management must then determine the outcome of each strategy, given a particular possible projection of future events. This information forms the basis for a decision analysis approach to determine the optimal course of action.

8.1 INTRODUCTION TO DECISION ANALYSIS

Throughout our day we are faced with numerous decisions, many of which require careful thought and analysis. In such cases, large sums of money might be lost or other severe consequences can result from the wrong choice. For example, you probably would do a careful analysis of the car you are going to purchase, the house you are going to buy, or the college you will attend.

Businesses continuously make many crucial decisions, such as whether or not to introduce a new product or where to locate a new plant. The outcome of these decisions can severely affect the firm's future profitability. The field of *decision analysis* provides the necessary framework for making these types of important decisions.

Decision analysis allows an individual or organization to *select a decision* from a set of possible *decision alternatives* when *uncertainties regarding the future* exist. The goal is to optimize the resulting return or *payoff* in terms of some *decision criterion*.

Consider an investor interested in purchasing an apartment building. Possible decisions include the type of financing to use and the building's rehabilitation plan. Unknown to the investor are the future occupancy rate of the building, the amount of rent that can be charged for each unit, and possible modifications in the tax laws associated with real estate ownership. Depending on the investor's decisions and their consequences, the investor will receive some payoff.

Although the criterion used in making a decision could be noneconomic, most business decisions are based on economic considerations. When probabilities can be assessed for likelihoods of the uncertain future events, one common economic criterion is maximizing expected profit. If probabilities for the likelihoods of the uncertain future events cannot be assessed, the economic criterion is typically based on the decision maker's attitude toward life.

Oftentimes, elements of risk need to be factored into the decision-making process. This is especially true if there is a possibility of incurring extremely large losses or achieving exceptional gains. *Utility theory* can provide a mechanism for analyzing decisions in light of these risks, as well as evaluating situations in which the criterion is noneconomic.

While decision analysis typically focuses on situations in which the uncertain future events are due to chance, there are business situations in which competition shapes these events. *Game theory* is a useful tool for analyzing decision making in light of competitive action.

We begin our discussion of decision analysis by focusing on the basic elements of decision making: (1) decision alternatives, (2) states of nature, and (3) payoffs.

8.2 PAYOFF TABLE ANALYSIS

PAYOFF TABLES

When a decision maker faces a finite set of discrete *decision alternatives* whose outcome is a function of a single future event, a **payoff table** analysis is the simplest way of formulating the decision problem. In a payoff table, the rows correspond to the possible decision alternatives and the columns correspond to the possible future events (known as *states of nature*). The states of nature of a payoff table are defined so that they are mutually exclusive (at most one possible state of nature will occur) and collectively exhaustive (at least one state of nature will occur). This way we know that exactly one state of nature must occur. The body of the table contains the *payoffs* resulting from a particular decision alternative when the corresponding state of nature occurs. Although the decision maker can determine which decision alternative to select, he or she has no control over which state of nature will occur.

To illustrate payoff table analysis, let us consider the following example.

Pub.daa
Pub.xls

PUBLISHERS CLEARING HOUSE

Publishers Clearing House is a nationwide firm that markets magazine subscriptions. The primary vehicle it uses to contact customers is a series of mailings known collectively as the Publishers Clearing House Sweepstakes. Individuals who receive these mailings can enter the sweepstakes even if they do not order any magazine subscriptions. Various prizes are available, the top prize being $10 million. Suppose you are one of the many individuals who are not interested in ordering magazines. You must decide whether or not to enter the contest.

SOLUTION

To help evaluate this problem we construct a payoff table. You have two possible *decision alternatives*:

D1: Spend the time filling out the contest application and pay the postage to mail it.

D2: Toss the letter in the recycling bin.

Obviously, if you knew the outcome in advance, your decision would be quite simple: Enter the contest if you are going to win something valuable; do not enter the contest if you are not. Unfortunately, winners are not known in advance, and you cannot win unless you enter. The act of winning or losing is something over which you have no control.

A number of different prizes are available. In a recent contest, these ranged from a flag to $10 million. The possible outcomes, or *states of nature*, for this problem are:

S1: The entry would be a losing one.

S2: The entry would win a flag.

S3: The entry would win $100.

S4: The entry would win $500.

S5: The entry would win $10,000.

S6: The entry would win $1 million.

S7: The entry would win $10 million.

Note that these states of nature are mutually exclusive and collectively exhaustive.

For each combination of decision alternative and state of nature there is a resulting payoff. For example, if you enter the contest and do not win, the loss is equivalent to the opportunity cost of the time spent completing the contest application plus the cost of the postage. Let's assume that these costs total $1.

If, on the other hand, you enter the contest and win $100, this results in a net payoff of $99 ($100 minus the $1 cost). Similarly, if the flag is worth $5, winning a flag will result in a net payoff of $4 ($5 − $1).

The $1 million and $10 million prizes are paid out over several years. To get the present value of these prizes you must calculate their discounted future cash flows. If you assume that the discounted present value of these prizes amounts to approximately 35% of their face amount, then the net payoff values for the $1 million and $10 million winners would be $349,999 and $3,499,999, respectively. The payoff table shown in Table 8.1 represents the particulars of this decision analysis problem. Once the payoff table is constructed, it can be utilized to determine which decision alternative should be pursued.

TABLE 8.1   PAYOFF TABLE FOR PUBLISHERS CLEARING HOUSE

Decision Alternatives	States of Nature						
	Do Not Win	Win Flag	Win $100	Win $500	Win $10,000	Win $1 Million	Win $10 Million
Enter contest	−$1	$4	$99	$499	$9,999	$349,999	$3,499,999
Do not enter contest	$0	$0	$0	$0	$0	$0	$0

CHOOSING THE STATES OF NATURE

Although determining the states of nature for the Publishers Clearing House example was rather straightforward, often the decision maker has a great deal of flexibility in defining them. Selecting the appropriate definition for the states of nature can require careful thought about the situation being modeled. To illustrate, consider the decision problem faced by Tom Brown, a senior at Iowa State University.

Tom.daa
Tom.xls

TOM BROWN INVESTMENT DECISION

Tom Brown has inherited $1000 from a distant relative. Since he still has another year of studies before graduation from Iowa State University, Tom has decided to invest the $1000 for a year. Literally tens of thousands of different investment possibilities are available to him, including growth stocks, income stocks, corporate bonds, municipal bonds, government bonds, futures, limited partnerships, annuities, and bank accounts.

Given the limited amount of money he has to invest, Tom has decided that it is not worthwhile to spend the countless hours required to fully understand these various investments. Therefore, he has turned to a broker for investment guidance.

The broker has selected five potential investments she believes would be appropriate for Tom: gold, a junk bond, a growth stock, a certificate of deposit, and a stock option hedge. Tom would like to set up a payoff table to help him choose the appropriate investment.

SOLUTION

The first step in constructing a payoff table is to determine the set of possible decision alternatives. For Tom, this is simply the set of five investment opportunities recommended by the broker.

The second step is to define the states of nature. One choice might be the percentage change in the gross national product (GNP) over the next year (rounded to the nearest percent). One principal drawback of this approach is the difficulty most people have determining the payoff for a given investment from the percentage change in the GNP. Even if Tom had a doctorate in economics, he might find it extremely difficult to assess how a 2% rise in GNP would affect the value of a particular investment.

Another possibility is to define the states of nature in terms of general stock market performance as measured by the Standard & Poor's 500 or Dow Jones Industrial Average. But even if he were to spend the time doing this, it is doubtful whether Tom or anyone else could correctly differentiate the return on an investment if, say, the Dow Jones Industrial Average goes up 87 points as opposed to 88 points.

What if Tom used, say, 100-*point* intervals? While this simplifies the problem of calculating payoffs, assuming a possible 2000-point increase or decrease in the Dow Jones Industrial Average, we would still be required to calculate 41 payoffs for each of the five investments. Instead, let us define the states of nature qualitatively as

S1: A large rise in the stock market over the next year

S2: A small rise in the stock market over the next year

S3: No change in the stock market over the next year

S4: A small fall in the stock market over the next year

S5: A large fall in the stock market over the next year

Since these states must be mutually exclusive and collectively exhaustive, there should be a clear understanding as to exactly what each of these terms means. In terms of the Dow Jones Industrial Average, for example, we might use the following correspondence:

State of Nature	Change in Dow Jones Industrial Average
S1: large rise	an increase of over 1000 points
S2: small rise	an increase of between 300 and 1000 points
S3: no change	a decrease or increase of less than 300 points
S4: small fall	a decrease of between 300 and 800 points
S5: large fall	a decrease of more than 800 points

Although the intervals corresponding to these states of nature are not of the same size, the states of nature are mutually exclusive and collectively exhaustive.

Using these definitions for the states of nature, as the final step in constructing the payoff table we determine the payoffs resulting from each decision alternative (investment) and state of nature. In doing so, we reason that stocks and bonds generally move in the same direction as the general market, whereas gold is an investment hedge that tends to move in the opposite direction from the market. The C/D account always pays 6% ($60 profit). The specific payoffs for the five different investments, based on the broker's analysis, are given in Table 8.2.

TABLE 8.2   PAYOFF TABLE FOR TOM BROWN

Decision Alternatives	States of Nature				
	Large Rise	Small Rise	No Change	Small Fall	Large Fall
Gold	−$100	$100	$200	$300	$ 0
Bond	$250	$200	$150	−$100	−$150
Stock	$500	$250	$100	−$200	−$600
C/D account	$ 60	$ 60	$ 60	$ 60	$ 60
Stock option hedge	$200	$150	$150	−$200	−$150

DOMINATED DECISIONS

It is worth comparing the payoffs associated with the stock option hedge investment to those associated with the bond investment. For each state of nature, Tom would do at least as well with the bond investment as with the stock option hedge and for several of the states of nature, the bond actually offers a higher return. In this case, the decision alternative to invest in the bond is said to *dominate* the stock option hedge decision alternative. A decision alternative that is dominated by another cannot be optimal under any criterion and can be dropped from further consideration. Thus the dominated decision alternative of "stock option hedge" can be eliminated, and the payoff table for Tom's decision problem simplified to include just the four remaining options. Now that a payoff table has been created for this decision problem, an optimization criterion can be applied to these data to determine the best decision for Tom.

8.3   DECISION-MAKING CRITERIA

In this section, we consider approaches for selecting an "optimal" decision based on some decision-making criterion. One way of categorizing such criteria involves the decision maker's knowledge of which state of nature will occur. The decision maker who knows "for sure" which state of nature will occur is said to be *decision making under certainty*.

Knowing which state of nature will occur makes choosing the appropriate decision alternative quite easy. For example, if you knew for certain that you were going to win the $10 million Publishers Clearing House grand prize, you would definitely enter the contest. Because few things in life are certain, however, you might wonder whether decision making under certainty is really ever done. The answer is an emphatic "yes!" Many management science models assume that the future is known with certainty.

For example, the linear programming model for Galaxy Industries discussed in Chapter 3 assumed that the unit profit and production time required per dozen Space Rays and Zappers, as well as the amount of plastic and available production time, were all known with certainty. Although we investigated relaxing these assumptions through sensitivity analysis, solving the problem as a linear program was, in effect, making a decision under certainty.

If the decision maker does not know with certainty which state of nature will occur, the model is classified as either decision making under uncertainty or decision making under risk. *Decision making under risk* assumes that the decision maker has at least some knowledge of the probabilities for the states of nature occurring; no such knowledge is assumed in *decision making under uncertainty*.

One method for making decisions under risk is to select the decision with the best expected payoff, which is calculated using the probability estimates for the states of nature. Since decision making under uncertainty assumes no knowledge of the probabilities for the states of nature, however, expected values cannot be calculated and decisions must be made based on other criteria. Because probability information regarding the states of nature is not always available, many decision problems are analyzed using decision making under uncertainty.

To contrast decision making under uncertainty and risk, let us return to the Publishers Clearing House example. In this case, the values of the prizes in the contest are known to participants. Because the chance of winning a prize depends on how many entries are received, however, the exact probabilities of winning a given prize are unknown; thus, decision making under uncertainty should be used to analyze this problem.

On the other hand, if you called Publishers Clearing House and learned that it receives an average of 1.75 million entries a day for its contest, you would be able to estimate the probability of winning each of the prizes offered. In this case, decision making under risk would be possible.

DECISION MAKING UNDER UNCERTAINTY

When using decision making under uncertainty to analyze a situation, the decision criteria are based on the decision maker's attitudes toward life. These include an individual being pessimistic or optimistic, conservative or aggressive.

Pessimistic or Conservative Approach— Maximin Criterion

A *pessimistic* decision maker believes that, no matter what decision is made, the worst possible result will occur. A *conservative* decision maker wishes to ensure a guaranteed minimum possible payoff, regardless of which state of nature occurs.

For either individual, the **maximin criterion** may be used to make decisions. Since this criterion is based on a worst-case scenario, the decision maker first finds the minimum payoff for each decision alternative. The optimal decision alternative is the one that *maximizes* the *minimum* payoff.

To illustrate, let us return to the Tom Brown investment problem. (Recall the dominated stock option hedge decision was eliminated.) From Table 8.3 we see that if Tom chooses to buy gold, the worst possible outcome occurs if there is a large rise in the stock market, resulting in a $100 loss. If he buys the bond or stock, the worst possible outcome occurs if the stock market has a large fall; in this case, his loss would be $150 for the bond and $600 for the stock. If Tom chooses the C/D account, he will earn $60 no matter which state of nature occurs.

TABLE 8.3   REVISED PAYOFF TABLE FOR TOM BROWN

Decision Alternatives	States of Nature				
	Large Rise	Small Rise	No Change	Small Fall	Large Fall
Gold	−$100	$100	$200	$300	$ 0
Bond	$250	$200	$150	−$100	−$150
Stock	$500	$250	$100	−$200	−$600
C/D account	$ 60	$ 60	$ 60	$ 60	$ 60

Table 8.4 summarizes the minimal payoffs for each decision alternative. If Tom is a conservative decision maker, he will try to maximize his returns under this worst-case scenario. Accordingly, he will select the decision that results in the best of these minimum payoffs—in this case, the C/D account.

TABLE 8.4   TOM BROWN INVESTMENT DECISION MINIMAL PAYOFFS

Decision Alternatives	Minimum Payoff	
Gold	−$100	
Bond	−$150	
Stock	−$600	
C/D account	$ 60	← maximum

In this problem, the numbers in the payoff table represent returns or profits. If the numbers in the payoff table represent costs rather than profits, however, the worst outcome for each decision alternative is the one with the maximum cost. A pessimistic or conservative decision maker would then select the decision alternative with the *minimum* of these *maximum* costs; that is, use a **minimax criterion**.

Maximin Approach for Profit Payoffs

1. Determine the minimum payoff for each decision alternative.
2. Select the decision alternative with the maximum minimum payoff.

Minimax Approach for Cost Payoffs

1. Find the maximum cost for each decision alternative.
2. Select the decision alternative with the minimum maximum cost.

Minimax Regret Criterion   Another criterion that pessimistic or conservative decision makers frequently use is the **minimax regret criterion**. This approach is identical to the minimax approach for cost data except that the optimal decision is based on "lost opportunity," or "regret," rather than costs. This approach involves calculating the regret or lost opportunity corresponding to each payoff and then using the minimax criterion on the calculated regret values.

In decision analysis, the decision maker incurs regret by failing to choose the "best" decision (the one with the highest profit or lowest cost). Of course, this best decision depends on the state of nature. For this problem, if there is a small rise in the stock market, the best decision is to buy the stock (yielding a return of $250). Tom will have no regret if this is his decision. If, instead, Tom purchases gold, his return will be only $100, resulting in a regret of $150 (=$250 − $100). Similarly, the regret associated with buying the bond for this state of nature is $50 (=$250 − $200), and from investing in the C/D it is $190 (=$250 − $60).

Calculation of Regret Values for a State of Nature

1. Determine the best value (maximum payoff or minimum cost) for the state of nature.
2. Calculate the regret for each decision alternative as the difference between its payoff value and this best value.

This process is repeated for each state of nature, giving the regret table shown in Table 8.5.

TABLE 8.5   REGRET TABLE FOR TOM BROWN

Decision Alternatives	States of Nature				
	Large Rise	Small Rise	No Change	Small Fall	Large Fall
Gold	$600	$150	$ 0	$ 0	$ 60
Bond	$250	$ 50	$ 50	$400	$210
Stock	$ 0	$ 0	$100	$500	$660
C/D account	$440	$190	$140	$240	$ 0

The minimax regret criterion is another conservative criterion that assumes the worst alternative for each decision. Here, the decision maker determines the maximum regret for each decision alternative and then chooses the one which has the minimum maximum regret.

Minimax Regret Approach

1. Determine the best value (maximum payoff or minimum cost) for each state of nature.
2. For each state of nature, calculate the regret corresponding to a decision alternative as the difference between its payoff value and this best value.
3. Find the maximum regret for each decision alternative.
4. Select the decision alternative that has the minimum maximum regret.

Table 8.6 shows the maximum regret for each decision alternative for the Tom Brown investment problem. Thus, if Tom uses the minimax regret criterion, he should decide to buy the bond.

TABLE 8.6   TOM BROWN INVESTMENT
DECISION—MAXIMUM REGRET

Decision Alternatives	Maximum Regret	
Gold	$600	
Bond	$400	← minimum
Stock	$660	
C/D account	$440	

The difference between the maximin and minimax regret criteria is as follows. When using the maximin criterion, the decision maker wishes to select the decision with the best possible assured payoff. Under the minimax regret criterion, the decision maker wishes to select the decision that minimizes the maximum deviation from the best return possible for each state of nature. In this case, it is not the return itself that is important, but rather how well a *given* return compares to the *best possible* return for that state of nature.

To complicate matters, when using the minimax regret criterion, the optimal decision can change by introducing a nonoptimal decision alternative. For example, suppose the broker had suggested that Tom consider the purchase of a put option instead of the stock option hedge, resulting in the payoff table shown in Table 8.7. In this case, the regret table and maximum regret for each decision are shown in Table 8.8.

TABLE 8.7   TOM BROWN INVESTMENT DECISION INCLUDING PUT OPTION

Decision Alternatives	States of Nature				
	Large Rise	Small Rise	No Change	Small Fall	Large Fall
Gold	−$100	$100	$200	$300	$ 0
Bond	$250	$200	$150	−$100	−$150
Stock	$500	$250	$100	−$200	−$600
C/D account	$ 60	$ 60	$ 60	$ 60	$ 60
Put option	−$200	−$600	$100	$350	$100

TABLE 8.8   REGRET TABLE FOR TOM BROWN INVESTMENT
DECISION INCLUDING PUT OPTION

Decision Alternatives	States of Nature					Maximum Regret	
	Large Rise	Small Rise	No Change	Small Fall	Large Fall		
Gold	$600	$150	$ 0	$ 50	$ 60	$600	
Bond	$250	$ 50	$ 50	$450	$210	$450	
Stock	$ 0	$ 0	$100	$550	$660	$660	
C/D account	$440	$190	$140	$290	$ 0	$440	← minimum
Put option	$700	$850	$100	$ 0	$ 40	$850	

We see that now Tom's optimal decision using the minimax regret criterion would be to invest his $1000 in the C/D account instead of his earlier decision to invest in the bond. This is because the addition of the put option investment increases the maximum regret for the bond from $400 to $450 which is now higher than that for the C/D.

Some may argue that it should be no surprise Tom's optimal decision could change since the introduction of the put option as a decision alternative changes his attitude toward the different investments. Others feel, however, that because a decision model frequently does not consider every possible alternative, changing the decision selection due to the introduction of additional nonoptimal decision alternatives is a major shortcoming of the minimax regret approach.

Optimistic or Aggressive
Approach—Maximax
Criterion

In contrast to a pessimistic decision maker, an optimistic decision maker feels that luck is always shining and whatever decision is made, the best possible outcome (state of nature) corresponding to that decision will occur.

Given a payoff table representing profits, an optimistic decision maker would use a **maximax criterion** that determines the maximum payoff for each decision alternative and selects the one which has the *maximum "maximum payoff."* The maximax criterion also applies to an aggressive decision maker looking for the decision with the best payoff.

Based on the data in Table 8.3, the maximum payoffs for each decision alternative in the Tom Brown investment problem are as shown in Table 8.9. If Tom were an optimistic or aggressive decision maker, he would choose the stock investment since it is the alternative with the maximum of the maximum payoffs.

TABLE 8.9   TOM BROWN INVESTMENT DECISION—MAXIMUM PAYOFF

Decision Alternatives	Maximum Payoff	
Gold	$300	
Bond	$200	
Stock	$500	← maximum
C/D account	$ 60	

Note that the alternative chosen using the maximax decision criterion is the one associated with the highest value in the payoff table. Hence, to use this criterion we need only locate the highest payoff in the table and select the corresponding decision.

If a payoff table represents costs rather than profits, an optimistic or aggressive decision maker would use the **minimin criterion** and select the alternative with the lowest possible, or *minimum minimum,* cost. In this case the optimal decision would be the one corresponding to the lowest entry in the payoff table.

Maximax Approach for Profit Payoffs

1. Find the maximum payoff for each decision alternative.
2. Select the decision alternative that has the maximum maximum payoff.

Minimin Approach for Cost Payoffs

1. Find the minimum cost for each decision alternative.
2. Select the decision alternative that has the minimum minimum cost.

Principle of
Insufficient Reason

Another decision criterion which can be used is the **principle of insufficient reason**. In this approach each state of nature is assumed to be equally likely. The optimal decision alternative can be found by adding up the payoffs for each decision alternative and selecting the alternative with the highest sum. (If the payoff table represents costs, we select the decision alternative with the lowest sum of costs.)

The principle of insufficient reason might appeal to a decision maker who is neither pessimistic nor optimistic. Table 8.10 gives the sum of the payoffs for each decision alternative for the Tom Brown investment problem. Thus, if Tom uses the principle of insufficient reason, he should invest in gold.

TABLE 8.10   TOM BROWN INVESTMENT DECISION—SUM OF PAYOFFS

Decision Alternatives	Sum of Payoffs	
Gold	$600	← maximum
Bond	$350	
Stock	$ 50	
C/D account	$300	

Table 8.11 summarizes the optimal decisions Tom would make using the four decision criteria. We note that each decision (except the dominated stock option hedge) is optimal for some decision criterion. Since the criterion depends on the decision maker's attitude toward life (optimistic, pessimistic, or somewhere in between), utilizing decision making under uncertainty can present a problem if these attitudes change rapidly.

TABLE 8.11   TOM BROWN INVESTMENT DECISION SUMMARY—OPTIMAL DECISIONS

Decision Criterion	Optimal Decision
Maximin	C/D account
Maximax	Stock
Minimax regret	Bond
Principle of insufficient reason	Gold

DECISION MAKING UNDER RISK

Expected Value Criterion

One way to avoid the difficulty of using subjective criteria is to obtain probability estimates for the states of nature and implement decision making under risk. If a probability estimate for the occurrence of each state of nature is available, it is possible to calculate an expected value associated with each decision alternative. This is done by multiplying the probability for each state of nature by the associated return and then summing these products. Using the **expected value criterion**, the decision maker would then select the decision alternative with the best expected value.

For the Tom Brown investment problem, suppose Tom's broker offered the following projections based on past stock market performance:

$$P(\text{large rise in market}) = .2$$
$$P(\text{small rise in market}) = .3$$
$$P(\text{no change in market}) = .3$$
$$P(\text{small fall in market}) = .1$$
$$P(\text{large fall in market}) = .1$$

Using these probabilities, we can calculate the expected value (EV) of each decision alternative as follows:

$$EV(gold) = .2(-100) + .3(100) + .3(200) + .1(300) + .1(0) = \$100$$
$$EV(bond) = .2(250) + .3(200) + .3(150) + .1(-100) + .1(-150) = \$130$$
$$EV(stock) = .2(500) + .3(250) + .3(100) + .1(-200) + .1(-600) = \$125$$
$$EV(C/D) = .2(60) + .3(60) + .3(60) + .1(60) + .1(60) = \$60$$

Since the bond investment has the highest expected value, it is the optimal decision.

Expected Value Approach

1. Find the expected payoff for each decision alternative.
2. Select the decision alternative that has the best expected payoff.

Expected Regret Criterion   The approach used in the expected value criterion can also be applied to a regret table. Because the decision maker wishes to minimize regret, under the **expected regret criterion**, he or she calculates the expected regret (ER) for each decision and chooses the decision with the smallest expected regret.

By applying this approach to the regret table for the Tom Brown investment problem (Table 8.5), the expected regrets for the decision alternatives are calculated as

$$ER(gold) = .2(600) + .3(150) + .3(0) + .1(0) + .1(60) = \$171$$
$$ER(bond) = .2(250) + .3(50) + .3(50) + .1(400) + .1(210) = \$141$$
$$ER(stock) = .2(0) + .3(0) + .3(100) + .1(500) + .1(660) = \$146$$
$$ER(C/D) = .2(440) + .3(190) + .3(140) + .1(240) + .1(0) = \$211$$

Using this approach, Tom would again select the bond investment since it is the decision alternative with the smallest expected regret.

Expected Regret Approach

1. Determine the best value (maximum payoff or minimum cost) for each state of nature.
2. For each state of nature, the regret corresponding to a decision alternative is the difference between its payoff value and this best value.
3. Find the expected regret for each decision alternative.
4. Select the decision alternative that has the minimum expected regret.

Note that the same optimal decision was found using the expected regret criterion and the expected value criterion. This is true for any decision problem because, for pairs of decision alternatives, the differences in expected regret values are the same as the differences in expected return values. Because the two approaches yield the same results, the expected value approach is generally used since it does not require the calculation of a regret table.

When to Use the
Expected Value Approach

Because the expected value and expected regret criteria base the optimal decision on the relative likelihoods that the states of nature will occur, they have a certain advantage over the criteria used in decision making under uncertainty. It is worth noting, however, that basing a criterion on expected value assures us only that the decision will be optimal in the long run when the same problem is faced over and over again. In many situations, however, such as the Tom Brown investment problem, the decision maker faces the problem a single time; in this case, basing an optimal decision solely on expected value may not be optimal.

Another drawback to the expected value criterion is that it does not take into account the decision maker's attitude toward possible losses. Suppose for example, you had a chance to play a game in which you could win $1000 with probability .51 but could also lose $1000 with probability .49. While the expected value of this game is .51($1000) + .49(−$1000) = $20, many people (perhaps even yourself) would decline the opportunity to play due to the possibility of losing $1000. As we will see in Section 8.7, utility theory offers an alternative to the expected value approach.

COMPUTER ANALYSIS

Payoff table analyses are very easy to perform using Excel. In addition the decision theory module of WINQSB can be used to determine the optimal decision alternative using various criteria. Figure 8.1 shows the WINQSB output for this problem.

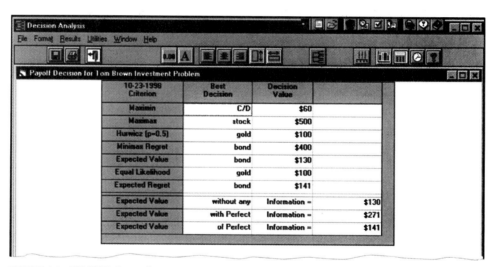

FIGURE 8.1   WINQSB Output for Tom Brown Decision Problem

8.4   EXPECTED VALUE OF PERFECT INFORMATION

Suppose it were possible to know with certainty the state of nature that was going to occur prior to choosing the decision alternative. The **expected value of perfect information (EVPI)** represents the *gain* in expected return resulting from this knowledge.

To illustrate this concept, recall that using the expected value criterion, Tom Brown's optimal decision was to purchase the bond. However, Tom can't be sure if this will be one of the 20% of the times that the market will experience a large rise, or one of the 10% of the times that the market will experience a large fall, or if some other state of nature will occur. If Tom repeatedly invested $1000 in the bond, under similar economic conditions (and assuming the same probabilities for the states of nature), we showed that in the long run he should earn an average of $130 per investment. The $130 is known as the **expected return using the expected value criterion** or **EREV**.

But suppose Tom could find out in advance which state of nature were going to occur. Each time Tom made an investment decision, he would be practicing decision making under certainty (see Section 8.3).

For example, if Tom knew the stock market were going to show a large rise, naturally he would choose the stock investment because it gives the highest payoff ($500) for this state of nature. Similarly, if he knew a small rise would occur, he would again choose the stock investment because it gives the highest payoff ($250) for this state of nature, and so on. These results are summarized as follows.

If Tom Knew in Advance the Stock Market Would Undergo	His Optimal Decision Would Be	With a Payoff of
a large rise	stock	$500
a small rise	stock	$250
no change	gold	$200
a small fall	gold	$300
a large fall	C/D	$ 60

(Interestingly, Tom would never choose the bond investment if he knew in advance which state of nature would occur.)

Under these conditions, since 20% of the time the stock market would experience a large rise, 20% of the time Tom would earn a profit of $500. Similarly, 30% of the time the market would experience a small rise and Tom would earn $250, 30% of the time the market would experience no change and he would earn $200; and so on.

The expected return from knowing for sure which state of nature will occur prior to making the investment decision is called the **expected return with perfect information (ERPI)**. For Tom Brown, ERPI = .2(500) + .3(250) + .3(200) + .1(300) + .1(60) = 271. This is a gain of $271 − $130 = $141 over the EREV. The difference ($141) is the **expected value of perfect information** (EVPI).

Another way to determine EVPI for the investment problem is to reason as follows: If Tom knows the stock market will show a large rise, he should definitely buy the stock, giving him $500, or *a gain of $250 over what he would earn from the bond investment* (the optimal decision without the additional information as to which state of nature would occur). Similarly, if he knows the stock market will show a small rise he should again buy the stock, earning him $250, or *a gain of $50 over the return from buying the bond*, and so on. These results are summarized as follows.

If Tom Knew in Advance the Stock Market Would Undergo	His Optimal Decision Would Be	With a Gain in Payoff of
a large rise	stock	$250
a small rise	stock	$ 50
no change	gold	$ 50
a small fall	gold	$400
a large fall	C/D	$210

Hence, to find the expected gain over always investing in the bond (i.e., the EVPI), we simply take the possible gains from knowing which state of nature will occur and weight them by the likelihood of that state of nature actually occurring:

$$EVPI = .2(250) + .3(50) + .3(50) + .1(400) + .1(210) = 141$$

This calculation of EVPI might look somewhat familiar since it is the same one we performed in order to calculate the expected regret for the bond investment.

Expected Value of Perfect Information

$$
\begin{pmatrix}
\text{Expected} \\
\text{Value of} \\
\text{Perfect} \\
\text{Information}
\end{pmatrix}
=
\begin{pmatrix}
\text{Expected return with} \\
\text{perfect information} \\
\text{as to which state of nature} \\
\text{will occur prior to} \\
\text{making decision}
\end{pmatrix}
-
\begin{pmatrix}
\text{Expected return without} \\
\text{additional information} \\
\text{as to which state of} \\
\text{nature will occur prior} \\
\text{to making decision}
\end{pmatrix}
$$

$$\text{EVPI} = \text{ERPI} - \text{EREV}$$

or

EVPI = Expected regret of the optimal decision as found using the expected value criterion. That is, it is the smallest expected regret of any decision alternative.

Having perfect information regarding the future for any situation is virtually impossible. However, often it *is* possible to procure imperfect, or *sample*, information regarding the states of nature. We calculate EVPI because it gives an upper limit on the expected value of any such sample information.

8.5 $\mathcal{B}$AYESIAN ANALYSES—DECISION MAKING WITH IMPERFECT INFORMATION

In Section 8.3 we contrasted decision making under uncertainty with decision making under risk. Some statisticians argue that it is unnecessary to practice decision making under uncertainty because one always has at least *some* probabilistic information that can be used to assess the likelihoods of the states of nature. Such individuals adhere to what is called **Bayesian statistics**.[1]

USING SAMPLE
INFORMATION TO AID
IN DECISION MAKING

Bayesian statistics play a vital role in assessing the value of additional *sample information* obtained from such sources as marketing surveys or experiments, which can assist in the decision-making process. The decision maker can use this input to revise or fine tune the original probability estimates and possibly improve decision making.

Making Decisions Using
Sample Information

To illustrate decision making using sample information, we again consider the Tom Brown investment problem.

Toma.daa
Tomb.daa
Toma.xls
Tomb.xls

TOM BROWN INVESTMENT DECISION (continued)

Tom has learned that, for only $50, he can receive the results of noted economist Milton Samuelman's multimillion dollar econometric forecast, which predicts either "positive" or "negative" economic growth for the upcoming year. Samuelman has offered the following verifiable statistics regarding the results of his model:

1. When the stock market showed a large rise, the forecast predicted "positive" 80% of the time and "negative" 20% of the time.

---

[1]Named for Thomas Bayes, an eighteenth-century British clergyman and mathematician.

2. When the stock market showed a small rise, the forecast predicted "positive" 70% of the time and "negative" 30% of the time.

3. When the stock market showed no change, the forecast was equally likely to predict "positive" or "negative."

4. When the stock market showed a small fall, the forecast predicted "positive" 40% of the time and "negative" 60% of the time.

5. When the stock market showed a large fall, the forecast always predicted "negative."

Tom would like to know whether it is worthwhile to pay $50 for the results of the Samuelman forecast.

SOLUTION

Tom must first determine what his optimal decision should be if the forecast predicts positive economic growth and what it should be if it predicts negative growth. If Tom's investment decision changes based on the results of the forecast, he must determine whether knowing the results of Samuelman's forecast would increase his expected profit by more than the $50 cost of obtaining the information.

Using the relative frequency method we have the following conditional probabilities based on the forecast's historical performance:

$$P(\text{forecast predicts ``positive''}|\text{large rise in market}) = .80$$
$$P(\text{forecast predicts ``negative''}|\text{large rise in market}) = .20$$

$$P(\text{forecast predicts ``positive''}|\text{small rise in market}) = .70$$
$$P(\text{forecast predicts ``negative''}|\text{small rise in market}) = .30$$

$$P(\text{forecast predicts ``positive''}|\text{no change in market}) = .50$$
$$P(\text{forecast predicts ``negative''}|\text{no change in market}) = .50$$

$$P(\text{forecast predicts ``positive''}|\text{small fall in market}) = .40$$
$$P(\text{forecast predicts ``negative''}|\text{small fall in market}) = .60$$

$$P(\text{forecast predicts ``positive''}|\text{large fall in market}) = 0$$
$$P(\text{forecast predicts ``negative''}|\text{large fall in market}) = 1.00$$

What Tom really needs to know, however, is how the results of Samuelman's economic forecast affect the probability estimates of the stock market's performance. That is, he needs probabilities such as P(large rise in market|forecast predicts "positive"). Unfortunately, in general, $P(A|B) \neq P(B|A)$, so it is incorrect to assume P(large rise in market|forecast predicts "positive") = .80.

One way to obtain the probabilities of this form from the above probabilities is to use a Bayesian approach, which enables the decision maker to revise initial probability estimates in light of additional information. The original probability estimates are known as the set of *prior* or *a priori* probabilities. A set of revised or *posterior probabilities* is obtained based on knowing the results of *sample* or *indicator* information:

Bayesian Analysis

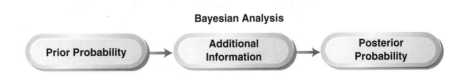

Prior Probability → Additional Information → Posterior Probability

BAYES' THEOREM

The Bayesian approach utilizes *Bayes' Theorem* to revise the prior probabilities.[2] This theorem states:

Given events B and A_1, A_2, A_3, . . . , A_n, where A_1, A_2, A_3, . . . , A_n are mutually exclusive and collectively exhaustive, posterior probabilities, $P(A_i|B)$ can be found by:

$$P(A_i|B) = \frac{P(B|A_i)\ P(A_i)}{P(B|A_1)\ P(A_1) + P(B|A_2)\ P(A_2) + \ldots + P(B|A_n)\ P(A_n)}$$

Although the notation of Bayes' Theorem may appear intimidating, a convenient way of calculating the posterior probabilities is to use a tabular approach. This approach utilizes five columns:

Column 1—States of Nature   A listing of the states of nature for the problem (the A_i's).

Column 2—Prior Probabilities   The prior probability estimates (before obtaining sample information) for the states of nature, $P(A_i)$.

Column 3—Conditional Probabilities   The known conditional probabilities of obtaining sample information given a particular state of nature, $P(B|A_i)$.

Column 4—Joint Probabilities   The joint probabilities of a particular state of nature and sample information occurring simultaneously, $P(B \cap A_i) = P(A_i)*P(B|A_i)$. These numbers are calculated for each row by multiplying the number in the second column by the number in the third column. The sum of this column is the marginal probability, $P(B)$.

Column 5—Posterior Probabilities   The posterior probabilities found by Bayes' Theorem, $P(A_i|B)$. Since $P(A_i|B) = P(B \cap A_i)/P(B)$, these numbers are calculated for each row by dividing the number in the fourth column by the sum of the numbers in the fourth column.

Table 8.12 gives the tabular approach for calculating posterior probabilities assuming that Tom responds to Milton Samuelman's offer and learns that Samuelman's economic forecast for next year is "positive."

TABLE 8.12   INDICATOR INFORMATION—"POSITIVE" ECONOMIC FORECAST FOR TOM BROWN

States of Nature S_i	Prior Probabilities $P(S_i)$	Conditional Probabilities $P(\text{positive}|S_i)$	Joint Probabilities $P(\text{positive} \cap S_i)$	Posterior Probabilities $P(S_i|\text{positive})$
Large rise	.20	.80	.16	.16/.56 = .286
Small rise	.30	.70	.21	.21/.56 = .375
No change	.30	.50	.15	.15/.56 = .268
Small fall	.10	.40	.04	.04/.56 = .071
Large fall	.10	0	0	0/.56 = 0
			$P(\text{positive}) = .56$	

As you can see, although the initial probability estimate of the stock market's showing a large rise was .20, after Samuelman's "positive" economic forecast Tom has revised this probability upward to .286. Similarly, based on this forecast Tom has revised his probability estimates for a small rise, no change, small fall, or large fall in the market

[2]Bayes' Theorem is a restatement of the conditional law of probability $[P(A|B) = P(A \cap B)/P(B)]$. In the parlance of decision theory, the A's correspond to the states of nature, and B is the sample or indicator information. We give a discussion of Bayes' Theorem in Supplement CD1 on the accompanying CD-ROM.

from .30, .30, .10, and .10 to .375, .268, .071, and 0, respectively. We also see that the probability that Samuelman's forecast will be "positive" is .56 (the sum of the values in Column 4). A similar procedure is used to obtain the posterior probabilities corresponding to a "negative" economic forecast, as shown in Table 8.13.

TABLE 8.13 INDICATOR INFORMATION—"NEGATIVE" ECONOMIC FORECAST FOR TOM BROWN

States of Nature S_i	Prior Probabilities $P(S_i)$	Conditional Probabilities $P(\text{negative}|S_i)$	Joint Probabilities $P(\text{negative} \cap S_i)$	Posterior Probabilities $P(S_i|\text{negative})$
Large rise	.20	.20	.04	.04/.44 = .091
Small rise	.30	.30	.09	.09/.44 = .205
No change	.30	.50	.15	.15/.44 = .341
Small fall	.10	.60	.06	.06/.44 = .136
Large fall	.10	1.00	.10	.10/.44 = 227
			$P(\text{negative}) = .44$	

As you can see, for a "negative" economic forecast the respective probability estimates for the states of nature have been revised to .091, .205, .341, .136, and .227. Also note that the probability that Samuelman's forecast will give a "negative" forecast is .44 (the sum of the values in Column 4).

These posterior probabilities can be easily calculated on an Excel spreadsheet or by using WINQSB. Figure 8.2 shows the results from WINQSB.

Posterior or Revised Probabilities for Tom Brown Investment Decision					
Indicator\State	Large Rise	Small Rise	No Change	Small Fall	Largel Fall
Predicts Positive	0.2857	0.3750	0.2679	0.0714	0
Predicts Negative	0.0909	0.2045	0.3409	0.1364	0.2273

FIGURE 8.2 Posterior or Revised Probabilities for Tom Brown

Expected Value of Sample Information

The Samuelman forecast generates two sets of probabilities for the states of nature, one based on a positive economic forecast and the other based on a negative economic forecast. We can now determine the optimal investment for each forecast using the expected value criterion.

If Samuelman forecasts positive economic growth, the revised expected values for the decision alternatives are:

$$EV(\text{gold}|\text{"positive"}) = .286(-100) + .375(100) + .268(200) + .071(300) + 0(0) = \$84$$
$$EV(\text{bond}|\text{"positive"}) = .286(250) + .375(200) + .268(150) + .071(-100) + 0(-150) = \$180$$
$$EV(\text{stock}|\text{"positive"}) = .286(500) + .375(250) + .268(100) + .071(-200) + 0(-600) = \$250$$
$$EV(\text{C/D}|\text{"positive"}) = .286(60) + .375(60) + .268(60) + .071(60) + 0(60) = \$60$$

If Samuelman's forecast is negative, the expected returns are:

$$EV(\text{gold}|\text{"negative"}) = .091(-100) + .205(100) + .341(200) + .136(300) + .227(0) = \$120$$
$$EV(\text{bond}|\text{"negative"}) = .091(250) + .205(200) + .341(150) + .136(-100) + .227(-150) = \$65$$
$$EV(\text{stock}|\text{"negative"}) = .091(500) + .205(250) + .341(100) + .136(-200) + .227(-600) = -\$37$$
$$EV(\text{C/D}|\text{"negative"}) = .091(60) + .205(60) + .341(60) + .136(60) + .227(60) = \$60$$

Thus, if Samuelman's forecast is positive, buying the stock would be optimal since it yields Tom the highest expected value ($250); if the forecast is negative, buying gold would be optimal since it yields the highest expected value ($120).

Table 8.14 summarizes the expected values that we have generated thus far for each decision alternative using the prior probabilities, the posterior probabilities assuming a positive forecast from Samuelman, and the posterior probabilities assuming a negative forecast from Samuelman.

TABLE 8.14   TOM BROWN INVESTMENT DECISION—EXPECTED VALUES WITH SAMPLE INFORMATION

Decision Alternative	States of Nature					EV Prior	EV "Positive"	EV "Negative"
	Large Rise	Small Rise	No Change	Small Fall	Large Fall			
Gold	−$100	$100	$200	$300	$ 0	$100	$ 84	$120
Bond	$250	$200	$150	−$100	−$150	$130	$180	$ 65
Stock	$500	$250	$100	−$200	−$600	$125	$250	−$ 37
C/D account	$ 60	$ 60	$ 60	$ 0	$ 60	$ 60	$ 60	$ 60
Prior Probability	.20	.30	.30	.10	.10	Probability		
Probability given "Positive"	.286	.375	.268	.071	0		.56	
Probability given "Negative"	.091	.205	.341	.136	.227			.44

We see that information regarding Samuelman's forecast dramatically changes the probability estimates for the states of nature and, therefore, the optimal decision. But is knowing the results of the Samuelman forecast worth $50? To answer this question, Tom must calculate his expected gain from making decisions based on the forecast results. This expected gain is known as the **expected value of sample information (EVSI)**.

To determine the EVSI, we compare the expected return available *with* the sample information (ERSI) to the expected return available *without* the additional sample information (EREV). The difference is the EVSI.

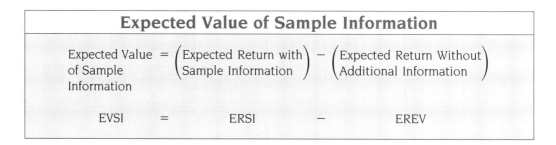

The investment with the largest expected return for a positive forecast is the stock (expected return = $250); for a negative forecast, it is the gold (expected return = $120). The probability Samuelman's forecast will be positive is .56; the probability his forecast will be negative is .44. Hence,

$$\text{ERSI} = .56(250) + .44(120) = \$193$$

Since the expected return without Samuelman's forecast, EREV, is the $130 obtained from buying the bond, the expected value of sample information is:

$$\$193 - \$130 = \$63$$

Because the expected gain from the Samuelman forecast is greater than its $50 cost, Tom should acquire it.

It is important to note that the Samuelman forecast gives additional, but not perfect, information. If the forecast could perfectly predict the future, the gain from the information would be the expected value of perfect information (EVPI) discussed earlier. If the same decision would be made regardless of the results of the indicator information, the value of the information would be 0. Thus,

$$0 \leq \text{EVSI} \leq \text{EVPI}$$

Efficiency

The measure of the relative value of sample information is its **efficiency**, which is simply the ratio of the EVSI to the EVPI.

Efficiency
$\text{Efficiency} = \dfrac{\text{EVSI}}{\text{EVPI}}$

Since $0 \leq \text{EVSI} \leq \text{EVPI}$, efficiency is a number between 0 and 1. For Tom Brown's problem, the efficiency of the Samuelman information is:

$$\text{Efficiency} = \text{EVSI}/\text{EVPI} = 63/141 = .45$$

Efficiency provides a convenient method for comparing different forms of sample information. Given that two different types of sample information could be obtained at the same cost, the one with the higher efficiency is preferred.

8.6 DECISION TREES

Although the payoff table approach is quite handy for some problems, its applicability is limited to situations in which the decision maker needs to make a single decision. Many real-world decision problems consist of a sequence of dependent decisions. For these, a decision tree can prove useful.

A **decision tree** is a chronological representation of the decision process by a network that utilizes two types of nodes: *decision nodes* (represented by squares) and *state of nature nodes* (represented by circles). The root of the tree corresponds to the present time, and the tree is constructed outward into the future.

Each branch emanating from a decision node corresponds to a decision alternative and includes the cost or benefit value associated with that decision. Each branch emanating from a state of nature node corresponds to a particular state of nature. Associated with these branches are the probabilities that the state of nature will occur, given all previous occurrences (decisions and states of nature) prior to the state of nature node. To illustrate, consider the following situation faced by the Bill Galen Development Company:

Billg.daa

BILL GALEN DEVELOPMENT COMPANY

The Bill Galen Development Company (BGD) needs a variance from the city of Kingston, New York, in order to do commercial development on a property whose asking price is a firm $300,000. BGD estimates that it can construct the shopping center for an additional $500,000 and sell the completed center for approximately $950,000.

A variance application costs $30,000 in fees and expenses, and there is only a 40% chance that the variance will be approved. Regardless of the outcome, the variance process takes two months. If BGD purchases the property and the variance is denied, the company will sell the property for a net return of $260,000. BGD can also purchase a three-month option on the property for $20,000, which would allow it to apply for a variance. Finally, for $5000 an urban planning consultant can be hired to study the situation and render an opinion as to whether the variance will be approved or denied. BGD estimates the following conditional probabilities:

P(consultant predicts approval|approval granted) = .70
P(consultant predicts denial|approval denied)   = .80

BGD wishes to determine the optimal strategy regarding this parcel of property.

SOLUTION

Initially, the company faces two decision alternatives: (1) hire the consultant and (2) do not hire the consultant. Figure 8.3 shows the initial tree construction corresponding to this decision. Note that the root of the tree is a decision node, two branches lead out from that node. The value on the "do not hire consultant" branch is 0 (there is no cost to this decision), while the −$5000 value on the "hire consultant" branch is the cash flow associated with hiring the consultant.

Let us consider the decision branch corresponding to "do not hire consultant." If the consultant is not hired, BGD faces three possible decisions: (1) do nothing; (2) buy the land; or (3) purchase the option. Thus, we find a decision node at the end of this branch and three branches (corresponding to the three decision alternatives) leaving the node. As shown in Figure 8.4, the values on the three decision branches—0, −$300,000, and −$20,000—correspond to the cash flows associated with each action.

If BGD does not hire the consultant and decides to do nothing, the total return to the company is 0. If, on the other hand, it decides to buy the land, it must then decide whether or not to apply for a variance. Clearly, if BGD were not going to apply for a variance, it would not have bought the land in the first place. Therefore, there is only one logical decision following "buy land" and that is to "apply for variance."

Extrapolating this path further into the future, BGD will next learn whether the variance will be approved or denied. This is a chance or state of nature event, signified

FIGURE 8.3   Bill Galen Development Company

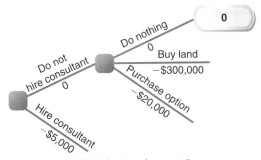

FIGURE 8.4   Bill Galen Development Company

by a round node at the end of the "apply for variance" branch. This node leads to two branches—"variance approved" or "variance denied"—on which the values, .4 and .6, respectively, are the corresponding state of nature probabilities.

At the end of each path through the tree is the total profit or loss connected with that particular set of decisions and outcomes, calculated by adding the cash flows on the decision branches, making up the path. This is shown in Figure 8.5. For example, if BGD does not hire the consultant, buys the land, gets the variance approved, builds the shopping center, and sells it, the profit will be 0 − $300,000 − $30,000 − $500,000 + $950,000 = $120,000. If, after buying the land, the variance is denied, BGD will sell the property for $260,000, and the total profit will be 0 − $300,000 − $30,000 + $260,000 = − $70,000; i.e., a net loss of $70,000.

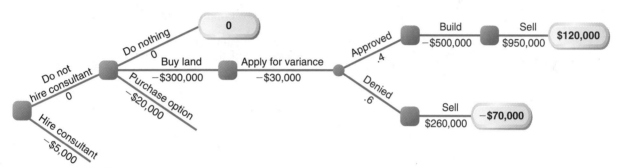

FIGURE 8.5   **Bill Galen Development Company**

Now if BGD decides to purchase the option, it would apply for the variance, which would then be either approved or denied. If the variance is approved, BGD will exercise the option and buy the property for $300,000, construct the shopping center for $500,000, and sell it for $950,000. If the variance is denied, BGD will simply let the option expire. Figure 8.6 shows the complete decision tree emanating from the decision not to hire the consultant.

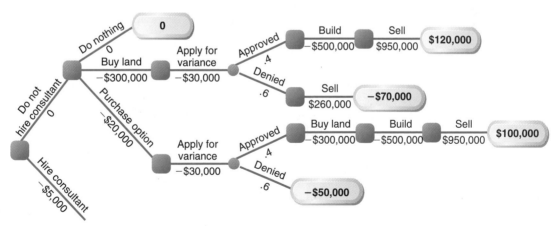

FIGURE 8.6   **Bill Galen Development Company**

Let us now consider the decision process if BGD does hire the consultant. The consultant will predict that the variance will either be approved or denied. This chance event is represented by a round state of nature node. The probability that the consultant will predict approval or denial is not readily apparent but can be calculated using Bayes' Theorem.

Let us first determine the posterior probabilities for approval and denial assuming that the consultant predicts that the variance will be *approved*.

Since:

$$P(\text{consultant predicts approval}|\text{approval granted}) = .70$$

then

$$P(\text{consultant predicts denial}|\text{approval granted}) = 1 - .70 = .30$$

Similarly, since

$$P(\text{consultant predicts denial}|\text{approval denied}) = .80$$

then

$$P(\text{consultant predicts approval}|\text{approval denied}) = 1 - .80 = .20$$

Tables 8.15 and 8.16 detail the Bayesian approach; Table 8.15 corresponds to the consultant's prediction of approval, and the second corresponds to the consultant's prediction of denial.

TABLE 8.15   INDICATOR INFORMATION—CONSULTANT PREDICTS APPROVAL OF VARIANCE

States of Nature	Prior Probabilities	Conditional Probabilities	Joint Probabilities	Posterior Probabilities
Variance approved	.40	.70	.28	.28/.40 = .70
Variance denied	.60	.20	.12	.12/.40 = .30
	P(consultant predicts approval)		.40	

TABLE 8.16   INDICATOR INFORMATION—CONSULTANT PREDICTS DENIAL OF VARIANCE

States of Nature	Prior Probabilities	Conditional Probabilities	Joint Probabilities	Posterior Probabilities
Variance approved	.40	.30	.12	.12/.60 = .20
Variance denied	.60	.80	.48	.48/.60 = .80
	P(consultant predicts denial)		.60	

Once the consultant's prediction is known, BGD is faced with the same decision choices as when the consultant was not hired: (1) do nothing; (2) buy the land; or (3) purchase the option. The differences here are the probabilities for the states of nature and the fact that the firm has spent $5000 for the consultant. Using this information, we can complete the decision tree as shown in Figure 8.7.

To determine the optimal strategy we work backward from the ends of each branch until we come to either a state of nature node or a decision node.

At a state of nature node, we calculate the expected value of the node using the ending node values for each branch leading out of the node and the probability associated with that branch. The expected value is the sum of the products of the branch probabilities and corresponding ending node values. This sum becomes the value for the state of nature node.

At a decision node, the branch that has the highest ending node value is the optimal decision. This highest ending node value, in turn, becomes the value for the decision node. Nonoptimal decisions are indicated by a pair of lines across their branches.

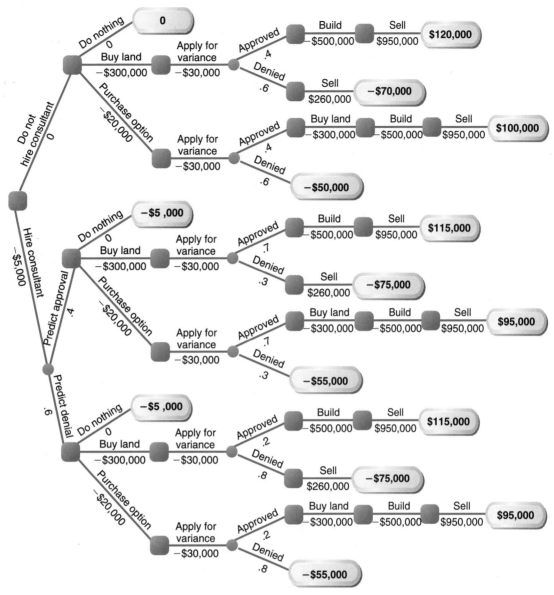

FIGURE 8.7   **Bill Galen Development Company**

To illustrate, consider in Figure 8.7 the possible paths reached if BGD does not hire the consultant. If BGD decides to buy the property and applies for the variance, two outcomes (branches) are possible: (1) the variance is approved and BGD earns $120,000; or (2) the variance is denied and BGD loses $70,000. The expected return at this state of nature node is found by (Probability Variance Is Approved)*(Expected Return If Variance Is Approved) + (Probability Variance Is Denied)*(Expected Return If Variance Is Denied) = .4($120,000) + .6(−$70,000) = $6000. This is the expected value associated with buying the land. The expected value associated with buying the option is .40($100,000) + .60(−$50,000) = $10,000.

Thus, if BGD decides not to hire the consultant, the corresponding expected values that result if it does nothing, buys the land, or purchases the option are $0, $6000, and $10,000, respectively; thus purchasing the option is the optimal decision. The expected return corresponding to the purchase option decision ($10,000) then becomes the expected return corresponding to the decision node not to hire the consultant. The remaining portion of the tree, in which BGD *does* hire the consultant, is calculated by working backwards in a similar fashion. The completed decision tree is given in Figure 8.8. As you can see, the optimal decision is to hire the consultant. Then if the consultant predicts approval, BGD should buy the property, but if the consultant predicts denial, BGD should do nothing.

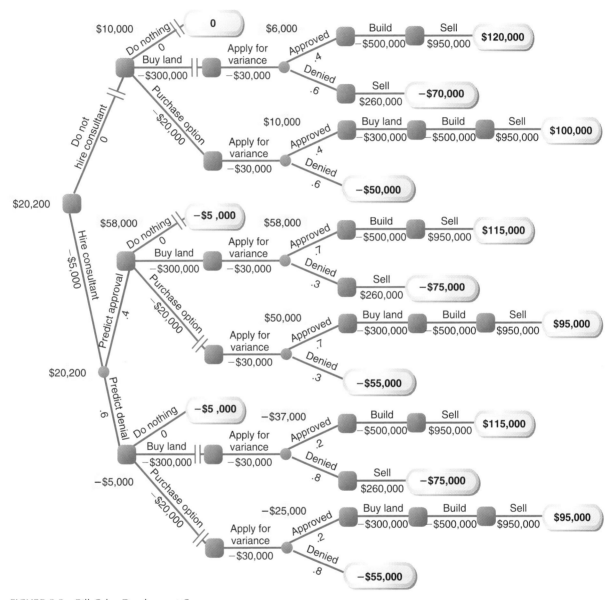

FIGURE 8.8   Bill Galen Development Company

This problem illustrates that the calculations required to analyze a problem using a decision tree can be lengthy and cumbersome. Fortunately computer modules, such as the one in WINQSB, have been written to expressly perform these computations. Figures 8.9a and 8.9b are the WINQSB outputs for the Bill Galen development problem. Here, the optimal strategy can be determined from the decision column in Figure 8.9b.

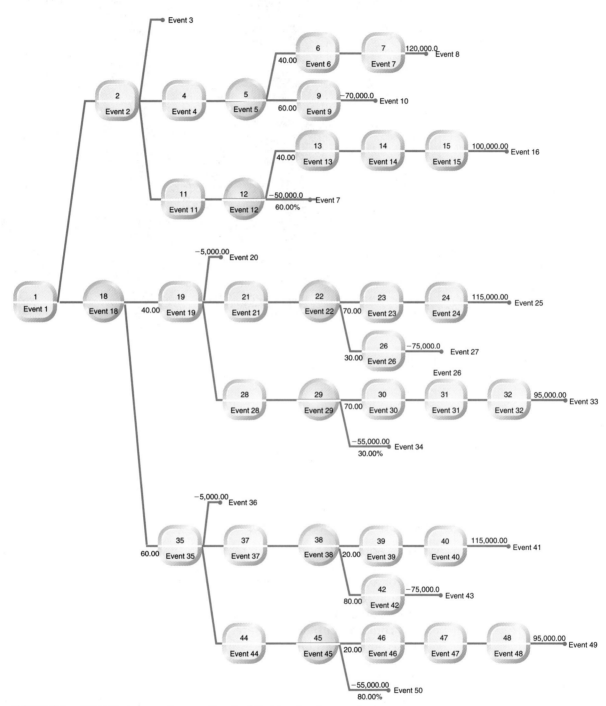

FIGURE 8.9a   **WINQSB Output—Decision Tree for Bill Galen Development Company**

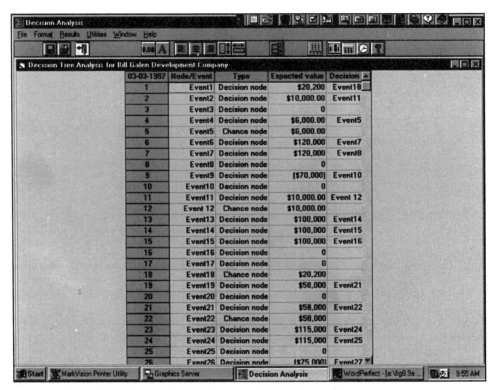

FIGURE 8.9*b* WINQSB Output—Decision Strategies for Bill Galen

A BUSINESS REPORT

Using this information, we can prepare the following business report to assist BGD in determining an optimal decision strategy. This memorandum cogently identifies the critical factors BGD should consider and highlights the possible risks the company may encounter.

M E M O R A N D U M

To: Bill Galen, President, Bill Galen Development Company

From: Student Consulting Group

Subj: 5th and Main Street Property

We have analyzed the situation regarding the parcel of property located at 5th and Main Streets in Kingston, New York, which your firm is interested in developing for a strip shopping center. The property is currently zoned residential and would require a variance in order to complete construction. Our analysis was completed assuming that BGD wishes to maximize the expected profit this project could potentially generate.

    Based on cost and revenue estimates supplied by management, the following table gives the returns available from different strategies the firm might pursue.

TABLE I   Expected Return Available from Different Possible Strategies

Strategy	Expected Return
Consultant not hired	
Do nothing	$0
Buy land	$6000
Buy option	$10,000

TABLE I Expected Return Available from Different Possible Strategies (continued)

Strategy	Expected Return
Consultant hired and predicts variance will be approved	
Do nothing	−$5000
Buy land	$58,000
Buy option	$50,000
Consultant hired and predicts variance will be denied	
Do nothing	−$5000
Buy land	−$37,000
Buy option	−$25,000

We analyzed this information using standard decision-making techniques and recommend the following strategy:

> Hire the consultant for $5000. If the consultant predicts that the variance will be approved, BGD should purchase the property for $300,000. If the consultant predicts that the variance will be denied, BGD should not proceed with this project. *Your expected return from this strategy is $20,200.*

Table II summarizes the potential maximum loss from each strategy and the probability that the firm will incur such a loss.

TABLE II Maximum Potential Loss and Likelihood of Such Loss from Different Possible Strategies

Strategy	Maximum Loss	Probability
Consultant not hired		
Do nothing	0	100%
Buy land	$70,000	40%
Buy option	$50,000	40%
Consultant hired and predicts variance will be approved		
Do nothing	$5000	40%
Buy land	$75,000	12%
Buy option	$55,000	12%
Consultant hired and predicts variance will be denied		
Do nothing	$5000	60%
Buy land	$75,000	48%
Buy option	$55,000	48%

If the consultant predicts that the variance will be approved and it is, in fact, *not* approved, BGD potentially will suffer a loss of $75,000. The likelihood of the consultant predicting approval is estimated to be 40%, and the possibility that the variance will be denied in this case is estimated to be 30%. Hence, there is approximately a 12% chance that BGD will incur a loss of $75,000 if this recommendation is followed.

If BGD feels that the potential loss from the recommended strategy is greater than the company can afford, instead of purchasing the property if the consultant predicts the variance will be approved, the company can buy the option. This lowers the expected return to $17,000 but will only expose BGD to a maximum potential loss of $55,000. Should this potential loss still be too large, we would be happy to meet with management to discuss alternative strategies.

8.7   DECISION MAKING AND UTILITY

The underlying basis for using the expected value criterion is that the decision maker wishes to choose the decision alternative that maximizes the expected return (or minimizes the expected cost). This criterion may not be appropriate, however, if the decision is a one-time opportunity with substantial risks.

For example, as pointed out in the BGD management memo, following the recommended strategy carries a potential loss of $75,000 for the company. If the maximum the company could currently afford to lose is $50,000, it may prefer to buy the option and not hire the consultant, even though this strategy has a lower expected return. The concept of utility has been developed to explain such behavior in a rational format.

Social scientists have long observed that individuals do not always choose decisions based on the expected value criterion, even when the payoffs and probabilities for the states of nature are known. For example, suppose you could play a coin toss game in which you will win $1 if the coin is heads and lose $1 if the coin is tails. If the coin is bent so that the probability of the coin landing heads is 55% and tails is 45%, your expected return from playing the game would be .55($1)+.45(−$1) = $.10. Given this expected return, you probably would wish to play this game.

Consider what happens, however, when the stakes increase so that you win $100,000 if the coin comes up heads and lose $100,000 if the coin comes up tails. Even though this game has an expected return of $10,000 [= .55($100,000) + .45(−$100,000)], you might be reluctant to play due to the potential of losing $100,000.

Playing state lottery games is an example of a case in which people do not base a decision on expected value. In most state lottery games, the expected return to the purchaser of a $1.00 lottery ticket is only about $0.50. Thus, if people decided whether or not to buy a lottery ticket based on expected value alone, lottery sales would be nonexistent.

Purchasing insurance is another such example. Insurance industry profits are predicated on the fact that, on the average, people will pay more for a policy than the expected present value of the loss for which they are insured. Again, if people's decisions were based solely on the expected value criterion, no one would buy insurance.

UTILITY APPROACH

In the utility approach to decision making, *utility values*[3] U(V) reflective of the decision maker's perspective are determined for each possible payoff. The optimal decision is then chosen by an *expected utility criterion*, which uses these values rather than the payoff values in the calculations.

DETERMINING UTILITY VALUES, U(V)

Although the following technique for finding utility values corresponding to payoffs may seem contrived, it does provide an insightful look into the amount of risk the decision maker is willing to take. The concept is based on the decision maker's preference to taking a sure thing (a particular payoff) versus risking receiving only the highest or lowest payoff.

---

[3]The utility of the least preferred outcome is given the lowest utility value (usually 0), whereas the most preferred outcome is given the highest utility value (usually 1).

Indifference Approach For Assigning Utility Values

1. List every possible payoff in the payoff table in ascending order, from lowest to highest value.

2. Assign a utility of 0 to the lowest value and a utility of 1 to the highest value.

3. For all other possible payoff values ask the decision maker, "Suppose you could receive this payoff for sure, or, alternatively, you could receive either the highest payoff with probability p and the lowest payoff with probability (1-p). What value of p would make you *indifferent* between the two situations?"

The answers to this question are known as the *indifference probabilities* for the payoffs and are used as the utility values. Obviously, larger payoffs have larger utility values, but the relative scale of utility values can differ vastly from that of the payoff values.

To illustrate the utility approach, let us consider once again the Tom Brown investment problem.

Tomc.daa
Tomc.xls

TOM BROWN INVESTMENT PROBLEM (continued)

We observed that the highest possible return for Tom in the payoff table calculated based on the broker's analysis was $500. Tom would achieve this payoff if he invested in the stock and there were a large rise in the market. The lowest possible payoff was a loss of $600, which Tom would incur if he invested in the stock and there were a large fall in the market.

The second highest possible return was $300. Tom would receive this sum if he invested in gold and there were a small fall in the market. We asked Tom, "If you could receive $300 for sure or you could receive $500 with probability p and lose $600 with probability (1-p), what value of p would make you indifferent between these two choices?"

Tom thought for a moment and replied, "I'd have to be pretty certain of receiving the $500 payoff to pass up a certain payoff of $300; say about 90%." We repeated this question for all possible outcomes from the payoff table, and Tom's responses were as follows:

Certain Payoff	Probability
−600	0
−200	.25
−150	.30
−100	.35
0	.50
60	.60
100	.65
150	.70
200	.75
250	.85
300	.90
500	1.00

In light of these preferences, Tom wishes to determine his optimal investment decision.

SOLUTION

The indifference preferences Tom gave in response to our questions are his utility values for the payoffs. To determine the optimal decision under the expected utility criterion, we substitute the corresponding utility values for the payoffs given in Table 8.3 and calculate the expected utility for each decision; this gives the results shown in Table 8.17.

TABLE 8.17 TOM BROWN INVESTMENT DECISION UTILITY PAYOFF TABLE

Decision Alternatives	States of Nature					Expected Utility	
	Large Rise	Small Rise	No Change	Small Fall	Large Fall		
Gold	.35	.65	.75	.90	.50	.63	
Bond	.85	.75	.70	.35	.30	.67	
Stock	1.00	.85	.65	.25	.0	.675	← maximum
C/D account	.60	.60	.60	.60	.60	.60	
Probability	.20	.30	.30	.10	.10		

Since the decision with the highest expected utility is the stock investment, it would be selected using the expected utility criterion. Comparing the expected utility of the stock investment to the bond investment, however, we note there is little difference in the two values. In fact, had the utility values been slightly different, the bond investment could have had the *higher* expected utility.

It is therefore important not to dismiss the bond investment from consideration. (Remember that in management science we are modeling in order to obtain insights into the optimal decision.) Tom may, in fact, wish to do some further investigation before making a final choice between the stock and the bond.

RISK-AVERSE, RISK-NEUTRAL, AND RISK-TAKING DECISION MAKERS

Within the context of utility theory, behavior can be classified as risk averse, risk taking, or risk neutral. A *risk-averse* decision maker prefers a certain outcome to a chance outcome having the same expected value. For example, suppose you have the choice of receiving $10,000 with probability .20 and $0 with probability .80. The expected value of this outcome is $2000 (= .20*$10,000 + .80*0). If you preferred receiving $2000 with certainty to the random outcome, you would be exhibiting risk-averse behavior. An example of risk-averse behavior is the purchase of an insurance policy. The concave utility curve depicted in Figure 8.10 is that of a risk-averse decision maker.

FIGURE 8.10 Risk-Averse Utility Curve

A *risk-taking* decision maker prefers a chance outcome to a certain outcome having the same expected value. Returning to the above example, if you were a risk-taking decision maker, you would prefer the chance outcome to receiving $2000. An example of risk-taking behavior is the purchase of a lottery ticket. The convex utility curve depicted in Figure 8.11 is that of a risk-taking decision maker.

A *risk-neutral* decision maker is indifferent between a chance outcome and a certain outcome having the same expected value. Using the above example once again, if you were a risk-neutral decision maker you would be indifferent between the two outcomes. Typically, large corporations are assumed to be risk neutral because they do not have a preference for or an aversion to risk with regard to the amounts of money involved in normal business situations. The linear utility curve depicted in Figure 8.12 is that of a risk-neutral decision maker.

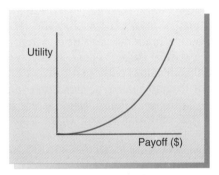

FIGURE 8.11   Risk-Taking Utility Curve

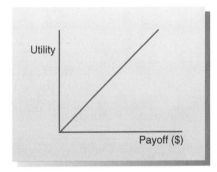

FIGURE 8.12   Risk-Neutral Utility Curve

The optimal decision for a risk-neutral decision maker can be determined using the expected value criterion on the payoff values. Therefore, the expected value criterion is generally used in decision making at large corporations.

Most individuals are not entirely risk averse, risk taking, or risk neutral. Social scientists have shown that, in general, people tend to be risk taking when dealing with small amounts of money while they tend to be risk averse when it comes to large amounts. Between large and small amounts of money, people are generally risk neutral. This explains why the same individual might purchase a lottery ticket as well as fire insurance. Figure 8.13 depicts Tom Brown's utility values. As you can see, Tom appears to exhibit such typical behavior.

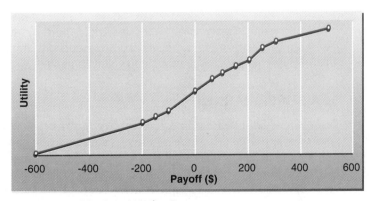

FIGURE 8.13   Tom Brown's Utility Curve

8.8   GAME THEORY

Playing games is a popular form of amusement. People typically play games such as poker, bridge, and chess, for the challenge and enjoyment they afford (and, if betting is allowed, for financial gain).

Similarly, the business environment provides numerous decision-making situations in which one firm or individual is "playing" against another. For example, an oil company bidding for exploration rights to a tract of land is, in a sense, playing a game against other oil companies bidding for the tract. When an airline lowers its fare on a particular route in order to capture a greater market share, it is playing a game against the other carriers serving that route.

Game theory can be used to determine the optimal decision in the face of other decision making players. In game theory, the payoff is based on the action taken by competing individuals who are also seeking to maximize their return. In decision theory, however, an individual (player) makes a decision and receives a payoff based on the outcome of a noncompetitive random event (the state of nature). You can therefore view decision theory as a special case of game theory in which the decision maker is playing against a single disinterested party (nature).

As shown in Table 8.18, games can be classified in a number of ways—by the number of players, the total return to all players, or the sequence of moves, to name a few.

TABLE 8.18   CLASSIFICATION OF GAMES

Classification	Description	Example
Number of Players		
Two player	Two competitors	Chess
Multiplayer	More than two competitors	Poker
Total Return		
Zero sum	The amount won by all players equals the amount lost by all players.	Poker among friends
Nonzero sum	The amount won by all players does not equal the amount lost by all players.	Poker in a casino; the "house" takes a percentage of each pot
Sequence of Moves		
Sequential	Each player gets a turn in a given sequence.	*Monopoly*
Simultaneous	All players make their decisions simultaneously.	Paper, rock, scissors

While game theory is an extensive topic, here we focus solely on two-person, zero-sum games in which all decisions are made simultaneously. The situation faced by IGA Supermarket can be modeled by such a game.

IGA SUPERMARKET

Iga.daa
Iga.lpp
Iga.xls

The town of Gold Beach, Oregon, is served by two supermarkets—IGA and Sentry. In a given week, the market share of the two supermarkets can be influenced by their advertising policies. In particular, the manager of each supermarket must decide weekly which area of operations to discount heavily and emphasize in the store's newspaper flyer. Both supermarkets have three areas of operation in common: meats, produce, and groceries. Sentry, however, has a fourth—an in-store bakery.

The weekly percentage gain to IGA in market share as a function of advertising emphasis of each store is indicated by the following payoff table (Table 8.19). Here it is assumed that a gain in market share to IGA will result in the equivalent loss in market share to Sentry, and vice versa.

TABLE 8.19   PERCENTAGE CHANGE IN IGA'S MARKET SHARE AS A FUNCTION OF ADVERTISING EMPHASIS

| | | Sentry's Emphasis | | | |
		Meat	Produce	Groceries	Bakery
IGA's Emphasis	Meat	2	2	−8	6
	Produce	−2	0	6	−4
	Groceries	2	−7	1	−3

Since the IGA manager does not know which operation Sentry will emphasize each week, she wishes to determine an optimal advertising strategy that will maximize IGA's expected change in market share *regardless* of Sentry's action.

SOLUTION

The IGA manager should vary the weekly advertising emphasis; otherwise the Sentry manager will always be able to select an advertising emphasis that ensures a loss of market share for IGA. Hence, the optimal strategy for the IGA manager is to change her advertising emphasis randomly. But what proportion of the time should the emphasis be on meat or produce or groceries?

Let us define:

$X1$ = the probability IGA's advertising focus is on meat

$X2$ = the probability IGA's advertising focus is on produce

$X3$ = the probability IGA's advertising focus is on groceries

The manager at IGA wants to maximize the store's expected change in market share, regardless of Sentry's advertising focus. This expected change, which we denote by V, is known as the *value* of the game.

Let us see what restrictions are placed on V. If Sentry's advertising focus is on meat, then the expected change in IGA's market share is expressed as $2X1 − 2X2 + 2X3$. This expected change must be at least V, since V represents IGA's change in market share regardless of Sentry's action. Thus, $2X1 − 2X2 + 2X3 \geq V$.

By using similar reasoning for Sentry's advertising emphasis on produce, groceries, and bakery, we arrive at the following conditional relationships:

Sentry's Advertising Emphasis	**Relationship**
Meat	$2X1 − 2X2 + 2X3 \geq V$
Produce	$2X1 \qquad − 7X3 \geq V$
Groceries	$−8X1 + 6X2 + X3 \geq V$
Bakery	$6X1 − 4X2 − 3X3 \geq V$

Because the sum of the probabilities of IGA's advertising focus must equal 1, we also know that $X1 + X2 + X3 = 1$. These conditions result in the following linear programming model, which IGA can use to determine its optimal advertising strategy:

$$\text{MAX} \qquad\qquad V$$
$$\text{ST}$$
$$2X1 - 2X2 + 2X3 - V \geq 0$$
$$2X1 \qquad - 7X3 - V \geq 0$$
$$-8X1 + 6X2 + X3 - V \geq 0$$
$$6X1 - 4X2 - 3X3 - V \geq 0$$
$$X1 + X2 + X3 \qquad = 1$$
$$X1, X2, X3 \geq 0, V \text{ unrestricted}$$

Solving this model using WINQSB gives the following solution X1 = .3889, X2 = .5000, X3 = .1111, and V = 0. Thus, IGA should focus its advertising on meat about 39% of the time, on produce 50% of the time, and on groceries about 11% of the time.

The average change in IGA's market share using this strategy is 0%, implying that, in the long run, the market shares of the two supermarkets will not change. When the value of a game is 0, it is known as a *fair game*.

Had the value of the game not been zero, then, on the average, each week the market share would change by that value. If this trend continued, at some point, the estimated percentage changes given in Table 8.17 would cease to be valid.

THE OPTIMAL STRATEGY FOR SENTRY MARKET

From Sentry's perspective, the model can be formulated by letting

Y1 = the probability Sentry's advertising focus is on meat
Y2 = the probability Sentry's advertising focus is on produce
Y3 = the probability Sentry's advertising focus is on groceries
Y4 = the probability Sentry's advertising focus is on bakery

Sentry also wishes to maximize its expected change in market share regardless of IGA's advertising focus. Since IGA's "gain" is Sentry's loss, this is equivalent to maximizing −V. Because the numbers in Table 8.19 are expressed as "gains" in market share to IGA, negatives of these numbers are the "gains" in market share for Sentry. Thus, −2Y1 − 2Y2 + 8Y3 − 6Y4 represents the expected gain in market share to Sentry if IGA focuses its advertising on meat.

Using the reasoning developed for the IGA model, we see that the following conditional relationships hold for the Sentry model:

IGA's Advertising Emphasis	Relationship
Meat	−2Y1 − 2Y2 + 8Y3 − 6Y4 ≥ −V
Produce	2Y1 − 6Y3 + 4Y4 ≥ −V
Groceries	−2Y1 + 7Y2 − Y3 + 3Y4 ≥ −V

Note that maximizing −V is equivalent to minimizing V. Multiplying the above expressions by −1 (allowing us to use the original numbers in Table 8.19), we can use the following linear programming model[4] to solve for Sentry's optimal advertising strategy:

$$\text{MIN} \qquad\qquad V$$
$$\text{ST}$$
$$2Y1 + 2Y2 - 8Y3 + 6Y4 - V \leq 0$$
$$-2Y1 \qquad + 6Y3 - 4Y4 - V \leq 0$$
$$2Y1 - 7Y2 + Y3 - 3Y4 - V \leq 0$$
$$Y1 + Y2 + Y3 + Y4 \qquad = 1$$
$$Y1, Y2, Y3, Y4 \geq 0, V \text{ unrestricted}$$

[4]This problem is known as the *dual* of the problem faced by IGA. Duality in linear programming is discussed in Supplement CD2 on the accompanying CD-ROM.

Solving this model using Excel or WINQSB indicates that Sentry's advertising focus should be on meat 60% of the time, on produce 20% of the time, and on groceries 20% of the time. Sentry should never focus its advertising on the bakery.

The Decision Analysis module of WINQSB has the ability to solve two-person zero-sum models without having to set them up as linear programs. Figure 8.14 gives the output from this module for the IGA Supermarket model.

Zero-sum Game Analysis for IGA Supermarket

08-25-1998	Player	Strategy	Dominance	Elimination Sequence
1	1	Meat	Not Dominated	
2	1	Produce	Not Dominated	
3	1	Groceries	Not Dominated	
4	2	Meat	Not Dominated	
5	2	Produce	Not Dominated	
6	2	Groceries	Not Dominated	
7	2	Bakery	Not Dominated	
	Player	Strategy	Optimal Probability	
1	1	Meat	0.3889	
2	1	Produce	0.5000	
3	1	Groceries	0.1111	
1	2	Meat	0.6000	
2	2	Produce	0.2000	
3	2	Groceries	0.2000	
4	2	Bakery	0	
	Expected	Payoff	for Player 1=	0

FIGURE 8.14   Zero-sum Game Analysis for IGA Supermarket

We would be remiss if we did not point out that using changes to market share as the decision criterion may not be appropriate. A business typically wishes to maximize its long-term weekly profit rather than its market share. If the cost structures for the two supermarkets are similar, however, it is probably not unreasonable to assume that a change in a store's market share is directly proportional to a change in its profitability.

8.9   SUMMARY

Decision analysis is useful for making decisions that have major profit or cost implications. Payoff tables, in which rows correspond to the decision alternatives and columns correspond to states of nature, are useful for analyzing problems that concern a single decision.

When probability information regarding the states of nature is not available, maximax, maximin, minimax regret, and principle of insufficient reason criteria can be used. The choice of criterion is a function of the decision maker's attitude. When probability information for the states of nature is available, the optimal decision can be determined using an expected payoff or expected regret approach.

Bayes' Theorem can be used to revise the probabilities for the states of nature based on additional experimentation. Using this information, the decision maker can determine the expected value of sample or indicator information. The expected value of perfect information provides an upper limit on the expected value of sample information.

For problems that are too complex to fit into the form of a payoff table, a decision tree approach can be utilized. Utility theory provides a rational basis for human behavior and to make optimal decisions incorporating risk attitudes. Game theory is an approach used for decision situations involving competitive play. The optimal strategy for a two-person zero-sum game can be determined using a linear programming approach.

$\mathcal{N}$OTATIONAL SUMMARY

$$Di = \text{decision alternative } i$$
$$EV(Di) = \text{expected value of decision alternative } i$$
$$EVPI = \text{expected value of perfect information}$$
$$EREV = \text{expected return without additional information}$$
$$ERPI = \text{expected return with perfect information}$$
$$ERSI = \text{expected return with sample information}$$
$$EVSI = \text{expected value of sample information}$$
$$P(A_i|B) = \text{conditional probability of } A_i \text{ given } B$$
$$Sj = \text{state of nature } j$$
$$U(V) = \text{utility of decision } V$$
$$V = \text{outcome of a particular decision or value of a game}$$

APPENDIX 8.1

Using WINQSB to Solve Decision Problems

WINQSB can be used to solve decision problems involving payoff tables or decision trees, or solve for the optimal solution to two person zero sum games. Exhibit 8.1 is the initial screen that we get when we open the Decision Analysis module of WINQSB.

EXHIBIT 8.1

On this screen we highlight the type of problem we wish to solve and name the problem. Additional informatioin is requested depending on the problem type we wish to solve. For example, in the above screen we indicated that we wished to solve a payoff table analysis and therefore WINQSB requests information on the number of states of nature and the number of decision alternatives. If we had indicated that we wished to solve a decision tree problem we would have been prompted for the number of nodes/events that make up the tree.

Payoff Table Analysis

After the initial information is given, we are next presented with a new screen requesting the necessary additional information in a spreadsheet type format. For example, the screen for the Tom Brown investment problem is shown in Exhibit 8.2.

Decision \ State	large rise	small rise	no change	small fall	large fall
Prior Probability	0.20	0.30	0.30	0.10	0.10
gold	-100	100	200	300	0
bond	250	200	150	-100	-150
stock	500	250	100	-200	-600
C/D	60	60	60	60	60

EXHIBIT 8.2

Once the additional information necessary for solving the problem has been entered, we solve the problem by selecting "Solve the Problem" from the "Solve and Analyze" option on the menu bar. This gives the screen in Exhibit 8.3.

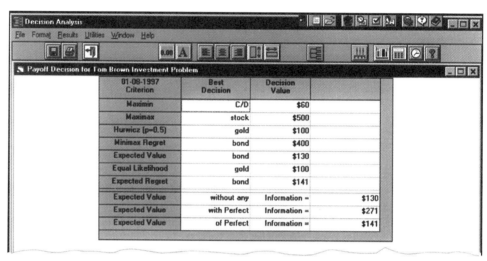

01-08-1997 Criterion	Best Decision	Decision Value	
Maximin	C/D	$60	
Maximax	stock	$500	
Hurwicz (p=0.5)	gold	$100	
Minimax Regret	bond	$400	
Expected Value	bond	$130	
Equal Likelihood	gold	$100	
Expected Regret	bond	$141	
Expected Value	without any	Information =	$130
Expected Value	with Perfect	Information =	$271
Expected Value	of Perfect	Information =	$141

EXHIBIT 8.3

WINQSB can also generate a decision tree such as that shown in Exhibit 8.4.

Decision Tree Analysis

To input data for a decision tree in WINQSB, we must specify the number of nodes (including the end points) and indicate for each node whether it is a decision or chance node; its preceding node number; and the profit, loss, or probability associated with it. By selecting "Draw the Decision Tree" from the "Solve and Analyze" option on the menu bar, we can generate decision tree output such as that given in Section 8.6.

Game Theory

To input data for a game theory problem in WINQSB, we specify the payoffs from the strategy combinations of Player 1 and Player 2. For example, Exhibit 8.5 gives the data input for the IGA Supermarket problem discussed in Section 8.8. The different advertising strategies for IGA and Sentry were entered by selecting "Player 1 Strategy Name" and "Player 2 Strategy Name" from the "Edit" option on the menu bar. The solution given in that section was attained by selecting "Solve the Problem" from the "Solve and Analyze" option on the menu bar.

EXHIBIT 8.4

EXHIBIT 8.5

PROBLEMS

1. The Campus Bookstore at East Tennessee State University must decide how many economics textbooks to order for the next semester's class. The bookstore believes that either seven, eight, nine, or ten sections of the course will be offered next semester; each section contains 40 students. The publisher is offering bookstores a discount if they place their orders early. If the bookstore orders too few texts and runs out, the publisher will air express additional books at the bookstore's expense. If it orders too many texts, the store can return unsold texts to the publisher for a partial credit. The bookstore is considering ordering either 280, 320, 360, or 400 texts in order to get the discount. Taking into account the discounts, air express expenses, and credits for returned texts, the bookstore manager estimates the following resulting profits.

Number of Textbooks to Order	Number of Introductory Economics Classes Offered			
	7	8	9	10
280	$2,800	$2,720	$2,640	$2,480
320	$2,600	$3,200	$3,040	$2,880
360	$2,400	$3,000	$3,600	$3,440
400	$2,200	$2,800	$3,400	$4,000

a. What is the optimal decision if the bookstore manager uses the maximax criterion?

b. What is the optimal decision if the bookstore manager uses the maximin criterion?

c. What is the optimal decision if the bookstore manager uses the minimax regret criterion?

d. What is the optimal decision if the bookstore manager uses the principle of insufficient reason criterion?

2. Consider the data given in Problem 1 for the Campus Bookstore at East Tennessee State University. Based on conversations held with the chair of the economics department, suppose the bookstore manager believes that the following probabilities hold:

$$P(7 \text{ classes offered}) = .10$$
$$P(8 \text{ classes offered}) = .30$$
$$P(9 \text{ classes offered}) = .40$$
$$P(10 \text{ classes offered}) = .20$$

a. Using the expected value criterion, determine how many economics books the bookstore manager should purchase in order to maximize the store's expected profit. Do you think the expected value criterion is appropriate for this problem?

b. Based on the probabilities given in part (a), determine the expected value of perfect information. Interpret its meaning.

3. National Foods has developed a new sports beverage it would like to advertise on Super Bowl Sunday. National's advertising agency can purchase either one, two, or three 30-second commercials advertising the drink and estimates that the return will be based on Super Bowl viewership. Viewership, in turn, is based on fans' perception of whether the game is "dull," "average," "above average," or "exciting."

   National Foods' ad agency has constructed the following payoff table giving its estimate of the expected profit resulting from purchasing one, two, or three advertising spots. (Another possible decision is for National Foods not to advertise at all during the Super Bowl.) The states of nature correspond to the game being "dull," "average," "above average," or "exciting."

Number of 30-Second Commercials Purchased	Perceived Game Excitement			
	Dull	Average	Above Average	Exciting
One commercial	$−200,000	$300,000	$700,000	$1,300,000
Two commercial	$−500,000	$600,000	$1,200,000	$1,800,000
Three commercial	$−900,000	$500,000	$1,300,000	$2,200,000

   a. What is the optimal decision if the National Foods advertising manager is optimistic?

   b. What is the optimal decision if the National Foods advertising manager is pessimistic?

   c. What is the optimal decision if the National Foods advertising manager wishes to minimize the firm's maximum regret?

4. Consider the data given in Problem 3 for National Foods. Based on past Super Bowl games, suppose the decision maker believes that the following probabilities hold for the states of nature:

$$P(\text{Dull Game}) = .20$$
$$P(\text{Average Game}) = .40$$
$$P(\text{Above-Average Game}) = .30$$
$$P(\text{Exciting Game}) = .10$$

   a. Using the expected value criterion, determine how many commercials National Foods should purchase.

   b. Based on the probabilities given here, determine the expected value of perfect information.

5. Consider the data given in Problems 3 and 4 for National Foods. The firm can hire the noted sport's pundit Jim Worden to give his opinion as to whether or not the Super Bowl game will be interesting. Suppose the following probabilities hold for Jim's predictions:

$$P(\text{Jim predicts game will be interesting}|\text{game is dull}) = .15$$
$$P(\text{Jim predicts game will be interesting}|\text{game is average}) = .25$$
$$P(\text{Jim predicts game will be interesting}|\text{game is above average}) = .50$$
$$P(\text{Jim predicts game will be interesting}|\text{game is exciting}) = .80$$
$$P(\text{Jim predicts game will not be interesting}|\text{game is actually dull}) = .85$$
$$P(\text{Jim predicts game will not be interesting}|\text{game is average}) = .75$$
$$P(\text{Jim predicts game will not be interesting}|\text{game is above average}) = .50$$
$$P(\text{Jim predicts game will not be interesting}|\text{game is exciting}) = .20$$

   a. If Jim predicts the game will be interesting, what is the probability the game will be dull?

   b. What is National's optimal strategy if Jim predicts the game will be i) interesting or ii) not interesting?

   c. What is the expected value of Jim's information?

6. Jeffrey William Company is considering introducing a new line of Christmas tree ornaments that glow in the dark and play melodies. If it introduces the product, it will back it up with a $100,000 advertising campaign using the slogan "Let your tree sing out in joy." The company estimates that sales will be a function of the economy and demand will be for either 10,000, 50,000, or 100,000 cases. Each case nets the company $24 and costs $18 to produce (not including the expense of the advertising campaign). Because the ornaments will be produced in a factory in Asia, the firm must order in multiples of 40,000 cases. Any unsold cases can be sold to a liquidator for $15 per case. If the company introduces the product and demand for the ornaments exceeds availability, management estimates it will suffer a goodwill loss of $1 for each case the company is short.

   a. Determine the payoff table for this problem.

   b. If the company president wishes to minimize the firm's maximum regret, what decision will she make regarding the ornaments?

   c. Suppose demand for 100,000 ornaments is twice as likely as demand for 10,000 ornaments, and demand for 50,000 ornaments is three times as likely as demand for 100,000 ornaments. What decision should the company make using the expected value criterion?

   d. Suppose the company can conduct a marketing survey to get a better idea of the demand for the ornaments. What is the most the company should pay for such a survey?

7. Southern Homes is a home builder located in a suburb of Atlanta. The company must decide whether to leave its model homes unfurnished, furnish them with minimal accessories, or completely furnish them using a custom decorator. The new-home market is generally quite profitable, but Southern is suffering cash-flow problems. The following table gives the expected profit per lot for Southern Homes based on how Southern furnishes its model homes and the overall demand for housing in the Atlanta market:

| Model Furnishing | Housing Market in Atlanta | | | |
	Weak	Moderate	Strong	Very Strong
Unfurnished	−$1,500	$1,000	$2,000	$3,000
Minimal Accessories	−$4,000	$ 500	$3,500	$6,000
Custom Decorated	−$7,000	$1,500	$2,500	$9,500

a. If Southern management is conservative, how should it decorate the model homes?

b. If Southern believes that each state of nature is equally likely, how should it decorate the model homes? What approach did you use?

8. Consider the data given in Problem 7 for Southern Homes. Although Southern management believes that each state of nature is equally likely, it is also considering hiring an economic forecaster to improve the probability estimates for the states of nature. The forecaster will predict whether there will be an above-average, average, or below-average rise in the GNP for the upcoming year. Based on past experience, the following conditional probabilities are believed to hold for the forecaster's predictions:

P(above average rise|Weak Housing Market) = .1
P(above average rise|Moderate Housing Market) = .3
P(above average rise|Strong Housing Market) = .6
P(above average rise|Very Strong Housing Market) = .9

P(average rise|Weak Housing Market) = .3
P(average rise|Moderate Housing Market) = .4
P(average rise|Strong Housing Market) = .2
P(average rise|Very Strong Housing Market) = .1

P(below average rise|Weak Housing Market) = .6
P(below average rise|Moderate Housing Market) = .3
P(below average rise|Strong Housing Market) = .2
P(below average rise|Very Strong Housing Market) = 0

a. How should Southern decorate the homes if the forecaster predicts: (i) an above-average rise in GNP? (ii) an average rise in GNP? (iii) a below-average rise in GNP?

b. What is the expected value of the forecaster's information?

c. What is the efficiency of the forecaster's information?

d. The data for this problem were constructed to illustrate the concept of the Bayesian decision process. Realistically, do you feel that GNP is a good indicator for housing sales in Atlanta? List some other indicators that might yield a higher efficiency.

9. TV Town must decide how many, if any, new Panasony 50-inch television sets to order for next month. The sets cost TV Town $1850 each and sell for $2450 each. Because Panasony is coming out with a new line of big-screen television sets in a month, any sets not sold during the month will have to be marked down to 50% of the normal retail price to be sold at the TV Town Clearance Center. TV Town estimates that if it does not have enough television sets on hand to satisfy demand, it will suffer a goodwill loss of $150 for each customer who cannot get a set. TV Town management feels that the maximum customer demand over the next month will be for three big-screen sets. If you define the states of nature to correspond to the number of sets demanded by customers, and the decision alternatives to the number of sets ordered, determine the payoff table for TV Town.

10. Consider the data given in Problem 9 for TV Town. Suppose the manager of TV Town estimates customer demand for next month as follows:

$$P(\text{demand} = 0 \text{ sets}) = .20$$
$$P(\text{demand} = 1 \text{ set}) = .30$$
$$P(\text{demand} = 2 \text{ sets}) = .30$$
$$P(\text{demand} = 3 \text{ sets}) = .20$$

   a. How many Panasony big-screen television sets should TV Town order?
   b. The manager of TV Town is considering conducting a telephone survey of 30 randomly selected customers. The survey will determine whether at least one of the 30 is likely to buy a big-screen set within the next month. What is the maximum amount TV Town should pay for the telephone survey?

11. Consider the data given in Problems 9 and 10 for TV Town. Suppose the manager of TV Town believes that the following conditional probabilities hold for the telephone survey being conducted on 30 randomly selected customers:

$$P(\text{At Least One Survey Customer Likely to Buy}|\text{Demand} = 0) = .1$$
$$P(\text{At Least One Survey Customer Likely to Buy}|\text{Demand} = 1) = .2$$
$$P(\text{At Least One Survey Customer Likely to Buy}|\text{Demand} = 2) = .4$$
$$P(\text{At Least One Survey Customer Likely to Buy}|\text{Demand} = 3) = .7$$

   a. If TV Town conducts the survey, what is the optimal strategy for ordering the Panasony big-screen television sets?
   b. What is the most amount of money TV Town should pay for this telephone survey?
   c. What is the efficiency of the telephone survey?
   d. Discuss in general terms how the results of the survey could be modified to result in improved efficiency.

12. Roney Construction Company is considering purchasing a home in the historic district of Lexington, Massachusetts, for restoration. The cost of the home is $150,000, and Roney believes that, after restoration, the home can be sold for $290,000. Roney will pay $2000 per month in finance charges until the project is completed.

   The company's architect has developed two sets of plans for the restoration. Plan A does not require changes to the front facade. Under this plan, the renovation will cost $120,000 and take three months to complete. Plan B does involve changes in the front facade of the building. Under this plan, Roney believes that it can do the restoration work in four months, at a cost of $80,000.

   Because Plan B changes the exterior of the house, it must be approved by the town's Historic Commission. The approval process takes two months and will cost $10,000. If Roney decides on Plan B, it can play it safe and wait to begin construction until after the plan has been approved by the Historic Commission. Alternatively, it can take a chance and begin construction immediately in the hopes that the commission will approve the plan.

   If the Historic Commission denies Plan B, Roney will have to resort to Plan A for the renovation work. If Roney begins construction under Plan B and the Historic Commission denies the plan, the company estimates that doing the construction work under Plan A will cost $140,000 and the project will take five additional months to complete.

   Roney estimates that there is a 40% chance that the Historic Commission will approve Plan B. However, if the firm were to contribute $6000 to the mayor's reelection campaign, Roney believes the chances for approval would increase to 50%. Determine an optimal strategy for the Roney Construction Company.

13. Steve Greene is considering purchasing fire insurance for his home. According to statistics for Steve's county, Steve estimates the damage from fire to his home in a given year is as follows:

Amount of Damage	Probability
0	.975
$10,000	.010
$20,000	.008
$30,000	.004
$50,000	.002
$100,000	.001

a. If Steve is risk neutral, how much should he be willing to pay for the fire insurance?

b. Suppose Steve's utility values are as follows:

	Amount of Loss ($1000s)						
	100	50	30	20	10	1	0
Utility	0	.65	.75	.8	.95	.995	1

What is the expected utility corresponding to fire damage?

c. Determine approximately how much Steve would be willing to pay for the fire insurance.

14. Wednesday Afternoon is a chain of stores that specialize in selling close-out merchandise. The firm has the opportunity to acquire either three, six, nine, or twelve store leases from the bankrupt In Focus chain. Each lease runs five years, and the profitability of these leases depends on the economy over this time period. The economists at Wednesday Afternoon believe that the average growth rate in GNP will be either 2, 3, 4, 5, or 6% per annum during the five-year period, with probabilities .1, .2, .2, .4, and .1, respectively. The following tables give the expected return to Wednesday Afternoon over the next five years (in $100,000s) as well as the utility values for these amounts.

	Average Annual Growth in GNP				
Number of Leases Acquired	2%	3%	4%	5%	6%
3	7	6	6	5	3
6	2	6	8	7	4
9	1	5	7	8	6
12	1	4	7	8	9

	Payoff (in $100,000s)								
	1	2	3	4	5	6	7	8	9
Utility	0	.05	.15	.30	.50	.65	.75	.90	1.0

Determine how many leases the company should acquire if its objective is to:

a. Maximize expected profit over the next five years.

b. Maximize expected utility over the next five years.

15. Craig Computer Company (CCC) manufactures supercomputers based on parallel processing technology. Next month the firm has scheduled demonstrations for its new Model 4365 with five potential customers. This model sells for $725,000, and CCC believes that the probability of each customer purchasing a computer is 30%. The company cannot completely shut down its assembly line over the next month and plans to manufacture at least one computer; it could manufacture as many as four. Production costs for the month are as follows:

Number of Computers Built	Total Production Costs
1	$ 800,000
2	$1,400,000
3	$1,800,000
4	$2,400,000

Any computers Craig manufactures during a given month but does not sell are exported overseas. Craig receives $500,000 for these computers and can sell as many as it is willing to export. If Craig sells more computers than it manufactures in a month, the customer must wait for delivery. In this case, Craig estimates it loses a total of $30,000 on the sale.

   a. Determine the payoff table for this problem.

   b. What decision alternatives are undominated?

   c. Determine the optimal strategy using the expected value criterion. (Hint: *The binomial distribution can be used to determine the probabilities for the states of nature.*)

16. The Post Office uses two freight carriers, Federal Parcel and Emery Express, to carry mail between New York and Boston. Federal Parcel has 30% of this business, and Emery Express has 70%. The Post Office is interested in signing an exclusive contract with one of the carriers to handle the mail between the cities. Federal Parcel is considering bidding either $0.02, $0.04, or $0.06 per ounce as the fee charged the Post Office. Emery Express is considering bidding either $0.02, $0.05, or $0.06 per ounce as the fee charged the Post Office. The carrier who submits the lower bid will get the contract; if both bids are the same, the Post Office will use the carriers to carry an equal amount of mail.

    The following table describes the change in market share that Federal Parcel will experience as a function of the amount that the two carriers bid.

		Emery Express's Bid		
		$.02	$.05	$.06
	$.02	+20%	+70%	+70%
Federal Parcel's Bid	$.04	−30%	+70%	+70%
	$.06	−30%	−30%	+20%

   a. What is Federal Parcel's optimal strategy if it wishes to maximize its expected change in market share?

   b. Suppose that Federal Parcel estimates that the total number of pounds the Post Office will be sending between the two cities this year will be 1.5 million pounds. Federal Parcel estimates that serving this route will cost it a fixed amount of $20,000 plus $0.01 per ounce. If Emery Express is believed to be equally likely to bid $0.02, $0.05, or $0.06 per pound, what should Federal Parcel's bid be in order to maximize its expected profit?

17. Little Trykes is considering offering a toy scooter that it will sell for $20 each. The company has two production options:

   a. Manufacture the scooters in their existing facilities

   b. Import the scooters from overseas

Little Trykes believes that the demand for the scooters will be between 100 and 300 units per day and has decided to model the situation as a decision analysis problem with three states of nature: demand = 100 units per day; demand = 200 units per day; and demand = 300 units per day. This was done because the company will either manufacture or import the units in lot sizes that are multiples of 100. The following table gives the per unit costs for the two production options.

	Amount Supplied Per Day		
Option	100	200	300
Use Existing Facilities	$18	$14	$10
Import	$15	$13	$ 9

If the company decides to import the scooters, there is a 30% chance that a tariff of $2 per unit will be imposed on the scooters. The company will learn whether there is a tariff only after it has made its decision on the source of its scooter production. The amount produced or imported will correspond to daily demand. The probability distribution for daily demand with no advertising versus spending $1000 a day on advertising is as follows:

Daily Demand	Probability with No Advertising	Probability with Spending $1000 a Day for Advertising
100	.3	.1
200	.5	.2
300	.2	.7

Determine Little Trykes's optimal course of action regarding manufacturing, importing, and advertising the scooters.

18. John Reynolds is planning to lease a new car. The car dealership offers three different two-year leasing plans:

Plan	Fixed Monthly Cost	Incremental Cost Per Mile
A	$200	$.098 per mile
B	$300	$.062 for first 5000 miles; $.052 thereafter
C	$180	first 6000 free; $.14 per mile thereafter

John estimates that he will drive between 20,000 and 36,000 miles during the two years, with the following probabilities:

$$P(\text{driving } 20{,}000) = .1$$
$$P(\text{driving } 24{,}000) = .2$$
$$P(\text{driving } 28{,}000) = .2$$
$$P(\text{driving } 32{,}000) = .3$$
$$P(\text{driving } 36{,}000) = .2$$

a. Construct a payoff table showing the costs to John of leasing the car under the three plans.

b. If John were optimistic, which plan would he choose?

c. If John bases his decision on the expected value criterion, which leasing plan would he choose?

19. Brenton Software Publishing Company (BSP) offers its sales representatives a choice of three compensation plans based on how many universities adopt Brenton's new statistical software package. The three plans are as follows:

Plan 1: A fixed salary of $2000 per month.

Plan 2: A fixed salary of $1000 per month plus a commission of $300 for each university that adopts the statistical package.

Plan 3: A commission of $700 for each university that adopts the statistical package.

Ted Benson is a new sales representative for BSP and must decide which compensation plan to accept. Experienced sales reps have told him that he can expect up to six universities per month to adopt the software. Ted is free to change his compensation plan at the beginning of any month.

a. Construct a payoff table showing Ted's monthly compensation as a function of the compensation plan he chooses and the monthly adoptions.

b. Which plan should Ted choose if he uses the minimax regret criterion?

c. Suppose Ted believes that the following probabilities hold regarding monthly adoptions for his first month with the firm:

$$P(0 \text{ adoptions}) = .10$$
$$P(1 \text{ adoption}) = .15$$
$$P(2 \text{ adoptions}) = .25$$
$$P(3 \text{ adoptions}) = .20$$
$$P(4 \text{ adoptions}) = .15$$
$$P(5 \text{ adoptions}) = .10$$
$$P(6 \text{ adoptions}) = .05$$

On the basis of these data, which compensation plan should Ted select for the upcoming month?

20. Midge Wallack has promised her parents that she will visit them over the summer. The normal round-trip airfare is $625, but the airline serving her parents' hometown is offering a reduced round-trip airfare of $300. The reduced fare tickets must be purchased within the next five days and are nonrefundable. Travel dates may be changed at a cost of $50 if the airline has space available.

Midge would really like to take advantage of the low airfare, but since summer is still four months away, she is concerned that she may not be able to get away from her job on the travel dates she selects. She estimates that there is a 30% chance that she will not encounter this difficulty. If she has to change her travel dates, Midge estimates there is a 50% chance that the airline will have space available. If space is not available, Midge will have to buy an additional full-fare ticket.

Another option is for Midge to wait two months to buy the tickets. By that time she will know exactly when she can take summer vacation. Midge estimates that there is a 60% chance that the airline will offer a reduced fare of $350 at that time and a 40% chance that the fare will be $625. Use a decision tree to represent this problem and determine whether Midge should purchase the $300 discount ticket.

21. John Deere is making a special offer on its model 603 riding mower. If ordered prior to May 1, the mower will cost Adams Hardware $820; after May 1 the cost rises to $920. Adams sells the mowers for $1150 and it incurs $100 in sales expenses on each mower. Any mower left in inventory at the end of the summer can be sold at Adams's end-of-season clearance sale and will net the firm only $750. Adams expects to sell between one and three of these mowers this summer. Management estimates that the probability of selling one mower is twice the probability of selling two mowers, and the probability of selling three mowers is .40. Using the expected value criterion, determine how many mowers Adams should purchase prior to May 1.

22. In order to increase tax revenue, residents of the town of Rocky Bluffs, Arkansas, are considering legalizing casino gambling. An election will be held in November on this issue. At present, the town's principal hotel, The Bluffs, is scheduled to be sold at a sealed bid auction. Jack Phillips, a local real estate speculator, is interested in bidding on the property and is considering bidding either $1.2 million, $1.4 million, or $1.8 million.

Jack estimates that if he bids $1.2 million, he will have a 25% chance of buying the property; if he bids $1.4 million, he will have a 40% chance of buying the property; and if he bids $1.8 million, he will have an 80% chance of buying the property. If he is successful in buying the property, and the town approves legalized gambling, he estimates he will be able to sell the Bluffs hotel for $2.1 million. If the town defeats legalized gambling, Jack estimates that the Bluffs could be sold for $1.1 million. Based on current polling data published in the *Rocky Bluffs Gazette*, he believes there is a 55% chance the town will vote to legalize gambling.

Jack is considering conducting his own survey to gain some insights into voter attitudes toward gambling, prior to placing his bid for the property. The poll will cost $20,000 to conduct and will indicate whether or not the majority of people polled favor gambling. Jack believes that the following conditional probabilities hold for the survey:

P(a majority favor gambling|legalized gambling approved) = .90
P(a majority do not favor gambling|legalized gambling defeated) = .70

That is, if the voters will approve legalized gambling, Jack believes there is a .90 probability that the majority of people surveyed will favor gambling; and, if the voters will defeat legalized gambling, there is a .70 probability that the majority of people surveyed will not favor gambling. Draw a decision tree for this problem and determine Jack's optimal decision strategy.

23. Ultima Electronics has just had its ManFriday robot selected for listing in the Neiman Marcus Christmas catalog. The catalog price is $28,000 per robot; Ultima sells the robots to Neiman Marcus for $16,000 each.

The Neiman Marcus marketing department has advised Ultima that the demand for the robots will be for between one and four units. The production cost for manufacturing the robots is estimated as follows:

Number Produced	Total Manufacturing Cost
1	$24,000
2	$31,500
3	$38,000
4	$43,500

Any robots produced but not sold by Neiman Marcus can be sold by Ultima to an overseas distributor at a price of $6000 each. If the store places orders for more robots than the company has produced, Ultima has agreed to substitute a more expensive model that the company has in stock but that costs $20,000 per unit to produce.

a. Construct the payoff table for this problem.

b. What decision alternatives are dominated?

c. If Ultima management uses the principle of insufficient reason to determine the production decision, how many ManFriday robots should be produced?

d. If Ultima management uses the minimax regret criterion to determine the production decision, how many ManFriday robots should be produced?

e. Suppose the company believes that the probability of demand for one robot will be twice as great as the probability of demand for three robots and four times as great as the probability of demand for four robots. The probability of demand for two robots is estimated to be .30. Using the expected value criterion, determine how many ManFriday robots Ultima should produce.

f. What is the most Ultima should pay for a marketing survey that could improve the probability estimates for the robot's demand?

24. Consider the Bill Galen Development Company problem discussed in Section 8.6. Suppose the utility function for the company corresponding to a return of x is $1-((x-120,000)/(195,000))^2$.

a. Given this utility function, would you characterize the company as risk averse, risk loving, or risk neutral?

b. Determine the optimal strategy for the company using the expected utility criterion.

25. Two airlines serve the city of Medford, Oregon: United and Alaska. Both airlines offer one morning flight to San Francisco. The United flight currently departs at 8 A.M., while the Alaska flight departs at 8:30 A.M. At present, United has 60% of the Medford to San Francisco market, and Alaska has 40% of the market.

Each month the FAA gives both airlines the chance to modify their flight departure times. Because of system schedule restrictions, however, United will only consider flights that depart on the hour, whereas Alaska will only consider flights that depart on the half hour.

The United Airlines management science group believes that only departures at 7:00, 8:00, 9:00, or 10:00 A.M. are reasonable possibilities and that Alaska will only consider departures at 7:30, 8:30, 9:30, and 10:30 A.M. The United team estimates that the change in market share with Alaska Airlines for the upcoming month can be modeled as a game theory problem. Suppose the following table provides the expected change in market share to United:

		Alaska Airlines Departure Time			
		7:30 A.M.	8:30 A.M.	9:30 A.M.	10:30 A.M.
United	7:00 A.M.	+1%	−2%	−1%	+4%
Airlines	8:00 A.M.	−5%	0	+7%	+3%
Departure	9:00 A.M.	+4%	+4%	−3%	+6%
Time	10:00 A.M.	−3%	−2%	+5%	+3%

a. Explain intuitively why Alaska Airlines would never select the 10:30 A.M. time slot.

b. Determine United's optimal strategy for selecting the morning flight departure time if its objective is to maximize its expected market share for the upcoming month. What will be the resulting expected market share?

c. Suppose the management science group at United Airlines decides to model this problem as a decision analysis problem in which the following probabilities are believed to hold for Alaska Airlines' choice of departure time for the upcoming month:

P(Alaska Airlines Selects a 7:30 A.M. Departure Time)   = .30
P(Alaska Airlines Selects an 8:30 A.M. Departure Time) = .50
P(Alaska Airlines Selects a 9:30 A.M. Departure Time)   = .20
P(Alaska Airlines Selects a 10:30 A.M. Departure Time) = 0

If United Airlines' objective is to maximize its expected market share for the upcoming month, at what time should it schedule the departure? What is United's expected market share for the upcoming month under this strategy?

d. Comment on the difference in the approaches taken in parts (b) and (c). Which approach do you think is more realistic?

CASE 1: *Swan Valley Farms*

Swan Valley Farms produces dried apricots, which it sells to two cereal producers—Kellogg's and General Foods. Swan Valley forecasts that for the upcoming year Kellogg's will want to purchase either 10, 20, or 30 tons of dried apricots, and General Foods will want to purchase either 10, 20, 30, or 40 tons. Kellogg's and General Foods order independently of each other. The following probability distributions are believed to hold:

Kellogg's Demand	Probability	General Food's Demand	Probability
10 tons	.20	10 tons	.20
20 tons	.50	20 tons	.30
30 tons	.30	30 tons	.30
		40 tons	.20

Swan Valley is currently contracting with local farmers for delivery of apricots for drying. It takes approximately four pounds of apricots to produce one pound of dried apricots. Swan Valley can purchase apricots at $0.15 per pound; it costs an additional $0.02 to produce one pound of dried apricots.

Swan Valley's contract with Kellogg's and General Foods calls for purchase in units of 10 tons at a price of $1500 per ton plus delivery costs.

The process of drying apricots takes several weeks; therefore, Swan Valley must sign its contract with growers before it knows the exact amount that Kellogg's and General Foods

will be ordering. If Swan Valley dries more apricots than its two customers demand, it will sell the surplus dried apricots to a food wholesaler at a price of $1100 per ton, plus delivery. If Swan Valley produces fewer dried apricots than the two cereal manufacturers demand, it can purchase additional dried apricots from a competitor at a price of $1400 per ton.

Swan Valley is considering offering one of two new pricing plans. Under the first plan, Swan Valley will lower its selling price to $1400 a ton if the cereal company agrees to order four months in advance of delivery. This will enable Swan Valley to know how many apricots will be demanded by a customer prior to its having to contract with growers. The company believes that there is a 30% chance that Kellogg's will accept this offer and a 40% chance that General Foods will accept this offer.

Under the second plan, Swan Valley will lower the selling price to $1375 a ton if the cereal company agrees to order four months in advance of delivery. Swan Valley believes there is a 60% chance that Kellogg's will accept this plan and an 80% chance that General Foods will accept.

Prepare a business report to Henry Swan, owner of Swan Valley Farms, giving your recommendation as to which of the two pricing plans, if any, the firm should adopt. Include in your report a recommendation for the number of pounds of apricots Swan Valley should purchase from farmers and the expected profit the company will earn.

CASE 2: *Pharmgen Corporation*

Pharmgen Corporation has developed a new medication for the treatment of high blood pressure. Tests on laboratory animals have been promising, and the firm is ready to embark on human trials in order to gain approval from the Food and Drug Administration (FDA). The firm estimates that it will cost an additional $4 million to do the required testing. Although the firm has this amount of money available, if the product turns out to be unsuccessful, the company will be virtually wiped out.

If the tests prove successful, the firm believes that the amount it will earn on the drug will be a function of the number of competing drugs of this type that also gain approval. If no other drugs gain approval, the firm estimates it will earn $50 million in present worth profits on the drug. For every

other drug that gains approval, Pharmgen believes the expected present worth profit will drop by $10 million. Based on industry publications, four other firms are working on similar drugs. Pharmgen's management estimates that the probability that its drug will gain FDA approval is 40% but that each of its four competitors' drugs only has a 20% chance of FDA approval.

Wyler Laboratories, a larger drug firm has approached Pharmgen about acquiring the rights to the drug. Wyler is willing to pay Pharmgen $5 million for a half interest in the drug (and split any costs or profits from the drug with Pharmgen) or $8 million for the full rights to the drug. Pharmgen's management has used the indifference approach to determine the following utility values:

Expected Present Worth Profit or Loss (in Millions)	−4	3	8	10	15	20	25	30	40	50
Utility	0	.30	.40	.45	.50	.55	.65	.75	.85	1.0

Prepare a business report to Dr. Joseph Wolf, president of Pharmgen, detailing your recommendation regarding the development of this drug.

FORECASTING

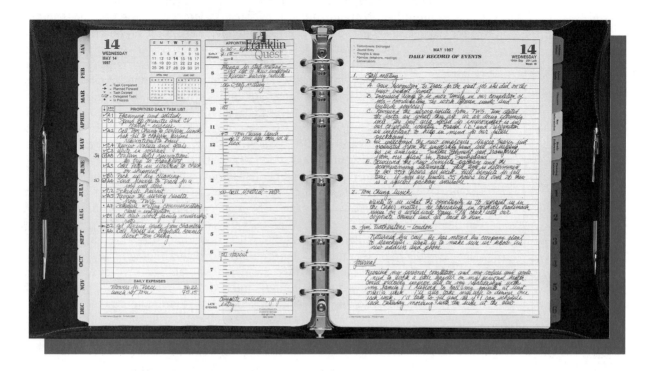

Franklin Quest is a manufacturer of pocket calendars and executive organizing systems. Since these systems are printed for a specific year, much of the firm's production has a limited shelf life. More than 80% of the retail sales' of the company's products occur from the middle of October through the middle of the following January. As a result, the firm's sales to distributors and national retail accounts are concentrated between August through November.

While Franklin Quest has been a leading manufacturer of such high-end products, due to a downturn in the economy and increased competition last year, the firm has found itself left with a substantial amount of unsold inventory. In order to plan production properly for the next calendar year, Franklin Quest management has proposed developing a system for forecasting retail demand for its products.

9.1 INTRODUCTION TO TIME SERIES FORECASTING

Forecasting is the process of predicting the future. It is an integral part of almost all business enterprises. Manufacturing firms forecast demand for their products in order to have the necessary manpower and raw materials to support production. Companies specializing in service operations forecast customer arrival patterns in an effort to maintain adequate staffing to serve customer needs. Security analysts forecast company revenues, profits, and debt ratios, as well as general trends in financial markets, in order to make investment recommendations. Numerous firms consider economic forecasts of indicators, such as housing starts and changes in the gross national profit, before deciding on capital investments.

Proper forecasting can result in reduced inventory costs, lower overall personnel costs, and increased customer satisfaction. By contrast, poor forecasting can result in decreased profitability or even outright collapse of the firm.

One way to perform a forecast is simply to venture an educated guess. An improvement upon guessing is to gather expert opinions from various sources and come to an overall consensus based on these opinions. Often, a past history of data values, known as a *time series*, is available and can be helpful in developing the forecast. For example, we may be able to predict future sales for a product by examining historic demands for that product, or we could forecast the customer arrival rate at a bank by examining how many customers actually arrived during similar time periods in prior weeks. In this chapter, we examine the use of such time series in performing forecasts.

COMPONENTS OF A TIME SERIES

A time series is comprised of one or more of the following four components: (1) long-term trend, (2) seasonal variation, (3) cyclical variation, and (4) random effects.

Long-Term Trend

A time series may be relatively stationary, or it may exhibit *trend* over time. Such trend may indicate that the time series is increasing or decreasing. A relatively new product might experience increasing demand over time, while demand for a mature product might be reasonably stationary or could even show a declining trend. Long-term trend in a time series is typically modeled as linear, quadratic, or exponential, but it can have some other functional form.

Seasonal Variation

A time series experiences *seasonal variation* if it is expected that, during certain time intervals, the time series increases or decreases due to calendar or climatic changes. For example, toy sales at Toys R Us typically are higher during the Christmas and Hanukkah season in December than in June; demand for bathing suits is higher during spring and summer than in fall or winter; and consumption of heating fuel is high in the winter and low in the summer months.

Seasonal variation is frequently tied to yearly cycles, but this need not be the case. A company that pays its bills at the beginning of each month shows seasonal variation in its bank balance; in this case, one "season" is the early part of each monthly cycle. At many grocery stores, shopping is typically higher on the weekends than during the middle of the week. In this case, one "season" is the weekend of a weekly cycle.

Cyclical Variation

In contrast to seasonal variation, a time series may experience *cyclical variation*, a temporary upturn or downturn that seems to follow no discernible pattern. Cyclical variation usually results from changes in economic conditions. The time series of demand for new cars typically has a cyclical component since such demand is linked to overall changes in the economy; sales of new cars are lower in recessionary periods than in nonrecessionary periods. But predicting when a recessionary period will occur is challenging, if not impossible.

Random Effects

Even if we were able to identify the trend, seasonal, and cyclical components of a time series correctly, it is still impossible to predict the exact value for some future time period because of the presence of a *random* component. For example, we might be able to measure fairly accurately the long-term trend, the seasonal variation, and the effects of cyclical components for sales of ice cream at a Baskin Robbins ice cream store. However, sales also differ simply because a few customers more or less choose to purchase ice cream on a day-to-day basis.

STEPS IN THE TIME SERIES FORECASTING PROCESS

The goal of a time series forecast is to identify those factors that *can* be predicted so that the forecast is as accurate as possible. This analysis can be thought of as a systematic approach involving the following steps:

Steps In The Time Series Forecasting Process
1. Hypothesize a form for the time series model
2. Select a forecasting technique
3. Prepare a forecast

Step 1: *Collect historic data, graph the data versus time to aid in hypothesizing a form for the time series model, and verify this hypothesis statistically.*

In this first step, we attempt to identify which of the time series components should be included in the model. One way to determine whether a time series exhibits trend, seasonal, or cyclical components is to plot a graph of data values over time. Based on this graph, a model for the time series can be hypothesized. Figures 9.1a–9.1d depict four situations of time series data plotted over time: (a) linear trend, (b) nonlinear trend, (c) trend and seasonality, and (d) a stationary pattern.

FIGURE 9.1a   Time Series with Linear Trend

FIGURE 9.1b   Time Series with Nonlinear Trend

c

FIGURE 9.1c   Time Series with Trend and Seasonality

d

FIGURE 9.1d   Stationary Time Series

Once a time series model has been hypothesized, it is important to test its validity statistically. In this chapter, we present several statistical tests that can be used to determine whether particular components of a time series are present.

Step 2: *Select an appropriate forecasting technique for the time series model and determine the values of its parameters.*

Once an appropriate model has been selected, a forecasting technique must be chosen to predict future values for the time series. These techniques may differ in the steps taken to perform the forecast or in the values of certain parameters that can be assigned at the decision maker's discretion.

Step 3: *Prepare a forecast using the selected forecasting technique.*

To perform a forecast, the appropriate data values must be substituted into the selected forecasting model. Key issues affecting the forecasted values include the number of past observations on which the forecast is based, and the initial forecast value used to begin the forecasting procedure.

9.2 $\mathcal{S}$TATIONARY FORECASTING MODELS

Perhaps the simplest time series forecasting model is one in which the mean value of the item being examined is assumed to be relatively constant, or *stationary*, over time. Since these time series do not exhibit any trend, seasonal, or cyclical components, the general form of such models can be expressed by:

Stationary Forecasting Model
$y_t = \beta_0 + \epsilon_t$

where: y_t = the value of the time series at time period t
β_0 = the unchanging mean value of the time series
ϵ_t = a random error term at time period t

The values of ϵ_t are assumed to be independent and to have a mean of 0. The independence assumption means that the value of the random error term at one time period has no effect on the value of the random error term at any other time period. In stationary models we assume that the error term has a mean value of 0 since the expected value of the time series at each period should be β_0. The purpose of the forecast is to determine a good estimate for the unknown value of β_0.

CHECKING THE ASSUMPTIONS—IS A STATIONARY MODEL APPROPRIATE?

We can use several forecasting methods to estimate β_0 in a stationary forecasting model. But before employing such methods, we should first determine whether or not a stationary model is, in fact, appropriate for our data. Obviously, if we get the results shown in Figures 9.1a–c when we plot the data, we should not expect a stationary model to reflect the true situation accurately.

Checking for Trend

One statistical technique commonly used to detect trend is to perform a regression analysis of the historical values of the time series versus the time period t. If linear trend exists over time, the time series can be represented by the following model:

$$y_t = \beta_0 + \beta_1 t + \epsilon_t$$

where the coefficient multiplying the time period t, β_1, is nonzero. If there were no linear trend, then $\beta_1 = 0$ and the model is that of a stationary time series. Thus, we can perform the following hypothesis test:

$$H_0: \beta_1 = 0 \text{ (no linear trend is present)}$$
$$H_A: \beta_1 \neq 0 \text{ (linear trend is present)}$$

This test is performed in almost all statistical and spreadsheet packages, including Excel and WINQSB. If we choose a significance level, α, which is the probability of falsely rejecting the null hypothesis (i.e., concluding that linear trend is present when it is not), all we need to do is compare the p-value for the test to α. (The p-value is usually found next to the t-value for the dependent variable (time period) on computer printouts.) If the p-value is greater than α, we will not reject H_0 and conclude that using a stationary model is acceptable.[1]

One difficulty with this approach is that we must assume that the random error terms, ϵ_t, are independently distributed normal random variables with a constant variance. If we suspect that at least *one* of these assumptions is not valid, nonparametric procedures, such as the Daniel's test (outlined in Appendix 9.2 on the accompanying CD-ROM) are preferred. Nonparametric tests generally are not as powerful as a parametric procedure such as regression analysis, however. Hence, in some cases, it may not be possible to detect trend in a time series when, in fact, such trend exists.

Checking for Seasonality Components

Autocorrelation is the measure of how the value at one time period affects the value at some subsequent time period. The correlation between time series values that are k periods apart is called autocorrelation of *lag k*. Generally, we check for autocorrelation between successive time periods (lag 1) and between time periods that correspond to possible seasonality (lag 7 for daily data; lag 12 for monthly data; lag 4 for quarterly data). Autocorrelation between successive periods is another indication that trend may be present in a time series, autocorrelation between time periods corresponding to seasons is a good indication of seasonality. In Appendix 9.3 on the accompanying CD-ROM, we present statistical procedures for determining whether or not autocorrelation exists for a given time series.

---

[1] Alternatively, if the computer package used does not print p-values, we would not reject H_0 if the absolute value of the t-statistic printed on the computer output did not exceed the critical value, $t_{\alpha/2}$, with $n - 2$ degrees of freedom (where n is the number of historical time periods).

Checking for Cyclical Components

As mentioned earlier, because cyclical components have no discernible pattern, they are often difficult to detect. Typically, cyclical components are identified solely by examining the graph of the time series.

MOVING AVERAGE METHODS FOR FORECASTING STATIONARY MODELS

If we conclude that a stationary model accurately reflects the time series data, we must choose a forecasting method appropriate for this model. Three of the simplest forecasting approaches for stationary models are the last period technique, the moving average method, and the weighted moving average method.

The Last Period Technique

Using the *last period technique*, our forecast for the next period of a stationary time series is simply the last observed value. Thus, given observed values for t time periods, y_1, y_2, . . . , y_t, using the last period technique, our forecasted value for time period t + 1, $\hat{y}_{t+1}$, is:

$$\hat{y}_{t+1} = y_t$$

The Moving Average Method

In the *moving average method*, the forecast for any time period is the average of the values for the immediately preceding n periods, where n is a value chosen by the modeler. For example, if we choose an n = 4 period moving average, the forecasted value for time period t + 1 is calculated by

$$\hat{y}_{t+1} = (y_t + y_{t-1} + y_{t-2} + y_{t-3})/4$$

By averaging over n periods, unusually high or low observed values will have a less radical effect on future predictions. Note that the last period technique is a special case of the moving average method, with n = 1.

The Weighted Moving Average Method

In the last period technique, all the weight of the forecast is placed on the most recent observed value of the time series. In the moving average method, the most recent observation is weighted equally with the previous n − 1 values. One might expect, however, that, although not all of the weight should be placed on the most recent observation, a forecast should reflect more heavily on more recent values.

One way to do this is by using a *weighted moving average technique*. In this procedure, the sum of the weights used must equal 1, and the weights given to observation values are nonincreasing with their age.[2] Thus, if w_i is the weight given to the ith previous observation, the w_i values should satisfy the following properties:

Properties Of Weights Used In Developing n Period Weighted Moving Average Forecasts

1. $\sum w_i = 1$
2. $w_1 \geq w_2 \geq w_3 \geq \ldots \geq w_n$

For example, a four-period weighted moving average technique might place a weight of .4 on the most recent value of the time series, .3 on the value at the previous time period, .2 on the value from two periods ago, and .1 on the value from three periods

[2]The simple moving average technique can be viewed as a special case of the weighted moving average technique, in which all weights equal 1/n.

ago. Then, the forecast for time period t + 1 using this four-period weighted moving average is determined by

$$\hat{y}_{t+1} = .4y_t + .3y_{t-1} + .2y_{t-2} + .1y_{t-3}$$

In the weighted moving average technique, both the number of periods, n, and the weights assigned to each period are chosen by the modeler.

FORECASTS FOR FUTURE TIME PERIODS

When we use a stationary model, our forecast for time period t + 1 is our forecast for all future time periods. The forecasts for these future periods are revised only when data from additional periods have been obtained.

To illustrate the concepts developed thus far for stationary models, consider the sales of YoHo brand of yo-yos at Galaxy Industries.

YOHO BRAND YO-YOS

Yoho.fcc
Yoho.xls

Galaxy Industries is interested in forecasting weekly demand for its YoHo brand yo-yos over the coming year so that it can properly allocate a budget for this division. Because YoHo yo-yos are a reasonably mature product, Galaxy believes that next year's demand for the yo-yos will be quite similar to the demand encountered this year; hence, the firm has decided to base its forecast on the past 52 weeks of demand. Weekly yo-yo demand (in boxes of 12) during the past 52 weeks is given in Table 9.1.

TABLE 9.1   WEEKLY YOHO YO-YO DEMAND

Week	Demand	Week	Demand	Week	Demand	Week	Demand
1	415	14	365	27	351	40	282
2	236	15	471	28	388	41	399
3	348	16	402	29	336	42	309
4	272	17	429	30	414	43	435
5	280	18	376	31	346	44	299
6	395	19	363	32	252	45	522
7	438	20	513	33	256	46	376
8	431	21	197	34	378	47	483
9	446	22	438	35	391	48	416
10	354	23	557	36	217	49	245
11	529	24	625	37	427	50	393
12	241	25	266	38	293	51	482
13	262	26	551	39	288	52[a]	484

[a]Week 52 corresponds to the most recent week.

If, in fact, a stationary model proves to be appropriate, one member of the Galaxy Industries management science team, Amy Chang, has suggested using the last period forecasting technique, while another member of the team, Bob Gunther, has suggested using a four-period moving average technique. A third member, Carlos Gonzalez, feels that a four-period weighted moving average technique using weights of .4, .3, .2, and .1 would better forecast demand.

Management wants to determine if it can use a stationary model to forecast demand, and, if so, what Amy's, Bob's and Carlos's forecast for demand would be for the next three weeks.

SOLUTION

We begin by constructing the time series plot of demand over the past 52 weeks, as shown in Figure 9.2.

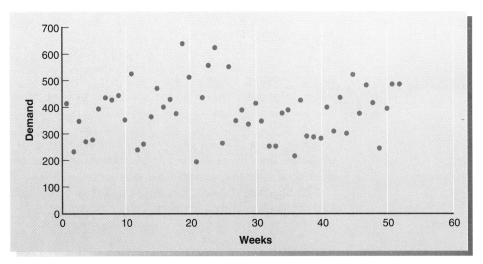

FIGURE 9.2   YoHo Yo-yo Demand

Checking the Assumptions

To check the assumption that no trend is present in this time series, we perform a regression analysis of these values versus the time period (labeled WEEKS). The regression module in Excel generated the following partial output:

	Coefficients	Standard Error	t Stat	P-value	Lower 95%	Upper 95%
Intercept	369.267	27.79436	13.28568	5E-18	313.4403	425.0936
WEEKS	0.333903	0.912641	0.365864	0.71601	−1.49919	2.166996

The p-value for the test of $\beta_1 = 0$ is the p-value associated with WEEKS, or .71601. This high p-value (much higher than a typical value for α, such as .05) indicates that there is little evidence that linear trend exists in the time series. We therefore conclude that a stationary model may be appropriate.

Visually checking for autocorrelation, we do not find any apparent seasonality by week, month, or quarter, nor does it appear that the time series exhibits cyclical variation. These assumptions can also be verified using the techniques described in Appendix 9.3 on the accompanying CD-ROM.

Forecasts for Week 53

Amy's forecast using the *last period forecasting technique* is:

$$\hat{y}_{53} = y_{52} = 484 \text{ boxes}$$

Bob's forecast using a *four-period moving average method* is:

$$\hat{y}_{53} = (y_{52} + y_{51} + y_{50} + y_{49})/4$$
$$= (484 + 482 + 393 + 245)/4 = 401 \text{ boxes}$$

Carlos's forecast using the *four-period weighted moving average method* with weights of .4, .3, .2, and .1 is:

$$\hat{y}_{53} = .4y_{52} + .3y_{51} + .2y_{50} + .1y_{49}$$
$$= .4(484) + .3(482) + .2(393) + .1(245)$$
$$= 441.3 \text{ boxes}$$

Because demand must be for full boxes, Carlos reports a demand forecast of 441 to management.

Forecasts for Weeks 54 and 55

Since a stationary model is used in each case, the forecast demand for weeks 54, 55, and beyond is the same as the forecast demand for week 53. Therefore, for weeks 54 and 55, Amy forecasts demand of 484 boxes, Bob of 401 boxes, and Carlos of 441 boxes. These forecasts will be revised pending observation of the actual demand in week 53.

THE EXPONENTIAL SMOOTHING METHOD FOR FORECASTING STATIONARY MODELS

While the n-period weighted moving average technique can be used to put greater weight on the more recent observations, it uses only the last n periods and ignores the history of the time series prior to that time. This prior history should not affect the prediction nearly as much as the more recent n data values, but many modelers feel that it is wrong to totally exclude their values in the analysis.

A problem that arises from using all prior historical data in forecasting, however, is that many companies must forecast demand for thousands or even hundreds of thousands of items on a regular basis. This could require them to keep huge databases dating back many years and involve lengthy calculations each time a new forecast is warranted. Such difficulties can be overcome by using *exponential smoothing*. This forecasting technique requires only two data values to forecast a value for the next time period: (1) the current value of the time series, y_i, and (2) and the forecast value for the current period, $\hat{y}_i$.

The idea behind the exponential smoothing method is to create the next period's forecast using a weighted average of the current period's actual value and the forecast value for the current period. The weight given to the current period's *actual value*, denoted by α, is called the *smoothing constant*. The weight applied to the current period's *forecast* value is $(1 - \alpha)$. Thus, the forecast for time period $t + 1$ using exponential smoothing is expressed by the following relationship.

Exponential Smoothing Forecasting Technique

$$\hat{y}_{t+1} = \alpha y_t + (1 - \alpha)\hat{y}_t$$

where: $\hat{y}_t$ = the forecast value for time t
y_t = the value of the time series at time t
α = smoothing constant $(0 \leq \alpha \leq 1)$

We indicated that the exponential smoothing approach considers all previous values of the historical time series. To illustrate, consider the equation for deriving the forecast value:

$$\hat{y}_{t+1} = \alpha y_t + (1 - \alpha)\hat{y}_t$$

Since the forecast at time period t, $\hat{y}_t$, is found using $\hat{y}_t = \alpha y_{t-1} + (1 - \alpha)\hat{y}_{t-1}$, we have:

$$\hat{y}_{t+1} = \alpha y_t + (1 - \alpha)(\alpha y_{t-1} + (1 - \alpha)\hat{y}_{t-1})$$
$$= \alpha y_t + \alpha(1 - \alpha)y_{t-1} + (1 - \alpha)^2\hat{y}_{t-1}$$

And since the forecast at time period $t - 1$, $\hat{y}_{t-1}$, is found using $\hat{y}_{t-1} = \alpha y_{t-2} + (1 - \alpha)\hat{y}_{t-2}$, we have:

$$\hat{y}_{t+1} = \alpha y_t + \alpha(1 - \alpha)y_{t-1} + (1 - \alpha)^2(\alpha y_{t-2} + (1 - \alpha)\hat{y}_{t-2})$$
$$= \alpha y_t + \alpha(1 - \alpha)y_{t-1} + \alpha(1 - \alpha)^2 y_{t-2} + (1 - \alpha)^3\hat{y}_{t-2}$$

Continuing in this fashion, we can express $\hat{y}_{t+1}$ by:

$$\hat{y}_{t+1} = \alpha y_t + \alpha(1-\alpha)y_{t-1} + \alpha(1-\alpha)^2 y_{t-2} + \alpha(1-\alpha)^3 y_{t-3}$$
$$+ \ldots + \alpha(1-\alpha)^k y_{t-k} + (1-\alpha)^{k+1}\hat{y}_{t-k}$$

Since $(1-\alpha)$ is a fraction, the weights given to past terms decrease as they become more distant from the present. Also, the last term of this equation, $\alpha(1-\alpha)^k$ (which represents the weight given to the forecast k periods in the past) approaches 0 as the value of k is increased.[3]

To begin an exponential smoothing process, a "first" forecast must be used to generate successive values. For example, the forecast for time period 2, $\hat{y}_2 = \alpha y_1 + (1-\alpha)\hat{y}_1$, implies that there was a forecast, $\hat{y}_1$ for time period 1. If no such forecast exists, the observed value y_1 is frequently used for $\hat{y}_1$, so that $\hat{y}_2 = \alpha y_1 + (1-\alpha)y_1 = y_1$. Another approach for finding a "first" forecast when a large number of historical values exist is to average the values for some initial i periods (say 10, 20, or 30 periods), use this average as the forecast for period $i + 1$, and begin using exponential smoothing from that time period onward.[4]

The forecasts generated from exponential smoothing depend on the modeler's choice for the smoothing constant, α. When α is large, greater weight is given to the current period's actual value, so the forecast tracks changes in the time series quite rapidly. When α is small, less weight is given to the current period's actual value, resulting in relatively small changes in the forecast; hence, the forecast tracks time series changes quite slowly.

To illustrate the concepts involved in exponential smoothing, let us return to the problem of forecasting demand of YoHo yo-yos at Galaxy Industries.

YOHO BRAND YO-YOS (continued)

Dick Gates, a recent hire at Galaxy Industries with a degree both in management science and statistics, has suggested forecasting sales using an exponential smoothing technique that puts a weight of .1 on the most recent observation. Management has asked Dick to forecast demand for weeks 53, 54, and 55.

SOLUTION

To perform the exponential smoothing analysis, Dick must use a "first" forecast. He decides to average the data values from the first 10 weeks and use the result as the forecast for week 11, $\hat{y}_{11}$. Thus, Dick uses $\hat{y}_{11} = (415 + 236 + 348 + \ldots + 354)/10 = 361.5$. Dick's forecast for week 12 is therefore:

$$\hat{y}_{12} = .1y_{11} + .9\hat{y}_{11} = .1(529) + .9(361.5) = 378.25$$

Similarly, his forecast for week 13 is:

$$\hat{y}_{13} = .1y_{12} + .9\hat{y}_{12} = .1(241) + .9(378.25) = 364.525$$

Using Excel to generate the forecast values, $\hat{y}_t$, for weeks 11 through 52 yields the results shown in Table 9.2:

---

[3]The term "exponential smoothing" is derived from the fact that the exponent of the term $(1-\alpha)$ increases for more distant data values of the time series.

[4]Since the weight placed on a very early forecast is so small, virtually any reasonable technique can be used to generate the "first" forecast without significantly affecting later forecast values.

TABLE 9.2   DICK'S FORECAST VALUES FOR WEEKS 11–52 USING EXPONENTIAL
SMOOTHING WITH $\alpha = .10$

Week t	Demand y_t	Forecast $\hat{y}_t$	Week t	Demand y_t	Forecast $\hat{y}_t$
11	529	361.5000	32	252	396.7596
12	241	378.2500	33	256	382.2836
13	262	364.5250	34	378	369.6552
14	365	354.2725	35	391	370.4897
15	471	355.3453	36	217	372.5407
16	402	366.9107	37	427	356.9867
17	429	370.4197	38	293	363.9880
18	376	376.2777	39	288	356.8892
19	363	376.2499	40	282	350.0003
20	513	374.9249	41	399	343.2003
21	197	388.7324	42	309	348.7802
22	438	369.5592	43	435	344.8022
23	557	376.4033	44	299	353.8220
24	625	394.4629	45	522	348.3398
25	266	417.5166	46	376	365.7058
26	551	402.3650	47	483	366.7352
27	351	417.2285	48	416	378.3617
28	388	410.6056	49	245	382.1255
29	336	408.3451	50	393	368.4130
30	414	401.1106	51	482	370.8717
31	346	402.3995	52	484	381.9845

Thus, Dick's forecast for week 53 is:

$$\hat{y}_{53} = .1y_{52} + .9\hat{y}_{52} = .1(484) + .9(381.9845) = 392.1861 \text{ boxes}$$

This quantity corresponds to a demand forecast of 392 boxes for week 53. Since this forecast is based on a stationary model, Dick's forecast for weeks 54 and 55 is also for 392 boxes.

RELATIONSHIP BETWEEN EXPONENTIAL SMOOTHING AND MOVING AVERAGES

As we have seen, both exponential smoothing and simple moving averages are special cases of the weighted moving average approach. We can, in a sense, equate simple moving averages with exponential smoothing by calculating the average age of the observations used in developing the two forecasts. For simple moving averages of length k, the average age of the data is $(1 + 2 + 3 + \ldots + k)/k = (k + 1)/2$ periods. For exponential smoothing, the average age of the data used in the forecast is $(1)\alpha + (2)\alpha(1 - \alpha) + (3)\alpha(1 - \alpha)^2 + (4)\alpha(1 - \alpha)^3 \ldots = 1/\alpha$.

Equating the two average ages, $(k + 1)/2$ and $1/\alpha$, gives us the following relationship:

$$k = (2 - \alpha)/\alpha \qquad (9.1)$$

Equation 9.1 can prove a useful guide to the appropriate value of the smoothing constant, α. For example, exponential smoothing with $\alpha = .10$ can be thought of as being, in a sense, equivalent to a moving average based on 19 periods of data (k = (2 − .1)/.1) = 19), while exponential smoothing with α = 1.0 is equivalent to a moving average based on only one period of data. If, therefore, we want the forecast to be based on a larger number of past data values, a smaller value of α is appropriate.

9.3 EVALUATING THE PERFORMANCE OF FORECASTING TECHNIQUES

Thus far, we have presented four different techniques for generating forecasts for stationary models; each has arrived at a different forecast for week 53 in the Galaxy Industries YoHo yo-yo problem. The obvious question is, "Which of these methods gives the *best* forecast?"

To answer this question, we must be able to evaluate forecasting techniques. One commonly used approach is to select a forecasting technique for which historic forecast errors are small. The *forecast error* for time period t, denoted as Δ_t, is the difference between the actual value of the time series for the period, y_t, and the value that would have been forecasted for the period using a particular forecasting approach, $\hat{y}_t$, i.e., $\Delta_t = y_t - \hat{y}_t$.

Four of the most popular measures used to evaluate forecast errors are the mean squared error (MSE), the mean absolute deviation (MAD), the mean absolute percent error (MAPE), and the largest absolute deviation (LAD). In the *mean squared error approach*, the squares of the Δ_t values are averaged, while in the *mean absolute deviation approach* the absolute values for Δ_t are averaged. In the *mean absolute percent error approach*, the absolute values for Δ_t are divided by the corresponding actual values, y_t; these values are then multiplied by 100% to give the absolute percentage the forecast varies from the actual value. Averaging these percentages gives the MAPE. To find the *largest absolute deviation*, we simply find the largest of the absolute values for Δ_t. These four measures are summarized in Table 9.3.

TABLE 9.3   MEASURES FOR EVALUATING FORECAST ERRORS

Measure	Description	Formula
Mean Squared Error (MSE)	Averages the squared differences of the forecasted values from the actual values	$\Sigma\Delta_t^2/n = \Sigma(y_t - \hat{y}_t)^2/n$
Mean Absolute Deviation (MAD)	Averages the absolute values of the differences of the forecasted values from the actual values	$\Sigma|\Delta_t|/n = \Sigma|y_t - \hat{y}_t|/n$
Mean Absolute Percent Error (MAPE)	Averages the absolute percentage differences of the forecasted values from the actual values	$\Sigma((|\Delta_t|/y_t) * 100\%)/n = \Sigma((|y_t - \hat{y}_t|/y_t) * 100\%)/n$
Largest Absolute Deviation (LAD)	Finds the largest absolute difference between the forecasted and actual values	$MAX|\Delta_t| = MAX|y_t - \hat{y}_t|$

Which Performance Measure Should Be Used?

The forecasting approach with the lowest MSE, MAD, MAPE, or LAD is the best one for that corresponding measure of performance. If one forecasting approach is superior to the others *using all four of these measures*, clearly this approach is the most reliable for forecasting future values. It is possible, however, that one forecasting approach may have the lowest value using one performance measure and that another approach may have the lowest value using another criterion. Therefore, it is important to know which performance measure to use to evaluate the forecasting approach.

Both the MSE and the MAD performance measures look at the total magnitude of the forecast error. The MSE approach gives greater weight to larger deviations, however, since the forecast errors are squared in calculating this total. Thus, the MSE is preferred over the MAD when the modeler wishes to give larger forecast errors proportionately more weight than smaller errors.

In contrast to the MSE and MAD, the MAPE considers the forecast errors relative to the corresponding values of the time series. Hence, a large error corresponding to a large time series value may count less than a small error based on a small time series value. The MAPE performance measure is generally used when the values of the time series show wide variations.

While the MSE, MAD, and MAPE performance measures consider all forecast errors in their calculations, the LAD performance measure is determined by the single largest absolute deviation. Therefore, it is used when we are interested in selecting a technique for which all forecast errors fall below some threshold value.

To illustrate these performance measures, we return to the situation for forecasting demand for YoHo yo-yos at Galaxy Industries.

YOHO BRAND YO-YOS (continued)

Management at Galaxy Industries is uncertain about which demand forecast it should accept for YoHo yo-yos for the next three weeks. They have asked the management science team to analyze the four forecast approaches suggested by Amy, Bob, Carlos, and Dick and to recommend which to use to forecast demand for yo-yos.

SOLUTION

The management science team has decided to evaluate each forecasting approach using the MSE, MAD, MAPE, and LAD approaches.

Amy's Forecast

Amy's forecast is based on the last period technique. Table 9.4 shows the actual values, the squared differences, the absolute differences, and the absolute percent differences. At the bottom of each column are the averages of these values, derived by summing the columns and dividing by 51. (We divide by 51 because there is no forecast for period 1.) Since Amy used the last period technique, the value in the column labeled "Forecasted Demand" ($\hat{y}_t$) is simply the observed value from the previous time period, y_{t-1}. The formulas for the other columns are exhibited. The LAD for Amy's forecast, is 359, corresponding to period 25.

TABLE 9.4 PERFORMANCE MEASURES FOR AMY'S FORECAST— LAST PERIOD TECHNIQUE

Week t	Actual Demand y_t	Forecasted Demand $\hat{y}_t$	Deviation $\Delta_t = y_t - \hat{y}_t$	Squared Deviation $(\Delta_t)^2$	Absolute Deviation $|\Delta_t|$	Absolute Percent Deviation $(|\Delta_t|/y_t)(100)$
1	415	—				
2	236	415	−179	32041	179	75.85
3	348	236	112	12544	112	32.18
4	272	348	−76	5776	76	27.94
5	280	272	8	64	8	2.86
6	395	280	115	13225	115	29.11
7	438	395	43	1849	43	9.82
8	431	438	−7	49	7	1.62
9	446	431	15	225	15	3.36
10	354	446	−92	8464	92	25.99

TABLE 9.4   (continued)

Week t	Actual Demand y_t	Forecasted Demand $\hat{y}_t$	Deviation $\Delta_t = y_t - \hat{y}_t$	Squared Deviation $(\Delta_t)^2$	Absolute Deviation $|\Delta_t|$	Absolute Percent Deviation $(|\Delta_t|/y_t)(100)$
11	529	354	175	30625	175	33.08
12	241	529	−288	82944	288	119.50
13	262	241	21	441	21	8.02
14	365	262	103	10609	103	28.22
15	471	365	106	11236	106	22.51
16	402	429	−69	4761	69	17.16
17	429	402	27	729	27	6.29
18	376	429	−53	2809	53	14.10
19	363	376	−13	169	13	3.58
20	513	363	150	22500	150	29.24
21	197	513	−316	99856	316	160.41
22	438	197	241	58081	241	55.02
23	557	438	119	14161	119	21.36
24	625	557	68	4624	68	10.88
25	266	625	−359	128881	359	134.96
26	551	266	285	81225	285	51.72
27	351	551	−200	40000	200	56.98
28	388	351	37	1369	37	9.54
29	336	388	−52	2704	52	15.48
30	414	336	78	6084	78	18.84
31	346	414	−68	4624	68	19.65
32	252	346	−94	8836	94	37.30
33	256	252	4	16	4	1.56
34	378	256	122	14884	122	32.28
35	391	378	13	169	13	3.32
36	217	391	−174	30276	174	80.18
37	427	217	210	44100	210	49.18
38	293	427	−134	17956	134	45.73
39	288	293	−5	25	5	1.74
40	282	288	−6	36	6	2.13
41	399	282	117	13689	117	29.32
42	309	399	−90	8100	90	29.13
43	435	309	126	15876	126	28.97
44	299	435	−136	18496	136	45.48
45	522	299	223	49729	223	42.72
46	376	522	−146	21316	146	38.83
47	483	376	107	11449	107	22.15
48	416	483	−67	4489	67	16.11
49	245	416	−171	29241	171	69.80
50	393	245	148	21904	148	37.66
51	482	393	89	7921	89	18.46
52	484	482	2	4	2	.41
			AVERAGE = SUM/51 =	19631.00 (MSE)	110.96 (MAD)	32.90 (MAPE)

Bob's Forecast

Table 9.5 provides equivalent information based on Bob's four-period moving average approach, because the first forecast does not occur until period 5, the MSE, MAD and MAPE are calculated by dividing the column sums by 48. The LAD for Bob's forecast, is 223.25, corresponding to period 21. Figures 9.3 and 9.4 show the first and last WINQSB output screens associated with Bob's forecast, respectively. These tables were obtained using the weighted moving average option in WINQSB, with four weights of .25 each.

TABLE 9.5 PERFORMANCE MEASURES FOR BOB'S FORECAST—FOUR-PERIOD MOVING AVERAGE

Week t	Actual Demand y_t	Forecasted Demand $\hat{y}_t$	Deviation $\Delta_t = y_t - \hat{y}_t$	Squared Deviation $(\Delta_t)^2$	Absolute Deviation $|\Delta_t|$	Absolute Percent Deviation $(|\Delta_t|/y_t)(100)$
1	415					
2	236					
3	348					
4	272					
5	280	317.75	−37.75	1425.06	37.75	13.48
6	395	284	111	12321	111	28.10
7	438	323.75	114.25	13053.06	114.25	26.08
8	431	346.25	84.75	7182.56	84.75	19.66
9	446	386	60	3600	60	13.45
10	354	427.5	−73.5	5402.25	73.5	20.76
11	529	417.25	111.75	12488.06	111.75	21.12
12	241	440	−199	39601	199	82.57
13	262	392.5	−130.5	17030.25	130.5	49.81
14	365	346.5	18.5	342.25	18.5	5.07
15	471	349.25	121.75	14823.06	121.75	25.85
16	402	334.75	67.25	4522.56	67.25	16.73
17	429	375	54	2916	54	12.59
18	376	416.75	−40.75	1660.56	40.75	10.84
19	363	419.5	−56.5	3192.25	56.5	15.56
20	513	392.5	120.5	14520.25	120.5	23.49
21	197	420.25	−223.25	49840.56	223.25	113.32
22	438	362.25	75.75	5738.06	75.75	17.29
23	557	377.75	179.25	32130.56	179.25	32.18
24	625	426.25	198.75	39501.56	198.75	31.8
25	266	454.25	−188.25	35438.06	188.25	70.77
26	551	471.5	79.5	6320.25	79.5	14.43
27	351	499.75	−148.75	22126.56	148.75	42.38
28	388	448.25	−60.25	3630.06	60.25	15.53
29	336	389	−53	2809	53	15.78
30	414	406.5	7.5	56.25	7.5	1.81
31	346	372.25	−26.25	689.06	26.25	7.59
32	252	371	−119	14161	119	47.22
33	256	337	−81	6561	81	31.64
34	378	317	61	3721	61	16.14
35	391	308	83	6889	83	21.23
36	217	319.25	−102.25	10455.06	102.25	47.12
37	427	310.5	116.5	13572.25	116.5	27.28
38	293	353.25	−60.25	3630.06	60.25	20.56
39	288	332	−44	1936	44	15.28
40	282	306.25	−24.25	588.06	24.25	8.60
41	399	322.5	76.5	5852.25	76.5	19.17
42	309	315.5	−6.5	42.25	6.5	2.10
43	435	319.5	115.5	13340.25	115.5	26.55
44	299	356.25	−57.25	3277.56	57.25	19.15
45	522	360.5	161.5	26082.25	161.5	30.94
46	376	391.25	−15.25	232.56	15.25	4.06
47	483	408	75	5625	75	15.53
48	416	420	−4	16	4	0.96
49	245	449.25	−204.25	41718.06	204.25	83.37
50	393	380	13	169	13	3.31
51	482	384.25	97.75	9555.06	97.75	20.28
52	484	384	100	10000	100	20.66
		AVERAGE = SUM/48 =		11037.16 (MSE)	88.75 (MAD)	25.61 (MAPE)

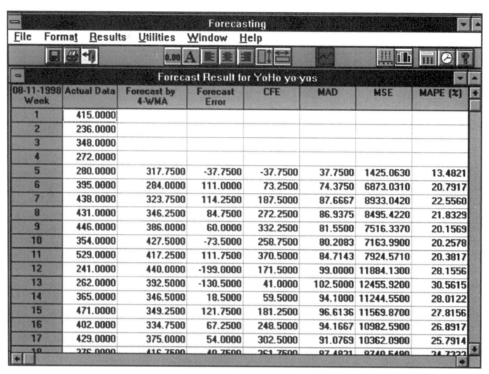

	Forecasting						
File	Format	Results	Utilities	Window	Help		

Forecast Result for YoHo yo-yos

08-11-1998 Week	Actual Data	Forecast by 4-WMA	Forecast Error	CFE	MAD	MSE	MAPE [%]
1	415.0000						
2	236.0000						
3	348.0000						
4	272.0000						
5	280.0000	317.7500	-37.7500	-37.7500	37.7500	1425.0630	13.4821
6	395.0000	284.0000	111.0000	73.2500	74.3750	6873.0310	20.7917
7	438.0000	323.7500	114.2500	187.5000	87.6667	8933.0420	22.5560
8	431.0000	346.2500	84.7500	272.2500	86.9375	8495.4220	21.8329
9	446.0000	386.0000	60.0000	332.2500	81.5500	7516.3370	20.1569
10	354.0000	427.5000	-73.5000	258.7500	80.2083	7163.9900	20.2578
11	529.0000	417.2500	111.7500	370.5000	84.7143	7924.5710	20.3817
12	241.0000	440.0000	-199.0000	171.5000	99.0000	11884.1300	28.1556
13	262.0000	392.5000	-130.5000	41.0000	102.5000	12455.9200	30.5615
14	365.0000	346.5000	18.5000	59.5000	94.1000	11244.5500	28.0122
15	471.0000	349.2500	121.7500	181.2500	96.6136	11569.8700	27.8156
16	402.0000	334.7500	67.2500	248.5000	94.1667	10982.5900	26.8917
17	429.0000	375.0000	54.0000	302.5000	91.0769	10362.0900	25.7914
18	376.0000	416.7500	40.7500	261.7500	87.4921	9740.5490	24.7222

FIGURE 9.3 First WINQSB Output Screen for YoHo Yo-yos Forecast Results

	Forecasting						
File	Format	Results	Utilities	Window	Help		

Forecast Result for YoHo yo-yos

08-11-1998 Week	Actual Data	Forecast by 4-WMA	Forecast Error	CFE	MAD	MSE	MAPE [%]
48	416.0000	420.0000	-4.0000	342.0000	87.3864	10644.1300	25.0361
49	245.0000	449.2500	-204.2500	137.7500	89.9833	11334.6600	26.3324
50	393.0000	380.0000	13.0000	150.7500	88.3098	11091.9300	25.8318
51	482.0000	384.2500	97.7500	248.5000	88.5106	11059.2300	25.7137
52	484.0000	384.0000	100.0000	348.5000	88.7500	11037.1600	25.6085
53		401.0000					
CFE		348.5000					
MAD		88.7500					
MSE		11037.1600					
MAPE		25.6085					
Trk.Signal		3.9268					
R-sqaure		0.2621					
		m=4					
		W[1]=0.2500					
		W[2]=0.2500					
		W[3]=0.2500					
		W[4]=0.2500					

FIGURE 9.4 Last WINQSB Output Screen for YoHo Yo-yos Forecast Results

The first column of the WINQSB output gives the period number. This information is followed by a column labeled "Actual Data," which lists the inputted time series values on which the forecast is based. The column labeled "Forecast by 4-WMA" gives the forecasted value for the period based on a four-period moving average.

The column labeled "Forecast Error" provides the difference between the actual data and the forecast. Next to it is a column labeled "CFE," which gives the cumulative forecast error (the sum of the values in the "Forecast Error" column), followed by columns for the MAD, MSE, and MAPE. Summary data for the CFE, MAD, MSE, and MAPE are provided at the bottom of the WINQSB analysis.

Figure 9.5 is a plot generated by WINQSB of the original time series data, together with the forecast obtained using the four-period moving average technique. As you can see, the forecast values track the actual time series data to a certain extent.

FIGURE 9.5   WINQSB Original and Forecast Time Series Data

Carlos's Forecast

Recall that Carlos is using a weighted moving average with weights $w_1 = .4$, $w_2 = .3$, $w_3 = .2$, and $w_4 = .1$ to forecast demand for YoHo yo-yos. Figure 9.6 shows the last WINQSB output screen associated with the weighted moving average technique. This technique results in an MSE of 11,992, an MAD of 92.39, and an MAPE of 26.78 for the 52 weeks of data. The LAD, in this case, is 258.4 corresponding to period 25.

Dick's Forecast

Recall that Dick is using exponential smoothing with $\alpha = .1$. His forecast begins in period 11; the initial forecast for that period equals the moving average over the first

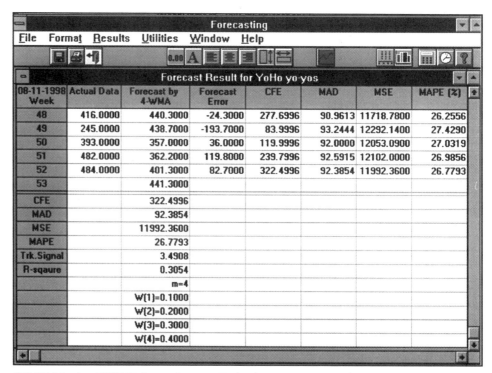

FIGURE 9.6   Last WINQSB Output Screen—Weighted Moving Average Technique

10 periods. Table 9.6, which can be calculated using Excel or WINQSB, gives the results for Dick's forecast. In Dick's forecast, the LAD is 230.54, which occurs in period 24. Table 9.7 summarizes these results.

TABLE 9.6   PERFORMANCE MEASURES FOR DICK'S FORECAST—EXPONENTIAL SMOOTHING WITH $\alpha = .10$

Week t	Actual Demand y_t	Forecasted Demand $\hat{y}_t$	Deviation $\Delta_t = y_t - \hat{y}_t$	Squared Deviation $(\Delta_t)^2$	Absolute Deviation $|\Delta_t|$	Absolute Percent Deviation $(|\Delta_t|/y_t)(100)$
1	415					
2	236					
3	348					
4	272					
5	280					
6	395					
7	438					
8	431					
9	446					
10	354					
11	529	361.50	167.50	28056.25	167.50	31.66
12	241	378.25	−137.25	18837.56	137.25	56.95
13	262	364.53	−102.53	10511.38	102.53	39.13
14	365	354.27	10.73	115.08	10.73	2.94
15	471	355.35	115.65	13376.02	115.65	24.56
16	402	366.91	35.09	1231.26	35.09	8.73
17	429	370.42	58.58	3431.66	58.58	13.66
18	376	376.28	−0.28	0.08	0.28	0.07
19	363	376.25	−13.25	175.56	13.25	3.65
20	513	374.92	138.08	19064.73	138.08	26.92
21	197	388.73	−191.73	36761.33	191.73	97.33

TABLE 9.6   (continued)

Week t	Actual Demand y_t	Forecasted Demand $\hat{y}_t$	Deviation $\Delta_t = y_t - \hat{y}_t$	Squared Deviation $(\Delta_t)^2$	Absolute Deviation $|\Delta_t|$	Absolute Percent Deviation $(|\Delta_t|/y_t)(100)$
22	438	369.56	68.44	4684.14	68.44	15.63
23	557	376.40	180.60	32615.18	180.60	32.42
24	625	394.46	230.54	53147.33	230.54	36.89
25	266	417.52	−151.52	22957.30	151.52	56.96
26	551	402.36	148.64	22092.37	148.64	26.98
27	351	417.23	−66.23	4386.21	66.23	18.87
28	388	410.61	−22.61	511.01	22.61	5.83
29	336	408.35	−72.35	5233.81	72.35	21.53
30	414	401.11	12.89	166.14	12.89	3.11
31	346	402.40	−56.40	3180.90	56.40	16.30
32	252	396.76	−144.76	20955.33	144.76	57.44
33	256	382.28	−126.28	15947.55	126.28	49.33
34	378	369.66	8.34	69.63	8.34	2.21
35	391	370.49	20.51	420.67	20.51	5.25
36	217	372.54	−155.54	24192.92	155.54	71.68
37	427	356.99	70.01	4901.87	70.01	16.40
38	293	363.99	−70.99	5039.30	70.99	24.23
39	288	356.89	−68.89	4745.72	68.89	23.92
40	282	350.00	−68.00	4624.04	68.00	24.11
41	399	343.20	55.80	3113.61	55.80	13.98
42	309	348.78	−39.78	1582.47	39.78	12.87
43	435	344.08	90.20	8135.64	90.20	20.74
44	299	353.82	−54.82	3005.45	54.82	18.34
45	522	348.34	173.66	30157.87	173.66	33.27
46	376	365.71	10.29	105.97	10.29	2.74
47	483	366.74	116.26	13517.50	116.26	24.07
48	416	378.36	37.64	1416.64	37.64	9.05
49	245	382.13	−137.13	18803.41	137.13	55.97
50	393	368.41	24.59	604.52	24.59	6.26
51	482	370.87	111.13	12349.50	111.13	23.06
52	484	381.98	102.02	10407.16	102.02	21.08
		AVERAGE = SUM/42 =		11062.67 (MSE)	87.32 (MAD)	25.14 (MAPE)

TABLE 9.7   COMPARISON OF THE FOUR PERFORMANCE MEASURES

Forecast	MSE	MAD	MAPE	LAD
Amy	19,631.00	110.96	32.90	359
Bob	11,037.16	88.75	25.61	223.25
Carlos	11,992.36	92.39	26.78	317.10
Dick	11,062.67	87.32	25.14	230.54

Since Bob's four-period moving average forecast and Dick's exponential smoothing forecast give lower forecast errors than Amy or Carlos's forecasts, either Bob's or Dick's approach should be used. Which of the two should be selected depends on the performance measure preferred by the decision maker.

SELECTING MODEL PARAMETERS

Often the modeler must select different parameters for a chosen technique. In the moving average technique, the modeler must select the number of periods to use in determining the forecast. In the weighted moving average technique, the modeler must select not only the number of periods to use, but also the weights to assign to each period. In the exponential smoothing technique, the modeler must determine the smoothing constant. Each of these parameters, in turn, influence the performance of the forecasting technique.

To illustrate, let us return to Bob's forecast. You may wonder whether the mean squared forecast error (the most commonly used performance measure for evaluating forecasting techniques) could be reduced even further by choosing a different value for n (the number of weeks used in calculating the moving average). Table 9.8 shows the value of mean squared forecast error for values of n between 1 and 10.

TABLE 9.8   MEAN SQUARED FORECAST ERRORS USING _n_ PERIOD MOVING AVERAGES

n	Mean Squared Forecast Error
1	19,007
2	12,996
3	12,467
4	11,037
5	11,756
6	11,332
7	11,104
8	10,737
9	10,791
10	11,400

While the eight-week moving average gives a slightly smaller mean squared forecast error than does the four-week moving average, the four-week moving average may still be preferred. This is because when the moving average is based on too many historical values, the forecast is not as responsive to changes in the time series. This is important because we are never certain what future time series values will be. Specifically, while historical values of the series may be stationary, future values could change quite rapidly.

Quick response is especially critical when there is evidence to indicate a positive autocorrelation exists or when the mean of the series is anticipated to shift at a future point in time. By using a moving average consisting of only a few past values, the forecasting procedure becomes much more sensitive to such changes.

For the exponential smoothing technique, WINQSB is capable of finding the best smoothing constant, α, to use based on either the MSE, the MAD, or the MAPE criteria. In general, if the time series does not exhibit significant autocorrelation, a low value of α (such as .10) is appropriate. If the time series shows significant autocorrelation, however, it is more desirable to track changes in the observation values quickly. In this case, a higher value of α should be used.

To summarize, the following are the key issues in determining which approach and parameters to use for forecasting a stationary time series:

Key Issues in Determining Which Forecasting Technique to Use for a Stationary Time Series

1. The degree of autocorrelation suspected in the data
2. The possibility of future shifts in time series values
3. The desired responsiveness of the forecasting technique
4. The amount of data that is required to calculate the forecast

9.4 $\mathscr{F}$ORECASTING TIME SERIES THAT EXHIBIT LINEAR TREND

In Section 9.2 we showed how to detect linear trend in a time series. If we suspect trend, we should assess whether the trend is linear or nonlinear (curvilinear). This determination is frequently based on the modeler's knowledge of the means by which the time series is generated. For example, an epidemiologist may know from theoretical analyses that the number of cases of a particular disease will grow initially at an exponential rate; an economist may believe that certain economic measures change logarithmically; or historical data may suggest that home use of natural gas has a quadratic relationship with daily low temperature readings.

Here, however, we restrict our attention to forecasting a time series that demonstrates linear trend. The model for such a time series is:

$$y_t = \beta_0 + \beta_1 t + \epsilon_t \tag{9.2}$$

In this model, β_0 represents the y-intercept and β_1 the slope of the time series. ϵ_t is the random error term at time t. Using linear regression, we can test whether the slope of the data values versus time is nonzero.

If we verify that a linear trend is present, the next step is to select a forecasting method. One technique is to use the regression equation based on the historical time series data to forecast future time series values. In this case the forecast for time period t is obtained by substituting t into the regression equation.

Another frequently used method, based on a generalization of exponential smoothing, is Holt's *linear exponential smoothing technique*. In this approach, forecasts are made for both the time series level, L_t, which corresponds to the constant in the regression equation (β_0), and its trend, T_t, which corresponds to the slope in the regression equation (β_1). Unlike regression, which generates a single forecasting equation, in Holt's method, forecasts for the level and trend are adjusted at each time period using the following two smoothing equations:

$$\text{Level: } \hat{L}_t = \alpha y_t + (1 - \alpha)\,\hat{y}_t \tag{9.3}$$
$$\text{Trend: } \hat{T}_t = \gamma\,(\hat{L}_t - \hat{L}_{t-1}) + (1 - \gamma)\,\hat{T}_{t-1} \tag{9.4}$$

In these equations,

α = smoothing constant for the time series level

γ = smoothing constant for the time series trend

$\hat{L}_t$ = estimate of the time series level for time t as of time t

$\hat{T}_t$ = estimate of the time series trend for time t as of time t

y_t = value of the time series at time t

$\hat{y}_t$ = forecast of the value of the time series for time t calculated at a period prior to time t

Thus, our forecast for time period t + 1, $\hat{y}_{t+1}$, based on data up to time period t, is:

$$\hat{y}_{t+1} = \hat{L}_t + \hat{T}_t \tag{9.5}$$

Until additional data are observed, the forecasts for future time periods are based on the current estimates of $\hat{L}_t$ and $\hat{T}_t$. Thus, the forecast for time period t + 2 is $\hat{y}_{t+2} = \hat{L}_t + 2\hat{T}_t$; for time period t + 3 it is $\hat{y}_{t+3} = \hat{L}_t + 3\hat{T}_t$; and, in general, for k periods from the current period, t, our forecast is $\hat{y}_{t+k} = \hat{L}_t + k\hat{T}_t$.

Comparing forecasting done by linear regression with that done by Holt's method, we note that the linear regression method treats all data points in the time series equally when developing the forecast equation. Holt's method, however, allows the modeler to give greater weight to more recent observations when developing the forecast, hence, it responds more rapidly to changes in time series values. Another advantage of Holt's method is that the modeler needs to keep track of fewer historical data values to obtain the forecast.

In order to perform exponential smoothing using Holt's method, we must not only choose appropriate values for the two smoothing constants, but also initial forecast values for both the time series level and trend. Since we need at least two points to forecast trend, the initial forecasts cannot begin until time period 2. One common approach for selecting the initial level and trend values at time period 2 is to begin with

$$\hat{L}_2 = y_2$$
$$\hat{T}_2 = y_2 - y_1$$

To illustrate these techniques, consider the year-end current asset data for American Family Products.

Amfam.fcc
Amfam.xls

AMERICAN FAMILY PRODUCTS CORPORATION

Hank Richards and Juanita Garcia, financial analysts with the bond rating firm of Standard and Poor's (S&P), are currently conducting an analysis of American Family Products Corporation (AFP) to determine whether the bond rating of the firm should be modified. One important factor in making this assessment is the projected year-end current assets of the firm. Table 9.9 provides information regarding American Family Products' year-end current assets (in millions of dollars) for the previous 10-year period (year 10 corresponds to the most recent year).

TABLE 9.9   AMERICAN FAMILY PRODUCTS'
YEAR-END CURRENT ASSETS

Year	Current Assets (in million $)
1	1990
2	2280
3	2328
4	2635
5	3249
6	3310
7	3256
8	3533
9	3826
10	4119

Hank and Juanita wish to forecast year-end current assets for American Family Products for years 11 and 12. Both feel that the company's assets have been increasing at a relatively constant rate over time. If this can be verified, Hank has decided to forecast year-end current assets for future years using a linear regression approach, whereas Juanita will use Holt's method to determine this forecast. S&P would like to determine a forecast for year-end current assets for AFP based on both approaches.

SOLUTION

Figure 9.7 is a graph generated by Excel showing the year-end current assets of American Family Products over the past 10 years. While the time series appears to exhibit a linear

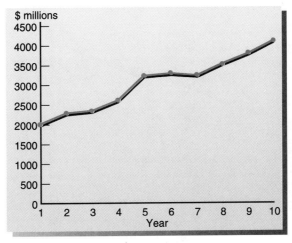

FIGURE 9.7   Year-end Current Assets of American Family Products

trend, we verify this statistically by regressing the year-end current assets against time. Table 9.10 shows the Excel output for this analysis.

TABLE 9.10   EXCEL SUMMARY OUTPUT—YEAR-END CURRENT ASSETS OF AMERICAN FAMILY PRODUCTS

Regression Statistics	
Multiple R	0.980225
R square	0.960842
Adjusted R square	0.955947
Standard error	149.0358
Observations	10

ANOVA

	df	SS	MS	F	Significance F
Regression	1	4360111	4360111	196.2981	6.53E-07
Residual	8	177693.4	22211.68		
Total	9	4537804			

	Coefficients	Standard Error	t-Stat	P-value	Lower 95%	Upper 95%
Intercept	1788.2	101.8109	17.56394	1.13E-07	1553.424	2022.976
Year	229.8909	16.4083	14.01064	6.53E-07	192.0533	267.7286

The p-value associated with the slope is $6.53\text{E-}07 = 6.53 \times 10^{-7} = 0.000000653$. Since this figure is far less than $\alpha = .05$, we conclude that the data show significant linear trend, and a linear forecasting model is appropriate.

Hank's Forecasts Using Linear Regression

From the Excel output, Hank observes that the following regression equation can be used to forecast future values of the time series:

$$\hat{y}_t = 1788.2 + 229.89t \tag{9.6}$$

Figure 9.8 shows the fit of this line to the time series.

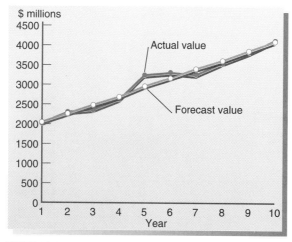

FIGURE 9.8 Hank's Forecasts Using Linear Regression

Using this model, Hank forecasts the current assets of American Family Products Corporation at the end of the next two fiscal years as follows:

$$\hat{y}_{11} = 1788.2 + 229.89 \,(11) = \$4317 \text{ million}$$
$$\hat{y}_{12} = 1788.2 + 229.89 \,(12) = \$4547 \text{ million}$$

Figure 9.9 gives the WINQSB output corresponding to these data, verifying the above forecast.

08-18-1998 Year	Actual Data	Forecast by LR	Forecast Error	CFE	MAD	MSE	MAPE (%)
1	1990	2018.091	-28.09131	-28.09131	28.09131	789.1216	1.411624
2	2280	2247.982	32.01782	3.926514	30.05457	907.1313	1.407957
3	2328	2477.873	-149.873	-145.9465	69.99406	8092.064	3.084586
4	2635	2707.764	-72.76367	-218.7102	70.68646	7392.687	3.003797
5	3249	2937.655	311.3455	92.63525	118.8183	25301.35	4.3196
6	3310	3167.545	142.4546	235.0898	122.7577	24466.67	4.31696
7	3256	3397.436	-141.4363	93.65356	125.426	23829.18	4.320804
8	3533	3627.327	-94.32715	-0.673584	121.5387	21962.73	4.114439
9	3826	3857.218	-31.21802	-31.8916	111.503	19630.71	3.74794
10	4119	4087.109	31.89111	882813E-04	103.5418	17769.35	3.45057
11		4317					
12		4546.891					
CFE		-4.882813E-04					
MAD		103.5418					
MSE		17769.35					
MAPE		3.45057					
Trk.Signal		-4.715786E-06					

FIGURE 9.9 WINQSB Output for Hank's Forecast

Juanita's Forecast Using
Holt's Technique

To begin the forecasting process in year 2, Juanita uses the value of the time series in year 2, y_2, as her estimate for $\hat{L}_2$, and the increase in the value of the series between years 1 and 2, $y_2 - y_1$, as her value for $\hat{T}_2$. Thus, $\hat{L}_2 = 2280$, and $\hat{T}_2 = 2280 - 1990 = 290$. Because she wants to track changes in the time series level and trend slowly, Juanita has selected the smoothing constant values of $\alpha = .10$ and $\gamma = .20$. The formulas give the following results for years 2, 3, and 4.

$$
\begin{aligned}
\text{Year 2:} \quad y_2 &= 2280 \\
\hat{L}_2 &= 2280.00 \\
\hat{T}_2 &= 290.00 \\
\hat{y}_3 &= 2280.00 + 290.00 = 2570.00 \\
\text{Year 3:} \quad y_3 &= 2328 \\
\hat{L}_3 &= (.1)2328 + (1 - .1)2570.00 = 2545.80 \\
\hat{T}_3 &= (.2)(2545.80 - 2280) + (1 - .2)290.00 = 285.16 \\
\hat{y}_4 &= 2545.80 + 285.16 = 2830.96 \\
\text{Year 4:} \quad y_4 &= 2635 \\
\hat{L}_4 &= (.1)2635 + (1 - .1)2830.96 = 2811.36 \\
\hat{T}_4 &= (.2)(2811.36 - 2545.80) + (1 - .2)285.16 = 281.24 \\
\hat{y}_5 &= 2811.36 + 281.24 = 3092.60
\end{aligned}
$$

We could continue in this fashion to generate values for all years up to year 10. Juanita actually used Excel to generate the values for periods 2 through 10. The results are shown in Table 9.11.

TABLE 9.11   JUANITA'S FORECAST—HOLT'S TECHNIQUE WITH $\alpha = .10$, $\gamma = .20$

Year t	Current Assets y_t	Level $\hat{L}_t$	Trend $\hat{T}_t$	Forecast $\hat{y}_t$	Forecast Error Δ_t
2	2280	2280.00	290.000		
3	2328	2545.80	285.160	2570.00	−242.00
4	2635	2811.36	281.240	2830.96	−195.96
5	3249	3108.24	284.368	3092.60	156.40
6	3310	3384.35	282.716	3392.61	−82.61
7	3256	3625.96	274.495	3667.07	−411.07
8	3533	3863.71	267.146	3900.46	−367.46
9	3826	4100.37	261.048	4130.86	−304.86
10	4119	4337.17	256.200	4361.42	−242.42

Thus, using Holt's technique, Juanita's forecasts for current assets for years 11 and 12 are:

$$
\begin{aligned}
\hat{y}_{11} &= 4337.17 + 256.20 = \$4593 \text{ million} \\
\hat{y}_{12} &= 4337.17 + 2(256.20) = \$4850 \text{ million}
\end{aligned}
$$

Referring to Table 9.11 Juanita observed that, in all but one year, the forecast error is negative; that is, the technique regularly forecasts values higher than the actual data values. The principal reason for this is that the initial value selected for the trend, 290, is too high. (Recall from the linear regression analysis that the slope of the regression line is only 229.89.)

Juanita can remedy this situation either by beginning with a lower initial forecast for the trend or using a faster tracking mechanism for the trend—that is, a larger value for γ. For example, if Juanita used a value of $\gamma = .80$, while keeping $\alpha = .10$, the results are those shown in Table 9.12. While the historic forecast errors are still predominantly negative, they are generally closer to 0 than those Juanita obtained using $\gamma = .20$.

TABLE 9.12   JUANITA'S FORECAST USING HOLT'S TECHNIQUE
WITH $\alpha = .10$, $\gamma = .80$

Year t	Assets y_t	Level $\hat{L}_t$	Trend $\hat{T}_t$	Forecast $\hat{y}_t$	Forecast Error Δ_t
2	2280	2280.00	290.000		
3	2328	2545.80	270.640	2570.00	−242.00
4	2635	2798.30	256.125	2816.44	−181.44
5	3249	3073.88	271.691	3054.42	194.58
6	3310	3342.01	268.846	3345.57	−35.57
7	3256	3575.37	240.457	3610.86	−354.86
8	3533	3787.55	217.831	3815.83	−282.83
9	3826	3987.44	203.480	4005.38	−179.38
10	4119	4183.73	197.727	4190.92	−71.92

Alternatively, if Juanita continued to use smoothing constants of $\alpha = .10$ and $\gamma = .20$ but selected an initial trend forecast of $\hat{T}_2 = 230$, the results are those shown in Table 9.13.

TABLE 9.13   JUANITA'S FORECAST USING HOLT'S TECHNIQUE
WITH $\alpha = .10$, $\gamma = .20$ and $\hat{T}_2 = 230$

Year t	Current Assets y_t	Level $\hat{L}_t$	Trend $\hat{T}_t$	Forecast $\hat{y}_t$	Forecast Error Δ_t
2	2280	2280.00	230.000		
3	2328	2491.80	226.360	2510.00	−182.00
4	2635	2709.84	224.697	2718.16	−83.16
5	3249	2965.99	230.986	2934.54	314.46
6	3310	3208.28	233.247	3196.97	113.03
7	3256	3422.97	229.536	3441.52	−185.52
8	3533	3640.56	227.146	3652.51	−119.51
9	3826	3863.53	226.312	3867.70	−41.70
10	4119	4092.76	226.895	3867.70	29.16

In this case, the forecast errors seem to be more equally divided between positive and negative values than they are in Juanita's previous two approaches. Juanita decided to use this model, and reported the following forecasts for years 11 and 12:

$$\hat{y}_{11} = 4092.76 + 226.895 = \$4320 \text{ million}$$
$$\hat{y}_{12} = 4092.76 + 2(226.895) = \$4547 \text{ million}$$

As you can see, Juanita's choice of smoothing parameters and the initial forecast values play a significant role in determining the accuracy of the forecast. As with the stationary models discussed earlier, performance measures such as MSE, MAD, MAPE, and LAD can be used to evaluate forecasting approaches for different values of α and γ. For a given performance measure, WINQSB can determine the best pair of smoothing constants given initial forecasts for the time series level and trend.

TRANSFORMING
MODELS WITH
NONLINEAR TREND
INTO MODELS WITH
LINEAR TREND

While the focus of our analysis has been on models with linear trend, it is worth noting that certain nonlinear trend models can be transformed into a linear time series. Therefore, the techniques discussed in this section are also applicable for these models.

For example, if the time series is suspected of being quadratic over time—that is, $y_t = \beta_0 + \beta_1 t + \beta_2 t^2 + \epsilon_t$—the difference between successive pairs of data values yields a linear model. We can than use a forecast based on these differences to determine the forecast for the original time series.

Another model that can be transformed into a linear model is an exponential model of the form $y_t = \beta_0 \beta_1^t \gamma_t$. If we take logarithms of both sides, we get the following linear model:

$$\log(y_t) = \log(\beta_0) + t \log(\beta_1) + \log(\epsilon_t) \qquad (9.7)$$

We can then obtain a forecast for $\log(y_t)$ and transform it back into a forecast for y_t using the relationship $y_t = e^{\log(y_t)}$.

OTHER FORECASTING TECHNIQUES FOR MODELS WITH LINEAR TREND

In addition to linear regression and Holt's method, a number of other techniques exist for forecasting time series with linear trend. Like Holt's technique, some of these methods are based on exponential smoothing. One method *not* based on exponential smoothing but on the difference between successive time series values is described in Appendix 9.4 on the accompanying CD-ROM.

9.5 TIME SERIES WITH TREND, SEASONAL, AND CYCLICAL VARIATION

In the previous section, we considered how to develop forecasting models that account for trend in the time series. Many time series, however, exhibit seasonal and cyclical variations along with trend. Such variation principally arises due to calendar, climatic, or economic factors. When these patterns can be anticipated, they should be accounted for in the forecasting model in order to improve the accuracy of the forecasts.

Two models that account for trend, seasonal, and cyclical variation are the *additive model* and the *multiplicative model*:

Additive Model

$$y_t = T_t + C_t + S_t + \epsilon_t \qquad (9.8)$$

Multiplicative Model

$$y_t = T_t C_t S_t \epsilon_t \qquad (9.9)$$

In these models,

$$y_t = \text{the time series value at time t}$$
$$T_t = \text{the trend component of the time series at time t}$$
$$S_t = \text{the seasonal component of the time series at time t}$$
$$C_t = \text{the cyclical component of the time series at time t}$$
$$\epsilon_t = \text{the random error component of the time series at time t}$$

The major difference between the two models is how one views the effects of the cyclical and seasonal variations on trend. An additive model is more appropriate when the seasonal and cyclical variations do not change in proportion to the time series values; whereas a multiplicative model is more appropriate if they do.

To illustrate this difference, consider a forecast of electricity consumption for a household that has electric baseboard heating and electric air conditioning. We would expect a seasonal variation in electricity usage due to heating in the winter and cooling in the summer. As measured in *kilowatt hours*, we expect seasonal effects to be additive because, while the overall electrical usage may increase over time (due to the family's purchase of more electrical appliances), the change in kilowatt usage during the winter and summer due to climatic variations does not vary in proportion to overall usage. In this case, an additive forecasting model may be appropriate.

On the other hand, if the *cost* of electricity is being forecast and the household is in a region in which the cost per kilowatt hour has been rising rapidly, the trend in cost data may be due primarily to the higher cost per kilowatt hour rather than the increase in the number of kilowatt hours used. If this is the case, the variation in utility cost in the summer and winter is proportional to the overall cost, and a multiplicative model is more appropriate.

In an additive model, the magnitude of the seasonal variations is reasonably constant over time, while in a multiplicative model the magnitude of the seasonal variations grows in proportion to the trend of the series. Because the effects of seasonality can usually be more appropriately modeled as a percentage of the trend (such as in the case of a time series dealing with the *cost* of electricity), multiplicative time series models are more frequently used to handle seasonal variation.

One technique often used to develop an additive or multiplicative forecasting model is *classical decomposition*. In this technique, the trend, cyclical, and seasonal components are isolated and forecast separately. The random error component is assumed to have a mean of 0 for additive models and a mean of 1 for multiplicative models. Once the trend, seasonal, and cyclical component forecasts have been determined, in additive models they are added together to obtain forecasts for the time series, while in multiplicative models they are multiplied together to obtain forecasts.

USING CLASSICAL DECOMPOSITION FOR MULTIPLICATIVE MODELS

In the following example, we illustrate the classical decomposition method using a multiplicative model. A similar approach can be used for an additive model.

Cfa.xls

CANADIAN FACULTY ASSOCIATION (CFA)

The Canadian Faculty Association (CFA) is the exclusive bargaining agent for the approximately 21,000 faculty members who teach in state-supported Canadian colleges and universities. Under Canadian law, membership in the organization is voluntary, but CFA is required to represent the interests of all full-time and part-time faculty, as well as librarians and coaches. Membership in the organization has grown gradually over the years. However, because approximately half the teaching faculty are lecturers who are hired on a year-to-year basis, membership in the organization tends to decline in the summer months and increase during the academic year.

While some 210 members pay dues to the organization directly, the vast majority pay through payroll deduction. Table 9.14 shows the CFA membership based on payroll deductions for the 48 periods (months) from June 1993 through May 1997.

TABLE 9.14   CANADIAN FACULTY ASSOCIATION MEMBERSHIP: JUNE 1993–MAY 1997

Period	Month	Membership	Period	Month	Membership
1	6/93	7245	15	8/94	7588
2	7/93	7107	16	9/94	7189
3	8/93	7038	17	10/94	7227
4	9/93	6748	18	11/94	7581
5	10/93	6901	19	12/94	7543
6	11/93	7170	20	1/95	7751
7	12/93	7282	21	2/95	7692
8	1/94	7379	22	3/95	7740
9	2/94	7401	23	4/95	7867
10	3/94	7456	24	5/95	7821
11	4/94	7592	25	6/95	7971
12	5/94	7619	26	7/95	7892
13	6/94	7737	27	8/95	7754
14	7/94	7694	28	9/95	7421

TABLE 9.14   CANADIAN FACULTY ASSOCIATION MEMBERSHIP: JUNE 1993–MAY 1997

Period	Month	Membership	Period	Month	Membership
29	10/95	7416	39	8/96	7987
30	11/95	7816	40	9/96	7765
31	12/95	7957	41	10/96	7783
32	1/96	8022	42	11/96	8157
33	2/96	7988	43	12/96	8234
34	3/96	8087	44	1/97	8296
35	4/96	8178	45	2/97	8275
36	5/96	8163	46	3/97	8392
37	7/96	8233	47	4/97	8431
38	7/96	8281	48	5/97	8486

To prepare the budget for the 1997–1998 fiscal year, the CFA treasurer requires a forecast of monthly membership over the period June 1997–May 1998.

SOLUTION

The first step is to graph the data over time to get an idea of the enrollment pattern, as shown in Figure 9.10. As you can see, membership in the organization exhibits both long term trend and a pattern of seasonal variation within each calendar year. Since it is believed that monthly changes in membership will increase as the general level of membership increases, we use a multiplicative model for the forecast of the form:

$$y_t = T_t \, S_t \, C_t \, \epsilon_t$$

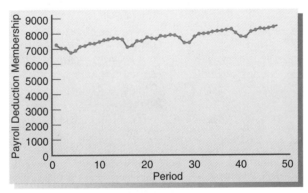

FIGURE 9.10   CFA Enrollment Pattern

We can use the following classical decomposition approach to obtain estimates for the trend, seasonal, and cyclical components of the model. These can then be used to forecast future values of CFA membership.

Step 1—Isolating Trend and Cyclical Components
Approach: Moving Averages

We begin by isolating the effects of the trend and cyclical components. Since we are dealing with monthly data, the "seasons" correspond to months. Taking 12-month moving averages of the data should eliminate the effects of seasonality and reduce the effects of the random error component to a negligible amount, leaving only the trend and cyclical components in the time series.

To illustrate this approach, we calculate the average membership of the first 12 periods (June 1993 to May 1994): (7245 + 7107 + 7038 + . . . + 7592 + 7619)/12 =

7244.83. Calculating the average associated with periods 2 through 13 (July 1993 through June 1994) yields $(7107 + 7038 + 6748 + \ldots + 7619 + 7737)/12 = 7285.83$. These values are associated with the time periods corresponding to the midpoints of these intervals: $(1 + 12)/2 = 6.5$, and $(2 + 13)/2 = 7.5$, respectively. While there is no period 6.5 or 7.5, averaging these two values gives a *centered moving average* corresponding to time period 7 of $(7244.83 + 7285.83)/2 = 7265.33$.

In Table 9.15, calculated using Excel, the moving averages and centered moving averages are presented in the fourth and fifth columns for each 12-month period.[5] We

TABLE 9.15 MOVING AVERAGES AND CENTERED MOVING AVERAGES

Period	Month	Membership	Twelve-Month Moving Average	Centered Moving Average	Seasonal/Random Error Factors $S_t \epsilon_t$	Deseasonalized Time Series
1	6/93	7245				7051.14
2	7/93	7107				6962.58
3	8/93	7038				7074.63
4	9/93	6748				7097.32
5	10/93	6901				7264.29
6	11/97	7170				7207.52
			7244.83			
7	12/93	7282		7265.33	1.00229	7289.78
			7285.83			
8	1/94	7379		7310.29	1.00940	7297.48
			7334.75			
9	2/94	7401		7357.67	1.00589	7369.72
			7380.58			
10	3/94	7456		7398.96	1.00771	7387.02
			7417.33			
11	4/94	7592		7430.92	1.02168	7433.95
			7444.5			
12	5/94	7619		7461.63	1.02109	7495.86
			7478.75			
13	6/94	7737		7489.63	1.03303	7529.98
			7500.50			
14	7/94	7694		7516.00	1.02368	7537.65
			7531.50			
15	8/94	7588		7543.63	1.00588	7627.50
			7555.75			
16	9/94	7189		7567.58	0.94997	7561.15
			7579.42			
17	10/94	7227		7590.88	0.95206	7607.45
			7602.33			
18	11/94	7581		7610.75	0.99609	7620.67
			7619.17			
19	12/94	7543		7628.92	0.98874	7551.05
			7638.67			
20	1/95	7751		7646.92	1.01361	7665.37
			7655.17			
21	2/95	7692		7662.08	1.00390	7659.49
			7669.00			
22	3/95	7740		7678.67	1.00799	7668.39
			7688.33			

[5] Taking moving averages results in only 36 12-month moving averages for the 48 months of data because the first and last six months of 12-month moving averages cannot be calculated.

TABLE 9.15   (continued)

Period	Month	Membership	Twelve-Month Moving Average	Centered Moving Average	Seasonal/Random Error Factors $S_t \, \epsilon_t$	Deseasonalized Time Series
23	4/95	7867		7696.20	1.02219	7703.22
			7704.08			
24	5/95	7821		7713.88	1.01389	7694.60
			7723.67			
25	6/95	7971		7740.92	1.02972	7757.72
			7758.17			
26	7/95	7892		7769.46	1.01577	7731.62
			7780.75			
27	8/95	7754		7793.08	0.99498	7794.36
			7805.41			
28	9/95	7421		7819.88	0.94899	7805.16
			7834.33			
29	10/95	7416		7847.29	0.94504	7806.40
			7860.25			
30	11/95	7816		7874.5	0.99257	7856.90
			7888.75			
31	12/95	7957		7899.67	1.00726	7965.50
			7910.58			
32	1/96	8022		7926.79	1.01201	7933.38
			7943.00			
33	2/96	7988		7952.71	1.00444	7954.24
			7962.42			
34	3/94	8087		7976.75	1.01382	8012.18
			7991.08			
35	4/96	8178		8006.38	1.02144	8007.75
			8021.67			
36	5/96	8163		8035.88	1.01582	8031.07
			8050.08			
37	6/96	8233		8061.63	1.02126	8012.71
			8073.17			
38	7/96	8281		8084.58	1.02430	8112.72
			8096.00			
39	8/96	7987		8107.96	0.98508	8028.57
			8119.92			
40	9/96	7765		8132.63	0.95480	8166.97
			8145.33			
41	10/96	7783		8155.88	0.95428	8192.72
			8166.42			
42	11/96	8157		8179.88	0.99720	8199.69
			8193.33			
43	10/96	8234				8242.79
44	1/97	8296				8204.35
45	2/97	8275				8240.02
46	3/97	8392				8314.36
47	4/97	8431				8255.48
48	5/97	8486				8348.85

illustrate that each moving average corresponds to the middle of each season (month), by placing these averages on a line midway between the corresponding periods. Figure 9.11 graphically depicts the centered moving averages over time.

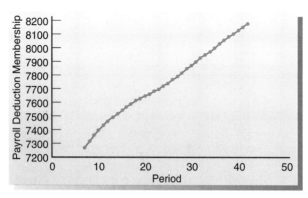

FIGURE 9.11 Centered Moving Averages for CFA Membership

Step 2—Determining Seasonal/Random Error Factors
Approach: Divide the Time Series Data by the Centered Moving Average Values

Because taking moving averages effectively eliminates seasonality and the random components, the centered moving averages only represent the product of the trend and cyclical components ($T_t C_t$) only. Since $Y_t = T_t S_t C_t \epsilon_t$, dividing the time series by the centered moving averages results in terms representing the product of the seasonal and random components, i.e., $Y_t/(T_t C_t) = S_t \epsilon_t$. These ratios, known as the seasonal/random error factors, are shown in column 6 of Table 9.15. For example, in time period 7, the seasonal/random error factor, $S_7 \epsilon_7$, is:

$$S_7 \epsilon_7 = 7282/7265.33 = 1.00229$$

Step 3—Determining Seasonal Factors
Approach: Average the Seasonal/Random Error Factors

For each month (season), we now average the corresponding seasonal/random error factors, $S_t \epsilon_t$, over the three years for which these values have been calculated. (Data are not available for the first and last six month periods.) Averaging the three different values for each seasonal factor substantially eliminates the random component, ϵ_t, giving a pure seasonal factor, S_t.[6] These average values are given in the second column of Table 9.16.

TABLE 9.16   SEASONAL FACTORS

Month	Seasonal Factor	Adjusted Seasonal Factor $=\dfrac{\text{Seasonal Factor}}{\text{Average Seasonal Factor}}$
December	0.999430	0.998933
January	1.011674	1.011171
February	1.004744	1.004245
March	1.009839	1.009338
April	1.021768	1.021261
May	1.016933	1.016428
June	1.028003	1.027493
July	1.021250	1.020743
August	0.995316	0.994822
September	0.951254	0.950781
October	0.950462	0.949990
November	0.995289	0.994794

[6]While a geometric average, rather than an arithmetic average, may be more appropriate, since the seasonal variations are values close to 1, there is little difference in the two approaches. Hence, we use an arithmetic average for simplicity.

For example, the seasonal/random error factors calculated for June 1994, 1995, and 1996 are 1.03303, 1.02972, and 1.02126, respectively. Thus, the seasonal factor for June is:

$$(1.03303 + 1.02972 + 1.02126)/3 = 1.028003$$

We also should adjust the seasonal factors so that they average 1. This is done by dividing each seasonal factor by the overall average of these factors. The average of the above set of 12 seasonal factors is $(0.99430 + 1.011674 + \ldots + 0.995289)/12 = 1.000497$. Therefore, we calculate the adjusted seasonal factors by dividing each seasonal factor in Table 9.1*b* by 1.000497. These values are given in the third column of Table 9.16.

Step 4—Identifying the Time Series Trend
Approach: Deseasonalize the Data By Dividing Series Values by Seasonal Factors

We now *deseasonalize* the data in Table 9.15 in order to identify the trend present in the time series. We do so by dividing each of the original time series values, $Y_t = T_t S_t C_t \epsilon_t$, by the corresponding adjusted seasonal factor, S_t. The resulting ratios comprise only the trend, cyclical, and irregular components of the time series ($T_t C_t \epsilon_t$).

For example, in period 1 (June 1993), we divide the number of members (7245) by the adjusted seasonal factor for June (1.027493), giving a deseasonalized value of $7245/1.027493 = 7051.14$. The last column of Table 9.15 shows the resulting deseasonalized data for all 48 periods. Figure 9.12 graphically depicts the deseasonalized time series.

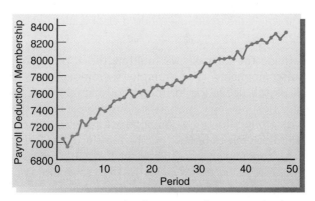

FIGURE 9.12   Deseasonalized Time Series for CFA Membership

Step 5—Identifying the Trend Component
Approach: Linear Regression

According to Figure 9.12, the time series data with the seasonal components eliminated exhibit a linear trend. Linear regression can therefore be used to determine the trend component in the deseasonalized time series[7] by regressing the deseasonalized time series values on the corresponding period number. Using the Excel output in Figure 9.13 the following regression equation was obtained.:

$$T_t = 7095.887 + 26.132t \tag{9.10}$$

For example, in period 50, the trend component of the time series forecast is $7095.887 + 26.132 (50) = 8402.487$.

Note that, if there had been no trend in the resulting data values calculated in Step 4, we could have used either a moving average or the exponential smoothing approach to forecast the level of the data. Alternatively, if the data values exhibited a nonlinear trend, we would use a forecasting technique appropriate for that functional form.

---

[7]While other techniques, such as Holt's method, can be used to forecast linear trend, linear regression is the method most frequently used in classical decomposition.

	df	SS	MS	F	Significance F
Regression	1	6290512	6290512	1869.944	6.63E-39
Residual	46	154740.4	3363.921		
Total	47	6445253			

	Coefficients	Standard Error	t-stat	P-value	Lower 95%	Upper 95%
Intercept	7095.887	17.00804	417.2078	5.93E-84	7061.651	7130.122
Time	26.1316	0.604291	43.24343	6.63E-39	24.91523	27.34798

FIGURE 9.13 Excel Regression Output for CFA Membership Data

Step 6—Identifying the Cyclical Factors

Approach: Divide the Deseasonalized Data by the Trend Component and Smooth

If cyclical variation is suspected, we divide the deseasonalized time series ratios, $T_t C_t \epsilon_t$, by the estimates of the trend component (T_t) found using the trend line determined in Step 5. The resulting ratios represent only the cyclical and random error components ($C_t \epsilon_t$). These ratios are then smoothed, using moving averages to eliminate the random error component. The result is an estimate for the cyclical component, C_t.

From Table 9.15 and Figure 9.12 we see, however, that the deseasonalized time series does not appear to exhibit any apparent cyclical variation. Hence, we shall assume that no cyclical variation is present in the time series and that all the cyclical factors are equal to 1. As a result, the ratios given in the last column of Table 9.15 represent solely the trend and random error components, $T_t \epsilon_t$.

Step 7—Performing the Forecast

Approach: Substitute the Values for T_t, S_t (and C_t)

To determine the forecast, we multiply the appropriate trend by the corresponding seasonal components.[8] For example, to forecast the membership that will be paid through payroll deduction for the period between June 1997 and May 1998, we must forecast corresponding to periods 49 through 60. Using the calculated regression equation to determine the trend component for these periods, we obtain the values given in the third column of Table 9.17. The fourth column gives the corresponding adjusted seasonal components we calculated in Table 9.16 for each of these 12 months. Multiplying the forecasted trend values by the seasonal components gives us the desired forecast, shown in the fifth column of Table 9.17.

TABLE 9.17   FORECASTED MEMBERSHIP PAID THROUGH PAYROLL DEDUCTION

Period t	Month	Trend T_t	Seasonal S_t	Forecast $T_t S_t$
49	6/97	8376.335	1.027493	8606.644
50	7/97	8402.487	1.020743	8576.778
51	8/97	8428.619	0.994822	8384.976
52	9/97	8454.751	0.950782	8038.621
53	10/97	8480.883	0.949990	8056.752
54	11/97	8507.015	0.994794	8462.730
55	12/97	8533.147	0.998934	8524.047
56	1/98	8559.279	1.011171	8654.897
57	2/98	8585.411	1.004245	8621.855
58	3/98	8611.543	1.009338	8691.959
59	4/98	8637.675	1.021261	8821.322
60	5/98	8663.807	1.016428	8806.134

[8]If cyclical factors are present in the time series, we multiply these also to obtain the forecast value.

Based on this analysis for CFA membership, the Student Consulting Group prepared the following memorandum to the treasurer of the CFA. In this memo, a graph of the membership over the four years is presented, and the forecasts are summarized in an easy-to-read table.

M E M O R A N D U M

To: Dr. Abigale Jarmon-Thomas, Treasurer—Canadian Faculty Association

From: Student Consulting Group

Subj: Forecasted Membership, June 1997–May 1998

We have prepared a forecast for the membership of the Canadian Faculty Association in each month of the fiscal year from June 1997 through May 1998 by separating the members who pay by payroll deduction from those who pay their dues directly to the organization. The reason for this distinction is that, while the membership paying dues directly has remained fairly constant, at approximately 210 members over the past five years, the number paying by payroll deduction has varied significantly from month to month. Hence, our approach is to add a constant 210 members to the forecasted number of members paying by payroll deduction in order to obtain a forecast of total membership.

In developing this forecast, we analyzed a historical pattern of membership to gain insights into its trend and variability. Figure I shows the membership pattern of payroll deduction members over the past four-year period.

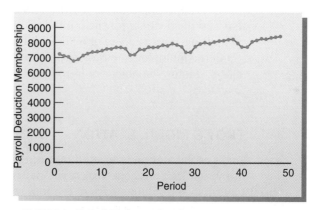

FIGURE I   Payroll Deduction Members over Four-year Period

Based on this pattern, we determined a forecasting model for members paying dues through payroll deduction. This model accounts for both the upward trend and periodic variation in membership and gives the following monthly forecast of total membership (including those who pay directly to the organization).

Month	Membership Forecast
June 1997	8817
July 1997	8787
Aug. 1997	8595
Sept. 1997	8249
Oct. 1997	8267

Month	Membership Forecast
Nov. 1997	8673
Dec. 1997	8734
Jan. 1998	8865
Feb. 1998	8832
Mar. 1998	8902
Apr. 1998	9031
May 1998	9016

It is important to realize that these forecasts implicitly assume that the historic trend in the past years' data will continue into the upcoming year. It is our understanding that the current fiscal difficulties experienced by a number of Canadian provinces may result in a decrease in the number of faculty employed by state-supported universities, which in turn, would be expected to have a negative impact on CFA membership.

If this situation does arise, it would be necessary to revise our forecast of membership downward. Hence, we recommend close monitoring of provincial budgets and, if there is a decrease in employment, we can modify the forecast appropriately.

We hope that this information has been of value to you. Should you have any questions, please do not hesitate to contact us.

THE ADDITIVE MODEL   We conclude this section by considering an additive forecasting model for time series that exhibit trend, seasonal, and cyclical components. If we believe that an additive model is appropriate for forecasting, we can use a decomposition approach similar to that described earlier for the multiplicative model. However, another technique, based on multiple regression, is often used for such models.

In the multiple regression approach to forecasting models with trend and seasonal effects, dummy variables are introduced to denote the seasons. We use this technique to analyze the situation at Troy's Mobil Station.

TROY'S MOBIL STATION

Troy.fcc
Troy.xls

Troy's Mobil station is located in the resort town of Liberty, New York. Over the past five years, Troy has kept track of his daily gasoline sales and noticed an apparent fluctuation in sales during each of the four seasons.

While the town has experienced a steady increase in the year-round population over this period, Troy feels that most of the seasonal variation in sales can be attributed to the varying number of tourists who visit the region throughout the year. Table 9.18 shows the average number of gallons of gasoline Troy has sold daily over the past five years during each of the four seasons. (Year 5 is the most recent year.)

TABLE 9.18   AVERAGE GALLONS OF GASOLINE SOLD DAILY AT TROY'S MOBIL STATION

Season	Year				
	1	2	3	4	5
Fall	3497	3726	3989	4248	4443
Winter	3484	3589	3870	4105	4307
Spring	3553	3742	3996	4263	4466
Summer	3837	4050	4327	4544	4795

Troy is interested in forecasting the average daily gasoline sales during each of the four seasons over the upcoming year in order to determine his inventory and personnel needs.

SOLUTION

Figure 9.14 shows the pattern of average gasoline sales over the five year period. Because the change in the number of tourists each season has been fairly constant over the past five years, an additive seasonality model may be appropriate. Multiple regression can be used to generate these forecasts.

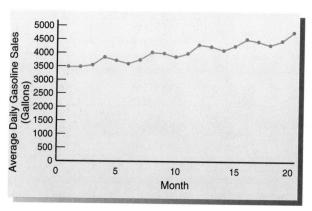

FIGURE 9.14   Troy's Average Daily Gasoline Sales over Five-year Period

In this approach, the item being forecasted (gasoline sales) is the dependent (y) variable. The independent variables are the period number and dummy variables that indicate the period's season. The dummy indicator variable for a season is 1 if the period corresponds to that season; otherwise, it is 0. Since there are four seasons, only three dummy variables are used; season 4 is indicated by assigning 0s to the other three.[9] Thus, the model (neglecting the cyclical component) is:

$$y_t = \beta_0 + \beta_1 t + S_1 x_1 + S_2 x_2 + S_3 x_3 + \epsilon_t \qquad (9.11)$$

where: t = period number
β_0 = level of the time series
β_1 = slope (trend) of the time series
S_1 = seasonal factor for fall
S_2 = seasonal factor for winter
S_3 = seasonal factor for spring
x_1 = indicator for fall
x_2 = indicator for winter
x_3 = indicator for spring
ϵ_t = random term in period t

That is, x_1, x_2, and x_3 are binary variables denoting the appropriate season (i.e., 1, if the period corresponds to that season and 0, if it does not. Summer is indicated by $x_1 = 0$, $x_2 = 0$, and $x_3 = 0$). The data for this problem are summarized in Table 9.19. Our objective is to obtain estimates for the parameters, β_0, β_1, S_1, S_2, and S_3, of the multiple regression model.

---

[9]In general, if there are N seasons, only N-1 dummy variables are needed in the model.

TABLE 9.19   QUARTERLY INPUT DATA FOR TROY'S MOBIL STATION PROBLEM

Year	Season	y_t	t	x_1	x_2	x_3
1	Fall	3497	1	1	0	0
	Winter	3484	2	0	1	0
	Spring	3553	3	0	0	1
	Summer	3837	4	0	0	0
2	Fall	3726	5	1	0	0
	Winter	3589	6	0	1	0
	Spring	3742	7	0	0	1
	Summer	4050	8	0	0	0
3	Fall	3989	9	1	0	0
	Winter	3870	10	0	1	0
	Spring	3996	11	0	0	1
	Summer	4327	12	0	0	0
4	Fall	4248	13	1	0	0
	Winter	4105	14	0	1	0
	Spring	4263	15	0	0	1
	Summer	4544	16	0	0	0
5	Fall	4443	17	1	0	0
	Winter	4307	18	0	1	0
	Spring	4466	19	0	0	1
	Summer	4795	20	0	0	0

Using Excel to solve this program gives us the output in (Figure 9.15). This output yields the regression equation

$$\hat{y}_t = 3611 + 58.3\, t - 155\, x_1 - 323\, x_2 - 248\, x_3 \qquad (9.12)$$

	df	SS	MS	F	Significance F
Regression	4	2710623	677655.7	685.3233	8.82E-17
Residual	15	14832.18	988.8117		
Total	19	2725455			

	Coefficients	Standard Error	t-stat	P-value	Lower 95%	Upper 95%
Intercept	3610.625	20.49988	176.1291	2.74E-26	3566.931	3654.319
Period	58.33125	1.242988	46.92826	1.08E-17	55.68188	60.98062
Fall	-155.006	20.23437	-7.66054	1.46E-06	-198.135	-111.878
Winter	-322.938	20.04257	-16.1126	7.04E-11	-365.657	-280.218
Spring	-248.269	19.92661	-12.4592	2.58E-09	-290.741	-205.796

FIGURE 9.15   Excel Regression Output for Troy's Mobil Station

The low p-value for the F test (denoted Significance F) indicates that the model has significant predictive ability. All the coefficients of this model are also statistically significant because of their low p-values (or, equivalently, the high absolute values of the t-ratios).

Using this model, Troy forecasts the following average gasoline sales during the upcoming four seasons:

Fall, year 6: This is period t = 21. The season is denoted by $x_1 = 1$, $x_2 = 0$, and $x_3 = 0$. Hence, $\hat{y}_t = 3611 + 58.3\,(21) - 155\,(1) - 323\,(0) - 248\,(0) = 4680$

Winter year 6: This is period 22 and $x_1 = 0$, $x_2 = 1$, and $x_3 = 0$.
   Hence, $\hat{y}_t = 3611 + 58.3\,(22) - 155\,(0) - 323\,(1) - 248\,(0) = 4571$

Spring year 6: This is period 23 and $x_1 = 0$, $x_2 = 0$, and $x_3 = 1$.
   Hence, $\hat{y}_t = 3611 + 58.3\,(23) - 155\,(0) - 323\,(0) - 248\,(1) = 4704$

Summer year 6: This is period 24 and $x_1 = x_2 = x_3 = 0$.
   Hence, $\hat{y}_t = 3611 + 58.3\,(24) - 155\,(0) - 323\,(0) - 248\,(0) = 5010$

9.6 OTHER FORECASTING TECHNIQUES

BOX–JENKINS METHOD

Often, the analyst may not know which model is the most appropriate for describing a time series. Ideally, we would like a technique that can help us select the appropriate underlying forecasting model. A popular advanced forecasting technique, known as the *Box–Jenkins method*, does just that. While the use of this method is beyond the scope of this text, a brief overview of how it works is worthwhile.

The Box–Jenkins method makes use of the autocorrelation function and a related function, known as the partial autocorrelation function, to identify the appropriate forecasting model. The technique bases its forecasts on a combined autoregressive and moving average model. It is called autoregressive because the forecast is based on historic time series values. In addition, n period differences between time series values are used in this forecasting model. These are known as ARIMA, or *autoregressive–integrated–moving average*, forecasting models.

FORECASTING USING MULTIPLE TIME SERIES

While we have focused on forecasting a single time series in this chapter, frequently, several time series are used to derive a forecast. For example, a video rental store may be able to forecast rental demand for a particular movie title based not only on past rental demand, but also on box office receipts during the movie's theatrical release. Similarly, a nationwide retailer selling replacement tires for automobiles could base its forecast of future tire demand not only on the time series of past sales of the tire brand, but also on the time series of past sales of new automobiles. Typically, a technique such as multiple regression is used for models in which more than one time series is used to derive the forecast.

Forecasting an item of interest may require the performance of several different forecasts. For example, a security analyst who wants to forecast a firm's upcoming quarterly profit typically forecasts not only revenues for each of the company's principal divisions or product lines, but also costs for major expense items, such as advertising, labor, and materials. In turn, forecasting revenue for a company's product line may require separate forecasts for both the total market for the product and the company's market share.

QUALITATIVE APPROACHES TO FORECASTING

Time series data may not always be available. For example, a new product has no past history on which to base sales forecasts. When historic time series data are not available (or when they are considered nonrepresentative of future values), we normally gather "expert" opinions on which to base a forecast.

One way to coalesce these opinions into a consensus is through a method known as the *Delphi Technique*. In this method, each member of a panel of experts is asked individually to give his or her forecast. The makeup of the expert panel is typically kept secret from the panel members. Forecasts are compiled into an anonymous list and returned to the experts so that panel members can revise their forecasts if necessary in light of the responses given by other panel members. After revision, the list is again circulated for possible additional revisions. The process continues until a reasonably consistent consensus is reached.

Another qualitative technique for generating forecasts is *scenario writing*. In this technique, we begin with a well-defined set of assumptions and build a scenario regarding the future based on these assumptions. Usually, several scenarios are developed based on different sets of assumptions. The decision maker then selects the scenario that corresponds to the set of assumptions believed most likely to occur.

9.7 SUMMARY

In this chapter, we have examined the process of generating a forecast. In particular, we have focused on how, based on time series data, we determine the appropriate forecasting model to use, and we have discussed techniques that can be applied to these various models in order to obtain forecasts.

Time series that exhibit a stationary pattern can be forecast using techniques such as simple or weighted moving averages or exponential smoothing. Of special concern when selecting the appropriate technique is the ability of the forecast model to respond quickly to changes so that future forecast errors are not too severe.

Some time series exhibit linear trend without seasonal or cyclical factors. Linear regression and double exponential smoothing are two techniques for forecasting such models. Other time series exhibit trend, seasonality, and cyclical factors. A multiplicative or an additive model may be appropriate for forecasting such time series. The multiplicative model relies on the classical decomposition technique, whereas a technique based on multiple regression is frequently used for forecasting an additive model.

The general method of classical decomposition for a multiplicative model is summarized in Table 9.20.

TABLE 9.20   SUMMARY OF THE CLASSICAL DECOMPOSITION PROCEDURE FOR MULTIPLICATIVE MODELS

Step 1. *Isolate Trend and Cyclical Components by Taking Moving Averages.* Calculate n-period centered moving averages (where n is the number of seasons) to give $T_t C_t$.

Step 2. *Determine Seasonal/Random Error Factors by Dividing the Time Series Data by the Centered Moving Average Values.* Divide the original time series values by the corresponding centered moving average to give $S_t \epsilon_t$.

Step 3. *Determine Seasonal Factors by Averaging the Seasonal/Random Error Factors.* Average the seasonal/random error factors for the time periods corresponding to that season. This eliminates the random error components, leaving S_t. Adjust the seasonal factors so that they average to 1 by dividing by the average seasonal factor.

Step 4. *Identify the Time Series Trend by Deseasonalizing the Data.* Divide each value of the time series by its corresponding seasonal factor. This results in ratios that reflect the combined effects of the trend, cyclical, and random error components ($T_t C_t \epsilon_t$).

Step 5. *Identify the Trend Component Using Linear Regression.* If the data values calculated in Step 4 show a linear trend, linear regression can be used to forecast the trend component. This is done by regressing the data values against their period number in order to calculate a regression equation. T_t is the value of the regression equation at time t.

Step 6. *Identify the Cyclical Component by Dividing the Deseasonalized Data by The Trend Component and Smoothing.* If it is suspected that a cyclical component is present in the data, divide the deseasonalized data by the estimated trend component (T_t). The resulting values then reflect only the cyclical and random error components ($C_t \epsilon_t$). Moving averages can then be used to eliminate the random error component, leaving estimates for the cyclical component, C_t.

Step 7. *Perform the Forecast.* To forecast future values of the time series, forecast the trend component (T_t) and multiply this value by the appropriate seasonal (S_t) and cyclical (C_t) components.

Other forecasting methods include advanced time series techniques and qualitative approaches that can be used when time series data are not available. Table 9.21 summarizes the principal time series forecasting techniques discussed in this chapter.

TABLE 9.21   PRINCIPLE FORECASTING TECHNIQUES

Time Series Model	Technique	Comments
Stationary	Last Period	*Pros*: Forecast is extremely easy to calculate; requires only one data value to perform forecast; tracks changes in the time series quickly. *Cons*: Past time series data are ignored; forecast errors may be large.
	Moving Average	*Pros*: Easy to calculate forecast; uses past time series values. *Cons*: Each historic period is given the same weight; data beyond a certain age are ignored; may be difficult to determine how many periods should be used; data for n periods must be stored in the system; tracks changes in the time series gradually.
	Weighted Moving Average	*Pros*: Uses past time series values but gives greater weight to more recent observations; useful for stationary time series that exhibit autocorrelation; can track changes in the time series quickly. *Cons*: May be difficult to determine how many periods to use and the weights to assign to each period; data beyond a certain age are ignored; data for n periods must be stored in the system.
	Exponential Smoothing	*Pros*: Fairly easy to calculate forecast; uses past time series values indirectly; only two data values must be stored in the system to perform the forecast; can track changes in the time series quickly; useful for stationary time series which exhibit autocorrelation. *Cons*: May be difficult to determine the appropriate smoothing constant and initial forecast value to use; the relative weight given to past observations is fixed by the choice of the smoothing constant.
Trend	Linear Regression	*Pros*: Determines the forecasting model that gives the smallest mean squared forecast error; uses as much historic data in developing the forecast as desired. *Cons*: May not be appropriate if the random error terms are not independent or if they do not have constant variance; data for n periods must be stored in the system; assumes linear trend will continue forever into the future; forecast will track changes quite slowly.
	Holt's Linear Exponential Smoothing	*Pros*: Forecast can respond rapidly to changes in the time series values; a small number of historical values must be stored in the system in order to perform the forecast. *Cons*: It may be difficult to determine the optimal values for the smoothing constants as well as the initial forecast values; forecast calculations are somewhat difficult to perform.

TABLE 9.21 (continued)

Time Series Model	Technique	Comments
Trend, Seasonal and Cyclical Component Models	Classical Decomposition for Multiplicative Models	*Pros:* The effects of the various factors on the forecast are clear; calculations are fairly straightforward. *Cons:* May be difficult to determine the cyclical factors; calculations may be time consuming; tracks changes in the time series components slowly.
	Multiple Regression for Additive Models	*Pros:* Easy to perform; the effects of seasonal and trend component on the time series are clear. *Cons:* May be difficult to incorporate cyclical variation; tracks changes in the time series components slowly.

It is important to realize that forecasting is not an exact science. No matter which technique is selected, the goal is the same: to develop a prediction regarding the future that is more accurate than simply guessing.

$\mathcal{N}$OTATIONAL SUMMARY

C_t = The cyclical component of the time series at time t

k = The number of periods used in calculating a weighted moving average

LAD = Largest absolute deviation

$\hat{L}_t$ = The estimate of the time series level for time t

MAD = Mean absolute deviation

MAPE = Mean absolute percent error

MSE = Mean squared error

n = The number of observations making up the time series

S_t = The seasonal component of the time series at time t for a multiplicative model

S_i = The seasonal factor for the ith season in an additive model

$\hat{T}_t$ = The estimate of the time series trend for time t

w_i = The weight given the time series value which is i periods old when calculating a weighted moving average

x_i = A dummy indicator for season i in an additive model

y_t = The value of the time series at time t

$\hat{y}_t$ = The forecasted value of the time series for period t

α = The smoothing constant used in exponential smoothing for the time series level

β_0 = The unchanging mean value of the time series

β_1 = The linear trend of the time series

Δ_t = The forecast error for period t

ϵ_t = The random error term at time t

γ = The smoothing constant for the time series trend

Using WINQSB *to Evaluate Forecasting Models*

On the initial data screen of the forecasting module of WINQSB we specify the problem name, the time unit, the number of periods of time series data, and the choice between times series forecasting and regression forecasting. Exhibit 9.1 shows the initial forecasting screen for the YoHo yo-yo problem discussed in Section 9.2.

EXHIBIT 9.1

We then enter the historic time series values on a data input screen and solve the problem by selecting "Perform Forecasting" from the "Solve and Analyze" menu. Exhibit 9.2, shows the screen we complete to determine the desired forecasting method, our choice between assigning

EXHIBIT 9.2

parameters or allowing WINQSB to search for the best parameters, the criteria we wish to use to evaluate the forecasting technique, and the number of periods we wish to forecast. To get the forecast we click OK.

If we select multiple regression analysis on the initial input screen, we input the problem name, the number of factors, and the number of observations. Exhibit 9.3 shows the initial screen for the additive model used by Troy's Mobil Station in Section 9.5. We enter the dependent variable as the first factor and the independent variables as the other factors. Exhibit 9.4 gives the data entry for the Troy's Mobile Station problem.

EXHIBIT 9.3

Observation	Factor 1	Factor 2	Factor 3	Factor 4	Factor 5
1	3497	1	1	0	
2	3484	2	0	1	
3	3553	3	0	0	
4	3837	4	0	0	
5	3726	5	1	0	
6	3589	6	0	1	
7	3742	7	0	0	
8	4050	8	0	0	
9	3989	9	1	0	
10	3870	10	0	1	
11	3996	11	0	0	
12	4327	12	0	0	
13	4248	13	1	0	
14	4105	14	0	1	
15	4263	15	0	0	
16	4544	16	0	0	
17	4443	17	1	0	

EXHIBIT 9.4

Once the data are entered, we select "Perform Linear Regression" from the "Solve and Analyze" option on the menu bar; this yields the screen shown in Exhibit 9.5. Clicking on OK gives the output shown in Exhibit 9.6.

EXHIBIT 9.5

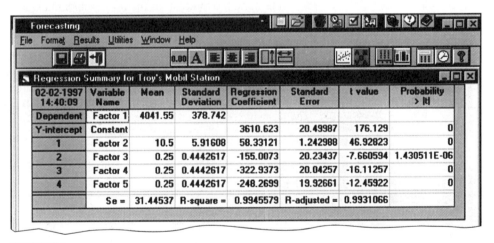

02-02-1997 14:40:09	Variable Name	Mean	Standard Deviation	Regression Coefficient	Standard Error	t value	Probability > |t|
Dependent	Factor 1	4041.55	378.742				
Y-intercept	Constant			3610.623	20.49987	176.129	0
1	Factor 2	10.5	5.91608	58.33121	1.242988	46.92823	0
2	Factor 3	0.25	0.4442617	-155.0073	20.23437	-7.660594	1.430511E-06
3	Factor 4	0.25	0.4442617	-322.9373	20.04257	-16.11257	0
4	Factor 5	0.25	0.4442617	-248.2699	19.92661	-12.45922	0
	Se =	31.44537	R-square =	0.9945579	R-adjusted =	0.9931066	

EXHIBIT 9.6

ℙROBLEMS

1. Monthly water usage at the Smith home for the past year, as measured in 100s of cubic feet, has been as follows:

Period	Month	Usage
1	January	17
2	February	24
3	March	21
4	April	20
5	May	17
6	June	21
7	July	21
8	August	19
9	September	17
10	October	18
11	November	20
12	December	21

a. Graph this time series. Does a stationary model seem appropriate?

b. Using regression, show that a stationary model is reasonable.

c. Using a four-month moving average, forecast water usage for the Smith family for both the upcoming month of January and the entire upcoming year.

d. What is the forecast for the upcoming month of January if a three-month weighted moving average with weights, $w_1 = .6$, $w_2 = .3$, and $w_3 = .1$ is used?

e. Which of the above two forecasting methods would you recommend based on the mean squared forecast error criterion?

2. Consider the data given for the Smith family water usage in Problem 1. Assume that the forecast procedure begins in February with an initial value equal to 17, the actual water usage (in 100s of cubic feet) in January.

a. Determine the forecast for the upcoming January if exponential smoothing is used with a smoothing constant of $\alpha = .1$.

b. Repeat part a using $\alpha = .6$.

c. Using the criterion of minimizing the mean squared forecast error which smoothing constant, $\alpha = .1$ or $\alpha = .6$, appears to give better results?

3. Curaid Company wishes to forecast monthly sales for the upcoming year of its line of designer bandages, introduced two years ago and advertised using the slogan "What the best-dressed cuts are wearing." Monthly sales (in gross) are as follows:

Month	Sales	Month	Sales
1	424	13	546
2	418	14	557
3	435	15	559
4	449	16	554
5	446	17	573
6	469	18	574
7	500	19	604
8	481	20	611
9	489	21	626
10	506	22	636
11	530	23	649
12	532	24	643

a. Graph this time series.

b. Show statistically that a linear trend forecasting model is appropriate.

c. Using a linear regression technique, forecast monthly sales for the next 12-month period (i.e., months 25–36).

4. Consider the data in Problem 3. Assume that the forecast procedure begins in month 2, with the initial forecast for the level being the sales in month 2, and the initial

forecast for the trend being the difference between the sales in months 1 and 2. Use Holt's technique with $\alpha = .2$ and $\gamma = .3$ to perform a forecast over the upcoming 12-month period.

5. Daily donut sales (in dollars) at Watson's Donuts for the past four weeks are as follows:

	Week			
Day	1	2	3	4
Sunday	291.59	310.57	285.28	307.43
Monday	346.86	336.89	358.67	361.30
Tuesday	319.47	335.68	331.77	342.59
Wednesday	375.34	365.19	369.82	381.43
Thursday	356.73	371.82	395.44	402.56
Friday	298.93	343.96	363.45	357.17
Saturday	327.05	338.05	352.02	354.63

Assume that Watson's wishes to forecast daily sales for weeks 5 and 6 and wants to use a multiplicative model to account for seasonal (daily) variations. Using classical decomposition, determine the forecast of daily demand for weeks 5 and 6.

6. Weekly sales (in hundreds) of PERT shampoo at the SaveMor drug chain for the past 16 weeks are as follows:

Week	Sales	Week	Sales
1	65	9	72
2	61	10	78
3	68	11	73
4	67	12	75
5	74	13	68
6	82	14	64
7	75	15	73
8	63	16	79

Management wishes to forecast the annual demand for PERT shampoo in order to determine an optimal order policy.

a. Graph this time series.

b. Verify statistically that a stationary model is appropriate for forecasting this time series.

c. Using a four-period moving average, forecast the annual demand for PERT shampoo. (Assume sales = demand.)

7. Consider the data given in Problem 6. Use exponential smoothing to forecast the annual demand for PERT shampoo. Let the forecast begin in week 10 with an initial forecast value equal to the average sales in the first 10 weeks and use a smoothing constant of $\alpha = .10$.

8. Dixon Glass manufactures mason jars for use in home canning. Quarterly sales for this division (in millions of dollars) over the past five years are as follows (year 5 is the most recent year):

	Year				
Quarter	1	2	3	4	5
1	7.8	7.2	6.8	6.6	6.3
2	12.1	10.7	11.4	10.3	10.2
3	9.4	8.5	8.2	7.4	8.6
4	5.3	4.9	4.3	5.2	4.2

Dixon management believes that an additive model incorporating seasonality is appropriate for forecasting upcoming quarterly sales. Using the multiple regression approach, forecast quarterly sales for year 6.

9. The Hillel Sandwich Shop is trying to estimate its profit for the upcoming month. In order to do this, it must forecast future sandwich sales. Below are the number of sandwiches sold each day of the five-day work week for the past four weeks (week 4 is the most recent week).

Day	Week			
	1	2	3	4
Monday	140	162	172	159
Tuesday	156	135	163	132
Wednesday	172	158	141	135
Thursday	144	174	162	151
Friday	112	146	138	142

a. Graph this time series.
b. Determine whether the time series exhibits any linear trend.
c. Using a five-day moving average, forecast the number of sandwiches that will be sold daily during the upcoming week.
d. What is the forecast of the number of sandwiches sold daily during the upcoming week if the firm uses exponential smoothing? (Assume that the smoothing constant is $\alpha = .10$ and the forecast begins on Tuesday in Week 1 with an initial forecast value of 140.)

10. Consider the data in Problem 9.

a. If the firm wishes to use exponential smoothing to forecast the number of sandwiches sold daily, use WINQSB to determine the smoothing constant that minimizes the mean squared forecast error. Assume that the forecast begins on Tuesday of week 1 with an initial forecast value of 140.
b. Determine how many days we would need to use in computing a moving average if we want the average age of the data to equal the average age of the data for the exponential smoothing technique found in part (a).

11. Net sales (in millions of dollars) for Armco Plastics over the past five years (year 5 is the most recent year) are as follows:

Year	Sales
1	107,742
2	112,346
3	122,168
4	125,598
5	126,610

Using the linear regression technique, forecast net sales of Armco Plastics for years 6 through 8.

12. Quarterly revenues (in $1000s) of the Gray Rabbit Hotel chain over the past five years have been as follows.

Quarter	Year				
	1	2	3	4	5
1	5108	4871	5248	5365	5423
2	6121	5907	6214	6323	6408
3	6394	6485	6582	6647	6586
4	4593	4798	4893	5021	5134

On the basis of these data, use a multiplicative forecasting model based on classical decomposition to forecast quarterly revenues for year 6.

13. Student enrollments in the management science core class offered at a major university have been as follows:

Period	Enrollment
Year 1	
Fall	756
Spring	723
Summer	143
Year 2	
Fall	823
Spring	745
Summer	157
Year 3	
Fall	834
Spring	752
Summer	158
Year 4	
Fall	836
Spring	765
Summer	164

Using an additive model based on linear regression to account for seasonality, determine the enrollment forecast for fall, spring, and summer of year 5.

14. Susan Wilson is considering purchasing an eight-unit apartment building as an investment. In order to determine her projected annual return, Susan must estimate the cost of natural gas used to provide hot water and heat to the building. The current owner has provided Susan with copies of the monthly gas bill over the past three years. These data are as follows (year 3 is the most recent year).

	Year		
	1	2	3
January	$396.87	$406.58	$429.04
February	$345.92	$429.56	$405.62
March	$287.56	$319.87	$347.29
April	$265.34	$306.45	$325.70
May	$194.13	$208.56	$254.55
June	$185.39	$196.49	$214.86
July	$156.43	$147.37	$187.72
August	$148.92	$174.63	$166.28
September	$239.58	$227.91	$245.18
October	$275.29	$269.02	$286.04
November	$295.06	$314.38	$337.91
December	$349.73	$319.34	$378.48

Using a multiplicative model based on classical decomposition, forecast the gas utility cost of the apartment building for the upcoming year.

15. The production manager for Bee's Candy Company is trying to decide whether he should purchase cocoa futures to satisfy the firm's cocoa requirements for the upcoming six-month period. The average cost of purchasing cocoa in this fashion is $0.46 per pound. The firm requires 140,000 pounds of cocoa in order to support production over this period.

The manager feels that purchasing futures contracts is worthwhile only if it costs an average of no more than $0.01 per pound over purchasing the cocoa on the spot market. Average spot market prices per pound over the past 20 weeks are given in the table below (week 20 is the most recent week):

Week	Cost/Pound	Week	Cost/Pound
1	$.42	11	$.48
2	.45	12	.49
3	.45	13	.48
4	.43	14	.47
5	.44	15	.47
6	.45	16	.46
7	.44	17	.46
8	.46	18	.45
9	.45	19	.44
10	.47	20	.45

a. Graph this time series.

b. Show statistically that a stationary forecasting model is appropriate. (Test at $\alpha = .05$.)

c. Suppose that the manager uses exponential smoothing with a smoothing constant, $\alpha = .2$. If this procedure begins with an initial cost/pound forecast of $0.42, forecast the firm's cost of buying its cocoa requirements for the next six months on the spot market.

d. On the basis of your answer to part (c), determine whether the firm should purchase futures contracts for the cocoa.

16. Consider the data given in Problem 15. Suppose the manager uses a four-period weighted moving average with weights, $w_1 = .4$, $w_2 = .3$, $w_3 = .2$, and $w_4 = .1$. On the basis of this forecasting procedure, would you recommend that the firm purchase the future contract? Explain your reasoning.

17. Year-end book value per share of Kerf Group was as follows:

Year	Book Value per Share
1993	$11.40
1994	11.29
1995	10.91
1996	10.43
1997	9.92

On the basis of these data, Matt Wallace, a security analyst, wishes to forecast the book value per share of Kerf in 2002. Using the linear regression technique, determine:

a. The book value per share for Kerf stock in 2002.

b. The book value per share for Kerf in 2030. Comment.

18. The manager of a recently opened branch of Home Fed Bank wishes to forecast the number of customers who will arrive at the bank between 10 A.M. and 11 A.M. so that he can determine how many tellers should be working during this time period. The number of customers who arrived at the bank during this period was recorded for the past four weeks, and the following data were obtained (week 4 is the most recent week).

Day	Week 1	2	3	4
Monday	45	47	46	45
Tuesday	36	35	39	43
Wednesday	42	44	46	50
Thursday	34	38	44	44
Friday	46	49	51	53

a. Graph this time series.

b. Forecast the number of customer arrivals in week 5 using an additive model to account for seasonality.

19. McCoy Motors offers customers a choice of several lease plans. The plan that will be least expensive for a customer depends on the expected number of miles the customer will drive over the first 12 months of the lease. Stan Bender is trying to decide which lease plan to choose and therefore wishes to forecast the number of miles he will drive the car over the lease period. He has reviewed his income tax records over the past two years and found that his monthly mileage is as follows (year 2 is the most recent year).

	Year	
	1	2
January	1051	1398
February	1145	1366
March	1076	1425
April	1344	1286
May	1276	1342
June	1286	1451
July	1157	1486
August	1398	1385
September	1339	1468
October	1291	1536
November	1365	1422
December	1528	1449

a. Graph this time series.

b. Verify statistically that this time series exhibits linear trend.

c. Using a linear regression approach, forecast Stan's mileage over the one-year lease period.

20. Consider the data in Problem 19. Suppose Stan uses Holt's method for forecasting mileage over the one-year period. Assume that the forecast procedure begins in January of year 2; the initial forecast for the level is the mileage driven in December of year 1, and the initial forecast for the trend is the average monthly mileage increase during year 1. If $\alpha = .1$ and $\gamma = .2$, what is the forecast of Stan's mileage over the one-year lease period?

21. Pat Young, manager of the Burger Barn restaurant in Logan, Utah, is interested in determining an optimal inventory policy for frozen french fries. The number of pounds of french fries used by the restaurant over the past 15 weeks is as follows:

Week	Pounds	Week	Pounds	Week	Pounds
1	16,400	6	14,800	11	17,300
2	15,500	7	16,100	12	16,800
3	18,200	8	15,600	13	17,200
4	17,400	9	16,900	14	15,700
5	16,100	10	17,700	15	16,200

a. Graph this time series.

b. Verify statistically that the time series is stationary.

c. Using a three-week moving average, calculate the forecasted weekly demand for frozen french fries at the restaurant for weeks 16 through 20.

d. Using a four-week moving average, calculate the forecasted weekly demand for frozen french fries at the restaurant for weeks 16 through 20.

Which moving average method gives the lower mean squared forecast error?

22. Consider the data in Problem 21. Suppose exponential smoothing is used to forecast weekly french fry demand; the procedure begins with an initial forecast in week 2 of 16,400 pounds.

   a. What is the forecast of the weekly french fry demand for weeks 16 through 20 using a smoothing constant of $\alpha = .10$?

   b. What is the forecast of the weekly french fry demand for weeks 16 through 20 using a smoothing constant of $\alpha = .20$?

   c. Which of the two smoothing constants gives the lower mean squared forecast error?

   d. Which of the two smoothing constants gives the lower mean absolute value of the forecast error?

   e. Which of the two smoothing constants gives the lower mean absolute percent of the forecast error?

   f. Which of the two smoothing constants gives the lower largest absolute deviation of the forecast error?

23. Consider the data in Problem 21. Suppose that exponential smoothing is used to forecast weekly french fry demand; for weeks 16 through 20 beginning with an initial forecast in week 2 of 16,400 pounds.

   a. Determine the value of α that minimizes the mean squared forecast error.

   b. Determine the value of α that minimizes the mean absolute value of the forecast error.

   c. Determine the value of α that minimizes the mean absolute percent of the forecast errors.

24. Carol Wright, Inc. specializes in direct mail coupon advertising for major food manufacturers. One client, Quaker Brands, has run 10 advertising campaigns using this medium. The response rate for the coupons for the 10 campaigns is as follows:

Campaign	Response
1	4.6%
2	5.2%
3	4.8%
4	5.3%
5	4.5%
6	5.9%
7	5.2%
8	5.4%
9	4.7%
10	4.9%

   a. Graph this time series.

   b. Determine statistically whether a stationary forecasting model is appropriate.

   c. Forecast the response rate for future advertising campaigns using exponential smoothing with a smoothing constant, $\alpha = .10$ and an initial forecast of 4.6%.

   d. Using WINQSB, determine the value for the smoothing constant that minimizes the mean squared forecast error (assume an initial forecast of 4.6%).

25. Consider the data given in Problem 24. Suppose the forecast for the future response rate is based on an n period moving average. Determine the forecast and mean squared forecasting error for:

   a. n = 1

   b. n = 2

   c. n = 3

   d. n = 4

   Which of the above four values of n would you recommend for use in forecasting the response rate? Explain your reasoning.

CASE 1: *Bubble Up Bottling Company*

The Bubble Up Bottling Company of Budapest, Hungary, is interested in forecasting sales of Bubble Up over the next two years. The company has analyzed Bubble Up's market share for its service area over the past 20 quarters. Market share has generally been growing as indicated in the following table:

Year	Season	Bubble Up's Market Share (in Percent)
1	Winter	6.42
1	Spring	6.58
1	Summer	6.99
1	Fall	6.82
2	Winter	6.64
2	Spring	6.46
2	Summer	6.70
2	Fall	7.00
3	Winter	6.70
3	Spring	6.84
3	Summer	6.78
3	Fall	6.48
4	Winter	6.93
4	Spring	6.79
4	Summer	6.83
4	Fall	7.21

Year	Season	Bubble Up's Market Share (in Percent)
5	Winter	7.73
5	Spring	8.16
5	Summer	8.36
5	Fall	8.23

During this same five-year period, total soft drink sales in the region (as measured in 100,000s of cases) have been as follows:

Season	Year 1	2	3	4	5
Winter	114	114	124	132	134
Spring	130	146	151	160	166
Summer	158	177	175	184	205
Fall	131	142	146	144	148

The company would like to forecast Bubble Up soft drink sales for years 6 and 7. To do so, use a linear trend model to forecast market share for each quarter of years 6 and 7 and classical decomposition to forecast total soft drink sales in these periods. Then multiply the forecast of total soft drink sales by Bubble Up's estimated market share in order to get a forecast of Bubble Up's sales during this period. Prepare a business report to Bubble Up management containing your forecast and explaining your approach.

CASE 2: *Oregon Chain Saw*

Oregon Chain Saw produces electric and gas-powered chain saws for the professional and do-it-yourself markets. The company purchases the engines from outside suppliers but produces all other components going into the chain saws at its factory in Portland, Oregon. Lee Spencer, manager of the Portland factory, is interested in scheduling next year's production of the chains used in these saws and would therefore like to have a forecast of chain demands over this period.

The two sizes of chains produced by the company at the Portland plant are 17 and 21 inch. Chains produced at the factory are packaged for the replacement parts market as well as used in producing new chain saws.

Monthly data over the past three years reveal the following chain demand:

17-Inch Chains

Total Chain Demand

Year	January	February	March	April	May	June	July	August	September	October	November	December
1	10059	10783	12865	12103	11892	11236	11621	12206	12708	12102	11615	11407
2	10789	12164	13958	13567	12960	12347	13174	13984	13991	13340	12924	12885
3	11991	13307	15219	15309	14752	13586	14725	15514	15705	15193	14578	14128

Chain Demand for Replacement Market

Year	January	February	March	April	May	June	July	August	September	October	November	December
1	3309	3345	3378	3480	3565	3654	3686	3720	3763	3860	3926	4045
2	4045	4159	4257	4320	4451	4593	4713	4802	4837	4873	5045	5099
3	5098	5215	5387	5558	5738	5818	5855	5943	6046	6095	6149	6353

Chain Demand for Production of New Products

Year	January	February	March	April	May	June	July	August	September	October	November	December
1	6750	7438	9487	8623	8327	7582	7935	8486	8945	8242	7689	7362
2	6744	8005	9701	9247	8509	7754	8461	9182	9154	8467	7879	7786
3	6893	8092	9832	9751	9014	7768	8870	9571	9659	9098	8429	7775

21-Inch Chains

Total Chain Demand

Year	January	February	March	April	May	June	July	August	September	October	November	December
1	4090	4168	4107	4118	4098	4085	3963	4031	4025	4110	4216	4381
2	4432	4380	4443	4445	4411	4466	4496	4586	4518	4579	4686	4798
3	4819	4738	4879	4771	4600	4556	4560	4599	4771	4720	4837	4879

Chain Demand for Replacement Market

Year	January	February	March	April	May	June	July	August	September	October	November	December
1	1215	1219	1226	1257	1262	1233	1226	1242	1226	1256	1235	1255
2	1254	1230	1217	1205	1211	1232	1214	1240	1247	1260	1245	1226
3	1226	1253	1226	1201	1195	1220	1216	1188	1208	1216	1216	1235

Chain Demand for Production of New Products

Year	January	February	March	April	May	June	July	August	September	October	November	December
1	2875	2949	2881	2861	2836	2852	2737	2789	2799	2854	2981	3126
2	3178	3150	3226	3240	3200	3234	3282	3346	3271	3319	3441	3572
3	3593	3485	3653	3570	3405	3336	3344	3411	3563	3504	3621	3644

It takes a worker approximately six minutes to produce a 17-inch chain and seven and a half minutes to produce a 21-inch chain.

On the basis of these data, prepare a business memorandum to Lee Spencer that gives a forecast for the total demand of 17- and 21-inch chains over the upcoming year (year 4). Include a forecast for the number of workers that will be needed in each month to produce these chains (assume that each worker is available for 12,000 minutes per month). As part of the report appendix, explain what techniques you used to perform these forecasts and your reasoning for selecting these techniques.

INVENTORY MODELS
BASED ON
STATIONARY DEMAND

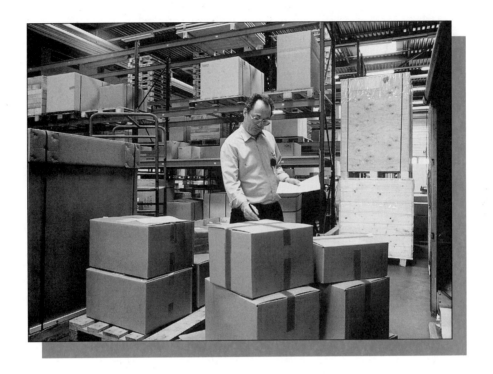

Dicom Appliances currently purchases the cases used in its line of microwave ovens from Wagner Industries. The amount Dicom pays for each case depends on the size of the order; larger orders receive discounted prices. The contract with Wagner calls for an allowable defect rate of 0.5%. Dicom incurs a cost each time it places an order with Wagner, which it estimates at $125 per order. It also estimates that its annual cost to keep a case in inventory averages 18% of its purchase price.

Dicom has warehouse space to store a maximum of 15,000 cases. If it wishes to take advantage of the lower prices for larger orders, it will have to build additional warehouse space, which will raise the annual holding cost rate from 18% to an estimated 20%.

Dicom is considering in-house production of the cases.

Management estimates that it can set up a production line capable of producing 20,000 cases per month and wants to determine if it is economically beneficial to change to in-house production.

To evaluate this option, Dicom management has proposed doing an inventory analysis that involves forecasting yearly demand for its products and obtaining estimates for the yearly operating cost of the production line, the fixed costs associated with each production run, and the decrease in the defect rate that would result from manufacturing its own cases. Once these estimates have been obtained, Dicom will be able to calculate an optimal production policy and determine whether this policy would yield a lower total annual cost than would purchasing the cases from Wagner Industries.

10.1 *O*VERVIEW OF INVENTORY ISSUES

Proper control of inventory is crucial to the success of an enterprise. Profitability can suffer if a firm has either too much or too little inventory. Companies that have excess inventory are frequently forced to offer substantial mark-downs in order to dispose of this merchandise. This situation is especially prevalent in industries affected by periodic style changes, such as the automobile industry. New-car dealerships are much more willing to deal on price at the end of the model year than at the beginning.

Not having enough inventory can also lead to problems. A retail store that is frequently out of stock of popular items will soon lose its customers to the competition. A manufacturing firm that runs out of a crucial component may have to shut down its production lines, resulting in great expense and lost opportunities.

Managers often use inventory models to develop an optimal **inventory policy**, consisting of an *order quantity* denoted Q and an inventory *reorder point* denoted R. Firms often have many thousands of different items known as *stock-keeping units or* SKUs in their inventories. Ideally, a firm would like to determine the inventory policy for each SKU which minimizes its total variable costs over a given (possibly infinite) time horizon.

Components of An Inventory Policy
Q = Inventory Order Quantity R = Inventory Reorder Point

In analyzing inventory models, we assess the costs associated with an inventory policy. If a firm orders in small amounts or produces in small batches, although the size (and cost) of the inventory may be relatively low, orders or production setups are more frequent, resulting in annual costs of ordering inventory or setting up production runs that are higher than those associated with larger quantities. If order or production sizes are larger, the number of orders or production runs and their associated fixed costs are less, but the costs associated with maintaining higher inventory levels are greater. Thus, inventory analyses can be thought of as cost-control techniques that strike a balance between having too much and too little inventory.

TYPES OF COSTS IN INVENTORY MODELS

The various costs in inventory models can be categorized into three broad areas: holding or carrying costs; procurement or production costs; and customer satisfaction costs.

Holding Costs

Holding, or **carrying, costs** are those incurred by a firm to maintain its inventory position. The typical annual holding cost of a firm's inventory is between 10% and 40% of the average inventory value. Given the high value of many firms' inventories, this rate can result in large annual expenditures. For example, the annual expense of a medium-sized lumberyard that has an inventory with an average value of a million dollars and a 30% annual holding cost rate is $300,000. If the lumberyard could cut this expense without affecting service, it could experience considerable savings.

Many factors affect a company's *holding cost rate*, not the least of which is the cost of capital. Firms typically must borrow money in order to finance their inventory, and few firms are able to borrow at the prime rate. For small businesses, the cost of capital is typically prime plus 1 to 3%. These costs may be even higher if the firm has financed its expansion through the issuance of "junk" bonds or if it lacks the creditworthiness necessary for standard banking relationships. Even if a firm has not had to borrow money to finance its inventory, it has foregone other investments that could have been made with available capital. Management must account for such *opportunity costs* when determining its holding cost rate.

Several other costs are associated with holding inventory. Since the product must be stored somewhere, the company must pay for rent, utilities, labor, insurance, and security of its inventory. In some localities, taxes must be paid based on the inventory's value. Other costs include theft and breakage of inventory (which are classified under the more polite term *shrinkage*).

Another factor in determining the inventory holding cost is deterioration or obsolescence. After a certain period of time, an item may lose some or all of its value. A car dealership stuck with last year's models will have to reduce its prices. A supermarket left with sour milk on its shelves may have to pay to dispose of it.

All these costs are difficult, if not impossible, to measure. Thus, the holding cost rate represents management's best judgment of their total net effect. An important factor in determining the optimal inventory policy for an item is the cost of holding one unit of the item in inventory for a full year. When the holding cost rate of an item is known, its annual holding cost per unit, C_h, can be calculated by multiplying the annual holding cost rate, H, of an item by its unit cost, C.

Holding Costs

C_h = Annual Holding Cost per Unit in Inventory (in $ per unit in inventory per year)
H = Annual Holding Cost Rate (in % per year)
C = Unit Cost of an Item (in $ per item)

Thus,

$$C_h = H * C$$

Procurement Costs

Procurement costs represent the cost of obtaining items for the inventory. Included are incremental costs, such as the actual cost of the units purchased or produced, as well as fixed costs, such as order or setup costs.

Order costs are incurred when a firm purchases goods from a supplier. These include postage, telephone charges, the expense to write up or phone in an order, the cost to check the order when it is received, and other fixed labor and transportation expenses that do not depend on the order size.

If the firm produces goods for sale to others, a production *setup cost* is normally incurred. This is the expense associated with beginning production of a particular item. For example, an ice cream manufacturer making a variety of flavors must clean out the machinery before it can begin producing a new flavor; machines producing ball bearings may need to be recalibrated when a new size is produced; and the staff at an aircraft manufacturer may need some refresher training prior to beginning a new production run. The procurement cost of placing an order or arranging a production setup, C_o, is *independent* of the order or production quantity. Because this cost is principally labor related, it can usually be readily measured.

Order or Setup Costs

C_o = Order or Production Setup Cost (in $ per order or $ per setup)

Customer Satisfaction
Costs

One possible inventory policy is to stock *no* inventory. Customers desiring the product simply place an order and wait for its arrival. In this case, customer satisfaction is likely to be lower than it would be if the item were readily available. Low customer satisfaction may result in declining revenue and profitability. *Customer satisfaction costs* measure the degree to which a customer is satisfied with the firm's inventory policy and the impact this has on long-term profitability.

In some cases, customer satisfaction costs are relatively easy to quantify. For example, if a retailer is out of stock of an item, the customer may be offered a more expensive substitute at the same price or a discount on the item if the customer is willing to wait. But what about a customer who is unwilling to wait, goes elsewhere for the item, and decides to stick with the competition for future purchases? It is extremely difficult to estimate the satisfaction cost in these cases.

For a customer who encounters an out-of-stock inventory situation and is willing to wait for the item, customer satisfaction costs have both a fixed and a variable component. The fixed component π, consists of costs that are independent of the length of time a customer must wait for an item, such as the administrative costs of issuing a "rain check," recording the order, and contacting the customer when the merchandise arrives. The variable component C_s, is a function of the length of time the customer must wait for goods to become available. Typically, the longer a customer waits for the item to arrive, the less satisfied the customer will be.

Customer Satisfaction Costs

π = the fixed administrative cost of an out-of-stock item
  (in $ per stockout unit)
C_s = the annualized cost of a customer waiting for an out-of-stock item
  (in $ per item out of stock per year)

Table 10.1 summarizes these various inventory costs.

TABLE 10.1 INVENTORY COSTS

Holding Costs (C_h)	Order/Setup Costs (C_o)	Satisfaction Costs (π, C_s)
Cost of capital	Labor	Goodwill
Rent	Communication	Loss in future sales
Utilities	Transportation	Labor
Insurance		Communication
Labor		
Taxes		
Shrinkage		
Spoilage		
Obsolescence		

DEMAND IN
INVENTORY MODELS

A key component affecting an inventory policy is the demand rate for a stock-keeping unit. Although future demand is generally not known with certainty, forecasting techniques (see Chapter 9) can generally provide good estimates for these values. Demand can be estimated for any future period; however, we will typically utilize the *annual demand* in developing our inventory models.

Perhaps the strongest factor influencing how we model a particular inventory situation is the demand pattern for the SKU in question. Demand that is projected to be reasonably constant over time must be modeled differently than demand that is highly variable. In this chapter, we limit our investigation to situations in which demand occurs at a known annual constant rate, D.

Demand in Inventory Models

D = Estimate of the Annual Demand for the Stock-Keeping Unit

INVENTORY CLASSIFICATIONS

Inventory can be classified in various ways, depending on the issues that concern management. Table 10.2 summarizes different inventory classifications.

TABLE 10.2   INVENTORY CLASSIFICATIONS

By Process	By Importance	By Life
Raw materials	A,B,C	Perishable
Work in progress		Nonperishable
Finished goods		

Process Classification

Accountants at manufacturing firms typically classify inventory into three categories as defined by the production process: raw materials, work in progress, and finished goods. This categorization enables management to track the production process and determine whether it has adequate inventory levels to support the projected demand. Financial analysts use such information to detect any changes in a firm's operations that might distort its profitability.

A,B,C Classification

A second way of classifying inventory is by the relative importance of the stock-keeping unit in terms of the firm's capital needs. For example, suppose we determine the annual inventory value for each stock-keeping unit by multiplying its unit cost by its annual demand. Normally, only 5% to 10% of the SKUs account for about 50% of a company's total inventory value. These SKUs are classified as A units. Another 40% to 50% of the SKUs account for all but a small percentage of the firm's total inventory value. These are classified as B units. The remaining nearly 50% of the SKUs usually account for a small percentage (less than 5) of the firm's total inventory value. These are classified as C units.

This A,B,C classification is useful in determining how much attention should be given to each stock-keeping unit in determining an inventory policy. A items are more carefully analyzed than B items. Because of the cost of inventory control, little, if any, analysis is done for C items.

Shelf Life Classification

Inventory models can also be classified by the shelf life of the inventory units. Certain perishable items, such as dairy products, baked goods, and periodicals, have a very short shelf life (no one wants to buy yesterday's news). Management of these inventory items is quite different than for items that can remain in inventory for long periods of time with no noticeable deterioration of quality. We discuss models with limited shelf life in Chapter 11.

REVIEW SYSTEMS

Two types of review systems are widely used in business and industry for controlling stock-keeping units. In a *continuous review system*, the inventory is constantly monitored, and a new order is placed when the inventory level reaches a certain critical point. In a *periodic review system*, the inventory position is investigated on a regular basis (once a day, twice a week, etc.), and orders are placed only at these times. Both systems are discussed in this chapter.

10.2 ECONOMIC ORDER QUANTITY MODEL

ASSUMPTIONS OF
THE EOQ MODEL

One of the most commonly used techniques for inventory optimization is the **economic order quantity (EOQ) model**. This model is useful for analyzing stock-keeping units that meet the following criteria:

- Demand for the item occurs at a known and reasonably constant rate
- The item has a sufficiently long shelf life (i.e. there is little or no spoilage)
- The item is monitored using a continuous review system

The EOQ model assumes that all parameters, including demand, remain constant forever—that is, over an *infinite time horizon*. Although no business will carry a stock-keeping unit indefinitely, by using an infinite time horizon we avoid the need to specify just how long the item will be stocked.

The *lead time*, L, for an order represents the time that elapses between placement of an order and its actual arrival. In a basic EOQ model, we initially make the (unrealistic) assumption that L is 0. (We will modify this assumption later.) Under these circumstances, it does not pay to order additional items until the exact instant we run out of stock. Furthermore, because demand is assumed to be constant over an infinite time horizon, whenever the firm runs out of inventory, it faces exactly the same future demand pattern as the previous time it ran out of inventory. For this model, a stationary inventory policy that orders the same amount each time must be optimal.

COST EQUATION FOR
THE EOQ MODEL

Figure 10.1 illustrates the inventory profile of ordering Q units each time. In this figure, the horizontal axis represents time, and the vertical axis represents the inventory level. The time between orders, T, is the *cycle time*. To build an EOQ model, we need to know the demand forecast, D, for a given period (typically one year), the unit holding cost, C_h, over the same period, and the ordering cost, C_o. We can then construct an equation for the total annual inventory cost consisting of annual holding costs, ordering costs, and procurement costs, expressed in terms of the order quantity, Q.

FIGURE 10.1   Inventory Profile—Ordering Q Units Each Time

Total Annual
Holding Costs

As Figure 10.1 illustrates, the inventory level for each cycle begins at level Q when the order arrives and is depleted at a constant rate to 0 just prior to the next order's arrival. Due to this constant demand rate, the average inventory level over time is Q/2. Thus, the annual holding cost associated with the policy of ordering Q units can be modeled as follows:

Total Annual Holding Cost for the EOQ Model

Total Annual Holding Cost
$$= \text{(Average Inventory Level)} * \text{(Annual Holding Cost per Unit)}$$
$$= (Q/2)C_h$$

Total Annual
Ordering Costs

If the annual demand is D and the order quantity is Q, the number of orders placed during the year is D/Q. Since the cost of placing each order is C_o, the total annual ordering cost is as follows:

Total Annual Ordering Cost for the EOQ Model

Total Annual Order Cost
$$= \text{(Average Number of Orders Per Year)} * \text{(Cost to Place an Order)}$$
$$= (D/Q)C_o$$

Total Annual Item Costs

Since we seek to satisfy demand, we will purchase D items during the year at a cost of $C each. Thus, the total annual item costs can be expressed as follows:

Total Annual Item Costs for an EOQ Model

Total Annual Item Cost
$$= \text{(Number of Items Purchased Per Year)} * \text{(Purchase Price per Item)}$$
$$= DC$$

Total Annual Inventory
Costs and the
EOQ Formula

Because the lead time for delivery of an order is assumed to be 0, there will never be any shortage costs. Thus, the total annual inventory costs, TC(Q), can be expressed by:

$$\begin{pmatrix} \text{Total Annual} \\ \text{Inventory Costs} \end{pmatrix} = \begin{pmatrix} \text{Total Annual} \\ \text{Holding Cost} \end{pmatrix} + \begin{pmatrix} \text{Total Annual} \\ \text{Ordering Cost} \end{pmatrix} + \begin{pmatrix} \text{Total Annual} \\ \text{Item Cost} \end{pmatrix}$$

or

$$TC(Q) = \left(\frac{Q}{2}\right)C_h + \left(\frac{D}{Q}\right)C_o + DC = TV(Q) + DC \qquad (10.1)$$

Here, TV(Q) represents the *total annual variable costs* that are dependent on Q; that is,

$$TV(Q) = \left(\frac{Q}{2}\right)C_h + \left(\frac{D}{Q}\right)C_o \qquad (10.1a)$$

We can find Q*, the value of Q that minimizes TC(Q) in Equation 10.1, using calculus (see Appendix 10.2 on the accompanying CD-ROM). The following relationship, known as the EOQ *formula*, gives the value for Q*.

$$Q^* = \sqrt{\frac{2DC_o}{C_h}} \qquad (10.2)$$

SENSITIVITY ANALYSIS
IN EOQ MODELS

Figure 10.2 shows a typical graph of TV(Q) versus Q. As you can see, at the point Q* where TV(Q) is minimized, the total annual holding and ordering costs are equal. The cost curve is also reasonably flat around Q*. Thus, small variations in Q* will not greatly affect total annual variable inventory costs. This is important because the optimal order quantity Q* is generally rounded off to an integer value or further modified owing to shipping restrictions. As long as these differences are not too large, the total annual variable cost will not be greatly affected.

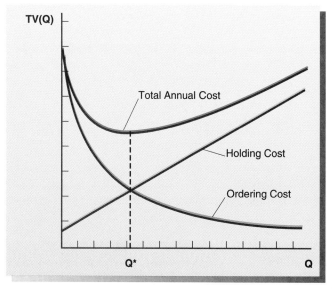

FIGURE 10.2   Total Annual Inventory Holding and Ordering Cost

Another factor that might affect the calculation of Q* is the variability in actual demand. If demand varies from the estimated forecast by a modest amount, however, the error in Q* is small and there is only a minor increase over the optimal cost. Accordingly, we disregard demand variability when calculating Q* for an EOQ model and assume that the annual demand is constant and known with certainty.

CYCLE TIME

The cycle time, T, represents the time that elapses between the placement of orders. It is calculated by dividing the order quantity by the annual demand:

$$T = Q/D \qquad (10.3)$$

Since the cycle time corresponds to the age of the last item sold from inventory, it can be compared to the shelf life to determine if items will go bad while in inventory. If the cycle time is greater than the shelf life, the model must be modified.

LEAD TIME AND THE REORDER POINT

In the preceding analysis, we assumed that the lead time was 0. In reality, lead time is always positive and must be accounted for when deciding when to place an order. The *reorder point*, R, is the inventory position of the item when an order is placed.

To determine the reorder point, we note that, since demand is constant at rate D, the total demand during lead time, L, is simply $L * D$, where L and D are expressed in the same time units (years, weeks, days, etc.). Hence, if an order is placed when the inventory level is at $L * D$, the order will arrive precisely when the inventory level is at 0. This gives the inventory profile shown in Figure 10.1.

> ## Reorder Point
>
> R = (Lead Time) * (Demand Rate)
> **R = L * D**
>
> L and D must be expressed in the same time units.

(10.4)

In some instances, the lead time may be of sufficient length that it exceeds the cycle time. In such cases, since $L > Q/D$, $L * D$ will exceed Q and it will be impossible to order the item for delivery during its current inventory cycle. Hence, this order would have to be placed during a previous cycle, and, as shown in Figure 10.3, there will be times when more than one order is outstanding. A company's stock on hand plus the size of any outstanding orders not yet delivered is known as its *inventory position*. At the reorder point, its inventory position is $L * D$.

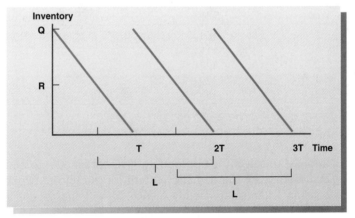

FIGURE 10.3   Lead Time Exceeding Cycle Time

Safety Stock

This calculation of the reorder point assumed that there is constant demand for the SKU and that there is a fixed lead time. In reality, demand usually fluctuates, and lead time varies. To account for these variations, most firms build a *safety stock* (SS) into their inventory policy. The safety stock acts as a buffer to handle higher than average lead time demand or longer than expected lead time. Including the safety stock, the reorder point is expressed by the following formula:

$$R = L * D + SS$$

(10.5)

The size of the safety stock is based on having a desired service level. Determining the safety stock size is the focus of Section 10.6.

To illustrate the concepts we have developed for solving an EOQ model, let us consider the case of the Allen Appliance Company.

ALLEN APPLIANCE COMPANY

Allen.its
Allen.xls

Allen Appliance Company (AAC) wholesales small appliances—toasters, mixers, blenders, and so on—to 90 retailers throughout Texas. One of its products, the Citron brand juicer, has shown a gradual decline in sales over the past several years. While this decline may be attributed to several factors, such as increased cost of fresh oranges, better availability of "fresh-squeezed" juice at grocery stores, or less time available to make juice by hand, the bottom line is that sales have been slipping.

Several years ago, Mr. Allen hired a consultant, who recommended an inventory policy of ordering 600 juicers whenever the inventory level reached 205. Although Mr. Allen has religiously followed this policy in the past, he wonders whether, given the reduction in sales, this policy is still optimal.

The juicers cost AAC $10 each and are sold to customers for $11.85 each. Mr. Allen is able to borrow money at a 10% annual interest rate. He estimates that storage and other miscellaneous costs amount to about 4% of the average inventory value per year.

Based on labor, postage, and telephone charges, Mr. Allen estimates that it costs $8 to place an order with the Citron Company. It takes a worker who earns $12 per hour 20 minutes to check the shipment when it arrives. AAC is open five days a week, 52 weeks a year. Lead time is approximately eight working days, and AAC monitors its inventory using a continuous review system. Over the past 10 weeks, demand for the juicers has been as shown in Table 10.3. Given this information, Mr. Allen wishes to know if he should revise his current inventory policy.

TABLE 10.3   SALES OF JUICERS OVER PREVIOUS 10 WEEKS

Week	Sales	Week	Sales
1	105	6	120
2	115	7	135
3	125	8	115
4	120	9	110
5	125	10	130

SOLUTION

In order to select the appropriate inventory model to analyze this situation, we must first investigate the demand pattern for the juicers. Weekly sales, though not exactly constant, do not vary greatly. Hence, we will analyze this situation using the economic order quantity model.[1]

To determine a representative value for weekly demand, we can use one of the various time series techniques appropriate for stationary models discussed in Chapter 9. After consulting with other members of the management science team, suppose we select a 10-week simple moving average approach to forecast future weekly demand. By averaging demand over the most recent 10 weeks, we forecast a weekly demand of (105 + 115 + . . . + 130)/10 = 120.

In an EOQ analysis, it is important to express all data values in the same time units. Mr. Allen collects data on an *annual* basis; therefore, he needs a forecast of *annual* demand for the juicer. Because he feels reasonably confident that demand for the juicers has bottomed out, our forecast for the annual demand is (120)(52) = 6240 units.

---

[1]In some situations, the only historic data a firm has are sales data. If sales patterns exhibit erratic behavior, underlying demand could be constant but the item might be frequently out of stock.

The annual holding cost rate for the juicers consists of the sum of the annual interest rate (10%) and the annual storage and miscellaneous costs (4%). Hence, using a holding cost rate of 10% + 4% = 14%, the annual holding cost of a juicer left in inventory for an entire year, C_h, is ($10)(.14) = $1.40. Note that we use AAC's *cost, not its selling price*, to determine the annual holding cost per unit.

Mr. Allen's ordering cost consists of the $8 cost of placing the order and the cost involved in checking the order upon its arrival. Since checking the shipment requires 20 minutes, and checkers make $12 per hour, the checking costs are (20/60)($12) = $4 per order. Hence, the total ordering cost, C_o, is $8 + $4 = $12. In summary, the following data exist for this problem:

$$D = 6240$$
$$C = \$10$$
$$H = 14\%$$
$$C_h = \$1.40$$
$$C_o = \$12$$

Analysis of Current Policy

Mr. Allen's current policy is to order 600 juicers at a time, yielding an annual holding cost of (600/2)($1.40) = $420 and an annual order cost of (6240/600)($12.00) = $124.80. Thus the total annual variable cost of this policy is:

$$TV(600) = \left(\frac{600}{2}\right)(\$1.40) + \left(\frac{6240}{600}\right)(\$12) = \$544.80$$

Including the total cost of the merchandise demanded during the year of (6240)($10) = $62,400, the total annual cost is:

$$TC(600) = \$544.80 + \$62,400 = \$62,944.80$$

Analysis of Optimal Policy

If we use the EOQ formula to determine the order quantity, we get:

$$Q^* = \sqrt{\frac{(2)(6240)(12)}{1.40}} = 327.065$$

Since Mr. Allen cannot order .065 of a juicer, we round this answer to an order quantity of 327.

Substituting $Q^* = 327$ into Equation 10.1 gives us:

$$TV(327) = \left(\frac{327}{2}\right)(\$1.40) + \left(\frac{6240}{327}\right)(\$12) = \$457.89$$

and

$$TC(327) = \$457.89 + \$62,400 = \$62,857.89$$

Thus adopting this policy will result in an annual savings of $544.80 − $457.89 = $86.91 in variable costs. This savings might seem small in absolute dollars, but on a percentage basis, it amounts to approximately 16% of the current annual variable costs for this one SKU. To put this in perspective, if AAC carries 2000 different SKUs in inventory and has total annual variable inventory costs of a quarter of a million dollars, a 16% savings in inventory holding and ordering costs for each SKU translates into approximately a $40,000 annual savings!

SENSITIVITY OF THE EOQ RESULTS—LOTS OF 100

Suppose Citron's policy requires AAC to purchase juicers in units of 100. In this case, AAC could not order 327 juicers and would modify its order quantity to, say, 300. The total annual inventory holding and ordering cost of a policy based on orders of 300 juicers at a time amounts to $459.60, an increase of only $1.71 (or less than one-half of 1% of the total variable costs) per year over the cost of ordering 327 juicers at a time. This cost increase is so slight that an order quantity of 300 might even be preferable just for the sake of operational convenience.

EFFECT OF CHANGES
IN INPUT PARAMETERS

One of the properties of the EOQ model is that the optimal total cost is relatively insensitive to small or even moderate changes to one of the input parameters of the model. To illustrate, suppose that, due to a "back to nature" craze, the actual annual demand for juicers turns out to be 7500 instead of the forecasted 6240 (an increase of over 20%). Using the EOQ formula, we find that AAC should have ordered $Q^* = 359$ juicers at a time rather than the 327 we calculated. The annual holding and ordering cost (excluding safety stock costs) associated with an annual demand of 7500 juicers and an order quantity of 359 is:

$$\text{TV}(359) = \left(\frac{359}{2}\right)(\$1.40) + \left(\frac{7500}{359}\right)(\$12) = \$502.00$$

If instead of ordering 359 juicers we used the order quantity of 327, the annual ordering and holding cost would be

$$\text{TV}(327) = \left(\frac{327}{2}\right)(\$1.40) + \left(\frac{7500}{327}\right)(\$12) = \$504.13$$

This is an increase of only $2.13, or 0.4% per year! Thus, a "mistake" of more than 20% in estimating demand has less than a 0.4% effect on the total annual variable cost.

CYCLE TIME

If AAC uses an order quantity of $Q^* = 327$, the cycle time is:

$$T = \frac{Q^*}{D} = \frac{327}{6240} = .0524 \text{ year}$$

$$= (.0524 \text{ year})(52 \text{ weeks/year})(5 \text{ days/week}) \approx 14 \text{ working days}$$

These calculations indicate that the juicers will be sold in a reasonably short period of time after they enter AAC's inventory. Thus, shelf life is not a factor. Since $T \approx 14$ working days, AAC will place orders for the juicers approximately every two and a half weeks. This information can be useful if Mr. Allen decides to coordinate orders for other items from Citron along with the juicers.

REORDER POINT

Since AAC is open five days a week, the average weekly demand of 120 juicers translates into an average demand of 120/5 = 24 juicers per working day. Given a lead time of eight working days, the reorder point should be:[2]

$$R = L * D = (8)(24) = 192$$

This calculation does not include any safety stock. Based on its current reorder point of 205 units, AAC has been using a safety stock of $205 - 192 = 13$ units. In Section 10.6 we will show that a safety stock of 27 juicers would be preferable under certain conditions. If AAC wishes to maintain a safety stock (SS) of 27 juicers, the reorder point will have to be increased to R = 192 + 27 = 219 juicers. The increased holding cost of maintaining an average of 27 units in safety stock would be $SS*C_h = (27)(\$1.40) = \$37.80$ per year.

---

[2]This calculation is based on L and D expressed in days. Expressed in years, L = 8/260 = .03077 and R = (.03077)(6240) = 192.

SOFTWARE RESULTS

Computer programs such as WINQSB can be used to generate optimal inventory policies. Figure 10.4 provides the WINQSB output for this problem. As you can see, the results coincide with those we generated by hand.

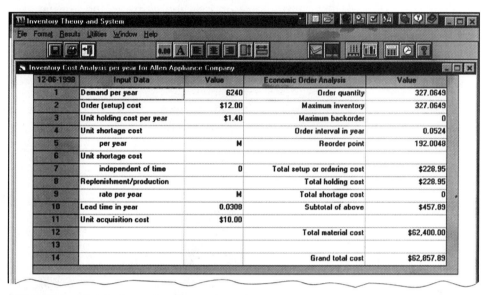

12-06-1998	Input Data	Value	Economic Order Analysis	Value
1	Demand per year	6240	Order quantity	327.0649
2	Order (setup) cost	$12.00	Maximum inventory	327.0649
3	Unit holding cost per year	$1.40	Maximum backorder	0
4	Unit shortage cost		Order interval in year	0.0524
5	per year	M	Reorder point	192.0048
6	Unit shortage cost			
7	independent of time	0	Total setup or ordering cost	$228.95
8	Replenishment/production		Total holding cost	$228.95
9	rate per year	M	Total shortage cost	0
10	Lead time in year	0.0308	Subtotal of above	$457.89
11	Unit acquisition cost	$10.00		
12			Total material cost	$62,400.00
13				
14			Grand total cost	$62,857.89

FIGURE 10.4   WINQSB Output for Allen Appliance Company*

On the basis of this analysis, the following memorandum was prepared. In this report, we outline an optimal inventory, policy for AAC and examine the sensitivity of these recommendations to changes in the annual demand and holding cost.

M E M O R A N D U M

To: Mr. James P. Allen, President—Allen Appliance Company

From: Student Consulting Group

Subj: Inventory Policy for Citron Juicers

Due to a gradual erosion in demand over the past several years, we have been asked to analyze the current inventory policy for Citron juicers and make policy recommendations that might help Allen Appliance Company lower its inventory costs. We have analyzed the inventory situation for these juicers and are pleased to report our findings.

Our analysis indicates that demand for the juicers is fairly constant and that the products have a shelf life in excess of three months. Based on the past 10 weeks of sales, we forecast the annual demand for juicers to be 6240 units. We assume that AAC will continue to operate five days a week, that lead time for delivery is estimated to be eight working days, and that the juicers must be ordered in multiples of 100 units from Citron.

The following cost data have been provided by Allen management and used in our analysis:

Unit cost per juicer:	$10
Ordering cost:	$12
Annual holding cost rate:	14%

Based on our analysis, of this data we recommend the following:

1. Lower the order quantity for Citron juicers from 600 to 300 units. This should result in a reduction in the annual holding and ordering costs from $544.80 to $459.60 (a savings of $85.20, or 15.6% per year).

2. Set the reorder point for the juicers at 219, including a safety stock of 27 units. Although changing the reorder point from 205 to 219 increases the annual safety stock holding costs by $20, this additional cost should be more than offset by the greater customer satisfaction generated from having fewer customers finding an out-of-stock situation.

Figure I compares the current and proposed policies.

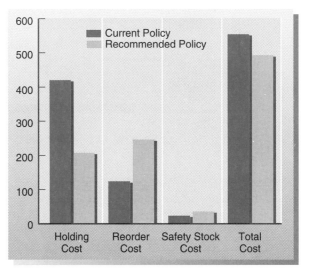

FIGURE I

While we are confident of the ordering cost data, management has indicated some uncertainty regarding both the value of $1.40 used for the annual holding cost per juicer and our forecast of 6240 for the annual juicer demand. We have therefore, considered different annual holding cost and demand amounts and examined the savings in total annual variable inventory costs of using our recommended policy versus AAC's current policy. Table I gives these percentage savings.

TABLE I   Percentage Improvement in Annual Variable Inventory Holding and Ordering Costs by Ordering 300 Versus 600 Juicers Per Order

		Annual Holding Cost per Unit			
		1.20	1.40	1.60	1.80
	5800	13.4	17.5	20.8	23.5
Annual	6000	12.5	16.7	20.0	22.7
Demand	6200	11.6	15.8	19.2	22.0
	6400	10.7	15.0	18.4	21.3

You can observe from this table that the recommended policy results in annual variable inventory cost savings of between 10.7% and 23.5%. If more precise information regarding the annual demand and annual holding cost per unit were available, we might be able to find a policy that gives even greater cost savings.

Should you have any further questions, please do not hesitate to contact us.

10.3 EOQ MODELS WITH QUANTITY DISCOUNTS

Quantity discounts are a common practice in business. By offering such discounts, sellers encourage buyers to order in amounts greater than they would ordinarily purchase, thereby shifting the inventory holding cost from the seller to the buyer. Quantity discounts also reflect the savings inherent in large orders. For example, when the Citron Company receives an order from AAC, a certain amount of work is required to process the order, independent of its size. By selling a larger quantity of juicers, Citron is able to amortize this fixed cost over a larger quantity and charge a lower price for the merchandise.

Perhaps the most important reason firms offer quantity discounts is federal legislation known as the Robinson-Patman Act, which states that a seller cannot discriminate among buyers when setting prices. This means that Citron cannot charge one price to AAC (which sells 6240 juicers a year) and a different price to a nationwide discount chain selling, say, 624,000 juicers a year. A quantity discount schedule does, however, enable a seller to reward its biggest customers with lower prices without violating the Robinson-Patman Act.

QUANTITY DISCOUNT SCHEDULES

A *quantity discount schedule* lists the discounted cost per unit corresponding to different purchase volumes. The quantities at which the prices change under a quantity discount schedule are called *breakpoints*. Each breakpoint corresponds to a particular *pricing level*. Normally, the price customers pay for the item declines as the order quantity increases. If C is the nondiscounted cost per unit, and C_i and B_i are the unit cost and breakpoint for the ith discount price level, respectively, then smaller values of C_i correspond to larger values for B_i.

Quantity discount schedules fall into two broad categories: *all units schedules* and *incremental schedules*. In an all units schedule, the price the buyer pays for *all the units purchased* is based on the total purchase volume. For example, suppose Citron uses an *all units* discount schedule and offers a discount price of $9.75 corresponding to a breakpoint of 300 juicers. If AAC orders 327 juicers, it will pay $9.75 per unit for each of the 327 juicers.

In an incremental discount schedule, the price discount applies only to the *additional units ordered beyond each breakpoint*. So if Citron uses an *incremental* discount schedule and offers a discount price of $9.75 corresponding to a breakpoint of 300 juicers, then if AAC orders 327 juicers, it will pay $10.00 per unit for the first 299 juicers and $9.75 per unit for the remaining 28 juicers. While some firms use incremental discount schedules, the all units discount schedule is more common.

ALL UNITS DISCOUNT SCHEDULE

Because the inventory unit cost is dependent on the quantity purchased, the all units discount inventory model must include the total cost of the goods purchased. The formula for TC(Q), therefore, is as follows:

$$TC(Q) = \left(\frac{Q}{2}\right)C_h + \left(\frac{D}{Q}\right)C_o + DC_i \qquad (10.6)$$

where C_i represents the unit cost at the ith pricing level corresponding to the order quantity, Q.

Since financing costs typically make up a major portion of the holding costs, it is reasonable to assume that the holding cost, C_h, will change proportionally to the unit cost. This assumption may not be totally accurate, however, because changes in the unit cost do not affect nonfinancing holding costs, such as storage costs. One way around this dilemma is to modify the holding cost by some fraction of the change in the unit cost reflecting the percentage of the holding cost represented by the inventory financing cost. Since the EOQ model is quite insensitive to minor changes in the parameters, however, the simplifying assumption that holding costs change proportionately to changes in the unit cost will have a minor effect on the optimal order quantity, Q^*.

Determining the Optimal Order Quantity

To illustrate how we determine the optimal order quantity under an all units discount schedule, let us return to the Allen Appliance Company example.

ALLEN APPLIANCE COMPANY (continued)

Allena.its
Allena.xls

Mr. Allen was quite impressed with our analysis. After reading the memorandum, however, he realized that we had not been given complete information concerning the Citron juicers. In particular, while the base price for the Citron juicers is $10 per unit, Citron offers its customers quantity discounts. The all units quantity discount schedule is given in Table 10.4.

TABLE 10.4   ALL UNITS QUANTITY DISCOUNT SCHEDULE

Amount Ordered	Price per Unit
1–299	$10.00
300–599	$ 9.75
600–999	$ 9.40
1000–4999	$ 9.50
5000 or more	$ 9.00

Mr. Allen wishes to determine whether he should order more than 300 units to take advantage of the discounts offered by Citron.

SOLUTION

There are four discount pricing levels for Citron juicers beyond the base price of C = $10 per unit. These are C_1 = $9.75, B_1 = 300; C_2 = $9.50, B_2 = 600; C_3 = $9.40, B_3 = 1000; and C_4 = $9.00, B_4 = 5000. Figure 10.5 shows five inventory cost curves for the juicer problem. Each represents the total cost TC(Q) as a function of the corresponding unit price, C_i, assuming that C_i is valid for all values of Q. The true total cost function, TC(Q), contains the pieces of each curve corresponding to the range of values for Q over which the corresponding discount price is valid, as highlighted in the figure.

Determining the optimal order quantity for an all units discount schedule is a straightforward process. For the original unit cost, as well as each discount pricing level, we use the EOQ formula

$$Q^* = \sqrt{\frac{2DC_o}{C_h}}$$

to determine the lowest total cost on each curve. Table 10.5 provides this information for the juicer problem. The Q^* values change slightly for each pricing level because C_h

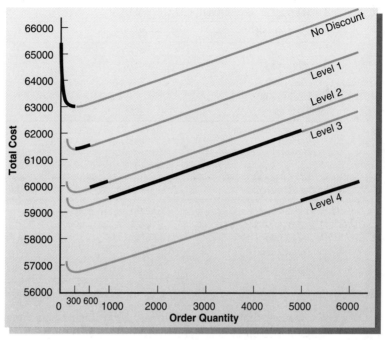

FIGURE 10.5   Inventory Cost Curves for AAC Juicer Problem—All Units Discount Policy

declines in proportion to the decrease in the price per unit for each pricing level. (If we had assumed a constant holding cost, Q* would have been the same for each pricing level.)

TABLE 10.5   LOWEST TOTAL COST ON EACH INVENTORY COST CURVE

Level	Amount Ordered	Price per Unit	Q*
0	1–299	$10.00	327
1	300–599	$ 9.75	331
2	600–999	$ 9.50	336
3	1000–4999	$ 9.40	337
4	5000 or more	$ 9.00	345

We see from Figure 10.5 that, for each pricing level, the cost curves increase as the order quantity increases beyond the Q* value. Hence, when the EOQ value for a curve is below the pricing level's breakpoint, the least expensive way to obtain the discount is to increase the order quantity up to that breakpoint.

When the Q* value is greater than the next pricing level's breakpoint, as it is for pricing level 0, the pricing level can be dropped from further consideration (since we would be ordering at the next pricing level anyway). Here we see that it does not make sense for Allen Appliance to order at pricing level 0 since its optimal order quantity, 327, falls within pricing level 1. But at level 1 the unit cost is $9.75, and the optimal order quantity is 331.

Table 10.6 lists the results of modifying the Q* values to take advantage of the discounts for the remaining pricing levels under consideration. Using the modified values for Q* for each remaining pricing level still under consideration, we then evaluate TC(Q*) using Equation 10.6. Table 10.7 gives the values of TC(Q*) for each remaining pricing level.

TABLE 10.6 MODIFIED Q* VALUES

Amount Ordered	Price per Unit	Modified Q*
1–299	$10.00	*
300–599	$ 9.75	331
600–999	$ 9.50	600
1000–4999	$ 9.40	1000
5000 or more	$ 9.00	5000

Q above breakpoint.

TABLE 10.7 TC(Q*) VALUES

Amount Ordered	Price per Unit	Modified Q*	TC(Q*)
1–299	$10.00	—	—
300–599	$ 9.75	331	$61,292.13
600–999	$ 9.50	600	$59,803.80
1000–4999	$ 9.40	1000	$59,388.88
5000 or more	$ 9.00	5000	$59,324.98

We see that AAC should order 5000 juicers at a time, since this value minimizes TC(Q*). The process is summarized as follows:

Determining the Optimal Order Quantity for an All Units Pricing Schedule

1. Calculate Q* for each discount level.

2. If Q* is less than the lower quantity limit for the discount level, increase Q* to this lower limit. If Q* is greater than the upper quantity limit for the discount level, eliminate this level from further consideration.

3. Substitute the modified Q* values into the formula:

$$TC(Q) = \left(\frac{Q}{2}\right)C_h + \frac{D}{Q}C_o + DC_i$$

4. Select the Q* value that minimizes TC(Q*).

Although quantity discounts may influence the order quantity, they do not affect the reorder point; this is determined in exactly the same way as for the nondiscounted EOQ problem.

Other Considerations

These results are based on a mathematical model that made certain simplifying assumptions, such as constant demand and a fixed holding cost rate. We should check to see if our results are consistent with these assumptions. For example, according to our analysis, the lowest total annual inventory cost is achieved when AAC orders 5000 juicers at a time. This quantity represents more than a nine-month supply of juicers and could raise some concerns among AAC management.

First, if AAC orders 5000 juicers it must have some place to store them. This could result in major additional expenses for new warehouse space. These additional costs would violate the fixed holding cost rate assumption.

Second, suppose Mr. Allen has heard rumors that Citron may be introducing a new improved juicer within the next three to four months. This plan could violate the constant demand assumption. AAC would rightfully be concerned about getting stuck with juicers that have been discontinued and need to be sold at drastically reduced prices.

Suppose, in fact, AAC's policy is to never order more than a three-month supply of any product in order to guard against such possibilities. Consequently, it would never order more than 6240/4 = 1560 juicers at a time. In this case, only the first three discount levels would be available, and, as we see from Table 11.7, AAC should order 1000 juicers at a time.

INCREMENTAL
DISCOUNT SCHEDULES

Figure 10.6 shows a graph of AAC's total annual juicer inventory cost as a function of the order quantity, assuming that Citron offers an incremental discount schedule. The procedure for determining the optimal order quantity for an incremental discount schedule is somewhat more complex than that used for the all units schedule. Details of this procedure are given in Appendix 10.4 on the accompanying CD-ROM.

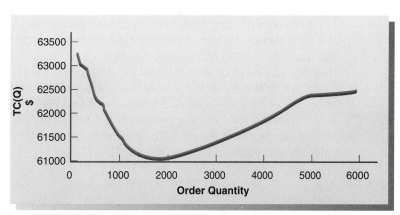

FIGURE 10.6   Total Annual Juicer Inventory Cost as a Function of Order Quantity—Incremental Discount Policy

10.4   PRODUCTION LOT SIZE MODEL

While the EOQ model is useful for determining an optimal inventory policy for goods obtained from other sources, in many instances the firm itself produces the items it sells. If demand for the item occurs at a constant rate, a **production lot size model** can be used to determine the item's optimal inventory policy.

A production lot size model is useful for manufacturers such as pharmaceutical companies, soft drink bottlers, cosmetics companies, ice cream manufacturers, furniture makers, and household goods producers. In all of these enterprises, a production line is not continuously used to manufacture the same product; rather, production of an item occurs in batches, or lots, that are added to the firm's inventory. Production does not resume until the item's inventory is nearly depleted, at which point another batch is produced. An ice cream producer, for example, does not continuously produce Heavenly Hash ice cream. It makes a batch of this flavor, cleans out its equipment, and moves on to produce another flavor.

Production lot size models assume that the production facility operates at a rate greater than the demand rate for the item. Clearly, if the production rate is less than the demand rate, the firm will not have any inventory problem since it will simply ship out all items as they are produced. This situation sometimes occurs with the introduction of an extremely popular children's toy or musical recording. Normally, this degree of popularity does not last long enough to warrant the firm expanding its production lines. Once demand declines below the production rate, a production lot size model may prove useful.

Our discussion focuses on determining the optimal production quantity for a single product. In the real world, where several products must share the same production line, it may be impossible to follow the resulting schedule for each product. Multiple scheduling problem are quite difficult to solve and are beyond the scope of this text.

Our approach parallels that of the EOQ model by developing a general expression for the annual inventory costs associated with producing and storing the stock-keeping unit. In a production process, however, a firm does not actually place an order; instead, it incurs a cost to begin production, known as the *setup cost*. We use the following notation in production lot size models:

D = Estimate of the Annual Demand for the Stock-Keeping Unit
C_h = Annual Holding Cost per Unit in Inventory
C_o = Production Setup Cost
P = Annual Production Rate Assuming Full and Continuous Operation

The goal of the optimal policy is to minimize total annual inventory costs. Because the production lot size model assumes that demand occurs at a constant rate, as with the EOQ model, we can show that, over an infinite time horizon, a stationary policy that produces the same quantity during each production run is optimal. Given a production lot size of Q, we can develop an equation for the total annual variable cost, $TV(Q)$, which represents the sum of the total annual holding cost plus production setup cost. Q^* denotes the value of Q which minimizes $TV(Q)$.

The total annual holding cost is the product of the average inventory level and the annual holding cost per unit. To determine the average inventory level, we need to calculate the *maximum inventory position*, M.

DETERMINING THE AVERAGE INVENTORY LEVEL

Unlike the EOQ model, in a production lot size model, the maximum inventory position is less than the production lot size, Q. This is because units are in demand while they are being produced. To determine the value of M, we refer to Figure 10.7, which profiles the inventory position over time. Here, we assume that the production process operates at a constant rate and that production resumes only when the inventory is depleted.

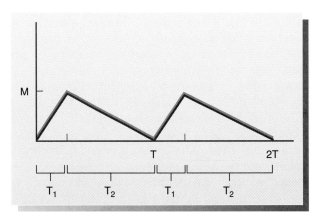

FIGURE 10.7   Production Lot Size Model—Inventory Position Over Time

The production cycle time, T, consists of two time periods, T_1 and T_2. T_1 represents the time during which the product is being produced and inventory is increasing, whereas T_2 represents the time during which the production line is being used for other purposes and the good is not being produced.

Since production of Q units takes place in time period T_1, then (assuming T and T_1 are expressed on a yearly basis),

$$Q = PT_1$$

or

$$T_1 = Q/P$$

Because Q units are demanded during each cycle T, Q can also be expressed by:

$$Q = DT$$

or

$$T = Q/D$$

As Figure 10.7 indicates, the inventory position reaches its highest point during a production cycle at time T_1. At this point, production ceases and the inventory accumulated during the production phase of the cycle begins to be depleted. Because PT_1 units have been produced and DT_1 units have been demanded during time T_1, the inventory position at this point is:

$$M = T_1(P - D) = (Q/P)(P - D) = Q(1 - D/P)$$

The average inventory level is, therefore:

$$\frac{M}{2} = \left(\frac{Q}{2}\right)(1 - D/P)$$

Total Annual Holding Costs

The annual inventory holding cost is then:

$$\left(\frac{Q}{2}\right)(1 - D/P)C_h$$

Total Annual Setup Costs

The annual production setup cost is found by multiplying the average number of production setups per year, D/Q, by the setup cost incurred for each production run, C_o:

$$\left(\frac{D}{Q}\right)C_o$$

Total Annual Variable Costs

Adding together the annual holding and production setup costs gives us the following formula for TV(Q):

$$TV(Q) = \frac{Q}{2}(1 - D/P)C_h + \left(\frac{D}{Q}\right)C_o \qquad (10.7)$$

In Appendix 10.2 on the accompanying CD-ROM, we show that the optimal production quantity is given by

$$Q^* = \sqrt{\frac{2DC_o}{(1 - D/P)C_h}} \qquad (10.8)$$

As in the EOQ model, at Q^* the annual holding costs equal the annual production setup costs.

Comparing Equations 10.1a and 10.2 for the EOQ model to Equations 10.7 and 10.8 for the production lot size model, we see that, if P equals infinity, D/P equals zero and the two sets of equations are identical. Hence, the EOQ model can be considered a special case of the production lot size model, in which goods can be supplied infinitely quickly.

To illustrate use of the production lot size model, let us consider the problem faced by the Farah Cosmetics Company.

FARAH COSMETICS COMPANY

Farah.its
Farah.xls

Management of the Farah Cosmetics Company is interested in determining the optimal production lot size for its most popular shade of lipstick, Autumn Moon. The factory operates seven days a week, 24 hours a day. The lipstick production line can produce 1000 tubes of lipstick per hour when operating at full capacity. Whenever the company changes production to a new shade of lipstick, it takes 30 minutes to clean out the machinery and do any necessary calibrations, and costs an estimated $150.

Demand for Autumn Moon lipstick has been reasonably constant, averaging 980 dozen tubes per week. Farah sells the lipstick to distributors for $.80 per tube, and the firm calculates its variable production cost at approximately $.50 per tube. Because lipsticks must be stored in an air-conditioned warehouse, the firm uses a relatively high annual holding cost rate of 40%.

Farah is currently producing Autumn Moon in batch sizes of 84,000 tubes and would like to determine if this policy is optimal.

SOLUTION

Weekly demand of 980 dozen units is equivalent to a daily demand of 140 dozen, or 1680, units. Thus, D = (1680)(365) = 613,200 per year. The annual holding cost, C_h, for a tube of Autumn Moon lipstick is (.40)($.50) = $.20, and the production setup cost, C_o, is $150. For Autumn Moon, the maximum production rate, P, is (1000)(24)(365) = 8,760,000 units. The unit selling price of the lipstick, $.80, does not enter into our analysis, since revenue is unaffected by the production lot size decision. In summary, we have:

$$D = 613,200$$
$$P = 8,760,000$$
$$C = \$.50$$
$$C_o = \$150$$
$$C_h = \$.20$$

Analysis of Current Policy   Farah currently schedules production runs of 84,000 tubes of Autumn Moon lipstick so that the time between production runs, T, is:

$$T = \frac{84,000 \text{ tubes/run}}{613,200 \text{ tubes/year}} = .1370 \text{ years } (\approx 50 \text{ days})$$

Since the production line can manufacture 8,760,000 tubes per year, the length of a production run is:

$$T_1 = \frac{84,000 \text{ tubes/run}}{613,20 \text{ tubes/year}} = .0096 \text{ years } (\approx 3.5 \text{ days})$$

Thus, the time during each production cycle for which the machine is not used to produce Autumn Moon lipstick is:

$$T_2 = T - T_1 = .1370 - .0096 = .1274 \text{ years } (\approx 46.5 \text{ days})$$

The total annual variable inventory cost for this policy is:

$$TV(84,000) = \left(\frac{84,000}{2}\right)\left(1 - \frac{613,200}{8,760,000}\right)(\$.20) + \left(\frac{613,200}{84,000}\right)(\$150) = \$8,907$$

Analysis of Optimal Policy

Using Equation 10.8 to determine the optimal production lot size, we find:

$$Q^* = \sqrt{\frac{2(613,200)(150)}{\left(1 - \frac{613,200}{8,760,000}\right)(.20)}} \approx 31,499$$

This quantity gives us a total annual variable inventory cost of

$$TV(31,449) = \left(\frac{31,449}{2}\right)\left(1 - \frac{613,200}{8,760,000}\right)(\$.20) + \left(\frac{613,200}{31,449}\right)(\$150) = \$5,850$$

This policy represents a variable inventory cost savings of $3057, or approximately 34%, over the policy of producing in batches of 84,000. Figure 10.8 shows the corresponding WINQSB output for this problem, verifying our hand calculations.

12-06-1998	Input Data	Value	Economic Order Analysis	Value
1	Demand per year	613200	Order quantity	31448.88
2	Order (setup) cost	$150.00	Maximum inventory	29247.46
3	Unit holding cost per year	$0.20	Maximum backorder	0
4	Unit shortage cost		Order interval in year	0.0513
5	per year	M	Reorder point	0
6	Unit shortage cost			
7	independent of time	0	Total setup or ordering cost	$2,924.75
8	Replenishment/production		Total holding cost	$2,924.75
9	rate per year	8.76E6	Total shortage cost	0
10	Lead time in year	0	Subtotal of above	$5,849.49
11	Unit acquisition cost	$0.50		
12			Total material cost	$306,600.00
13				
14			Grand total cost	$312,449.50

FIGURE 10.8   WINQSB Output for Autumn Moon Lipstick

From a practical standpoint, the firm probably would not wish to schedule a production run of exactly 31,449 tubes of lipstick. A more realistic approach is to round off Q^* and recommend a production quantity of 31,000 or 32,000, or even 30,000, tubes of lipstick. As in the EOQ model, small variations in Q^* have a minimal effect on the total annual inventory costs.

10.5 𝒫LANNED SHORTAGE MODEL

When you go to your local supermarket, you expect to find items like eggs, coffee, spaghetti, and ketchup readily available. If they aren't, you will probably begin shopping elsewhere. In other situations, however, we have become accustomed to waiting several days or even weeks or months to get the merchandise we want.

For example, if you wish to purchase a new car complete with a detailed list of specific options, and the car is not currently available at your local new car dealership, it may take the factory six or more weeks to produce and deliver the car. Other products we are typically willing to wait for include quality furniture, some major appliances, and specialty parts. What these items have in common are relatively high holding costs, due to either the high cost of the item or its low demand.

The phenomenon of waiting for merchandise to be delivered is known as *backordering*. If an item desired by a customer is not available, the customer either goes elsewhere for the good (a lost sale) or places a backorder for the item. When the next shipment of the item arrives, all backorders are filled immediately, and the remainder of the order is placed into inventory. One approach used to represent such situations is the planned shortage model.

In a **planned shortage model**, we assume that no customers will be lost due to an out-of-stock situation; all such customers will backorder. Although this assumption may not necessarily be true if the item or an appropriate substitute is readily available from another source, it might be appropriate if there is no alternative to waiting. Like the EOQ and production lot size models, this model deals with an item with a sufficiently long shelf life, whose demand occurs at a known constant rate over an infinite time horizon.

Naturally, customers prefer not to have to wait for their merchandise. To incorporate this preference, the planned shortage model includes a cost, C_s, of keeping a customer on backorder for an entire year. (The cost for waiting less than a year is simply prorated.) For example, if a store offers a $10 per week discount for each week a customer waits for merchandise, then $C_s = \$10(52) = \$520$. Hence, if a customer has to wait only four weeks for the item, the backorder cost for that customer is $(4/52)(\$520) = \$40$.

In general, C_s does not represent a customer discount, but, rather, an estimate of customer dissatisfaction known as *goodwill cost*. This cost translates into the future reduction in the firm's profitability associated with keeping a customer waiting. Goodwill costs are, at best, difficult to measure, but firms can sometimes get reasonable estimates of such costs from marketing surveys and focus groups.

In addition to the goodwill cost of keeping a customer waiting for the item, an administrative cost, π, may also be associated with writing up a backorder and contacting the customer whose item was on backorder when the order arrives. This cost differs from C_s because it is a fixed cost per backorder, independent of how long a customer waits for the item to arrive.

In a planned shortage model, the total annual inventory cost equation must account for not only annual holding and ordering costs, but also the annual cost of keeping customers on backorder. The decision maker can control two quantities in this model: Q, the order quantity, and S, the number of units on backorder at the time the next order arrives. Hence, the total variable inventory cost equation, TV(Q,S), is a function of both of these quantities:

TV(Q,S) = (Total Annual Holding Costs)
+ (Total Annual Ordering Costs)
+ (Total Annual Time-Dependent Shortage Costs)
+ (Total Annual Time-Independent Shortage Costs)

Figure 10.9 is useful in developing expressions for these terms. In this figure:

T_1 = the period in the inventory cycle during which inventory is available
T_2 = the period in the inventory cycle during which items are on backorder
T = the time of the complete inventory cycle = $T_1 + T_2$

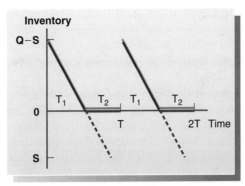

FIGURE 10.9   Planned Shortage Model—Inventory Profile Over Time

An inventory cycle begins when S units are on backorder and an order of size Q is received. Since the S backorders are filled immediately, the inventory position at the beginning of the cycle is brought to its maximum inventory position $M = Q - S$. We assume that items are demanded (thus, inventory is depleted) at a constant rate until the inventory level reaches 0 at time T_1. Then, during period T_2, backorders accumulate at the same constant demand rate until, at the end of the cycle, S units are on backorder. At that point the next cycle begins, and the process is repeated. Let us now evaluate the individual components of TV(Q,S).

ANNUAL HOLDING COST

The average inventory level is the average inventory level during the in-stock period, $(Q - S)/2$, times the proportion of time there is inventory in stock, (T_1/T). In Appendix 10.5 on the accompanying CD-ROM, we show that (T_1/T) equals $(Q - S)/Q$, so that

$$\text{Average Inventory Level} = \frac{(Q - S)^2}{2Q}$$

As in the previous models, the annual holding cost is the average inventory level times C_h. Thus,

$$\text{Annual Inventory Holding Costs} = \frac{(Q - S)^2}{2Q}C_h$$

ANNUAL ORDERING COST

The annual ordering cost is found by multiplying the average number of orders per year by the fixed ordering cost, C_o. Thus, the total annual ordering cost is:

$$\left(\frac{D}{Q}\right)C_o$$

ANNUAL TIME-DEPENDENT SHORTAGE COST

The average backorder level is the average number of stockouts during the out-of-stock period, $S/2$, times the proportion of time inventory is on backorder, (T_2/T). In Appendix 10.5 on the accompanying CD-ROM we show that (T_2/T) equals S/Q, so that

$$\text{Average Number of Customers on Backorder} = \frac{S^2}{2Q}$$

The annual time-dependent shortage cost equals the average backorder level times C_s. Thus,

$$\text{Annual Time-Dependent Backorder Cost} = \left(\frac{S^2}{2Q}\right)C_s$$

ANNUAL
TIME-INDEPENDENT
SHORTAGE COST

During each inventory cycle there are S backorders, and there are D/Q cycles per year, so that

$$\text{Total Number of Backorders During a Year} = \left(\frac{D}{Q}\right)S$$

The annual shortage cost that is incurred independent of the length of time customers are on backorder is π times the total number of backorders during the year. Thus,

$$\text{Annual Time-Independent Backorder Cost} = \left(\frac{D}{Q}\right)S\pi$$

TOTAL ANNUAL COSTS

Combining these terms gives us the following formula for TV(Q,S):

$$\text{TV(Q,S)} = \frac{(Q-S)^2}{2Q}C_h + \frac{D}{Q}(C_o + S\pi) + \frac{S^2}{2Q}C_s \qquad (10.9)$$

OPTIMAL INVENTORY
POLICY

Let Q^* and S^* represent the pair of values for Q and S that minimize TV(Q,S). While it is not always possible to obtain closed-form solutions for a pair of values such as Q^* and S^*, they can be obtained for this model provided that $C_s > 0$ and

$$\pi < \sqrt{2C_oC_h/D}$$

(See Appendix 10.2 on the accompanying CD-ROM.) These values are:

$$Q^* = \sqrt{\left(\frac{2DC_o}{C_h}\right)\left(\frac{C_h + C_s}{C_s}\right) - \frac{(D\pi)^2}{C_hC_s}} \qquad (10.10)$$

and

$$S^* = \frac{QC_h - D\pi}{C_h + C_s} \qquad (10.11)$$

REORDER POINT

To find the reorder point when there is a lead time of L years, we note that S^* represents the number of customers who should be on backorder when the new shipment arrives. If the annual demand is for D units, the lead time demand equals L * D. Hence, the reorder point, R, for this model is given by the following formula:

$$R = L * D - S^* \qquad (10.12)$$

The value of R can be negative, implying that the reorder point occurs when several units are already on backorder. If R = −5, for example, the order should be placed when five units are on backorder.

To illustrate the planned shortage model, consider the situation faced by the Scanlon Plumbing Corporation.

SCANLON PLUMBING CORPORATION

Scan.its
Scan.xls

Scanlon Plumbing Corporation is the exclusive North American distributor of a portable sauna manufactured in Sweden. The saunas cost Scanlon $2400 each, and the company estimates the annual holding cost per unit for this product is $525. Because the saunas must be shipped in a containerized vessel, the fixed ordering cost is fairly high, at $1250. Lead time for delivery is four weeks.

Scanlon receives orders for an average of 15 saunas per week. Customers are willing to place orders for the saunas when Scanlon is out of stock. However, the company estimates the goodwill cost of keeping a customer's sauna on backorder is $20 per week. There is also an administrative cost of $10 for each sauna placed on backorder.

Management wishes to determine an optimal inventory policy for ordering the saunas.

SOLUTION

For the Scanlon Plumbing model the parameters are:

$$D = 15(52) = 780$$
$$C_o = \$1{,}250$$
$$C_h = \$525$$
$$C_s = \$20(52) = \$1{,}040$$
$$\pi = \$10$$

Substituting these quantities into Equations 10.10 and 10.11 gives:

$$Q^* = \sqrt{\left(\frac{2(780)(1250)}{525}\right)\left(\frac{525 + 1040}{1040}\right) - \frac{((780)(10))^2}{(525)(1040)}} \approx 74$$

and

$$S^* = \frac{(74)(525) - (780)(10)}{525 + 1040} \approx 20$$

Since lead time is four weeks, $L = 4/52 = .07692$ years. Orders should therefore be placed when the inventory level reaches:

$$R = .07692(780) - 20 = 40 \text{ units}$$

PRACTICAL
CONSIDERATIONS

Again, we must check the validity of the assumptions we used to generate Q^* and S^*. For example, the planned shortage model assumes that goodwill costs are linear; that is, the cost of keeping a customer on backorder for four months is assumed to be four times the cost of keeping a customer on backorder for one month. This is probably not the case in most real-world situations. Customers may be reasonably tolerant of short delays, but long delays can result in a tremendous loss in customer goodwill. Hence, the decision maker should analyze the model results to see whether the assumed backorder cost is realistic.

In this case, we assumed that the backorder cost for saunas is $20 per week. Although management feels that this cost is realistic for delays of a week or less, it believes that delays greater than a week are actually more costly. The maximum delay experienced by any customer can be found by dividing S^* by D. For Scanlon Plumbing, the maximum backorder delay encountered by a customer (in weeks) is $S^*/D = 20/15 = 1\frac{1}{3}$ weeks.

As a result of this analysis, management might feel that a $25 per week backorder cost is more realistic. This variation changes C_s from $1040 to $1300 and, using Equations 10.10 and 10.11, suggests a revised inventory policy of ordering 72 units when the inventory level reaches 44 units. In this case, the maximum number of customers on backorder is approximately 16, and the longest time a customer will spend on backorder is just slightly more than one week.

ECONOMIC
IMPLICATIONS

It is worth examining the implications of the formulas for Q^* and S^* on inventory control. (To simplify, let us assume π equals 0.) If C_h is quite large relative to C_s (as it is for custom or big-ticket items for which the buyer expects delays), the ratio $C_h/(C_h + C_s)$ is close to 1 and S^* is approximately Q^*. That is, whenever an inventory order arrives, nearly all units have already been presold and the firm carries virtually no inventory. The optimal order quantity in this case is given approximately by the formula

$$Q^* \approx \sqrt{\frac{2DC_o}{C_s}}$$

In this case, the holding cost plays no role in determining Q^*.

On the other hand, suppose that C_s is quite large relative to C_h, as it is for products for which customer goodwill costs are quite high if the item is not available for purchase (such as daily staples like bread, milk, and eggs). In this case, $C_h/(C_h + C_s)$ is close to 0 and the firm almost always wants the good to be in stock. Therefore, customers are never intentionally placed on backorder. Furthermore, because $(C_h + C_s)/C_s$ is effectively 1, the formula for Q^* reduces to the EOQ formula (Equation 10.2). Hence, we can view the EOQ model as a special case of the planned shortage model for which C_s equals infinity and π equals 0.

Thus if an item has a high holding cost relative to its backorder cost, the firm will carry little, if any, inventory, while if its backorder cost is high relative to its holding cost, the firm generally tries to keep the item in inventory and avoid running out of stock.

SPECIAL CASES

A special case of the planned shortage model occurs when the value of π is high relative to the value of C_s. In particular, when $\pi > \sqrt{2C_oC_h/D}$, the optimal solution is to allow no shortages ($S^* = 0$), and Q^* equals the EOQ value.

To understand why this is the case, note that, for the EOQ solution, $Q^* = \sqrt{2DC_o/C_h}$. Substituting this value into the total annual variable cost formula (Equation 10.1) gives us:

$$\text{TV}(Q^*) = \sqrt{2DC_oC_h} \tag{10.13}$$

Dividing $\text{TV}(Q^*)$ by the annual demand, D, results in the variable inventory cost per unit under the EOQ policy, $\sqrt{2C_oC_h/D}$. Hence, if the administrative backorder cost, π, is greater than this amount, it must be more expensive to allow backorders than not to allow them.

Another special case of the model occurs when $C_s = 0$. If the value of C_s is 0 and $\pi \leq \sqrt{2C_oC_h/D}$, the model does not make any sense because the optimal policy is to keep all customers on backorder for an infinitely long period of time.

10.6 $\mathcal{D}$ETERMINING SAFETY STOCK LEVELS

The discussion in Section 10.5 dealt with situations in which firms intentionally run out of stock during the inventory cycle. As we saw earlier for the EOQ model, when businesses want to avoid stockouts, they incorporate safety stock requirements when determining the reorder point.

One approach for determining the appropriate safety stock level for an item is for management to specify a desired *service level*. This can represent one of two quantities:

1. the likelihood or probability of not incurring a stockout during an inventory cycle, or

2. the percentage of demands that are filled without incurring any delay

The first approach, known as the *cycle service level*, is appropriate when the firm is concerned about the *likelihood* of a stockout and not its magnitude. It is used, for example, in manufacturing settings in which *any* stockout affects production.

The second approach known as the *unit service level*, is appropriate when the firm is interested in controlling the *percentage* of unsatisfied demands. It corresponds to the term *fill rate* and is what managers commonly mean when they state a service level.

To illustrate the difference between these two service levels, we return to the Allen Appliance Company example described in Section 10.2. Table 10.8 shows the juicer demand and number of units on backorder during the last five inventory cycles at AAC when the policy was to order 600 units whenever the inventory level reached 205 units.

TABLE 10.8   JUICER DEMAND AND UNITS ON BACKORDER

Cycle Number	Demand	Number of Units on Backorder
1	585	0
2	610	0
3	628	15
4	572	0
5	605	0

We see that, during this time period, the cycle service level is 80% since 4 out of 5 cycles experienced no stockouts. At the same time the unit service level is 99.5% since only 15 of 3000 units were backordered.

THE CYCLE SERVICE LEVEL APPROACH

Stockouts occur only if demand during the lead time exceeds the reorder point. For example, if AAC uses a reorder point of 205, a stockout occurs only when demand during the lead time exceeds 205 units. Hence, if the lead time demand distribution is known, a statistical analysis can be used to determine the service level corresponding to a given reorder point or the safety stock required to maintain a given cycle service level.

In many cases, we can assume that demand during the lead time follows a normal distribution with estimated mean, $\mu = L * D$, and standard deviation, σ. In such instances, the reorder point R is calculated using the formula:

$$R = \mu + z\sigma$$

where z represents the number of standard deviations above the average lead time demand required to maintain the desired cycle service level. The value for z is found by looking in the standard normal random variable table (Appendix A) and finding the z value corresponding to a tail area equal to 1-(cycle service level). In this formula, $z\sigma$, the amount above the mean lead time demand, μ, is the *safety stock*.

For example, recall that the lead time for delivery of juicers at AAC is eight working days and that demand over the past 10 weeks is that given in Table 10.3. From these data, we can calculate the sample mean and variance, which can be used as estimates for the population mean and variance for weekly demand:

$$\mu \approx \bar{x} = \frac{(105 + 115 + \ldots + 130)}{10} = 120$$

$$\sigma^2 \approx s^2 = \frac{(105^2 + 115^2 + \ldots + 130^2) - 10(120^2)}{9} = 83.33$$

We can find the estimates of the mean, μ_L, and variance, σ_L^2 of the lead time demand by multiplying the weekly demand estimates by the length of the lead time (expressed in weeks). Since the lead time is eight days, or $8/5 = 1.6$ weeks,

$$\mu_L \approx 1.6(120) = 192$$
$$\sigma_L^2 \approx 1.6(83.33) = 133.33$$

Thus

$$\sigma_L \approx \sqrt{133.33} = 11.55$$

Analysis of Current Policy

If we can assume that lead time demand follows a normal distribution,[3] a reorder point of R = 205 implies:

$$205 = 192 + z(11.53)$$

---

[3]This can be verified by performing a standard goodness-of-fit test as described in Appendix 12.2 on the accompanying CD-ROM.

Solving for z we find:

$$z = (205 - 192)/11.53 = 1.13$$

We see from Appendix A, the area in the tail above $z = 1.13$ is $.5 - .3708 = .1292$. Thus as shown in Figure 10.10 this policy corresponds approximately to an 87% cycle service level.

FIGURE 10.10   Determining a Cycle Service Level for AAC

Analysis of Optimal Policy

Now suppose that AAC management wants to improve its cycle service level from 87% to 99%. In this case, the z value corresponding to a 99% shaded area (1% tail area) is 2.33. As illustrated in Figure 10.11, the reorder point is $R = (192 + 2.33 * 11.55) = 219$ units, requiring a safety stock of $219 - 192 = 27$ units.

FIGURE 10.11   Reorder Point for AAC Corresponding to a 99% Cycle Service Level

Another way of expressing a cycle service level is to specify an acceptable value for the likelihood of being out of stock for a given average number of cycles per year. For example, suppose AAC is willing to run out of juicers an average of at most one cycle per year. If the firm uses an order quantity of 327 units, it will average $6240/327 = 19.08$ lead times during each year, and the desired probability of a stockout during a lead time is $1/19.08 = .0524$, which corresponds to a 94.76% service level. Referring to Appendix A, this gives us a z value equal to approximately 1.62. In this case, the safety stock, $z\sigma$, equals $1.62(11.55) \approx 19$. Thus, the reorder point should be $R = 192 + 19 = 211$ units.

THE UNIT SERVICE LEVEL APPROACH

Finding the reorder point corresponding to a desired *unit* service level is a bit more complicated than finding the reorder point corresponding to a desired *cycle* service level. Appendix 10.3 on the accompanying CD-ROM contains the general formula used to find this value. When lead time demand follows a normal distribution with estimated mean μ and standard deviation σ, the reorder point, R, can be determined as follows:

1.   Determine the value of z that satisfies the relationship:

$$L(z) = \frac{(1 - \text{service level})Q^*}{\sigma}$$

(Here L(z) represents the partial expected value for the standard normal random variable between some value z and infinity. Values of the L(z) function are given in Appendix B.)

2. Solve for R using the formula $R = \mu + z\sigma$.

For example, suppose AAC desires a 99% unit service level. Based on values $\mu = 192$, $\sigma = 11.55$, and $Q^* = 327$, for a 99% unit service level, $L(z) = (1 - .99)(327/11.55) = .2831$. Referring to Appendix B a value of $L(z) = .2831$, corresponds to $z \approx .26$. Therefore, $R = 192 + .26(11.55) = 195$. This results in a safety stock of $195 - 192 = 3$ units.

It is interesting to compare the safety stock requirements between a cycle and a unit service level. For the Allen Appliance example, the safety stock equals only three units for a 99% unit service level, compared to 27 units for a 99% cycle service level. The safety stock requirements are lower for the unit service level because the calculations include the nonlead time portions of the inventory cycle. Since it is impossible to be in an out-of-stock situation during these times, fewer safety stock units are necessary. Another way to view this is to recognize that, when we select a reorder point based on a desired unit service level, the corresponding cycle service level will be lower.

10.7 REVIEW SYSTEMS

CONTINUOUS REVIEW SYSTEMS

The EOQ model, the production lot size model, and the planned shortage model are all examples of continuous review systems because we implicitly assume that the inventory position is *continuously* monitored and an order is placed at the instant the inventory level reaches the reorder point.

(R,Q) Policies

For the EOQ, production lot size, and planned shortage models, an order of size Q is placed whenever the inventory level reaches the reorder point, R. Hence, these models are sometimes known as *order point, order quantity*, or (R,Q) *policies*.

There are several ways to implement such policies. If inventory is tracked by a point-of-sale (POS) computerized cash register system, as it is in many retail establishments (department stores and supermarkets), the computer can be programmed to carry out the recommended policy. Because the computer does not record shrinkage (theft and breakage), however, this method is not foolproof. This shortcoming is generally not too severe, however, and can be overcome by introducing a shrinkage factor into the computer program.

If the inventory is not tracked by computer, it may appear impossible, from a practical standpoint, to continuously review the firm's inventory position. Fortunately, there is a fairly easy way of implementing an (R,Q) policy, known as the *two-bin system*. This system, which is used in a number of factories and supply houses, operates as follows.

For a given product, a small bin holds R units and a larger bin holds up to Q units. When a new order arrives, the small bin is filled and tagged, and the remaining inventory from the order is placed in the large bin. Employees are instructed to remove units from the large bin until that bin is depleted. Once the large bin is empty, the small bin is opened up and items are supplied from that bin. At the time the small bin is opened, an order tag is removed and given to the inventory foreman. The order tag alerts the foreman that it is time to place an order for an additional Q units.

(R,M) Policies

Implicit in the development of our previous models is the fact that the firm sells stockkeeping units one at a time. In many businesses, however, the typical customer order may consist of multiple units of the same item. When such an order triggers the reorder point, problems can arise in an (R,Q) system.

For example, suppose that Citron did not offer quantity discounts and AAC adopted the policy recommendation to order 327 units when the inventory level reaches 219. If the inventory level is 224 and one of AAC's customers purchases 60 juicers, this purchase triggers a new order. If AAC only orders 327 juicers, it may find itself out of stock again faster than anticipated because only $224 - 60 = 164$ juicers are in stock when the order is placed.

One way to avoid the potential problem caused by exceptionally large orders is to use an *order point, order up to level*, or (R,M) *policy*. Under this system, while a new order is placed whenever the inventory level falls to R or below, the order size must be sufficient to bring the inventory level back up to an anticipated level of M. This system effectively amends the (R,Q) policy to account for situations in which the inventory level may be substantially below the reorder point when the order is placed.

For example, suppose AAC uses an (R,M) policy with reorder point R = 219, and maximum inventory level M = 354 (the order quantity of 327 plus the safety stock of 27). If a customer orders 60 juicers when the inventory level is at 224, a reorder is triggered and the reorder amount is 382 juicers instead of 327. The extra 55 units account for the fact that, when the reorder is placed, the inventory level is 55 units below the desired reorder point of 219.

In the long run, an (R,M) policy typically has a lower average costs than a comparable (R,Q) policy. (R,M) systems are more complicated to monitor than (R,Q) systems, however. For example, implementing an (R,M) policy in a two-bin system requires the employee who removes the tag from the smaller bin to record how many units are being removed from that bin at the time it is opened. This extra control cost is not always worth the savings achieved by the (R,M) system.

PERIODIC REVIEW SYSTEMS

Continuous review systems are not practical for many businesses. Some establishments may not have the resources available to purchase computerized cash register systems or the space available to adopt a two-bin system. Others may order many different items from the same vendor and find it impractical to place separate purchase orders at different time periods for the numerous SKUs. In such instances, many firms resort to *periodic review inventory systems* in which the inventory position for each SKU is observed periodically.

(T,M) Policies

In *replenishment cycle* or (T,M) *policies*, the inventory position is reviewed every T time units (days, weeks, etc.), and an order is placed to bring the inventory level for the stockkeeping unit back up to a maximum inventory level, M. This maximum level is determined by forecasting the number of units demanded during the review period and adding the desired safety stock to this amount. Replenishment cycle policies are typically used by rack jobbers who have a scheduled plan for servicing customers. The following formulas can then be used to find the order quantity, Q, and the value of M, for a (T,M) policy:

$$Q = (T+L) * D + SS - SH$$
$$M = T * D + SS$$

where: T = review period
           L = lead time
           D = demand
          SS = safety stock
           Q = order quantity
           M = maximum inventory level
          SH = stock on hand

(*Note*: T, L, and D must be in the same time units.)

To illustrate this technique, let us return to the situation at the Allen Appliance Company.

ALLEN APPLIANCE COMPANY (continued)

Allen Appliance Company has begun selling several different products from Citron in addition to its juicers and has decided to implement a periodic review system for controlling inventory. Citron makes regular deliveries to AAC every three weeks, based on orders it has received eight days before shipment. Thus, AAC reviews its inventory every three weeks, eight days before it expects a shipment, and faxes an order to Citron. It is now time for AAC to place an order, and it finds that 210 juicers are in stock. AAC wants to know how many juicers to order if it now desires a safety stock of 30 units.

SOLUTION

Since AAC reviews its position and places an order with Citron every three weeks, $T = 3/52 = .05769$ years. Recall that demand for juicers averages 6240 units per year. Hence, over the three-week review period, approximately $.05769 * 6240 = 360$ juicers are demanded. Because AAC desires a safety stock of 30 juicers, the maximum inventory, M, is:

$$M = 360 + 30 = 390 \text{ juicers}$$

The lead time for juicers is eight days, or $L = 8/260 = .03077$ years. Since AAC has 210 juicers in stock, the order quantity, Q, should be:

$$Q = (.05769+.03077) * 6240 + 30 - 210 = 372 \text{ juicers}$$

(T,R,M) Policies

One shortcoming of a (T,M) policy arises when there has been little demand for the stock-keeping unit during the previous review period. Under these circumstances, it may not even pay to place a new order. We can modify the (T,M) policy by introducing a threshold inventory level R, meaning that orders for the stock-keeping unit are placed only if the current inventory level is R or less. This policy, known as a (T,R,M) *policy*, has a lower long-run cost than a simple (T,M) policy. How we determine optimal values for T and R is beyond the scope of this text. However, this problem can be analyzed using the simulation approach detailed in Chapter 13.

CONTROL COSTS OF AN INVENTORY POLICY

We should not overlook the control cost associated with an inventory policy. Although the inventory techniques we've discussed in this chapter may reduce a firm's annual inventory expense, there are costs associated with determining inventory policies and controlling the inventory to conform with such policies. Consequently, the methods discussed here generally apply only to A and B type inventory items. For C items, the expense of inventory control generally exceeds the cost savings such control carries.

10.8 SUMMARY

In this chapter, we have examined a class of inventory models useful for analyzing goods for which demand occurs at a known and reasonably constant rate. In situations in which a firm purchases goods from a supplier, the economic order quantity (EOQ) model can be used to determine the amount to order. The EOQ solution is quite robust; small errors in estimating parameter values have only minor effects on the EOQ solution.

Firms often offer their customers quantity discounts. Two frequently used discount schedules are the all units schedule and the incremental schedule. For the all units discount schedule, simple modifications to the EOQ analysis help determine the optimal order quantity.

In many manufacturing settings, the production lot size model can be used to determine the optimal production quantity for a good. The EOQ model can be considered a special case of the production lot size model, in which goods are supplied at an infinitely rapid rate.

The planned shortage model incorporates a backorder cost into the EOQ model. Items that have a relatively high shortage cost are most likely carried in stock, while items with a relatively high holding cost are most likely to be on backorder.

While some backorders are planned, many are not. In order to determine the necessary safety stock to accommodate a desired service level, a firm can undertake a statistical analysis. The appropriate safety stock is based on whether a cycle service level or a unit service level is desired.

There are several methods firms can use to control their inventories. Review of inventory may be done on a continuous or periodic basis. Order quantities may be fixed or adjusted to bring the inventory up to a specified level. The control costs associated with an inventory model should be accounted for when selecting an appropriate policy.

$\mathcal{N}$OTATIONAL SUMMARY

B_i = i^{th} Quantity Breakpoint for a Discount Schedule
C = Cost per Unit
C_s = Cost to Keep a Customer on Backorder for a Year
C_h = Annual Holding Cost per Unit
C_i = Cost per Unit at the ith Breakpoint of a Discount Schedule
C_o = Ordering or Production Setup Cost
D = Annual Demand
H = Annual Holding Cost Rate
L = Lead Time (expressed on an annual basis)
M = Maximum Inventory Model
P = Annual Production Capacity
Q = Inventory Order Quantity
Q^* = Optimal Inventory Order Quantity
R = Reorder Point
S = Number of Units on Backorder When Inventory Arrives
S^* = Optimal Number of Units on Backorder When Inventory Arrives
SH = Stock on Hand
SS = Safety Stock
T = Length of an Inventory Cycle (expressed on an annual basis)
$TC(Q)$ = Total Annual Inventory Costs
$TV(Q)$ = Total Annual Variable Inventory Costs
μ = Mean Lead Time Demand
σ = Standard Deviation of Lead Time Demand
π = Fixed Administrative Cost per Backorder

Using WINQSB to Solve Inventory Models Based on Stationary Demand

The inventory module of WINQSB can be used to solve problems involving stationary demand. Exhibit 10.1 shows the initial screen for this module. For EOQ, production lot size, and planned shortage models, we click on "Deterministic Demand Economic Order Quantity (EOQ) Problem." For EOQ models involving quantity discounts we click on "Deterministic Demand Quantity Discount Analysis Problem." We can determine safety stock requirements by clicking on "Continuous Review Fixed-Order-Quantity (s,Q) Systems," while the "Periodic Review Fixed-Order-Interval (R,S) System" option is used to analyze the periodic review models covered in the chapter.

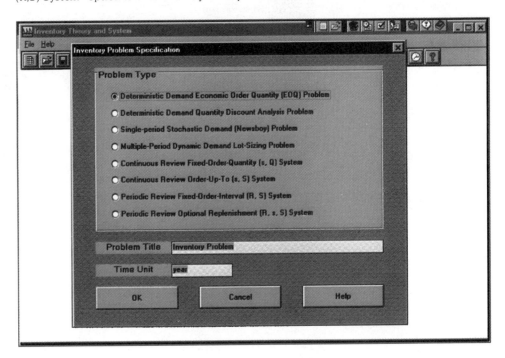

EXHIBIT 10.1

EOQ Models

To solve the EOQ problem faced by Allen Appliance Company, we click on "Deterministic Demand Economic Order Quantity (EOQ) Problem" and complete the data input screen as shown in Exhibit 10.2. We then solve the problem by selecting "Solve the Problem" from the "Solve and

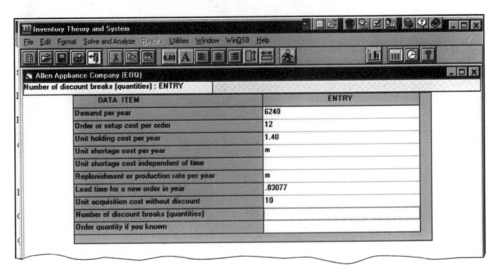

EXHIBIT 10.2

Analyze" option on the menu bar. Exhibit 10.3 shows the screen for the Allen Appliance Company problem.

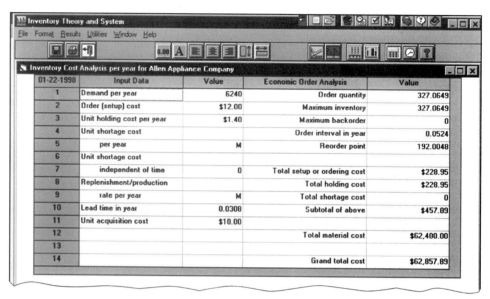

EXHIBIT 10.3

Quantity Discount Models

To solve a quantity discount problem, after clicking on "Deterministic Demand Quantity Discount Analysis Problem," the initial data entry screen is the same as that used for EOQ problems. Now, select Discount Characteristics from the Edit menu and check to see that the button labeled "Also discounted" for Holding Costs is selected. Then, enter the number of discount breaks by choosing the "Discount Breaks" option from the Edit menu. Exhibit 10.4 shows the discount break input screen for the Allen Appliance problem.

EXHIBIT 10.4

We can now solve the problem by selecting "Solve the Problem" from the "Solve and Analyze" option on the menu bar, which gives us the screen shown in Exhibit 10.5.

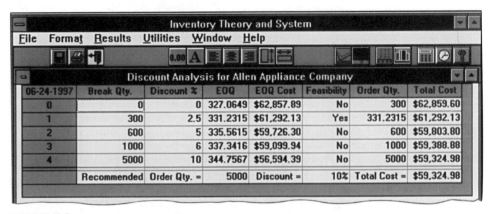

Inventory Theory and System
File   Format   Results   Utilities   Window   Help

Discount Analysis for Allen Appliance Company							
06-24-1997	Break Qty.	Discount %	EOQ	EOQ Cost	Feasibility	Order Qty.	Total Cost
0	0	0	327.0649	$62,857.89	No	300	$62,859.60
1	300	2.5	331.2315	$61,292.13	Yes	331.2315	$61,292.13
2	600	5	335.5615	$59,726.30	No	600	$59,803.80
3	1000	6	337.3416	$59,099.94	No	1000	$59,388.88
4	5000	10	344.7567	$56,594.39	No	5000	$59,324.98
	Recommended	Order Qty. =	5000	Discount =	10%	Total Cost =	$59,324.98

EXHIBIT 10.5

$\mathcal{P}$ROBLEMS

1. Demand for STICK disposable razors at Buyright Drugs averages seven packages per day. The razors cost Buyright $0.80 per package and sell for $1.49. Buyright uses a 20% annual holding cost rate and estimates the cost to place an order for additional razors at $25. Buyright is open 365 days a year and desires a safety stock of 15 packages. The lead time for delivery is five days. Determine the following:
   a. The optimal order quantity of STICK razors.
   b. The reorder point for these razors.
   c. The number of days between orders (cycle time).
   d. The total annual inventory cost (holding, ordering, and procurement) of this policy.
   e. The projected annual net profit of this policy.
   What assumptions did you make regarding demand in solving this problem?

2. How would your answers to Problem 1 change if STICK requires its customers to purchase razors in gross units (multiples of 144) and Buyright desires a safety stock of 20 razors?

3. OfficeHQ is a discount retailer of office goods. One of its most popular products is the STICK brand pen, packaged six to a box and retailing for $1.29. Each box costs OfficeHQ $0.95. OfficeHQ is open five days a week, 52 weeks a year.

   Daily demand for STICK pens is reasonably constant, averaging 65 boxes. The cost for OfficeHQ to place an order is $30, and the firm uses an annual inventory holding cost rate of 22%. Lead time for delivery is one week, and OfficeHQ desires a safety stock of 100 boxes of pens. If OfficeHQ must order in increments of 100 boxes, determine the following:
   a. The optimal order quantity of STICK pens
   b. The reorder point for these pens.
   c. The number of calendar days between orders (cycle time).
   d. The total annual inventory cost (holding, ordering, safety stock, and procurement) of this policy.
   e. The projected annual net profit of this policy.

4. Suppose that in Problem 3 the daily demand for STICK pens averages 75 boxes (instead of 65).
   a. What is the optimal order quantity for STICK pens?
   b. If OfficeHQ uses the order policy determined in Problem 3, determine the difference in total annual variable inventory costs between this policy and the optimal policy found in part (a).

5. OfficeHQ carries boxes of Disco floppy diskettes. Because the diskettes come in different formats, OfficeHQ has decided to use a periodic review policy, in which it places an order with Disco once every three weeks.

   Weekly demand for Disco $3\frac{1}{2}''$ diskettes at OfficeHQ averages 45 boxes. The lead time for delivery is approximately one week, and OfficeHQ desires a safety stock of 30 boxes. OfficeHQ uses an annual holding cost rate of 20% for the diskettes. If the inventory level at the time OfficeHQ places its next order with Disco is 55 boxes, determine its optimal order quantity.

6. Scanlon Plumbing Corporation distributes American Consolidated lavatories. Demand for the basic China White Oval Model 2634 averages 19 units a week. The lavatories cost Scanlon $22.50 each and sell for $35.75. Unfortunately, approximately 5% of the lavatories ordered by Scanlon are either defective or damaged during shipment. Therefore, Scanlon needs 20 (= 19/.95) units a week to meet its demand.

   The company uses a periodic review policy with American Consolidated and orders once every four weeks. Lead time for delivery is two weeks, and Scanlon desires a safety stock of 50 units. If the inventory level of the lavatories at the time of the next order is 35 units, determine the optimal inventory policy.

7. GROW Garden Center sells Raincloud automatic sprinkler valves. The valves cost GROW $8.75 each, and GROW uses an annual holding cost rate of 24%. The cost to place an

order with Raincloud is approximately $30. Demand over the past eight weeks has been as follows:

Week	Demand	Week	Demand
1	24	5	18
2	20	6	22
3	16	7	28
4	22	8	18

GROW uses a simple eight-week moving average to forecast average annual demand and average lead time demand. Lead time for delivery is two weeks, and GROW desires a cycle service level of 96%. GROW estimates that lead time demand follows a normal distribution with a standard deviation of 5.45 units. On the basis of this information, determine:

a. The optimal order quantity of sprinkler valves.

b. The reorder point for the sprinkler valves.

c. The number of calendar days between orders (cycle time).

d. The total annual inventory cost (holding, ordering, procurement) for this policy.

8. Bryan's Office Supply sells the Harrington 2000 automatic stapler. Demand for the staplers averages 24 units per week. The staplers cost Bryan's $17.25 each, and Bryan's uses a 22% annual holding cost rate. The cost to place an order with Harrington is $45, and the lead time for delivery is two weeks. Bryan's desires a safety stock of 15 staplers.

Harrington offers its customers the following all unit quantity discount pricing schedule:

Number Ordered	Discount
1–199	none
200–399	4%
400–699	6%
700–999	8%
1000–4999	11%
5000+	15%

Bryan's never orders an amount greater than a 35-week supply for any product. Assuming that holding costs are discounted, determine the following:

a. The optimal order quantity of Harrington staplers.

b. The reorder point for the staplers.

c. The number of calendar days between orders (cycle time).

d. The total annual inventory cost (holding, ordering, procurement, and safety stock) for this policy.

What assumptions did you make to solve this problem?

9. Archer Pharmaceuticals manufactures Tranquility brand sleeping pills, which have an average weekly demand of 25,000 bottles. The Archer factory operates 10 hours a day, six days a week. The production line at Archer Pharmaceuticals can produce 10,000 bottles of Tranquility daily. Archer's policy is to make a batch of Tranquility and, after building up sufficient inventory, use the production line to produce other products.

The company estimates that the production setup for producing tranquility pills takes about two hours and costs $325. It also estimates that the annual holding cost for a bottle of Tranquility is $0.55.

a. What is the optimal production batch size?

b. What is the total annual inventory holding and production setup cost of this policy?

c. What is the length of a production run in hours (including setup time)?

d. What is the number of calendar days between the start times of successive production runs?

What assumptions did you make in solving this problem?

10. Bee's Candy manufactures a variety of candy bars in a number of different sizes. One of its more popular products is the three-ounce Smirk bar. Bee's forecasts that demand for this product should be fairly constant over the next year, totalling 21 million bars.

The candy production line, which operates 24 hours a day, 365 days a year, is capable of producing two candy bars per second. A production setup for the three-ounce Smirk bar takes 50 minutes and costs approximately $450. The annual holding cost of a three-ounce Smirk bar is estimated as $0.12.

a. What is the optimal production batch size?

b. What is the total annual inventory holding and production setup cost for this policy?

c. What is the length of a production run in hours (including setup time)?

d. What is the number of days between the start times of successive production runs?

e. How would your answer to part (a) change if the annual holding cost decreased to $0.10 per bar?

11. Click Pix, a large discount camera shop in New York City is open six days a week, 52 weeks a year. The store has recently begun carrying Sonic model PS58 camcorders which cost $520.00 each and retail for $649.99. Sales average 60 units per week.

The cost of placing an order with Sonic is $90, and the lead time is seven working days. The store estimates that the lead time demand follows a normal distribution with a mean of 70 units and a standard deviation of 15 units. Click Pix uses an annual holding cost rate of 18% for the camcorders. Ideally, it would like to run out of the camcorders during at most one inventory cycle per year. Given this goal, determine the following:

a. The optimal order quantity for Sonic camcorders.

b. The reorder point for camcorders.

c. The number of working days between orders (cycle time).

d. The total annual inventory cost (holding, ordering, procurement, and safety stock) for this policy.

e. The projected annual profit for this policy.

12. How would your answers to Problem 11 change if Sonic offered Click the following all units discount schedule?

Order Quantity	Discount
200–599	5.0%
600–999	7.5%
1,000 or more	9.0%

13. Scott Stereo sells personal tape players. One of its more popular sellers is the Sonic Walkperson. These units cost Scott $18.55 each and retail for $32.95. Weekly demand averages 12 units. The cost of placing an order with Sonic is $25, and lead time is two weeks. Scott uses a 26% annual inventory holding cost rate.

If Scott is out of stock of the Walkperson, it estimates that it will suffer a customer goodwill cost of $2 for each week a customer must wait for the Walkperson to arrive. A fixed administrative cost of $0.50 is associated with each backordered customer. Determine the following:

a. The optimal order quantity of Walkpersons.

b. The reorder point for the Walkpersons.

c. The number of calendar days between orders (cycle time).

d. The percentage of customers who will be placed on backorder.

e. The total annual inventory cost (holding, ordering, shortage, and procurement) for this policy.

f. The projected total annual profit for this policy.

14. Scott Stereo orders Dutch brand cassette tapes once every three weeks. Weekly demand for the T-60 format is approximately normal with a mean of 200 units and a standard deviation of 30 units. The tapes cost Scott $0.65 each and sell for $1.25. Lead time for delivery is one week, Scott desires a safety stock that will give the store a cycle service level of 98%. If Scott's inventory level for the Dutch T-60 tapes is at 230 units when it places an order, determine:

a. The order quantity for the tapes.

b. The desired safety stock.

15. Pete's Coffee is a local shop that roasts and packages its own coffee. The store purchases its Colombian coffee beans from Valdez Importing Company (VIC). VIC offers its customers the following discount pricing schedule for Colombian coffee:

Order Quantity	Price per Pound
under 1000 lbs.	$3.25
1000–3000 lbs.	$3.12
3000–6000 lbs.	$3.055
6000–9000 lbs.	$2.99
over 9000 lbs.	$2.925

Pete's estimates its annual demand for Colombian coffee beans at 62,000 pounds. The annual holding cost rate for a pound of unroasted coffee beans is estimated at 30%. The cost to place an order with VIC is $125 and the lead time is four weeks. Pete's desires a safety stock of 1000 pounds.

   a. What is the optimal order quantity if the discount pricing schedule is an all units schedule?

   b. What is the optimal order quantity if the discount pricing schedule is an incremental schedule?

   c. What is the reorder point for Colombian coffee?

   What assumptions did you make in solving this problem?

16. The coffee roaster at Pete's Coffee can roast 600 pounds of coffee per day. Pete's is open 310 days per year and, because of freshness requirements, the store never roasts more than a 10-day supply of any type of coffee it sells.

   Daily demand for French Roast coffee averages 75 pounds, while daily demand for Amaretto Cream averages 20 pounds. The annual holding cost for a pound of roasted coffee is $1.28, and the production setup cost for roasting a new variety of coffee is $25. Determine the optimal production batch sizes for French Roast and Amaretto Cream coffees.

17. Pete's Coffee is planning to stock the Melvitta brand espresso maker. Pete's estimates the annual demand for this coffee maker to be 180 units. The machines, which retail for $189 each, are imported from Italy and cost Pete's $95 each. The cost to place an order with Melvitta is $150, and the lead time is an estimated five weeks. Pete's uses a 30% annual holding cost rate for the coffee makers.

   Pete's is considering using one of two customer satisfaction plans to deal with the possibility of stockouts of the espresso maker. Under the first plan, Pete's will offer backordered customers one free pound of coffee. This will cost $4.25, and Pete's estimates an additional customer goodwill loss of $15 for each week a customer must wait for the espresso maker.

   Under the second plan, Pete's will offer backordered customers three free pounds of coffee. This will cost $12.75 but reduce additional goodwill loss to $3 for each week a customer must wait for the espresso maker.

   a. Which customer satisfaction plan should Pete's adopt?

   b. What is the optimal order quantity and reorder point under this plan?

   c. Using this policy, what is Pete's expected annual profit on the espresso machines?

18. Business Supply Company, Inc. (BSC) is a local distributor of the NCQ electronic cash register. The cash registers cost BSC $320 each, and (neglecting inventory costs) BSC estimates it earns a profit of $80 on each cash register sold. The cost of ordering the cash registers from NCQ is $100, and BSC uses an annual inventory holding cost rate of 20%.

   If BSC runs out of the cash registers, it estimates it will suffer a customer goodwill cost of $50 for each week a customer must wait. There is also a fixed administrative cost of $1.50 to process a backorder. Weekly demand averages 75 units, and the delivery lead time is two weeks. Determine the following:

   a. The optimal order quantity for NCQ cash registers.

   b. The reorder point for these cash registers.

   c. The number of weeks between cash register orders.

   d. The percentage of customers who will be placed on backorder.

   e. BSC's annual profit on the cash registers.

19. The Circle 7 convenience store has been receiving deliveries of Royal Cola once a week. Weekly demand for the cola averages 60 cases and follows a normal distribution with a standard deviation of 12 cases. When the delivery truck arrives the store orders enough cola so that the cycle service level is 99%. Because the orders arrive on a regular basis, there is no ordering cost to Circle 7. The annual holding cost rate for a case of cola is estimated at 25%.

     Royal Cola has just instituted a quantity discount schedule. Instead of charging stores like Circle 7 the normal price of $4.25 per case, Royal is offering the following all units discount schedule:

Number of Cases Ordered	Price per Case
under 100	$4.25
101–199	$4.00
200–499	$3.80
500–899	$3.70
900 or more	$3.60

     If Circle 7 wants to take advantage of the quantity discounts being offered by Royal Cola, it will have to cancel its regular delivery schedule. In this case, it estimates that the cost to place an order with Royal Cola will be $35 and lead time will be one week. Circle 7 will continue to desire a cycle service level of 99%.

     a. If Circle 7 continues with the regular delivery schedule and has 22 cases in inventory when the next delivery arrives, how many cases will be delivered to the store?

     b. What is the annual inventory cost (holding, safety stock, and procurement) of the regular delivery schedule?

     c. If Circle 7 decides to take advantage of the quantity discount schedule, how many cases should it order each time?

     d. What is the reorder point for the answer in part (c)?

     e. What is the annual inventory cost (holding, ordering, safety stock, and procurement) associated with the firm using the quantity discount schedule?

     f. Do you recommend that Circle 7 take advantage of the quantity discount schedule? Why or why not?

     g. How would your answers to parts (c), (d), (e), and (f) change if Circle 7 had enough room to store only 250 cases of Royal Cola?

20. Clark Equipment distributes the Clanton Model 406 bread slicer used in bakeries. The slicers cost $250 each, and Clark sells them to net $306 after marketing and related expenses. The company estimates that the annual demand for this product is 450 units.

     The policy at Clark has been never to allow stockouts intentionally, and the company has carried a safety stock of 30 units in order to protect against such occurrences. Because of mounting fiscal pressure, however, Clark is considering eliminating the safety stock for the bread slicers and adopting a policy that allows for stockouts.

     Clark estimates that it will suffer a customer goodwill loss of $25 per week for each week a customer must wait for a backordered bread slicer. Clark also believes that there is an administrative cost of $30 in handling a backorder and that adopting such a policy would result in a 4% decrease in annual sales of the bread slicer.

     Clark uses a 15% annual inventory holding cost rate, and the cost of ordering slicers from Clanton is $90. Delivery lead time is 10 working days, and Clark is open 250 days a year.

     a. Determine the optimal order quantity, reorder point, and annual profit under the current policy of not intentionally allowing backorders.

     b. Determine the optimal order quantity, reorder point, and annual profit if Clark intentionally allows for backorders.

     c. What is your recommendation to management as to whether Clark should intentionally allow for backorders? Justify this recommendation?

21. Microvision currently purchases a particular computer chip from IMTEL for $12.42 each, for use in its PC computers. Microvision's annual demand for the chip is estimated at 140,000 units, and it has a safety stock requirement of 600 chips. Because of high security expense, the cost to place an order with IMTEL is estimated at $1300 and lead time is 20 working days.

Instead of purchasing from IMTEL, Microvision can sign a licensing agreement to manufacture the chips itself. The licensing agreement will cost Microvision $5000 per year. If Microvision signs the agreement, it estimates it can produce the chips on its own assembly line at a cost of $11.60 per chip (not including the licensing or inventory costs). Setup time will take two days.

The production setup cost for making these chips is $15,000, and the production line is capable of manufacturing 2000 chips a day, 310 days a year. If the company produces the chips in-house, it will no longer require any safety stock. Microvision uses a 24% annual holding cost rate.

a. What are the optimal order quantity, reorder point, number of days between orders (cycle time), and total annual inventory cost (holding, ordering, safety stock, and procurement) if Microvision purchases the chips from IMTEL?

b. What are the optimal batch size, length of a production run in days (including production setup time), number of days between the start of successive production runs, and total annual inventory cost (holding, setup, licensing, and production) if Microvision begins producing the chips in-house?

c. What is your recommendation to management as to whether Microvision should begin in-house production of the chips? Justify this recommendation.

22. Consider the data from Problem 21. Suppose IMTEL has decided to offer incremental price discounts on chips sold to Microvision. In particular, the new pricing schedule is as follows:

Order Quantity	Discount
1–4,999	none
5,000–24,999	5%
25,000–49,999	8%
50,000–99,999	10%
100,000 or more	13%

a. What is Microvision's optimal order quantity for chips under this pricing policy if it continues to purchase chips from IMTEL?

b. Determine the total annual cost of this policy to Microvision.

23. United Parcel Delivery (UPD) owns a fleet of 1800 delivery trucks serving the metropolitan Chicago area. All trucks are maintained at a central garage. On the average, three trucks a week require a new engine.

Engines cost $900 each, and the delivery time is two weeks. There is a fixed order cost of $130, and UPD uses an annual inventory holding cost rate of 30%. For each week a truck is out of service, UPD estimates it suffers a loss of $80.

a. What is UPD's optimal inventory policy for engines?

b. What is the annual inventory (holding, ordering, backordering, and procurement) of this policy?

24. Bridgecross Foods is a major producer of frozen bread products. The company has decided to broaden its product line by manufacturing its own brand of frankfurters. Annual demand potential for its frankfurters is an estimated 1.2 million pounds.

Bridgecross has a choice of two machines to lease for manufacturing the frankfurters. Annual lease cost and daily production capacity for the two machines are as follows:

Machine	Annual Lease Cost	Daily Production Capacity
I	$40,000	2,750
II	$45,000	11,000

The factory is open 365 days a year. Production setup cost is estimated at $4000, while the holding cost is estimated at $0.10 per pound per year. Bridgecross estimates that it will earn $0.20 on each pound of frankfurters produced.

Because of the perishable nature of the product, Bridgecross cannot keep the frankfurters in inventory for more than three weeks after they are produced. Prepare a brief management report that recommends to Bridgecross management which machine to lease. Include in this report your supporting analysis as well as a discussion of any assumptions you made in solving this problem.

25. Mercury Corporation manufactures running shoes. The factory is open 10 hours a day, 260 days a year. Mercury currently buys its laces from Tiright Company but is considering manufacturing the laces in-house. Mercury's contract with Tiright specifies a base price per lace of $.036; however, Tiright offers the following all units discount schedule:

Order Quantity	Discount
50,000–149,999	3%
150,000–499,999	4%
500,000 or more	5%

Annual demand for laces at Mercury is an estimated 450,000 (225,000 pairs). Approximately 4% of the laces supplied by Tiright are defective; therefore, Mercury must order 468,750 ($= 450{,}000/.96$) laces. The cost to place an order with Tiright is $150, and lead time for delivery is 10 working days. Mercury desires a safety stock of 2000 laces if it buys from Tiright.

If Mercury begins in-house production of the laces, it will have to lease a lace-making machine at an annual fixed cost of $1800. The machine can produce 2 million laces per year at an incremental production cost of $0.032 per lace. The defect rate on laces produced in-house is expected to be only 2%. Production setups will take four hours and cost $800. If Mercury produces the laces in-house, it will not require any safety stock. Mercury uses an annual holding cost rate of 15% for laces.

a. What are the optimal order quantity, reorder point, number of days between orders (cycle time), and total annual inventory cost (holding, ordering, safety stock, and procurement) if Mercury purchases the laces from Tiright?

b. What are the optimal batch size, length of a production run in hours (including production setup time), number of days between the start of successive production runs, and total annual inventory cost (holding, setup, production, and machine leasing) if Mercury begins producing the laces in-house?

c. What is your recommendation to management as to whether Mercury should begin in-house production of the laces? Justify this recommendation? What assumptions did you make to solve this problem.

CASE 1: *TexMex Foods*

TexMex Foods operates a plant in Irving, Texas, for manufacturing taco sauce used in fast-food restaurants. The sauce, which is packaged in plastic containers, is made from a special recipe that includes tomato concentrate, onions, and chile peppers that TexMex purchases from various suppliers. The plant operates 365 days a year, and TexMex uses an annual holding cost rate of 18%.

Tomato Concentrate

TexMex Foods purchases its tomato concentrate from Hunt Farms. The company requires 2500 gallons of concentrate per day to manufacture this sauce. Hunt Farms offers customers the following all units price discount schedule:

Number of Gallons Ordered	Price per Gallon
1–9999	$3.12
10,000–49,999	$3.08
50,000–124,999	$3.02
125,000–249,999	$3.01
250,000 or more	$2.96

The shelf life of the concentrate is 80 days, and the ordering cost is $750. Orders must be placed in 1000-gallon increments. The company desires a safety stock of 10,000 gallons and the lead time for delivery is 10 days. Management wishes to determine the optimal order quantity for the concentrate as well as the reorder point.

Onions

In the cooking process, TexMex requires 6000 pounds of onions daily. Onions cost the company $0.15 per pound, and the ordering cost is $180. Lead time for delivery is three days, and the company desires a safety stock equal to one day's usage. Management wants to determine the optimal order quantity for onions as well as the reorder point.

Chile Peppers

TexMex also needs an estimated 2000 pounds of chile peppers daily. The peppers cost TexMex $0.37 per pound. Order cost, including transportation, is $1500. Lead time is normally two weeks but may vary somewhat. Because of this variability, the company estimates that the lead time demand for chile peppers follows approximately a normal distribution, with a mean of 28,000 pounds and a standard deviation of 4000 pounds. Management wants to determine the optimal order quantity, reorder point, and safety stock for chile peppers to meet a desired cycle service level of 99.5%.

Plastic Containers

TexMex packages the sauce in one-ounce plastic containers it buys from Union Chemical at $0.003 per unit. The ordering cost is $120. TexMex is contemplating leasing a machine to make the containers. The yearly lease cost of the machine is $45,000, and the production setup cost is $260. The machine can produce 1 million containers per day at a per unit cost of $0.0027 (excluding leasing, inventory holding, and production setup costs). The company estimates that it requires 450,000 containers per day. Management wants to determine whether it should continue purchasing containers from Union Chemical or begin in-house production and what the optimal order quantity or production lot size should be.

Prepare a detailed management report addressing each of the concerns facing TexMex Foods. Include in your report supporting graphs and charts as well as appropriate "what-if" analyses.

CASE 2: *Rodman Industries*

Rodman Industries of Barstow, California, sells, among other items, specialized tires for off-road vehicles (ORV). A new ORV model requiring tires slightly larger than normal is being developed by Pacific Star Enterprises in nearby Apple Valley. Pacific Star and Rodman have done business together for years, and Rodman has contracted with Pacific Star to supply tires for the new vehicle.

Rodman's staff analyst has estimated that Pacific Star's weekly demand will follow approximately a normal distribution, with a mean of 2000 tires and a standard deviation of 100 tires. Rodman charges Pacific Star $25 per tire and Rodman's holding costs are figured at 20% per year, or, in weekly terms, 0.4%.

Manufacturing/Purchasing Options

Rodman has three choices available to it for supplying the tires to Pacific Star:

1. Rodman can convert production line 3 to manufacture the tires. The equipment on this line can be converted at a cost of $150,000 to produce the new tire. This production line will have a maximum production rate of 4000 tires per week. It takes roughly one week to set up between production runs, and each setup costs approximately $4000. Unit production costs (raw materials and labor) are $12 per tire.

2. Rodman can convert production line 5 to manufacture the tires. This line is capable of producing only 1800 tires per week. It is very reliable, however, and, after a conversion cost of $75,000, the line is expected to run without failure. Although this option means that Rodman could supply Pacific Star with only 1800 tires per week, Pacific Star has indicated that it would accept this quantity, if necessary. Again, unit production costs (raw materials and labor) are $12 per tire.

3. Rodman can purchase tires from Hiro Inc., a Japanese firm and import them to its San Pedro warehouse for distribution directly to Pacific Star. Reorder costs, which include some substantial shipping fees, are estimated at

$10,000 per order, and shipping time is consistently two weeks from the time an order is placed. Hiro charges $14 per tire but offers the following all units discount pricing schedule:

Order Quantity	Discount
under 5000	none
5000–9999	7.5%
10,000 or more	15.0%

Safety Stock

While selecting option 2 allows Rodman to maintain no safety stock, for options 1 and 3 Rodman should have enough safety stock to maintain at least a 90% cycle service level.

The Report

On the basis of the given information, prepare a business report for Rodman suggesting a policy that will optimize total weekly profit for the company. Assume that this is a three-year project (156 weeks) and that conversion costs can be amortized at a constant rate over this time period. Include in your report any assumptions you made (or model assumptions you violated) in doing your analysis. The report should contain a table giving, for each option, the optimal order or production quantity, the reorder or setup point, and the total weekly revenue, costs, and profit.

CHAPTER 11

INVENTORY MODELS BASED ON NONSTATIONARY DEMAND

Lucifer Technologies produces several models of notebook computers at its manufacturing facility in Singapore. Although each model has certain unique features, many contain common elements. For example, six models use the same power supply system and battery, whereas eight others use the same hard disk drive. The computers are assembled from subcomponents, some of which Lucifer produces itself; others, such as the batteries, are purchased from outside suppliers.

The marketing department has projected sales for the different models over the next three months. Using these data, the production department schedules the amount of each subcomponent it should produce and when they should be manufactured. It also generates order amounts and dates at which the orders should be placed for the items Lucifer is purchasing from outside suppliers. Its goal is to ensure that the necessary materials are on hand to support production of the finished goods, while keeping inventory costs to a minimum. To deter-

mine this information, Lucifer has installed an MRP (Materials Requirement Planning) system at the factory.

Lucifer management also wants to ensure that adequate shipping capacity is available to transport the finished goods from the factory back to its Seattle warehouse. The company can obtain the lowest shipping cost by prebooking space on cargo vessels four months in advance. Unfortunately, this far in advance Lucifer does not have an exact projection of its requirements. It does, however, have past shipping records, which can be used to approximate a probability distribution for its capacity requirements.

If Lucifer prebooks too little cargo space, it can obtain additional cargo space on the spot market, which is expected to cost approximately 20% more than prebooked space. Conversely, if it books too much space, the firm can sell the unused space to a transportation broker for approximately 70% of cost. Lucifer uses a single-period inventory model to determine the amount of cargo space it should prebook.

11.1   SINGLE-PERIOD INVENTORY MODEL

The inventory models developed in Chapter 10 assumed that demand occurs at a known and reasonably constant rate and that the shelf life of the stock-keeping units is long enough that the goods will not spoil or deteriorate in value while in inventory. In many situations, however, demand is stochastic, and the inventory shelf life or selling season is quite short; consequently, the stock-keeping unit cannot be carried in inventory beyond a certain time period. In such cases, we can use the **single-period inventory model** to determine the optimal order quantity. This model assumes that demand varies according to a specified probability distribution and deals with a stock-keeping unit that has a limited shelf life of one period. Hence, no inventory is stored from period to period.

A common example is a newsstand where newspapers that are unsold at the end of a day are not kept in inventory, but are disposed of to make room for delivery of the next day's papers. For this reason, the single-period inventory model is frequently referred to as the *newsboy problem*. Other commodities that have a limited shelf life include magazines, Christmas trees, Valentine's Day candy, Halloween costumes, baked goods, concert tickets, chemicals, seasonal clothing, and dairy products. The basic assumptions of the single-period inventory model are given in Table 11.1.

TABLE 11.1   ASSUMPTIONS OF THE SINGLE-PERIOD INVENTORY MODEL

1. Inventory is saleable only within a single time period.
2. During each time period, inventory is delivered only once.
3. Customer demand during each period is stochastic (random) but follows a known probability distribution.
4. At the end of each period, unsold inventory is disposed of for some salvage value (which may be positive, negative, or zero).
5. The salvage value is less than the cost of the good.
6. If customer demand exceeds available supply, the firm may encounter a goodwill or shortage cost for each unsatisfied customer demand.

To determine the optimal order quantity in a single-period inventory model, we must strike a balance between overordering, which would create excess inventory left at the end of the period, and underordering, which would result in unsatisfied customer demand. We use the following notation for single-period inventory models:

$$p = \text{per unit selling price of the good}$$
$$c = \text{per unit cost of the good}$$
$$s = \text{per unit salvage value of unsold goods}$$
$$g = \text{goodwill or shortage cost for each unsatisfied customer}$$
$$K = \text{fixed purchasing costs}$$
$$Q = \text{order quantity}$$
$$EP(Q) = \text{expected profit if } Q \text{ units are ordered}$$

DEVELOPMENT OF THE SINGLE-PERIOD MODEL

We begin our analysis by developing an expression for $EP(Q)$. Two scenarios are possible depending on whether the actual demand, x, is (1) less than the order quantity; or (2) greater than or equal to the order quantity. Each leads to a different expression for the profit.

Case 1: Demand, x, Is Less than the Units Stocked, Q: In this case, x units are sold at a price of p each, and the remaining (Q − x) units will have to be disposed of for a salvage value of s each. Hence, total revenue is px + s(Q − x). Since demand is less than the available inventory, no goodwill costs are incurred. The cost of stocking the Q units is cQ + K. Accordingly, profit is given by the following expression:

$$\text{Profit} = px + s(Q - x) - cQ - K$$

Case 2: Demand, x, Is Greater than or Equal to the Units Stocked, Q: In this case, all Q units are sold at a price of p each, and no inventory is left to dispose of for salvage value. Hence, the total revenue is pQ. As demand exceeds the available inventory, (x − Q) customer demands are unsatisfied at a goodwill cost of g each. The cost of supplying the Q units is cQ + K, bringing total costs to g(x − Q) + cQ + K. Hence, the profit is:

$$\text{Profit} = pQ - g(x - Q) - cQ - K$$

Note that, in either case, the profit varies according to the actual demand, x. To determine the expected profit, given an order quantity of Q, we must find the weighted average profit over all possible values of x. When demand follows a discrete probability distribution, p(x), this is done by multiplying the profit corresponding to a demand of x by the probability that x units are demanded and then summing these products over all possible values of x:

$$EP(Q) = \sum_x (\text{profit given demand} = x) * p(x)$$

Substituting the formulas for the profit in the two demand cases yields a straightforward, but rather messy, formula for EP(Q).

If demand is assumed to follow a continuous probability distribution with density function f(x), the expected profit function can be determined as follows:

$$EP(Q) = \int (\text{profit given demand} = x) * f(x)dx$$

Our objective is to determine the value, Q*, that maximizes this expected profit function. Appendix 11.2 on the accompanying CD-ROM contains detailed formulas for EP(Q) as well as the derivation of Q* for both discrete and continuous probability demand distributions. There we show that when demand follows a discrete probability distribution with cumulative probability P(x), Q* is the smallest value of Q, such that:

$$P(D \le Q^*) \ge \frac{p - c + g}{p - s + g} \tag{11.1}$$

When demand follows a continuous probability distribution with cumulative distribution F(x), Q* satisfies the following relationship:

$$F(Q^*) = \frac{p - c + g}{p - s + g} \tag{11.2}$$

Note that the fixed cost, K, plays no role in determining the optimal order quantity.

The ratio (p − c + g)/(p − s + g) is known as the *optimal service level*. It represents the long-run percentage of periods in which inventory is sufficient to satisfy all customer demands. This does *not* imply that in any given period the proportion of customer demands that will be satisfied is (p − c + g)/(p − s + g).

SINGLE PERIOD
MODELS WITH A
DISCRETE DEMAND
DISTRIBUTION

Sent.its

To help motivate the single-period inventory model when demand can be modeled by a discrete distribution, consider the situation faced by the *Sentinel* newspaper.

THE SENTINEL NEWSPAPER

Company management at the *Sentinel* newspaper wishes to determine how many papers should be placed in each of several vending machine locations. The newspapers sell for $0.30 each. Although they cost the company $0.38 each to produce, *Sentinel* receives approximately $0.18 in advertising revenue for each paper printed. Hence, the net production cost per paper is $0.20.

Any unsold papers are delivered to a newspaper recycling firm and net the *Sentinel* $0.01 per copy. The company estimates that if a vending machine runs short of papers, it will suffer a goodwill loss of $0.10 for each unsatisfied customer. The cost of filling a vending machine averages $1.20.

Based on many prior weeks of sales data, the circulation manager for the *Sentinel* estimates that demand for the Tuesday paper at the sixth and Main vending machine location approximately follows a discrete uniform distribution with demand between 30 and 49 papers. Management would like to know the optimal number of papers to stock at this location.

SOLUTION

In terms of our notations, we have

$$p = \$0.30$$
$$c = \$0.20$$
$$s = \$0.01$$
$$g = \$0.10$$
$$K = \$1.20$$

To illustrate the two profit expressions, suppose the *Sentinel* puts 40 newspapers in a vending machine. If demand is only 32 newspapers (Case 1), the profit would be $0.30 (32) + $0.01(40 − 32) − $0.20(40) − $1.20 = $0.48. On the other hand, if demand is 45 newspapers (Case 2), the profit would be $0.30(40) − $0.10(45 − 40) − $0.20(40) − $1.20 = $2.30.

Our objective is to determine the optimal number of newspapers, Q*, to stock at the 6th and Main location. Substituting the values of the parameters for the *Sentinel* newspaper into the right side of Equation 11.1 gives us the following optimal service level:

$$\frac{p + g - c}{p + g - s} = \frac{.30 + .10 - .20}{.30 + .10 - .01} = \frac{.20}{.39} = .513$$

Hence, Q* is the smallest value for Q such that P(D ≤ Q*) ≥ .513. Because demand is uniformly distributed between 30 and 49 papers, demand will equally likely be 30, 31, 32, . . . , 48, or 49. For these 20 possible values, p(x = 30) = p(x = 31) = p(x = 32) = . . . = p(x = 49) = 1/20 = .05; therefore, P(x ≤ 30) = .05, P(x ≤ 31) = .10, P(x ≤ 32) = .15, and so on. Proceeding in this fashion, P(x ≤ 39) = .50 and P(x ≤ 40) = .55.

Since P(x ≤ 39) is less than .513 and P(x ≤ 40) is greater than .513, the *Sentinel* should put 40 newspapers in the vending machine. Note that, given the discrete nature of the probability distribution, stocking the vending machine with 40 papers actually results in a 55% service level.

SINGLE PERIOD
MODELS WITH A
CONTINUOUS
DEMAND
DISTRIBUTION

Wend.its

We now illustrate these concepts when there is a continuous probability distribution for demand, we consider the case of Wendell's Bakery.

WENDELL'S BAKERY

State University has given Wendell's Bakery the concession to sell glazed donuts in the School of Business during evening classes. It costs the bakery $0.15 to produce each donut, and Wendell's sells the donuts to students for $0.35 each. Any donuts that are unsold at the end of the evening are donated to a local charity, and the bakery obtains a tax credit equal to $0.05 per donut. If Wendell's produces too few donuts and does not have enough to satisfy all its customers, it incurs a customer goodwill cost of $0.25. The bakery hires a student to operate the concession and pays the student $15 per evening.

After several months of operations, the bakery has determined that demand for glazed donuts on weekday evenings approximately follows a normal distribution with a mean of 120 and a standard deviation of 20. Wendell's wishes to determine the optimal number of donuts to prepare for weekday evenings.

SOLUTION

For this problem,

$$p = \$0.35$$
$$c = \$0.15$$
$$s = \$0.05$$
$$g = \$0.25$$
$$K = \$15.00$$

Hence, Q^* should be chosen so that: $F(Q^*) = (.35 + .25 - .15)(.35 + .25 - .05) = .8182$. That is, the bakery should produce enough donuts so that the probability of satisfying all demands during the evening is .8182.

To determine values for the normal distribution, we use the standard normal random variable, z. Recall that z represents the number of standard deviations that a variable, x, is from its mean; z is related to x by the formula $z = (x - \mu)/\sigma$, or $x = \mu + z\sigma$.

A cumulative probability of .8182 corresponds to an area of .3182 between 0 and the appropriate z value (Figure 11.1). Referring to Appendix A, the closest entry in the table to .3182 is .3186, corresponding to a z value of .91. Thus, using z = .91, we conclude that the number of donuts the bakery should deliver to the School of Business is:

$$Q^* = \mu + z\sigma = 120 + .91 * 20 \approx 138$$

FIGURE II.I   Optimal Order Quantity for Wendell's Bakery

If demand follows a normal distribution with a mean of μ and a standard deviation of σ, it can be shown that the equation for the expected per period profit, assuming that Q* units are ordered, is:

$$EP(Q^*) = (p - s)\mu - (c - s)Q^* - (p + g - s)\sigma L \left(\frac{Q^* - \mu}{\sigma}\right) - K \quad (11.3)$$

In this expression, L(z) represents the partial expected value for the standard normal random variable between some value z and infinity. Values for L(z) are given in Appendix B.

For the Wendall's Bakery the expected profit per period is:

$$EP(138) = (.35 - .05)(120) - (.15 - .05)(138)$$
$$- (.35 + .25 - .05)(20)L \left(\frac{138 - 120}{20}\right) - 15$$
$$= .30(120) - .10(138) - .55(20)L(.9) - 15$$
$$= 36 - 13.8 - 11(.1004) - 15 = \$6.10$$

Computer programs such as WINQSB that solve the single-period inventory problem require the values of p, c, s, g, and K, as well as the probability distribution for x. Figure 11.2 shows the WINQSB output for this problem.

Inventory Analysis for Wendell's Bakery: Newsboy Problem

10-23-1998	Input Data or Result	Value
1	Demand distribution (in day)	Normal
2	Demand team	120
3	Demand standard deviation	20
4	Order or setup cost	$15.00
5	Unit cost	$0.15
6	Unit selling price	$0.35
7	Unit shortage (opportunity) cost	$0.25
8	Unit salvage value	$0.05
9	Initial inventory	0
10		
11	Optimal order quantity	138.1691
12	Optimal inventory level	138.1691
13	Optimal service level	81.8182%
14	Optimal expected profit	$6.10

FIGURE II.2   WINQSB Inventory Analysis for Wendell's Bakery

The single period model can also be used to determine the impact of alternative compensation plans. To illustrate, let us return to the Wendell's Bakery problem.

WENDELL'S BAKERY (continued)

As an alternative strategy, suppose the bakery is considering paying the student a commission of $0.13 for each donut sold, rather than a fixed wage of $15 per evening. Wendell's wishes to determine how this compensation will affect its inventory decision and whether its daily profits will increase.

SOLUTION

In this case, the analysis must be done in a slightly different fashion. In particular, the unit selling price from the bakery's standpoint is not the full $0.35, but the difference between the $0.35 selling price and the $0.13 commission, or $0.22. For p = $0.22, the optimal inventory quantity, Q^*, is chosen so that

$$F(Q^*) = \frac{.22 + .25 - .15}{.22 + .25 - .05} = \frac{.32}{.42} = .7619$$

This corresponds to a z value of approximately .71 and results in an optimal production quantity of

$$x = \mu + z\sigma = 120 + .71 * 20 \approx 134 \text{ donuts}$$

To see whether this quantity will increase the bakery's expected profits, we substitute the modified values into the expected profit equation, giving the following expected per period profit:

$$\begin{aligned}
EP(134) &= (.22 - .05)(120) - (.15 - .05)(134) \\
&\quad - (.22 + .25 - .05)(20)L\left(\frac{134 - 120}{20}\right) \\
&= .17(120) - .10(134) - .42(20)L\,(.7) = 20.4 = 13.4 - 8.4\,(.1429) \\
&= \$5.80
\end{aligned}$$

Under this plan, we can find the student's expected compensation by using Equation 11.3, recognizing that from the student's perspective p = .13, c = s = g = K = 0, $Q* = 134$, $\mu = 120$, and $\sigma = 20$. Making the appropriate substitutions gives an expected compensation of $15.23. It is worth noting that the increase in the student's expected compensation is less than the decrease in the bakery's expected profit.

However this analysis does not account for the possibility that the student's sales motivation may be greater if compensation is based on commission. If this is the case the increase in mean donut demand should somehow be estimated and incorporated into the analysis. Based on this observation, the Student Consulting Group has prepared the following business report, which investigates the effects of changes in mean demand and goodwill cost on profitability.

M E M O R A N D U M

To: Mr. Steve Wendell, Owner—Wendell's Bakery

From: Student Consulting Group

Subj: Inventory Policy for Glazed Donuts at State University

We have been asked to analyze Wendell's production of glazed donuts for sale in the School of Business at State University on weekday evenings. We focused our investigation on two objectives: (1) determining an optimal production quantity of donuts, and (2) recommending a compensation scheme for the student selling the donuts. Our ultimate objective is to determine strategies that will maximize Wendell's expected profits.

After meeting with the firm's accountant, we have determined that the cost of producing a glazed donut is approximately $0.15. The accountant also informed us that, because Wendell's donates unsold baked goods to a local food bank, it receives a tax credit of $0.05 for every unsold donut.

The agreement with State University specifies that Wendell's will sell the donuts to students for $0.35 each. Hence, we did not investigate the possibility of raising the donuts' selling price or the impact such an action would have on profitability.

After analyzing prior weeks' sales data, we determined a probability distribution for demand that had an average of 120 donuts. Since the estimate may be slightly in error, we have prepared an analysis for four possible values of the average donut demand: 115, 120, 125, and 130 units.

In determining the optimal inventory policy, we account for the shortage (goodwill) cost, which represents the present worth decrease in future profitability associated with not having enough donuts on hand for all customers who desire one. We estimated this amount as follows: Wendell's earns approximately $0.20 on each donut produced and sold. A marketing study we conducted showed that the typical student purchases an average of 18 donuts per year and has two years of studies at State University remaining. Thus, the present value of the average future profit per customer is approximately $6.45. We estimate that Wendell's will permanently lose 4% of the customers who encounter a donut stockout. Hence, the shortage cost per customer is approximately $0.25. We realize this estimate is quite inexact. Our analysis, therefore, considers four possible values of the goodwill cost: $0, $0.25, $0.50, and $1.00.

We analyzed the problem using a single-period inventory model and the WINQSB software package. Table I contains our recommendations for the quantity of donuts Wendell's should produce for delivery to State University given various possible combinations of values for goodwill cost and mean donut demand. For example, if the goodwill cost is estimated at $0.25 per unsatisfied customer, and the average demand is for 125 donuts, the optimal strategy is to produce 143 donuts to sell to students.

TABLE I Optimal Production Quantities for Glazed Donuts Given $15 per Evening Worker Salary

		Average Customer Demand			
		115	120	125	130
Goodwill Cost	$0	124	129	134	139
	$0.25	133	138	143	148
	$0.50	138	143	148	153
	$1.00	144	149	154	159

In addition to the production and possible goodwill costs, Wendell's must also compensate the student who sells the donuts. Wendell's has been paying this student $15 per evening. Accounting for these costs, Table II shows the expected profit per day if Wendell's uses the production quantities recommended in Table I. If, for example, the goodwill cost is $0.25 and average customer demand is 125 donuts, Wendell's should produce 143 donuts (the amount recommended in Table I) and will earn an expected daily profit of $7.10. As you might expect, the lower the goodwill cost and the higher the average demand, the higher Wendell's expected profit.

TABLE II Expected Daily Profit From Selling Glazed Donuts Given $15 per Evening Worker Salary

		Average Customer Demand			
		115	120	125	130
Goodwill Cost	$0	$5.82	$6.82	$7.82	$8.82
	$0.25	$5.10	$6.10	$7.10	$8.10
	$0.50	$4.71	$5.71	$6.71	$7.71
	$1.00	$4.25	$5.25	$6.25	$7.25

Given this information, we also considered the compensation paid to the student worker. In our discussions, the student indicated a willingness to accept a commission of $0.13 per donut instead of the fixed wages of $15. Assuming this compensation scheme is adopted, the optimal production quantities for donuts are given in Table III. The expected daily profit to Wendell's resulting from the production quantities of Table III is given in Table IV.

TABLE III Optimal Production Quantities for Glazed Donuts Given $0.13 Commission per Donut Sold

		Average Customer Demand			
		115	120	125	130
	$0	110	115	120	125
Goodwill	$0.25	129	134	139	144
Cost	$0.50	136	141	146	151
	$1.00	142	147	152	157

TABLE IV Expected Daily Profit From Selling Glazed Donuts Given $0.13 Commission per Donut Sold

		Average Customer Demand			
		115	120	125	130
	$0	$6.73	$7.08	$7.43	$7.78
Goodwill	$0.25	$5.45	$5.80	$6.15	$6.50
Cost	$0.50	$4.94	$5.29	$5.64	$5.99
	$1.00	$4.39	$4.74	$5.09	$5.44

Comparing the data in Tables II and IV, we see that if the commission compensation scheme does not change the average customer demand or goodwill cost, Wendell's should continue paying the student worker a fixed wage of $15 per evening. However, if placing the worker on commission increases average demand by five or more donuts, it may be a viable strategy. Expected profits could be further enhanced by a decrease in goodwill costs.

Should you have any further questions, please do not hesitate to contact us.

PRACTICAL CONSIDERATIONS OF USING THE SINGLE-PERIOD INVENTORY MODEL

Whereas the single-period inventory model is easy to solve given the required data inputs, determining the appropriate values for the parameters of a problem is frequently quite difficult. Many businesses do not have any idea what the goodwill cost for an unsatisfied customer might be. Determining the appropriate probability distribution for demand can also be daunting because we usually observe only sales data, which are limited by the amount of inventory available.

Advanced techniques exist for dealing with these difficulties, but one simplified approach is to solve the problem for a number of different scenarios and determine a "range" of optimal solutions. Once this range has been established, management can select the policy with which it feels most comfortable. This is essentially the approach we used in the preceding analysis for Wendell's Bakery.

11.2 MATERIAL REQUIREMENTS PLANNING

Typically, a manufacturer produces many different finished goods. For example, a television set manufacturer may produce several different models, with variations in screen size and options such as remote control or stereo. Many of these finished goods share the same components (e.g., speakers, picture tubes). Further complicating the process is the fact that a finished product can consist of components that need assembly themselves. Thus, several layers or hierarchies might be involved in the assembly of the finished good, resulting in dependence among component demands.

Material requirements planning (MRP) is a computer-based technique used for controlling inventory in such cases. While we will demonstrate the concepts of MRP using manual records rather than a computer approach, it is important to realize that real-world applications of MRP are nearly always implemented using a computer.

MRP INPUTS

The key inputs into the MRP process are: (1) the master production schedule, (2) the bill of materials, and (3) the inventory records file.

The *master production schedule* is a forecast of the finished goods demand over a particular *planning horizon*, consisting of several weeks or even months of production. The *bill of materials* details how the finished good is to be assembled. The *inventory records file* contains information about the inventory status of each component for each period of time, as well as the component vendors, required lead time for delivery, and specified lot size. Included in the inventory information are the quantity on hand and on order for each component. Table 11.2 summarizes the key elements of the MRP system.

TABLE 11.2   KEY ELEMENTS OF AN MRP SYSTEM

Master Production Schedule	Bill or Materials	Inventory Records File
A forecast of demands for the finished good over a particular planning horizon	A detailed listing of how the finished good is assembled	Information on the inventory status of each component

An MRP systems "translates" finished good demands into demands for their individual components, allowing the firm to properly manage its inventory records file. Although an MRP system looks at finished good demands over a given planning horizon, decisions that need to be made in the current period are of utmost importance to the manager. Because of component lead times, however, decisions made regarding components in the current period must be based on future demand projections for finished goods. Therefore, in implementing an MRP system, it is essential to extend the finished good planning horizon sufficiently far into the future to adequately account for such lead times.

To incorporate possible changes in demand forecasts, most firms use *rolling updates* of their master production schedule. That is, whenever changes are made to the master production schedule forecasts, the MRP reevaluates the inventory policy to determine the impact of such changes on the current period's inventory policy.

To illustrate the concepts of an MRP system, we consider the manufacturing decisions faced by Little Trykes Toys, Inc.

LITTLE TRYKES TOYS, INC.

Little Trykes Toys, Inc. (LTT) manufactures children's tricycles and wagons. Figure 11.3 shows the components required to make these two products. The components required for final assembly of a tricycle are a frame, seat, front wheel assembly, and small wheel set for the rear wheels. A front wheel assembly consists of a handle bar, a large wheel, and a pedal. The small wheel set consists of an axle and two small wheels. Each small wheel is purchased fully assembled, but the company produces the large wheels using a rim and a tire. The wagon assembly consists of a handle, wagon body, and two small wheel sets. Both the tricycles and wagons use the same small wheel sets.

FIGURE II.3 Products Manufactured by Little Trykes Toys, Inc., and Their Level I Components

LTT has received an order for delivery of 1000 tricycles 10 weeks from now and would like to schedule production and ordering of the subcomponents to meet this demand.

SOLUTION

Product Trees

One way to represent the bill of materials pictorially is by a *product tree*. Figures 11.4 and 11.5 give the product trees for the tricycle and wagon produced by LTT, respectively. The "root" of the product tree corresponds to the finished good and is placed at the top of the diagram; it is known as hierarchical level 0. Immediately below the root are

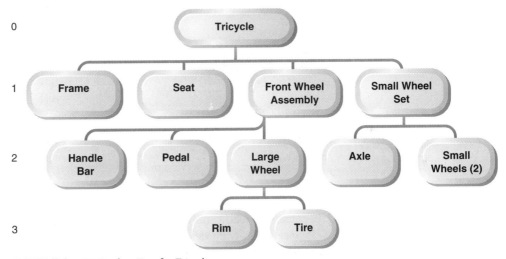

FIGURE II.4 LTT Product Tree for Tricycles

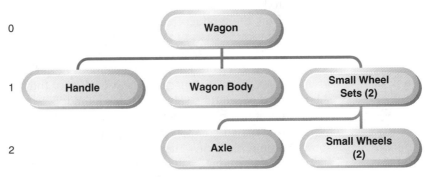

FIGURE II.5 LTT Product Tree for Wagons

the components or subassemblies required to produce the finished good. For the tricycle, (Figure 11.4) this consists of the frame, seat, front wheel assembly, and small wheel set. These items correspond to hierarchical level 1.

Similarly, below each level 1 subassembly are the hierarchical level 2 components for the level 1 subassemblies. For example, below the tricycle front wheel assembly in Figure 11.4 are the handle bars, pedals, and large wheels. Below the small wheel set assembly are the axles and small wheels. Because each small wheel set requires two small wheels, we place the number 2 in parentheses within the box representing small wheels. The process continues in this fashion until all the components have been delineated.

Since the small wheel sets that Little Trykes uses for the wagon are the same as those used for the rear wheels of the tricycle, Little Trykes must keep track of a total of 15 different components, subassemblies, or finished goods. The lead times for each of these items have been determined and are summarized in Table 11.3.

TABLE 11.3   LEAD TIMES FOR TRICYCLE AND WAGON COMPONENTS

Item	Lead time
Tricycles	2 weeks
Frames	3 weeks
Seats	4 weeks
Front Wheel Assemblies	1 week
Handle Bars	2 weeks
Pedals	3 weeks
Large Wheels	1 week
Rims	2 weeks
Tires	1 week
Small Wheel Sets	2 weeks
Axles	2 weeks
Small Wheels	3 weeks
Wagons	1 week
Handles	5 weeks
Wagon Bodies	4 weeks

Because the lead time for assembling the tricycles is two weeks, LTT must begin tricycle assembly at the beginning of week 8 (= 10 − 2). The tricycles cannot be produced unless the frames, seats, front wheel assemblies, and small wheel sets are available. Each of these level 1 components must therefore be available by the start of week 8. Continuing this analysis, because frames have a lead time of three weeks, in order for them to be available by week 8, the firm must order them by week 5 (= 8 − 3).

Modifying the product tree to include the intended delivery date and component lead times provides an easy way to determine the order date for each component. We place the component's lead time (in weeks) in square brackets ([ ]) inside each component's box (see Figure 11.6). Then, beginning at the top of the tree with the intended *delivery date*, (week 10 in this case) the *order date* for the finished good can be found by subtracting the lead time value from this intended delivery date.

We repeat this procedure for subsequent hierarchical levels, with the intended delivery date for each component being equal to the ordering date of the component above it in the hierarchy. The order date for each component can then be found by subtracting its lead time value (found in that component's box) from the component's

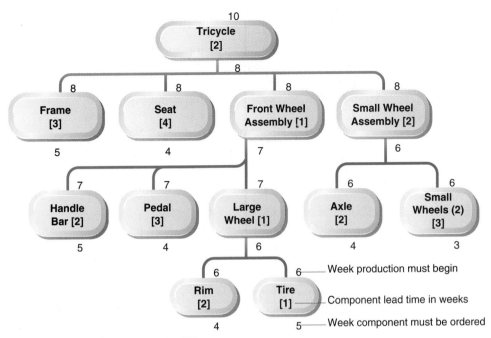

FIGURE II.6   Tricycle Component Lead Times

intended delivery date. The order dates necessary to support production in week 10, therefore, are as given in (Table 11.4).

TABLE 11.4   ORDER DATES FOR TRICYCLE COMPONENTS

Item	Order Date
Tricycles	week 10 − 2 = 8
Frames	week 8 − 3 = 5
Seats	week 8 − 4 = 4
Front Wheel Assemblies	week 8 − 1 = 7
Handle Bars	week 7 − 2 = 5
Pedals	week 7 − 3 = 4
Large Wheels	week 7 − 1 = 6
Rims	week 6 − 2 = 4
Tires	week 6 − 1 = 5
Small Wheel Sets	week 8 − 2 = 6
Axles	week 6 − 2 = 4
Small Wheels	week 6 − 3 = 3

Thus, if LTT wishes to produce tricycles beginning in week 10, it must order small wheels at the beginning of week 3, seven weeks prior to the intended completion date. Any planning cycle for a given week's tricycle production should include at least seven weeks if LTT is to account for all components properly.

NET INVENTORY REQUIREMENTS PER ORDER

If LTT does not have any inventory in stock for any of the components, it is fairly easy to determine how many of each component should be ordered. For example, if the firm wishes to produce 1000 tricycles, since each tricycle needs one seat, one frame, one front wheel assembly, and one rear wheel set, LTT will need a *gross inventory requirement* of 1000 units of each of these components.

Suppose, however, that LTT has an *available inventory* of 200 front wheel assemblies and 400 small wheel sets. As a result, it only needs to order $1000 - 200 = 800$ front wheel assemblies and $1000 - 400 = 600$ small wheel sets. These are the *net inventory requirements* for the hierarchical level 1 assemblies.

We see that to determine the net component requirements at each hierarchical level, we use the following relationship:

$$\begin{pmatrix} \text{Net Inventory} \\ \text{Requirements} \end{pmatrix} = \begin{pmatrix} \text{Gross Inventory} \\ \text{Requirements} \end{pmatrix} - \begin{pmatrix} \text{Available} \\ \text{Inventory} \end{pmatrix}$$

Continuing with hierarchical level 2, the 800 front wheel assemblies require 800 handle bars, 800 pedals, and 800 large wheels. The 600 small wheel sets require 600 axles but, since each small wheel set involves two wheels, a total of $2(600) = 1200$ wheels are needed. Similarly, at hierarchical level 3, a total of 800 large tires and 800 rims are required for the 800 large wheels.

The product tree can also be modified, providing an easy way to determine the net requirements for each component by including the current inventory level for each component in brackets ([ ]) inside each component box and the desired production level (1000 units) at the top of the tree. The desired production level corresponds to the gross component requirements for the finished good.

The gross requirements for a component are found by multiplying the net component requirements for the component at the hierarchical level directly above it by the number of units of the component going into the product. The component's net requirements are found by subtracting its current inventory from its gross requirements (a negative value corresponds to a net requirement of 0). For example, suppose LTT has the inventory in stock shown in Table 11.5 to support the production of 1000 tricycles in week 10. The net requirements of each component are calculated using the product tree depicted in Figure 11.7.

TABLE 11.5   AVAILABLE TRICYCLE COMPONENT INVENTORY

Item	Inventory Level
Tricycles	200 units
Frames	100 units
Seats	400 units
Front Wheel Assemblies	none
Handle Bars	150 units
Pedals	300 units
Large Wheels	250 units
Rims	600 units
Tires	350 units
Small Wheel Sets	300 units
Axles	250 units
Small Wheels	400 units

To illustrate just one branch of the tree, we note that, to support the production of 1000 tricycles, since 200 are in stock, 800 should be produced. Thus, 800 small wheel sets are required. Since 300 small wheel sets are currently in inventory, 500 small wheel sets are needed. Each small wheel set requires an axle and, since 250 axles are in

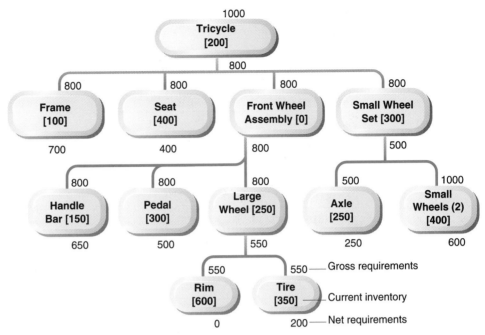

FIGURE II.7   Tricycle Net Requirements

inventory, 250 additional axles are required. Each small wheel set also requires two small wheels. Thus, the gross requirements for small wheels are 2(500) = 1000. Subtracting the available inventory of 400 small wheels from the gross requirements of 1000 yields a net requirement of 600 small wheels. Given the preceding product tree, Table 11.6 summarizes the net component requirements.

TABLE 11.6   NET COMPONENT REQUIREMENTS

Item	Net Component Requirements
Tricycles	1000 − 200 = 800 units
Frames	800 − 100 = 700 units
Seats	800 − 400 = 400 units
Front Wheel Assemblies	800 − 0 = 800 units
Handle Bars	800 − 150 = 650 units
Pedals	800 − 300 = 500 units
Large Wheels	800 − 250 = 550 units
Rims	550 − 600 = none
Tires	550 − 350 = 200 units
Small Wheel Sets	800 − 300 = 500 units
Axles	500 − 250 = 250 units
Small Wheels	2(500) − 400 = 600 units

THE MRP PLANNING WORKSHEET

Although we have calculated the net component requirements and order dates for the components separately, the interaction between the two pieces of information over time is also important. One convenient way to record this information is on an MRP *planning worksheet* containing relevant information for each component over a given planning horizon. The MRP planning worksheet for a 10-period planning horizon is shown in Table 11.7.

TABLE 11.7   MRP PLANNING WORKSHEET

ITEM NAME	LEAD TIME	TIME PERIODS									
INVENTORY RULE	SAFETY STOCK	1	2	3	4	5	6	7	8	9	10
GROSS REQUIREMENTS											
SCHEDULED RECEIPTS											
BALANCE AVAILABLE											
NET REQUIREMENTS											
PLANNED ORDER RECEIPTS											
PLANNED ORDER RELEASES											

The item name and known lead time for the item are entered in the upper left corner of the MRP Worksheet. The "inventory rule" entry provides information concerning requirements on the inventory order size. For some components, the firm may specify a *lot size* rule that designates a certain required order quantity. This quantity may be set to take advantage of quantity discounts or to simplify the production scheduling. For other components, the firm may use a *lot-for-lot* rule, by which the firm orders only the amount needed for a given period.

The "safety stock" entry designates the average inventory quantity the firm desires to keep in stock to cover losses due to shrinkage and to meet shortages that could result from unexpected delays in production or delivery of the component.

For each time period over the planning horizon,[1] we determine the "gross requirements" for the component from the net component requirements for the assemblies that use it. Because an MRP analysis is a dynamic process that uses a rolling time horizon, deliveries of the component may already be scheduled for some of the time periods in the planning horizon under analysis. These are accounted for in the "scheduled receipts" row of the worksheet.

The "balance available" row keeps a running total of the number of inventory units that will be available at the *end* of each time period. This number is equivalent to the balance available at the *beginning of the next period*. The entry to the left of the first period corresponds to the inventory balance at the *beginning* of the first period. The rest of the entries in this row are calculated after determining the net requirements row, the planned order receipt row, and the planned order release row.

"Net requirements" refer to the amount of the component required to satisfy the gross requirements and safety stock for the period after accounting for any scheduled receipts and are calculated by:

(Net Requirements) = (Gross Requirements) + (Safety Stock) − (Scheduled Receipts) − (Balance Available from Previous Time Period)

---

[1]In practice, we substitute the actual dates for the numerical time periods (i.e., week 1 might be June 11, week 2, June 18, etc.).

If this calculation results in a negative difference (i.e., the scheduled receipts plus the balance available exceed the gross requirements plus the safety stock), then the net requirements are simply 0. If the net requirements for a given period are positive, "planned order receipts" of inventory are needed for that period, which are at least equal to the net requirements. If a lot-for-lot rule is used for ordering the inventory, then the planned order receipts for the period are the net requirements for the period. If a lot size rule is used, however, the planned order receipts equal the smallest multiple of the lot size necessary to meet the net requirements.

The "planned order release" date takes into account the inventory lead time. For periods that carry planned order receipts, corresponding planned order releases must exist L periods earlier, L being the inventory lead time. For example, if there is a planned order receipt of 800 units for a component in week 8, and the component has a lead time of three weeks, there must be a planned order release in week 5 (=8 − 3).

We can therefore use the following formula to determine the entries in the balance available row of the MRP worksheet:

$$\text{(Balance Available at End of Period)} = \text{(Balance Available at Beginning of Period)} - \text{(Gross Requirements)} + \text{(Scheduled and Planned Order Receipts)}$$

Given this background, we can now extend our MRP analysis for the production of tricycles at Little Trykes over a multiperiod planning horizon. Because the production process for making tricycles spans seven weeks, our planning begins seven weeks into the future, starting at week 8.

LITTLE TRYKES TOYS, INC. (continued)

Little Trykes Toys, Inc. has forecast the following demand for tricycles between weeks 8 and 16:

Week	8	9	10	11	12	13	14	15	16
Demand	90	75	85	100	80	60	70	80	95

Company policy is to produce tricycles in lot sizes of 250 and require 30 units of safety stock. The lead time for assembly of tricycles is two weeks.

Based on previous planning, LTT expects an available balance of 150 tricycles at the beginning of week 8, and receipt of 250 tricycles is scheduled at the beginning of week 9. Management wishes to determine the MRP worksheet for tricycles in order to properly plan production during this time frame.

SOLUTION

Accounting for the demand data and other problem information, the initial MRP worksheet is shown in Table 11.8.

TABLE 11.8   INITIAL MRP WORKSHEET FOR TRICYCLES

TRICYCLES	LEAD TIME 2 WEEKS	TIME PERIODS								
LOT SIZE 250	SAFETY STOCK 30	8	9	10	11	12	13	14	15	16
GROSS REQUIREMENTS		90	75	85	100	80	60	70	80	95
SCHEDULED RECEIPTS			250							
BALANCE AVAILABLE	150									
NET REQUIREMENTS										
PLANNED ORDER RECEIPTS										
PLANNED ORDER RELEASES										

The following analysis completes the tricycle MRP worksheet for balance available, net requirements, planned order receipts, and planned order releases on a week-by-week basis.

Week 8

Net Requirements: Although no receipts are scheduled for week 8, the balance available at the beginning of week 8 (150) exceeds the sum of the gross requirements for that week (90) plus the safety stock of 30. Hence, the net requirements for week 8 are 0, and no planned order receipts are required.

Balance Available at End of Week 8 (Beginning of Week 9)

$$\begin{pmatrix} \text{Balance Available} \\ \text{at End of Week 8} \end{pmatrix} = \begin{pmatrix} \text{Balance Available} \\ \text{at Beginning of Week 8} \end{pmatrix} - \begin{pmatrix} \text{Gross Requirements} \\ \text{in Week 8} \end{pmatrix}$$
$$+ \begin{pmatrix} \text{Scheduled and Planned} \\ \text{Order Receipts} \end{pmatrix}$$
$$= 150 - 90 + 0 = 60$$

This allows the MRP worksheet to be updated as in Table 11.9.

TABLE 11.9   MRP WORKSHEET FOR TRICYCLES—WEEK 8

TRICYCLES	LEAD TIME 2 WEEKS	TIME PERIODS								
LOT SIZE 250	SAFETY STOCK 30	8	9	10	11	12	13	14	15	16
GROSS REQUIREMENTS		90	75	85	100	80	60	70	80	95
SCHEDULED RECEIPTS			250							
BALANCE AVAILABLE	150	60								
NET REQUIREMENTS		0								
PLANNED ORDER RECEIPTS										
PLANNED ORDER RELEASES										

Week 9

Net Requirements: The sum of the balance available at the beginning of the week (60) plus the scheduled receipts in week 9 (250) again exceeds the gross requirements (75) plus the safety stock (30). Hence, there are no net requirements.

Balance Available at End of Week 9 (Beginning of Week 10)

$$\begin{pmatrix} \text{Balance Available} \\ \text{at End of Week 9} \end{pmatrix} = \begin{pmatrix} \text{Balance Available} \\ \text{at Beginning of Week 9} \end{pmatrix} - \begin{pmatrix} \text{Gross Requirements} \\ \text{in Week 9} \end{pmatrix}$$

$$+ \begin{pmatrix} \text{Scheduled and Planned} \\ \text{Order Receipts} \end{pmatrix}$$

$$= 60 - 75 + 250 = 235$$

Weeks 10 and 11

Net Requirements: Net requirements for weeks 10 and 11 remain at 0.

Balance Available at End of Week: The balances available at the end of weeks 10 and 11 equal the balances available at the beginning of the respective weeks, reduced by the gross requirements of 85 and 100, respectively, giving rise to the worksheet in Table 11.10.

TABLE 11.10   MRP WORKSHEET FOR TRICYCLES—THROUGH WEEK 11

TRICYCLES	LEAD TIME 2 WEEKS	TIME PERIODS								
LOT SIZE 250	SAFETY STOCK 30	8	9	10	11	12	13	14	15	16
GROSS REQUIREMENTS		90	75	85	100	80	60	70	80	95
SCHEDULED RECEIPTS			250							
BALANCE AVAILABLE	150	60	235	150	50					
NET REQUIREMENTS		0	0	0	0					
PLANNED ORDER RECEIPTS										
PLANNED ORDER RELEASES										

Week 12

Net Requirements: In week 12, the gross requirements are 80, and the safety stock requirements are 30. Thus, there is a need for 110 units. Because the balance available from week 11 is only 50, however, the net requirements for week 12 are for $80 + 30 - 50 = 60$ units.

Planned Order Receipts: Since LTT uses a production lot size of 250 units, there must be a planned order receipt of 250 for week 12.

Planned Order Releases: Given that the lead time for assembling the tricycles is two weeks, to meet a planned order receipt in week 12, there must be a planned order release of 250 in week 10 $(12 - 2)$.

Balance Available at End of Week 12

$$\begin{pmatrix} \text{Balance Available} \\ \text{at End of Week 12} \end{pmatrix} = \begin{pmatrix} \text{Balance Available} \\ \text{at Beginning of Week 12} \end{pmatrix} - \begin{pmatrix} \text{Gross Requirements} \\ \text{for Week 12} \end{pmatrix}$$

$$+ \begin{pmatrix} \text{Planned Order Receipt} \\ \text{for Week 12} \end{pmatrix}$$

$$= 50 - 80 + 250 = 220 \text{ units}$$

The worksheet at this point is given in Table 11.11.

TABLE 11.11   MRP WORKSHEET FOR TRICYCLES—THROUGH WEEK 12

TRICYCLES	LEAD TIME 2 WEEKS	TIME PERIODS								
LOT SIZE 250	SAFETY STOCK 30	8	9	10	11	12	13	14	15	16
GROSS REQUIREMENTS		90	75	85	100	80	60	70	80	95
SCHEDULED RECEIPTS			250							
BALANCE AVAILABLE	150	60	235	150	50	220				
NET REQUIREMENTS		0	0	0	0	60				
PLANNED ORDER RECEIPTS						250				
PLANNED ORDER RELEASES				250						

Weeks 13 and 14

The gross requirements of 60 and 70 units for weeks 13 and 14, respectively, plus the 30 units of safety stock are covered by the available balances for these weeks. Thus, there are no net requirements during this period, as reflected in Table 11.12.

TABLE 11.12   MRP WORKSHEET FOR TRICYCLES—THROUGH WEEK 14

TRICYCLES	LEAD TIME 2 WEEKS	TIME PERIODS								
LOT SIZE 250	SAFETY STOCK 30	8	9	10	11	12	13	14	15	16
GROSS REQUIREMENTS		90	75	85	100	80	60	70	80	95
SCHEDULED RECEIPTS			250							
BALANCE AVAILABLE	150	60	235	150	50	220	160	90		
NET REQUIREMENTS		0	0	0	0	60	0	0		
PLANNED ORDER RECEIPTS						250				
PLANNED ORDER RELEASES				250						

Weeks 15 and 16

Net Requirements: In week 15, there are gross requirements for 80 units. Although the balance available at the beginning of week 15 is 90 units, this quantity is not sufficient to meet the requirements for week 15 owing to the desired safety stock of 30 units. Hence, the net requirements for week 15 are for $80 + 30 - 90 = 20$ units.

Planned Order Receipts: Given that LTT uses a production lot size of 250 units, there is a planned order receipt of 250 for week 15.

Planned Order Releases: Since the lead time for assembling the tricycles is two weeks, for a planned order release to be available in week 15 there must be a planned order release of 250 in week 13 $(15 - 2)$.

Balance Available at End of Week 15

$$\begin{pmatrix} \text{Balance Available} \\ \text{at End of Week 15} \end{pmatrix} = \begin{pmatrix} \text{Balance Available} \\ \text{at Beginning of Week 15} \end{pmatrix} - \begin{pmatrix} \text{Gross Requirements} \\ \text{for Week 15} \end{pmatrix}$$
$$+ \begin{pmatrix} \text{Planned Order Receipt} \\ \text{for Week 15} \end{pmatrix}$$
$$= 90 - 80 + 250 = 260 \text{ units}$$

Incorporating the gross requirements of 95 units for week 16 gives the completed MRP worksheet for week 8 through week 16 shown in Table 11.13.

TABLE 11.13   COMPLETED MRP WORKSHEET FOR TRICYCLES— WEEKS 8–16

TRICYCLES	LEAD TIME 2 WEEKS	TIME PERIODS								
LOT SIZE 250	SAFETY STOCK 30	8	9	10	11	12	13	14	15	16
GROSS REQUIREMENTS		90	75	85	100	80	60	70	80	95
SCHEDULED RECEIPTS			250							
BALANCE AVAILABLE	150	60	235	150	50	220	160	90	260	165
NET REQUIREMENTS		0	0	0	0	60	0	0	20	0
PLANNED ORDER RECEIPTS						250			250	
PLANNED ORDER RELEASES			250		250					

MRP PLANNING WORKSHEET FOR SUBCOMPONENTS

Once we have determined the planned order releases for one hierarchical level, we can generate the MRP planning worksheets for the next lower hierarchical level. For example, in the Little Trykes problem, once we have determined the planned order releases for tricycles (hierarchical level 0), we can generate the MRP worksheets for all hierarchical level 1 components (frames, seats, front wheel assemblies, and small wheel sets). Because of space limitations, we illustrate this process only for the small wheel sets. Note that, since the lead time for small wheel sets is two weeks, the MRP planning worksheet for small wheel sets covers a period two weeks earlier than that considered for the tricycles, namely, week 6 through week 14.

LITTLE TRYKES TOYS, INC. (continued)
SMALL WHEEL SETS

Little Trykes Toys, Inc. uses a lot-for-lot inventory rule for producing the small wheel sets. It requires a safety stock of 50 sets and projects that a balance of 80 small wheel sets will be available at the beginning of week 6. Management would like to develop an MRP worksheet for the small wheel sets used in the production of the tricycles over the nine-week planning period.

SOLUTION

Based on the MRP planning worksheet for the tricycle production, we see that 250 small wheel sets must be available by weeks 10 and 13 in order for Little Trykes to support the planned order releases for the tricycles. This quantity becomes the gross requirements for the small wheel sets. (Note that the 250 small wheel sets required in week 7 to support the scheduled receipt of 250 tricycles in week 9 are excluded from the MRP planning worksheet because this amount would have been previously accounted for in an earlier planning horizon.) The initial worksheet is given in Table 11.14.

TABLE 11.14   INITIAL MRP WORKSHEET FOR SMALL WHEEL SETS

SMALL WHEEL SETS	LEAD TIME 2 WEEKS	TIME PERIODS								
LOT FOR LOT	SAFETY STOCK 50	6	7	8	9	10	11	12	13	14
GROSS REQUIREMENTS		0	0	0	0	250	0	0	250	0
SCHEDULED RECEIPTS										
BALANCE AVAILABLE	80									
NET REQUIREMENTS										
PLANNED ORDER RECEIPTS										
PLANNED ORDER RELEASES										

Week 6 through Week 9

Because the gross requirements for week 6 through week 9 are 0, net requirements and planned order receipts are 0 for this time period, and the balance available remains at 80.

Week 10

Net Requirements: The gross requirements of 250 units imply net requirements of $250 + 50 - 80 = 220$.

Planned Order Receipts: Because we use a lot-for-lot rule for the small wheel sets, a planned order receipt equal to the net requirements of 220 for week 10 is required.

Planned Order Releases: Because there is a two-week lead time for small wheel sets, a planned order release of 220 units is scheduled for week 8 ($=10 - 2$).

Balance Available

$$\begin{pmatrix} \text{Balance Available} \\ \text{at End of Week 10} \end{pmatrix} = \begin{pmatrix} \text{Balance Available} \\ \text{at Beginning of Week 10} \end{pmatrix} - \begin{pmatrix} \text{Gross Requirements} \\ \text{for Week 10} \end{pmatrix}$$
$$+ \begin{pmatrix} \text{Planned Order Receipt} \\ \text{for Week 10} \end{pmatrix}$$
$$= 80 - 250 + 220 = 50 \text{ units}$$

This is the required safety stock. At this point, the MRP planning worksheet for small wheel sets is as shown in Table 11.15.

TABLE 11.15   MRP WORKSHEET FOR SMALL WHEEL SETS—THROUGH WEEK 10

SMALL WHEEL SETS	LEAD TIME 2 WEEKS	TIME PERIODS								
LOT FOR LOT	SAFETY STOCK 50	6	7	8	9	10	11	12	13	14
GROSS REQUIREMENTS		0	0	0	0	250	0	0	250	0
SCHEDULED RECEIPTS										
BALANCE AVAILABLE	80	80	80	80	80	50				
NET REQUIREMENTS						220				
PLANNED ORDER RECEIPTS						220				
PLANNED ORDER RELEASES				220						

The balance available stays at 50 through the remaining time periods. In week 13, the gross demand of 250 units implies net requirements of 250 units. Hence, there must be a planned order receipt of 250 in week 13 and a planned order release of 250 in week 11 (= 13 − 2). The completed worksheet for small wheel sets is given in Table 11.16.

TABLE 11.16　COMPLETED WORKSHEET FOR SMALL WHEEL SETS—WEEKS 6–14

SMALL WHEEL SETS	LEAD TIME 2 WEEKS	TIME PERIODS								
LOT FOR LOT	SAFETY STOCK 50	6	7	8	9	10	11	12	13	14
GROSS REQUIREMENTS		0	0	0	0	250	0	0	250	0
SCHEDULED RECEIPTS										
BALANCE AVAILABLE	80	80	80	80	80	50	50	50	50	50
NET REQUIREMENTS						220			250	
PLANNED ORDER RECEIPTS						220			250	
PLANNED ORDER RELEASES				220			250			

A similar process is used for hierarchical level 2 components. To illustrate, consider the small wheels that go into the small wheel sets.

LITTLE TRYKES TOYS, INC. (continued)
SMALL WHEELS

Management wishes to determine the MRP planning worksheet for small wheels over the nine-week planning period between week 3 and week 11. The company has determined that it needs a safety stock of 200 small wheels; in order to obtain quantity discounts from its supplier, it orders small wheels in lots of 800. A balance of 225 wheels is expected to be available at the beginning of week 3.

SOLUTION

Recall that each small wheel set requires two small wheels and that the lead time for delivery of the small wheels is three weeks. Hence, the appropriate time frame for the MRP planning worksheet is from week 3 through week 11. Table 11.17 shows the completed MRP worksheet for this component.

TABLE 11.17　COMPLETED MRP WORKSHEET FOR SMALL WHEELS

SMALL WHEELS	LEAD TIME 3 WEEKS	TIME PERIODS								
LOT SIZE 800	SAFETY STOCK 200	3	4	5	6	7	8	9	10	11
GROSS REQUIREMENTS		0	0	0	0	0	440	0	0	500
SCHEDULED RECEIPTS										
BALANCE AVAILABLE	225	225	225	225	225	225	585	585	585	885
NET REQUIREMENTS							415			115
PLANNED ORDER RECEIPTS							800			800
PLANNED ORDER RELEASES				800			800			

We can determine the inventory planning worksheets for each of the other components making up the tricycle in a similar manner.

GOODS SHARING THE SAME COMPONENTS

One important aspect of the MRP process that has been ignored thus far is the impact on inventory of several finished goods sharing the same components. For LTT, this occurs with the small wheel sets, used both in tricycles and wagons. To illustrate, let us examine the effect of wagon demand on the MRP worksheet for the small wheel sets.

LITTLE TRYKES TOYS, INC. (continued)
WAGONS AND SMALL WHEEL SETS

LTT has forecasted the following demand for wagons during the period from week 7 through 15:[2]

Week	7	8	9	10	11	12	13	14	15
Demand	80	55	75	110	90	70	100	90	95

Wagons are produced in lot sizes of 300 and require no safety stock. The company would like to determine the MRP worksheet for the wagons during this period, given a projected balance of 140 units at the beginning of week 7. It would also like to investigate the effect this demand will have on the MRP worksheet for the small wheel sets.

SOLUTION

Applying the same analysis as that performed for tricycles results in the completed MRP planning worksheet for wagons given in Table 11.18.

TABLE 11.18   COMPLETED MRP WORKSHEET FOR WAGONS

WAGONS	LEAD TIME I WEEK	TIME PERIODS								
LOT SIZE 300	SAFETY STOCK 0	7	8	9	10	11	12	13	14	15
GROSS REQUIREMENTS		80	55	75	110	90	70	100	90	95
SCHEDULED RECEIPTS										
BALANCE AVAILABLE	140	60	5	230	120	30	260	160	70	275
NET REQUIREMENTS		0		70	0	0	40	0	0	25
PLANNED ORDER RECEIPTS				300			300			300
PLANNED ORDER RELEASES			300			300			300	

As you can see by the planned order releases, 300 small wheel sets are required for wagon production in weeks 8, 11, and 14. Recall that we previously determined that 250 small wheel sets are required in weeks 10 and 13 to support tricycle production

_____

[2]We consider a one-week earlier period than that used for the tricycles because the lead time for wagon assembly is one week less than that for tricycles.

over its planning period. Incorporating this information into the planning worksheet gives us the revised MRP planning worksheet for the small wheel sets shown in Table 11.19. This new worksheet differs from the MRP planning worksheet for small wheel sets in Table 11.16 due to the additional gross requirements of 300 units in weeks 8, 11, and 14.

TABLE 11.19   REVISED MRP WORKSHEET FOR SMALL WHEEL SETS

SMALL WHEEL SETS	LEAD TIME 2 WEEKS	TIME PERIODS								
LOT FOR LOT	SAFETY STOCK 50	6	7	8	9	10	11	12	13	14
GROSS REQUIREMENTS		0	0	300	0	250	300	0	250	300
SCHEDULED RECEIPTS										
BALANCE AVAILABLE	80	80	80	50	50	50	50	50	50	50
NET REQUIREMENTS			0	270		250	300		250	300
PLANNED ORDER RECEIPTS				270		250	300		250	300
PLANNED ORDER RELEASES		270		250	300		250	300		

Analysis of Orders

Over the nine-week period, five orders will be placed for small wheel sets if Little Trykes uses a lot-for-lot rule in producing these units. In particular, orders for 300 wheel sets immediately follow the orders for 250 wheel sets. On a practical basis, this does not seem particularly efficient.

One way of avoiding these extra production setups is simply to specify a given production lot size. Because demand for wheel sets is not constant over time, however, such a strategy will not necessarily yield an optimal policy. In the next section, we address the problem of determining the inventory order policy in situations in which future demand forecasts vary over time.

11.3 𝓘NVENTORY MODELS WITH TIME VARYING DEMAND

In Chapter 10 we saw that, when demand is reasonably constant over time, the EOQ model may be used to determine an optimal inventory policy. If demand varies greatly from period to period, however, an EOQ solution may be far from optimal.

Demands can vary significantly over time because of fluctuations in consumer preferences. Even when demand for a finished good does not vary significantly, as we saw earlier, component demand need not be stationary. The **Wagner-Whitin algorithm**[3] can be used to determine the optimal inventory policy if the following assumptions hold:

1. Demand is known for each period over some time horizon.

2. While demand may vary from period to period, within each period, demand occurs at a relatively constant rate.

3. If an order is placed for arrival during a given period, it arrives at the beginning of the delivery period.

4. Holding costs are incurred at a known fixed rate. The holding cost for a period is a function of the average inventory level during that period.

---

[3]Named for Harvey Wagner and Thomas Whitin, who developed the algorithm in 1958.

Although assumptions 2 and 4 are not critical to developing the inventory model, we include them in the set of assumptions to clarify how the inventory holding costs are being incurred.

THE WAGNER-WHITIN ALGORITHM

The Wagner-Whitin algorithm uses a dynamic programming technique to determine an optimal inventory policy. As discussed in Chapter 16 on the accompanying CD-ROM, dynamic programming is a family of management science techniques that take advantage of the fact that certain problems can be solved by breaking them into smaller, more manageable subproblems.

The Wagner-Whitin algorithm makes use of two important concepts:

1. If there is an order in some period, an optimal inventory policy orders an amount exactly equal to the sum of the next k period's future demands (where k is an integer determined by the algorithm).

2. There is an upper limit to the value of k.

To illustrate these two concepts, let us consider the situation faced by Golden West Homes, a manufacturer of modular housing.

GOLDEN WEST HOMES

Golden West Homes purchases kitchen ranges for its homes from Admiral Appliance Company at a cost of $325 each. Golden West uses a 16% annual holding cost rate, and the cost to place an order with Admiral is $100. Golden West forecasts the following requirements for Admiral kitchen ranges over the next 10 weeks:

Week	1	2	3	4	5	6	7	8	9	10
Demand	120	40	80	60	90	30	20	90	60	130

Management would like to determine the optimal ordering policy for the ranges over this planning horizon.

SOLUTION

According to concept 1, if an order is placed to arrive at the beginning of week 1, it is for either 120 units (to satisfy the demand for week 1), 160 units (to satisfy the demand for weeks 1 and 2), 240 units (to satisfy the demand for week 1 through week 3), and so on. An order of say, 200, would *not* be placed since it would cover demand for two *and a half* weeks.

Because Golden West uses a 16% annual holding cost rate and the ranges cost the company $325 each, the annual holding cost for the SKU is $C_h = .16(\$325) = \$52$. Thus, the weekly holding cost per unit is $1. In period 1, if 120 units are ordered (to satisfy the demand for that period only), the average inventory is 120/2 = 60. The inventory cost, which equals the sum of the order cost and the holding cost, is therefore $100 + 60(\$1) = \$160$.

If Golden West orders enough ranges to satisfy the demand for weeks 1 and 2 (160), then the inventory level at the beginning of week 1 would be 160, decrease to 40 $(=160 - 120)$ by the end of that week, and further decrease from 40 to 0 during week 2. Hence, the average inventory level during week 1 is 100 units $[= (160 + 40)/2]$ and, during week 2, it is 20 $[= (40 + 0)/2]$ units. Figure 11.8 shows the inventory profile of

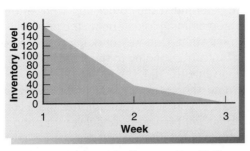

FIGURE II.8   Inventory Profile—over Two Weeks

ordering 160 units in week 1. The cost of supplying inventory to cover the demand for weeks 1 and 2 is the sum of the $100 order cost, the holding cost for week 1 (100 ∗ $1), and the holding cost for week 2 (20 ∗ $1), a total of $220.

Now consider ordering enough inventory in week 1 to satisfy the first three weeks of demand, 240 ranges. If an extra 80 ranges are ordered to satisfy the demand for week 3, however, these 80 units have to be kept in inventory for a full two weeks, costing an extra $160 (= $2 ∗ 80). Since it costs only $100 to place an order, it is clearly cheaper to delay ordering these 80 units until week 3. Hence, in week 1, it does not pay to order inventory to satisfy the demand beyond week 2. This is an illustration of concept 2 of the algorithm.

Summarizing, we have the following rule:

> If the marginal cost of ordering inventory for an extra week exceeds the cost of placing an order, it is not economical to place an order for that week or beyond.

Repeating this analysis for week 2 through week 10 gives us the values found in Table 11.20. The formulas for obtaining these values are given in Appendix 11.3 on the accompanying CD-ROM. The values, designated $T(j, j + k)$, represent the cost of ordering an amount for delivery in week j (the row value) sufficient to satisfy the demand up to the beginning of week $j + k$ (the column value). For example, the cost of ordering inventory for delivery in week 5, which is sufficient to last up to the beginning of week 7, is $190.

TABLE 11.20   INVENTORY ANALYSIS—GOLDEN WEST HOMES

| Week | Order up to the Beginning of Week ($j + k$): | | | | | | | | | |
(j)	2	3	4	5	6	7	8	9	10	11
1	160	220								
2		120	240							
3			140	230						
4				130	265	340	410			
5					145	190	240			
6						115	145			
7							110	245		
8								140	230	
9									130	
10										165

Once we have determined the "order up to" inventory cost values, T(j, j + k), we can use dynamic programming to determine the optimal inventory ordering policy over the time frame in question. One way of doing this is by constructing a network, with nodes (1, 2, 3, . . . , n) corresponding to the n time periods and the arcs between nodes j and j + k equal in value to T(j, j + k).

We can then find the optimal inventory policy by identifying the shortest path through this network. In particular, if the shortest path contains an arc from period j to period j + k, an order will be placed for delivery at period j that is of sufficient size to handle the demand *up to, but not including, period j + k*.

Figure 11.9 shows the network corresponding to this problem. Using the shortest path approach developed in Chapter 6, we find that the shortest path through this network begins at node 1 and proceeds through nodes 3, 5, 8, and 10. Thus, the optimal inventory policy for Golden West Homes is as follows:

Week	Order Amount	Order for Weeks
1	120 + 40 = 160	1,2
3	80 + 60 = 140	3,4
5	90 + 30 + 20 = 140	5,6,7
8	90 + 60 = 150	8,9
10	130	10

FIGURE 11.9   Inventory Cost Network for Golden West Homes

The total cost of this policy—is $1085. Figure 11.10 summarizes the inventory profile corresponding to this solution over the 10-week (70-day) period.

FIGURE 11.10   Inventory Profile for Golden West Homes' Over 10-Week Period

WINQSB has the capability of solving for the optimal inventory policy using the Wagner-Whitin algorithm. The WINQSB output corresponding to this problem is given in Figure 11.11.[4]

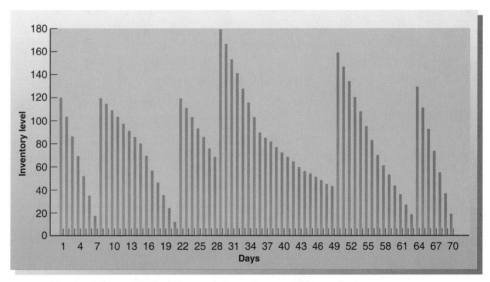

11-25-1998 week	Demand	Production (Lot Size)	Setup	Expected Inventory	Expected Backorder	Cumulative Cost
Initial				0		
1	120.0000	160.0000	Yes	40.0000	0	$140.00
2	40.0000	0	No	0	0	$140.00
3	80.0000	140.0000	Yes	60.0000	0	$300.00
4	60.0000	0	No	0	0	$300.00
5	90.0000	140.0000	Yes	50.0000	0	$450.00
6	30.0000	0	No	20.0000	0	$470.00
7	20.0000	0	No	0	0	$470.00
8	90.0000	150.0000	Yes	60.0000	0	$630.00
9	60.0000	0	No	0	0	$630.00
10	130.0000	130.0000	Yes	0	0	$730.00
	Solution	Method:	WW		Total Cost =	$730.00

FIGURE 11.11   Golden West Homes—WINQSB Output for Wagner Whitten Algorithm

It is interesting to contrast the recommended solution to the EOQ solution. The average weekly demand over the 10-week period is 72 units. If we use this value for the weekly demand, D, then, since C_h is $1/week and C_o is $100, the EOQ order quantity is:

$$Q^* = \sqrt{\frac{2(72)\,(100)}{1}} = 120$$

Using an order quantity of 120 units, the firm would have to place six orders (in weeks 1, 2, 4, 5, 7, and 9), resulting in the inventory profile given in Figure 11.12. The average

FIGURE 11.12   Inventory Profile Based on 120-Unit Order Quantity (Six Orders)

---

[4]The solution derived using WINQSB is the same policy as that developed manually, but the cost of the policy is different. This is because WINQSB calculates inventory holding costs based solely on the inventory level at the beginning of the period, rather than the average inventory level during the period. While the two approaches might give different policy recommendations, in cases in which the holding cost is small relative to the ordering cost, the results generally will be in agreement.

weekly inventory level under this policy is given in Table 11.21.

TABLE 11.21   AVERAGE WEEKLY INVENTORY LEVEL—GOLDEN WEST HOMES

Week	1	2	3	4	5	6	7	8	9	10
Average Inventory Level	60	100	40	90	135	75	50	115	40	65

Since C_h is $1/per item per week, the sum of the holding costs over the 10-week period under the EOQ policy is $60 + $100 + $40 + \ldots + $65 = $770. Adding the cost of placing six orders ($600) to the inventory holding cost ($770) gives a total inventory cost of $1370 over the 10-week period; this is $285 (or 26%) greater than the solution found using the Wagner-Whitin algorithm.

THE SILVER-MEAL
HEURISTIC

The Wagner-Whitin algorithm gives the lowest-cost solution for an inventory problem when the forecasted demand is known but varies over time. Yet the solution is far more difficult to obtain than simply using the EOQ formula. To reduce the computational complexities of the Wagner-Whitin algorithm, management scientists began looking for a heuristic solution technique that was easier to implement and would give an answer close to optimal. One such technique is the **Silver-Meal heuristic**,[5] which utilizes the same cost data, $T(j, j + k)$, as the Wagner-Whitin algorithm but avoids the need to construct a cost network and solve a shortest path problem. Instead, the procedure uses the following steps.

Silver-Meal Heuristic

Start at Period 1.

1. Calculate the per period average inventory holding and ordering cost of satisfying demand for the next k periods.
2. Order enough inventory to satisfy demand out to the period that has the lowest average cost.
3. If demand for the final period has not been satisfied, return to step (1) using the period found in step (2).

We illustrate the Silver-Meal heuristic using the cost data from the Golden West Homes example. In week 1, satisfying demand for one week costs $160, while satisfying demand for two weeks costs $220 (see Table 11.20). Hence, the *per period* average inventory cost of satisfying demand for one period is $160 and for two periods $110 (= $220/2). Since $110 is less than $160, demand is satisfied for two weeks. The heuristic then returns to step (1) beginning at week 3. (As discussed earlier, we do not have to look beyond two weeks because the marginal cost of carrying inventory for additional weeks exceeds the cost of placing an order.)

From Table 11.20 we see that satisfying demand for week 3 only gives a per period average inventory cost of $140, while satisfying demand for weeks 3 and 4 gives a per period average inventory cost of $115 (= $230/2). Hence, Golden West Homes should place an order in week 3 which satisfies demand for two more weeks. The heuristic then returns to step (1) beginning at week 5.

---

[5]Named for Edward Silver and Harlan Meal, who proposed this technique in 1973.

Continuing in this fashion using the data from Table 11.20, gives:

	Number of Periods	Average per Period Cost
Week 5	1	$145/1 = $145
	2	$190/2 = $95
	3	$240/3 = $80

Satisfy demand for the next three periods

	Number of Periods	Average per Period Cost
Week 8	1	$140/1 = $140
	2	$230/2 = $115

Satisfy demand for the next two periods

	Number of Periods	Average per Period Cost
Week 10	1	$165/1 = $165

Satisfy demand for this period only.

In this case, the Silver-Meal heuristic indicates that Golden West Homes should place orders in periods 1, 3, 5, 8, and 10. This is exactly the same solution achieved with the Wagner-Whitin algorithm.

Although the Silver-Meal heuristic may not always yield the same solution as the Wagner-Whitin algorithm, in general, it gives a solution that either is optimal or differs in cost from the optimal solution by only a few percent.

11.4 CURRENT TRENDS IN INVENTORY CONTROL

JUST-IN-TIME SYSTEMS

During the past few years, management scientists have paid a great deal of attention to Japanese management techniques. An inventory/production control technique pioneered in Japan, known as **just-in-time**, or **JIT**, can reduce work-in-process inventories to the lowest possible level by keeping production lot sizes small. Although an MRP or EOQ inventory control system can also utilize small production lot sizes, JIT differs in the way in which production decisions are made and in the movement of inventory from one hierarchial level to another.

Traditional inventory systems, such as MRP, are referred to as *push systems*. Decisions are made regarding the production schedule for the subcomponents based on the forecast demand for the finished good. Once these subcomponents have been produced, they are "pushed up" to the next level of assembly. By contrast, a just-in-time system is characterized as a *pull system*. A subcomponent is produced only on request from the work center that utilizes the subcomponent in assembly. Hence, the inventory is "pulled" through the system.

The size of the lot that is pulled from one hierarchical level to the next is intentionally kept small, with a minimum buildup of safety or buffer stock. Consequently, if there is a failure in the production process at some point in the system, the entire production system may have to shut down because once production of a component ceases two things happen. First, the assemblies that utilize that component quickly run out of inventory for the component and have to stop production. Second, the assemblies that go into making the component quickly find themselves with a sufficient inventory buildup and, therefore, also have to stop production.

Although it may appear quite inefficient that an entire system shuts down whenever there is a problem with the production of a single component, this policy immediately focuses attention on the problem area. As a result, great efforts are made to correct problems quickly. Workers typically learn to handle more than one task so that the labor necessary to correct production deficiencies is readily available and shut-downs usually do not last long. The necessity of avoiding problems and quickly solving whatever difficulties arise results in a general improvement in total product quality.

For a just-in-time system to operate properly, the factory and its suppliers must be completely coordinated. Because work stoppages can result in idling the entire factory, the quality of the components supplied by vendors is of crucial importance. In addition, the small lot sizes require frequent deliveries on a reliable schedule. Accordingly, a factory normally selects only one supplier for a particular component. This *single sourcing* allows the supplier and the factory to develop a full partnership in the production process. On the downside, the factory is left vulnerable to any production problems that might occur with the supplier. From the supplier's standpoint, it can be dangerous to rely too greatly on a single customer because downturns in customer demand can have a devastating effect on the supplier's profitability. Perhaps for these reasons, JIT has not yet won the same degree of acceptance in the United States as it has in Japan.

KANBAN SYSTEMS

The ordering of inventory from one production level to the next in JIT systems is frequently done using a **kanban** system. This ticket-based system (*kanban* is the Japanese word for these tickets) keeps track of the flow of components through the factory as described below.

Kanban System

1. A component is produced in a small batch, each of which is attached to a *production ordering kanban*. The batches are then shipped to an intermediary storage location known as the *store*, where they are held until needed for production in some assembly.

2. The assembly that utilizes this component collects the component from the store and brings it to a *holding area*. When the component is picked up from the store, a worker removes the production ordering kanbans from the component and returns them to the component production area. At the same time, the worker attaches a *withdrawal kanban* to the component.

3. When the component is removed from the holding area for use in production, the withdrawal kanban is collected and placed on a *kanban post*. When the number of withdrawal kanbans on the kanban post reaches a sufficient level, a worker returns to the store with the withdrawal kanbans to initiate another delivery to the holding area.

4. The production ordering kanbans removed from the component at the store and returned to the component production area are also placed on a kanban post. When the number of production ordering kanbans on this post reaches a predetermined amount, production of the component is resumed.

Management science techniques can be used to determine optimal batch sizes and the optimal number of kanbans required to trigger a resumption of production or a visit to the store to obtain additional inventory.

Although kanbans are typically used in JIT applications, they are not essential. As the cost of computing power decreases, we should expect to see the functions performed by kanbans increasingly taken over by computers. An integrated computer control system is able to identify problem areas more quickly and allow dynamic determination of optimal production lot sizes and safety stocks.

FLEXIBLE MANUFACTURING SYSTEMS

Another production/inventory approach that is gaining popularity is the notion of a **flexible manufacturing system**, or **FMS**, in which computer-controlled machines are capable of performing several different operations used in the production process. The goods to be manufactured are placed on pallets and their movements in the factory are controlled by a computer. Because a single machine may have many different functions, an item may visit a particular machine on more than one occasion during the manufacturing process.

Flexible manufacturing systems are most appropriate in factories that produce a moderate variety of goods, none of which has the sales volume to warrant mass production. By necessity, retooling and setup times for the machines have to be short enough that machine efficiency is not sacrificed. Management science techniques such as queuing theory (see Chapter 12) have been used in flexible manufacturing systems to determine the optimal movement of a good among the different machines making up the manufacturing process.

A flexible manufacturing system offers several advantages over a conventional assembly-line system in which each machine has a dedicated function. These include: (1) reduced work-in-progress inventory, (2) reduced manufacturing lead times, (3) reduced labor costs, (4) reduced plant space requirements, (5) increased machine utilization, and (6) increased number of different products the factory can produce.

Although these advantages are substantial, flexible manufacturing systems are far more costly than traditional assembly-line systems because of the higher cost of the sophisticated machinery required. Hence, even though FMS has found acceptance in some industries (such as metal-working), the cost barrier has limited the degree to which this technology has been embraced. As costs decrease, however, we should see an increase in the use of these systems.

11.5 SUMMARY

The inventory techniques discussed in this chapter have been developed for models in which the assumption of demand occurring at a known constant rate is not appropriate. When items have stochastic demand and a shelf life of one period, the single-period inventory model can be used to determine an optimal inventory policy.

A Material Requirements Planning (MRP) inventory control system can be used to translate finished goods demands into demands for the subcomponents making up the finished goods. One consequence of this system is that component demands, though deterministic, typically do not occur at a constant rate.

In situations in which demands are deterministic but vary substantially from period to period, the Wagner-Whitin algorithm can be used to determine an optimal inventory policy. The Silver-Meal heuristic is another procedure for solving such problems; it requires fewer calculations than the Wagner-Whitin algorithm and generally gives results that are optimal or near optimal.

Two inventory/production management systems that are gaining increased acceptance are just-in-time (JIT) and flexible manufacturing systems (FMS). As the cost of computers continues to decline, we should expect to see greater utilization of management science techniques incorporated in such systems.

Notational Summary

$$c = \text{Per unit cost}$$
$$d_j = \text{Demand in period j}$$
$$f(x) = \text{Probability density function}$$
$$F(x) = \text{Cumulative probability function}$$
$$g = \text{Per unit goodwill cost}$$
$$K = \text{Fixed costs}$$
$$p = \text{Probability that demand equals x}$$
$$p(x) = \text{Per unit selling price}$$
$$P(D \leq Q) = \text{Probability that demand is less than or equal to Q}$$
$$s = \text{Per unit salvage value}$$
$$T(j, j + k) = \text{Inventory holding and ordering cost of placing an order in period j,}$$
which will satisfy demand up to, but not including, period $j + k$
$$Y = \text{Number of periods in a year}$$

Using WINQSB to Solve Inventory Models Based on Nonstationary Demand

We can use the inventory module of WINQSB to solve problems utilizing the single period inventory model, and multiple-period inventory models using the Wagner-Whitin algorithm and Silver-Meal heuristic.

Single-Period Inventory Model

To solve a single period inventory model, we click on "Single-period Stochastic Demand (Newsboy) Problem" from the initial Inventory Module data entry screen and indicate the problem name and time units; this takes us to a data input screen. Exhibit 11.1 shows this screen for the Wendell's Bakery problem presented in Section 11.1. By selecting "Solve the Problem" from the "Solve and Analyze" option on the menu bar, WINQSB returns a screen that includes the input data and values for the optimal order quantity and the optimal expected profit.

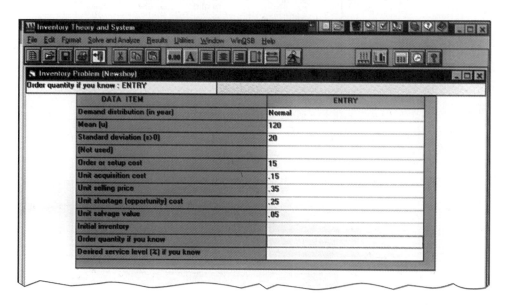

EXHIBIT 11.1

Multiple-Period Inventory Models

To conduct a multiple-period inventory analysis, we click on "Multiple-Period Dynamic Demand Lot-Sizing Problem" and indicate the problem name, the time units, and number of periods; this takes us to a data input screen. Exhibit 11.2 shows the data input for the Golden West Homes problem presented in Section 11.3.

EXHIBIT 11.2

To solve the problem we select "Solve the Problem" from the "Solve and Analyze" option on the menu bar. The screen that arises allows us to select the solution procedure to be used. Two options are the Wagner-Whitin algorithm and the Silver-Meal heuristic procedure. WINQSB then solves the problem for the method selected. Exhibit 11.3 shows the WINQSB output obtained by selecting the Wagner-Whitin option for this problem.

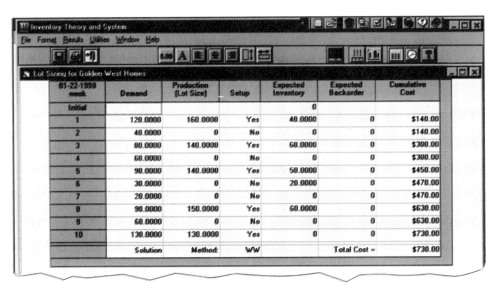

01-22-1998 week	Demand	Production (Lot Size)	Setup	Expected Inventory	Expected Backorder	Cumulative Cost
Initial				0		
1	120.0000	160.0000	Yes	40.0000	0	$140.00
2	40.0000	0	No	0	0	$140.00
3	80.0000	140.0000	Yes	60.0000	0	$300.00
4	60.0000	0	No	0	0	$300.00
5	90.0000	140.0000	Yes	50.0000	0	$450.00
6	30.0000	0	No	20.0000	0	$470.00
7	20.0000	0	No	0	0	$470.00
8	90.0000	150.0000	Yes	60.0000	0	$630.00
9	60.0000	0	No	0	0	$630.00
10	130.0000	130.0000	Yes	0	0	$730.00
Solution		Method:	WW		Total Cost =	$730.00

EXHIBIT 11.3

PROBLEMS

1. Masks-R-Us sells Halloween masks at a kiosk in the local mall. The store is open only during the month of October. Masks are imported from Asia and cost the store $3.45 each; they retail for $9.95 each. Any masks left in inventory after Halloween are sold to a merchandise closeout specialist at a price of $1.80 each. Masks-R-Us estimates that if it runs out of Halloween masks, it will suffer a customer goodwill loss of $15. The company further estimates the cost of rent, utilities, labor, insurance, and so on, to operate the kiosk is approximately $4000 for the month.

   Based on past sales, Masks-R-Us estimates that demand for its masks during the month of October will be approximately normally distributed with a mean of 900 masks and a standard deviation of 100 masks. Because the masks are imported from Asia, Masks-R-Us must place its order with the mask manufacturer in May.

   Determine the number of masks Masks-R-Us should order and the expected profit or loss it can expect to earn if it follows this policy.

2. Jackson Mint produces collectible plates. It has recently contracted with the estate of well-known artist, Skip Gunther, to produce a series of five commemorative plates bearing copies of the artist's most famous pictures. The plates will be sold by subscription at a cost of $275 plus shipping and handling for the entire five-plate series. Jackson estimates the cost of producing each plate in the series at $12.50 plus a $9.75 royalty. Jackson has agreed to pay the Gunther estate.

   Jackson intends to mount a $175,000 nationwide advertising campaign promoting these plates as a "limited edition"; that is, Jackson will specify the number of plates it will produce and limit production to that amount. Any unsold plates will be destroyed. Based on its previous experience with such products, Jackson estimates that customer demand for the series will be approximately normally distributed, with a mean of 1800 and a standard deviation of 250.

   If Jackson has more subscribers than plate series, it will refund subscribers' money with a note explaining that the series has been oversubscribed. Reasoning that the unsatisfied customers will be more willing to subscribe to Jackson's future offerings, it estimates that each unsatisfied customer will earn the company an average of $40 in discounted future profits.

   a. What is the optimal number of Skip Gunther plate series Jackson should produce?

   b. What expected profit or loss will Jackson earn if it follows the production policy found in part (a)?

   c. Comment on any assumptions you made to solve this problem.

3. Consider Little Trykes Toys production of wagons during week 16 through week 23, discussed in Section 11.3. Suppose Little Trykes management forecasts the following demand for the wagons:

Week	16	17	18	19	20	21	22	23
Demand	65	120	95	80	140	170	125	80

   Recall that wagons have a one-week lead time. Little Trykes uses a production lot size of 300, and no safety stock is desired. If Little Trykes has a balance available of 200 wagons at the beginning of week 16, determine the MRP planning worksheet for the period from week 16 through week 23.

4. Consider the following MRP planning worksheet for Little Trykes tricycles for week 8 through week 16:

TRICYCLES	LEAD TIME 2 WEEKS	TIME PERIODS								
LOT SIZE 250	SAFETY STOCK 30	8	9	10	11	12	13	14	15	16
GROSS REQUIREMENTS		90	75	85	100	80	60	70	80	95
SCHEDULED RECEIPTS			250							
BALANCE AVAILABLE	150	60	235	150	50	220	160	90	260	165
NET REQUIREMENTS		0	0	0	0	60	0	0	20	0
PLANNED ORDER RECEIPTS						250			250	
PLANNED ORDER RELEASES				250			250			

Little Trykes produces front wheel assemblies in lot sizes of 200 units and desires a safety stock of 60 units. There is a scheduled receipt of 200 front wheel sets in week 10, and a balance of 90 front wheel assemblies is available at the beginning of week 7. Recall that the lead time for assembling front wheel assemblies is one week. Using this information, determine the MRP planning worksheet for front wheel assemblies for week 7 through week 15.

5. Golden West Homes manufactures mobile homes. Requirements for ovens over a 10-week planning period are as follows:

Week	1	2	3	4	5	6	7	8	9	10
Demand	130	160	60	50	40	80	120	140	70	150

The company purchases the ovens from the Swiss Maid Appliance Company. The estimated cost to place an order with Swiss Maid is $800, and Golden West estimates the weekly holding cost at $2 per oven. The company had been using the EOQ model to determine its ordering policy but is considering using the Wagner-Whitin algorithm instead. Golden West management has calculated the following values for T(j,j + k), the inventory cost of ordering in week j to supply demand up to the beginning of week j + k:

Week j	Order up to the Beginning of Week j + k									
	2	3	4	5	6	7	8	9	10	11
1	930	1410	1710	2060	2420					
2		960	1140	1390	1670	2390				
3			860	1010	1210	1770				
4				850	970	1370				
5					840	1080	1680			
6						880	1240	1940	2430	
7							920	1340	1690	
8								940	1150	1900
9									870	1320
10										950

a. If Golden West forecasts its annual demand based on a simple 10-week moving average, determine the EOQ value for ovens.

b. If Golden West uses the Wagner-Whitin algorithm, what is the optimal inventory policy for ovens over the 10-week period?

c. If Golden West uses the Silver-Meal heuristic, what is the inventory policy for ovens over the 10-week period?

6. Consider the data given in Problem 5. Determine the total inventory cost over the 10-week period for
   a. the EOQ policy
   b. the Wagner-Whitin policy
   c. the Silver-Meal policy

7. Little Trykes is considering importing a children's pedal car to sell under the Little Trykes brand name. The company estimates the demand for the cars over the next eight-week planning period to be as follows.

Week	1	2	3	4	5	6	7	8
Demand	210	160	190	80	300	130	110	260

   The cost to order the cars is an estimated $160, and the annual holding cost per car is approximately $13 (weekly cost of $0.25).

   a. Determine the inventory policy for the cars over this eight-week period using the Silver-Meal heuristic.
   b. How much cheaper is the Silver-Meal inventory policy than the EOQ policy over the eight-week period? (Assume that an eight-week simple moving average is used to forecast annual demand.)

8. Flavan Faucet manufactures a designer line of bathroom faucets. The following product tree represents the bill of materials for the Athena 242 faucet set.

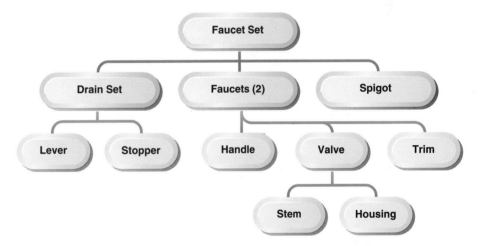

The lead time and current inventory for each component are as follows.

Item	Lead Time (in weeks)	Current Inventory
Faucet Set	1	200
Drain Set	3	300
Lever	4	500
Stopper	3	400
Faucets	2	500
Handle	6	100
Valve	3	500
Stem	5	800
Housing	2	300
Trim	7	1200
Spigot	7	600

   Suppose the company wishes to schedule production for 1000 units of the Athena 242 faucet set and wants the production completed in 10-weeks. Determine the order quantity and the latest date the order can be initiated for each component of the faucets.

9. Consider Flavan Faucet's production of Athena 242 faucet sets in Problem 8. Suppose the company forecast the following demand between week 12 and week 18:

Week	12	13	14	15	16	17	18
Demand	800	600	400	200	600	400	500

The company estimates that the production setup cost to produce the Athena 242 faucet is $1400 and the annual holding cost per unit is $12. Flavan Faucet has a safety stock requirement of 200 faucets and a balance of 200 faucets available at the beginning of week 12. If Flavan Faucet uses the EOQ formula to determine the production lot size, determine the MRP planning worksheet over the period from week 11 through week 18. (Assume that annual demand is forecast based on a seven-week simple moving average and that demand in week 11 has already been addressed through previous analysis and is 0.)

10. Consider the data of Problem 9. Suppose Flavan Faucet uses the Silver-Meal heuristic to schedule production of the faucet sets. Determine the MRP planning worksheet over the period from week 11 through week 18 in this case. (Assume that demand in week 11 has already been addressed through previous analysis and is 0.)

11. Consider the data of Problem 9. If Flavan Faucet uses a lot-for-lot rule to schedule faucet set production, the MRP planning worksheet for week 11 through week 18 is as follows.

FAUCET SETS	LEAD TIME I WEEK	TIME PERIODS							
LOT FOR LOT	SAFETY STOCK 200	11	12	13	14	15	16	17	18
GROSS REQUIREMENTS		0	800	600	400	200	600	400	500
SCHEDULED RECEIPTS									
BALANCE AVAILABLE	200	200	200	200	200	200	200	200	200
NET REQUIREMENTS			800	600	400	200	600	400	500
PLANNED ORDER RECEIPTS			800	600	400	200	600	400	500
PLANNED ORDER RELEASES		800	600	400	200	600	400	500	

Recall that the lead time for the drain sets is three weeks. Flavan Faucet uses a production lot size of 1200 for the drain sets and desires a safety stock of 400 units. If there is a balance available of 500 drain sets at the end of week 10 and a scheduled receipt of 1200 drain sets in week 11, determine the MRP planning worksheet for drain sets during the period from week 8 through week 17.

12. Consider the data from Problem 11. Recall that the lead time for faucets is two weeks. Flavan Faucet is considering using a production lot size of 3000 for the faucets with no safety stock. If no balance is available at the end of week 10, but there is a scheduled receipt of 3000 faucets in week 11, determine the MRP planning worksheet for faucets during the period from week 9 through week 17.

13. Clothesline, Inc. is a retailer of moderately priced women's clothing. Clothesline's policy is to give customers a $5 gift certificate if they request an out-of-stock advertised item. This certificate is estimated to cost the company only $3, but it avoids a loss in customer goodwill.

Clothesline is considering selling a line of scarves produced by a noted fashion designer. Because of long lead times, Clothesline can only place one order for the scarves. The scarves cost Clothesline $6.25, and it plans to retail them for $10.95. Clothesline estimates that total demand at its 55 stores during the selling season will follow approximately a normal distribution, with a mean of 8000 units and a standard deviation of 1500 units. Any scarves left in inventory at the end of the selling season will be marked down to a clearance price of $4.95 and sold quickly.

On the basis of this information, determine how many scarves Clothesline should order. Comment on any assumptions you made to solve this problem.

14. Stefani Foods produces fresh pasta products for sale through local supermarkets. One product that is quite popular is fresh linguini and clam sauce. This item has a shelf life of two weeks and costs Stefani $1.19 per unit to produce. The product retails at a suggested price of $1.99 and is sold to supermarkets at a wholesale price of $1.46.

Many supermarkets receive only one delivery per week of Stefani products. In these instances, the delivery route agent is instructed to pick up any unsold linguini to return to the company. The supermarkets receive full credit on these returns, and the returned merchandise is sold in the Stefani owned Thrift Store at a retail price of $1.05. Such sales are estimated to net the company $0.83 per unit.

Van's Supermarket estimates that weekly demand for the linguini follows a uniform distribution between 160 and 239 units. Stefani delivers to Van's once a week. Determine the optimal stocking quantity for the linguini if the goodwill cost to Stefani associated with the supermarket's running out of inventory is:

a. $0.10

b. $0.50

c. $1.00

d. $5.00

15. Barnett Furniture Company (BFC) manufactures bedroom furniture for sale through mass merchandise retailers. One of its more popular products is a white laminate four-drawer dresser. The bill of materials for this dresser is represented by the following product tree.

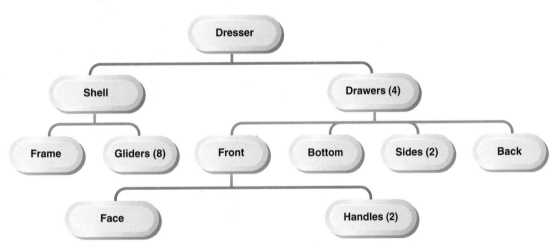

The company has just received a rush order for 2500 of these dressers. Lead times and the current inventory position of each component are as follows.

Item	Lead Time (in days)	Current Inventory
Dresser	5	300
Shell	5	50
Frame	10	100
Gliders	15	1600
Drawers	10	0
Front	5	200
Face	5	600
Handles	10	24000
Bottom	10	800
Sides	10	4000
Backs	5	3000

a. If Barnett wants to complete the order in 40 days, determine how many of each component should be ordered and the latest possible day to order each component.

b. What is the shortest amount of time required for Barnett to complete this order?

16. Barnett Furniture Company (see Problem 15) is open five days a week. The lead time to complete the final assembly of white laminate four-drawer dressers is one week. BFC desires a safety stock of 200 dressers and produces in lot sizes of 2400 units. The company has forecast the demand over the planning period from week 7 through week 13 as follows.

Week	7	8	9	10	11	12	13
Demand	500	1000	1500	3000	1800	2200	1800

If BFC has a balance available of 100 dressers at the end of week 6 and a scheduled receipt of 2400 dressers in week 7, determine the MRP planning worksheet for dressers during the period from week 7 through week 13.

17. Consider the situation at Barnett Furniture Company given in Problems 15 and 16. Based on an MRP analysis, BFC estimates the following gross requirements for dresser-drawer fronts over the planning period from week 4 through week 10:

Week	4	5	6	7	8	9	10
Gross Requirements	7500	0	14,500	0	0	13,500	10,000

The company has 2500 drawer fronts available at the end of week 3 and desires a safety stock of 100 units. Lead time for drawer fronts is one week, and the components are produced in lot sizes of 10,000 units. Determine the MRP planning worksheet for drawer fronts over the planning period from week 3 through week 10.

18. BFC (see Problems 15 through 17) orders handles in lot sizes of 25,000. The lead time for handles is two weeks, and the company desires a safety stock of 4000 handles. If 6000 handles are available at the end of week 2, determine the MRP planning worksheet for handles over the period from week 1 through week 10. Base your gross requirements for handles on the answer you obtained in Problem 17.

19. Johansen's Ice Cream Shoppe purchases fresh-baked waffle cones from the Myra Cone Company. The cones cost Johansen $0.28 each and are delivered once each day. Johansen's charges customers who want their ice cream in a waffle cone an extra $0.40. If Johansen's runs out of waffle cones, it estimates that it suffers a customer goodwill loss of $0.75 for each additional customer request for a waffle cone. Unsold waffle cones are ground up and used as toppings on the frozen yogurt sold by the company. Johansen's therefore estimates the salvage value of unsold cones at $.06. Johansen's also estimates that daily demand for the waffle cones follows approximately a normal distribution with a mean of 70 units and a standard deviation of 16 units. Determine how many waffle cones Johansen's should purchase each day from Myra Cone.

20. Frank's Garden Center sells McMurray riding mowers. McMurray has found itself with an excess inventory of Model 412 mowers and is temporarily offering dealers a discount of $75 off its normal wholesale price of $725. Frank's sells the Model 412 at a retail price of $895 and estimates that its demand during the upcoming selling season will be between one and five units, with the following probabilities:

$$P(\text{Demand} = 1 \text{ unit}) = .25$$
$$P(\text{Demand} = 2 \text{ units}) = .20$$
$$P(\text{Demand} = 3 \text{ units}) = .10$$
$$P(\text{Demand} = 4 \text{ units}) = .30$$
$$P(\text{Demand} = 5 \text{ units}) = .15$$

Unfortunately, Frank's must decide how many mowers to purchase at the temporary price discount before the selling season begins. Once the selling season starts, if demand for the McMurray mower at Frank's exceeds the number ordered at the discounted price, Frank's must pay the normal wholesale price of $725 per unit. Any purchased mowers that Frank's is not able to sell during the normal selling season can be sold for $595 at the annual clearance sale. How many mowers should Frank's purchase from McMurray at the temporary price discount?

21. Frank's Garden Center forecasts demand for its products based on the previous year's sales. The demand for McMurray snow blowers over the same 10-week winter selling season last year was as follows.

Week	1	2	3	4	5	6	7	8	9	10
Demand	6	12	16	18	12	8	6	6	4	2

The store currently has one McMurray snow blower in stock and would like to have two left at the end of week 10. The cost of placing an order with McMurray for snow blowers is $50, and the cost of holding a snow blower in inventory is an estimated $1 per week.

a. Determine the inventory policy and inventory cost over the 10-week period if Frank's uses the EOQ formula for determining the order quantity. (Assume that annual demand is forecast to be 90 units.)

b. Determine the inventory policy and inventory cost over the 10-week period if Frank's uses the Silver-Meal heuristic for determining order quantities.

c. Determine the inventory policy and inventory cost over the 10-week period if Frank's uses the Wagner-Whitin algorithm for determining order quantities.

22. Whirling Blender manufactures electric blenders for sale to commercial customers. Whirling estimates the following customer demand over the eight-week planning cycle from week 10 through week 17.

Week	10	11	12	13	14	15	16	17
Demand	1200	1400	800	1000	700	1500	1200	900

The following product tree represents the bill of materials for the electric blender:

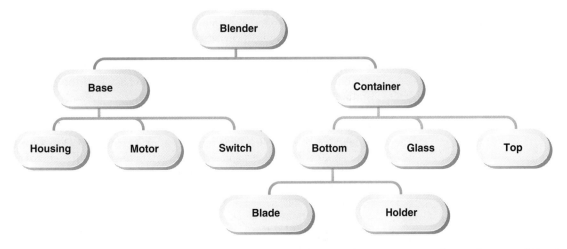

Whirling produces the blenders in batch sizes of 3000 units. Lead time for assembling the finished product is one week. Whirling desires a safety stock of 500 units and estimates that 800 blenders will be in inventory at the beginning of week 10.

a. Construct the MRP planning worksheet for blenders during the period from week 9 through week 17.

b. Whirling produces bases in lots of 2000 units and desires no safety stock. The lead time for base assembly is two weeks. If there is a balance of 500 bases in inventory at the beginning of week 9, determine the MRP planning worksheet for bases during the period from week 7 through week 17.

c. Whirling orders motors on a lot-for-lot basis. Motors have a lead time of three weeks. If the company desires a safety stock of 400 motors, and a balance of 600 motors is available at the beginning of week 7, determine the MRP planning worksheet for motors during the period from week 4 through week 17.

23. Consider the data given in Problem 22 for Whirling blenders. The lead time and current inventory for each of the components are as follows.

Item	Lead Time (in weeks)	Current Inventory
Blender	1	300
Base	2	200
Housing	4	100
Motor	3	300
Switch	2	1000
Container	1	700
Bottom	2	200
Blade	5	500
Holder	3	100
Glass	6	400
Top	4	600

a. Determine the latest order date for each component in order to satisfy the demand in week 10.

b. Determine how much of each component should be ordered to satisfy the demand in week 10.

24. Each year a local landowner allows Scout Troop 819 of Tustin, California, to set up a Christmas tree lot during the period between December 12 and December 24. The troop has contracted with a Christmas tree grower in Oregon, who will make one delivery of trees on December 12.

The grower charges the troop $12 per tree, and the troop retails the trees for $25 each. Any trees that are unsold by December 25 must be hauled away to the local landfill, at a cost of approximately $1 per tree.

If the troop runs short of Christmas trees, it feels that there is a small likelihood that customers encountering an out-of-stock situation will not revisit the Christmas tree lot in future years. Accordingly, the troop has decided to assign a shortage cost of $2.50 per customer who visits the tree lot after it is sold out of trees. If the troop feels that the total demand for the Christmas trees over the 12-day selling period will be almost uniformly distributed between 150 and 249 trees, determine the optimal number of trees the scout troop should purchase and the expected profit from this venture.

25. *Business Daily* sells its newspapers for $0.75 in coin-operated kiosks, each of which is designed to hold up to 60 papers. The production and delivery costs of each newspaper equal $0.60, but *Business Daily* receives approximately $0.23 in advertising revenue for each paper sold. Any newspapers that remain unsold at the end of the day are sold to a recycling center. *Business Daily* estimates that the revenue it receives from the recycling center will only cover the cost of transporting the papers to the center.

Management at *Business Daily* estimates that the goodwill cost of not having enough papers in the kiosk to satisfy customer demand is $1.50 per unsatisfied customer. Demand for the Thursday paper at a particular kiosk is estimated to follow a Poisson distribution with a mean $\lambda = 36$ units. Determine how many newspapers *Business Daily* should place in the kiosk. (Hint: The Poisson distribution can be approximated by a normal distribution with $\mu = \lambda$ and $\sigma = \sqrt{\lambda}$.)

CASE 1: *Mr. Pretzel*

Mr. Pretzel sells soft pretzels to movie theaters, skating rinks, and snack bars. The company bakes the pretzels in its factory and delivers them fresh daily to its various accounts. Mr. Pretzel has recently signed a contract to purchase 50 pretzel vending machines. Management feels that these machines will enable the company to sell its pretzels in new locations, thus expanding company revenue.

Mr. Pretzel's marketing department is busy trying to determine suitable locations for the vending machines. It has decided that, at a minimum, pretzel demand at a vending machine location must average at least 25 units per day. Each vending machine is capable of holding 140 pretzels. The marketing department is interested in determining what compensation it should offer the owners of the sites at which the vending machines will be placed.

According to the company's accounting department, the cost of producing a soft pretzel (fixed and variable) is approximately $0.32. The pretzels to be sold in the vending machines are sealed in plastic, adding $0.005 to their cost. They are delivered daily and sell for $0.75. Any pretzels left in the vending machine from the previous day are removed and returned to the factory. There they are ground up and sold for use in cattle feed, for which the company receives approximately $0.02 in net revenue from each returned pretzel. The cost of delivering new pretzels and removing old ones is estimated to be $4.20 per vending machine per day. An additional capital cost of $2.50 per day is associated with each vending machine.

If the vending machine runs out of pretzels, there is some likelihood that a dissatisfied customer may kick the machine, causing some damage. Since the company has not had any operating history regarding these machines, it is uncertain of the goodwill and potential damage cost of not having enough pretzels in the machine to satisfy all customers.

The company has three different compensation schemes for site owners:

1. Pay the site owner a fixed revenue of $3 per day.
2. Pay the site owner a commission of $0.08 per pretzel sold.
3. Lease the vending machine to the site owner with the stipulation that Mr. Pretzel will service the machine. Mr. Pretzel will charge the site owner $3.25 per day for leasing the machine and $0.45 apiece for the pretzels. Mr. Pretzel will give no credit for unsold pretzels, and the pretzels have no salvage value to the site owner.

Prepare a management report indicating the expected daily profit to Mr. Pretzel for each compensation plan, assuming daily demand follows a Poisson distribution with means, λ, of either 25, 50, 75, or 100 units. Use the normal distribution approximation to the Poisson distribution ($\mu = \lambda$ and $\sigma = \sqrt{\lambda}$). Assume that if Mr. Pretzel leases the vending machine to the site owner, the site owner will order the optimal number of pretzels from the company. Do the analysis for at least three possible goodwill costs, including $0.05, $0.25, and $0.75.

CASE 2: **SWITCH** *Watch Company*

SWITCH Watch Company manufactures watches with exchangeable fronts that customers can switch depending on their fashion mood. The company is planning its production of the men's 4320 Dual Display watch, which has two displays to enable the wearer to tell the time in two different parts of the world. The principal market for this watch is the business traveler; hence, it is heavily advertised in airline magazines.

The following product tree represents the bill of materials for this watch.

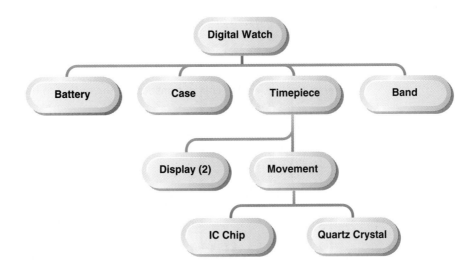

Safety stock requirements, lead times, and production lot sizes for the components are as follows.

Item	Safety Stock	Lead Time	Lot Size
Digital watches	200 units	1 week	500
Batteries	400 units	3 weeks	800
Cases	none	2 weeks	lot for lot
Timepieces	none	1 week	400
Displays	300 units	4 weeks	1200
Movements	100 units	2 weeks	lot for lot
IC chips	150 units	3 weeks	800
Quartz crystals	450 units	2 weeks	1400
Watch bands	500 units	5 weeks	2000

Demand for the watch over the planning period (week 8 through week 14) has been forecast as follows:

Week	8	9	10	11	12	13	14
Demand	350	500	400	650	800	400	300

Prepare a management report including MRP planning worksheets for each component over the relevant time period up to week 14. Discuss the ramifications of the watch's having two displays instead of a single display.

CHAPTER 12

QUEUING THEORY

C arl's Jr. is planning to open a new restaurant in Logan, Utah. The company has narrowed down its location choices to three potential sites. A principal concern is that the restaurant must be designed to adequately handle the drive-thru business during lunch hour.

One of the sites is quite small and can only accommodate a single drive-thru window with space for up to six cars to wait in line. The second site is somewhat larger and can handle a single drive-thru line with space for up to nine cars to wait. If the site is built with two windows (the customer pays at the first and the food is delivered at the second), the waiting line will accommodate a maximum of only eight cars. The third site is quite large and has enough room for two separate drive-thru

lines. Each line can handle a maximum of either nine cars (when there is a single service window) or eight cars (when there are separate windows for the cashier and food delivery).

The asking prices for the three sites differ, and construction costs will vary, depending on the configuration selected. Labor costs will be higher if there are separate windows for the cashier and food server; at the same time, using two windows will speed up service.

To choose a site and configuration, Carl's Jr. management proposes conducting an analysis of the drive-thru waiting lines, known as a *queuing analysis*. Of principal importance is the effect the lines will have on the potential profitability of each site.

12.1 $\mathcal{I}$NTRODUCTION

Every day it seems we spend some amount of time waiting in lines. When we shop at the supermarket we wait in line to check out; when we go to the bank, we wait in line to see a teller; and when we call a business, we are sometimes put on hold for several minutes until a real person answers the phone. Even when we have a confirmed appointment with a doctor, a lawyer, or an accountant, we frequently wait for service.

Queuing theory is the study of waiting lines, or *queues*. The objective of a queuing analysis is to design systems that enable an organization to perform optimally according to some criterion.

One possible criterion is to maximize profit. We must be careful to include all relevant factors in this criterion, however. For example, a store may be able to lower staffing costs by reducing the number of clerks. But this action may also increase the time customers must wait in line. If the waiting time becomes too long, customers may take their business elsewhere, which could result in lower revenues and potentially lower profits for the store. Thus, when determining staffing requirements, the store must also account for the loss in customer goodwill attributed to longer waiting lines.

In other cases, an organization's objective is to meet a certain desired level of service at minimum cost. For example, a municipal hospital may wish to determine the minimum number of ambulances it should have on call so that an ambulance will be immediately available for dispatch at least 99% of the time.

The effects of poorly designed queuing systems can range from inconvenience (waiting too long in a bank teller line) to death (needing an ambulance and not having one available). In order to analyze queuing systems properly, it is necessary to have a clear understanding of how service is to be measured. The average time a customer spends in line, the average length of the line, and the probability that an arriving customer must wait for service are some of the measures of queuing performance we consider in this chapter.

12.2 $\mathcal{E}$LEMENTS OF THE QUEUING PROCESS

As illustrated in Figure 12.1, a queuing system consists of three basic components:

Components of a Queuing System

1. *Arrivals*: Customers arrive at a system according to some arrival pattern.
2. *Waiting in a Queue*: Arriving customers may have to wait in one or more queues for service.
3. *Service*: Customers receive service and leave the system.

Let us briefly examine each of these.

THE ARRIVAL PROCESS   In certain situations, customers arrive according to a set schedule. For example, medical patients scheduled for nonemergency treatment may not arrive at the precise moment for which their appointments have been made, but the facility will have a pretty good idea of the number of patients who need to be treated and approximately when each will arrive. We can therefore model this system using a *deterministic arrival process*.

FIGURE 12.1   Three Server Queuing System

By contrast, when you need a loaf of bread or a gallon of milk, you don't call ahead to the supermarket to schedule an appointment to come in. Similarly, customers generally show up at a bank or post office or call an airline when they have a particular need, not according to a set schedule. Since a manager does not know when the next customer will arrive, the arrival of customers is a *random process*. Although deterministic arrivals exist for certain situations, a random customer arrival process is more common for most businesses.

In order to analyze a random process, we must have some idea of the probability distribution for the arrivals. One way to estimate an arrival distribution might be to station ourselves outside the business and record the time between customer arrivals or the number of customers who arrive in a given time interval. Then, using statistical analysis, we can attempt to "fit" a probability distribution to the data.

Such a laborious analysis is not always necessary, however. For instance, if a customer arrival process satisfies conditions known as orderliness, stationarity, and independence, it can be modeled by a **Poisson distribution**.[1] Fortunately, these conditions are quite unrestrictive and are approximately satisfied in a great many situations.

The *orderliness* condition states that, during any split second of time, at most one customer will arrive at the service facility. This condition is violated in certain circumstances (such as the instant the doors open for a department store's after-Christmas clearance sale), but, for most business situations, customers do arrive in an orderly fashion—namely, one at a time.

The *stationarity* condition requires that, within some time frame, the probability of customer arrivals remains the same for each incremental time epoch. This does not mean that the probability of an arrival is constant for *all* time periods. For example, the arrival rate of customers at a bank typically is higher on Friday afternoons than on Tuesday mornings. But if the probability of an arrival at the bank on Friday afternoon in the time period between 3:38 and 3:39 is the same as the probability of an arrival in the time period between 3:39 and 3:40, then the stationarity assumption is satisfied for the time frame between 3:38 and 3:40. The stationarity assumption generally holds if the time frame under consideration is small enough.

The *independence* condition is satisfied if the arrival of one customer has no influence on the arrival of another. For example, if Mary Smith decides to go to the local supermarket at 4:45 P.M., her action will not affect when, if ever, Paul Robinson will go to the same supermarket. Although the independence condition is not highly restrictive, it is violated if customers arrive in groups (such as tour groups arriving on a bus to a res-

---

[1]Named for the nineteenth-century French mathematician Simeon Denis Poisson.

taurant)[2] or if the population of potential customers is small (such as the arrival of squad cars from a 10-car police department to the department's repair garage).

Conditions for a Poisson Arrival Process

1. *Orderliness*—In any time instant, at most one customer will arrive at the service facility.
2. *Stationarity*—For a given time frame, the probability that a customer will arrive within a certain time interval is the same for all time intervals of equal length.
3. *Independence*—Customers arrive independently of one another; that is, an arrival during a given time interval does not affect the probability of an arrival during other time intervals.

If the modeler can verify or is willing to accept these conditions, then the probability of k arrivals during any time period of length t can be expressed by the random variable X having the following Poisson distribution:

Poisson Arrival Distribution

Probability of k Arrivals Within Time t

$$P(X = k) = \frac{(\lambda t)^k e^{-\lambda t}}{k!}$$

Here,

λ = the mean arrival rate per time unit
t = the length of the time interval
e = 2.7182818 (the base of the natural logarithm)
$k! = k(k - 1)(k - 2)(k - 3) \ldots (3)(2)(1)$

In this expression, λ and t must be expressed in the same time units; that is, if λ is expressed in customers *per hour*, t must be expressed in *hours*.

The Poisson arrival distribution is illustrated in the following situation faced by Hank's Hardware.

HANK'S HARDWARE

Customers arrive at Hank's Hardware according to a Poisson distribution. The store opens at 8:00 A.M., and on Tuesday mornings between 8:00 and 9:00, an average of six customers arrive at the store. Hank was out late partying on Monday evening and would like to sleep an extra half hour on Tuesday. He is concerned, however, that if he opens the store a half hour late, he might lose too much business. Hence, Hank would like to know the probability that 0, 1, 2, 3, etc., customers will arrive between 8:00 and 8:30 on Tuesday morning.

---

[2]Although the buses may arrive independently, the number of customers on the bus can vary. This is an example of a *compound Poisson process*.

SOLUTION

To find the probability that a specific number of customers will arrive during the half-hour interval in question, we use the formula for the Poisson distribution, with $\lambda = 6$ per hour and $t = 30$ minutes $= .5$ hour. This gives us a value of $\lambda t = 6(.5) = 3$. Substituting $\lambda t = 3$ into the Poisson formula gives:

$$P(X=0) = 3^0 e^{-3}/0! = e^{-3} \qquad = .049787$$
$$P(X=1) = 3^1 e^{-3}/1! = 3e^{-3} \qquad = .149361$$
$$P(X=2) = 3^2 e^{-3}/2! = 9e^{-3}/2 \quad = .224042$$
$$P(X=3) = 3^3 e^{-3}/3! = 27e^{-3}/6 = .224042$$
$$P(X=4) = 3^4 e^{-3}/4! = 81e^{-3}/24 = .168031$$

and so on. Although, theoretically, 10, 100, or even 1 million customers could arrive during this half-hour period, as we see from the histogram of the arrival probability distribution in Figure 12.2, the probability of the number of customer arrivals in the half-hour period decreases rapidly after reaching a peak at three. In fact, the probability of more than eight customers arriving during this time interval is less than .004.

FIGURE 12.2   Histogram for the Poisson Distribution with $\lambda = 6$ and $t = .5$

In reviewing this analysis, Hank observed that since the probability of no arrivals during the period is about .050 and of one arrival is about .149, the probability that he would miss two or more customers if he opened the store a half hour late is about $1 - .050 - .149 = .801$. Hence, Hank decided it would be best to open on time. (He also resolved not to stay out so late partying in the future!)

THE WAITING LINE

Many factors influence how the actual waiting lines, or queues, are modeled, including:

1. Line configuration (one long line or several smaller ones)
2. Jockeying (line switching among customers)
3. Balking (not joining the queue if it is too long)
4. Priority (the service order of customers)
5. Tandem queues (if a second service is required)
6. Homogeneity (all customers require the same service)

Line Configuration

Figure 12.3 illustrates a number of commonly used queuing system *line configurations*. For example, the line configuration illustrated in (c) is a queuing system found at a typical

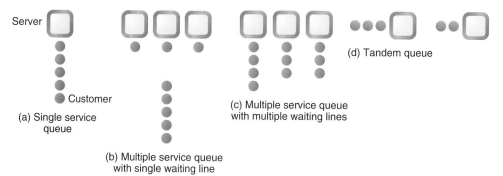

FIGURE 12.3   Commonly Used Queuing System Configurations

supermarket, where a separate line forms at each checkstand[3] whereas the line configuration in (b) is that found at most banks or post offices, where one line forms and the next person designated to be served goes to a server when one becomes available.

Jockeying

Jockeying occurs when customers switch between lines when they perceive that another line is moving faster. Another example of jockeying is when lines are long and a new server begins working. In this case customers in line typically make a mad dash to reach that server first. If customers do, in fact, jockey, there will never be an idle server while customers are in line waiting to begin service.

You might think that a single waiting line is more efficient than multiple lines. In some sense this is true, because using a single line reduces the variance of the amount of time customers wait in line. If customers are smart enough to jockey, however, either line configuration results in the same average performance measures. Because this is typically how multiple line queuing systems behave, the performance measure results presented in this chapter for systems with a single waiting line will normally hold true for systems with multiple waiting lines.

Balking

Although a single waiting line reduces the variance of waiting time over a multiple line configuration, it does have its disadvantages. For example, if a bank has only three tellers working on a Friday afternoon, and 30 customers are present in the bank, 27 people are waiting in a single waiting line. Customers perceiving the waiting line as too long may *balk* (not join the queue) and decide to take their business elsewhere. If too many customers balk, the long-term profitability of the business will suffer. On the other hand, if there were an individual line for each teller, the average number of customers waiting in each line for service would be nine. While a line length of nine is certainly long, it is not as intimidating as 27, and customers may be less likely to balk.

Priority Rules

When a server becomes available, a customer from the waiting line goes to that server to begin service. The *priority rule* most commonly used to select the next customer for service is *first come, first served* (FCFS). This means that the first person in the waiting line will be the next one to be served. Other priority rules also exist, however. A clerk processing orders from the top of her "in basket" is using a *last-come, first-served* (LCFS) priority rule. Computer centers often prioritize jobs for processing based on the esti-

---

[3]Many supermarkets have designated "express" checkstands for customers purchasing fewer than a given number of items (say, 10 or less) or for cash purchases. In this chapter, we focus on developing queuing models only for the case where all servers work at the same average rate.

mated length of the job run and the resources required for the job. At airports, flight controllers use sophisticated rules for determining the order in which planes should land, including the type of plane requesting landing clearance. The priority rule might even be random, as in the case of a telephone operator selecting which of eight incoming lines to answer when all are ringing simultaneously. Although the priority rule used to choose the next customer affects the waiting time variance, it has no effect on the average customer waiting time.

Tandem Queues

Customers usually need to see only one server in order to complete their necessary business. In some systems, however, multiple servers must be visited, typically in a distinct order. Such systems are known as *tandem queues*. For example, an airline may have separate agents for ticket sales and baggage check-in. If you need to purchase a ticket and check baggage, you will visit two servers; however, you could not check bags for a flight until you first purchase a ticket.

Homogeneity

Although many queuing models assume a *homogeneous* population of arriving customers, each requiring essentially the same type of service, some queuing models categorize customers according to different arrival patterns or different service treatments. For example, patients needing emergency treatment at a doctor's office are treated differently from those needing routine physical examinations. Such differences, which can influence performance of the system, must be accounted for when developing the queuing model.

THE SERVICE PROCESS

Since it always takes about the same fixed amount of time to dispense a cup of coffee from a vending machine, its service time can be modeled by a constant, or deterministic, service time distribution. In most business situations, however, service times vary widely and are best modeled by a random variable.

Given its mathematical simplicity, the *exponential probability distribution* is sometimes used to model customer service time. This distribution has the following probability density function.

Exponential Service Time Distribution

$$f(X) = \mu e^{-\mu X}$$

Here,

μ = the average number of customers who can be served per time period

---

In this expression, μ is the *mean service rate* for the server and is expressed in terms of customers per hour, per day, etc. $1/\mu$ is the *average service time*. If we know the average service time, then 1/(average service time) is the average service rate. Thus, if the average service time is 10 minutes, the average service rate is 1/10 per minute, or 6 customers per hour.

For the exponential distribution, the average customer service time and the standard deviation of the customer service time both equal to $1/\mu$. Using the exponential distribution, we can calculate the probability that the service time, X, is less than some value t as follows.

Probability Service Will Be Completed Within Time t

$$P(X \le t) = 1 - e^{-\mu t}$$

In this expression, μ and t must be expressed in the same time units; that is, if t is in *hours*, μ must be in customers *per hour*. Furthermore, the service rate, μ, should be expressed in the same time units as the arrival rate, λ.

To illustrate the exponential distribution, let us return to the situation at Hank's Hardware.

HANK'S HARDWARE (continued)

Hank estimates that it takes an average of four minutes to serve a customer at his store, and service times follow an exponential distribution. Hank has an important luncheon date, so he wishes to find the probability that it will take less than three minutes to serve the next customer.

SOLUTION

Since the average service time, $1/\mu$, is 4 minutes, the average service rate, μ, equals 1/4 per minute, or $60(1/4) = 15$ per hour. Because service times follow an exponential distribution, the probability that a service will take less than 3 minutes = 3/60 = .05 hour is:

$$P(X < .05) = 1 - e^{-15^*.05} = 1 - e^{-.75} = 1 - .47237 = .52763$$

The density function for the exponential distribution when $\mu = 15$ appears in Figure 12.4. The area under the curve between 0 and some time, t, represents the probability that service is completed by time t. As you can see, this distribution is skewed to the right; that is, the mean of the distribution, $1/\mu$, exceeds its median value, $(\ln 2)/\mu$. For Hank's Hardware, the mean service time is 1/15 hour (4 minutes) and the median is $\ln2/15$ hours = 2.77 minutes. Therefore, while the average service time is 4 minutes, 50% of all customers will be served in less than 2.77 minutes.

FIGURE 12.4 Exponential Distribution for $\mu = 15$/hour

Memoryless Property
of the Exponential
Distribution

The exponential distribution is a *memoryless* distribution, which means that no additional information regarding the probability distribution is gained from observing the service time already expended. In the Hank's Hardware example, this implies that if a customer has already had two minutes of service but the service is not yet completed, the probability that the customer's remaining *additional* service time will be less than 3 minutes is .52763, the same probability as if we had just started observing the customer. Such memoryless distributions are sometimes referred to as *Markovian distributions*.[4]

The Relationship Between
the Poisson and
Exponential Distributions

The exponential distribution is the "flip side" of the Poisson distribution. That is, if customer arrivals follow a Poisson distribution with arrival rate λ, the time between such arrivals, known as the *interarrival time*, follows an exponential distribution with average interarrival time $1/\lambda$. (Hence, the Poisson distribution also possesses the memoryless property.)

Note that the Poisson distribution describes the probability of a specific number of events, whereas the exponential distribution describes the time between such events. This interrelationship between the Poisson and exponential distributions allows us to obtain simple formulas for queuing performance measures when the customer arrival process is Poisson and the service time distribution is exponential. Table 12.1 summarizes the properties for arrivals and services in a Markovian queuing process in which the time units are hours.

TABLE 12.1 SUMMARY OF FORMULAS FOR A POISSON EXPONENTIAL PROCESSES

Arrivals		Services	
Arrival Rate = Average number of arrivals per hour	λ customers/hour	Service Rate = Average number of services[a] per hour	μ customers/hour
Probability of k arrivals in t hours	$\dfrac{(\lambda t)^k e^{-\lambda t}}{k!}$	Probability of k services[a] in t hours	$\dfrac{(\mu t)^k e^{-\mu t}}{k!}$
Average time between arrivals	$1/\lambda$ hours	Average service time	$1/\mu$ hours
Probability that an arrival will occur within t hours	$1 - e^{-\lambda t}$	Probability that service will be completed within t hours	$1 - e^{-\mu t}$
Probability that the next arrival will not occur within t hours	$e^{-\lambda t}$	Probability that service time will be greater than t hours	$e^{-\mu t}$

[a]This assumes that customers are there to be served. Thus, μ is actually the average number of *potential services per hour*.

In this chapter, we present "closed form" performance measure results for a number of systems, including those with arrival patterns that can be modeled by a Poisson process and exponential service times. Appendix 12.2 on the accompanying CD-ROM discusses how statistical goodness-of-fit tests can be used to determine whether or not these assumptions are reasonable.

[4]Named for A. A. Markov, a Russian mathematician who introduced this concept in 1907.

If an exponential distribution is not appropriate for modeling service times (due to the failure of the memoryless property), one alternative is the *Erlangian distribution*. Formulas for the probability density function and cumulative probability distribution, as well as the mean and standard deviation for the Erlangian distribution, are given in Appendix 12.3 on the accompanying CD-ROM.

12.3 MEASURES OF QUEUING SYSTEM PERFORMANCE

In a queuing model, performance can be measured by focusing on customers in the *queue* or customers in the entire *system* (the system includes both those in the queue and those being served). Which measure is more relevant is a function of the decision criterion.

To illustrate, suppose you are a supermarket customer who has a choice of two checkout lines. One has an extremely fast checker, who takes an average of two minutes to check out each customer, and you estimate that you will have to spend four minutes waiting in line before being served by this checker. The other has a slower checker who takes an average of three minutes to wait on each customer, but you estimate you will spend only three minutes waiting in line before service begins. In either case, you figure you will spend six minutes in the *system*, so does it make a difference which line you select?

The answer depends on how you feel about waiting in line, since you expect to wait four minutes in the first line but only three minutes in the second. You might welcome the additional time in the first line (perhaps to catch up with the latest sighting of Elvis in the *National Enquirer* or *Star*), or you might appreciate the extra service time of the second line (perhaps to hear the checker give the latest neighborhood gossip). To account for possible preferences, queuing system performance measures are expressed both in terms of the waiting line and the system.

TRANSIENT AND STEADY STATE PERIODS

One complicating factor in assessing queuing performance is that most queuing systems experience *start-up bias* at the beginning of the observation period. In this *transient period*, initial system behavior is not representative of long-run performance. This transient period can last minutes, hours, or even days (depending on the service operation).

Following this transient period, the system settles down to what is known as steady state. In *steady state*, the long-run probabilities of there being 0, 1, 2, 3, or, in general, n customers in the system remain constant over time. Steady state assumes that the queuing system operates over a theoretically infinite time horizon. While no real-life system operates forever, by concentrating on steady state results, we avoid start-up bias. In practice, most real-life queuing systems quickly approach steady state performance.

In order to achieve steady state, the effective arrival rate of customers must be less than the sum of the effective service rates of all servers.[5] This condition is stated for various queuing systems as follows:

---

[5]If there are k servers and the arrival rate λ exactly equals $\mu_1 + \mu_2 + \ldots + \mu_k$, this queue will not reach steady state. The combined service rate must be strictly greater than the arrival rate in order to achieve steady state.

Requirement to Achieve Steady State

System	Requirement
One server	$\lambda < \mu$
k servers, possibly with different service rates	$\lambda < \mu_1 + \mu_2 + \ldots + \mu_k$
k servers, each with service rate μ	$\lambda < k\mu$

If this condition is violated, the queue will ultimately become infinitely large and steady state will never be achieved. For example, suppose customers arrive at the rate of $\lambda = 20$ per hour and there are k = 3 servers, each serving an average of 4 customers per hour. On the average, only 3(4) = 12 customers can be served per hour; therefore, an average of 20 − 12 = 8 customers will be added to the waiting line each hour. Hence, steady state will never be reached as, over time, the waiting line will continue to lengthen.

In this chapter, we present steady state performance measures for queuing systems with one or more servers. For systems with more than one server, we restrict our attention to models in which all servers work at the same rate, μ. If this is not an appropriate assumption, simulation methods can be employed to approximate steady state queuing performance measures (see Chapter 13).

STEADY STATE PERFORMANCE MEASURES

The following steady state performance measures can be calculated directly for many queuing systems:

P_0 = Probability that there are no customers in the system

P_n = Probability that there are n customers in the system

L = Average number of customers in the system

L_q = Average number of customers in the queue

W = Average time a customer spends in the system

W_q = Average time a customer spends in the queue

P_w = Probability that an arriving customer must wait for service

ρ = Utilization rate of each server (the percentage of time that each server is busy)

LITTLE'S FORMULAS

Important relationships, known as **Little's Formulas**,[6] exist between the average number of customers in the system, L, and the average customer waiting time in the system, W, as well as between the average number of customers waiting for service, L_q, and the average time a customer spends waiting for service, W_q. These formulas state that if a queuing system has a single waiting line, customers arrive at some finite mean rate, λ, and the necessary condition for steady state exists, then the following relationships hold:

Little's Formulas

$$L = \lambda W$$
$$L_q = \lambda W_q$$

---

[6]Named for John D.C. Little, the first to rigorously prove the results in 1961.

For steady state models that involve a potentially infinite customer population, if all servers perform at the same rate, μ, then λ/μ represents the average number of customers being served. Hence, $L = L_q + \lambda/\mu$. Therefore, knowing one of the values for L, L_q, W, or W_q allows us to calculate the other three.

QUEUING SYSTEM NOTATION

Different assumptions about arrival and service processes and the number of servers give rise to different queuing system configurations. So that we can easily refer to a particular queuing situation, we use the following shorthand notation to identify the model:[7]

Classification of Queues
Arrival Process/Service Process/Number of Servers

Commonly used notations for the arrival and service distributions include:

M *Markovian*—For arrivals, customers arrive according to a Poisson process at a mean rate of λ or have an interarrival time that follows an exponential distribution with mean $1/\lambda$. For services, service times are exponential, with an average service time of $1/\mu$.

D *Deterministic*—For arrivals, customers arrive at a constant rate of λ. For service, service times are constant at $1/\mu$.

G *General*—For arrivals or departures, G signifies a general probability distribution for arrivals or services having a known mean and variance.

For example, a G/D/5 queue refers to a system in which the arrival process follows a general probability distribution, the service time is constant, and there are five servers.

Sometimes two additional designations are added to the notation to indicate situations in which there is a maximum limit for the number of customers in the system and/or a maximum number of customers in the population. Thus, an M/G/6/10/20 model refers to a queuing system for which the interarrival time of customers is exponential, the service time follows a general distribution, there are 6 servers, the maximum number of customers who can be in the system at any one time is 10, and the population of potential customers is 20. An M/G/6//20 model would refer to the same system but with no limit for the maximum number of customers who can be present.

12.4   M/M/1 QUEUING SYSTEMS

As stated earlier, the arrival process in many business situations follows a Poisson distribution. If, in addition, the service times can be appropriately modeled using the

---

[7]The notation used to identify queuing models was first proposed by D. G. Kendall in 1951 and has come to be called *Kendall's notation*.

exponential distribution and there is a single server, we have an **M/M/1 queuing system**. Examples of queues modeled as M/M/1 systems include some small banks, rural post offices, and convenience stores.

The following formulas give the steady state performance measures for the M/M/1 queuing system. Recall that the requirement for steady state to exist is $\lambda < \mu$, λ being the average arrival rate and μ the average service rate. These results are derived using a technique known as *balance equations* (see Appendix 12.4 on the accompanying CD-ROM).

Performance Measures for the M/M/1 Queue

$$P_0 = 1 - (\lambda/\mu)$$
$$P_n = (1 - (\lambda/\mu))\,(\lambda/\mu)^n$$
$$L = \lambda/(\mu - \lambda)$$
$$L_q = \lambda^2/(\mu(\mu - \lambda))$$
$$W = 1/(\mu - \lambda)$$
$$W_q = \lambda/(\mu(\mu - \lambda))$$
$$P_w = \lambda/\mu$$
$$\rho = \lambda/\mu$$

For the M/M/1 queue we can also show that the distribution of waiting time in the system follows an exponential distribution with mean $1/(\mu - \lambda)$. This implies that the probability that a customer will wait more than t hours is $e^{-(\mu-\lambda)t}$ and less than t hours, $1 - e^{-(\mu-\lambda)t}$.

To illustrate these formulas, consider the situation faced by Mary's Shoes.

Mary.qaa
Mary.xls

MARY'S SHOES

Customers arrive at Mary's Shoes on the average of once every 12 minutes, according to a Poisson process. The store is staffed by Dale Bandy who estimates that he can serve a customer in an average of eight minutes and that his service times follow an exponential distribution. Dale always finishes serving one customer before waiting on the next one.

Mary's management has received an anonymous letter of complaint regarding service at the store and is interested in determining the performance measures for this system.

SOLUTION

Based on the data provided, the average arrival rate is $\lambda = 1/12$ per minute, or $60/12 = 5$ per hour. Since it takes Dale an average of eight minutes to serve a customer, he can serve an average $\mu = 1/8$ per minute, or $60/8 = 7.5$ customers per hour. Substituting these values into the steady state formulas for the M/M/1 queue yields the following performance measures:

$$P_0 = 1 - (\lambda/\mu) = 1 - 5/7.5 = 1 - .66667 = .33333$$
$$P_n = (1 - (\lambda/\mu))(\lambda/\mu)^n = (.33333)(.66667)^n$$
$$L = \lambda/(\mu - \lambda) = 5/(7.5 - 5) = 5/2.5 = 2$$
$$L_q = \lambda^2/(\mu(\mu - \lambda)) = 5^2/(7.5(7.5 - 5)) = 25/((7.5)(2.5)) = 1.33333$$
$$W = 1/(\mu - \lambda) = 1/(7.5 - 5) = 1/2.5 = .4 \text{ hour} = 24 \text{ minutes}$$
$$W_q = \lambda/(\mu(\mu - \lambda)) = 5/(7.5(7.5 - 5)) = 5/((7.5)(2.5)) = .26667 \text{ hour} = 16 \text{ minutes}$$
$$P_w = \lambda/\mu = 5/7.5 = .66667$$
$$\rho = \lambda/\mu = 5/7.5 = .66667$$

Note that the difference between W, the average time a customer spends in the store (24 minutes), and W_q, the average time a customer spends waiting before being served by Dale Bandy (16 minutes), is the average service time of 8 minutes. The difference between L, the average number of customers in the store (2), and L_q, the average number of customers waiting to be served by Dale Bandy (1.3333), is .66667. This is the average number of customers being served, ρ.

You may wonder why the difference between L and L_q is .66667, rather than 1. The reason is because one-third of the time (.33333) no customers are present and Dale is serving 0 customers, whereas two-thirds of the time (.66667) one or more customers are present and Dale is serving one customer. Thus, the weighted average number of customers being served is .33333(0) + .66667(1) = .66667. These observations give rise to the following relationships:

Relationship Between System and Queue Performance Measures

Average waiting time in system =
Average waiting time in queue + Average service time
$$W = W_q + 1/\mu$$
Average number of customers in system =
Average number of customers in queue + Average number of customers being served
$$L = L_q + \lambda/\mu$$

Customer waiting time in the system for Mary's Shoes follows an exponential distribution with an average rate of $(\mu - \lambda) = 7.5 - 5 = 2.5$ per hour. Hence, the probability that a customer will wait less than 10 minutes (10/60 hours) is $1 - e^{-2.5(10/60)} = 1 - e^{-.417} = .341$. The probability that a customer will wait less than 20 minutes (20/60 hours) is $1 - e^{2.5(20/60)} = 1 - e^{-.833} = .565$, and the probability that a customer will wait less than 30 minutes (30/60 hours) is $1 - e^{-2.5(30/60)} = 1 - e^{-1.25} = .713$.

If Dale's average service time could be reduced to 6 minutes and 40 seconds, μ would be 9 per hour. Hence, the distribution of customer waiting time in the system would now be exponential with an average rate $(\mu - \lambda) = 9 - 5 = 4$. In this case, the probability that a customer will wait less than 10 minutes (10/60 hours) is $1 - e^{-4(10/60)} = 1 - e^{-.667} = .487$; less than 20 minutes (20/60 hours) is $1 - e^{-4(20/60)} = 1 - e^{-1.333} = .736$; and less than 30 minutes (30/60 hours) is $1 - e^{-4(30/60)} = 1 - e^{-2} = .865$.

While we could write formulas for performance measures into cells of a spreadsheet package, the queuing module in WINQSB can be used to quickly generate performance measures for most elementary queuing systems. Figures 12.5a and 12.5b show the WINQSB output for an M/M/1 queue with $\lambda = 5$ and $\mu = 9$.

On the basis of this information, the following business report was prepared for Mary Hanes, president of Mary's Shoes. The memo focuses on current performance

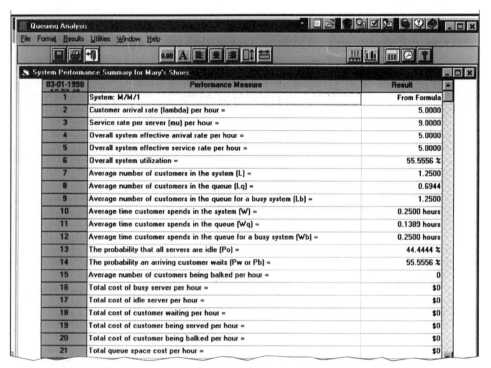

03-01-1998	Performance Measure	Result
1	System: M/M/1	From Formula
2	Customer arrival rate (lambda) per hour =	5.0000
3	Service rate per server (mu) per hour =	9.0000
4	Overall system effective arrival rate per hour =	5.0000
5	Overall system effective service rate per hour =	5.0000
6	Overall system utilization =	55.5556 %
7	Average number of customers in the system (L) =	1.2500
8	Average number of customers in the queue (Lq) =	0.6944
9	Average number of customers in the queue for a busy system (Lb) =	1.2500
10	Average time customer spends in the system (W) =	0.2500 hours
11	Average time customer spends in the queue (Wq) =	0.1389 hours
12	Average time customer spends in the queue for a busy system (Wb) =	0.2500 hours
13	The probability that all servers are idle (Po) =	44.4444 %
14	The probability an arriving customer waits (Pw or Pb) =	55.5556 %
15	Average number of customers being balked per hour =	0
16	Total cost of busy server per hour =	$0
17	Total cost of idle server per hour =	$0
18	Total cost of customer waiting per hour =	$0
19	Total cost of customer being served per hour =	$0
20	Total cost of customer being balked per hour =	$0
21	Total queue space cost per hour =	$0

FIGURE 12.5a   WINQSB Output: Performance Measures for Gary's Shoes

03-01-1998 12:30:21 n	Probability of n Customers in the System (P(n))	Cumulative Probability
0	0.4444	0.4444
1	0.2469	0.6914
2	0.1372	0.8285
3	0.0762	0.9047
4	0.0423	0.9471
5	0.0235	0.9706
6	0.0131	0.9837
7	0.0073	0.9909
8	0.0040	0.9950
9	0.0022	0.9972
10	0.0012	0.9984
11	0.0007	0.9991
12	0.0004	0.9995
13	0.0002	0.9997
14	0.0001	0.9999
15	0.0001	0.9999
16	0.0000	1.0000
17	0.0000	1.0000
18	0.0000	1.0000
19	0.0000	1.0000
20	0.0000	

FIGURE 12.5b   WINQSB Output: Steady State Probabilities for Gary's Shoes

measures. A graphical breakdown showing customer waiting time as a percentage of total customers clearly indicates that a large proportion of customers are spending too much time in the store under the present systems. The report also analyzes the impact of increases in the arrival rate and suggests improvements to service.

M E M O R A N D U M

To: Mary Hanes, President
Mary's Shoes

From: Student Consulting Group

Subj: Operations at the New Market Mall Store

At your request, we have conducted an analysis of operations at your New Market Mall store to determine whether company performance measures are being met. While, at one time, the store had sales volume to support a staff of three shoe salespersons, since the recent construction of a nearby mall, sales have declined dramatically. Currently, only one shoe salesperson is employed at the store, Mr. Dale Bandy. Two issues in particular seem to be of concern:

1. Many customers are encountering a long wait before service begins. This may exacerbate the sales decline that has been prevalent since the competing mall opened.

2. Mr. Bandy appears to be idle for excessive periods of time.

To evaluate these potential problems, we have conducted a queuing analysis. We collected data on customer arrival times and Mr. Bandy's service times over 40 days. A study of these arrival and service patterns indicates that the average time between customer arrivals is approximately 12 minutes and that Mr. Bandy spends an average of about 8 minutes with each customer.

Statistical analyses of the data indicate that distributions based on the following assumptions closely approximate the observed data: (1) no two arrivals or departures occur simultaneously; (2) the arrival and service patterns do not vary significantly throughout the day; (3) the arrival of a customer has no effect on the time to the next customer arrival; and (4) the remaining time for Mr. Bandy to complete a service is not affected by the amount of time he has already spent with the customer. Although this last assumption may appear counterintuitive, the statistical analysis verifies that the observed service times mirror those generated by such an assumption.

GENERAL CONCLUSIONS

Based on these data, we developed a queuing model for operations at your New Market Mall store and derived the following estimates of its current operation.

Waiting Time   The average customer waiting time is 16 minutes. With an average service time of 8 minutes, a customer spends an average total of 24 minutes in the store. Figure I shows customer waiting time as a percentage of total cus-

FIGURE I   Customer Waiting Time Assuming an Average Service Time of 8 Minutes tomers. As you can see, 43% of customers spend longer than 20 minutes in the store; 29% spend over 30 minutes, and 8% spend more than an hour.

Dale Bandy's Idle Time   The model indicates that Dale Bandy averages 20 minutes of idle time per hour. Furthermore, if Mr. Bandy's average service time does not change, any decrease in his idle time would result in a simultaneous increase in the average time a customer waits for service. For example, if store traffic increases by 20%, although Mr. Bandy's idle time will decrease from 20 minutes to 12 minutes per hour, the average customer waiting time will double from 16 to 32 minutes.

RECOMMENDATIONS

To improve customer satisfaction, Mr. Bandy's service time must decrease. While conducting the study, we observed that much of Mr. Bandy's service time is spent trying to locate the right size shoes from the store's inventory. We believe that a reorganization of the shoe inventory can reduce Mr. Bandy's average service time by one-sixth, from 8 minutes to about 6 minutes 40 seconds.

   Table I summarizes the effect of such a reorganization on various factors that may be of concern to you. As you can see, performance will greatly improve under this plan. Also, Mr. Bandy's idle time should increase from about 20 to $26\frac{2}{3}$ minutes per hour, and hence, we do not expect him to voice any opposition to implementing this policy.

TABLE I   Impact on Performance of Proposed Inventory Reorganization

	Current Operations	Operations After Inventory Reorganization
Average service time	8 minutes	$6\frac{2}{3}$ minutes
Average customer time in store	24 minutes	15 minutes
Average time waiting for service	16 minutes	$8\frac{1}{3}$ minutes
Average number of customers in store	2	1.25
Average number of customers waiting for service	1.53	.69
Average time Mr. Bandy will be idle/hour	20 minutes	$26\frac{2}{3}$ minutes

Figure II shows the revised percentages for customer time in the store for the inventory reorganization plan. In this case, fewer than 15% of the customers

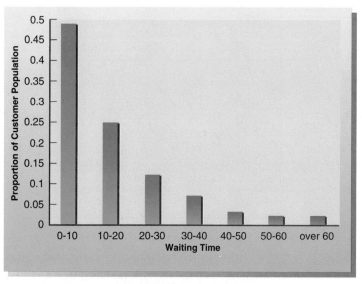

FIGURE II   Customer Waiting Time Assuming an Average Service Time of $6\frac{2}{3}$ Minutes

will spend more than 30 minutes in the store, and the percentage of customers spending longer than an hour in the store will decrease to about 2%.

Based on the preceding projections, we recommend that you consider such an inventory reorganization. If performance still does not meet your expectations, we regretfully suggest that you consider replacing Mr. Bandy.

12.5   M/M/K QUEUING SYSTEMS

An **M/M/k queuing system** assumes

1. Customers arrive according to a Poisson process at mean rate λ.

2. Service times follow an exponential distribution.

3. Each of the k servers works at an average rate μ (with $k\mu > \lambda$).

Typical examples of M/M/k queuing systems include banks with several tellers, post offices with several service windows, and fast-food restaurants with several cashiers.

 Appendix 12.5 on the accompanying CD-ROM contains a derivation of the performance measure formulas for the M/M/k queuing system found using the balance equation approach. The appropriate formulas are as follows:

Performance Measures for an M/M/k Queuing System

$$P_0 = \frac{1}{\left[\sum_{n=0}^{k-1} \frac{1}{n!} \left(\frac{\lambda}{\mu}\right)^n\right] + \frac{1}{k!}\left(\frac{\lambda}{\mu}\right)^k \left(\frac{k\mu}{k\mu - \lambda}\right)}$$

$$P_n = \frac{(\lambda/\mu)^n}{n!} P_0 \quad \text{for } n \le k$$

$$P_n = \frac{(\lambda/\mu)^n}{k! k^{(n-k)}} P_0 \quad \text{for } n > k$$

$$L = \frac{(\lambda/\mu)^k \lambda\mu}{(k-1)! \, (k\mu - \lambda)^2} P_0 + \frac{\lambda}{\mu}$$

$$W = \frac{(\lambda/\mu)^k \mu}{(k-1)! \, (k\mu - \lambda)^2} P_0 + \frac{1}{\mu}$$

$$L_q = \frac{(\lambda/\mu)^k \lambda\mu}{(k-1)! \, (k\mu - \lambda)^2} P_0$$

$$W_q = \frac{(\lambda/\mu)^k \mu}{(k-1)! \, (k\mu - \lambda)^2} P_0$$

$$P_w = \frac{1}{k!}\left(\frac{\lambda}{\mu}\right)^k \left(\frac{k\mu}{k\mu - \lambda}\right) P_0$$

$$\rho = \frac{\lambda}{k\mu}$$

Although these formulas are more intimidating than those for an M/M/1 queuing system, their values can be easily obtained from many management science software packages (including WINQSB) or calculated using a spreadsheet package such as Excel.

To illustrate the use of an M/M/k queuing system, let us consider Saturday operations at the Littletown Post Office.

LITTLETOWN POST OFFICE

Little.qaa
Little.xls

The Littletown Post Office is open on Saturdays from 9:00 A.M. to 1:00 P.M. On the average, 100 customers per hour visit the post office during this period. Three postal clerks are on duty, and the mean time to serve each customer is 1.5 minutes. Previous studies have shown that a Poisson arrival distribution and an exponential service time distribution provide relatively good approximations of the post office's arrival and service operations.

The Littletown Postmaster has received a number of complaints concerning the length of time required for customers to receive service on Saturdays. In addition, the three postal clerks have filed a grievance alleging excessive workloads during this period. The Postmaster is interested in determining the relevant service measures for the post office on Saturdays in order to respond to these issues. There has also been talk about the need for a budget cut, and the Postmaster would like to know whether reducing the number of clerks on Saturday morning duty to two is feasible.

SOLUTION

The Littletown Post Office is an M/M/3 queuing system with $\lambda = 100$ customers per hour and an average hourly service rate, μ, equal to $60/1.5 = 40$ customers per hour. Since $\lambda < k\mu$ ($100 < 3(40) = 120$), we can use the steady state formulas for an M/M/3 model:

$$
P_0 = \frac{1}{\left[\sum_{n=0}^{k-1} \frac{1}{n!}\left(\frac{\lambda}{\mu}\right)^n\right] + \frac{1}{k!}\left(\frac{\lambda}{\mu}\right)^k \left(\frac{k\mu}{k\mu - \lambda}\right)}
$$

$$
= \frac{1}{\left[\sum_{n=0}^{2} \frac{1}{n!}\left(\frac{100}{40}\right)^n\right] + \frac{1}{3!}\left(\frac{100}{40}\right)^3 \left(\frac{3(40)}{3(40) - 100}\right)}
$$

$$
= \frac{1}{\left[\sum_{n=0}^{2} \frac{1}{n!}(2.5)^n\right] + \frac{1}{6}(15.625)\left(\frac{120}{20}\right)}
$$

$$
= \frac{1}{\left[1 + 2.5 + \frac{6.25}{2} + 15.625\right]} = \frac{1}{22.25} = .045
$$

Either Excel or WINQSB can be used to calculate the probability of having any number of customers present in the system. For up to 10-customers, these data are as follows:

$P_0 = .045 \quad P_1 = .112 \quad P_2 = .140 \quad P_3 = .117 \quad P_4 = .098 \quad P_5 = .081$

$P_6 = .068 \quad P_7 = .056 \quad P_8 = .047 \quad P_9 = .039 \quad P_{10} = .033$

For example, if the Postmaster wants to know the probability that *exactly two* people are waiting in line to be served, the solution will be equivalent to the probability of five people in the system (since three people are being served while two are waiting in line), $P_5 = .081$. If the Postmaster wants to determine the probability that *three or fewer* people are waiting in line, we will need to calculate the probability that six or fewer people are in the system: $P_0 + P_1 + P_2 + P_3 + P_4 + P_5 + P_6 = .045 + .112 + .140 + .117 + .098 + .081 + .068 = .661$.

Using Excel or a queuing model such as that contained in WINQSB to evaluate the performance measures, the Postmaster will see that the average time a customer spends at the post office is 3.6 minutes (W = .06 hour) and that approximately 70% of the time (P_W =.702) an arriving customer will have to wait in line before he can begin being served. Evaluating the other performance measure formulas yields the following additional information.

1. The average number of customers present in the post office is L = 6.01.
2. The average number of customers present in the waiting line is L_q = 3.51.
3. A customer spends an average W_q = 2.1 minutes waiting in line.

With regard to the workload grievance, the analysis indicates that each postal clerk is serving customers only 83.33% of the time (ρ = .8333), or about 50 minutes out of each hour. In addition, approximately 4.5% of the time all three clerks are idle (P_0 = .044944); approximately 11.2% of the time two of the clerks are idle (P_1 = .112); and approximately 14.0% of the time one of the clerks is idle (P_2 = .140). After discussing the grievance with representatives from the Postal Union, the postal clerks agreed that their workload was reasonable and the grievance was withdrawn.

In terms of the budget cutting issue, we note that reducing the number of postal clerks on Saturday mornings to two would result in $\lambda > k\mu$ (100 > 2(40)). Hence, the queue would not achieve steady state, and the two remaining postal clerks would eventually never have a spare moment. Thus, the Postmaster should consider cost savings measures other than laying off a clerk.

12.6   M/G/1 QUEUING SYSTEMS

Although the assumption of a Poisson arrival process is appropriate for a large number of studies, frequently, the exponential distribution does not adequately model the service time. When there is a single server, although P_0 = 1 − λ/μ and ρ = λ/μ, we cannot use the results based on balance equations to analyze formulas for the P_n values. Instead, a different approach based on Markov Chains (see Chapter 15 on the accompanying CD-ROM) gives rise to the following expression, known as the *Pollaczek-Khintchine formula*, for L:

$$L = \frac{(\lambda\sigma)^2 + (\lambda/\mu)^2}{2\,(1 - \lambda/\mu)} + \frac{\lambda}{\mu}$$

Here, λ is the mean arrival rate, $1/\mu$ is the mean service time, and σ is the standard deviation of the service time expressed in the same units as the service time. For an **M/G/1 queue**, only the mean and standard deviation for the service time need to be known to calculate the performance measures; it is not necessary to identify the particular service time distribution.

L_q can still be calculated by L_q = L − λ/μ, and, using Little's formulas, we can determine W = L/λ and W_q = L_q/λ. The formulas for the performance measures for the M/G/1 queue are given in Table 12.12 at the conclusion of the chapter. As we stated above we cannot obtain formulas for the P_n values for this model.

In comparing the formula for L in an M/G/1 queuing system to the formula for L in an M/M/1 queuing system, we see that the value for L is larger for an M/G/1 system if $\sigma > 1/\mu$. (Recall that $1/\mu$ is the standard deviation for an exponential service time distribution.) If $\sigma = 1/\mu$, however, the performance measure formulas for the M/G/1 system are identical to those derived for the M/M/1 system.

Two special cases of M/G/1 queues occur when the service time is (1) deterministic (M/D/1) and (2) Erlangian (M/E_n/1). In an M/D/1 *system*, customers are served at a constant (deterministic) rate. This system is equivalent to an M/G/1 system with σ = 0.

Substituting $\sigma = 0$ into the M/G/1 steady state formulas yields the performance measure formulas listed in Table 12.12. Examples of M/D/1 queuing systems include vending machines and automated information systems that have constant service times.

When customer service is made up of several independent tasks, service time can often be modeled using an *Erlangian distribution*. An Erlangian random variable is made up of the sum of n independent exponentially distributed random variables, each with a mean equal to $1/n\mu$. Thus, an $M/E_n/1$ system is equivalent to an M/G/1 system, having a mean service time $1/\mu$ and service time standard deviation equal to $1/\mu\sqrt{n}$. Performance measure formulas for the $M/E_n/1$ system are listed in Table 12.12. Examples of businesses for which service is frequently modeled using an Erlangian distribution include retail establishments such as grocery stores, service stations, and restaurants. To illustrate the use of an M/G/1 queuing system, let us consider the situation faced by Ted's TV Repair Shop.

Teds.qaa
Tedsa.qaa
Teds.xls
Tedsa.xls

TED'S TV REPAIR SHOP

Ted's TV Repair is a sole proprietorship that repairs television sets and VCRs. Ted currently takes an average of 2.25 hours to repair a set, with a standard deviation of 45 minutes. Customers arrive at the shop according to a Poisson process on the average of once every 2.5 hours.

Ted works nine hours a day and has no other employees. He is considering purchasing a new piece of testing equipment he believes will reduce the average time required to repair a set to two hours, with a standard deviation of 40 minutes.

Ted wants to know how using this equipment will affect the average number of sets in the shop needing repair work, as well as the average length of time a customer will have to wait to have a set repaired.

SOLUTION

Since service times do not exhibit the memoryless property of an exponential distribution, we will use an M/G/1 queuing model to calculate the service measures. Currently, for Ted's TV Repair, $\lambda = 1/2.5 = .4$ per hour, and $\mu = 1/2.25 = .444444$ per hour. The standard deviation of the service time, σ, is 45 minutes, or .75 hours. If Ted invests in the new testing equipment, μ will be $1/2 = .5$ per hour, and σ will be $40/60 = .666667$ hours.

Using WINQSB, we can derive the performance measures for both the current and the new testing equipment. These are summarized in Table 12.2. As you can see, currently the average time a customer has a set in the repair shop is 13.5 hours, or 1.5 working days, and, while an average of 5.4 sets are in the shop needing repair, 10% of the time Ted will have no sets to work on.

TABLE 12.2   PERFORMANCE MEASURES FOR TED'S TV REPAIR SHOP

Performance Measure	Current Testing Equipment	New Testing Equipment
Overall system effective utilization factor (ρ)	0.9	0.8
Average number of customers in the system (L)	5.40	2.58
Average number of customers in the queue (Lq)	4.50	1.78
Average time (in hours) a customer is in the system (W)	13.50	6.44
Average time (in hours) a customer is in the queue (Wq)	11.25	4.44
The probability that all servers are idle (Po)	0.1	0.2
The probability an arriving customer waits (Pw)	0.9	0.8

The new testing equipment will reduce the average number of sets in the shop to 2.58. It will also reduce the average time required to repair a customer's set by more than 50%, to 6.44 hours, resulting in greater customer satisfaction and potentially more business. At the same, time the probability that Ted will not have any sets in his shop to work on doubles to 20%. This may be desirable if Ted has other activities. If he does not, the increased probability that he is idle may be highly undesirable. Ted should consider this information, together with the cost of the testing equipment, before making his purchase decision.

12.7   M/M/к/F QUEUING SYSTEMS (FINITE QUEUE LENGTH)

Almost all queuing systems have design or physical characteristics that limit their size. For example, the fire code may limit a fast-food restaurant to a maximum of 150 people at any one time. A telephone switchboard that has three incoming lines will only be able to handle a maximum of three customer calls at any one time.

Often as in the case of the fast-food restaurant that can hold 150 people the potential queue size is large enough so that models assuming an infinite queue length give accurate performance measures. When the number of customers who can be accommodated in the system is small, however (like the telephone switchboard with three lines), such models do not give accurate results. In addition to telephone switchboards, finite queuing models are also appropriate in retail establishments that have a limited capacity for customers, such as drive-thru windows at fast-food restaurants and hospital emergency rooms. In such cases, the limitation on the potential number of customers who can be present in the system at any given time must be explicitly accounted for in the model.

An **M/M/k/F model** assumes a Poisson arrival process at mean rate λ, k servers, each having an exponential service time distribution with mean rate μ; and an upper limit of F customers who can be present *in the system* at any one time. Customers attempting to enter when F people are already present (when the system is full) are denied entry, or *blocked*. The model assumes that blocked customers will leave the system forever.[8]

The implication of blocking arriving customers is that, although an average of λ customers per hour may *attempt to join* the system, some will be turned away. Hence, only a fraction of these λ potential arrivals make it through to the system. This *effective arrival rate* is denoted by λ_e. It is λ_e that must be used in Little's formulas for the M/M/k/F case.

Arriving customers are blocked only if F customers are already in the system. Since the probability of F customers in the system is P_F, the following relationship exists between λ_e and λ:

Effective Arrival Rate for Finite Queues

$$\lambda_e = \lambda (1 - P_F)$$

For finite queues with Markovian arrival and service processes, balance equations can be used to determine formulas for the steady state performance measures. Because

[8]In reality, some customers will probably try to reenter the system at a later time. This can be accounted for in the model by increasing the arrival rate of customers by the proportion estimated to return after being blocked.

the queue is finite, the restriction that $\lambda < k\mu$ does not have to hold in order to achieve steady state results. Appendix 12.6 on the accompanying CD-ROM contains a network representation of this queuing system.

Table 12.12 at the conclusion of the chapter gives performance measure formulas for the M/M/k/F system. When there are multiple servers, the performance measure formulas are quite complex. Fortunately, computer software packages such as WINQSB can be used or spreadsheet packages such as Excel can be programmed to calculate these values for the general model.

In two special cases, however, the formulas are reasonably easy to evaluate: (1) when there is a single server (an M/M/1/F queuing system), and (2) when the maximum number of customers permitted in the system equals the number of servers (an M/M/k/k queuing system). Interestingly, the performance measure formulas for the M/M/k/k queuing system are identical to those for the M/G/k/k queuing system. Performance measure formulas for the M/M/1/F and M/G/k/k queuing systems are also given in Table 12.12. Birthing stations in a hospital maternity ward is one example of a situation that can be modeled by an M/G/k/k system. An example of an M/M/1/F system is that faced by the by Ryan Roofing Company.

RYAN ROOFING COMPANY

Ryan.qaa

Ryan Roofing Company is a full-service residential roofer. Although some of its business comes from referrals, the vast majority of business is derived from customers who see Ryan's advertisement in the Yellow Pages. The roofing business is quite competitive, and most customers who need a roofer need one as soon as possible. Hence, management believes that if a customer calls Ryan and gets a busy signal, the customer will select another firm.

Ryan has three telephone lines and one appointments secretary who answers the phone. Because the appointments secretary must get all the relevant details on the potential job, the average length of each phone call is three minutes.

Ryan estimates that an average of 10 customers per hour call the company. The phone system has a music-on-hold feature, and if a customer calls while the appointments secretary is busy with another call, it is assumed that the customer will hold until the appointments secretary becomes available. It is further believed that the arrival process follows a Poisson distribution and that service time follows an exponential distribution.

Ryan's management is concerned that it may be losing too much potential business as a result of customers getting a busy signal. It would like to design a system that has the fewest lines necessary so that, at most, 2% of all callers will get a busy signal. In selecting this system, management would like to know the percentage of time the appointments secretary is speaking to customers, the average number of customers who are on hold, the average time a customer spends on hold, and the actual percentage of callers who encounter a busy signal.

SOLUTION

Based on these data, this queuing system can be modeled as an M/M/1/3 system with $\lambda = 10$ per hour and $\mu = 1/3$ per minute $= 60/3 = 20$ per hour. WINQSB gives the following probabilities for this M/M/1/3 queuing system:

$$P_0 = .533 \quad P_1 = .267 \quad P_2 = .133 \quad P_3 = .067$$

As you can see, with three telephone lines, 6.7% of the time three customers are in the system and any additional customers calling Ryan Roofing will encounter a busy signal. Because this probability is greater than the stated goal of 2%, Ryan should consider increasing the number of telephone lines to four. The following are the probabilities for such an M/M/1/4 queuing system:

$$P_0 = .516 \quad P_1 = .258 \quad P_2 = .129 \quad P_3 = .065 \quad P_4 = .032$$

For this system there is still a 3.2% chance (P(4)) that a customer will get a busy signal. Increasing the number of telephone lines to five yields the following probabilities:

$$P_0 = .508 \quad P_1 = .254 \quad P_2 = .127$$
$$P_3 = .063 \quad P_4 = .032 \quad P_5 = .016$$

In this case, the stated service goal is met, since only 1.6% of customers will encounter a busy signal. Thus, a minimum of five lines should be used.

The performance measures for a system with five lines are as follows:

Overall system effective utilization factor (ρ) = 0.492
Average number of customers in the system (L) = 0.905
Average number of customers in the queue (L_q) = 0.413
Average time a customer is in the system (W) = 0.092 hour
Average time a customer is in the queue (W_q) = 0.042 hour
The probability that all servers are idle (P_o) = 0.508
The probability that an arriving customer will wait (P_w) = 0.492

From these data, we see that, with five telephone lines:

1. The appointments secretary is on the telephone 49.2% of the time.
2. The average number of customers on hold is .413.
3. The average time a customer spends on hold is .042 hour, or 2.52 minutes.

12.8 M/M/1//M QUEUING SYSTEMS (FINITE CUSTOMER POPULATION)

All the models we have discussed thus far have assumed that the number of potential customers is large enough that the queuing system can be modeled assuming an infinite customer population. If there is a small number of potential customers, however, the number of customers present in the system will affect the rate at which new customers arrive. This situation is frequently referred to as the *machine repair problem*.

In an **M/M/1//m system**, we assume that there is a single server; that the service time for each customer follows an exponential distribution with mean $1/\mu$; and that there are m potential customers. If n of the m customers are already in the system, the interarrival time of the next customer follows an exponential distribution with mean $1/((m-n)\lambda)$.

 Appendix 12.7 on the accompanying CD-ROM shows the queuing network used to determine the balance equations for finding P_n, L, and L_q. The values for W and W_q are calculated with Little's formulas using the effective arrival rate of $\lambda_e = \lambda(m - L)$, L being the average number of customers in the system. Table 12.12 gives these performance measure formulas.

To illustrate a finite population system, let us consider the problem faced by Keith Cooke, vice president for construction at Pacesetter Homes.

PACESETTER HOMES

Pace.qaa
Pacea.qaa
Pace.xls
Pacea.xls

Pacesetter Homes is developing four housing tracts in the greater Las Vegas area. While each tract has a construction supervisor situated on site, company policy dictates that any work stoppages arising from labor disputes, governmental regulations, or problems with suppliers must be handled personally by the firm's vice president for construction, Keith Cooke.

Keith believes that each of the four projects will average one work stoppage every 20 working days and that it will take him an average of 16 hours (two days) to solve each problem (including the travel time between sites). The time between work stoppages occurring at a particular construction site as well as the time required to handle such a stoppage are expected to follow exponential distributions. Keith handles work stoppages one at a time, and work remains halted until he can personally resolve the problem.

Keith would like the company to purchase him a new Jaguar automobile to drive among the job sites. He claims that having this car will enable him to travel faster, reducing the average time to handle a dispute to 15 hours (1.875 days). The company president feels that a new car is worthwhile only if it reduces the average time a job site is shut down by at least two hours. Keith would like to determine if this is the case.

SOLUTION

Since the number of potential customers (the housing tracts) is only 4, this problem can be modeled as an M/M/1//4 queue. Because the mean time between work stoppages is 20 days, $\lambda = 1/20 = .05$ per day. Assuming Keith uses his current car, it takes him an average of two days to solve each problem. Thus his mean service rate, μ is $1/2 = .5$ per day. If the company purchases the Jaguar for Keith, the value of μ increases to $1/1.875 = .533$. The performance measures for both cases, generated using WINQSB, are given in Table 12.3.

TABLE 12.3   PERFORMANCE MEASURES FOR PACESETTER HOMES

Performance Measure	Using Current Car	Using New Car
Overall system effective utilization factor (ρ)	0.353	0.334
Average number of customers in the system (L)	0.467	0.435
Average number of customers in the queue (Lq)	0.113	0.100
Average number of days a customer is in the system (W)	2.641	2.437
Average number of days a customer is in the queue (Wq)	0.641	0.562
The probability that all servers are idle (Po)	0.647	0.666
The probability that an arriving customer will wait (Pw)	0.353	0.334

Giving Keith a new Jaguar will reduce the average time a job is stopped from 2.64 days to 2.44 days, a savings of .2 days or only 1.6 hours. Because the company president feels that this savings is not sufficient to justify the purchase of the new car, Keith must continue traveling between job sites using his existing vehicle.

12.9 ECONOMIC ANALYSIS OF QUEUING SYSTEMS

Throughout this chapter, we have developed performance measure formulas for a number of different queuing models and have obtained results for specific cases using either WINQSB or Excel. In this section, we present two analyses that illustrate the use of such performance measures to determine a minimal cost queuing system.

Let us first see how we can use queuing models to determine an optimal staffing level for the Wilson Foods Talking Turkey Hot Line.

WILSON FOODS TALKING TURKEY HOT LINE

Wils.qaa
Wils.xls

Wilson Foods has an 800 phone number consumers can call if they have questions about cooking a Wilson *Butterbaster* turkey. With the exception of busy holiday periods, such as Thanksgiving and Christmas, an estimated 225 customers per hour call the number. The average phone call is estimated to last 1.5 minutes.

Wilson has arranged sufficient phone lines with the telephone company so that if all customer service representatives are busy, a recorded message asks the caller to stay on the line until the next representative becomes available. Wilson believes that, as long as the average waiting time to speak to a representative is under three minutes, nearly all callers will stay on the line.

Wilson pays its customer service representatives $16 per hour in wages and benefits. The phone company charges Wilson $.18 for each minute a customer is either on hold or speaking to a customer service representative. Based on focus group studies, Wilson has concluded that there is a customer goodwill cost of approximately $.20 for each minute a caller is on hold. While a caller is speaking to a customer service representative, the goodwill cost drops to $.05 per minute.

Wilson would like to determine the number of customer service representatives it should use to minimize the hourly cost of operating the 800 phone line during non-holiday periods.

SOLUTION

In order to solve this problem, we need a model for total hourly costs. We will use the following notation:

k = number of customer service representatives
c_w = hourly compensation paid to each customer service representative
c_t = hourly telephone charge for each customer using the 800 line
g_w = goodwill cost per hour for a customer while waiting on hold
g_s = goodwill cost per hour for a customer while speaking to a customer service representative
$TC(k)$ = total average hourly cost of employing k customer service representatives

The average hourly cost consists of three basic components: wages, telephone charges, and goodwill costs. Thus,

$$TC(k) = (\text{wages of employees}) + (\text{telephone charges}) + (\text{goodwill costs})$$

We now analyze each of these hourly costs.

Wages

If there are k employees, and each employee earns c_w per hour, then:

$$(\text{Total hourly wages}) = C_w k$$

Telephone Charges

The average number of customers on hold and being served is the average number of customers in the queuing system, L. Since the cost per hour for a single customer using this line is c_t, then the total average hourly telephone charge is $c_t L$.

$$(\text{Total average hourly telephone charge}) = C_t L$$

Goodwill Charges

There are two different goodwill charges in this scenario, depending on whether the caller is on hold or speaking to a customer service representative. Since the goodwill cost per hour for a customer on hold is g_w and the average number of customers on hold is L_q, the average hourly goodwill cost for customers on hold is $g_w L_q$.

Because L equals the average number of customers in the system and L_q is the average number of customers waiting on hold, the average number of customers speaking to customer service representatives must be $L - L_q$. Since the goodwill cost per hour for each of these customers is g_s, the average hourly goodwill cost of customers speaking to customer service representatives is $g_s(L - L_q)$. Thus, the total average customer goodwill cost per hour is $g_w L_q + g_s(L - L_q)$.

$$(\text{Total average customer good will cost per hour}) = g_w L_q + g_s (L - L_q)$$

Total Average
Cost Per Hour

Summing the three cost categories gives us the following equation for the total average hourly cost:[9]

$$TC(k) = c_w k + c_t L + g_w L_q + g_s(L - L_q) = c_w k + (c_t + g_s)L + (g_w - g_s)L_q$$

For the Wilson Talking Turkey Hot Line, $c_w = \$16$, $c_t = \$.18 * 60 = \$10.80$, $g_w = \$.20 * 60 = \$12.00$, and $g_s = \$.05 * 60 = \$3.00$. The total average hourly cost is:

$$TC(k) = 16k + (10.8 + 3)L + (12 - 3)L_q = 16k + 13.8L + 9L_q$$

Assuming that callers to the 800 number follow a Poisson arrival process and that service times follow an exponential distribution, the system can be modeled as an M/M/k queuing system. Based on the information provided, $\lambda = 225$ per hour and $\mu = 60/1.5 = 40$ per hour. Since steady state is achieved only if $\lambda < k\mu$, the smallest value of k for which this condition holds is k = 6.

WINQSB was used to generate the results for k = 6, 7, 8, 9 and 10 shown in Table 12.4. The values for TC(k) were calculated using the formula derived above. According to this chart, Wilson should employ eight customer service representatives in order to minimize total average hourly costs.[10] With eight representatives the average time a caller will spend on hold is .0029 hours, or 10.4 seconds.

TABLE 12.4   SERVICE MEASURES AND COSTS FOR WILSON FOODS BASED ON NUMBER OF CUSTOMER SERVICE REPRESENTATIVES

k	L	L_Q	W_Q	TC(k)
6	18.1249	12.5000	.05556	$458.62
7	7.6437	2.0187	.00897	$235.62
8	6.2777	.6527	.00290	$220.50
9	5.8661	.2411	.00107	$227.12
10	5.7166	.0916	.00041	$239.71

We now consider a different queuing model for determining the optimal number of servers.

---

[9]Note that if $c_t = 0$, since $L - L_q = \lambda/\mu$, the total cost equation can be simplified as: $TC(k) = c_w k + g_w L_q + g_s (\lambda/\mu)$. Alternatively, if the goodwill cost for waiting in line is the same as the goodwill cost of being served ($g_w = g_s = g$), the expression becomes $TC(k) = c_w k + (c_t + g)L$.

[10]Once total average costs begin increasing, they will continue to increase.

HARGROVE HOSPITAL MATERNITY WARD

Hargrove Hospital is experiencing cutbacks in funding and revenues. One suggestion for saving money is to eliminate one of its two birthing stations. The hospital estimates that this cut will save $25,000 per year in direct expenses.

The hospital is also considering building additional birthing stations at an annual cost of $30,000 per station because when all birthing stations are occupied, women in labor are sent to one of the hospital's surgery rooms. The estimated cost per hour for the use of a surgery room for maternity purposes is $400 (due to the need to reschedule surgeries). Hence, the expense of additional birthing stations may be more than offset by the savings from a decreased use of the hospital's surgery rooms.

Studies have indicated that an average of six women a day go into labor at the hospital and that the average time spent in a birthing station is two hours. Women who need a birthing station arrive at the hospital according to a Poisson process. The hospital wishes to determine the number of birthing stations that will minimize its costs.

SOLUTION

Analysis of Current Situation

Initially, Hargrove Hospital needs to know the daily cost savings associated with cutting back the number of birthing stations from two to one. The current situation can be modeled as an M/G/2/2 queuing system. WINQSB generates the following performance measures:

Overall system effective utilization factor $(\rho) = 0.231$
Average number of customers in the system (L) = 0.462
Average time a customer in the system (W) = 0.083 day
The probability that all servers are idle $(P_o) = 0.615$
The probability that an arriving customer will wait $(P_w) = 0.077$

The probability that a woman will need to use a birthing station and will not find one available is .077. Hence, 7.7% of all women who arrive to use a birthing station will be sent to a surgery room instead. Since an average of six women per day need to use a birthing center, the expected number of women who will give birth in a surgery room is 6(.077) = .462 per day.

The average time each woman spends in a birthing station is two hours; hence, the average number of hours the surgery rooms will be used for delivery each day is 2(.462) = .924 hour. At a cost per hour of $400, the average daily cost is .924($400) = $369.60.

Analysis of Elimination of One Birthing Station

If the number of birthing stations is reduced to one, we have an M/G/1/1 queue with λ = 6 and μ = 12, resulting in a probability of .333 (from WINQSB) that a woman will need to use a surgery room to deliver. Hence, an average of 6(.333) = 2 women a day will deliver in a surgery room, and the average time spent there is 2(2) = 4 hours per day. The average daily cost of using the surgery rooms therefore increases to 4($400) = $1600.

While reducing the number of birthing stations by one results in a daily savings of $25,000/365 = $68.49, the expense associated with using the surgery rooms increases by $1600 − $369.60 = $1230.40. Thus, rather than saving money, this policy actually increases average daily costs by $1230.40 − $68.49 = $1161.91, and annual costs by $424,097!

Analysis of Adding One
Birthing Station

Let us now consider the option of adding birthing stations. If k stations are available, the average daily cost of women using a surgery room to give birth is $(P_k)(\lambda)(24/\mu)(c_h)$, where c_h is the hourly cost to use a surgery room.

For this problem, $\lambda = 6$, $\mu = 12$, and $c_h = \$400$. Hence, the average daily cost is 4800 P_k. In addition, we must account for the daily cost of the additional birthing stations, which amounts to $\$30,000/365 = \$82.19$ per station. Based on these data, Table 12.5 details the costs of having between one and four birthing stations. As you can see, the total average daily cost is minimized when the maternity ward has three birthing stations. As a result, in this case a surgery room would be used for approximately 1.3% of all births.

TABLE 12.5   HARGROVE HOSPITAL AVERAGE DAILY COST BASED ON NUMBER OF BIRTHING STATIONS

k	P_k	$4800 P_k	Additional Daily Cost of Stations	Total Net Average Daily Cost
1	.333	$1,600	$(68.49)	$1,531.51
2	.077	$ 369.60	$ 0	$ 369.60
3	.013	$ 62.40	$ 82.19	$ 144.59
4	.002	$ 9.60	$164.38	$ 173.98

12.10   TANDEM QUEUING SYSTEMS

Thus far, we have only considered queuing models in which a customer leaves the system immediately after obtaining service. In many situations, however, a customer must visit several different servers before service is completed. Such systems are called *tandem queuing systems*.

An example of a tandem queue is a customer at a "soup and salad" cafeteria-style restaurant who may wait in one line for soup, move to a second line to select a salad, then proceed to a third line for a beverage, before waiting in a fourth line to pay a cashier. A second example is a business phone system in which a secretary answers all incoming phone calls, determines the purpose of the call, and then transfers the call to the appropriate party. Callers may have to wait to speak to both the secretary and the desired party.

Tandem queuing models can also be used to model a production setting in which an item is worked on at several different stations before completion. This topic, known as assembly-line balancing, is discussed in Section 12.11.

Although tandem queues can be difficult to solve, for cases in which customers arrive according to a Poisson process and customer service times at each station follow exponential distributions, the total average time a customer spends in the system can be calculated by simply summing the average times a customer spends at each of the individual stations. This is possible because if customers arrive at station i according to a Poisson process at an average rate of λ_i per hour, with $\lambda_i < k\mu_i$, the departure process from station i will also have Poisson distribution with average rate λ_i.

If all customers from this station proceed to the next station, arrivals at the next station also follow a Poisson distribution with an average rate of λ_i per hour. If, however, a certain proportion of those from the previous station fail to move on to the next station, the arrival process to the next station is still Poisson, but the rate is reduced proportionately.

To illustrate a tandem queuing situation, let us consider the operations of Big Boys Sound, Inc.

BIG BOYS SOUND, INC.

Big1.qaa
Big2.qaa
Big3.qaa
Big.xls

Big Boys Sound, Inc. is a chain of discount audio stores whose sales personnel wait on customers and take orders. After an order has been written up, the customer goes to a cashier to pay for the merchandise. Once payment has been made, the customer is sent to the merchandise pickup desk to obtain the goods.

On Saturday, the store is staffed with eight sales clerks, three cashiers, and two workers assigned to the merchandise pickup desk. Studies have shown that the average time a salesperson waits on a customer is ten minutes (regardless of whether or not the customer makes a purchase); the average time required to pay for merchandise is three minutes; and the average time it takes a customer to receive the merchandise from the merchandise pickup desk is two minutes. The service times for each of these three operations is distributed approximately exponentially.

Customers arrive according to a Poisson distribution, and an average of 40 customers an hour visit the store each Saturday, 75% of whom make a purchase. Management would like to know the average amount of time a customer who makes a purchase spends in the store.

SOLUTION

This problem can be modeled as a three-station tandem queuing system. Operations at the first station, where a customer works with a sales clerk to select merchandise, can be modeled by an M/M/8 queue with $\lambda_1 = 40$ per hour and $\mu_1 = 60/10 = 6$ per hour. Using WINQSB, we find that the average time a customer spends waiting for and being served by a sales clerk, W_1, is .233252 hour or 14.00 minutes.

Because the steady state condition holds ($40 < 8(6)$), the departure process from the sales clerks will follow a Poisson distribution with an average rate of $\lambda_1 = 40$ per hour. Since only 75% of customers actually purchase merchandise, however, the arrival process of customers to the cashiers (the second station) is a Poisson distribution with an average arrival rate of $\lambda_2 = (.75)(40) = 30$ per hour. Because the service distribution at this station is also exponential, the second phase in this tandem system is an M/M/3 system with $\lambda_2 = 30$ per hour and $\mu_2 = 60/3 = 20$ per hour. WINQSB shows that the average waiting and service time at the cashiers is $W_2 = .057895$ hour, or 3.47 minutes.

At the merchandise pickup desk (the third station), customers arrive according to a Poisson distribution with a rate of $\lambda_3 = 30$ per hour. This station is an M/M/2 system with an average service rate of $\mu_3 = 60/2 = 30$ per hour. Using WINQSB, we find that the average customer waiting and service time at the pickup desk is $W_3 = .044444$ hour, or 2.67 minutes. Thus, the average time customers who make purchases spend in the store is:

$$W = W_1 + W_2 + W_3 = 14.00 + 3.47 + 2.67 = 20.14 \text{ minutes}$$

12.11 ASSEMBLY LINE BALANCING—AN APPLICATION OF TANDEM QUEUES

Analyzing production assembly lines is an important management science task. In an assembly line, a product visits a series of workstations in a given sequence. We can therefore envision an assembly line as a tandem queue in which the workstations correspond to servers, and the items being produced correspond to arriving customers. In most assembly line situations, products arrive at the workstations at regularly defined intervals, not according to a Poisson process, and service times at each work station are relatively constant.

In order for an assembly line to operate efficiently, the length of time a product spends at any one workstation should be approximately the same as it spends at any other. Otherwise, large imbalances in workload would occur, resulting in decreased overall productivity and declining employee morale, as overburdened workers may become jealous of the less strenuous jobs held by some of their peers. Hence, it is important to define the work tasks so that the time at each station is relatively balanced.

A key to assembly line balancing is the proper definition of worker jobs. A typical product assembly operation consists of tens or even hundreds of separate tasks. Generally, an individual worker is responsible for several of these tasks. The objective is to allocate these tasks to workers so that production throughput is maximized or, equivalently, so that the *cycle time* needed to produce a unit is minimized.

Most assembly lines have a precedence ordering of some tasks. For example, at an automobile assembly plant, a worker cannot put tires on a car until both the axles and the wheels are attached. It also might not be possible to do certain tasks at the same workstation. For instance, automobile assemblers might not be able to work on the right and left sides of the car at a given workstation. This constraint is known as a *zoning restriction*. In other instances, some tasks may have to be done together. Still others may involve several workers. As you can see, because of all these factors, assembly line balancing can be quite a difficult problem to solve and implement.

To illustrate the concepts of assembly line balancing, let us consider the production line at McMurray Machine Company.

McMURRAY MACHINE COMPANY

McMurray Machine Company is a small manufacturer of lawn mowers and snow blowers. The company has set up an assembly line to produce its 21-inch rear bagger rotary mower. The assembly operation currently consists of four workstations, as detailed in Table 12.6.

TABLE 12.6   MCMURRAY MACHINE'S WORKSTATIONS

Station	Operations	Average Job Time (Minutes)
1	Stamp mower body and handle; attach control bar to handle	2
2	Mount engine unit to body; attach backstop; blade, wheels, and handle latches	4
3	Attach mower handle, control bar, cables, grass bag collar	3
4	Connect control bar; insert spark plug; quality inspection; packaging	3

Thus, the entire production operation takes $2 + 4 + 3 + 3 = 12$ minutes. Since, at present, the lawn mower spends the greatest amount of time at station 2, this station is, in effect, a bottleneck for the assembly process. The four minutes spent at station 2 means that the maximum number of lawn mowers that can be produced each hour is $60/4 = 15$. Management would like to determine if it can increase productivity through better balancing of the tasks.

SOLUTION

One way to balance the line is to schedule the operations so that the work at each station takes three minutes. This might be accomplished by switching some of the work done at station 2 to station 1. If this were possible, McMurray could produce $60/3 = 20$

lawn mowers per hour, or one lawn mower every three minutes. Hence, proper assembly-line balancing has the potential to reduce the cycle time from four to three minutes (a 33.33% increase in productivity) using the same resources.

But suppose McMurray needed to produce only 15 mowers per hour (a cycle time of four minutes). Then, if it is possible to divide the work equally between any number of workstations, only three workstations, with four minutes of work each, are necessary (instead of the four workstations currently being used). Unfortunately, it is not always possible to divide the tasks equally among workstations.

Another way to balance the line is to place a different number of workers at each station in an effort to equalize the production rates among the stations. While the reduction in job time at a workstation achieved by adding more workers may or may not be proportional to the number of workers, a reduction in average job time at the station can be expected.

Still another way to achieve equality in the output of the operations assigned to various workstations is to assign multiple workstations to perform the same operations. For example, suppose business expanded and McMurray needed to produce 60 mowers per hour. Station 1 can work on 60/2 = 30 units per hour, station 2 60/4 = 15 units per hour, and stations 3 and 4 60/3 = 20 units per hour. The assembly line can then be balanced by setting up two station 1 locations, four station 2 locations, three station 3 locations, and three station 4 locations, as shown in Figure 12.6. The total output for the 12 workstations is the required 60 units per hour.

FIGURE 12.6   Balanced Assembly Line to Produce 60 Units/Hour

Although McMurray can achieve a production rate of 60 mowers per hour by setting up 4 separate assembly lines, because of equipment and floor space considerations, increasing the number of individual workstations to equalize the production rate is generally the less costly alternative.

The Ranked Position Weight Technique

A typical approach taken in assembly-line balancing is to specify a desired cycle time and determine the smallest number of workstations necessary to produce goods within that amount of time. Another objective is to minimize the total amount of idle time at all workstations. Techniques such as integer (see Chapter 5) and dynamic programming (see Chapter 16 on the accompanying CD-ROM) can be used to determine an optimal solution to assembly-line balancing problems. Because of the computational complexity of these methods, however, heuristic techniques are frequently used instead.

One such heuristic method that has proven successful is the *ranked position weight technique*, as described below:

Ranked Position Weight Technique

1. For each task find the total job time as well as the time for all tasks for which that task is a predecessor.
2. Rank the jobs in descending order of these *total* times.
3. Consider workstation 1 the current workstation.
4. Assign the lowest ranked task not already assigned to the current workstation, unless by adding this task the time at the current workstation would exceed the desired cycle time. In this latter case, designate a new workstation as the current workstation and assign the task as the first one done at this workstation.
5. Repeat step 4 until all tasks have been assigned to workstations.

To demonstrate this method, let us return to the McMurray lawn mower example.

McMURRAY MACHINE COMPANY (continued)

Demand for the McMurray 21-inch rear bagger rotary mower has increased to the point at which the company desires a cycle time of three minutes. Table 12.7 gives the completion times and precedence relations of the 17 tasks required to manufacture the lawn mower.

TABLE 12.7   TASKS REQUIRED TO MANUFACTURE A LAWN MOWER

Tasks	Must Follow Job	Job Time (seconds)
A—Stamp out mower body	—	40
B—Stamp out mower handle	—	50
C—Bolt engine to mower body	A	55
D—Attach back stop to mower body	A	30
E—Attach left wheels and handle latch	C	65
F—Attach right wheels and handle latch	C	65
G—Attach grass bag collar	E	30
H—Attach blade	C	25
I—Attach throttle cable to engine	F, G	35
J—Attach control bar cable to engine	I	50
K—Insert spark plug	H	20
L—Attach control bar to handle	B	30
M—Attach handle to mower	L	20
N—Attach throttle cable to handle	M	50
O—Attach control bar cable to control bar	N	45
P—Test mower	D, J, K, O	50
Q—Pack mower	P	60

Figure 12.7 gives the project graph corresponding to this work flow, with the activities corresponding to arcs. The company would like to balance its assembly line using the smallest number of workstations.

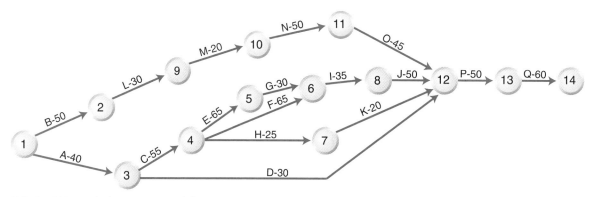

FIGURE 12.7   Work Flow Project Graph for McMurray Lawn Mowers

SOLUTION

Table 12.8 summarizes the total remaining times for each task corresponding to step 1 of the rank position weight heuristic. For example, task A is the predecessor for tasks C, D, E, F, G, H, I, J, K, P, and Q. Thus, the total remaining time for task A is the time needed to do tasks A, C, D, E, F, G, H, I, J, K, P, and Q, or 525 seconds. By contrast, task P is the predecessor only for job Q. Hence, the total remaining time corresponding to task P is the time to do jobs P and Q, or 110 seconds. The lowest rankings are assigned to those tasks with the highest remaining times. Note that a ranking ending in .5 denotes a tie in the rank ordering.

TABLE 12.8   RANKING FOR TASKS REQUIRED TO MANUFACTURE A LAWN MOWER

Tasks	Time	Remaining Tasks	Total Time (seconds)	Rank
A—Stamp out mower body	40	C, D, E, F, G, H, I, J, K, P, Q	525	1
B—Stamp out mower handle	50	L, M, N, O, P, Q	305	3
C—Bolt engine to mower body	55	E, F, G, H, I, J, K, P, Q	455	2
D—Attach back stop to mower body	30	P, Q	140	14
E—Attach left wheels and handle latch	65	G, I, J, P, Q	290	4
F—Attach right wheels and handle latch	65	I, J, P, Q	260	5
G—Attach grass bag collar	30	I, J, P, Q	225	6.5
H—Attach blade	25	K, P, Q	155	12.5
I—Attach throttle cable to engine	35	J, P, Q	195	10
J—Attach control bar cable to engine	50	P, Q	160	11
K—Insert spark plug	20	P, Q	130	15
L—Attach control bar to handle	30	M, N, O, P, Q	255	6.5
M—Attach handle to mower	20	N, O, P, Q	225	8
N—Attach throttle cable to handle	50	O, P, Q	205	9
O—Attach control bar cable to control bar	45	P, Q	155	12.5
P—Test mower	50	Q	110	16
Q—Pack mower	60	—	60	17

In step 3, workstation 1 is made the current workstation. The first assignment to this station in step 4 is the task with the lowest ranking, task A (rank 1). The time allotted for this task is 40 seconds. Task C (rank 2) takes 55 seconds. Adding this task to workstation 1 results in a total time of 95 seconds, which does not exceed the desired cycle time of 3 minutes (180 seconds). Adding task B (rank 3) increases the time at workstation 1 to 95 + 50 = 145 seconds, which is still less than 180 seconds. The next lowest ranked task is task E (Rank 4). But adding its time of 65 seconds brings the total time of workstation 1 to 210 seconds. Since this exceeds the desired 180-second cycle time, task E is instead assigned as the first task of a new workstation 2.

Tasks continue to be assigned to workstation 2 in rank order until adding another task results in a total time greater than the desired cycle time. In doing so, tasks E, F, and G (ranks 4, 5, and 6.5) are assigned to workstation 2, requiring 65 + 65 + 30 = 160 seconds. Task L (rank 6.5) would then be the first task assigned to workstation 3. Following this procedure for the remaining tasks and workstations results in the workstation assignment given in Table 12.9.

TABLE 12.9 WORKSTATION ASSIGNMENTS FOR LAWN MOWER PRODUCTION

Workstation	Tasks	Total Task Time (seconds)	Total Idle Time (seconds)
1	A, B, C	145	35
2	E, F, G	160	20
3	I, L, M, N	135	45
4	D, H, J, K, O	170	10
5	P, Q	110	70

In this solution, the cycle time is actually 170 seconds. There is, however, a wide variance in the amount of idle time among the different workstations. Unfortunately, finding an equal allocation to the workstations for the tasks that make up the assembly of a lawn mower is impossible. To achieve a cycle time of 170 seconds, five workstations are necessary. By using five workstations, however, it is possible to reduce the cycle time below 170 seconds. Table 12.10 shows how task assignments to five workstations result in a cycle time of only 160 seconds. This assignment also results in more than a 50% reduction in total idle time, as well as a more equal balance of idle time among the workstations than the assignment given in Table 12.9.

TABLE 12.10 WORKSTATION ASSIGNMENTS FOR LAWN MOWER PRODUCTION

Workstation	Tasks	Total Task Time (seconds)	Total Idle Time (seconds)
1	A, B, C	145	15
2	E, F, G	160	0
3	I, L, M, N	135	25
4	D, H, J, O	150	10
5	K, P, Q	130	30

If McMurray management were willing to accept a cycle time of 200 seconds, by applying the ranked position weight technique, the assembly line would require only four workstations, as shown in Table 12.11.

TABLE 12.11   WORKSTATION ASSIGNMENTS FOR LAWN MOWER PRODUCTION

Workstation	Tasks	Total Task Time (seconds)	Total Idle Time (seconds)
1	A, B, C	145	55
2	E, F, G, L	190	10
3	I, J, M, N, O	200	0
4	D, H, K, P, Q	185	15

Although this heuristic method is easy to employ, it does not address many practical issues concerning assembly-line balancing, such as the degree of job interest and skill level necessary to perform the tasks assigned to each workstation. It makes little sense, for example, to assign a highly paid worker to a workstation at which some of the tasks require extensive expertise, while others are tedious and of a lower skill level. By incorporating such concerns into the assignment process, firms can often realize significant increases in productivity. Such issues frequently are the subject of human factors and industrial engineering studies.

12.12 SUMMARY

The proper design of a queuing system has an important impact on the service provided by an enterprise. Steady state measures can be obtained when the overall service rate exceeds the arrival rate. Measures such as the average time a customer spends in the system and queue, the average number of customers in the system and queue, the system utilization rate, and the probability of a given number of customers being present in the system can provide useful information in assessing service and developing optimal queuing systems.

If the arrival process is random and possesses the properties of orderliness, stationarity, and independence, it can be modeled by a Poisson process. In this case, formulas exist for the service measures of a wide range of queuing models.

If there is only one server and queue length is unlimited, steady state solutions for models with a Poisson arrival process can be derived for any service distribution. Such solutions can also be derived in the case of multiple servers all working at the same rate if no waiting line is permitted.

When the arrival process can be modeled by a Poisson distribution and the service time by an exponential distribution, and all servers work at the same rate, steady state results can be derived for models in which the potential queue length is either finite or unlimited. Steady state results can also be obtained for other models, including those characterized by a single server and a finite customer population and in which both the interarrival times of customers and the service times follow an exponential distribution. Figure 12.8 is a flow chart we can use to guide us in selecting the appropriate modeling technique.

Tandem queuing systems, in which the arrival process at each station is Poisson, the servers at each station work at the same rate, and the service time follows an exponential distribution, can be analyzed by focusing on the individual stations. One

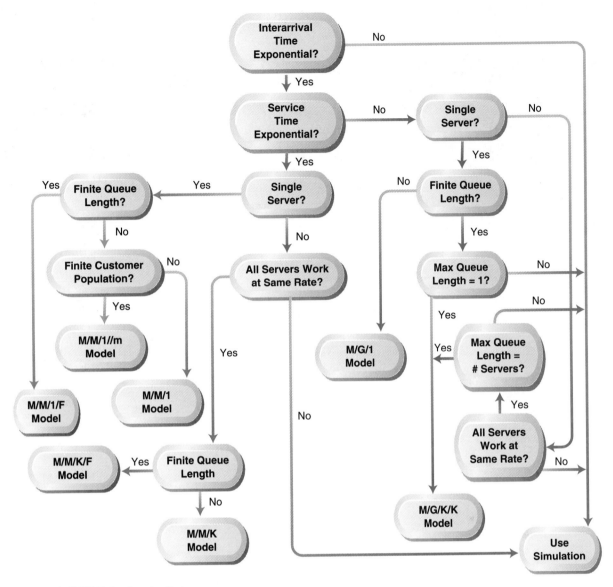

FIGURE 12.8   Queuing Systems

type of tandem queue frequently found in a manufacturing setting is an assembly line. Balancing such a line ensures that production rates are optimized.

Because of space limitations, we have discussed only a limited set of queuing models and performance measures in this chapter. Table 12.12 gives performance measures formulas for each of these models. Results for other systems exist and are found in advanced texts on queuing analyses. When performance measures cannot be obtained analytically, simulation can be used to approximate these values. Such analyses are discussed in the next chapter.

TABLE 12.12 PERFORMANCE MEASURE FORMULAS FOR QUEUING MODELS

Performance Measure	Queue	
	M/M/l	M/M/k
P_0	$1 - (\lambda/\mu)$	$\dfrac{1}{\left[\displaystyle\sum_{n=0}^{n=k-1} \dfrac{1}{n!}\left(\dfrac{\lambda}{\mu}\right)^n\right] + \dfrac{1}{k!}\left(\dfrac{\lambda}{\mu}\right)^k \dfrac{k\mu}{k\mu - \lambda}}$
P_n	$(1 - (\lambda/\mu))(\lambda/\mu)^n$	$P_n = \dfrac{(\lambda/\mu)^n}{n!}P_0 \quad$ for $n \le k$ $\quad$ $P_n = \dfrac{(\lambda/\mu)^n}{k!k^{(n-k)}}P_0 \quad$ for $n > k$
L	$\lambda/(\mu - \lambda)$	$\dfrac{(\lambda/\mu)^k \lambda\mu}{(k-1)!\,(k\mu - \lambda)^2}P_0 + \dfrac{\lambda}{\mu}$
L_q	$\lambda^2/(\mu(\mu - \lambda))$	$\dfrac{(\lambda/\mu)^k \lambda\mu}{(k-1)!\,(k\mu - \lambda)^2}P_0$
W	$1/(\mu - \lambda)$	$\dfrac{(\lambda/\mu)^k \mu}{(k-1)!\,(k\mu - \lambda)^2}P_0 + \dfrac{1}{\mu}$
W_q	$\lambda/(\mu(\mu - \lambda))$	$\dfrac{(\lambda/\mu)^k \mu}{(k-1)!\,(k\mu - \lambda)^2}P_0$
P_w	λ/μ	$\dfrac{1}{k!}\left(\dfrac{\lambda}{\mu}\right)^k\left(\dfrac{k\mu}{k\mu - \lambda}\right)P_0$
ρ	λ/μ	$\lambda/k\mu$

Performance Measure	Queue		
	M/G/l	M/D/l	M/E$_n$/l
P_0	$1 - \lambda/\mu$	$1 - \lambda/\mu$	$1 - \lambda/\mu$
P_n			
L	$\dfrac{(\lambda\sigma)^2 + (\lambda/\mu)^2}{2(1 - \lambda/\mu)} + \dfrac{\lambda}{\mu}$	$\dfrac{(\lambda/\mu)^2}{2(1 - \lambda/\mu)} + \dfrac{\lambda}{\mu}$	$\left(\dfrac{n+1}{2n}\right)\dfrac{\lambda^2}{\mu(\mu - \lambda)} + \dfrac{\lambda}{\mu}$
L_q	$\dfrac{(\lambda\sigma)^2 + (\lambda/\mu)^2}{2(1 - \lambda/\mu)}$	$\dfrac{(\lambda/\mu)^2}{2(1 - \lambda/\mu)}$	$\left(\dfrac{n+1}{2n}\right)\dfrac{\lambda^2}{\mu(\mu - \lambda)}$
W	$\dfrac{\lambda\sigma^2 + \lambda/\mu^2}{2(1 - \lambda/\mu)} + \dfrac{1}{\mu}$	$\dfrac{\lambda/\mu^2}{2(1 - \lambda/\mu)} + \dfrac{1}{\mu}$	$\left(\dfrac{n+1}{2n}\right)\dfrac{\lambda}{\mu(\mu - \lambda)} + \dfrac{1}{\mu}$
W_q	$\dfrac{\lambda\sigma^2 + \lambda/\mu^2}{2(1 - \lambda/\mu)}$	$\dfrac{\lambda/\mu^2}{2(1 - \lambda/\mu)}$	$\left(\dfrac{n+1}{2n}\right)\dfrac{\lambda}{\mu(\mu - \lambda)}$
P_w	λ/μ	λ/μ	λ/μ
ρ	λ/μ	λ/μ	λ/μ

(continued)

TABLE 12.12   PERFORMANCE MEASURE FORMULAS FOR QUEUING MODELS
(*continued*)

Performance Measure	Queue M/M/k/F
P_0	$$\dfrac{1}{\left[1 + \sum_{n=1}^{k}\dfrac{(\lambda/\mu)^n}{n!} + \dfrac{(\lambda/\mu)^k}{k!}\sum_{n=k+1}^{F}\left(\dfrac{\lambda}{k\mu}\right)^{n-k}\right]}$$
P_n	$$\dfrac{(\lambda/\mu)^n}{n!}P_0 \quad n=1,2,3,\ldots,k$$ $$\dfrac{(\lambda/\mu)^n}{k!k^{n-k}}P_0 \quad n=k+1,k+,2,k+3,\ldots,F$$
L	$$\dfrac{P_0(\lambda/\mu)^k(\lambda/k\mu)\,[1-(\lambda/k\mu)^{F-k}-(F-k)\,(\lambda/k\mu)^{F-k}\,(1-(\lambda/k\mu))]}{k!\,(1-(\lambda/k\mu))^2}$$ $$+\sum_{n=0}^{k-1}nP_n + k\left(1-\sum_{n=0}^{k-1}P_n\right)$$
L_q	$$L-\left(\sum_{n=0}^{k-1}nP_n + k\left(1-\sum_{n=0}^{k-1}P_n\right)\right)$$
W	$$\dfrac{L}{\lambda\sum_{n=0}^{F-1}P_n}$$
W_q	$$\dfrac{L_q}{\lambda\sum_{n=0}^{F-1}P_n}$$
P_w	$$1-\sum_{n=0}^{k-1}P_n$$
ρ	$$\dfrac{\lambda\sum_{n=0}^{F-1}P_n}{k\mu}$$

Performance Measure	Queue M/M/1/F $\lambda\neq\mu$	M/M/1/F $\lambda=\mu$
P_0	$\dfrac{1-(\lambda/\mu)}{1-(\lambda/\mu)^{F+1}}$	$\dfrac{1}{F+1}$
P_n	$P_0\,(\lambda/\mu)^n \quad n=1,2,3,\ldots,F$	$\dfrac{1}{F+1} \quad n=1,2,3,\ldots,F$
L	$\dfrac{(\lambda/\mu)}{1-(\lambda/\mu)}-\dfrac{(F+1)\,(\lambda/\mu)^{F+1}}{1-(\lambda/\mu)^{F+1}}$	$F/2$
L_q	$L-(1-P_0)$	$L-(1-P_0)$
W	$\dfrac{L}{\lambda\,(1-P_F)}$	$\dfrac{L}{\lambda\,(1-P_F)}$
W_q	$\dfrac{L_q}{\lambda\,(1-P_F)}$	$\dfrac{L_q}{\lambda\,(1-P_F)}$
P_w	$1-P_0$	$1-P_0$
ρ	$1-P_0$	$1-P_0$

TABLE 12.12   PERFORMANCE MEASURE FORMULAS FOR QUEUING MODELS
(*continued*)

Performance Measure	Queue	
	M/G/k/k	M/M/l//m
P_0	$\dfrac{1}{\displaystyle\sum_{n=0}^{k} \dfrac{(\lambda/\mu)^n}{n!}}$	$\dfrac{1}{\left[\displaystyle\sum_{n=0}^{m} \dfrac{m!}{(m-n)!}\left(\dfrac{\lambda}{\mu}\right)^n\right]}$
P_n	$\dfrac{(\lambda/\mu)^n}{n!}\, P_0 \quad n = 1, 2, 3, \ldots, k$	$\dfrac{m!}{(m-n)!}\left(\dfrac{\lambda}{\mu}\right)^n P_0$
L	$\dfrac{\lambda}{\mu}(1 - P_k)$	$m - \left(\dfrac{\mu}{\lambda}\right)(1 - P_0)$
L_q	0	$m - \left(\dfrac{\lambda + \mu}{\lambda}\right)(1 - P_0)$
W	$\dfrac{1}{\mu}$	$\dfrac{L}{\lambda(m - L)}$
W_q	0	$\dfrac{L_q}{\lambda(m - L)}$
P_w	0	$1 - P_0$
ρ	$\dfrac{\lambda}{k\mu}(1 - P_k)$	$1 - P_0$

$\mathcal{N}$OTATIONAL SUMMARY

D = deterministic arrival or service distribution
E_n = Erlangian distribution
F = maximum number of customers allowed in the system
g = goodwill cost per hour for a customer while in the system
G = general arrival or service distribution
k = specific number of servers in the system
L = average number of customers in the system
L_q = average number of customers in the queue
m = size of the customer population if finite
M = Markovian arrival or service distribution
N = number of servers in the system
P_0 = probability that there are no customers in the system
P_n = probability that there are n customers in the system
W = average time a customer spends in the system
W_q = average time a customer spends in the queue
P_w = probability that an arriving customer must wait for service
λ = mean arrival rate per time unit
μ = service rate per server
ρ = utilization rate of each server (this is the percentage of time that each server is busy)

APPENDIX 12.1

Using WINQSB and Excel to Solve Queuing Problems

The queuing analysis module of WINQSB can be used to solve numerous queuing models, and Excel can be programmed to evaluate the steady state formulas given in the chapter. Here we focus on how to use WINQSB or program Excel to solve the M/M/k model. The approach is similar for other queuing models.

Solving M/M/k Queuing Models Using WINQSB

To solve an M/M/k queuing model, we click on "Simple M/M System" from the initial data entry screen and indicate the problem title and time units; this takes us to a data input screen. Exhibit 12.1 shows this screen for the Littletown Post Office problem presented in Section 12.5.

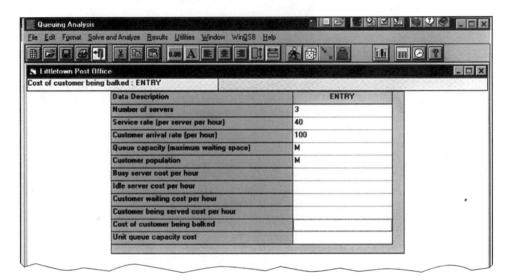

EXHIBIT 12.1

When we select "Solve the Performance" from the "Solve and Analyze" option on the menu bar, WINQSB returns a screen that includes the input data and values for the steady state performance measures. If we input cost data, the cost per period for different system components and the total cost per period are also calculated. Exhibit 12.2 provides this information for the Littletown Post Office problem.

We can find the probabilities of having from 1 to n customers in the system by selecting "Probability Summary" from the "Results" option on the menu bar.

Using WINQSB to Solve M/G/1 Queuing Models

To solve an M/G/1 queuing model using WINQSB, we click on "General Queuing System" from the initial data entry screen and indicate the problem title and time units. The data input screen for these systems is similar to that used by WINQSB for the M/M/k systems. To input a service or arrival distribution other than exponential, simply position the mouse over the word "exponential" and double click. You will find a menu of different possible distributions. You would choose the last choice on this menu, "General/Arbitrary," to find the service time distribution for an M/G/1 system.

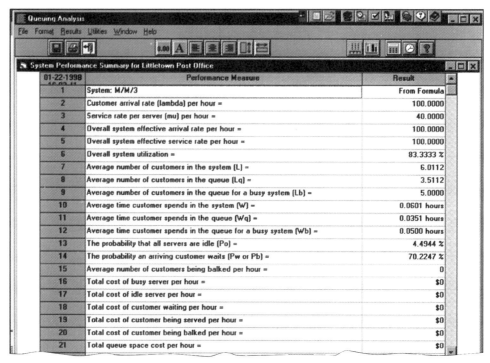

EXHIBIT 12.2

Using Excel to Solve M/M/k Queuing Models

We can use Excel to solve for the performance measures and the steady state probabilities for the number of customers in the system by programming the formulas for these measures into individual cells of the spreadsheet. Here we show a spreadsheet that provides these values for an M/M/k queuing situation with an infinite calling population and no limit on the size of the queue. Since an M/M/1 system is a special case of an M/M/k system, these formulas apply to that situation as well.

Exhibit 12.3 shows the Excel screen for the Littletown Post Office problem; in this case, $\lambda =$ 100 per hour, $\mu = 40$ per hour, and k = 3 servers. These input data are placed in cells B3, B4, and B5, respectively.

In Section 12.5, we introduced the following formulas for the M/M/k system:

Calculating P_0

P_0 is calculated in cell B14 by the formula:

$$P_0 = \frac{1}{\sum_{n=0}^{k-1} \frac{(\lambda/\mu)^n}{n!} + \frac{(\lambda/\mu)^k}{k!}\left(\frac{k\mu}{k\mu - \lambda}\right)}$$

One difficulty with evaluating the summation term in the denominator is that it is a function of the input parameter, k, which is not known in advance. While a simple macro in Visual Basic can be written to perform this calculation, here we show how we use the Excel command, VLOOKUP, to perform this summation.

To get the screen in Exhibit 12.3, we begin by inputting a column of ascending values of n—0, 1, 2, 3, etc., in Column E. We want to enter enough numbers so that the last value of n in the column exceeds the largest possible value of k we would consider. Here we input values of n from n = 0 in cell E3 to n = 15 in cell E18 by:

Cell	Entry
E3	0
E4	1
E5–E18	Highlight E3 and E4 and drag to E18

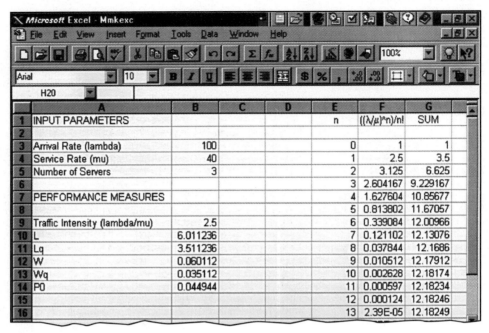

EXHIBIT I2.3

In Column F we put the values of $(\lambda/\mu)^n/n!$ for the corresponding values of n in Column E:

Cell	Formula
F3	$= \$B\$9\,\hat{}\,E3/FACT(E3)$
F4–F18	Highlight F3 and drag to cell F18

In Column G we keep the running total of the sum of these numbers:

Cell	Formula	
G3	1	(This is $(\lambda/\mu)^0/0!$)
G4	$= G3 + F4$	
G5–G18	Highlight G4 and drag to cell G18	

The appropriate summation term to be used in the denominator of the formula for P_0 in cell B14 is VLOOKUP(B5-1,E3:G18,3). To summarize, this command does the following:

1. Finds the entry in B5 and subtracts I

2. Finds the same value as B5-I in the first Column of the block from E3 to G18 (i.e., matches a number in Column E)

3. Returns the entry from the same row of the third column of the block from E3 to G18 (i.e., from Column G) of the matched entry;

Thus, the formula for P_0 in cell B14 is:

$$I/(VLOOKUP(B5\text{-}1,E3{:}G18,3) + VLOOKUP(B5,E3{:}G18,2)*(B5*B4/(B5*B4{=}B3))$$

Using the value of P_0 to calculate L, the other performance measures can be generated in cells B9-B13 as follows:

Cell	Expression	Formula
B9	λ/μ	$= B3/B4$
B10	$((\lambda/\mu)^k \lambda\mu P_0/((k-1)!(k\mu-\lambda)^2)) + \lambda/\mu$	See below
B11	$L - \lambda/\mu$	$= B10 - B9$
B12	L/λ	$= B10/B3$
B13	L_q/λ	$= B11/B3$

Formula For Cell B10:

$$= ((B9\,\hat{}\,B5)*B3*B4*B14)/(FACT(B5-1)*(B5*B4-B3)\,\hat{}\,2)) + B9$$

PROBLEMS

1. Customers arrive at Pete's Coffee Shop on the average of one every five minutes, according to a Poisson distribution. The average time Pete spends serving a customer is three minutes, and the service times are believed to follow an exponential distribution. The shop is run entirely by Pete, and customers are served on a first-come, first-served basis.

   a. What is the probability that exactly two customers will arrive at Pete's in a 15-minute period?

   b. What is the probability that more than three customers will arrive in a 30-minute period?

   c. What is the probability that the service time for a customer is under two minutes?

   d. On the average, how long does a customer spend waiting for service at Pete's?

   e. What is the probability that a customer spends less than five minutes at Pete's?

   f. What is the average number of customers present at Pete's?

   g. What percentage of Pete's time is spent serving customers?

2. At Dolly Foods, customers spend an average of 25 minutes selecting their groceries and checking out by entering a single-line queue served by two cashiers. The service times required for the cashiers to check out customers follow an exponential distribution and average four minutes. Customers arrive at the cashier counter according to a Poisson distribution at the average rate of eight customers per hour.

   a. Determine: (i) the average time a customer spends in the store; (ii) the average number of customers waiting in line prior to being checked out; (iii) the proportion of customers who will have to wait in line.

   b. What assumptions did you make in part (a)?

3. Consider the information given in Problem 2 for Dolly Foods. For the same amount that Dolly is paying the two cashiers, she can lay off one cashier and use the savings to lease an optical scanning system. The resulting checkout times will then follow a distribution, with a mean service time of three minutes and a standard deviation of one minute.

   a. If Dolly opts for the optical scanning system, determine: (i) the average time a customer would spend in the store; (ii) the average number of customers waiting in line prior to being checked out; (iii) the proportion of customers who would have to wait in line.

   b. Compare the results from part (a) of Problems 2 and 3. Would you recommend that Dolly Foods lease the optical scanning system? Justify your answer.

4. INFOSERVE, Inc. is a 900 line telephone service that supplies various kinds of obscure information. The company is expanding its service to Monmouth County, New Jersey, and has allocated $60,000 to purchase the computer systems necessary to handle customer calls. INFOSERVE has received bids from two computer suppliers: Infotechnologies and Compufact. The system from Infotechnologies sells for $20,000 and can handle an average customer inquiry in three minutes. Compufact's database system sells for $30,000 and can handle an average customer inquiry in two minutes. INFOSERVE can therefore purchase three of the Infotechnologies systems or two of the Compufact systems.

   INFOSERVE estimates that an average of 40 customers per hour will call its service and that customer phone calls will arrive according to a Poisson process. If no computer system is available, callers remain on hold until a system is free. Service times are believed to follow an exponential distribution. If INFOSERVE's objective is to minimize the average time a caller must wait on hold to get information, which supplier should it select?

5. Muncie State University runs its registration line by dividing the student population into three equal groups based on student ID numbers. A student will enter the appropriate line to register, and jockeying among lines is *not* permitted. The arrival rate of students for each line follows a Poisson process, with a mean rate of 30 students per

hour. Service of a student follows an exponential distribution, and the average time it takes to serve a student is 90 seconds.

   a. Determine the average time required for a student to wait in line and register.

   b. Determine the total average number of students waiting to be served in the three lines.

   c. Muncie State University is contemplating eliminating the three-line system and replacing it by a single line staffed by two clerks supported by a microcomputer system. This would reduce the average service time to 72 seconds and save $2.60 per hour in labor costs. Muncie State estimates that the goodwill cost of a student's being in the system is $4 per hour. Assuming service times continue to follow an exponential distribution and students arrive according to a Poisson process at a mean rate of 90 per hour, should the university switch to the single-line system?

6. The Atlas Health Club has one tanning booth for its customers. Users of the tanning booth spend *exactly* five minutes in the facility. Customers arrive at the booth according to a Poisson process at the mean rate of eight per hour.

   a. What is the average time a customer must wait in line to use the tanning booth?

   b. What is the average number of customers waiting to use the tanning booth?

   c. What is the probability that there is no waiting line at the tanning booth?

   d. What assumptions did you make in parts (a)–(c)?

7. Harry's Variety Store has two checkstand locations—one at the front entrance to the store, the other at the rear. The checkstand locations are so far apart it is reasonable to expect that customers will *not* jockey between them. The checkstand in the front has two cashiers, while the checkstand in the rear has four. The service times for each cashier follow an exponential distribution, with a mean time of 2.5 minutes.

    Customers arrive at the checkstand locations according to a Poisson process. Because there is more parking at the rear of the store, the arrival rate of customers at that checkstand averages 66 customers per hour, while the arrival rate at the front entrance checkstand averages 20 customers per hour.

   a. What is the average time a customer spends waiting in line prior to beginning service at each of the two checkstand locations?

   b. What is the average number of customers both waiting in line and being served at each of the two checkstand locations?

   c. What is the probability that there are exactly two people waiting in line at the rear entrance checkstand?

   d. What is the probability that there are three or fewer people waiting in line at the front entrance checkstand?

   e. As a customer, would you prefer to check out at the front or the rear of the store? Justify your answer.

8. Consider the situation at Harry's Variety Store (Problem 7). Harry is considering consolidating the two checkstands into one centralized location in the middle of the store. Harry estimates that the combined average of 86 customers per hour would arrive at the centralized location. Cashiers will continue to check customers out in an average of two and a half minutes and earn $16 per hour in salary and benefits. Harry feels that the goodwill cost of having a customer waiting in line is $20 per hour, while the goodwill cost during a customer's service is $10 per hour. Determine the optimal number of cashiers Harry should use at the centralized location.

9. Pat Smith and Chris Brown are two applicants for the position of telephone receptionist at Taylar Industries. Both applicants can handle a phone call in an average of one minute. The standard deviation of Pat's service time is 10 seconds, while the standard deviation of Chris's service time is 20 seconds. The interarrival time of customer calls is expected to follow an exponential distribution, with a mean of 90 seconds. On the average, how much longer will a caller wait on hold to speak to a receptionist if Chris were hired than if Pat were hired?

10. Mr. Chips manufactures an automated vending machine that can prepare a single order of french fries in exactly 45 seconds. The company has placed one of its machines in the student union building of a local community college, where it believes customers will arrive according to a Poisson process at the mean rate of 40 per hour. Determine the average amount of time an arriving customer will have to wait before ordering french fries from the vending machine.

11. Steve Jackson is responsible for maintaining a fleet of eight school buses. On the average, a bus will need repair work every 20 days. The average time required to perform this work is one day. Both the time between needed repairs and the time to perform repairs are expected to follow exponential distributions.

  a. What is the average amount of time a bus will be out of service for a needed repair?

  b. On the average, how many buses will be waiting for repair at any given time?

  c. What proportion of the time will all buses be operational?

12. The telephone system at WAVY Radio has six incoming phone lines and two operators to take listener requests for music. If both operators are busy, a customer is normally placed on hold. If all six phone lines are busy, however, callers will get a busy signal and probably not call back. Customer calls to WAVY can be modeled by a Poisson process, with a mean rate of 50 per hour. The service times follow an exponential distribution, with a mean of 90 seconds.

  a. What is the probability that a caller will be placed on hold?

  b. On the average, how many callers are on hold?

  c. If a caller does not get a busy signal, what is the average total time spent waiting on hold and speaking to an operator?

  d. What is the probability that there is exactly one caller on hold?

13. Hotspot Appliance Company is planning an assembly line for its new model 4321 electric dryer. The tasks making up the dryer assembly, together with their estimated times and predecessors, are as follows.

Tasks	Must Follow Job	Job Time (seconds)
A—Build chassis	—	45
B—Attach heating coil to front panel	—	35
C—Attach sides to front panel	B	45
D—Attach top to sides and front	C	30
E—Attach control unit to control panel	D	25
F—Attach control panel to dryer top	E	35
G—Attach thermostat to drum	—	20
H—Attach drum to chassis	A, G	35
I—Attach motor to chassis	A, G	35
J—Attach motor switch to chassis	I	15
K—Attach dryer belt to motor	H, J	10
L—Wire motor to control unit	K, F	30
M—Wire drum to control unit	L	30
N—Attach panel assembly to chassis	M	40
O—Attach leveling screws to dryer	A, G	30
P—Attach heat discharge vent to dryer	N	40
Q—Insert lint filter in dryer drum	H, J	10
R—Attach dryer back	P	35
S—Attach front door to dryer	B	30
T—Test dryer	O, Q, R, S	40
U—Pack dryer	T	45

Using the ranked position weight technique, determine which tasks should be assigned to which workstations if Hotspot desires a cycle time of (i) four minutes; (ii) three minutes.

14. Bronco Burger has a drive-thru window for take-out orders. Because of space limitations, the restaurant has been designed to allow a maximum of five cars in the drive-

thru window line (including the car being served). If the line is full, cars will not stop at Bronco Burger, but will instead drive to a competing restaurant.

Cars attempt to arrive to Bronco Burger's drive-thru window at an average of one every 80 seconds. Interarrival times are assumed to follow an exponential distribution. Service times also follow an exponential distribution, with a mean service time of one minute.

a. What is the average number of cars waiting in line for service?

b. What is the average time a car spends in line, including the service?

c. What is the probability that there are no cars at the drive-thru window?

d. Comment on the appropriateness of modeling the service time at Bronco Burger by an exponential distribution.

15. Consider the data in Problem 14 for Bronco Burger. How would your answers change for Bronco Burger if it added a second drive-thru window? Assume there is a single line for the two drive-thru windows and that the maximum number of cars in this line remains at five (including the two cars being served).

16. Soup Herman is a restaurant that serves soup and salad. Customers first line up in a cash register line to pay for their meals. After paying, they proceed to one of four salad bars. While all customers purchase salad, only 60% of customers go on to take the soup from one of the two soup stations.

During the hours between 6:15 and 8:00 P.M., an average of 140 customers arrive at the restaurant. Assume that the arrival process can be modeled by a Poisson distribution. The time it takes to pay the cashier, get salad, and get soup each follows an exponential probability distribution. If the cashier takes an average of 40 seconds to collect money from a customer, and the customer averages two minutes to get a salad and one minute to get soup, determine the average time a customer spends paying for and getting food if: (i) the customer is getting salad only; and (ii) the customer is getting both soup and salad.

17. Circle J convenience store has two check-out counters. Customers arrive according to a Poisson process at an average rate of one every 90 seconds. On the average, each of the two checkers serves 50 customers per hour, and service times follow an exponential distribution.

Circle J is considering eliminating one of the two check-out counters and having the two employees work together, one ringing up the merchandise, the other bagging it. How fast would their combined average service time have to be if the average time a customer spends in the store is to remain unchanged?

18. Gameland is a combination miniature golf course and video arcade. One of the most popular games in the arcade is Thunderblaster, a virtual reality space trip. The playing time for Thunderblaster is exactly two minutes. An additional 30 seconds is required for a player to put on the virtual reality helmet. Customers arrive to play the game according to a Poisson process at an average rate of once every three minutes.

a. What is the average time a player waits in line to play Thunderblaster?

b. On the average, how many people are playing or waiting to play Thunderblaster?

19. Littletown Hospital has two ambulances. Calls for the ambulances are received according to a Poisson process. The mean time between calls is 45 minutes. If a call comes in when both ambulances are out, another hospital is contacted to send out an ambulance. The time it takes a Littletown ambulance to respond to a call and get the patient to the hospital averages 25 minutes and has a standard deviation of 15 minutes.

a. Determine the probability that both Littletown ambulances are available to answer calls.

b. Determine the probability that a call must be answered by an ambulance from another hospital.

c. Determine the utilization rate for each ambulance.

d. If Littletown Hospital buys a third ambulance, what proportion of the time would it be used?

20. At the merchandise return department at Bull's Eye Department Store, customers wait in line to have their merchandise checked in by a refund clerk. The clerk determines if the store will accept the merchandise and, if appropriate, issues a refund credit. The store accepts and issues refund credits on 95% of the merchandise returned by customers. Approximately 60% of customers go to the cashier for the cash refund, while the other 40% use the credit for shopping in the store.

After Christmas, an average of 100 customers arrive each hour at the Bull's Eye merchandise return department, where three clerks are positioned to check over returned merchandise. Service times for each clerk follow an exponential distribution, with a mean of 1.5 minutes. Bull's Eye uses one cashier to issue cash refunds. Issuing a cash refund averages 50 seconds and has a standard deviation of 20 seconds. For those customers who return merchandise and desire a cash refund, determine the average number of minutes it will take them to get their refund.

21. Customers arrive at Dave & Steve's Ice Cream Shop according to a Poisson process at a mean rate of 48 per hour. The store pays its sales clerks $7.50 per hour in wages and benefits. Dave & Steve's estimates the goodwill cost of a customer waiting to be served at $6 per hour and the goodwill cost of a customer being served at only $1.00 per hour. Customer service times follow an exponential distribution and average two minutes.

a. Determine the number of sales clerks Dave & Steve's should employ to minimize the store's total average hourly costs.

b. If the customer arrival rate increases by 50% and the goodwill cost of a customer waiting to be served and being served were doubled, determine how many sales clerks Dave & Steve's should employ to minimize the store's total average hourly costs.

22. Lyle Scott, an employee at South Coast Distributors, is responsible for delivering and stocking wine at eight grocery stores in Broward County, Florida. Each grocery store calls Lyle with an order approximately once every five days. If Scott is free, it takes him approximately a half day to deliver and stock an order. If Scott is already working on orders, the customer's order joins a first-come, first-served queue. The time between Scott's stocking a grocery store and the store's placing an order can be approximated by an exponential distribution, and an exponential distribution can also be used to model the service time for Scott to deliver and stock an order.

a. Determine the proportion of time Scott is working on orders.

b. On the average, how many orders does Scott have waiting to be filled?

c. What is the average time a store waits for an order to be stocked?

23. K & J Sport Boating, located in Wailea, Hawaii, specializes in individualized scuba diving and wind surfing lessons. Four instructors are available to teach wind surfing. Because most customers are tourists, if K & J does not have an instructor available, potential customers either go to another company for the lessons or do some other activity. They *do not* wait for an instructor to become available. On the average, customers arrive at K & J for windsurfing lessons every 20 minutes according to a Poisson process. Lessons average 1.5 hours, with a standard deviation of 15 minutes.

a. What is the probability that all four instructors are busy?

b. What is the probability that all four instructors are idle?

c. What is the utilization rate of each instructor? Explain what the utilization rate means in the context of this problem.

24. K & J Sport Boating (see Problem 23) charges customers $46 for each lesson and pays each instructor $18 per hour in wages and benefits. It also pays $6 per hour in insurance, boat rental, and overhead costs. K & J operates 10 hours a day.

a. Determine K & J's average daily profit or loss.

b. K & J is thinking about hiring another instructor at $18 per hour. Should the instructor be hired? Justify your answer.

25. Panasony has an assembly line for manufacturing 19-inch color stereo television sets. The following table lists the tasks, average task time, and predecessor information of the operations involved in their production.

Tasks	Must Follow Job	Job Time (seconds)
A—Stamp out chassis body	—	25
B—Attach transformer to chassis	A	30
C—Attach picture circuit board to chassis	A	30
D—Attach sound circuit board to chassis	B	25
E—Attach antenna gain circuit to chassis	C	25
F—Attach antenna to chassis	A	30
G—Attach tuner circuit to chassis	D, E	45
H—Attach speakers to console	B	45
I—Attach infrared R/C unit to chassis	D, E	35
J—Attach picture tube to chassis	F, G	50
K—Attach electrical cord to transformer	I, J	20
L—Attach control knobs	K	40
M—Insert chassis in console	H, K	30
N—Attach back of set to console	M	25
O—Test set	N	35
P—Pack set	O	50

Using the ranked position weight technique, determine the assignment of tasks to workstations if Panasony wants a cycle time of (i) three minutes; and (ii) two minutes.

26. Suppose you are designing rest-room facilities at a campground and believe that 120 men and 120 women per hour will need to use these facilities. Estimates indicate that men spend an average of 1.5 minutes in rest rooms, while women average four minutes. If you want the average time a man or a woman has to wait in line to use the facility to be approximately the same, how many rest rooms should be built for women if you build four rest rooms for men? (Assume a Poisson arrival process to the rest rooms and assume that rest-room usage times follow an exponential distribution.)

27. The Hillel Sandwich Shop specializes in delivery of sandwiches in New York's financial district. Customers phone or fax Hillel their orders, which are then delivered directly to the customer's place of business. From 11:30 A.M. to 1:00 P.M. Hillel receives an average of 180 orders, which arrive according to a Poisson process. The time required to make a sandwich by Joe Hillel or either of his two assistants averages 75 seconds, and preparation times follow an exponential distribution. Once an order has been filled, it is given to one of five delivery persons. Delivery times also follow an exponential distribution and average two minutes.

   On the average, how many minutes does it take a customer to get a sandwich delivered from the Hillel Sandwich Shop after placing an order?

28. During the 1991 Persian Gulf War, Apache helicopters had certain reliability problems. Battalion 436 had 11 Apache helicopters assigned to its unit. The helicopters flew an average of nine hours between failures, and the time between failures was distributed approximately exponentially. The battalion had one repair crew, and repairs were made to helicopters on a first-come, first-served basis. Repair times for servicing a failed helicopter also followed an exponential distribution with a mean of two hours.

   a. What was the mean number of helicopters available for flight missions at any point in time for Battalion 436?

   b. What was the probability that Battalion 436 had seven or more helicopters available to go on flight missions?

   c. What was the average time required to repair a helicopter?

29. R & S Plumbing and Heating Contractors is a two-person partnership. The two plumbers occasionally work on a big job together, but nearly all the calls are handled by a single plumber. Calls come into R & S according to a Poisson process. The average time between calls is 45 minutes. The time required for each plumbing job follows an exponential distribution, and each job takes an average of two hours to perform.

   In order to ensure customer satisfaction, R & S will not keep more than four plumbing jobs waiting for repair at a given time. Hence, once the backlog of jobs reaches four, the company stops answering the telephone. The firm resumes answering the phone when the backlog falls below four jobs.

a. For a customer who gets through to R & S, determine the average elapsed time from when the call is placed until R & S completes its work on the plumbing problem.

b. What is the probability that a calling customer will not receive an answer from R & S Plumbing?

c. What is the average number of jobs R & S has waiting to be worked on?

d. R & S nets an average of $88 per plumbing job. If it can hire an additional plumber for $20 per hour, should it do so? (Assume the plumber works at the same rate as the two partners, so that a job is completed in an average of two hours.) Justify your answer.

30. Littletown is considering building an airport to handle two types of aircraft—large and small. City managers are evaluating three options: (1) build one runway to handle all types of traffic; (2) build two runways, each of which can handle all types of traffic; and (3) build two runways and restrict traffic on one to small aircraft and restrict traffic on the other to large aircraft. Under options 1 and 2, a runway can handle an average of 55 aircraft landings per hour. Under option 3, the small aircraft runway can handle 80 aircraft landings per hour, and the large aircraft runway can handle 40 aircraft landings per hour.

Large aircraft arrive at random at a mean rate of 20 per hour, and small aircraft arrive at random at a mean rate of 25 per hour. Both the interarrival time of aircraft and the time required for an aircraft to land follow an exponential distribution. Because of safety concerns and fuel costs, waiting costs are figured at $10 per minute for both large and small aircraft. Amortized cost for a runway is an estimated $350 per hour.

a. For each option, determine the average number of planes waiting in the system.

b. Determine the hourly operating cost for each of the three options.

c. Which option would you recommend? Justify your answer.

CASE 1: *Saveway Supermarkets*

Saveway Supermarkets is a major food retailer in upstate New York. The chain has over 60 stores that receive merchandise from their Rochester, New York, warehouse. The warehouse receives shipments of merchandise throughout the day from the various vendors and manufacturers with whom Saveway does business.

The Rochester warehouse has eight loading docks available for delivery of goods. Trucks arrive at the warehouse approximately once every six minutes according to a Poisson process. If all the loading docks are occupied, an arriving truck waits in a queue until a dock becomes available.

Currently, each dock is staffed by a single worker, who unloads a truck in an average of 30 minutes. Saveway management has been getting complaints from some of its suppliers that their truckers are spending too much time unloading merchandise at the Rochester warehouse. Hence, Saveway has come up with a number of possible strategies to address this problem: (1) hire a second worker for each loading dock, reducing the average time to unload a truck to 18 minutes (workers earn $16 per hour in salary and benefits); (2) equip each loading dock with an electric forklift that can be leased for $5 per hour and reduce the time required to unload a truck to an average of 24 minutes; or (3) build up to two more loading docks (accounting for capital costs, each dock will cost Saveway $6 per hour to build).

While strategies 1 and 2 are mutually exclusive, the firm may decide to implement strategy 3 either alone or in combination with 1 or 2. Saveway estimates the goodwill cost of a delivery truck being in the system at $60 per hour.

Prepare a business report recommending a course of action to Saveway management assuming the objective is to minimize total system costs. Assume that service times for each option follow exponential distributions. Include in your report a comparison of the system parameters of your recommendation to those of current operations.

CASE 2: *Boone Travel Agency*

Having run a successful travel agency in Denver, Colorado, Jan Hall has decided to open a branch in Boone, Colorado. She must decide where to locate her office and which and how many employees to hire.

Jan has narrowed her choice of office to two locations. The one on Main Street is a large office with space for virtually any number of employees and customers. Jan estimates that the agency can attract an average of 12 customers per day at this location. Rent for this office is $1300 per month. Utilities, insurance, and other expenses should average an additional $500 per month.

The second choice for an office is on Frontier Street, approximately two blocks off Main Street. This is a much smaller office that can effectively hold only one worker and at most four customers (including the one being served). It rents for $400 per month. Utilities, insurance, and other expenses should average an additional $200 per month. This out-of-the-way location would reduce the number of potential customers by 20%, and any arriving customer finding the office full will presumably take his or her business to the other travel agency in town.

Jan has decided that if she opens the Main Street office, she will hire one or more local employees to staff the office.

If she opens the Frontier Street office, however, she will hire either Wendy Brown, an experienced travel agent from the Denver area, or a local employee to staff the office. Jan would have to pay Wendy a monthly salary (including benefits) of $2100, whereas she could hire local employees for $1200 per month (including benefits). Because of her experience, Wendy's average customer service time is approximately 20 minutes, compared to 48 minutes for local employees.

Jan estimates that each customer served by the Boone Travel Agency will result in an average commission of $35. She also estimates a goodwill cost to the firm of $15 per hour for the time a customer spends waiting in the office for service to begin. In addition, goodwill costs of $50 are associated with any customers who find the Frontier Street location full and leave to go to another travel agency.

The travel agency will be open an average of 20 days per month, eight hours each day. Customers arrive according to a Poisson process, and customer service times follow an exponential distribution.

Prepare a business report for Jan Hall detailing her various options and your recommendation as to her best course of action. Include in your report the financial information on which you base your recommendation.

CHAPTER 13

SIMULATION

Hunt Wesson is one of the world's largest food processing companies. One of its principal product lines is Wesson Oil, which is made from a variety of vegetable oils and packaged in various-sized bottles. Management is particularly concerned about the operation of the production line used to bottle the oil.

The bottling process begins by using a decaser to remove empty plastic bottles from their shipping cases and place them on the bottling line. The bottles are then air cleaned and moved onto a conveyer belt for transport to the filling station. After filling, they are sealed and capped and proceed to a labeler. A caser places the filled bottles in cases. Finally, the cases are sealed using a case sealer and loaded on pallets by a palletizer.

Management conducted a simulation study to develop procedures for ensuring that the bottling line operates at a sufficient capacity to meet sales projections. They gathered data on the frequency, length, and repair cost of breakdowns for each workstation on the bottling line and determined the cost and effects of modifications to the existing equipment. They also investigated different line speeds as well as the placement of buffer areas (accumulation tables) between workstations.

As a result of the simulation analysis, management was able to redesign the bottling process to meet the firm's production requirements and to develop procedures for dealing with future breakdowns which will minimize the variation in production rates.

13.1 OVERVIEW OF SIMULATION

In the preceding chapters, we have studied many analytical models. Often, however, the underlying assumptions necessary for these models to provide good results are not met. For example, in a single-server queuing system if service time does not follow an exponential distribution or if customers do not arrive according to a Poisson process we cannot expect the M/M/1 queuing formulas to accurately describe steady state results. Inventory systems for which demand varies greatly from period to period cannot be adequately analyzed using the EOQ formula. In cases such as these, we may use a simulation approach to perform the desired analysis.

A **simulation** develops a model to evaluate a system numerically over some time period of interest. Its purpose is to estimate characteristics for the system, which can then be used to select the best policy from a set of alternatives under consideration. Unlike many analytical techniques, a simulation does not rely on an algorithm to solve for the optimal solution; instead, a computer program known as a **simulator** is used to evaluate each option.

It is important for the simulator to be as accurate as possible in capturing the important aspects of the operation of the system. A challenging aspect of developing a simulation, therefore, is to identify the relevant factors affecting system performance. For example, if we are interested in determining a customer's average waiting time in a queuing system, the arrival process, the service time, the number of servers, and the priority rule for selecting the next customer are all important attributes. By contrast, the hair color of an arriving customer does not affect waiting time and is ignored.

Other attributes, such as the gender of a customer, may or may not be a factor. If we are modeling a queuing system for a bank, for example, a customer's gender is probably not a factor. But if we are modeling the waiting line at a campground rest room, a customer's gender probably is an important factor, since the time men and women spend in a rest room generally differs.

Simulation is used for many purposes in business and industry. Airlines use flight simulators to train prospective pilots; the weather service uses simulation analysis to predict future weather patterns; and process engineers use simulation to determine the operating characteristics of projects, such as a proposed oil refinery. These are all examples of *continuous simulation systems*, in which the state of the system changes continuously over time. For example, a plane rises continuously as a pilot moves the throttle; weather changes from instant to instant; and oil flows continuously through the refining process. Since in many cases, continuous simulation systems require the use of differential equations to model changes in system parameters, these systems are beyond the scope of this text.

Other simulation models, such as those involving queuing or inventory systems, monitor changes that occur at discrete points in time. Still other simulation models are hybrids of continuous and discrete simulation systems. For example, in simulating jet fuel inventory at an airport, customers (airplanes) arrive on a discrete basis, while the fuel going into each airplane is a continuous flow. It is the analysis of *discrete simulation systems* that is the focus of this chapter.

Although simple simulation models may be solved by hand, simulation of most practical problems requires the use of a computer program. Computer simulations can be written in any computer language or performed by using a spreadsheet program, such as Excel. While many simulations have been written in general-purpose programming languages, such as FORTRAN, PL/1, Pascal, and BASIC, specialized computer languages have been developed to assist in writing the computer code. Among the more popular simulation languages are GPSS, SIMSCRIPT, SIMAN, and SLAM.

The principal advantage of using specialized languages is that compared to a general purpose language, fewer lines of computer code are required, allowing the program to be written and debugged more quickly and easily. In addition, many specialized languages include an animation ability, enabling the user to view the effects of the simulation as the program is running.

Even though these specialized languages share many similarities, they also have certain differences that may make one language more appropriate than another for a particular application. Deciding whether learning a particular simulation language is worthwhile depends on how frequently the modeler develops simulation models. For the infrequent modeler, such specialized languages may prove to be more of a time investment than the return in programming ease justifies. Since most students are unfamiliar with these specialized languages, the computer simulations used in this chapter are performed using either Excel or specially written BASIC programs.[1]

While the concept of simulation is quite intuitive, great care must be taken not only in modeling the system, but also in conducting the simulation. As we will see in this chapter, simulation requires good modeling and programming skills. A knowledge of statistics is also important for determining the overall design of the simulation and other critical factors, such as the required length of individual simulation runs and the number of runs that should make up the simulation study.

13.2 MONTE CARLO SIMULATION

If the system being simulated includes data inputs that are random variables, the simulation model should reflect them as accurately as possible. One way of doing so is to use a technique known as **Monte Carlo simulation**, in which a computer program called a *simulator* is designed so that the **simulated events** both occur randomly and reflect the theoretical frequencies being modeled.

Monte Carlo simulation uses *random numbers*, which can either be generated by a computer or taken from a random number table (Appendix C), to generate simulated events. The process for matching random numbers to simulated events is called *random number mapping*. We illustrate how random number mappings are developed and how random numbers are used in a Monte Carlo simulation by analyzing the situation faced by Bill Jewel, owner of the Jewel Vending Company.

Jewel.lxs

JEWEL VENDING COMPANY

Bill Jewel is the owner of the Jewel Vending Company (JVC), which installs and stocks gum and novelty vending machines in supermarkets, discount stores, and restaurants. Bill is considering installing a Super Sucker jaw breaker dispenser at the new Saveway Supermarket on Lincoln Avenue. The vending machine holds 80 jaw breakers. Ideally, Bill would like to fill the machine whenever it becomes half empty. (Bill does not want the machine to appear too empty, because he fears that potential customers will believe the jaw breakers are not fresh and so will elect not to make a purchase.)

Based on performance of similar vending machine placements, Bill has estimated the following distribution for daily jaw breaker demand:

P(daily demand = 0 jaw breakers) = .10
P(daily demand = 1 jaw breaker) = .15
P(daily demand = 2 jaw breakers) = .20
P(daily demand = 3 jaw breakers) = .30

---

[1]WINQSB includes modules for simulating queuing and inventory systems. But, since our focus is on understanding the concepts underlying simulation rather than obtaining results, these modules will not be illustrated in this chapter.

$$P(\text{daily demand} = 4 \text{ jaw breakers}) = .20$$
$$P(\text{daily demand} = 5 \text{ jaw breakers}) = .05$$

Bill would like to estimate the expected number of days it takes for a filled machine to become half empty (i.e., the average number of days it takes to sell 40 jaw breakers). This information will help him determine how often to refill the machine.

SOLUTION

Bill might consider estimating the expected time between refills by calculating the average (expected) daily demand based on the assumed probability distribution and dividing this value into 40. This gives us:

$$\frac{\text{Expected time}}{\text{between refills}} = \frac{40}{.10(0) + .15(1) + .20(2) + .30(3) + .20(4) + .05(5)}$$

$$= \frac{40}{2.5} = 16 \text{ days}$$

Bill is not certain that this method yields the true average number of days required to sell 40 or more jaw breakers, but he feels it probably yields a good approximation. To test it, Bill has decided to employ a simulation approach.

SIMULATION OF THE
DAILY DEMAND FOR
JAW BREAKERS

To properly simulate the JVC system, let us define the random variable:

$$X = \text{daily demand for jaw breakers at the Saveway store}$$

Based on Bill's estimates, the probability distribution function for X is:

$$P(X = 0) = .10$$
$$P(X = 1) = .15$$
$$P(X = 2) = .20$$
$$P(X = 3) = .30$$
$$P(X = 4) = .20$$
$$P(X = 5) = .05$$

The theory behind generating a *random event*, such as daily demand, is that the event outcomes should not occur in any particular pattern, but, in the long run, they should occur with relative frequencies equal to the probability distribution being modeled. In particular, the probability distribution for each day's demand should follow the same distribution as that given above for X, regardless of the results of the simulated demand generated for any other day.

For example, if we simulated 1000 days of demand at JVC, we would expect demand to be zero on approximately 100 days (since $P(X = 0) = .10$), one on approximately 150 days (since $P(X = 1) = .15$), two on approximately 200 days (since $P(X = 2) = .20$) and so on. However, there should be no pattern, such as demand of zero on days 1, 11, 21, etc.

To simulate demand on a particular day, we might imagine 100 balls put into a box. Of these 100 balls, 10 are marked with the number 0, 15 the number 1, 20 the number 2, 30 the number 3, 20 the number 4, and five the number 5. Once the balls have been thoroughly mixed, one is chosen at random from the box. If it is marked with the number "3," for this one simulated day, demand for the jaw breakers is 3. To simulate demand for the next day, the ball is replaced in the box, the balls are mixed, and another random draw is made. This process can be repeated to simulate demand for as many days as desired.

But suppose Bill changes his probability estimates slightly so that $P(X = 0) = .12$ and $P(X = 1) = .13$, with the other demand probabilities remaining the same. Now two more balls marked "0" have to be added, while two balls marked "1" have to be removed from the box.

Random Number
Mappings

One way of generating the daily demands which avoids having to change the numbers on the balls is to label each of the 100 balls with a distinct two-digit number, 00, 01, 02, 03, . . . , 98, 99. Each of the 100 numbers now corresponds to a given daily demand in proportion to the desired probability distribution. For example, since P(X = 0) = .10, 10% of the 100 numbers, or 10 numbers, correspond to the event that demand is 0 on a given day. Similarly, 15 of the numbers correspond to a demand of 1, 20 to a demand of 2, and so on. To generate the simulated demand for several days, therefore, a sequence of random balls are selected and the corresponding demands determined.

The easiest way to simulate this process is to let the first 10 numbers correspond to the event "daily demand = 0," the next 15 numbers correspond to the event "daily demand = 1," and so on. This process is called a *random number mapping* because it "maps" a random number (the number corresponding to the ball selected) to the outcome of a simulated event (the daily demand for jaw breakers). Table 13.1 shows the random number mapping for JVC.[2]

TABLE 13.1   RANDOM NUMBER MAPPING FOR JVC

Daily Demand (X)	Corresponding Random Numbers
0	00–09
1	10–24
2	25–44
3	45–74
4	75–94
5	95–99

Now if P(X = 0) is changed to .12 and P(X = 1) to .13, we simply change the mapping so that random numbers 00 through 11 correspond to a daily demand of 0 and random numbers 12 through 24 correspond to a daily demand of 1.

The Cumulative
Distribution Approach
for a Random
Number Mapping

While this approach works well for discrete random variables, a more comprehensive approach is required for continuous distributions. One approach that can be used for both discrete and continuous distributions involves the use of the cumulative distribution function for the random variable, X. A cumulative distribution, F(x), gives the probability that X is less than or equal to some value, x; that is, F(x) = P(X ≤ x). Table 13.2 provides the cumulative distribution function for customer arrivals in the JVC problem, which is illustrated graphically in Figure 13.1

TABLE 13.2   CUMULATIVE DISTRIBUTION
FOR CUSTOMER ARRIVALS

$$F(0) = P(X \le 0) = .10$$
$$F(1) = P(X \le 1) = .25$$
$$F(2) = P(X \le 2) = .45$$
$$F(3) = P(X \le 3) = .75$$
$$F(4) = P(X \le 4) = .95$$
$$F(5) = P(X \le 5) = 1.00$$

---

[2]We need to use two-digit numbers because the probability distribution for X is accurate to two decimal places. If the probabilities were accurate to three decimal places, we would use three-digit numbers, that is, 000–999. Similarly, if the probabilities were accurate to only one decimal place, we would use one-digit numbers, 0–9.

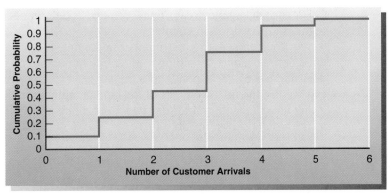

FIGURE 13.1   Cumulative Distribution for Customer Arrivals

Now if we choose a random number Y (between 0 and 1), we can determine the value for the event by finding the smallest value for x such that $F(x) \geq Y$. For example, suppose the ball marked number 34 is chosen. Since we are using only two-digit probabilities, we convert the number 34 to the two-digit decimal .34. Referring to the cumulative distribution function in Figure 13.1, we see that the smallest value of x such that $F(x) = P(X \leq x) \geq .34$ is $x = 2$. This is the same value for demand obtained using the random number mapping given in Table 13.1.

Generating Random Numbers

Thus far, we have generated random numbers by selecting one ball from 100 at random. Since each ball is equally likely to be drawn on any one draw, this process results in a *uniform distribution* of two-digit numbers between 00 and 99.

Of course, in practice, we do not select balls out of a box. Instead, we mimic this process as closely as possible on a computer by using a *random number generator*. A random number generator actually generates what are called *pseudo-random numbers* ("pseudo" means false) because the numbers are not *truly* random but are obtained using a mathematical formula.

A random number generator begins with a starting value, known as a *seed* (which the user can supply), and produces a sequence of numbers that meets the following statistical properties for randomness:

1. Each number has an equally likely chance of occurring.

2. There is no apparent correlation between the numbers generated by the mathematical formula.

 Appendix 13.2 on the accompanying CD-ROM describes a commonly used technique for generating pseudo-random numbers, known as the *linear congruential method*.

SIMULATION OF THE JVC PROBLEM

Given the random number mapping in Table 13.1, we can use the set of pseudo-random numbers in Appendix C to conduct a fixed time simulation for the JVC problem. Each iteration of the simulation corresponds to a fixed time period of one day.

Beginning with day 1, a random number is selected to determine the demand for jaw breakers on that day. The demand value will be used to update the total demand to date. The simulation is repeated for a second day, then a third day; it stops once total demand to date reaches 40 or more. The number of "simulated" days required for the total demand to reach 40 or more is then recorded.

Since only two-digit random numbers are needed to generate jaw breaker demands, we begin the simulation using the first two digits in the top row of column 1 in Appendix

C. For each subsequent day, a new demand is determined using the two-digit number in the next row down in column 1.

As you can see, the first number in column 1 is 6506. The first two digits of this number are 65, and, according to the random number mapping in Table 13.1, the random number 65 corresponds to a demand of three jaw breakers on day one. For day two, we use the first two digits of the random number in the next row of column 1 (77), giving us a demand of 4 for day two. Continuing down column 1 in this fashion gives us the results shown in Table 13.3.

TABLE 13.3   A TYPICAL SIMULATION FOR JVC

Day	Random Number	Demand	Total Demand to Date
1	65	3	3
2	77	4	7
3	61	3	10
4	88	4	14
5	42	2	16
6	74	3	19
7	11	1	20
8	40	2	22
9	03	0	22
10	62	3	25
11	54	3	28
12	10	1	29
13	16	1	30
14	69	3	33
15	16	1	34
16	02	0	34
17	31	2	36
18	79	4	40

In this simulation, it took 18 days to sell 40 jaw breakers, two days more than the 16 days Bill had originally estimated. It is difficult, however, to draw any firm conclusions based on only one simulation run. To get a better estimate, we should run additional simulations and average the results.

Let us now perform a second simulation run by using the random numbers in column 15. Table 13.4 gives the results. This time, it took 14 days to sell 40 or more jaw breakers. Note, also, that by day 14 the total demand was 41 jaw breakers rather than 40.

TABLE 13.4   A SECOND SIMULATION FOR JVC

Day	Random Number	Demand	Total Demand to Date
1	42	2	2
2	74	3	5
3	93	4	9
4	84	4	13
5	89	4	17
6	89	4	23
7	12	1	24
8	64	3	25
9	64	3	28
10	38	2	30
11	61	3	33
12	53	3	36
13	12	1	37
14	76	4	41

Using Simulation Results to Conduct Hypothesis Tests

The purpose of performing the simulation runs is to determine if the average number of days required to sell 40 jaw breakers is, in fact, 16. Neither run gave a value of 16; however, the *average* of the times of the two runs, 18 and 14, is 16. As we conduct additional simulation runs, the laws of probability suggest that our calculated average should become closer and closer to the true average. Thus, for the JVC problem, to test whether or not $\mu = 16$, we conduct the following two-tailed hypothesis test:

$$\text{Null hypothesis:} \qquad H_O\text{: } \mu = 16$$
$$\text{Alternative hypothesis:} \quad H_A\text{: } \mu \neq 16$$

If we assume that the distribution of the number of days to sell 40 jaw breakers, x, is approximately normal, then since the population variance is unknown, we would perform a t-test with n − 1 degrees of freedom (df), where n is the number of simulation runs. To conduct this test, we must select a level of significance, α, which is the probability of concluding that the alternative hypothesis, H_A, is true when it in fact is *not*.

For a two-tailed test, we construct the interval $-t_{\alpha/2,\text{d.f.}}$ to $+t_{\alpha/2,\text{d.f.}}$. If the test statistic t lies outside this interval, we conclude that the alternative hypothesis is true (and the null hypothesis is false). If the test statistic lies within this interval, there is *not* enough evidence to conclude that the alternative hypothesis is true.

Programmers often use flow charts to guide the development of a computer program for problem solving. Figure 13.2 shows a possible flow chart that could be used to perform the JVC jaw breaker simulation. A BASIC program listing for doing this simulation is given in Appendix 13.3 on the accompanying CD-ROM.

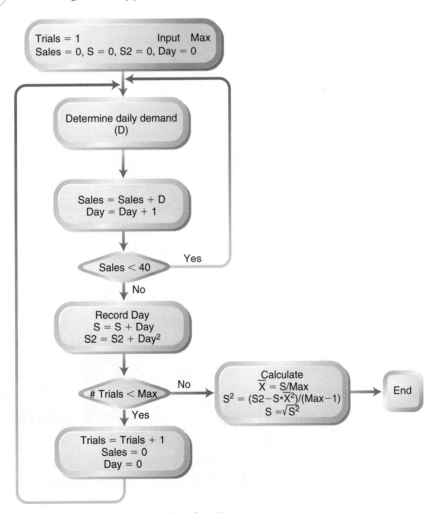

FIGURE 13.2   Flow Chart for Jewel Vending Company

The simulation can also be done using Excel. Figure 13.3 is an example of the output of a simulation run for the JVC problem done using Excel. The formulas used to generate this spreadsheet are given in Figure 13.4.

FIGURE 13.3   Excel Output—Simulation Run For JVC

FIGURE 13.4   Formulas Used to Generate JVC Excel Spreadsheet

To illustrate how the t-distribution is used to conduct an hypothesis test for μ, let us perform a total of 10 simulation runs (replications) using the Excel spreadsheet. The number of days it takes to sell 40 or more jaw breakers on each replication are listed in Table 13.5.

TABLE 13.5   NUMBER OF DAYS TO SELL 40 OR MORE JAW BREAKERS

Replication	Jaw Breakers
1	18
2	14
3	16
4	16
5	16
6	14
7	14
8	19
9	19
10	20

One value typically chosen for α is .05. For 10 observations (nine degrees of freedom) and $\alpha = .05$, we see from Appendix D that $t_{.025,9} = 2.262$. Hence, if the t-statistic yields a value greater than 2.262 or less than -2.262, there is enough evidence to conclude that the average number of days it takes to sell 40 or more jaw breakers differs from 16. From these 10 observations, we can calculate

$$\bar{x} = (18 + 14 + 16 + 16 + 16 + 14 + 14 + 19 + 19 + 20)/10 = 16.6$$
$$s^2 = ((18 - 16.6)^2 + (14 - 16.6)^2 + \ldots + (20 - 16.6)^2)/9 = 5.1556$$
$$s = \sqrt{s^2} = \sqrt{5.1556} = 2.2706$$

Thus, the t-statistic is:

$$t = \frac{(16.6 - 16)}{2.2706/\sqrt{10}} = \frac{.6}{.7180} = .836$$

Since .836 lies within the interval $(-2.262, +2.262)$, there is not enough evidence from these 10 simulation runs to conclude that the average number of days required to sell 40 or more jaw breakers differs from 16. The fact that the alternative hypothesis is not accepted in this case does not mean, of course, that μ is exactly 16. It simply means that, based on these 10 replications, the evidence is not strong enough to conclude otherwise. Collecting additional sample evidence may, in fact, lead to a different conclusion.

ESTIMATING THE AVERAGE NUMBER OF DAYS BEFORE A REFILL IS NEEDED

Conducting additional simulations using Excel can become quite tedious. Fortunately, an add-on program called @RISK[3] is available for Excel, which can be used to repeat the simulation easily for any desired number of replications. Alternatively, the BASIC program listed in Appendix 13.3 can be used to conduct as many simulation runs of the Jewel Vending problem as desired.

Table 13.6 gives the average number of days, $\bar{x}$, it took to sell 40 or more jaw breakers, the value of the standard deviation, s, and the t-statistic, based on 10, 50, 100, 500, 2500, and 10,000 simulation runs.

---

[3]@RISK is published by Palisade Corporation. If you are interested in learning more about @RISK you may contact the company by phone at (800) 432-7475 or visit its web site at http://www.palisade.com.

TABLE 13.6   AVERAGE TIME IT TAKES TO SELL 40 OR MORE JAW BREAKERS

Number of Simulation Runs (n)	Average Number of Days	Standard Deviation	t
10	16.60	2.2706	.836
50	17.04	2.2035	3.337
100	16.66	2.2026	2.996
500	16.39	2.2423	3.889
2500	16.52	2.2449	11.582
10,000	16.46	2.2131	20.785

Recall that when n ≥ 30, we can find a close approximation to critical values for the t-distribution by using the standard normal distribution.[4] Thus, for large values of n and $\alpha = .05$, the interval $(-t_{.025,d.f.}, +t_{.025,d.f.})$ can be closely approximated by the interval $(-z_{.025}, +z_{.025})$ or $(-1.96, +1.96)$.

Referring to Table 13.6, we see that in samples based on 50 or more simulation runs, the value of the t-statistic lies well outside this interval. In these cases, we reject the null hypothesis and conclude that the true average number of days to sell 40 or more jaw breakers differs from 16.

DETERMINING CONFIDENCE INTERVALS FOR THE POPULATION MEAN

What, then, is our best estimate for μ, the true average number of days to sell 40 or more jaw breakers? To answer this question, we might use a $(1 - \alpha)$ confidence interval to estimate the population mean, μ, given by

$$\left(\bar{x} - t_{\alpha/2,n-1} \frac{s}{\sqrt{n}}, \bar{x} + t_{\alpha/2,n-1} \frac{s}{\sqrt{n}} \right) \qquad (13.1)$$

When the number of replications is large (n ≥ 30), this can be approximated by

$$\left(\bar{x} - z_{\alpha/2} \frac{s}{\sqrt{n}}, \bar{x} + z_{\alpha/2} \frac{s}{\sqrt{n}} \right) \qquad (13.2)$$

For example, the 95% confidence interval for μ based on the simulation consisting of 10,000 replications is:[5]

$$\left(16.46 - 1.96 \left(\frac{2.2131}{\sqrt{10000}} \right), 16.46 + 1.96 \left(\frac{2.2131}{\sqrt{10000}} \right) \right) = (16.42, 16.50)$$

As a result of this analysis, Bill concludes that the average number of days it takes to sell 40 or more jaw breakers is likely to be between 16.4 and 16.5.

13.3 RANDOM NUMBER MAPPINGS FOR CONTINUOUS RANDOM VARIABLES

In the previous section we illustrated two methods for generating random variables corresponding to discrete probability distributions; one used the probability distribu-

---

[4]When n ≥ 30, the central limit theorem states that a normal distribution closely approximates the distribution for the sample mean, regardless of the true underlying distribution for the random variable.

[5]This confidence interval does not mean that there is a 95% probability that this interval contains the true population mean. Rather, the interpretation is that if we construct numerous confidence intervals in this fashion, in the long run 95% of the intervals will contain the true population mean.

tion itself, the other used the cumulative distribution function, F(x). In this section, we illustrate a number of techniques for simulating continuous random variables.

THE EXPLICIT INVERSE DISTRIBUTION METHOD

In the **explicit inverse distribution method** we use the cumulative distribution function, F(x), to determine a value for the random variable. In particular, we develop an equation, known as the *inverse distribution function*, which expresses x in terms of F(x). A pseudo-random number, Y, which corresponds to a uniformly distributed random variable between 0 and 1 is then selected, and the inverse distribution function is used to find the value of x that corresponds to Y = F(x). For example, if a random number, say Y = .37268, is generated, the event simulated has a value x, such that F(x) = .37268.

To illustrate this technique, we consider the M/M/k queuing system discussed in Chapter 12. In this model, a continuous exponential distribution describes customer interarrival times. A different exponential distribution describes customer service times.

The probability density function for the exponential distribution of the service time is:

$$f(x) = \mu e^{-ux} \qquad \text{for } x \geq 0 \tag{13.3}$$

and the cumulative distribution is:

$$F(x) = 1 - e^{-\mu x} \tag{13.4}$$

In these expressions, μ is the server's mean service rate and $1/\mu$ is the server's mean service time.

If Y is a random number generated from a uniform distribution over the interval from 0 to 1, we can determine a simulated service time, x, by finding the value of x such that

$$Y = 1 - e^{-\mu x} \tag{13.5}$$

Rearranging these terms gives us:

$$e^{-\mu x} = 1 - Y \tag{13.6}$$

Taking logarithms of both sides of Equation 13.6 to solve for x gives us:

$$-\mu x = \ln(1 - y) \tag{13.7}$$

or

$$x = \frac{-\ln(1 - Y)}{\mu} \tag{13.8}$$

In Equation 13.8, the time units for x are the same as those for μ. Thus, if μ is expressed in terms of customers per minute, x is in terms of minutes.

To illustrate the use of Equation 13.8, consider a queuing process that has an exponential service time distribution with an average service time of $1/\mu = .5$ minute. The service rate, therefore, is $\mu = 2$ per minute. To simulate the service times, we use the *second* column of Appendix C and put a decimal point in front of these numbers. Moving down column 2, we see that the first value is .3338; hence, using Equation 13.8 we get the following service time, x:

$$x = \frac{-\ln(1 - .3338)}{2} = .203 \text{ minute}$$

The simulation of 10 service times using the first 10 numbers of column 2 in Appendix C is summarized in Table 13.7.

TABLE 13.7   SIMULATION OF 10 SERVICE TIMES

Replication i	Random Number Y_i	Service Time x_i
1	.3338	.203
2	.9874	2.187
3	.2631	.153
4	.9139	1.226
5	.9651	1.678
6	.4883	.335
7	.8260	.874
8	.2781	.163
9	.9636	1.657
10	.4696	.317

Notice that, while the mean value for the service time is .5 minute, the values generated using the first 10 numbers of column 2 in Appendix C range from a low of .153 to a high of 2.187 minutes.

OTHER TRANSFORMATION METHODS

Although it is easy to map pseudo-random numbers in the case of the exponential distribution, such mapping is not always so simple, because it may not be possible to obtain a closed-form solution for x in terms of F(x). In such cases, the *interpolation method* can be used instead of the explicit inverse method. This method is described in Appendix 13.4 on the accompanying CD-ROM.

Another method uses a Taylor series expansion for the inverse distribution function. (Recall that a Taylor series provides a way of expressing a mathematical relationship as an equivalent sum of an infinite series of terms.) This approach is useful when we are not able to find the inverse distribution function for a given cumulative distribution, but we can find the inverse distribution for the individual terms of the equivalent Taylor series.

Still another approach exploits special properties of the random variable's distribution. As an example, consider generating random variables that follow a normal distribution. According to the central limit theorem, the sum of a large number of independent random variables approximately follows a normal distribution, with a mean equal to the sum of the random variable means and a variance equal to a sum of the random variable variances. Therefore, one way to generate normally distributed random variables is to take the sum of n uniformly distributed pseudo-random numbers. Since uniformly distributed numbers between 0 and 1 have a mean of 1/2 and a variance of 1/12, the sum of n such numbers is approximately normally distributed, with a mean equal to n/2 and a variance equal to n/12.

13.4 SIMULATION OF A QUEUING SYSTEM

Management scientists frequently use simulation to analyze queues. While we presented closed-form solutions for operating characteristics of several queuing situations in Chapter 12, these models were based on a number of simplifying assumptions. For example, we assumed that if a system has multiple servers, all servers work at the same rate. In many businesses (such as supermarkets that operate express check-out lines), this assumption is not valid. The queuing models also assumed that the interarrival times of customers follow an exponential distribution and that no customer balks. If this is not the case, the model results presented in Chapter 12 would not be valid.

When the underlying assumptions necessary to obtain closed-form solutions are not met, simulation can be used to estimate the steady state values. In this section we discuss the background and basic concepts behind many queuing simulations.

NEXT EVENT SIMULATION

The simulation conducted for the Jewel Vending Company problem in Section 13.2 is an example of a *fixed time simulation*—each iteration of the simulation represents a fixed time period (one day of operation). For many practical simulation problems, such as queuing systems, however, time itself is a random variable, and a fixed time simulation is either impossible or quite inefficient to perform. In these cases, we can use a *next-event simulation*, in which the simulated data are updated when a particular event occurs (such as the arrival or departure of a customer) rather than after a specific period of time.

Next-event simulations can be modeled using a *process-interaction approach*, in which each iteration traces all relevant processes incurred by an item in the system under study. For example, a queuing system simulation considers everything that happens to a particular customer as he or she moves through the system. This includes arrival time, waiting time, selection of server(s), and service time(s).

Simulation of an M/M/1 System

Although an M/M/1 system would never actually be simulated (because we know the closed-form steady state results for this model), we simulate one here to illustrate the approach and accuracy of a next-event queuing simulation.

In a process-interaction approach, the arrival time for each customer is determined by adding a random interarrival time to the time of the previous customer's arrival. If an arriving customer finds no other customers in the system service begins immediately, otherwise it begins when the previous customer has completed service. The time at which a customer completes service equals the time service begins plus a random service time. We can then estimate the average waiting time in the queue or system by keeping track of the time each simulated customer spends in the system.

To illustrate this concept, consider the following situation faced by the Lanford Sub Shop.

LANFORD SUB SHOP

Lanf.xls

The Lanford Sub Shop is a small sandwich shop serving downtown Dayton, Ohio. The sole employee is the owner, Frank Lanford, who makes a customer's sandwich in an average time of one minute.

During the lunch hour period (11:30 A.M. to 1:30 P.M.), an average of 30 customers an hour arrive at the Sub Shop. Frank believes that the customer arrival process is Poisson and that his service time follows an exponential distribution. He is interested in using simulation to determine the average time a customer must wait for service.

SOLUTION

The Lanford Sub Shop can be modeled as an M/M/1 queue (see Chapter 12) with an arrival rate $\lambda = 30$ customers per hour (.5 per minute) and a service rate $\mu = 60$ customers per hour (1 per minute). We perform a simulation for this operation by generating the following data:

1. The number of the arriving customer (C#).
2. The random number used to determine the interarrival time (R#1).
3. The interarrival time (IAT).
4. The arrival time for the customer (AT).

5. The time at which service begins for the customer (TSB).
6. The waiting time a customer spends in line (WT).
7. The random number used to determine the service time (R#2).
8. The service time (ST).
9. The time at which service ends for the customer (TSE).

The simulation "clock" begins at time t = 0, which corresponds to 11:30 A.M. We use the explicit inverse method to generate the interarrival times (IAT) and service times (ST). The AT, TSB, and TSE columns are times measured from time t = 0 on the simulation clock.

Using random numbers from column 1 to generate both R#1 for the interarrival times and R#2 for Frank's service times gives us the simulation in Table 13.8 for the first 10 customers (times given are in minutes).

TABLE 13.8 LANFORD SUB SHOP SIMULATION FOR FIRST 10 CUSTOMERS

C#	R#1	IAT	AT	TSB	WT	R#2	ST	TSE
1	.6506	2.10	2.10	2.10	0	.7761	1.50	3.60
2	.6170	1.92	4.02	4.02	0	.8800	2.12	6.14
3	.4211	1.09	5.11	6.14	1.03	.7452	1.37	7.51
4	.1182	.25	5.36	7.51	2.15	.4012	.51	8.02
5	.0335	.07	5.43	8.02	2.59	.6299	.99	9.01
6	.5482	1.59	7.02	9.01	1.99	.1085	.11	9.12
7	.1698	.37	7.39	9.12	1.73	.6969	1.19	10.31
8	.1696	.37	7.76	10.31	2.55	.0267	.03	10.34
9	.3175	.76	8.52	10.34	1.82	.7959	1.59	11.93
10	.4958	1.37	9.89	11.93	2.04	.4281	.56	12.49

Let us show how we obtained the entries for customer 3 in this table. At this point we would have already used four random numbers (two for the interarrival times and two for the service times of customers 1 and 2). Thus, we select the fifth random number from column 1, (.4211) to determine the interarrival time for customer 3. Using the explicit inverse method, generates an interarrival time of x = −ln(1 − .4211)/30 = .0182 hours = 1.09 minutes. Hence, customer 3 arrives 1.09 minutes after customer 2. Since the arrival time for customer 2 occurred at a simulated clock time of 4.02 minutes, the arrival time for customer 3 is 4.02 + 1.09 = 5.11 minutes.

Customer 2 did not complete service until 6.14 minutes. Since customer 3 cannot begin service until customer 2 leaves, the customer must wait in line 6.14 − 5.11 = 1.03 minutes.

We then select the sixth random number from column 1 (.7452) to determine the service time for customer 3. Using the explicit inverse method .7452 generates a service time of x = −ln(1 − .7452)/60 = .0228 hours = 1.37 minutes. Hence, since customer 3's service begins at clock time 6.14 and lasts 1.37 minutes, his or her service ends at time 6.14 + 1.37 = 7.51 minutes.

From this limited simulation run, we can estimate the average waiting time for a customer in the queue by averaging the 10 customers' waiting times:

(Average waiting time for this 10 customer simulation) =
[0 + 0 + 1.03 + 2.15 + 2.59 + 1.99 + 1.73 + 2.55 + 1.82 + 2.04]/10 = 1.59 minutes

The true steady state value for the average customer waiting time at the Lanford Sub Shop derived from the formula for W_q in Chapter 12 is:

$$W_q = \frac{\lambda}{\mu(\mu - \lambda)} = \frac{30}{60(60 - 30)} = \frac{1}{60} \text{ hours} = 1 \text{ minute}$$

It should be no surprise that the value calculated for W_q based on a single simulation run of only 10 customers is quite different from the steady state value. However, as the number of customers used to calculate the average waiting time increases, we expect the calculated value for W_q to become closer to the steady state value.

Figure 13.5 shows the simulation of an M/M/1 queue based on 10 customer arrivals using Excel. Figure 13.6 gives the formulas used to generate this simulation.

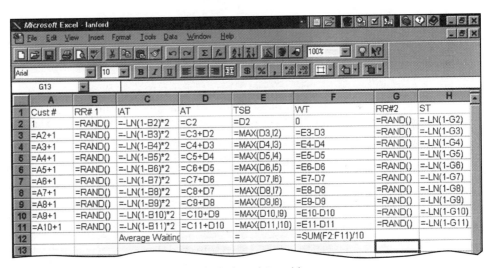

Cust #	RR# 1	IAT	AT	TSB	WT	RR#2	ST	TSE		
1	0.211762	0.475909	0.475909	0.475909	0	0.922119	2.552571	3.028481		
2	0.528358	1.503069	1.978978	3.028481	1.049503	0.340452	0.418201	3.444681		
3	0.201539	0.450139	2.429117	3.444681	1.015564	0.791092	1.565862	5.010543		
4	0.069951	0.145036	2.574153	5.010543	2.43639	0.526541	0.747691	5.758233		
5	0.248331	0.570918	3.145072	5.758233	2.613162	0.373312	0.467306	6.22554		
6	0.880566	4.24998	7.395052	7.395052	0	0.508367	0.710023	8.105075		
7	0.556936	1.628082	9.023134	9.023134	0	0.884584	2.159211	11.18235		
8	0.418017	1.082628	10.10576	11.18235	1.076583	0.709324	1.235545	12.41789		
9	0.544568	1.57302	11.67878	12.41789	0.739108	0.478755	0.651535	13.06942		
10	0.372399	0.931702	12.61048	13.06942	0.45894	0.062259	0.064281	13.13371		
		Average Waiting Time =			0.938925					

FIGURE 13.5   Excel Simulation of An M/M/1 Queue Based on 10 Customer Arrivals

Cust #	RR# 1	IAT	AT	TSB	WT	RR#2	ST
1	=RAND()	=-LN(1-B2)*2	=C2	=D2	0	=RAND()	=-LN(1-G2)
=A2+1	=RAND()	=-LN(1-B3)*2	=C3+D2	=MAX(D3,I2)	=E3-D3	=RAND()	=-LN(1-G3)
=A3+1	=RAND()	=-LN(1-B4)*2	=C4+D3	=MAX(D4,I3)	=E4-D4	=RAND()	=-LN(1-G4)
=A4+1	=RAND()	=-LN(1-B5)*2	=C5+D4	=MAX(D5,I4)	=E5-D5	=RAND()	=-LN(1-G5)
=A5+1	=RAND()	=-LN(1-B6)*2	=C6+D5	=MAX(D6,I5)	=E6-D6	=RAND()	=-LN(1-G6)
=A6+1	=RAND()	=-LN(1-B7)*2	=C7+D6	=MAX(D7,I6)	=E7-D7	=RAND()	=-LN(1-G7)
=A7+1	=RAND()	=-LN(1-B8)*2	=C8+D7	=MAX(D8,I7)	=E8-D8	=RAND()	=-LN(1-G8)
=A8+1	=RAND()	=-LN(1-B9)*2	=C9+D8	=MAX(D9,I8)	=E9-D9	=RAND()	=-LN(1-G9)
=A9+1	=RAND()	=-LN(1-B10)*2	=C10+D9	=MAX(D10,I9)	=E10-D10	=RAND()	=-LN(1-G10)
=A10+1	=RAND()	=-LN(1-B11)*2	=C11+D10	=MAX(D11,I10)	=E11-D11	=RAND()	=-LN(1-G11)
		Average Waiting		=	=SUM(F2:F11)/10		

FIGURE 13.6   Formulas Used to Generate Lanford Excel Spreadsheet

Start-Up Bias

One problem associated with obtaining accurate estimates for the steady state operating characteristics from the simulation is the fact that, in this simulation, the system starts with no customers in the system. Thus, the results calculated for W_q are somewhat biased.

One way to eliminate this "start-up" bias is to ignore the values of the first few customers. This allows the system to settle down to approximately a steady state operation before we begin to record data values. Determining the number of customers to ignore until the system reaches steady state is not an exact science. Although guidelines have been developed for some cases, this determination is often left to the analyst's best judgment.

Table 13.9 shows the estimated values of W_q for the Lanford Sub Shack problem using different combinations for the number of customers run (k) and the number of customers who are ignored (m) in the simulation before calculating the operating characteristic, W_q. For each of these cases, we calculate the average customer waiting time in the queue for 10 simulation runs. We then average these 10 values, to obtain an overall estimate for W_q. We then determine the standard deviation for these 10 values. While these simulations were performed using a specially written BASIC program, they could have just as easily been done using the Excel spreadsheet approach demonstrated in Figures 13.5 and 13.6.

TABLE 13.9   AVERAGE TIME A CUSTOMER WAITS IN LINE TO BEGIN SERVICE

Run Number	k = 100 m = 0	k = 100 m = 9	k = 1000 m = 0	k = 1000 m = 9	k = 1000 m = 99	k = 5000 m = 9
1	.953	.969	.923	.925	.919	.902
2	.609	.625	.927	.933	.967	1.009
3	.726	.792	.792	.799	.778	1.141
4	.655	.695	1.038	1.045	1.032	.910
5	.359	.395	1.144	1.151	1.176	1.064
6	.561	.611	.915	.918	.895	.947
7	.833	.910	1.011	1.016	1.055	1.105
8	.461	.477	1.157	1.166	1.218	1.049
9	1.002	1.083	.842	.850	.785	1.029
10	.870	.798	1.146	1.152	1.217	.852
Average estimate of W_q						
$\bar{x}$	.703	.735	.990	.995	1.004	1.000
Standard deviation of W_q						
s	.212	.217	.131	.131	.165	.095

The column labeled "k = 100, m = 0" in Table 13.9 corresponds to a simulation of 100 customers with all 100 customer waiting times used to calculate the average waiting time. In the column labeled "k = 100, m = 9," the average waiting time in each run is based only on the 91 waiting times of customers 10 through 100.

Note that when k = 100, the set of simulation runs for which data are collected beginning with the tenth customer arrival (m = 9) gives a mean value closer to the steady state value of $W_q = 1$ than the set for which data are collected for all customer arrivals (m = 0). This difference is due, in part, to the fact that the system is closer to being in steady state after 10 customer arrivals; that is, start-up bias has been reduced.

When k = 100, neither set of simulation runs gives a very good estimate for the value of W_q. Furthermore, since each set has a relatively large sample standard deviation, a larger number of runs is required to give a more precise estimate for W_q.

The three sets of runs based on 1000 customer arrivals provide results that are much closer to the steady state value. Again, better estimates for W_q are obtained when the first nine customers are ignored (m = 9) than when all the customers are counted (m = 0). Ignoring even more customers (m = 99), however, seems to make little difference in the accuracy of the value calculated for W_q. We can conclude, therefore, that for simulation runs of size 1000, ignoring the results of the first nine customers is enough to eliminate most of the start-up bias.[6]

The last column of Table 13.9 gives the results obtained when the steady state value is based on 10 runs of 5000 customers each and data are recorded beginning with the

---

[6]Actually, although the start-up bias remains present, because the average is based on 1000 customers its effect becomes negligible.

tenth customer. In this case, the average estimate for W_q when measured to three decimal places is indeed equal to the steady state value for W_q.

Calculating Confidence Intervals from the Simulation

The calculated values of $\bar{x}$ and s can be used to determine confidence intervals for the true value of W_q. The formula for a $(1 - \alpha)$ confidence interval for W_q based on n simulation runs is:

$$\left(\bar{x} - t_{\alpha/2,n-1} \frac{s}{\sqrt{n}}, \bar{x} + t_{\alpha/2,n-1} \frac{s}{\sqrt{n}} \right) \tag{13.9}$$

Here, n is the number of simulation runs that make up the data set, and $\bar{x}$ and s are, respectively, the overall sample average and standard deviation of the average waiting times as calculated from the n runs. For example, based on the data in the column corresponding to $k = 1000$ and $m = 99$ in Table 13.9, the 95% confidence interval for the steady state value of W_q is:

$$\left(1.004 - 2.262 \left(\frac{.165}{\sqrt{10}} \right), 1.004 + 2.262 \left(\frac{.165}{\sqrt{10}} \right) \right) = (.886, 1.122)$$

Other Methods to Eliminate Start-Up Bias

One shortcoming of the above approach for calculating steady state values is the amount of data that must be disregarded in an attempt to eliminate start-up bias. For example, by using values of $k = 1000$ and $m = 99$, we ignore almost 10% of the data values in the calculation of the sample mean.

Appendix 13.5 on the accompanying CD-ROM details two techniques that can be used to estimate confidence intervals while ignoring far less data. These methods are commonly classified as *variance reduction techniques* because they result in a lower variance and, therefore, tighter confidence intervals.

Selecting the Best Queuing Configuration

While this section has focused on using simulation to estimate steady state values for a queuing system, simulation of such systems is generally done in order to determine an optimal system configuration. When comparing configurations, we should use the same set of random number inputs for data generation whenever possible to ensure that the decision alternatives are evaluated under similar circumstances. Using pseudo-random numbers, rather than pure random numbers, facilitates this comparison in that we can generate the same set of numbers simply by using the same "seed value." Excel,[7] @RISK, and WINQSB are all capable of beginning random number generation with a predetermined seed value.

13.5 SIMULATION MODELING OF INVENTORY SYSTEMS

In Chapters 10 and 11, we presented a number of inventory models for which analytical solutions exist, each based on a particular set of assumptions. As in queuing situations, when these assumptions are not met, those models may not provide reasonable solutions. In such cases, simulation can predict the outcome of inventory policies.

By supplying the simulation with the values of parameters, such as the order and holding cost as well as the lead time and demand distributions, we can calculate an

---

[7]One simple way to use the same set of random numbers in different Excel simulations without the use of a common seed value is to generate an initial set of random numbers using the RAND( ) function. Then this set of numbers can be copied into a new worksheet using the Paste Special command, making sure to check the "Values" box. This set of numbers can then be recopied into new worksheets using the standard Copy and Paste commands.

average total inventory cost for a particular inventory policy. While simulation cannot be used to determine an optimal policy, it can be used to test which policy appears to yield the best results from the set of policies being considered.

One way to simulate inventory systems is to use the *next-event* approach we applied to the Lanford Sub Shack queuing model. Here, the "events" correspond to the arrival of customers, the placement of orders for future delivery, and the arrival of additional inventory from suppliers.

Frequently, however, a *fixed-time* approach is more appropriate for simulating inventory systems. In this approach, the system is monitored and updated at fixed-time intervals (daily, weekly, monthly). During each time period, activity associated with demands, orders, and shipments is determined and the system is updated accordingly.

To illustrate the fixed-time simulation approach, we consider the inventory situation faced by the Allen Appliance Company.

ALLEN APPLIANCE COMPANY

Allenb.its
Allenrq.xls
Allenrm.xls

Allen Appliance Company is a small appliance wholesaler that stocks the Doughboy electric bread maker. Each unit costs Allen $200; Allen, in turns sells them for $260 each. Allen uses an annual holding cost rate for the bread makers of 26%. Orders are placed at the end of the week and management estimates the cost of placing an order is about $45.

Management believes that if the company runs out of bread makers, all customers will backorder. Allen estimates that it will suffer a weekly goodwill cost due to future lost sales of $5 per backordered unit. The company also incurs a fixed administrative cost of $2 for each unit backordered, regardless of the length of time it is backordered.

Allen believes that the number of retailers who wish to purchase Doughboy bread makers each week approximately follows a Poisson distribution with a mean of two retailers and that the number of machines that each retailer wishes to purchase can be estimated by the following distribution:

$$P(\text{demand} = 1) = .10$$
$$P(\text{demand} = 2) = .15$$
$$P(\text{demand} = 3) = .40$$
$$P(\text{demand} = 4) = .35$$

The lead time for delivery of the bread makers from the manufacturer varies between one and three weeks and can be approximated by the following distribution:

$$P(\text{lead time} = 1 \text{ week}) = .2$$
$$P(\text{lead time} = 2 \text{ weeks}) = .6$$
$$P(\text{lead time} = 3 \text{ weeks}) = .2$$

Orders arrive at the beginning of a week. (For example, an order placed at the end of week 2 with a two-week lead time arrives at the beginning of week 5.) Allen wishes to determine the optimal inventory policy for the Doughboy bread maker.

SOLUTION

Suppose we wished to apply the planned shortage model discussed in Chapter 10. We are given values for the order cost, $C_o = \$45$, the weekly per unit backorder cost, $C_b = \$5$, and the administrative backorder cost, $\pi, = \$2$. But we also need estimates for the average weekly demand, D, the per unit weekly holding cost, C_h, and the lead time, L.

To estimate the average weekly demand, we note that, for each retailer who purchases bread makers, demand is between one and four units, and the average retailer demand is equal to:

$$.10(1) + .15(2) + .40(3) + .35(4) = 3 \text{ units}$$

We can then find the average weekly demand by multiplying the average retailer demand of three units by the average number of retailers who order per week, two. Hence, average weekly demand is estimated at six units.

The unit *weekly* holding cost, C_h, is:

$$C_h = \frac{(\text{annual holding cost rate}) * (\text{wholesale cost per unit})}{52 \text{ weeks per year}}$$

$$= (.26 * \$200/52) = \$1 \text{ per unit per week}$$

and the average lead time for delivery is:

$$.2(1) + .6(2) + .2(3) = 2 \text{ weeks}$$

Thus, if we were to model this problem by assuming that demand and lead time are constant, then, using these average values for the quantities required for the planned shortage model we obtain the WINQSB output shown in Figure 13.7.

Inventory Cost Analysis per week for Allen Appliance Company

12-24-1998	Input Data	Value	Economic Order Analysis	Value
1	Demand per week	6	Order quantity	24.8837
2	Order (setup) cost	$45.00	Maximum inventory	22.7364
3	Unit holding cost per week	$1.00	Maximum backorder	2.1473
4	Unit shortage cost		Order interval in week	4.1473
5	per week	$5.00	Reorder point	9.8527
6	Unit shortage cost			
7	independent of time	$2.00	Total setup or ordering cost	$10.85
8	Replenishment/production		Total holding cost	$10.39
9	rate per week	M	Total shortage cost	$1.50
10	Lead time in week	2	Subtotal of above	$22.74
11	Unit acquisition cost	$200.00		
12			Total material cost	$1,200.00
13				
14			Grand total cost	$1,222.74

FIGURE 13.7   WINQSB Weekly Inventory Cost Analysis for Allen Appliance Company

The output indicates an optimal inventory policy of ordering 25 bread makers when the inventory on hand reaches 10 units. Because both the weekly demand and lead time are random quantities, however, Allen has some concern that the solution generated by the planned shortage model may not be the optimal policy.

Selecting the Inventory System

Allen is considering implementing a continuous review system to monitor its inventory position. As we discussed in Chapter 10, two types of continuous review systems are (1) the order point, order up to level ((R,M)) inventory system, and (2) the order point, order quantity ((R,Q)) inventory system.[8]

---

[8]WINQSB refers to (R,M) systems as (s,S) systems and (R,Q) systems as (s,Q) systems.

Under both systems, orders are placed when the inventory level reaches R units or less. In an (R,M) system, the firm orders enough inventory to bring the inventory level back up to a projected level of M when the order arrives. In an (R,Q) system, the firm simply orders Q units each time an order is placed.

Allen is initially interested in determining whether an (R,M) system will result in a lower average cost than an (R,Q) system. To investigate this, the company has decided to conduct a fixed-time simulation. The simulation model for this inventory problem requires the construction of random number mappings for the number of retailers who arrive each week, the number of bread makers each retailer wishes to purchase, and the lead time in weeks after an order has been placed.

Random Number Mappings

To construct the random number mapping for the number of retailers who order in a week, we first generate the probabilities that 0, 1, 2, 3, etc. retailers place orders. The probability distribution for the number of retailers placing orders in a week is given by the Poisson distribution:

$$P(X = k) = \frac{(\lambda t)^k e^{-\lambda t}}{k!} \tag{13.10}$$

where λ is the mean number of retailers who order per week ($\lambda = 2$) and t is the interval under consideration (t = 1 week).

For Allen Appliance, $\lambda t = 2(1) = 2$. Substituting $\lambda t = 2$ into Equation 13.10 gives us the probabilities for the number of retailers who actually place orders in a week. These values are summarized in Table 13.10.

TABLE 13.10   PROBABILITIES FOR NUMBER OF RETAILERS WHO PLACE ORDERS IN A WEEK

P(0 retailers order)	= .135
P(1 retailer orders)	= .271
P(2 retailers order)	= .271
P(3 retailers order)	= .180
P(4 retailers order)	= .090
P(5 retailers order)	= .036
P(6 retailers order)	= .012
P(7 retailers order)	= .003
P(8 retailers order)	= .001
P(9 retailers order)[a]	= .001

[a]In calculating these probabilities, there is a small possibility that the number of retailers who order in a week will be greater than 9. To compensate for this fact, the probability that nine retailers order has been assigned a value of .001 when the actual value is only .0002.

Because these probabilities are accurate to three decimal places, we shall use the three-digit random number mapping in Table 13.11 and the pseudo-random numbers from Column 1 in Appendix C to determine the number of retailers who order from Allen each week. Since the number of bread makers demanded by a retailer is independent of the number of retailers who order each week, we must use a separate random number for each retailer in order to generate that retailer's demand. Given that the probability distribution of retailer demand is accurate to two decimal places, we use the two-digit random number mapping given in Table 13.12 and pseudo-random numbers from Column 2 to generate individual retailer demand. Finally, because the probability distribution for lead time is only accurate to one decimal place, we use the one-digit random number mapping in Table 13.13 to determine lead times and pseudo-random numbers from Column 3 to generate lead times.

TABLE 13.11 RANDOM NUMBER MAPPING FOR NUMBER OF RETAILERS ORDERING IN A WEEK

Number of Retailers Ordering During a Week	Random Number Mapping
0	000–134
1	135–405
2	406–676
3	677–856
4	857–946
5	947–982
6	983–994
7	995–997
8	998
9	999

TABLE 13.12 TWO-DIGIT RANDOM NUMBER MAPPING FOR RETAILER BREADMAKER DEMAND

Retailer Demand	Random Number Mapping
1	00–09
2	10–24
3	25–64
4	65–99

TABLE 13.13 RANDOM NUMBER MAPPING FOR LEAD TIME AT ALLEN APPLIANCE COMPANY

Lead Time	Random Number Mapping
1 week	0–1
2 weeks	2–7
3 weeks	8–9

Calculating Inventory Costs

We shall assume that if there are *no* backorders at the beginning or end of a week, the weekly inventory holding cost is as follows:

weekly holding cost = (average inventory level during the week) $* C_h$

For example, if the inventory level at the start of a week is 20 and the inventory level at the end of the week is 13, the average inventory level *during* the week is $(20 + 13)/2 = 16.5$. Since the weekly holding cost per unit is $C_h = \$1$, the simulated holding cost for that week is:

$$16.5(\$1) = \$16.50$$

Similarly, if units are on backorder at both the beginning *and* the end of a week, the weekly backorder cost is as follows:

weekly backorder cost =
(average number of units on backorder during the week) $* C_s$
+ (the number of units that go on backorder during the week) $* \pi$

For example, if the number of units on backorder at the start of a week is 6, and 9 more units are demanded and placed on backorder during the week, the number of units on backorder at the end of the week is 15 and the average number of backorders for the week is $(6 + 15)/2 = 10.5$. Recall that $C_s = \$5$ and $\pi_t = \$2$; thus, the total backorder cost for the week is:

$$(10.5)(\$5) + (9)(\$2) = \$70.50$$

When a company has inventory at the beginning of a week and backordered units at the end of the week, we shall make the simplifying assumption for the fixed-time simulation that demand occurs at a constant rate during the week. While this is not quite the case for Allen Appliance, the effect of such an assumption on the overall simulation is negligible.

For example, if Allen has three bread makers in stock at the beginning of a particular week and experiences a demand for eight bread makers during the week, the number of backorders at the end of the week is five. Our assumption is that, during the week, Allen will experience an "in-stock" period for 3/8 of the week and an "out-of-stock" period for 5/8 of the week.

During the "in-stock" period, since the beginning inventory is three and the ending inventory is zero, the average inventory is 1.5. Of course, during the "out-of-stock" period the average inventory is zero. Thus, the average inventory level for the week is calculated by

$$\begin{pmatrix} \text{Average} \\ \text{Inventory} \\ \text{Level} \end{pmatrix} = \begin{pmatrix} \text{Proportion} \\ \text{of Time} \\ \text{"In Stock"} \end{pmatrix} * \begin{pmatrix} \text{Average} \\ \text{Inventory} \\ \text{Level} \\ \text{During} \\ \text{"In Stock"} \\ \text{Period} \end{pmatrix} + \begin{pmatrix} \text{Proportion} \\ \text{of Time} \\ \text{"Out of} \\ \text{Stock"} \end{pmatrix} * \begin{pmatrix} \text{Average} \\ \text{Inventory} \\ \text{Level} \\ \text{During} \\ \text{"Out of} \\ \text{Stock"} \\ \text{Period} \end{pmatrix} \quad (13.11)$$

$$= .375 * (1.5) + .625 * 0 = .5625 \text{ units}$$

The holding cost for the week is then:

$$.5625(\$1) = \$0.5625$$

Similarly, during the "out-of-stock" period, the number of backorders starts at 0 and ends at 5, for an average of 2.5. During the "in-stock" period, there are, of course, no backorders; thus, the average backorder level for the week is:

$$\begin{pmatrix} \text{Average} \\ \text{Backorder} \\ \text{Level} \end{pmatrix} = \begin{pmatrix} \text{Proportion} \\ \text{of Time} \\ \text{"In Stock"} \end{pmatrix} * \begin{pmatrix} \text{Average} \\ \text{Backorder} \\ \text{Level} \\ \text{During} \\ \text{"In-Stock"} \\ \text{Period} \end{pmatrix} + \begin{pmatrix} \text{Proportion} \\ \text{of Time} \\ \text{"Out of} \\ \text{Stock"} \end{pmatrix} * \begin{pmatrix} \text{Average} \\ \text{Backorder} \\ \text{Level} \\ \text{During} \\ \text{"Out-of-} \\ \text{Stock"} \\ \text{Period} \end{pmatrix} \quad (13.12)$$

$$= .375 * (0) + .625 * 2.5 = 1.5625 \text{ units}$$

The total backorder cost for this week is then:

$$1.5625 * (\$5) + 5 * (\$2) = \$17.8125$$

THE INVENTORY SIMULATION FOR ALLEN APPLIANCE

To simulate the Allen Appliance problem, we first determine the number of retailers who will order. Then, for each retailer that places an order, we determine the number of bread makers demanded. The sum of these demands gives us the total weekly demand. The inventory of bread makers on hand at the end of the week equals the inventory on hand at the beginning of the week less this weekly demand. Note that a negative quantity implies a backorder situation.

If the inventory on hand at the end of the week is at or below the reorder point and *no orders are outstanding*, a new order is placed and the lead time for the order is determined. Note that if an order arrives at the start of a week, the inventory level increases by the size of the order quantity. Then we calculate the total costs for a simulated week by adding the week's holding, ordering, and backordering costs.

Simulation Information for Inventory Problems

Suppose that Allen wishes to evaluate the policy of reordering 25 units whenever inventory reaches 10 or less [that is, an (R,Q) system with R = 10 and Q = 25]. When performing the simulation, we must keep track of demands, inventories, backorder levels, lead times, and costs. The following column headings correspond to the information required:

	Inventory/Demand							Backorders/Reordering						Costs				
WK	BI	R#1	#O	R#2	#D	EI	AI	BB	#B	EB	AB	R#3	LT	HC	BC	AC	RC	TC

Number of Retailers Who Order: At the start of a week (WK), Allen has a beginning inventory (BI). During the week, a certain number of retailers order, (#O), generated by a random number (R#1) from column 1 of Appendix C.

Demand from the Retailers: For each retailer who orders, a demand (#D) is generated by a random number (R#2) from column 2. These individual demands are summed to give us the total demand for the week (#D).

Ending Inventory/Backorder Position: If the total weekly demand (#D) is less than the beginning inventory (BI), then the ending inventory (EI) is the beginning inventory less the weekly demand (EI = BI − #D), and the number of backorders during the week (#B) is 0. If, however, the weekly demand (#D) exceeds the beginning inventory (BI), then the ending inventory (EI) is 0 and the number of backorders during the week (#B) is the difference between the weekly demand and the beginning inventory (#B = #D − BI). The ending number of backorders during the week (EB) is the number of backorders incurred (#B). From these values we can use Equations 13.11 and 13.12 to calculate the average inventory level for the week (AI) and the average backorder level for the week (AB).

If the beginning inventory for the week (BI) is 0, then the ending inventory for the week (EI) will also be 0. The ending number of backorders for the week (EB) is the sum of the beginning backorders for the week (BB) and the week's demand (EB = BB + D).

Placing Orders/Delivery Time: When there are no orders pending and inventory falls to or below the reorder point of 10, an order is placed. We then select a random number from column 3 (R#3) to generate the lead time (LT). If an order is pending a new order is not placed, rather the LT is reduced by 1 from the previous week's value.

Weekly Costs: The total costs (TC) for the week may include holding costs (HC), time-dependent backorder costs (BC), administrative backorder costs (AC), and reorder costs (RC):

$$HC = C_h * (\text{Average Inventory}) = \$1 * AI$$

$$BC = C_s * (\text{Average Backorders}) = \$5 * AB$$

$$AC = \pi, * (\text{Number of New Backorders}) = \$2 * \#B$$

$$RC = C_o * (\text{Number of Orders Placed}) = \$45 \text{ if an order is placed}$$
$$= \$0 \text{ if no order is placed}$$

$$TC = \text{Total Weekly Costs} = HC + BC + AC + RC$$

Updating the System for the Next Week: At the start of the week, the beginning inventory (BI) and beginning number of backorders (BB) for that week are, respectively, the ending inventory (EI) and ending number of backorders (EB) from the previous week, unless an order arrives. The simulation detects that an order has arrived if there has been a pending order and the lead time (LT) for the previous week has reached 0. Once an order arrives, any backorders are filled immediately, and the remainder of the order is added to the ending inventory (EI) of the previous week to give us the beginning inventory (BI) for the week. Unless any unfilled backorders remain, the number of backorders at the beginning of the week (BB) is reset to 0.

Simulation of the Order Point, Order Quantity Policy for AAC

Table 13.14 shows a 10-week manual simulation of the policy of recording Q = 25 units when the inventory reaches R = 10 units or less. We assume that Allen begins with an inventory of 25 units and that there is, at most, one outstanding order at any point in time.

TABLE 13.14   REORDERING 25 UNITS WHEN THE INVENTORY LEVEL REACHES 10 OR LESS

		Inventory/Demand						Backorders/Reordering						Costs				
Wk	Bi	R#1	#O	R#2	#D	EI	AI	BB	#B	EB	AB	R#3	LT	HC	BC	AC	RC	TC
1	25	650	2	33	3			0										
				98	4													
				Total = 7		18	21.5		0	0	0	—	—	$21.50	0	0	0	$21.50
2	18	776	3	26	3			0										
				91	4													
				96	4													
				Total = 11		7	12.5		0	0	0	2	2	$12.50	0	0	$45	$57.50
3	7	617	2	48	3			0										
				82	4													
				Total = 7		0	3.5		0	0	0	—	1	$ 3.50	0	0	0	$ 3.50
4	0	880	4	27	3			0										
				96	4													
				46	3													
				20	2													
				Total = 12		0	0		12	12	6	—	0	0	$30	$24	0	$54.00
5	13	421	2	44	3			0										
				84	4													
				Total = 7		6	9.5		0	0	0	9	3	$ 9.50	0	0	$45	$54.50
6	6	745	3	94	4			0										
				66	4													
				63	3													
				Total = 11		0	1.64		5	5	1.14	—	2	$ 1.64	$5.70	$10	0	$17.34
7	0	118	0		—	0	0	5	0	5	5	—	1	0	$25	0	0	$25.00
8	0	401	1	75	4			5										
				Total = 4		0	0		4	9	7	—	0	0	$35	$ 8	0	$43.00
9	16	033	0		—	16	16	0	0	0	0	—	—	$16.00	0	0	0	$16.00
10	16	629	2	05	1			0										
				10	2													
				Total = 3		13	14.5		0	0	0	—	—	$14.50	0	0	0	$14.50

Analysis of this Simulation

A brief run-through of the simulation reveals the follows:

Week	Events
1	Two retailers demand a total of 7 units. Hence, inventory is reduced to 18. Since this quantity is greater than 10, no order is placed. Only holding costs are incurred.
2	11 units are demanded, so ending inventory reaches 7. Since this quantity is below 10, an order for 25 units is placed which will take 2 weeks to arrive. Both holding and ordering costs are incurred.
3	Demand exactly equals supply, so only a holding cost is incurred. One week has passed since the placement of an order, so lead time is reduced to 1 week.

4	There is no inventory during this entire period, and 12 units are demanded; these are all placed on backorder. Both backorder and administrative costs are incurred. Lead time is reduced by 1 week to 0 so that the order of 25 is available at the beginning of the next week.
5	The order of 25 units arrives and the 12 backorders are filled, leaving a beginning inventory for the week of 13. Demand is 7, leaving only 6 items at the end of the week. Thus, another order for 25 units is placed. This order takes 3 weeks to arrive. Both holding and ordering costs are incurred.
6	11 items are demanded, but only 6 are in inventory. The average inventory during the "in-stock" period is $6/2 = 3$, and the average number of backorders during the "out-of-stock" period is $5/2 = 2.5$. Thus, the average inventory (AI) equals $(6/11) * 3 + (5/11) * 0 = 1.64$, and the average number of backorders (AB) equals $(6/11) * 0 + (5/11) * 2.5 = 1.14$. Holding, backorder, and administrative costs are all incurred. Lead time is reduced by 1 week to 2.
7	There is no demand. The only cost incurred is the backorder cost. Lead time is reduced to 1 week.
8	The week starts with no inventory and 5 units on backorder. Demand is for 4 units increasing the number of backorders to 9. Thus, the average number of units on backorder for the period is 7. Both backorder and administrative costs are incurred. Lead time is reduced by 1 week to 0 so that the order will arrive at the start of week 9.
9	The order of 25 arrives, and the 9 backorders are filled, resulting in a beginning inventory of 16. Since there is no demand, ending inventory for the week is 16 and no order is placed. Only holding costs are incurred.
10	Demand totals three units, reducing inventory to 13. Since ending inventory is greater than 10, no order is placed. Only holding costs are incurred.

The average weekly cost of this 10-day simulation is:

$$\frac{21.50 + 57.50 + 3.50 + 54.00 + 54.50 + 17.34 + 25.00 + 43.00 + 16.00 + 14.50}{10} = \$30.68$$

Longer simulation runs would provide a more accurate estimate of the average weekly cost for this policy.

Simulation of the Order Point, Order Up to Level Policy for AAC

Let us now consider an order point, order up to level policy using the same reorder point, $R = 10$. From the WINQSB printout shown in Figure 13.7, we note that, under deterministic conditions, the order quantity is 25. Hence, an order point order up to level policy would be to order 35 $(= 25 + 10)$ less the stock on hand.

Thus, for example, if the inventory level is at 10 units when an order is placed, Allen will, in fact, order 25 units; however, only seven units are left in inventory when an order is placed, the order is for $25 + 10 - 7 = 28$ units.

To determine the average cost of this policy, we can conduct another 10-day simulation under the same sequence of demands and lead times used for the simulation of the order point, order quantity policy given above. In this simulation, shown in Table 13.15, we add another column for the variable order quantity, $Q = 35 -$ (stock on hand when an order is placed). The differing order quantities arrived at using this policy (28 in week 2; 26 in week 5) have an effect on the inventory levels and the number of backorders. Based on the 10-day simulation, the average weekly cost for this policy is:

$$\frac{21.50 + 57.50 + 3.50 + 54.00 + 57.50 + 8.58 + 10.00 + 28.00 + 20.00 + 18.50}{10} = \$27.91$$

TABLE 13.15   ORDER 35 UNITS LESS STOCK ON HAND WHEN SUPPLY REACHES 10

		Inventory/Demand						Backorders/Reordering							Costs				
Wk	Bi	R#1	#O	R#2	#D	EI	AI	BB	#B	EB	AB	Q	R#3	LT	HC	BC	AC	RC	TC
1	25	650	2	33	3			0											
				98	4														
				Total = 7		18	21.5		0	0	0	—	—	—	$21.50	0	0	0	$21.50
2	18	776	3	26	3			0											
				91	4														
				96	4														
				Total = 11		7	12.5		0	0	0	28	2	2	$12.50	0	0	$45	$57.50
3	7	617	2	48	3			0											
				82	4														
				Total = 7		0	3.5		0	0	0	—	—	1	$ 3.50	0	0	0	$ 3.50
4	0	880	4	27	3			0											
				96	4														
				46	3														
				20	2														
				Total = 12		0	0		12	12	6	—	—	0	0	$30	$24	0	$54.00
5	16	421	2	44	3			0											
				84	4														
				Total = 7		9	12.5		0	0	0	26	9	3	$12.50	0	0	$45	$57.50
6	9	745	3	94	4			0											
				66	4														
				63	3														
				Total = 11		0	3.68		2	2	18	—	—	2	$ 3.68	$ 0.90	$ 4	0	$ 8.58
7	0	118	0		—	0	0	2	0	2	2	—	—	1	0	$10	0	0	$10.00
8	0	401	1	75	4			2											
				Total = 4		0	0		4	6	4	—	—	0	0	$20	$ 8	0	$28.00
9	20	033	0		—	20	20	0	0	0	0	—	—	—	$20.00	0	0	0	$20.00
10	20	629	2	05	1		0												
				10	2														
				Total = 3		17	18.5		0	0	0	—	—	—	$18.50	0	0	0	$18.50

Comparing Inventory Costs

Using this one pair of 10-week simulations, we estimate that the order point, order up to level policy has an average weekly cost savings of $30.68 − $27.91 = $2.77 or ($2.77/$30.68) ∗ 100% = 9% over the order point, order quantity policy. While it appears that the order up to level policy results in a significant cost savings, this difference may simply be due to the random numbers selected for the simulation. In fact, there may be no real difference in the true average cost between the two policies. Unfortunately, we cannot verify this possibility on the basis of a single pair of simulation runs of only 10 weeks duration. In the next section, we introduce two tests designed to determine whether one of these policies does, in fact, yield better results.

13.6 TESTS FOR COMPARING SIMULATION RESULTS

Different policies or choices for the input parameters can result in different performance for the simulated system. For example, in the Lanford Sub Shack example discussed in Section 13.4, if the server had a different service time distribution, we would expect the simulation to generate different values for the average waiting times.

As we saw in the previous section, a change in the way in which the order quantity is determined results in different estimated values for the average weekly costs. Conclusions based on a single set of simulation runs, however, are risky at best and can in fact, be misleading.

To test the effect of different values for the parameters or different policy decisions, we should conduct multiple simulation runs. We can then employ standard statistical tests to determine whether there are, in fact, significant differences in the observed simulation outputs. To illustrate these testing procedures, let us reconsider the Allen Appliance Company situation described in the previous section.

Suppose that Allen wishes to consider inventory policies in which orders are placed when the inventory level reaches 10 units or less at the end of a week. The company specifically wishes to compare the order point, order quantity policy of ordering exactly 25 bread makers versus the order point, order up to level policy of ordering an amount equal to 35 less the stock on hand at the time of reordering.

To compare these two policies, we perform 10 simulation runs of 100 weeks duration for each policy. Files for running these simulations using Excel are included on the accompanying CD-ROM under the file names Allenrq.xls for the order point, order quantity policy and Allenrm.xls for the order point, order up to level policy. The results of the 10 pairs of simulations are summarized in Table 13.16.

TABLE 13.16   AVERAGE WEEKLY INVENTORY COST

Run	Order 25 When Supply Reaches 10 or Less Mean Cost Over 100 Weeks	Order 35 Less Stock on Hand When Supply Reaches 10 or Less Mean Cost Over 100 Weeks
1	$29.19	$35.51
2	$28.77	$26.42
3	$30.05	$32.52
4	$40.46	$27.15
5	$36.33	$29.39
6	$31.33	$25.82
7	$27.79	$32.20
8	$45.31	$29.21
9	$36.28	$31.07
10	$31.32	$27.91

MANN–WHITNEY TEST

One method used to determine whether there is a statistical difference in the output of the two policies is the **Mann–Whitney test**. For this test we consider the two data sets as a single set, and rank order them with rank 1 corresponding to the lowest cost, and rank 20 corresponding to the highest cost. We then sum the rankings of the *first* data set and denote this sum by r. Table 13.17 contains the rank values for the data in the two sets as well as the rank sum for each set. As you can see, r = 126.

TABLE 13.17   MANN–WHITNEY TEST FOR COMPARING INVENTORY POLICIES

Run	Order 25 When Supply Reaches 10 or Less — Mean Cost Over 100 Weeks	Rank	Run	Order 35 Less Stock on Hand When Supply Reaches 10 or Less — Mean Cost Over 100 Weeks	Rank
1	$29.19	7	1	$35.51	16
2	$28.77	6	2	$26.42	2
3	$30.05	10	3	$32.52	15
4	$40.46	19	4	$27.15	3
5	$36.33	18	5	$29.39	9
6	$31.33	13	6	$25.82	1
7	$27.79	4	7	$32.20	14
8	$45.31	20	8	$29.21	8
9	$36.28	17	9	$31.07	11
10	$31.32	12	10	$27.91	5
	RANK SUM	r = 126			84

The total sum of the rankings is $(1 + 2 + 3 + \ldots + 19 + 20) = 210$.[9] Were there no difference between the two data sets, we would expect the rank sums of the two sets to be approximately equal to one-half the total rank sum, or 105 each. The Mann–Whitney test procedure works by comparing the value of r to the expected rank sum of 105.

If the two data sets are drawn from populations with the same distribution, then the random variable R, representing the rank sum of the first data set, is distributed approximately normally with the following mean and standard deviation:

$$\mu = n^2 + \frac{n}{2} \qquad (13.13)$$

$$\sigma = n\sqrt{\frac{2n + 1}{12}} \qquad (13.14)$$

where n is the number of simulation runs conducted for each policy.

Since we used n = 10 observations, the rank sum of the first data set, R, should be approximately normally distributed with mean,

$$\mu = (10)^2 + \frac{10}{2} = 105$$

and standard deviation,

$$\sigma = 10\sqrt{\frac{2(10) + 1}{12}} = 13.23$$

To determine whether the calculated value for r, 126, is significantly different from the expected value of 105 (indicating that we should reject the hypothesis that there is no difference between the two sets of runs), we use the following testing procedure:

Mann–Whitney Test

H_0: The data sets are drawn from the same population.

H_A: The data sets are drawn from different populations.

Test: Reject H_0 if $|z| > z_{\alpha/2}$, where the test statistic $z = (r - \mu)/\sigma$.

Applying the Mann–Whitney Test to the Allen Appliance Company Problem

For the Allen Appliance Company simulation data, if we use a value of $\alpha = .05$, the test becomes:

$$\text{Reject } H_0 \text{ if } |z| > z_{.025} = 1.96$$

Here, the test statistic is:

$$z = (r - \mu)/\sigma = (126 - 105)/13.23 = 1.44$$

Since z = 1.44 ≯ 1.96, we do not reject H_0; that is, there is not enough evidence to statistically conclude that the data sets are drawn from different populations. The differences between the data values in one set of 10 simulation runs and the other set of 10 simulation runs may simply be due to chance.

The two principal advantages of the Mann–Whitney test over other tests used to determine whether there is a statistical difference in the two outputs are: (1) the data

---

[9]In general, if each set contains n observations, the total rank sum of the 2n observations is $2n^2 + n$.

sets themselves need not follow a normal distribution; and (2) the test works well with small samples.

The major difficulty with the test, however, is that, because it utilizes only data rankings (rather than their actual values), it is not a particularly powerful testing procedure. That is, even if the data sets are from different populations, the Mann–Whitney test may not detect this fact.

MATCHED-PAIR TEST

An alternative to the Mann–Whitney test which *does* take into account the actual data values is a **matched-pair test**. In this procedure, the observations are, in some sense, "matched," and the differences in the paired values form the basis for calculating the test statistic. The most obvious way of matching simulation run results is to use the same set of random number inputs for data generation so that we can compare policies under the same set of conditions.

Table 13.18 shows the differences in the mean weekly costs for the order point, order quantity and order point, order up to level policies based on 10 simulation runs of 100 weeks duration. For each run, the two policies in question are evaluated with identical sets of random numbers. That is, in the first pair of runs, the same set of random numbers that generated $29.19 for the order point, order quantity policy are used to generate $26.58 for the order point, order up to level policy. Similarly, in the second pair of runs, the same set of random numbers that give us $28.77 for the order point, order quantity policy yield $28.86 for the order point, order up to level policy, etc.

TABLE 13.18   MATCHED-PAIR TEST FOR COMPARING INVENTORY POLICIES

Run	Order 25 When Supply Reaches 10 or Less Mean Cost Over 100 Weeks	Order 35 Less Stock on Hand When Supply Reaches 10 or Less Mean Cost Over 100 Weeks	Difference
1	$29.19	$26.58	2.61
2	$28.77	$28.86	−0.09
3	$30.05	$29.64	0.41
4	$40.46	$34.79	5.67
5	$36.33	$32.39	3.94
6	$31.33	$28.85	2.48
7	$27.79	$27.20	0.59
8	$45.31	$32.98	12.33
9	$36.28	$31.05	5.23
10	$31.32	$29.74	1.58
Sample mean $\bar{x}$	$33.68	$30.21	$\bar{x}_D = $ 3.48
Sample Standard Deviation s	$ 5.76	$ 2.594	$s_D = $ 3.69

In a matched-pair hypothesis test, we determine whether the mean of the random variable D (the differences between corresponding pairs of data set values) is significantly different from zero. For our experiment, D represents the difference between the mean weekly costs for the order point, order quantity and order point, order up to level policies. The "Difference" column in Table 13.18 gives us the observed values of D for the 10 matched pairs. We calculate the mean difference, $\bar{x}_D$, and the standard deviation for the difference, s_D, based on the difference for the 10 pairs of runs, as shown at the bottom of the table. These statistics form the basis for the matched-pair test.

The matched-pair test is the following t-test for μ_D:[10]

---

[10]We present a two-tailed test here because we are interested in simply determining whether there is any difference in the average weekly costs between the two policies. If we wished to test whether one policy has a lower cost than another, we would use a single-tail test, and the critical value for t would be $t_{\alpha, n-1}$.

Matched-Pair Hypothesis Test

H_0: $\mu_D = 0$ (the two populations have the same mean)

H_A: $\mu_D \neq 0$ (the two populations have different means)

Test: Reject H_0 if $|t| > t_{\alpha/2, n-1}$ where the test statistic $t = (x_D - 0)/(s_D/\sqrt{n})$

Applying the Matched-Pair Test to the Allen Appliance Company Problem

For the Allen Appliance Company simulations, using $\alpha = .05$, with $n = 10$, the critical t-value is $t_{.025,9} = 2.262$. Thus, we should reject H_0 if $|t| > 2.262$, where

$$t = (\bar{x}_D - 0)/(s_D/\sqrt{n}) = (3.48 - 0)/(3.69/\sqrt{10}) = 3.93$$

Since $t = 3.93 > 2.262$, the matched-pair test provides enough evidence for us to conclude that a difference exists between the true mean weekly cost of the order point, order quantity and order point, order up to level policies considered. Furthermore, because $\bar{x}_D$ is positive, we infer that this difference is due to there being a lower cost for the order point, order up to level policy.

DETERMINING AN OPTIMAL POLICY

As a result of the matched-pair test, Allen has decided to focus on the order point, order up to level policy. It now wishes to determine optimal values for Doughboy bread makers for both the order point and the order up to level. To accomplish this, Allen is interested in evaluating the effect of increasing and decreasing the reorder point, R, by one unit while keeping the order quantity for the order up to level, Q, at 25 plus the difference between the reorder point and the inventory level at the time at which the order is placed. Allen conducted 10 simulation runs for reorder points of R = 9, R = 10, and R = 11, each based on 2000 weeks of operation in order to reduce the sample variance corresponding to the different policy sets. The mean weekly costs are given in Table 13.19. Using these data, Allen is interested in determining whether μ_1, μ_2, and μ_3, the mean costs for each of the three policies, are the same or different.

TABLE 13.19   AVERAGE WEEKLY COST WITH AN ORDER UP TO LEVEL OF 35 LESS STOCK ON HAND

Run	R = 9 Mean Cost Over 2000 Weeks	R = 10 Mean Cost Over 2000 Weeks	R = 11 Mean Cost Over 2000 Weeks
1	$30.09	$30.39	$30.41
2	$31.56	$30.04	$29.43
3	$30.41	$29.55	$29.51
4	$31.37	$30.18	$30.52
5	$30.78	$29.98	$29.92
6	$31.31	$30.71	$29.88
7	$28.92	$30.55	$30.46
8	$31.06	$30.57	$31.14
9	$31.04	$31.13	$29.78
10	$31.75	$30.66	$29.51
Sample Mean $\bar{x}$	$30.83	$30.38	$30.06
Sample Variance s^2	.7360	.2831	.3431

From Table 13.19 it appears that a reorder point of R = 11 yields a lower overall weekly cost; at least it did for these 10 simulation runs. But to test if $\mu_1 = \mu_2 = \mu_3$, we use a technique known as a one-way **analysis of variance (ANOVA)**.

ANOVA bases its test statistic on the sample variances of the three data samples. While it may seem strange to use variances when testing for equality of means, this method does make intuitive sense. The idea behind ANOVA is that if the data values are from the same population, the variance between data values within a sample should be proportionally the same as the variance between samples.

To perform an analysis of variance test, we assume the following two conditions:

1. Data must be drawn from normally distributed populations with identical variances.[11]

2. Data values must be independently selected, both within each data set and between data sets.[12]

A summary of the steps required using the ANOVA approach to test whether the average weekly inventory costs under each of the three reorder policies differ follows.

Analysis of Variance (ANOVA) Approach

1. Perform n simulation runs for each of the k cases (policies).
2. Calculate the sample mean, $\bar{x}$, and sample variance, s^2, for each case based on the data values obtained from the n simulations.
3. Calculate the *within-treatment variability* by averaging the variances calculated for each of the k cases. This yields the "pooled" variance, denoted by s_p^2.
4. Calculate the *between-treatment variability*, s_m^2, by determining the sample variance between the k sample means.
5. Calculate the F-statistic:

$$F = ns_m^2/s_p^2 \qquad (13.19)$$

6. Perform the following hypothesis test:

$H_0: \mu_1 = \mu_2 = \ldots = \mu_k$ (the average total weekly costs are the same for each of the k policies)

$H_A:$ at least one μ_i differs from the others (there is a difference in the average total weekly costs among the k policies)

Reject H_0 if $F > F_{\alpha, D1, D2}$
where the degrees of freedom for the critical F-value are

$$D1 = k - 1$$
$$D2 = k(n - 1)$$

The following steps correspond to the ANOVA test applied to the three policies under consideration by Allen.

1. Ten simulation runs are made for each of the three policies (Table 13.19). Each simulation run represents 2000 weeks of operation, and the average weekly cost is

---

[11]While the normality result generally holds if the data values represent means of a large number of observations (due to the central limit theorem), the population variances are not always identical. We can verify this assumption before using ANOVA by conducting a standard F-test for equality of variances.

[12]Use of a common seed to generate the data values in the three sets is allowable, but, in such instances, the test is based on what is known as a randomized block design. The interested reader should consult a statistics text for a discussion of this procedure.

determined for each run. For the ith simulation run and j^{th} policy, denote this value as $x_{i,j}$ (for instance, $x_{6,2} = 30.71$).

2. For each policy, calculate the average total weekly cost for the set of 10 simulation runs. For the jth policy, the sample mean is designated as $\bar{x}_j$ and is calculated by

$$\bar{x}_j = \frac{\sum_{i=1}^{10} x_{i,j}}{10}$$

These values are given in the "Sample Mean" row of Table 13.19.

The sample variance for the jth policy, s_j^2, is calculated using the formula:

$$s_j^2 = \frac{\sum_{i=1}^{10} (x_{i,j} - \bar{x}_j)^2}{9}$$

These values are given in the "Sample Variance" row of Table 13.19.

3. Calculate s_p^2 by

$$s_p^2 = (s_1^2 + s_2^2 + s_3^2)/3$$
$$= (.7360 + .2831 + .3431)/3 = .4541$$

4. Calculate s_m^2 by

$$s_m^2 = (\Sigma \bar{x}_i^2 - ((\Sigma \bar{x}_i)^2/k))/(k - 1)$$
$$= (((30.83)^2 + (30.38)^2 + (30.06)^2) - ((91.27)^2)/3)/2 = .1496$$

5. Calculate the F-statistic by

$$F = n\,(s_m^2/s_p^2)$$
$$= 10\,(.1496/.4541) = 3.294$$

6. The critical F-value for $\alpha = .05$ with $D1 = (k - 1) = 2$ degrees of freedom and $D2 = k(n - 1) = 3(10 - 1) = 27$ degrees of freedom, found in Appendix F, is:

$$F_{\alpha,\ D1,\ D2} = F_{.05,\ 2,\ 27} = 3.35$$

Since $F = 3.294 \not> 3.35$ (with $\alpha = .05$), there is not enough evidence to *conclude* that there is a difference in the total average weekly costs among the three policies. Three possible reasons for the insufficient evidence are:

1. The simulation runs did not consider a large enough quantity of weeks (2000) in calculating the average weekly cost.

2. The number of total simulation runs used for comparing policies ($n = 10$) was too small.

3. There really is very little difference between the mean values.

By increasing the number of weeks that make up each simulation run or the number of simulation runs for each policy, we might attain more accurate results. Rather than attempt this, however, let us investigate the effect of different combinations of order point and order up to level values on the average weekly cost.

INVESTIGATING ALTERNATIVE ORDER POINT, ORDER UP TO LEVEL VALUES—A TRIAL-AND-ERROR APPROACH

In trying to identify the best combination of values for the order point and order up to level, we use a trial-and-error approach of varying the reorder point from 9 to 14 and the order up to level from 24 to 31. For each of these 48 possible combinations, we conduct 10 simulations runs, each representing 2000 weeks of operations. Table 13.20 shows the average weekly cost calculated based on these 10 simulation runs.

The lowest average weekly cost from these runs, $29.10, occurs when ordering up to an amount based on Q = 26 when the inventory level reaches R = 12. Several other

TABLE 13.20   AVERAGE WEEKLY COST BASED ON SIMULATION RUNS OF 2000 WEEKS

		R					
		9	10	11	12	13	14
	24	$31.62	$30.76	$31.21	$29.47	$29.57	$29.40
	25	$30.83	$30.38	$30.06	$29.34	$29.38	$29.37
	26	$30.35	$30.15	$29.91	$29.10	$29.33	$29.43
Q	27	$30.25	$29.91	$29.56	$29.18	$29.26	$29.25
	28	$30.17	$29.89	$29.35	$29.26	$29.30	$29.24
	29	$29.89	$29.81	$29.58	$29.16	$29.44	$29.46
	30	$29.91	$29.83	$29.30	$29.31	$29.43	$29.36
	31	$29.92	$29.79	$29.32	$29.36	$29.60	$29.45

policies give average weekly values very close to this amount, however. The standard deviation associated with the set of simulation runs for $Q = 26$, $R = 12$ is, in fact, $0.5530. Thus a 95% confidence interval for the true mean weekly cost of this policy, the interval is $28.70 to $29.50. Since many of the cells corresponding to reorder points R between 12 and 14 and order up to level quantities Q between 26 and 30 have values within this range, we might consider performing lengthier simulation runs for such combinations of Q and R in order to obtain tighter confidence intervals for the true average weekly cost corresponding to these policies. Table 13.21 summarizes the mean weekly costs for these combinations based on simulations of 10,000 weeks.

TABLE 13.21   AVERAGE WEEKLY COST BASED ON SIMULATION RUNS OF 10,000 WEEKS

		R		
		12	13	14
	26	$29.30	$29.18	$29.19
	27	$29.28	$29.20	$29.24
Q	28	$29.13	$29.09	$29.18
	29	$29.23	$29.22	$29.33
	30	$29.18	$29.21	$29.36

The lowest sample average now occurs when $Q = 28$ and $R = 13$. Thus, Allen should order an amount equal to 41 minus its current stock on hand when the inventory level at the end of a week reaches 13 or less. For this policy, a 95% confidence interval for the average weekly cost is between $28.92 and $29.26. Since nearly all the values in Table 13.21 fall within this range, the differences in the average weekly costs for the 15 policy combinations are minimal at best. Potential savings do not appear to warrant further simulation runs.

On the basis of this analysis, the Student Consulting Group prepared the following report for Allen management recommending an inventory policy. One important issue included in the report is the sensitivity of the inventory policy to the assumed goodwill cost. The consulting group used simulation analysis to investigate the sensitivity of the results and determine the appropriate policy recommendations.

M E M O R A N D U M

To: James P. Allen, President—Allen Appliance Company

From: Student Consulting Group, Inc.

Subj: Inventory Policy for Doughboy Bread Makers

At your request, we conducted an analysis of the inventory policy for Dough-boy bread makers at Allen Appliance Company. Based on historical data, we observed that both customer arrival and demand patterns and the lead time possess a high degree of variability. We concluded that the problem could best be analyzed using a simulation approach.

We held meetings with personnel in the accounting and marketing departments to gain information about relevant costs and demands for the product. On the basis of these meetings, we utilized the following data and assumptions in developing the simulation model:

1. Doughboy bread makers cost Allen $200 per unit.
2. A 26% annual holding cost rate is used for this product.
3. The cost of placing an order with Doughboy is $45.
4. If Allen runs short of bread machines due to a higher-than-expected lead time demand, all potential customers place backorders for the item, incurring an administrative cost of $2 per unit.
5. The company suffers a goodwill cost of $5 per unit per week for each week that a unit is on backorder.
6. Orders are placed at the end of a week while delivery occurs at the beginning of a week.

   Based on the data we collected, we developed probability distributions for:

1. Customer arrivals
2. Customer demands
3. Lead time for the arrival of orders

Using only average values for these quantities, a simplified model indicates that Allen should implement an inventory policy of ordering 25 bread makers when the supply reaches 10 or less. Using this policy as a starting point, we tested different inventory policies using simulation. Based on repeated runs simulating thousands of weeks (equivalent to approximately 200 years of operation), we recommend the following policy:

> 1. Reorder when the supply of Doughboy bread makers at the end of a week reaches 13 units or less.
> 2. Order an amount equal to 41 less the stock on hand at the end of the week in which the order is placed.

Under this policy, Allen can expect to incur an average total weekly inventory cost of approximately $29.09 for the Doughboy bread makers. This total includes all holding, backorder, and ordering costs but does not include the cost of the machines themselves. The analysis also reveals that small changes from the recommended inventory policy do not greatly affect the average weekly inventory cost. For example, inventory policies for which the reorder point is changed by ± 1 unit and order up to level quantities vary by ± 2 units increase the average total weekly inventory cost by less than 1%. Figure I shows the range in these weekly costs.

FIGURE I   Range in Average Weekly Inventory Costs

Since management is somewhat unsure of the assumed $5 goodwill cost per unit per week, we performed a sensitivity analysis to examine the effect that changing this cost to $1 and to $10 will have on the optimal inventory policy.

For a goodwill cost of $1 per week, we recommend a policy of ordering 33 units minus the stock on hand when supply reaches three units or less. We estimate the average weekly cost of this policy at $23.62. In contrast, using the recommended policy of ordering 41 units less the stock on hand when supply reaches 13 or less results, in this case, in an average weekly cost of $26.03.

If the goodwill cost is $10 per week, we recommend ordering 47 units less the stock on hand when supply reaches 17 units or less. We estimate the average weekly cost of this policy at $32.15. In contrast, using the recommended policy of ordering 41 units less the stock on hand when supply reaches 13 or less results, in this case, in an average weekly cost of $32.93.

Hence, if the goodwill cost is actually $1/unit/week, the original recommended policy yields average weekly costs that are more than 10% greater than the optimal policy. If, however, the goodwill cost is actually $10/unit/week, the recommended policy yields an average weekly cost within 2.5% of the optimal policy. Because a significantly different policy results if the goodwill cost per unit per week is substantially less than the estimated $5 amount, we recommend that management undertake a focus group analysis to obtain firm estimates for the goodwill cost. We would be happy to assist you in this endeavor.

13.7 ADVANTAGES AND DISADVANTAGES OF SIMULATION

Simulation as an analysis tool has several important advantages and disadvantages. The following are some of the principal advantages:

Advantages of Simulation Analysis	

1. Simulation provides insight into the problem solution when other management science methods fail.

2. Simulation enables us to project the performance of an existing system under a proposed set of modifications without disrupting current system performance. Such performance may be analyzed over any time horizon.

3. Simulation models assist in the design of proposed systems by providing a convenient experimental laboratory for conducting "what if" analyses.

These advantages do not come without a price, however. Some of the principal disadvantages of simulation are summarized as follows.

Disadvantages of Simulation

1. Simulation models are generally time consuming and expensive to develop.

2. Simulation models provide only an estimate of a model's true parameter values.

3. There is no guarantee that the policy shown to be optimal by the simulation is in fact, optimal.

The last disadvantage listed is an important one. We have illustrated that simulation works by evaluating the results from different policies. Performance measures are calculated for each policy, and the "best" policy from this set is selected on the basis of such measures. If the true optimal policy is not one of the policies evaluated, however, or if a nonrepresentative set of random numbers occurs in the simulation, the optimal policy will not be found by the simulation. While we can protect against the second possibility by basing the results on enough trials, there is no way to be sure that the optimal policy has been included in the list of policies evaluated.

For example, when we used simulation to study the Allen inventory problem in Sections 13.5 and 13.6, we restricted our attention to a limited set of possible alternatives in order to make the analysis manageable. We first used the EOQ model to get a rough idea of what the order quantity and reorder point should be and then considered policy alternatives close to these. We did not, however, consider a policy such as ordering 40 units when the inventory level reaches 20 units. If this policy were indeed optimal, the simulation analysis would not have been able to detect it.

13.8 SUMMARY

Simulation can be used to model many complex business models, including problems in queuing and inventory. In Monte Carlo simulation, a random number mapping is developed to ensure that random variable inputs to the simulation correspond to the desired probability distribution.

Fixed-time simulations are used when the simulation is set up so that each iteration corresponds to a set time period. When events do not correspond to exact time periods, a next event approach is used in developing the simulation model.

Proper statistical design and analysis is critical for estimating system parameters and determining optimal policies from the simulation runs. The length of a simulation run, the number of runs needed to achieve a particular level of confidence, and the number of iterations that should be discarded before recording data from the simulation are addressed using statistics.

Some statistical tests that are useful in simulation analysis include the Mann–Whitney test for comparing the means of two populations using independent simulation runs, the matched-pair test for comparing the means of two populations using paired simulation runs, and ANOVA for comparing the means of several populations using independent simulation runs.

One purpose of developing a simulation is to identify a recommended policy. When standard analytical models cannot be used to determine an optimal policy, a simulation model can identify a best course of action from the set considered. The simulation model also frequently provides a convenient laboratory for performing "what-if" analyses.

While the concepts behind simulation analysis are relatively straightforward, the execution can be fairly complex. Not only must one develop appropriate models for the system being simulated, but one must also write and debug computer code to carry out the analysis. Because the costs involved in developing simulation models are typically high, they are generally used only in cases in which the payoff from the analysis is considerable.

$\mathcal{N}$OTATIONAL SUMMARY

D = A random variable representing differences in paired values

$f(x)$ = The probability density function

$F(x)$ = The cumulative probability distribution

r = rank sum for the first data set in the Mann-Whitney test

s_D = The sample standard deviation for the differences in a matched-pair test

$\bar{x}_D$ = The sample mean difference in a matched-pair test

α = The significance level for the hypothesis test

Using Excel and WINQSB to Perform Simulations

Using Excell to Perform Simulations

All of the simulations in this chapter can be done using EXCEL. The command used to generate random numbers in EXCEL is RAND ( ); the commands used to generate the random number mapping are IF, VLOOKUP, and HLOOKUP. If the random variable being simulated cannot assume too many different values, we typically use the IF statement to generate the random number mapping. This is the approach we used to conduct the simulation for JVC in Section 13.2 (see Figure 13.4). If, however, the random variable can assume a large number of possible values, the VLOOKUP or HLOOKUP commands are better alternatives for generating random number mappings.

To use VLOOKUP (HLOOKUP works in a similar fashion except that the mapping is done horizontally instead of vertically), we set aside three columns for the input. We put the probability distribution for the random variable in the second column and the corresponding random variable value in the third column. We enter the cumulative probability distribution into the first column by entering a value of 0 in the first row. For the next row, the cell value is equal to the value in the cell directly above plus the value in the column next to the cell directly above. We then drag down this formula for all rows in which a probability value is found in the second column.

For example, if we wished to simulate the number of customers who arrive each day to purchase bread makers for the Allen Appliance Company example discussed in Section 13.5, we might put the probability for demand in column B and the corresponding demand in Column C of the spreadsheet. We calculate the cumulative probability values in Column A using the values in Column B. If the week number is in Column D and random numbers are in Column E, we use the command VLOOKUP (E2, $A$2:$C$5,3) to generate the demand for week 1, as shown in Exhibits 1 and 2.

In this VLOOKUP formula, the first argument, E2, indicates that the random number is found in cell E2. The second argument, $A$2:$C$5, indicates that there is an array in that block of values giving the cumulative probability distribution for the random number mapping. The value of the third argument, 3, indicates that the value of the random variable is found in the third column of the array (the C column).

	A	B	C	D	E	F
1	Cum. Prob	Prob.	# Cust.	Week	Rand. #	Demand
2	0	0.1	1	1	0.601865	3
3	0.1	0.15	2	2	0.906567	4
4	0.25	0.4	3	3	0.484237	3
5	0.65	0.35	4	4	0.475234	3
6				5	0.555775	3
7				6	0.345621	3
8				7	0.149795	2
9				8	0.450559	3
10				9	0.280749	3
11				10	0.069043	1
12				11	0.911909	4
13				12	0.776469	4
14				13	0.278644	3
15				14	0.807257	4
16						

EXHIBIT 13.1

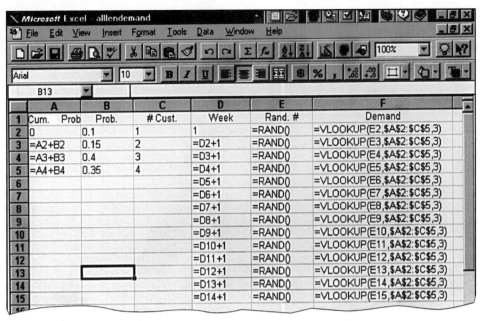

EXHIBIT 13.2

VLOOKUP (E2,$A$2:$C$5,3) will return the value from column C in the same row as the largest value in column A that does not exceed E2; i.e., the appropriate demand corresponding to the random number is E2.

Using WINQSB to Perform Simulations

We can use the Queuing System Simulation module of WINQSB to simulate complex queuing systems. We can perform simulations of simple queuing systems by selecting general queuing systems within the Queuing Analysis module and choosing "Simulate the System" from the "Solve and Analyze" option on the menu bar.

We simulate inventory systems using WINQSB by selecting one of the continuous review or periodic review system options on the initial data screen of the Inventory Theory and Systems module. To perform a simulation, we select "Perform Simulation" from the "Solve and Analyze" option on the menu bar.

PROBLEMS

Note: *The Excel file corresponding to Appendix C is included on the accompanying CD-ROM. If you are using Excel to solve these problems you may wish to import these values into your spreadsheet.*

1. Price changes of shares of the Saveway Stores, Inc. have been recorded over the past 50 days. The frequency distribution is as follows:

Price Change	Frequency
−1/2	3 days
−3/8	4 days
−1/4	5 days
−1/8	6 days
0	10 days
+1/8	12 days
+1/4	4 days
+3/8	3 days
+1/2	3 days

a. Develop a relative frequency distribution for the price change of Saveway stock.

b. Using the relative frequency distribution developed in part (a), determine the mean daily change in the price of shares of Saveway Stores, Inc. If the current stock price is 32, what would be the expected stock price 30 days from now?

c. If the current price of Saveway stock is 32, use the first two numbers in column 1 of Appendix C to simulate the price of the stock over the next 30 trading days.

d. Compare the answer in part (c) with the expected stock price after 30 days calculated in part (b). Comment on the difference between the two values.

2. It has been estimated that customers arrive at the Quick Stop Convenience store during the evening according to a Poisson process at a mean rate of 40 per hour. Each customer buys between zero and five lottery tickets according to the following probability distribution:

Number of Lottery Tickets Purchased	Probability
0	.45
1	.30
2	.15
3	.03
4	.02
5	.05

If Quick Stop has 30 lottery tickets available at 6 P.M., use simulation to determine the time at which the store will sell out of the lottery tickets. Use column 1 of Appendix C to determine the interarrival times of customers and column 2 to determine the number of lottery tickets each customer will purchase.

3. Management scientists developed a simulation of the queuing situation at Bravo Dry Cleaners in order to consider operational procedures that might improve customer service. The simulation model assumed a single-server queuing system in which customers arrive according to a Poisson process at a mean rate of 30 customers per hour, and service time is uniformly distributed between zero and two minutes.

The management scientists conducted 10 simulation runs of 1000 customers each and recorded the data beginning with the tenth customer. The average time (in minutes) that a customer waited in line prior to beginning service is as follows:

Run	Average Waiting Time	Run	Average Waiting Time
1	.6448	6	.6893
2	.6754	7	.7581
3	.6166	8	.7030
4	.5797	9	.5572
5	.7813	10	.6016

For the 10 runs, the overall average waiting time is .6607 minute and the standard deviation is .0744 minute.

a. On the basis of these data, determine a 95% confidence interval for the average waiting time of this queuing system.

b. For this problem, $\lambda = .5$ per minute, $\mu = 1$ per minute, and $\sigma^2 = 1/3$. Compare the answer you obtained in part (a) with the result you would obtain using the M/G/1 queuing formula for W_q.

4. An analysis of operations at the Frosty Freeze Drive Thru Window indicates that the customer waiting line can be modeled by a single server queuing system in which customer interarrival times are uniformly distributed between 0 and 4 minutes and customer service time is exponentially distributed with a mean of 1 minute. Management developed a simulation program based on this model, conducting 10 simulation runs of 1000 customers each. Data were recorded beginning with the tenth customer; the average time (in minutes) that a customer waits in line prior to beginning service is as follows:

Run	Average Waiting Time	Run	Average Waiting Time
1	.5642	6	.5455
2	.6402	7	.4305
3	.5762	8	.6323
4	.5608	9	.7018
5	.6143	10	.5718

The overall average waiting time for the 10 runs is .5837 minutes, and the standard deviation is .0718 minutes.

a. On the basis of these data, determine a 95% confidence interval for the average waiting time of this queuing system.

b. In comparing the data in problems 3 and 4, can you conclude that the average waiting times for the two queuing systems are different? Test at the $\alpha = .05$ level.

5. Consider the following PERT network used to describe the planning of regional sales meetings by Craig Computer Corporation:

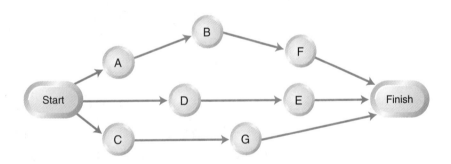

The expected completion time for each job is as follows:

Job	Expected Completion Time in Weeks
A	6
B	4
C	9
D	7
E	8
F	3
G	5

a. Determine the critical path(s) and the expected completion time for the project.

b. Suppose each job has a 25% chance of being completed two weeks early, a 25% chance of being completed on time, and a 50% chance of being completed two weeks late. Using the first two digits in column 4 of Appendix C to determine the job times, calculate the project completion time for five different sets of job times. On the basis of these five simulations, determine the probability that each job is on the critical path.

c. Calculate a 95% confidence interval for the expected project completion time.

6. Taks Home Furnishing is currently having its year-end appliance clearance sale. The store has 12 18-cubic-foot whirlpool refrigerators on sale; five are white, 4 are almond, and 3 are harvest gold. Each day, the company expects between 0 and 4 customers interested in buying a refrigerator to arrive at the store according to the following probability distribution:

$$P(0 \text{ arrivals}) = .15$$
$$P(1 \text{ arrival}) = .25$$
$$P(2 \text{ arrivals}) = .30$$
$$P(3 \text{ arrivals}) = .20$$
$$P(4 \text{ arrivals}) = .10$$

For each of these customers, there is a 60% chance that the person will want to purchase one of the sale-priced Whirlpools.

Taks knows that 40% of customers desire a white refrigerator, 25% desire an almond refrigerator, and 35% desire a harvest gold refrigerator. If the store is sold out of a particular color choice, the customer will leave without making a purchase.

Use random numbers from column 1 of Appendix C to determine the number of customer arrivals, column 2 to determine whether an arriving customer will wish to purchase an 18-cubic-foot Whirlpool refrigerator, and column 3 to determine the choice of color. How many days it will take for Taks to sell all 12 refrigerators?

7. In order to evaluate the possible effects of offering a special tenth anniversary sale on soft drinks, Joe's Beverage Barn has decided to conduct a simulation, modeling the check-out line as an M/M/1 queuing system with $\lambda = 57$ per hour and $\mu = 60$ per hour. Two sets of simulation runs were performed for analyzing operations; each used the same random number seed values and consisted of 10 runs of 1000 customers. The following data are the average waiting time in minutes for each of the 10 runs for the two sets of data. In Set A, data were collected beginning with the tenth customer; in Set B, data were collected beginning with the two hundredth customer.

Run	Set A	Set B	Run	Set A	Set B
1	7.336	8.079	6	11.373	11.520
2	9.736	10.673	7	13.186	15.574
3	3.647	3.426	8	8.369	9.295
4	9.501	9.819	9	8.426	6.407
5	27.967	33.100	10	17.408	19.978

On the basis of these data, is the estimated value for the waiting time different for the two sets? Test at the 5% significance level.

8. Consider the data for Joe's Beverage Barn in Problem 7. For Set A, the data have a mean value of 11.695 minutes and a standard deviation of 6.782 minutes; for Set B, the mean value is 12.787 minutes and the standard deviation is 8.496 minutes.

a. Determine a 95% confidence interval for W_q on the basis of the data in Set A.

b. Determine a 95% confidence interval for W_q on the basis of the data in Set B.

c. Compare the answers in parts (a) and (b) with the value of W_q as calculated using the M/M/1 formula given in Chapter 12.

9. Consider the Allen Appliance problem described in Section 13.5. Suppose that the company wants to use an order point, order quantity policy with $Q = 35$. Three sets of 10 simulation runs are conducted using values for the reorder point, R, of 10, 15, and 20. Each run lasts 1000 weeks, and the average weekly costs are as given below.

Can you conclude that the average weekly cost was different for the three values of R? Test at an $\alpha = .05$ significance level.

R = 10	R = 15	R = 20
30.35	30.99	32.76
31.34	31.68	33.12
30.11	30.42	32.70
29.23	29.88	33.09
29.10	29.82	32.30
31.94	31.04	33.24
29.20	29.88	32.63
30.00	30.29	32.94
29.12	28.73	31.50
28.87	29.46	32.49

10. Hervis Rentals is a small rental agency that rents various pieces of equipment. The company owns three wallpaper removal machines that rent for a net price of $12 per day. When there is a demand for a machine and none is available, the firm offers a discount certificate good for $15 off a future rental. The firm estimates that the certificate costs it $12 in lost profits. Each day a wallpaper rental machine goes unrented costs the firm $1 in storage costs. The owner of the agency estimates the following statistics:

Number of Wallpaper Removal Machines Demanded Daily	Probability	Length of Rental	Probability
0	.25	1 day	.60
1	.20	2 days	.25
2	.30	3 days	.10
3	.15	4 days	.05
4	.10		

a. Conduct a 10-day simulation of this business, using column 5 of Appendix C to determine the daily demand and column 6 to determine the length of each rental.

b. Suppose the company could obtain another wallpaper removal machine at a cost of $5 per day. On the basis of a 10-day simulation, should the company obtain the additional machine?

11. Dizzy Izzy is a discount appliance store specializing in home entertainment equipment. The firm carries two brands of satellite antenna systems: Panasony and ChannelMaster. Due to the high cost of ordering these systems and the rapid changes in the technology, Dizzy Izzy's policy is to not reorder additional systems until the store is completely sold out of both brands.

Presently, the store has six Panasony and four ChannelMaster systems in stock. The number of customers who arrive each day intending to buy a satellite system follows a Poisson distribution with a mean of 2. Forty percent of customers want to purchase a Panasony system, 50% want to purchase a ChannelMaster system, and 10% want to purchase a brand that Dizzy Izzy does not carry and therefore leave without making a purchase.

If a customer wants to purchase a Panasony system but Izzy is sold out, there is a 25% chance that the customer will buy the ChannelMaster system instead, a 35% chance of placing a backorder for the Panasony system, and a 40% chance that the sale will be lost.

If a customer wants to purchase a ChannelMaster system but Izzy is sold out, there is a 45% chance that the customer will buy a Panasony system instead, a 40% chance of placing a backorder, and a 15% chance that the sale will be lost.

Using simulation, determine how many days it will take for Dizzy Izzy to completely sell out of the existing inventory of satellite antennae systems. Determine the number of backordered systems and lost sales as of that date. Use column 3 of Appendix C to determine the number of customers who arrive each day to purchase satellite systems, column 4 to determine the choice of system, and column 5 to determine, what will happen if the customer's selection is sold out.

12. At Steve's Super Scooper, two employees serve customers during the lunch hour. One employee gets the customer's ice cream selection, while the other receives payment. Customers arrive at Steve's according to a Poisson process, having a mean interarrival

time of 1.5 minutes. The time it takes to get an ice cream selection follows an exponential distribution with a mean of one minute. The service time for the second employee follows a uniform distribution between 30 and 80 seconds.

Using simulation, determine the average time a customer spends waiting in line to get and pay for ice cream. Base your results on a simulation of 20 customer arrivals using column 1 of Appendix C to determine the customer interarrival time, column 2 to determine the time a customer spends with the employee getting ice cream, and column 3 to determine the time a customer spends with the cashier.

13. Albright's Hardware sells Security brand dead-bolt locks in single packages and two-packs (one key fits both locks). Single packages sell for $12 each, while two-packs sell for $30. Albright's cost is one-half the retail selling price.

Albright's is open seven days a week and receives a delivery from Security once a week. If Albright runs out of single packages but still has two-packs available, the store will break open a two-pack and sell each of the two at the single-package price. If the store is out of stock of the type of dead-bolt set the customer wants to purchase, Albright management believes that it will suffer a goodwill loss of $10.

Each day, between zero and three customers arrive to purchase dead-bolt locks with the following distribution:

$$P(0 \text{ arrivals}) = .30$$
$$P(1 \text{ arrival}) = .35$$
$$P(2 \text{ arrivals}) = .20$$
$$P(3 \text{ arrivals}) = .15$$

Sixty percent of purchasers want a single set, while 40% want a two-pack. The store's policy is to order sufficient dead bolts to bring the beginning-of-the-week inventory up to five single sets and five two-packs.

Neglecting holding and ordering costs, determine a 95% confidence interval for Albright's mean weekly profit based on four weeks of simulation. Use column 1 of Appendix C to determine the daily number of arriving customers and column 2 to determine whether a customer wants to purchase a single set or a two-pack.

14. Consider the data given in Problem 13 for Albright's Hardware. The company is considering changing its inventory policy so that it begins each week with six single sets and only four two-packs. Conduct a four-week simulation using the same random numbers as in Problem 13 to determine whether there is any difference in the mean weekly profit. Test at a 5% significance level.

15. Attendees at the annual Orange County Small Business Administration Conference register by standing in line to pay their registration fee and then proceeding to a designated line based on their business interest to collect their materials. The conference addresses four types of small businesses: Manufacturing, Retailing, Import/Export, and Financial Services.

The registration period lasts from 8:30 A.M. to 9:30 A.M. During this period, the conference organizers estimate that the interarrival time of attendees approximately follows an exponential distribution with a mean time of one minute. The time to register an attendee is anticipated to be 30 seconds if the attendee pays by cash or check, or 90 seconds if the attendee pays by a credit card. The organizers estimate that 60% of attendees will use a credit card.

Based on similar conferences, the organizers estimate that 40% of attendees will be interested in manufacturing, 30% in retailing, 10% in import/export, and 20% in financial services. The time required to obtain materials for the manufacturing and retailing lines an estimated to be exactly two minutes, while the time to obtain materials for the import/export and financial services lines is estimated to be exactly three minutes.

Simulate the arrival of the first 20 customers at the conference using appropriate random number selections from Appendix C. For this simulation, determine:

a. The time it takes for the twentieth customer to complete registration.

b. The average waiting time in each of the five lines (registration, manufacturing, retailing, import/export, and financial services).

16. The Treasure Trove Casino in Las Vegas has a free telephone booth that allows customers to make a one-minute telephone call anywhere in the United States at no charge. Customers arrive to make their free calls according to a Poisson process at a mean rate of $\lambda = 40$ per hour. The time each customer is allowed to be in the phone booth is a constant 72 seconds. Management is interested in using simulation to determine the average waiting time for a customer at the free telephone both.

    Conduct the simulation for 20 customer arrivals assuming that there is no one initially present at the phone booth. Use column 5 of Appendix C to determine the customer interarrival times. Based on these 20 arrivals, calculate the average time a customer spends waiting in line to use the phone. Compare this result to that obtained for W_q using the formula for the M/G/1 queue.

17. Ricon, Inc. uses an assembly line to produce its office copiers. The final step in the assembly process is quality control inspection. Copiers arrive at the quality inspection area exactly every 90 seconds. The time it takes to perform a quality control inspection follows an exponential distribution, with a mean of 72 seconds. Ricon management is interested in using simulation to determine the average time it takes a copier to complete its quality control inspection.

    Conduct a simulation for 20 copier arrivals assuming that the system starts empty. Use column 6 of Appendix C to determine the inspection times. Calculate the average time a copier spends in the system based on these 20 arrivals.

18. Shari Winslow has gone to Atlantic City to play roulette. Her strategy is to place $10 bets on red. She has $30 and will quit either when she loses all her money or wins $20.

    If the roulette wheel is operating properly, the chance of landing on red is 18/38, the chance of landing on black is 18/38, and the chance of landing on green is 2/38. Hence, Shari's chance of winning her bet is 18/38 (approximately .4737) and of losing her bet is 20/38 (approximately .5263).

    Use simulation to determine the number of spins it will take before Shari will stop playing roulette. Conduct four simulation runs and determine a 95% confidence interval for the average number of plays based on these four simulations.

19. Terry Moore has three alternative routes to travel from his home in Tustin to his office in Anaheim. He can take the Santa Ana Freeway to the Orange Freeway; the Costa Mesa Freeway to the Riverside Freeway; or the Garden Grove Freeway to the Orange Freeway.

    The travel time (in minutes) on each of the five freeways follows the following probability distribution:

Santa Ana	Probability	Orange	Probability	Costa Mesa	Probability	Riverside	Probability	Garden Grove	Probability
8	.30	6	.25	7	.35	5	.20	3	.20
9	.25	7	.35	8	.20	6	.30	4	.10
10	.30	8	.20	9	.10	7	.25	5	.20
11	.10	9	.20	10	.25	8	.10	6	.50
12	.05			11	.10	9	.15		

    For each of the three routes, conduct 10 simulation runs and calculate the average commuting time. Which route appears to take the least travel time?

20. Harvest Supermarket has one loading dock for receiving deliveries. During any half-hour interval, either 0, 1, 2, or 3 delivery trucks arrive with the following probabilities:

$$P(0 \text{ arrivals}) = .60$$
$$P(1 \text{ arrival}) = .25$$
$$P(2 \text{ arrivals}) = .10$$
$$P(3 \text{ arrivals}) = .05$$

Eighty percent of the delivery trucks can be unloaded in a half hour, while 20% of the trucks take a full hour to unload. Using fixed-time simulation, determine the average number of trucks waiting to unload during a 10-hour period. Assume that the simulation starts with the loading dock empty. Use column 6 of Appendix C to determine the number of trucks that arrive in a half-hour period and column 7 to determine how long it will take to unload a truck.

21. Customers arrive at the Blinkies Donut shop between 6:30 A.M. and 8:30 A.M. according to a Poisson process with a mean rate of one every minute. Seventy percent of the arriving customers purchase one or two donuts, while 30% purchase the Blinkies Dozen pack. For customers purchasing one or two donuts, the service time is uniformly distributed between 30 and 50 seconds. For customers purchasing the Blinkies Dozen pack, the service time is exponentially distributed with a mean of 90 seconds.

    Blinkies employs a single clerk to help customers. Simulate the arrival of the first 20 customers into the store during the 6:30 A.M. to 8:30 A.M. time period. Determine the maximum number of customers who will wait in line to begin service during this period. Use appropriate random number selections from Appendix C.

22. The Quick Stop Convenience Store has two gas pump islands, one for full service and one for self service. Cars arrive at the gas pumps according to a Poisson process at a mean rate of 20 per hour. Sixty percent of the cars want self serve, while 40% want full serve. The service time for the self-serve pump follows an exponential distribution with a mean of four minutes. The service time for the full-serve pump follows an exponential distribution with a mean of five minutes.

    If more than two cars are in line waiting for self serve, but no one is using the full-serve pump, an arriving car wanting self serve will join the self-serve queue with probability .3, balk (immediately leave without service) with probability .5, or go to the full-serve pump with probability .2. If more than two cars are in line waiting for self serve and the full-serve pump is occupied, an arriving car wanting self serve will join the self-serve pump queue with probability .4 and balk with probability .6.

    Simulate this system for 20 car arrivals. Use column 1 of Appendix C to determine the interarrival time of cars, column 2 to determine whether the car will want self serve or full serve, column 3 to determine the service time for obtaining the gasoline, and column 4 to determine whether an arriving car wanting self serve will join the queue, balk, or switch to full serve. What observations can you make based on this simulation?

23. Ontario, California, is a suburb of Los Angeles. Its airport serves primarily domestic air traffic; however, occasionally an international flight is diverted to Ontario if Los Angeles International Airport is fogged in. If an international flight arrives at Ontario, two customs inspectors set up operations to process the passengers.

    Passengers line up to have their passports and visas checked by the first customs inspector. The time required to do this follows a uniform distribution with times between 20 and 70 seconds. Passengers then claim their baggage. The time it takes to retrieve baggage follows an exponential distribution with a mean of three minutes. Finally, the passengers join a line to have their baggage inspected by the second customs inspector. Forty percent of the passengers are waived through without inspection, 50% experience a cursory inspection of one minute duration, and 10% experience a full inspection of three minutes duration.

    Use simulation to determine how long it takes a plane load of 20 passengers to get through customs. Use column 1 of Appendix C to determine the time required to check a passenger's passport and visa, column 2 to determine the time required to obtain baggage, and column 3 to determine the type of baggage inspection a passenger experiences (none, cursory, or full).

24. Family Appliance specializes in selling major appliances for use in kitchen remodeling. One of its more popular items is the SubZero refrigerator. Over the past 40 weeks, the store has collected data regarding the weekly demand for this refrigerator. On the basis of these data, the following demand distribution has been estimated:

Weekly Demand	Probability
0	.25
1	.15
2	.15
3	.25
4	.10
5	.10

The store's policy is to reorder up to 15 refrigerators whenever the inventory on hand reaches five or fewer at the end of a week. The holding cost for each refrigerator is $2 per week, and the cost of reordering is $50. If a customer wants a SubZero refrigerator and Family is out of stock, the customer will go elsewhere and the sale is lost. The company estimates that it suffers a goodwill cost of $40 for each lost sale. Current inventory is seven refrigerators.

Lead time for delivery can be described by the following distribution:

Lead Time	Probability
1 week	.30
2 weeks	.50
3 weeks	.20

a. Conduct a 10-week simulation of Family's inventory situation regarding the SubZero refrigerator to determine the total cost for this period. Use column 3 of Appendix C to determine the weekly demand and column 4 to determine the lead time.

b. SubZero is offering Family a new policy of automatically delivering five refrigerators every two weeks. The administrative cost of this policy is $5 per week, and the first delivery will be in two weeks. Conduct a 10-week simulation of Family's inventory situation under this plan and determine the total cost for the 10-week period.

c. On the basis of your answers to parts (a) and (b), what would you recommend to Family management regarding the supplier's offer?

25. Marv Portney is a salesman for Craftco Comfort Beds. Marv gets his leads when customers call the Craftco 800 number to arrange an in-house demonstration. (Customers receive a free clock-radio for agreeing to this demonstration.) Of the customers with whom Marv makes appointments, 10% turn out to be not at home. Of the others, 10% are single women, 30% are single men, and 60% are married couples.

Craftco offers four sizes of beds: king, queen, double, and twin. The list price of the king is $4000, the queen $3000, the double $2500, and the twin $2000. Marv can discount each bed up to 50% in order to make a sale, however; therefore, he estimates that his commission is uniformly distributed within the following ranges:

Bed Size	Commission Uniformly Distributed Between
King	$400 and $1000
Queen	$300 and $800
Double	$200 and $600
Twin	$250 and $500

Marv has found that, among the single women he calls upon, he makes a sale 70% of the time; 40% want to buy a twin bed, 50% want a double, 5% want a queen, and 5% want a king. Marv makes a sale to 65% of the single men he calls on. Of these, 30% want a twin bed, 40% want a double, 25% want a queen, and 5% want a king. Among the married couples, Marv makes a sale 55% of the time. Ten percent of the couples want to buy a single twin bed, 20% want two twin beds, 15% want a double, 40% want a queen, and 15% want a king.

Marv makes one, two, or three sales calls per day with the following probabilities:

Number of Sales Calls per Day	Probability
1	.50
2	.40
3	.10

a. Simulate Marv's activity over a 10-day period using an appropriate random number selection from Appendix C.

b. Calculate Marv's earnings over this 10-day period.

CASE 1: *Office Central*

Office Central is a nationwide mail-order firm specializing in selling office supplies. One of the items the company carries is the Ricon 436 copier. The copiers cost the firm $1825 each, and Office Central sells them for $2499 each. The firm uses a 20% annual holding cost rate so that the daily holding cost per unit is approximately $1. The cost of placing an order with Ricon is $150, and orders have a lead time between three and six working days (the store is open six days a week). The following distribution holds for the lead time:

$$P(\text{lead time} = 3 \text{ days}) = .2$$
$$P(\text{lead time} = 4 \text{ days}) = .4$$
$$P(\text{lead time} = 5 \text{ days}) = .3$$
$$P(\text{lead time} = 6 \text{ days}) = .1$$

If Office Central is out of Ricon copiers, it offers customers a $150 discount off the price and agrees to airfreight the copier to the customer as soon as it arrives. Airfreight costs Office Central an additional $95. Eighty percent of customers agree to place a backorder, while 20% go elsewhere to buy their copier. The company has been considering eliminating the out-of-stock discount and estimates that the percentage of customers who will place a backorder will decline from 80% to 50%.

Daily demand for the copiers follows a Poisson distribution with a mean of three units. Office Central has decided to use an order point, order up to level policy for the copiers and wishes to determine an optimal policy.

Conduct a simulation to analyze this problem. From the output of this model, prepare a business report to Joe Dixon, Operations Manager of Office Central, with your recommendation regarding the inventory policy for the Ricon 436 copier under the current discount policy. Include in your report a recommendation regarding eliminating the discount as well as a discussion regarding the effect a 10% decrease in the holding cost would have on your inventory policy recommendations.

CASE 2: *Four Wheel Tire Shop*

Four Wheel Tire Shop is a single bay tire store located in Eugene, Oregon. The interarrival time of cars in need of tires follows a uniform distribution with times between 10 and 50 minutes. Twenty percent of arriving customers want a single tire replaced, 40% want two tires replaced, 5% want three tires replaced, and 35% want all four tires replaced. Customer service time approximately follows a uniform distribution that varies with the number of tires that need to be replaced. The following statistics hold:

Number of Tires Needing Replacement	Service Time Is Uniformly Distributed Between
1	10 minutes and 20 minutes
2	15 minutes and 35 minutes
3	20 minutes and 40 minutes
4	25 minutes and 50 minutes

The owner of the store, Ben Stern, is considering leasing a new computerized tire balancing machine, which will reduce the average service time, resulting in the following uniform service distributions:

Number of Tires Needing Replacement	Service Time Is Uniformly Distributed Between
1	8 minutes and 18 minutes
2	12 minutes and 32 minutes
3	15 minutes and 35 minutes
4	20 minutes and 40 minutes

The machine lease cost averages $1.50 per hour. Mr. Stern estimates that the goodwill cost of a customer's being in the tire shop (either being served or waiting on line) is $4.00.

After using Excel to perform a simulation analysis, prepare a business report for Mr. Stern recommending whether or not he should lease the machine. Include in your report relevant service statistics, such as the average time a customer spends waiting to begin service as well as time in the system using both the existing tire balancing machine and the proposed computerized balancing machine.

Statistical Tables

Standard Normal Distribution P(0 < Z < z)

z	0.00	0.01	0.02	0.03	0.04	0.05	0.06	0.07	0.08	0.09
0.00	.0000	.0040	.0080	.0120	.0160	.0199	.0239	.0279	.0319	.0359
0.10	.0398	.0438	.0478	.0517	.0557	.0596	.0636	.0675	.0714	.0753
0.20	.0793	.0832	.0871	.0910	.0948	.0987	.1026	.1064	.1103	.1141
0.30	.1179	.1217	.1255	.1293	.1331	.1368	.1406	.1443	.1480	.1517
0.40	.1554	.1591	.1628	.1664	.1700	.1736	.1772	.1808	.1844	.1879
0.50	.1915	.1950	.1985	.2019	.2054	.2088	.2123	.2157	.2190	.2224
0.60	.2257	.2291	.2324	.2357	.2389	.2422	.2454	.2486	.2517	.2549
0.70	.2580	.2611	.2642	.2673	.2704	.2734	.2764	.2794	.2823	.2852
0.80	.2881	.2910	.2939	.2967	.2995	.3023	.3051	.3078	.3106	.3133
0.90	.3159	.3186	.3212	.3238	.3264	.3289	.3315	.3340	.3365	.3389
1.00	.3413	.3438	.3461	.3485	.3508	.3531	.3554	.3577	.3599	.3621
1.10	.3643	.3665	.3686	.3708	.3729	.3749	.3770	.3790	.3810	.3830
1.20	.3849	.3869	.3888	.3907	.3925	.3944	.3962	.3980	.3997	.4015
1.30	.4032	.4049	.4066	.4082	.4099	.4115	.4131	.4147	.4162	.4177
1.40	.4192	.4207	.4222	.4236	.4251	.4265	.4279	.4292	.4306	.4319
1.50	.4332	.4345	.4357	.4370	.4382	.4394	.4406	.4418	.4429	.4441
1.60	.4452	.4463	.4474	.4484	.4495	.4505	.4515	.4525	.4535	.4545
1.70	.4554	.4564	.4573	.4582	.4591	.4599	.4608	.4616	.4625	.4633
1.80	.4641	.4649	.4656	.4664	.4671	.4678	.4686	.4693	.4699	.4706
1.90	.4713	.4719	.4726	.4732	.4738	.4744	.4750	.4756	.4761	.4767
2.00	.4772	.4778	.4783	.4788	.4793	.4798	.4803	.4808	.4812	.4817
2.10	.4821	.4826	.4830	.4834	.4838	.4842	.4846	.4850	.4854	.4857
2.20	.4861	.4864	.4868	.4871	.4875	.4878	.4881	.4884	.4887	.4890
2.30	.4893	.4896	.4898	.4901	.4904	.4906	.4909	.4911	.4913	.4916
2.40	.4918	.4920	.4922	.4925	.4927	.4929	.4931	.4932	.4934	.4936
2.50	.4938	.4940	.4941	.4943	.4945	.4946	.4948	.4949	.4951	.4952
2.60	.4953	.4955	.4956	.4957	.4959	.4960	.4961	.4962	.4963	.4964
2.70	.4965	.4966	.4967	.4968	.4969	.4970	.4971	.4972	.4973	.4974
2.80	.4974	.4975	.4976	.4977	.4977	.4978	.4979	.4979	.4980	.4981
2.90	.4981	.4982	.4982	.4983	.4984	.4984	.4985	.4985	.4986	.4986
3.00	.4987	.4987	.4987	.4988	.4988	.4989	.4989	.4989	.4990	.4990
3.10	.4990	.4991	.4991	.4991	.4992	.4992	.4992	.4992	.4993	.4993
3.20	.4993	.4993	.4994	.4994	.4994	.4994	.4994	.4995	.4995	.4995
3.30	.4995	.4995	.4995	.4996	.4996	.4996	.4996	.4996	.4996	.4997
3.40	.4997	.4997	.4997	.4997	.4997	.4997	.4997	.4997	.4997	.4998
3.50	.4998	.4998	.4998	.4998	.4998	.4998	.4998	.4998	.4998	.4998

Generated from Excel using the z-row as row 1 and the z-column as column A. The entires in cell (i,j) are:
=NORMSDIST($Aj+i$1) − .5.

Partial Expectations of the Standard Normal Distribution L(Z)

z	.00	.01	.02	.03	.04	.05	.06	.07	.08	0.09
−2.90	2.9005	2.9105	2.9205	2.9305	2.9405	2.9505	2.9604	2.9704	2.9804	2.9904
−2.80	2.8008	2.8107	2.8207	2.8307	2.8407	2.8506	2.8606	2.8706	2.8806	2.8906
−2.70	2.7011	2.7110	2.7210	2.7310	2.7409	2.7509	2.7609	2.7708	2.7808	2.7908
−2.60	2.6015	2.6114	2.6214	2.6313	2.6413	2.6512	2.6612	2.6712	2.6811	2.6911
−2.50	2.5020	2.5119	2.5219	2.5318	2.5418	2.5517	2.5617	2.5716	2.5816	2.5915
−2.40	2.4027	2.4126	2.4226	2.4325	2.4424	2.4523	2.4623	2.4722	2.4821	2.4921
−2.30	2.3037	2.3136	2.3235	2.3334	2.3433	2.3532	2.3631	2.3730	2.3829	2.3928
−2.20	2.2049	2.2147	2.2246	2.2345	2.2444	2.2542	2.2641	2.2740	2.2839	2.2938
−2.10	2.1065	2.1163	2.1261	2.1360	2.1458	2.1556	2.1655	2.1753	2.1852	2.1950
−2.00	2.0085	2.0183	2.0280	2.0378	2.0476	2.0574	2.0672	2.0770	2.0868	2.0966
−1.90	1.9111	1.9208	1.9305	1.9402	1.9500	1.9597	1.9694	1.9792	1.9890	1.9987
−1.80	1.8143	1.8239	1.8336	1.8432	1.8529	1.8626	1.8723	1.8819	1.8916	1.9013
−1.70	1.7183	1.7278	1.7374	1.7470	1.7566	1.7662	1.7758	1.7854	1.7950	1.8046
−1.60	1.6232	1.6327	1.6422	1.6516	1.6611	1.6706	1.6801	1.6897	1.6992	1.7087
−1.50	1.5293	1.5386	1.5480	1.5574	1.5667	1.5761	1.5855	1.5949	1.6044	1.6138
−1.40	1.4367	1.4459	1.4551	1.4643	1.4736	1.4828	1.4921	1.5014	1.5107	1.5200
−1.30	1.3455	1.3546	1.3636	1.3727	1.3818	1.3909	1.4000	1.4092	1.4183	1.4275
−1.20	1.2561	1.2650	1.2738	1.2827	1.2917	1.3006	1.3095	1.3185	1.3275	1.3365
−1.10	1.1686	1.1773	1.1859	1.1946	1.2034	1.2121	1.2209	1.2296	1.2384	1.2473
−1.00	1.0833	1.0917	1.1002	1.1087	1.1172	1.1257	1.1342	1.1428	1.1514	1.1600
−0.90	1.0004	1.0086	1.0168	1.0250	1.0333	1.0416	1.0499	1.0582	1.0665	1.0749
−0.80	.9202	.9281	.9360	.9440	.9520	.9600	.9680	.9761	.9842	.9923
−0.70	.8429	.8505	.8581	.8658	.8734	.8812	.8889	.8967	.9045	.9123
−0.60	.7687	.7759	.7833	.7906	.7980	.8054	.8128	.8203	.8278	.8353
−0.50	.6978	.7047	.7117	.7187	.7257	.7328	.7399	.7471	.7542	.7614
−0.40	.6304	.6370	.6436	.6503	.6569	.6637	.6704	.6772	.6840	.6909
−0.30	.5668	.5730	.5792	.5855	.5918	.5981	.6045	.6109	.6174	.6239
−0.20	.5069	.5127	.5186	.5244	.5304	.5363	.5424	.5484	.5545	.5606
−0.10	.4509	.4564	.4618	.4673	.4728	.4784	.4840	.4897	.4954	.5011
−0.00	—	.4040	.4090	.4141	.4193	.4244	.4297	.4349	.4402	.4456

Generated from Excel using row 1 for the z-row and column A for the z-column. The cell entries are:

=EXP(−(($Aj−i$1)*($Aj−i$1))/2)/((2*PI())^0.5)−($Aj−i$1)*(1−NORMSDIST($Aj−i$1)))

z	.00	.01	.02	.03	.04	.05	.06	.07	.08	0.09
0.00	.3989	.3940	.3890	.3841	.3793	.3744	.3697	.3649	.3602	.3556
0.10	.3509	.3464	.3418	.3373	.3328	.3284	.3240	.3197	.3154	.3111
0.20	.3069	.3027	.2986	.2944	.2904	.2863	.2824	.2784	.2745	.2706
0.30	.2668	.2630	.2592	.2555	.2518	.2481	.2445	.2409	.2374	.2339
0.40	.2304	.2270	.2236	.2203	.2169	.2137	.2104	.2072	.2040	.2009
0.50	.1978	.1947	.1917	.1887	.1857	.1828	.1799	.1771	.1742	.1714
0.60	.1687	.1659	.1633	.1606	.1580	.1554	.1528	.1503	.1478	.1453
0.70	.1429	.1405	.1381	.1358	.1334	.1312	.1289	.1267	.1245	.1223
0.80	.1202	.1181	.1160	.1140	.1120	.1100	.1080	.1061	.1042	.1023
0.90	.1004	.0986	.0968	.0950	.0933	.0916	.0899	.0882	.0865	.0849
1.00	.0833	.0817	.0802	.0787	.0772	.0757	.0742	.0728	.0714	.0700
1.10	.0686	.0673	.0659	.0646	.0634	.0621	.0609	.0596	.0584	.0573
1.20	.0561	.0550	.0538	.0527	.0517	.0506	.0495	.0485	.0475	.0465
1.30	.0455	.0446	.0436	.0427	.0418	.0409	.0400	.0392	.0383	.0375
1.40	.0367	.0359	.0351	.0343	.0336	.0328	.0321	.0314	.0307	.0300
1.50	.0293	.0286	.0280	.0274	.0267	.0261	.0255	.0249	.0244	.0238
1.60	.0232	.0227	.0222	.0216	.0211	.0206	.0201	.0197	.0192	.0187
1.70	.0183	.0178	.0174	.0170	.0166	.0162	.0158	.0154	.0150	.0146
1.80	.0143	.0139	.0136	.0132	.0129	.0126	.0123	.0119	.0116	.0113
1.90	.0111	.0108	.0105	.0102	.0100	.0097	.0094	.0092	.0090	.0087
2.00	.0085	.0083	.0080	.0078	.0076	.0074	.0072	.0070	.0068	.0066
2.10	.0065	.0063	.0061	.0060	.0058	.0056	.0055	.0053	.0052	.0050
2.20	.0049	.0047	.0046	.0045	.0044	.0042	.0041	.0040	.0039	.0038
2.30	.0037	.0036	.0035	.0034	.0033	.0032	.0031	.0030	.0029	.0028
2.40	.0027	.0026	.0026	.0025	.0024	.0023	.0023	.0022	.0021	.0021
2.50	.0020	.0019	.0019	.0018	.0018	.0017	.0017	.0016	.0016	.0015
2.60	.0015	.0014	.0014	.0013	.0013	.0012	.0012	.0012	.0011	.0011
2.70	.0011	.0010	.0010	.0010	.0009	.0009	.0009	.0008	.0008	.0008
2.80	.0008	.0007	.0007	.0007	.0007	.0006	.0006	.0006	.0006	.0006
2.90	.0005	.0005	.0005	.0005	.0005	.0005	.0004	.0004	.0004	.0004

Generated from Excel using row 1 for the z-row and column A for the z-column. The cell entries are:

$$=EXP(-((\$Aj+i\$1)*(\$Aj+i\$1))/2)/((2*PI())^{0.5})-(\$Aj+i\$1)*(1-NORMSDIST(\$Aj+i\$1)))$$

Table of Pseudo-Random Numbers

	1	2	3	4	5	6	7	8	9	10	11	12	13	14	15
1	6506	3338	2197	8927	6320	1094	1995	5971	5147	3620	0582	2982	8731	6037	4231
2	7761	9874	9834	8848	4630	7371	7971	6600	1296	5299	1374	9517	8177	2403	7443
3	6170	2631	6268	9089	8657	2809	3554	4814	7401	9983	8613	3199	6005	1879	9339
4	8800	9139	8305	2605	0030	5148	6300	1762	2499	5417	2607	7111	9892	3703	8408
5	4211	9651	0051	7982	5624	9115	5495	2710	2888	9620	5078	6541	5066	9082	8981
6	7452	4883	5619	5541	6728	1469	5165	1908	9619	2043	9221	6405	6559	6343	8920
7	1182	8260	3367	2624	5925	6480	9339	5104	7435	4121	9234	9031	3506	6230	1202
8	4012	2781	6140	1603	2829	2447	6997	4947	3343	3125	1070	2998	1236	9821	6438
9	0335	9636	1645	4063	7939	7031	1443	7610	9665	3357	6415	4994	3780	8437	6475
10	6299	4696	8036	6519	6476	8442	3574	4978	7911	0759	7991	2677	4401	9996	3878
11	5482	2016	7017	6106	3319	7387	0150	7166	7336	2121	1006	4066	5675	8784	6141
12	1085	4426	4988	6807	8134	1788	0933	7209	3054	0107	0033	2795	9978	4542	5388
13	1698	8464	8208	7589	1712	4891	7082	3021	4519	2000	7987	4122	8150	3058	1281
14	6969	9424	1524	6590	6317	1149	5025	8181	0013	1805	7521	6735	1511	4255	7643
15	1696	6693	9525	0882	6605	8822	4081	0772	8234	9257	3985	5061	2021	9265	9641
16	0267	6317	1051	3193	2734	9451	4100	1471	3270	1065	6001	4366	7642	2800	5026
17	3175	7529	1759	2084	0432	2990	7190	4648	8760	9085	4591	3874	7636	3983	7406
18	7959	0515	8149	4053	3441	8314	6822	0714	7731	6648	3007	5625	8682	8699	3711
19	4958	1069	0318	9941	0726	7176	5053	5177	6950	9598	0640	0297	7153	5376	3610
20	4281	1877	8785	0967	6969	2766	8284	2528	0194	2496	4152	9645	3200	8762	1574
21	2231	0382	7782	7890	3434	5391	2022	6820	9294	8609	6437	3848	0668	2868	7085
22	0002	0786	2889	1522	0059	1313	9858	1336	4964	3223	3010	9118	6072	6432	1895
23	8434	7236	3686	8333	0617	1821	4297	9250	5737	2599	3785	4356	6943	1461	6921
24	8959	5886	9020	7247	5586	7136	0595	2432	0685	1058	6967	0202	8565	1423	6268
25	8975	6480	9478	5140	0996	6483	0881	4444	5587	4517	5402	4436	1516	8855	1132
26	1288	8758	5711	0916	1114	2046	2564	4713	5154	7742	1653	2428	8366	7530	8709
27	6412	0141	9310	7329	6063	4279	8996	6782	5013	1565	8090	8400	6118	5830	6202
28	6463	0315	2277	3642	4400	5030	9321	6107	8498	7838	8209	4891	8378	8816	2156
29	3856	1780	5371	1981	8971	2679	7859	1416	8795	4004	1302	2802	1445	8578	0356
30	6117	4088	7219	2557	6612	3386	2724	8737	6412	5548	5214	6804	4716	2134	6811
31	5396	2510	3168	9061	5963	2243	6824	6614	1074	6839	5576	8077	9191	2406	8859
32	1281	1710	4009	5721	5830	1755	1225	6382	4148	1870	3651	5876	9282	4682	6765
33	7644	0296	2395	7493	8626	4617	9388	2845	1363	4705	6759	2983	7857	8906	1027
34	8608	3656	0659	6827	2183	9893	4989	1855	9358	1041	4488	3197	1723	4120	6987
35	9359	0331	6735	1301	7891	5985	1119	8374	1817	4825	8017	2728	7241	6119	0439
36	4233	0282	0397	0646	0527	9247	2280	6931	3963	3227	9732	9148	6735	5047	0981
37	3871	1294	9059	7680	5964	5402	6068	1781	6103	3768	1999	2403	3006	3742	2539

A similar table can be generated in Excel by entering for each cell: =INT(RAND()*10000).

APPENDIX D

t Distribution Value of t_α That Puts α in the Tail

Degrees of Freedom	Values of α							
	.10	0.05	0.025	0.01	0.005	0.0025	0.001	0.0005
1	3.0777	6.3137	12.7062	31.8210	63.6559	127.3211	318.2888	636.5776
2	1.8856	2.9200	4.3027	6.9645	9.9250	14.0892	22.3285	31.5998
3	1.6377	2.3534	3.1824	4.5407	5.8408	7.4532	10.2143	12.9244
4	1.5332	2.1318	2.7765	3.7469	4.6041	5.5975	7.1729	8.6101
5	1.4759	2.0150	2.5706	3.3649	4.0321	4.7733	5.8935	6.8685
6	1.4398	1.9432	2.4469	3.1427	3.7074	4.3168	5.2075	5.9587
7	1.4149	1.8946	2.3646	2.9979	3.4995	4.0294	4.7853	5.4081
8	1.3968	1.8595	2.3060	2.8965	3.3554	3.8325	4.5008	5.0414
9	1.3830	1.8331	2.2622	2.8214	3.2498	3.6896	4.2969	4.7809
10	1.3722	1.8125	2.2281	2.7638	3.1693	3.5814	4.1437	4.5868
11	1.3634	1.7959	2.2010	2.7181	3.1058	3.4966	4.0248	4.4369
12	1.3562	1.7823	2.1788	2.6810	3.0545	3.4284	3.9296	4.3178
13	1.3502	1.7709	2.1604	2.6503	3.0123	3.3725	3.8520	4.2209
14	1.3450	1.7613	2.1448	2.6245	2.9768	3.3257	3.7874	4.1403
15	1.3406	1.7531	2.1315	2.6025	2.9467	3.2860	3.7329	4.0728
16	1.3368	1.7459	2.1199	2.5835	2.9208	3.2520	3.6861	4.0149
17	1.3334	1.7396	2.1098	2.5669	2.8982	3.2224	3.6458	3.9651
18	1.3304	1.7341	2.1009	2.5524	2.8784	3.1966	3.6105	3.9217
19	1.3277	1.7291	2.0930	2.5395	2.8609	3.1737	3.5793	3.8833
20	1.3253	1.7247	2.0860	2.5280	2.8453	3.1534	3.5518	3.8496
21	1.3232	1.7207	2.0796	2.5176	2.8314	3.1352	3.5271	3.8193
22	1.3212	1.7171	2.0739	2.5083	2.8188	3.1188	3.5050	3.7922
23	1.3195	1.7139	2.0687	2.4999	2.8073	3.1040	3.4850	3.7676
24	1.3178	1.7109	2.0639	2.4922	2.7970	3.0905	3.4668	3.7454
25	1.3163	1.7081	2.0595	2.4851	2.7874	3.0782	3.4502	3.7251
26	1.3150	1.7056	2.0555	2.4786	2.7787	3.0669	3.4350	3.7067
27	1.3137	1.7033	2.0518	2.4727	2.7707	3.0565	3.4210	3.6895
28	1.3125	1.7011	2.0484	2.4671	2.7633	3.0470	3.4082	3.6739
29	1.3114	1.6991	2.0452	2.4620	2.7564	3.0380	3.3963	3.6595
30	1.3104	1.6973	2.0423	2.4573	2.7500	3.0298	3.3852	3.6460
99	1.2902	1.6604	1.9842	2.3646	2.6264	2.8713	3.1746	3.3915
199	1.2858	1.6525	1.9720	2.3452	2.6008	2.8387	3.1317	3.3401
499	1.2833	1.6479	1.9647	2.3338	2.5857	2.8196	3.1067	3.3101

Generated from Excel using row 2 for the values of α and column A for the degrees of freedom. The entries in cell (i,j) are: =TINV(2*j$2,$Ai).

χ^2 Distribution
Value of χ^2_α That Puts α in the Tail

Degrees of Freedom	Value of α							
	.10	0.05	0.025	0.01	0.005	0.0025	0.001	0.0005
1	2.7055	3.8415	5.0239	6.6349	7.8794	9.1404	10.8274	12.1153
2	4.6052	5.9915	7.3778	9.2104	10.5965	11.9827	13.8150	15.2014
3	6.2514	7.8147	9.3484	11.3449	12.8381	14.3202	16.2660	17.7311
4	7.7794	9.4877	11.1433	13.2767	14.8602	16.4238	18.4662	19.9977
5	9.2363	11.0705	12.8325	15.0863	16.7496	18.3854	20.5147	22.1057
6	10.6446	12.5916	14.4494	16.8119	18.5475	20.2491	22.4575	24.1016
7	12.0170	14.0671	16.0128	18.4753	20.2777	22.0402	24.3213	26.0179
8	13.3616	15.5073	17.5345	20.0902	21.9549	23.7742	26.1239	27.8674
9	14.6837	16.9190	19.0228	21.6660	23.5893	25.4625	27.8767	29.6669
10	15.9872	18.3070	20.4832	23.2093	25.1881	27.1119	29.5879	31.4195
11	17.2750	19.6752	21.9200	24.7250	26.7569	28.7291	31.2635	33.1382
12	18.5493	21.0261	23.3367	26.2170	28.2997	30.3182	32.9092	34.8211
13	19.8119	22.3620	24.7356	27.6882	29.8193	31.8830	34.5274	36.4768
14	21.0641	23.6848	26.1189	29.1412	31.3194	33.4262	36.1239	38.1085
15	22.3071	24.9958	27.4884	30.5780	32.8015	34.9494	37.6978	39.7173
16	23.5418	26.2962	28.8453	31.9999	34.2671	36.4555	39.2518	41.3077
17	24.7690	27.5871	30.1910	33.4087	35.7184	37.9462	40.7911	42.8808
18	25.9894	28.8693	31.5264	34.8052	37.1564	39.4220	42.3119	44.4337
19	27.2036	30.1435	32.8523	36.1908	38.5821	40.8847	43.8194	45.9738
20	28.4120	31.4104	34.1696	37.5663	39.9969	42.3358	45.3142	47.4977
21	29.6151	32.6706	35.4789	38.9322	41.4009	43.7749	46.7963	49.0096
22	30.8133	33.9245	36.7807	40.2894	42.7957	45.2041	48.2676	50.5105
23	32.0069	35.1725	38.0756	41.6383	44.1814	46.6231	49.7276	51.9995
24	33.1962	36.4150	39.3641	42.9798	45.5584	48.0336	51.1790	53.4776
25	34.3816	37.6525	40.6465	44.3140	46.9280	49.4351	52.6187	54.9475
26	35.5632	38.8851	41.9231	45.6416	48.2898	50.8291	54.0511	56.4068
27	36.7412	40.1133	43.1945	46.9628	49.6450	52.2152	55.4751	57.8556
28	37.9159	41.3372	44.4608	48.2782	50.9936	53.5939	56.8918	59.2990
29	39.0875	42.5569	45.7223	49.5878	52.3355	54.9662	58.3006	60.7342
30	40.2560	43.7730	46.9792	50.8922	53.6719	56.3325	59.7022	62.1600
99	117.4069	123.2252	128.4219	134.6415	138.9869	143.0945	148.2297	151.9312
199	224.9568	232.9118	239.9598	248.3284	254.1350	259.5940	266.3860	271.2568
499	539.8898	552.0747	562.7896	575.4189	584.1246	592.2692	602.3506	609.5466

Generated from Excel using row 2 for the values of α and column A for the degrees of freedom. The entries in cell (i,j) are: =CHIINV(j$2,$Ai).

F Distribution
Value of F That Puts .01 in the Tail

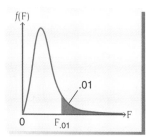

Denominator Degrees of Freedom	Numerator Degrees of Freedom												
	1	2	3	4	5	6	7	8	9	10	11	12	13
1	4052	4999	5404	5624	5764	5859	5928	5981	6022	6056	6083	6107	6126
2	98.50	99.00	99.16	99.25	99.30	99.33	99.36	99.38	99.39	99.40	99.41	99.42	99.42
3	34.12	30.82	29.46	28.71	28.24	27.91	27.67	27.49	27.34	27.23	27.13	27.05	26.98
4	21.20	18.00	16.69	15.98	15.52	15.21	14.98	14.80	14.66	14.55	14.45	14.37	14.31
5	16.26	13.27	12.06	11.39	10.97	10.67	10.46	10.29	10.16	10.05	9.96	9.89	9.82
6	13.75	10.92	9.78	9.15	8.75	8.47	8.26	8.10	7.98	7.87	7.79	7.72	7.66
7	12.25	9.55	8.45	7.85	7.46	7.19	6.99	6.84	6.72	6.62	6.54	6.47	6.41
8	11.26	8.65	7.59	7.01	6.63	6.37	6.18	6.03	5.91	5.81	5.73	5.67	5.61
9	10.56	8.02	6.99	6.42	6.06	5.80	5.61	5.47	5.35	5.26	5.18	5.11	5.05
10	10.04	7.56	6.55	5.99	5.64	5.39	5.20	5.06	4.94	4.85	4.77	4.71	4.65
11	9.65	7.21	6.22	5.67	5.32	5.07	4.89	4.74	4.63	4.54	4.46	4.40	4.34
12	9.33	6.93	5.95	5.41	5.06	4.82	4.64	4.50	4.39	4.30	4.22	4.16	4.10
13	9.07	6.70	5.74	5.21	4.86	4.62	4.44	4.30	4.19	4.10	4.02	3.96	3.91
14	8.86	6.51	5.56	5.04	4.69	4.46	4.28	4.14	4.03	3.94	3.86	3.80	3.75
15	8.68	6.36	5.42	4.89	4.56	4.32	4.14	4.00	3.89	3.80	3.73	3.67	3.61
16	8.53	6.23	5.29	4.77	4.44	4.20	4.03	3.89	3.78	3.69	3.62	3.55	3.50
17	8.40	6.11	5.19	4.67	4.34	4.10	3.93	3.79	3.68	3.59	3.52	3.46	3.40
18	8.29	6.01	5.09	4.58	4.25	4.01	3.84	3.71	3.60	3.51	3.43	3.37	3.32
19	8.18	5.93	5.01	4.50	4.17	3.94	3.77	3.63	3.52	3.43	3.36	3.30	3.24
20	8.10	5.85	4.94	4.43	4.10	3.87	3.70	3.56	3.46	3.37	3.29	3.23	3.18
21	8.02	5.78	4.87	4.37	4.04	3.81	3.64	3.51	3.40	3.31	3.24	3.17	3.12
22	7.95	5.72	4.82	4.31	3.99	3.76	3.59	3.45	3.35	3.26	3.18	3.12	3.07
23	7.88	5.66	4.76	4.26	3.94	3.71	3.54	3.41	3.30	3.21	3.14	3.07	3.02
24	7.82	5.61	4.72	4.22	3.90	3.67	3.50	3.36	3.26	3.17	3.09	3.03	2.98
25	7.77	5.57	4.68	4.18	3.85	3.63	3.46	3.32	3.22	3.13	3.06	2.99	2.94
26	7.72	5.53	4.64	4.14	3.82	3.59	3.42	3.29	3.18	3.09	3.02	2.96	2.90
27	7.68	5.49	4.60	4.11	3.78	3.56	3.39	3.26	3.15	3.06	2.99	2.93	2.87
28	7.64	5.45	4.57	4.07	3.75	3.53	3.36	3.23	3.12	3.03	2.96	2.90	2.84
29	7.60	5.42	4.54	4.04	3.73	3.50	3.33	3.20	3.09	3.00	2.93	2.87	2.81
30	7.56	5.39	4.51	4.02	3.70	3.47	3.30	3.17	3.07	2.98	2.91	2.84	2.79
31	7.53	5.36	4.48	3.99	3.67	3.45	3.28	3.15	3.04	2.96	2.88	2.82	2.77
32	7.50	5.34	4.46	3.97	3.65	3.43	3.26	3.13	3.02	2.93	2.86	2.80	2.74
33	7.47	5.31	4.44	3.95	3.63	3.41	3.24	3.11	3.00	2.91	2.84	2.78	2.72
34	7.44	5.29	4.42	3.93	3.61	3.39	3.22	3.09	2.98	2.89	2.82	2.76	2.70
35	7.42	5.27	4.40	3.91	3.59	3.37	3.20	3.07	2.96	2.88	2.80	2.74	2.69
36	7.40	5.25	4.38	3.89	3.57	3.35	3.18	3.05	2.95	2.86	2.79	2.72	2.67
37	7.37	5.23	4.36	3.87	3.56	3.33	3.17	3.04	2.93	2.84	2.77	2.71	2.65
38	7.35	5.21	4.34	3.86	3.54	3.32	3.15	3.02	2.92	2.83	2.75	2.69	2.64
39	7.33	5.19	4.33	3.84	3.53	3.30	3.14	3.01	2.90	2.81	2.74	2.68	2.62
49	7.18	5.07	4.21	3.73	3.42	3.19	3.03	2.90	2.79	2.71	2.63	2.57	2.52
59	7.08	4.98	4.13	3.65	3.34	3.12	2.96	2.83	2.72	2.64	2.56	2.50	2.45
69	7.02	4.93	4.08	3.60	3.29	3.08	2.91	2.78	2.68	2.59	2.52	2.45	2.40
79	6.97	4.88	4.04	3.57	3.26	3.04	2.87	2.75	2.64	2.55	2.48	2.42	2.36
89	6.93	4.85	4.01	3.54	3.23	3.01	2.85	2.72	2.61	2.53	2.45	2.39	2.34
99	6.90	4.83	3.99	3.51	3.21	2.99	2.83	2.70	2.59	2.51	2.43	2.37	2.32
199	6.76	4.71	3.88	3.41	3.11	2.89	2.73	2.60	2.50	2.41	2.34	2.28	2.22
499	6.69	4.65	3.82	3.36	3.05	2.84	2.68	2.55	2.44	2.36	2.28	2.22	2.17

Generated from Excel using row 2 for the numerator degrees of freedom and column A for the denominator degrees of freedom. The entries in cell (i,j) are: =FINV(0.01,j$2,$Ai).

F Distribution
Value of F That Puts .01 in the Tail (cont.)

Denominator Degrees of Freedom	Numerator Degrees of Freedom												
	14	15	19	24	29	39	49	59	69	79	89	99	199
1	6143	6157	6201	6234	6257	6285	6301	6313	6320	6326	6330	6334	6350
2	99.43	99.43	99.45	99.46	99.46	99.47	99.48	99.48	99.48	99.48	99.49	99.49	99.49
3	26.92	26.87	26.72	26.60	26.52	26.42	26.36	26.32	26.29	26.27	26.25	26.24	26.18
4	14.25	14.20	14.05	13.93	13.85	13.75	13.69	13.66	13.63	13.61	13.59	13.58	13.52
5	9.77	9.72	9.58	9.47	9.39	9.30	9.24	9.20	9.18	9.16	9.14	9.13	9.08
6	7.60	7.56	7.42	7.31	7.24	7.15	7.10	7.06	7.03	7.01	7.00	6.99	6.93
7	6.36	6.31	6.18	6.07	6.00	5.91	5.86	5.83	5.80	5.78	5.77	5.76	5.70
8	5.56	5.52	5.38	5.28	5.21	5.12	5.07	5.03	5.01	4.99	4.98	4.96	4.91
9	5.01	4.96	4.83	4.73	4.66	4.57	4.52	4.49	4.46	4.44	4.43	4.42	4.36
10	4.60	4.56	4.43	4.33	4.26	4.17	4.12	4.08	4.06	4.04	4.03	4.01	3.96
11	4.29	4.25	4.12	4.02	3.95	3.87	3.81	3.78	3.75	3.74	3.72	3.71	3.66
12	4.05	4.01	3.88	3.78	3.71	3.63	3.57	3.54	3.51	3.49	3.48	3.47	3.41
13	3.86	3.82	3.69	3.59	3.52	3.43	3.38	3.34	3.32	3.30	3.29	3.27	3.22
14	3.70	3.66	3.53	3.43	3.36	3.27	3.22	3.18	3.16	3.14	3.12	3.11	3.06
15	3.56	3.52	3.40	3.29	3.23	3.14	3.09	3.05	3.02	3.01	2.99	2.98	2.92
16	3.45	3.41	3.28	3.18	3.11	3.02	2.97	2.94	2.91	2.89	2.88	2.86	2.81
17	3.35	3.31	3.19	3.08	3.01	2.93	2.87	2.84	2.81	2.79	2.78	2.77	2.71
18	3.27	3.23	3.10	3.00	2.93	2.84	2.79	2.75	2.73	2.71	2.69	2.68	2.62
19	3.19	3.15	3.03	2.92	2.86	2.77	2.71	2.68	2.65	2.63	2.62	2.60	2.55
20	3.13	3.09	2.96	2.86	2.79	2.70	2.65	2.61	2.58	2.56	2.55	2.54	2.48
21	3.07	3.03	2.90	2.80	2.73	2.64	2.59	2.55	2.52	2.50	2.49	2.48	2.42
22	3.02	2.98	2.85	2.75	2.68	2.59	2.54	2.50	2.47	2.45	2.44	2.42	2.36
23	2.97	2.93	2.80	2.70	2.63	2.54	2.49	2.45	2.42	2.40	2.39	2.37	2.32
24	2.93	2.89	2.76	2.66	2.59	2.50	2.44	2.41	2.38	2.36	2.34	2.33	2.27
25	2.89	2.85	2.72	2.62	2.55	2.46	2.40	2.37	2.34	2.32	2.30	2.29	2.23
26	2.86	2.81	2.69	2.58	2.51	2.42	2.37	2.33	2.30	2.28	2.27	2.25	2.19
27	2.82	2.78	2.66	2.55	2.48	2.39	2.33	2.30	2.27	2.25	2.23	2.22	2.16
28	2.79	2.75	2.63	2.52	2.45	2.36	2.30	2.27	2.24	2.22	2.20	2.19	2.13
29	2.77	2.73	2.60	2.49	2.42	2.33	2.28	2.24	2.21	2.19	2.17	2.16	2.10
30	2.74	2.70	2.57	2.47	2.40	2.31	2.25	2.21	2.18	2.16	2.15	2.13	2.07
31	2.72	2.68	2.55	2.45	2.37	2.28	2.23	2.19	2.16	2.14	2.12	2.11	2.04
32	2.70	2.65	2.53	2.42	2.35	2.26	2.20	2.16	2.14	2.11	2.10	2.08	2.02
33	2.68	2.63	2.51	2.40	2.33	2.24	2.18	2.14	2.11	2.09	2.08	2.06	2.00
34	2.66	2.61	2.49	2.38	2.31	2.22	2.16	2.12	2.09	2.07	2.05	2.04	1.98
35	2.64	2.60	2.47	2.36	2.29	2.20	2.14	2.10	2.07	2.05	2.04	2.02	1.96
36	2.62	2.58	2.45	2.35	2.28	2.18	2.12	2.08	2.06	2.03	2.02	2.00	1.94
37	2.61	2.56	2.44	2.33	2.26	2.17	2.11	2.07	2.04	2.02	2.00	1.99	1.92
38	2.59	2.55	2.42	2.32	2.24	2.15	2.09	2.05	2.02	2.00	1.98	1.97	1.90
39	2.58	2.54	2.41	2.30	2.23	2.14	2.08	2.04	2.01	1.99	1.97	1.95	1.89
49	2.47	2.43	2.30	2.19	2.12	2.02	1.96	1.92	1.89	1.87	1.85	1.84	1.77
59	2.40	2.36	2.23	2.12	2.05	1.95	1.89	1.85	1.81	1.79	1.77	1.76	1.69
69	2.35	2.31	2.18	2.07	2.00	1.90	1.84	1.79	1.76	1.74	1.72	1.70	1.63
79	2.32	2.27	2.14	2.03	1.96	1.86	1.80	1.75	1.72	1.70	1.68	1.66	1.58
89	2.29	2.25	2.12	2.01	1.93	1.83	1.77	1.72	1.69	1.66	1.64	1.63	1.55
99	2.27	2.22	2.09	1.98	1.91	1.81	1.74	1.70	1.66	1.64	1.62	1.60	1.52
199	2.17	2.13	2.00	1.89	1.81	1.70	1.64	1.59	1.55	1.52	1.50	1.48	1.39
499	2.12	2.07	1.94	1.83	1.75	1.64	1.57	1.52	1.48	1.45	1.43	1.41	1.31

Generated from Excel using row 2 for the numerator degrees of freedom and column A for the denominator degrees of freedom. The entries in cell (i,j) are: =FINV(0.01,j$2,$Ai).

F Distribution
Value of F That Puts .05 in the Tail

Denominator Degrees of Freedom	Numerator Degrees of Freedom												
	1	2	3	4	5	6	7	8	9	10	11	12	13
1	161.4	199.5	215.7	224.6	230.2	234.0	236.8	238.9	240.5	241.9	243.0	243.9	244.7
2	18.51	19.00	19.61	19.25	19.30	19.33	19.35	19.37	19.38	19.40	19.40	19.41	19.42
3	10.13	9.55	9.28	9.12	9.01	8.94	8.89	8.85	8.81	8.79	8.76	8.74	8.73
4	7.71	6.94	6.59	6.39	6.26	6.16	6.09	6.04	6.00	5.96	5.94	5.91	5.89
5	6.61	5.79	5.41	5.19	5.05	4.95	4.88	4.82	4.77	4.74	4.70	4.68	4.66
6	5.99	5.14	4.76	4.53	4.39	4.28	4.21	4.15	4.10	4.06	4.03	4.00	3.98
7	5.59	4.74	4.35	4.12	3.97	3.87	3.79	3.73	3.68	3.64	3.60	3.57	3.55
8	5.32	4.46	4.07	3.84	3.69	3.58	3.50	3.44	3.39	3.35	3.31	3.28	3.26
9	5.12	4.26	3.86	3.63	3.48	3.37	3.29	3.23	3.18	3.14	3.10	3.07	3.05
10	4.96	4.10	3.71	3.48	3.33	3.22	3.14	3.07	3.02	2.98	2.94	2.91	2.89
11	4.84	3.98	3.59	3.36	3.20	3.09	3.01	2.95	2.90	2.85	2.82	2.79	2.76
12	4.75	3.89	3.49	3.26	3.11	3.00	2.91	2.85	2.80	2.75	2.72	2.69	2.66
13	4.67	3.81	3.41	3.18	3.03	2.92	2.83	2.77	2.71	2.67	2.63	2.60	2.58
14	4.60	3.74	3.34	3.11	2.96	2.85	2.76	2.70	2.65	2.60	2.57	2.53	2.51
15	4.54	3.68	3.29	3.06	2.90	2.79	2.71	2.64	2.59	2.54	2.51	2.48	2.45
16	4.49	3.63	3.24	3.01	2.85	2.74	2.66	2.59	2.54	2.49	2.46	2.42	2.40
17	4.45	3.59	3.20	2.96	2.81	2.70	2.61	2.55	2.49	2.45	2.41	2.38	2.35
18	4.41	3.55	3.16	2.93	2.77	2.66	2.58	2.51	2.46	2.41	2.37	2.34	2.31
19	4.38	3.52	3.13	2.90	2.74	2.63	2.54	2.48	2.42	2.38	2.34	2.31	2.28
20	4.35	3.49	3.10	2.87	2.71	2.60	2.51	2.45	2.39	2.35	2.31	2.28	2.25
21	4.32	3.47	3.07	2.84	2.68	2.57	2.49	2.42	2.37	2.32	2.28	2.25	2.22
22	4.30	3.44	3.05	2.82	2.66	2.55	2.46	2.40	2.34	2.30	2.26	2.23	2.20
23	4.28	3.42	3.03	2.80	2.64	2.53	2.44	2.37	2.32	2.27	2.24	2.20	2.18
24	4.26	3.40	3.01	2.78	2.62	2.51	2.42	2.36	2.30	2.25	2.22	2.18	2.15
25	4.24	3.39	2.99	2.76	2.60	2.49	2.40	2.34	2.28	2.24	2.20	2.16	2.14
26	4.23	3.37	2.98	2.74	2.59	2.47	2.39	2.32	2.27	2.22	2.18	2.15	2.12
27	4.21	3.35	2.96	2.73	2.57	2.46	2.37	2.31	2.25	2.20	2.17	2.13	2.10
28	4.20	3.34	2.95	2.71	2.56	2.45	2.36	2.29	2.24	2.19	2.15	2.12	2.09
29	4.18	3.33	2.93	2.70	2.55	2.43	2.35	2.28	2.22	2.18	2.14	2.10	2.08
30	4.17	3.32	2.92	2.69	2.53	2.42	2.33	2.27	2.21	2.16	2.13	2.09	2.06
31	4.16	3.30	2.91	2.68	2.52	2.41	2.32	2.25	2.20	2.15	2.11	2.08	2.05
32	4.15	3.29	2.90	2.67	2.51	2.40	2.31	2.24	2.19	2.14	2.10	2.07	2.04
33	4.14	3.28	2.89	2.66	2.50	2.39	2.30	2.23	2.18	2.13	2.09	2.06	2.03
34	4.13	3.28	2.88	2.65	2.49	2.38	2.29	2.23	2.17	2.12	2.08	2.05	2.02
35	4.12	3.27	2.87	2.64	2.49	2.37	2.29	2.22	2.16	2.11	2.07	2.04	2.01
36	4.11	3.26	2.87	2.63	2.48	2.36	2.28	2.21	2.15	2.11	2.07	2.03	2.00
37	4.11	3.25	2.86	2.63	2.47	2.36	2.27	2.20	2.14	2.10	2.06	2.02	2.00
38	4.10	3.24	2.85	2.62	2.46	2.35	2.26	2.19	2.14	2.09	2.05	2.02	1.99
39	4.09	3.24	2.85	2.61	2.46	2.34	2.26	2.19	2.13	2.08	2.04	2.01	1.98
49	4.04	3.19	2.79	2.56	2.40	2.29	2.20	2.13	2.08	2.03	1.99	1.96	1.93
59	4.00	3.15	2.76	2.53	2.37	2.26	2.17	2.10	2.04	2.00	1.96	1.92	1.89
69	3.98	3.13	2.74	2.50	2.35	2.23	2.15	2.08	2.02	1.97	1.93	1.90	1.86
79	3.96	3.11	2.72	2.49	2.33	2.22	2.13	2.06	2.00	1.95	1.91	1.88	1.85
89	3.95	3.10	2.71	2.47	2.32	2.20	2.11	2.04	1.99	1.94	1.90	1.86	1.83
99	3.94	3.09	2.70	2.46	2.31	2.19	2.10	2.03	1.98	1.93	1.89	1.85	1.82
199	3.89	3.04	2.65	2.42	2.26	2.14	2.06	1.99	1.93	1.88	1.84	1.80	1.77
499	3.86	3.01	2.62	2.39	2.23	2.12	2.03	1.96	1.90	1.85	1.81	1.77	1.74

Generated from Excel using row 2 for the numerator degrees of freedom and column A for the denominator degrees of freedom. The entries in cell (i,j) are: =FINV(0.05,j$2,$Ai).

F Distribution
Value of F That Puts .05 in the Tail (cont.)

Denominator Degrees of Freedom	Numerator Degrees of Freedom												
	14	15	19	24	29	39	49	59	69	79	89	99	199
1	245.4	245.9	247.7	249.1	250.0	251.1	251.7	252.2	252.5	252.7	252.9	253.0	253.7
2	19.42	19.43	19.44	19.45	19.46	19.47	19.48	19.48	19.48	19.48	19.48	19.49	19.49
3	8.71	8.70	8.67	8.64	8.62	8.60	8.58	8.57	8.57	8.56	8.56	8.55	8.54
4	5.87	5.86	5.81	5.77	5.75	5.72	5.70	5.69	5.68	5.67	5.67	5.66	5.65
5	4.64	4.62	4.57	4.53	4.50	4.47	4.45	4.43	4.42	4.42	4.41	4.41	4.39
6	3.96	3.94	3.88	3.84	3.81	3.78	3.76	3.74	3.73	3.72	3.72	3.71	3.69
7	3.53	3.51	3.46	3.41	3.38	3.34	3.32	3.31	3.29	3.29	3.28	3.28	3.25
8	3.24	3.22	3.16	3.12	3.08	3.05	3.02	3.01	3.00	2.99	2.98	2.98	2.95
9	3.03	3.01	2.95	2.90	2.87	2.83	2.80	2.79	2.78	2.77	2.76	2.76	2.73
10	2.86	2.85	2.79	2.74	2.70	2.66	2.64	2.62	2.61	2.60	2.59	2.59	2.56
11	2.74	2.72	2.66	2.61	2.58	2.53	2.51	2.49	2.48	2.47	2.46	2.46	2.43
12	2.64	2.62	2.56	2.51	2.47	2.43	2.40	2.39	2.37	2.36	2.36	2.35	2.32
13	2.55	2.53	2.47	2.42	2.39	2.34	2.32	2.30	2.29	2.28	2.27	2.26	2.23
14	2.48	2.46	2.40	2.35	2.31	2.27	2.24	2.22	2.21	2.20	2.19	2.19	2.16
15	2.42	2.40	2.34	2.29	2.25	2.21	2.18	2.16	2.15	2.14	2.13	2.12	2.10
16	2.37	2.35	2.29	2.24	2.20	2.15	2.13	2.11	2.09	2.08	2.08	2.07	2.04
17	2.33	2.31	2.24	2.19	2.15	2.11	2.08	2.06	2.05	2.04	2.03	2.02	1.99
18	2.29	2.27	2.20	2.15	2.11	2.07	2.04	2.02	2.00	1.99	1.99	1.98	1.95
19	2.26	2.23	2.17	2.11	2.08	2.03	2.00	1.98	1.97	1.96	1.95	1.94	1.91
20	2.22	2.20	2.14	2.08	2.05	2.00	1.97	1.95	1.93	1.92	1.91	1.91	1.88
21	2.20	2.18	2.11	2.05	2.02	1.97	1.94	1.92	1.90	1.89	1.88	1.88	1.84
22	2.17	2.15	2.08	2.03	1.99	1.94	1.91	1.89	1.88	1.87	1.86	1.85	1.82
23	2.15	2.13	2.06	2.01	1.97	1.92	1.89	1.87	1.85	1.84	1.83	1.82	1.79
24	2.13	2.11	2.04	1.98	1.95	1.90	1.86	1.84	1.83	1.82	1.81	1.80	1.77
25	2.11	2.09	2.02	1.96	1.93	1.88	1.84	1.82	1.81	1.80	1.79	1.78	1.75
26	2.09	2.07	2.00	1.95	1.91	1.86	1.83	1.80	1.79	1.78	1.77	1.76	1.73
27	2.08	2.06	1.99	1.93	1.89	1.84	1.81	1.79	1.77	1.76	1.75	1.74	1.71
28	2.06	2.04	1.97	1.91	1.88	1.82	1.79	1.77	1.75	1.74	1.73	1.73	1.69
29	2.05	2.03	1.96	1.90	1.86	1.81	1.78	1.76	1.74	1.73	1.72	1.71	1.67
30	2.04	2.01	1.95	1.89	1.85	1.80	1.76	1.74	1.73	1.71	1.70	1.70	1.66
31	2.03	2.00	1.93	1.88	1.83	1.78	1.75	1.73	1.71	1.70	1.69	1.68	1.65
32	2.01	1.99	1.92	1.86	1.82	1.77	1.74	1.72	1.70	1.69	1.68	1.67	1.63
33	2.00	1.98	1.91	1.85	1.81	1.76	1.73	1.70	1.69	1.68	1.67	1.66	1.62
34	1.99	1.97	1.90	1.84	1.80	1.75	1.72	1.69	1.68	1.66	1.65	1.65	1.61
35	1.99	1.96	1.89	1.83	1.79	1.74	1.71	1.68	1.67	1.65	1.64	1.64	1.60
36	1.98	1.95	1.88	1.82	1.78	1.73	1.70	1.67	1.66	1.64	1.63	1.63	1.59
37	1.97	1.95	1.88	1.82	1.77	1.72	1.69	1.66	1.65	1.63	1.62	1.62	1.58
38	1.96	1.94	1.87	1.81	1.77	1.71	1.68	1.66	1.64	1.63	1.62	1.61	1.57
39	1.95	1.93	1.86	1.80	1.76	1.70	1.67	1.65	1.63	1.62	1.61	1.60	1.56
49	1.90	1.88	1.80	1.74	1.70	1.64	1.61	1.58	1.56	1.55	1.54	1.53	1.49
59	1.86	1.84	1.77	1.70	1.66	1.60	1.57	1.54	1.52	1.51	1.50	1.49	1.44
69	1.84	1.81	1.74	1.68	1.63	1.57	1.54	1.51	1.49	1.48	1.46	1.45	1.41
79	1.82	1.79	1.72	1.66	1.61	1.55	1.51	1.49	1.47	1.45	1.44	1.43	1.38
89	1.80	1.78	1.70	1.64	1.59	1.53	1.50	1.47	1.45	1.43	1.42	1.41	1.36
99	1.79	1.77	1.69	1.63	1.58	1.52	1.48	1.45	1.43	1.42	1.40	1.39	1.34
199	1.74	1.72	1.64	1.57	1.52	1.46	1.42	1.39	1.37	1.35	1.33	1.32	1.26
499	1.71	1.69	1.61	1.54	1.49	1.42	1.38	1.35	1.32	1.31	1.29	1.28	1.21

Generated from Excel using row 2 for the numerator degrees of freedom and column A for the denominator degrees of freedom. The entries in cell (i,j) are: =FINV(0.05,j$2,$Ai).

F Distribution
Value of F That Puts .10 in the Tail

Denominator Degrees of Freedom	Numerator Degrees of Freedom												
	1	2	3	4	5	6	7	8	9	10	11	12	13
1	39.86	49.50	53.59	55.83	57.24	58.20	58.91	59.44	59.86	60.19	60.47	60.71	60.90
2	8.53	9.00	9.16	9.24	9.29	9.33	9.35	9.37	9.38	9.39	9.40	9.41	9.41
3	5.54	5.46	5.39	5.34	5.31	5.28	5.27	5.25	5.24	5.23	5.22	5.22	5.21
4	4.54	4.32	4.19	4.11	4.05	4.01	3.98	3.95	3.94	3.92	3.91	3.90	3.89
5	4.06	3.78	3.62	3.52	3.45	3.40	3.37	3.34	3.32	3.30	3.28	3.27	3.26
6	3.78	3.46	3.29	3.18	3.11	3.05	3.01	2.98	2.96	2.94	2.92	2.90	2.89
7	3.59	3.26	3.07	2.96	2.88	2.83	2.78	2.75	2.72	2.70	2.68	2.67	2.65
8	3.46	3.11	2.92	2.81	2.73	2.67	2.62	2.59	2.56	2.54	2.52	2.50	2.49
9	3.36	3.01	2.81	2.69	2.61	2.55	2.51	2.47	2.44	2.42	2.40	2.38	2.36
10	3.29	2.92	2.73	2.61	2.52	2.46	2.41	2.38	2.35	2.32	2.30	2.28	2.27
11	3.23	2.86	2.66	2.54	2.45	2.39	2.34	2.30	2.27	2.25	2.23	2.21	2.19
12	3.18	2.81	2.61	2.48	2.39	2.33	2.28	2.24	2.21	2.19	2.17	2.15	2.13
13	3.14	2.76	2.56	2.43	2.35	2.28	2.23	2.20	2.16	2.14	2.12	2.10	2.08
14	3.10	2.73	2.52	2.39	2.31	2.24	2.19	2.15	2.12	2.10	2.07	2.05	2.04
15	3.07	2.70	2.49	2.36	2.27	2.21	2.16	2.12	2.09	2.06	2.04	2.02	2.00
16	3.05	2.67	2.46	2.33	2.24	2.18	2.13	2.09	2.06	2.03	2.01	1.99	1.97
17	3.03	2.64	2.44	2.31	2.22	2.15	2.10	2.06	2.03	2.00	1.98	1.96	1.94
18	3.01	2.62	2.42	2.29	2.20	2.13	2.08	2.04	2.00	1.98	1.95	1.93	1.92
19	2.99	2.61	2.40	2.27	2.18	2.11	2.06	2.02	1.98	1.96	1.93	1.91	1.89
20	2.97	2.59	2.38	2.25	2.16	2.09	2.04	2.00	1.96	1.94	1.91	1.89	1.87
21	2.96	2.57	2.36	2.23	2.14	2.08	2.02	1.98	1.95	1.92	1.90	1.87	1.86
22	2.95	2.56	2.35	2.22	2.13	2.06	2.01	1.97	1.93	1.90	1.88	1.86	1.84
23	2.94	2.55	2.34	2.21	2.11	2.05	1.99	1.95	1.92	1.89	1.87	1.84	1.83
24	2.93	2.54	2.33	2.19	2.10	2.04	1.98	1.94	1.91	1.88	1.85	1.83	1.81
25	2.92	2.53	2.32	2.18	2.09	2.02	1.97	1.93	1.89	1.87	1.84	1.82	1.80
26	2.91	2.52	2.31	2.17	2.08	2.01	1.96	1.92	1.88	1.86	1.83	1.81	1.79
27	2.90	2.51	2.30	2.17	2.07	2.00	1.95	1.91	1.87	1.85	1.82	1.80	1.78
28	2.89	2.50	2.29	2.16	2.06	2.00	1.94	1.90	1.87	1.84	1.81	1.79	1.77
29	2.89	2.50	2.28	2.15	2.06	1.99	1.93	1.89	1.86	1.83	1.80	1.78	1.76
30	2.88	2.49	2.28	2.14	2.05	1.98	1.93	1.88	1.85	1.82	1.79	1.77	1.75
31	2.87	2.48	2.27	2.14	2.04	1.97	1.92	1.88	1.84	1.81	1.79	1.77	1.75
32	2.87	2.48	2.26	2.13	2.04	1.97	1.91	1.87	1.83	1.81	1.78	1.76	1.74
33	2.86	2.47	2.26	2.12	2.03	1.96	1.91	1.86	1.83	1.80	1.77	1.75	1.73
34	2.86	2.47	2.25	2.12	2.02	1.96	1.90	1.86	1.82	1.79	1.77	1.75	1.73
35	2.85	2.46	2.25	2.11	2.02	1.95	1.90	1.85	1.82	1.79	1.76	1.74	1.72
36	2.85	2.46	2.24	2.11	2.01	1.94	1.89	1.85	1.81	1.78	1.76	1.73	1.71
37	2.85	2.45	2.24	2.10	2.01	1.94	1.89	1.84	1.81	1.78	1.75	1.73	1.71
38	2.84	2.45	2.23	2.10	2.01	1.94	1.88	1.84	1.80	1.77	1.75	1.72	1.70
39	2.84	2.44	2.23	2.09	2.00	1.93	1.88	1.83	1.80	1.77	1.74	1.72	1.70
49	2.81	2.41	2.20	2.06	1.97	1.90	1.84	1.80	1.76	1.73	1.71	1.68	1.66
59	2.79	2.39	2.18	2.04	1.95	1.88	1.82	1.78	1.74	1.71	1.68	1.66	1.64
69	2.78	2.38	2.16	2.03	1.93	1.86	1.81	1.76	1.72	1.69	1.67	1.64	1.62
79	2.77	2.37	2.15	2.02	1.92	1.85	1.79	1.75	1.71	1.68	1.65	1.63	1.61
89	2.76	2.36	2.15	2.01	1.91	1.84	1.79	1.74	1.70	1.67	1.64	1.62	1.60
99	2.76	2.36	2.14	2.00	1.91	1.83	1.78	1.73	1.70	1.66	1.64	1.61	1.59
199	2.73	2.33	2.11	1.97	1.88	1.80	1.75	1.70	1.66	1.63	1.60	1.58	1.56
499	2.72	2.31	2.09	1.96	1.86	1.79	1.73	1.68	1.64	1.61	1.58	1.56	1.54

Generated from Excel using row 2 for the numerator degrees of freedom and column A for the denominator degrees of freedom. The entries in cell (i,j) are: =FINV(0.10,j$2,$Ai).

F Distribution
Value of F That Puts .10 in the Tail (cont.)

Denominator Degrees of Freedom	Numerator Degrees of Freedom												
	14	15	19	24	29	39	49	59	69	79	89	99	199
1	61.07	61.22	61.66	62.00	62.23	62.51	62.68	62.79	62.86	62.92	62.97	63.00	63.17
2	9.42	9.42	9.44	9.45	9.46	9.47	9.47	9.47	9.48	9.48	9.48	9.48	9.49
3	5.20	5.20	5.19	5.18	5.17	5.16	5.16	5.15	5.15	5.15	5.15	5.14	5.14
4	3.88	3.87	3.85	3.83	3.82	3.80	3.80	3.79	3.79	3.78	3.78	3.78	3.77
5	3.25	3.24	3.21	3.19	3.18	3.16	3.15	3.14	3.14	3.13	3.13	3.13	3.12
6	2.88	2.87	2.84	2.82	2.80	2.78	2.77	2.76	2.76	2.75	2.75	2.75	2.73
7	2.64	2.63	2.60	2.58	2.56	2.54	2.52	2.51	2.51	2.50	2.50	2.50	2.48
8	2.48	2.46	2.43	2.40	2.39	2.36	2.35	2.34	2.33	2.33	2.32	2.32	2.31
9	2.35	2.34	2.30	2.28	2.26	2.23	2.22	2.21	2.20	2.20	2.19	2.19	2.17
10	2.26	2.24	2.21	2.18	2.16	2.13	2.12	2.11	2.10	2.10	2.09	2.09	2.07
11	2.18	2.17	2.13	2.10	2.08	2.05	2.04	2.03	2.02	2.01	2.01	2.01	1.99
12	2.12	2.10	2.07	2.04	2.01	1.99	1.97	1.96	1.95	1.95	1.94	1.94	1.92
13	2.07	2.05	2.01	1.98	1.96	1.93	1.92	1.91	1.90	1.89	1.89	1.88	1.86
14	2.02	2.01	1.97	1.94	1.92	1.89	1.87	1.86	1.85	1.84	1.84	1.83	1.82
15	1.99	1.97	1.93	1.90	1.88	1.85	1.83	1.82	1.81	1.80	1.80	1.79	1.77
16	1.95	1.94	1.90	1.87	1.84	1.81	1.79	1.78	1.77	1.77	1.76	1.76	1.74
17	1.93	1.91	1.87	1.84	1.81	1.78	1.76	1.75	1.74	1.74	1.73	1.73	1.71
18	1.90	1.89	1.84	1.81	1.79	1.76	1.74	1.72	1.71	1.71	1.70	1.70	1.68
19	1.88	1.86	1.82	1.79	1.76	1.73	1.71	1.70	1.69	1.68	1.68	1.67	1.65
20	1.86	1.84	1.80	1.77	1.74	1.71	1.69	1.68	1.67	1.66	1.66	1.65	1.63
21	1.84	1.83	1.78	1.75	1.72	1.69	1.67	1.66	1.65	1.64	1.63	1.63	1.61
22	1.83	1.81	1.77	1.73	1.71	1.67	1.65	1.64	1.63	1.62	1.62	1.61	1.59
23	1.81	1.80	1.75	1.72	1.69	1.66	1.64	1.62	1.61	1.61	1.60	1.59	1.57
24	1.80	1.78	1.74	1.70	1.68	1.64	1.62	1.61	1.60	1.59	1.58	1.58	1.56
25	1.79	1.77	1.73	1.69	1.66	1.63	1.61	1.59	1.58	1.58	1.57	1.56	1.54
26	1.77	1.76	1.71	1.68	1.65	1.62	1.60	1.58	1.57	1.56	1.56	1.55	1.53
27	1.76	1.75	1.70	1.67	1.64	1.61	1.58	1.57	1.56	1.55	1.54	1.54	1.52
28	1.75	1.74	1.69	1.66	1.63	1.60	1.57	1.56	1.55	1.54	1.53	1.53	1.50
29	1.75	1.73	1.68	1.65	1.62	1.59	1.56	1.55	1.54	1.53	1.52	1.52	1.49
30	1.74	1.72	1.68	1.64	1.61	1.58	1.55	1.54	1.53	1.52	1.51	1.51	1.48
31	1.73	1.71	1.67	1.63	1.60	1.57	1.55	1.53	1.52	1.51	1.50	1.50	1.47
32	1.72	1.71	1.66	1.62	1.59	1.56	1.54	1.52	1.51	1.50	1.49	1.49	1.46
33	1.72	1.70	1.65	1.61	1.59	1.55	1.53	1.51	1.50	1.49	1.49	1.48	1.46
34	1.71	1.69	1.65	1.61	1.58	1.54	1.52	1.51	1.49	1.49	1.48	1.47	1.45
35	1.70	1.69	1.64	1.60	1.57	1.54	1.51	1.50	1.49	1.48	1.47	1.47	1.44
36	1.70	1.68	1.64	1.60	1.57	1.53	1.51	1.49	1.48	1.47	1.46	1.46	1.43
37	1.69	1.68	1.63	1.59	1.56	1.52	1.50	1.49	1.47	1.47	1.46	1.45	1.43
38	1.69	1.67	1.62	1.58	1.56	1.52	1.50	1.48	1.47	1.46	1.45	1.45	1.42
39	1.68	1.67	1.62	1.58	1.55	1.51	1.49	1.47	1.46	1.45	1.45	1.44	1.41
49	1.65	1.63	1.58	1.54	1.51	1.47	1.45	1.43	1.42	1.41	1.40	1.39	1.36
59	1.62	1.61	1.56	1.51	1.48	1.44	1.42	1.40	1.39	1.38	1.37	1.36	1.33
69	1.60	1.59	1.54	1.49	1.46	1.42	1.40	1.38	1.36	1.35	1.34	1.34	1.30
79	1.59	1.58	1.52	1.48	1.45	1.41	1.38	1.36	1.35	1.34	1.33	1.32	1.29
89	1.58	1.57	1.51	1.47	1.44	1.40	1.37	1.35	1.33	1.32	1.31	1.31	1.27
99	1.57	1.56	1.51	1.46	1.43	1.39	1.36	1.34	1.32	1.31	1.30	1.30	1.26
199	1.54	1.52	1.47	1.42	1.39	1.34	1.31	1.29	1.27	1.26	1.25	1.24	1.20
499	1.52	1.50	1.45	1.40	1.36	1.32	1.28	1.26	1.24	1.23	1.22	1.21	1.16

Generated from Excel using row 2 for the numerator degrees of freedom and column A for the denominator degrees of freedom. The entries in cell (i,j) are: =FINV(0.10,j$2,$Ai).

Constants for Quality Control Charts

Number of Observations per Group, n	d_2	d_3	D_3	D_4
2	1.128	.853	.000	3.267
3	1.693	.888	.000	2.574
4	2.059	.880	.000	2.282
5	2.326	.864	.000	2.114
6	2.534	.848	.000	2.004
7	2.704	.833	.076	1.924
8	2.847	.820	.136	1.864
9	2.970	.808	.184	1.816
10	3.078	.797	.223	1.777
11	3.173	.787	.256	1.744
12	3.258	.778	.283	1.717
13	3.336	.770	.307	1.693
14	3.407	.762	.328	1.672
15	3.472	.755	.347	1.653
16	3.532	.749	.363	1.637
17	3.588	.743	.378	1.622
18	3.640	.738	.391	1.608
19	3.689	.733	.403	1.597
20	3.735	.729	.415	1.585
21	3.778	.724	.425	1.575
22	3.819	.720	.434	1.566
23	3.858	.716	.443	1.557
24	3.895	.712	.451	1.548
25	3.931	.709	.459	1.541

Source: ASTM Manual on the Presentation of Data Collection and Control Analysis (Philadelphia, Pa.: American Society for Testing Materials, 1976), pp 134–136.

Critical Values of Spearman's Rank Correlation Coefficient

The α values in this table correspond to a one-tailed test; they must be doubled for two-tailed tests.

n	α					
	.001	.005	.010	.025	.050	.100
4	—	—	—	—	.8000	.8000
5	—	—	.9000	.9000	.8000	.7000
6	—	.9429	.8857	.8286	.7714	.6000
7	.9643	.8929	.8571	.7450	.6786	.5357
8	.9286	.8571	.8095	.7143	.6190	.5000
9	.9000	.8167	.7667	.6833	.5833	.4667
10	.8667	.7818	.7333	.6364	.5515	.4424
11	.8364	.7545	.7000	.6091	.5273	.4182
12	.8182	.7273	.6713	.5804	.4965	.3986
13	.7912	.6978	.6429	.5549	.4780	.3791
14	.7670	.6747	.6220	.5341	.4593	.3626
15	.7464	.6536	.6000	.5179	.4429	.3500
16	.7265	.6324	.5824	.5000	.4265	.3382
17	.7083	.6152	.5637	.4853	.4118	.3260
18	.6904	.5975	.5480	.4716	.3994	.3148
19	.6737	.5825	.5333	.4579	.3895	.3070
20	.6586	.5684	.5203	.4451	.3789	.2977
21	.6455	.5545	.5078	.4351	.3688	.2909
22	.6318	.5426	.4963	.4241	.3597	.2829
23	.6186	.5306	.4852	.4150	.3518	.2767
24	.6070	.5200	.4748	.4061	.3435	.2704
25	.5962	.5100	.4654	.3977	.3362	.2646
26	.5856	.5002	.4564	.3894	.3299	.2588
27	.5757	.4915	.4481	.3822	.3236	.2540
28	.5660	.4828	.4401	.3749	.3175	.2490
29	.5567	.4744	.4320	.3685	.3113	.2443
30	.5479	.4665	.4251	.3620	.3059	.2400

Source: G. J. Glasser and R. F. Winter (1961), "Values of Rank Correlation for Testing the Hypothesis of Independence," Biometrika 48 (1961): 444–448, including corrections of W. J. Conover, Practical Nonparametric Statistics (New York: Wiley, 1971).

GLOSSARY

A

absorbing state a state that is never left after it is entered (15)

activities the tasks of a project (7)

activity on arc (AOA) network a network representation that reflects activity precedence relations, in which arcs correspond to activities and nodes represent specific time points (events) denoting the completion of a set of activities (7)

activity on node (AON) network a network representation that reflects activity precedence relations, in which nodes designate activities and arcs describe the precedence relations between activities (7)

additivity assumption an assumption in linear programming that implies that the total value of some function can be found simply by adding the linear terms (3)

algorithm a structured series of steps involving simple, repetitious mathematical operations (2)

all units schedule a quantity discount schedule in which the price the buyer pays for all the units purchased is based on the total purchase volume (10)

analysis of variance (ANOVA) a statistical procedure that uses the variances of the data samples to test for equality of population means (13)

arc a linkage of nodes, or entities, in a network model (6)

assignment problem a network model designed to find the minimum cost assignment of objects to tasks (6)

autocorrelation the measure of how the value at one time period affects the value at some subsequent time period (9)

autoregressive-integrated-moving average (ARIMA) forecasting model a forecasting model based on historic time series values and n period differences between time series values (9)

B

backordering the phenomenon of waiting for merchandise to be delivered (10)

balking a phenomenon that occurs when customers perceive that a waiting line is too long and decide to leave the system (12)

Bayesian statistics a mathematical approach that argues that it is unnecessary to practice decision making under uncertainty since there is always at least *some* probabilistic information that can be used to assess the likelihoods of the states of nature (8)

Bellman's principle of optimality the underlying principle of dynamic programming that states that from a given state at a given stage, the optimal solution for the remainder of the process is independent of any previous decisions made to that point (16)

Beta distribution a statistical distribution useful in approximating distributions with limited data and fixed end points (7)

bill of materials the details of how a finished good is to be assembled (11)

binary integer linear program (BILP) a model applied to any situation that can be represented by "yes/no," "good/bad," "right/wrong," or "0/1"; also called 0/1 *programs* (5)

binding constraint a constraint that is satisfied with equality at the optimal point (3)

binomial distribution function a distribution that can be used to determine the probability that k out of n sample items is defective (14)

Box-Jenkins method a forecasting technique that assists in selecting the appropriate underlying forecasting model by basing its forecasts on a combined autoregressive and moving average model (9)

branch and bound algorithm a mathematical approach for solving integer, mixed integer, and binary linear programs (5, SCD4)

breakpoint the quantity at which the price changes under a quantity discount schedule (10)

buffer stock inventory that acts as a buffer to handle a firm's higher-than-average lead time demand or longer-than-expected lead time; also called *safety stock* (10)

C

canonical form a system of equations in which for each equation there exists a variable that appears only in that equation and its coefficient in that equation is +1 (SCD3)

capacitated transshipment model a transshipment problem in which an upper limit is placed on the amount of flow along one or more arcs in the network; also called a *general network model* (6)

carrying costs the costs incurred by a firm to maintain its inventory position; also called *holding costs* (10)

certainty assumption an assumption in linear programming that asserts that all parameters of the problem are fixed, known constants (3)

classical decomposition a forecasting technique in which the trend, cyclical, and seasonal components are isolated and forecast separately (9)

complementary slackness a linear programming property that states that, at the optimal solution, either the variable is 0 or the reduced cost for the variable is 0 and that either the slack and surplus on a constraint is 0 or its shadow price is 0 (3)

constant returns to scale assumption an assumption in linear programming that prohibits a "learning curve" or different unit values for lesser quantities (3)

constrained mathematical model a mathematical model with an objective and one or more constraints (2)

constraint a restrictive condition that may affect the optimal value for an objective function (2)

continuous review system an inventory system in which the inventory is constantly monitored and a new order placed when the inventory level reaches a certain critical point (10)

continuous simulation system a simulation in which the state of the system changes continuously over time (13)

continuity assumption an assumption in linear programming that implies that decision variables can take on any value within the limits of the functional constraints (3)

control chart   a graphical display that provides a view of the production process over time by plotting data based on samples selected from the process (14)

controllable input   a factor over which the decision maker has control; also called a *decision variable* (2)

convex programming problems   a class of non-linear programming models whose objective is to maximize a concave function or minimize a convex function and whose constraints form a convex set (16)

cost overrun   the amount that the actual expenditures of a project exceed the value of the work (7)

cost underrun   the amount that the value of the work of a project exceeds the actual expenditures (7)

critical activity   an activity that has no slack time and must be rigidly scheduled to start and finish at its earliest start and finish times, respectively, to ensure that the project completion time is not delayed (7)

critical path   the longest path in the directed network made up of critical activities from a project's start to finish nodes (7)

critical path method (CPM)   a deterministic approach to cost analysis in project planning based on the assumption that an activity's completion time can be determined with certainty based on the amount spent on the activity (7)

customer satisfaction costs   the measure of the degree to which a customer is satisfied with the firm's inventory policy and the impact this has on long-term profitability (10)

cutting plane approach   a mixed integer linear programming approach in which integer restrictions are initially ignored and the problem solved as a linear program; if the optimal solution fails to provide integer values, a new constraint is added to make the solution infeasible without eliminating any feasible point that provides integer values for these variables (5)

cycle   a circuitous path that starts at some node and returns to the same node without using any arc twice (6)

cycle time   the time that elapses between orders (10)

D

decision analysis   a process that allows an individual or organization to select from a set of possible alternatives when uncertainties regarding the future exist, with the goal of optimizing the resulting payoff in terms of some decision criterion (7)

decision making under certainty   a decision-making situation in which the decision maker knows for sure which state of nature will occur (8)

decision making under risk   a decision-making situation in which the decision maker has at least some knowledge of the probabilities of the states of nature occurring (8)

decision making under uncertainty   a decision-making situation in which the decision maker has no knowledge of the probabilities of the states of nature occurring (8)

decision tree   a chronological representation of the decision process by a network that utilizes decision nodes and state of nature nodes (8)

decision variable   a factor over which the decision maker has control; also called a *controllable input* (2)

definitional variable   an additional decision variable not part of the original set of decision variables in a linear programming problem which is used to define some relationship between the variables (4)

Delphi technique   a method of coalescing different expert opinions into a consensus (9)

deterministic model   a mathematical model in which the profit, cost, and resource data are assumed to be known with certainty (2)

diet problem   a linear programming model with a minimization objective function and "$\geq$" constraints (3)

Dijkstra algorithm   an algorithm used to find the shortest path from a start node to a terminal node in a network (SCD5)

directed arc   a linkage that indicates that flow occurs in only one direction in a network model (6)

directed graph (digraph)   a graphic representation of a network made up entirely of directed arcs (6)

discrete simulation system   a simulation that studies changes that occur at discrete points in time (13)

dual simplex method   an approach that can be used for solving linear programs by generating a new optimal solution when a change in a right-hand side coefficient extends beyond its range of feasibility or when a new constraint is added to a problem after an optimal solution has been found (SCD3)

dual price   the change to the optimal value of the objective function resulting from a one-unit increase in the right-hand side of a constraint; also expressed as *shadow price* (3)

duality   a condition that exists when a linear programming problem called the primal has an associated linear programming problem called the dual (SCD3)

dynamic programming (DP) model   a multistage problem in which a set of decisions is made "in sequence" (16)

E

economic order quantity (EOQ) model   a model for inventory optimization which involves analyzing stock keeping units, assuming that all parameters remain constant forever (over an infinite time horizon) (10)

efficiency   a measure of the relative value of sample information (8)

80/20 rule   a rule of thumb which states a client settles for 80% of the optimal solution at 20% of the cost to obtain it (2)

Erlangian distribution   a probability distribution which can be viewed as arising from the sum of n independent exponentially distributed random variables; often used to describe a service time distribution (12)

expected regret criterion   a decision-making criterion that determines the optimal decision by selecting the one with the minimum expected regret (8)

expected utility criterion   a decision-making criterion that determines the optimal decision by selecting the one with the highest expected utility (8)

expected value criterion   a decision-making criterion that determines the optimal decision by selecting the one that has the best expected payoff (8)

expected value of perfect information (EVPI)   the expected gain in return from knowing for sure which state of nature will occur (8) expected value of sample information (EVSI)   the expected gain from making decisions based on sample or indicator information (8)

explicit inverse distribution method   a technique used in simulation that utilizes the cumulative distribution function to determine a value for the random variable (13)

exponential smoothing method   a forecasting technique that creates the next period's forecast using a weighted average of the current period's actual value and the current period's forecasted value (9)

extreme point   a feasible point at the intersection of two lines in a two-dimensional feasible region or the intersection of three planes in a three-dimensional feasible region, etc. that would be the last point touched in a feasible region by some linear objective function (3)

F

facility location problem   a linear programming model that determines which of several possible locations to operate in order to maximize or minimize some objective function (5)

feasible region   the set of points that satisfy all the constraints of a linear programming model (3)

fishbone diagram   a cause-and-effect diagram that graphically relates the factors that affect quality to their results (14)

fixed-charge problem   a linear programming model that includes in the objective function the fixed costs of operating a facility if the facility is, in fact, operating (5)

fixed time simulation   a simulation in which each iteration represents a fixed time period (e.g., one day of operation) (13)

flexible manufacturing system (FMS)   a production system in which machines do several different operations, and goods to be manufactured are placed on pallets with their movements about the factory controlled by a computer (11)

flow   the amount of a resource that is delivered on an arc(s) between nodes in a network (6)

forecast error   the difference between the actual time series for a period and

the value forecasted for the period using a particular forecasting technique (9)

forecasting   the process of predicting the future (9)

functional constraint   "$\leq$," "$\geq$," or "$=$" restrictions that involve expressions with one or more variables (2)

G

game theory   an approach that uses competitive play to determine the optimal decision in the face of other decision-making players (8)

Gantt chart   a bar chart used to display activities of a project and monitor their progress (7)

general network model   a transshipment problem in which an upper limit can be placed on the amount of flow along one or more arcs in the network; also called a *capacitated transshipment model* (6)

general non-linear programming (NLP) model   a non-linear model in which the objective function and constraints (if any) may be non-linear relationships (16)

goal programming problem   a linear programming model that involves prioritized objectives (5,16)

goodwill cost   the future reduction in the firm's profitability associated with not having an item readily available for purchase (10)

Greedy algorithm   an algorithm which sequentially selects the best course of action for a minimal spanning tree model (SCD5)

H

heuristic   a "rule of thumb," or common-sense procedure (2)

holding costs   the costs incurred by a firm to maintain its inventory position; also called *carrying costs* (10)

Holt's technique   a linear exponential smoothing technique that forecasts the time series' level and its trend, both of which are adjusted at each time period (9)

Hungarian algorithm   an algorithm used to solve the assignment problem of a least cost assignment of m workers to m jobs based on the fact that the assignment cost matrix can be reduced to

a point at which a 0 cost assignment is optimal (SCD5)

I

included costs   the cost of the resources that is included in the calculation of objective function coefficients of a linear programming model (3)

incremental discount schedule   a quantity discount schedule in which the price discount applies only to the additional units ordered beyond each breakpoint (10)

infeasible linear program   a linear program that has no feasible solutions (3)

infeasible point   a point lying outside the feasible region of a mathematical programming model (3)

integer linear programming   a model for which some or all of the decision variables are restricted to integer values (5)

interior point   a feasible solution to a mathematical programming model that satisfies none of the constraints with equality (3)

interior point method   a linear programming solution procedure that ultimately approaches the optimal extreme point by starting from an interior point of the feasible region (3)

inventory policy   a policy that consists of an order quantity and an inventory reorder point (10)

inventory position   the stock on hand plus the size of any outstanding orders not yet delivered (10)

inventory records file   information about the inventory status of each component for each period of time, the component vendors, required lead time for delivery, and specified lot sizes (11)

J

jockeying   a phenomenon that occurs when customers switch between lines when they perceive that another line is moving faster (12)

just-in-time (JIT)   an inventory/production control technique that reduces raw material and work-in-process inventories to the lowest possible level by keeping production lot sizes small (11)

K

kanban system   a ticket-based inventory system that keeps track of the flow of components through the factory (11)

Kendall's notation the notation used to identify queuing models (12)

knapsack problem a resource allocation problem that is equivalent to the problem faced by a hiker carrying a knapsack with limited space for items, each with a weight or volume and a value; the objective is to fill the knapsack so that it contains the highest possible value of goods (16)

L

largest absolute deviation (LAD) the largest absolute difference between the forecasted and actual values (9)

last period technique a forecasting technique in which the forecast of the value for the next period of a stationary time series is the last observed value (9)

lead time the time that elapses between when an order is placed and when it arrives (10)

limiting transition matrix a matrix that gives the eventual likelihood that a Markov process will move from a transient state to an absorbing state (15)

linear assumption of CPM the assumption that if any amount between the normal cost and crash cost is spent to complete an activity, the percentage decrease in the activity's completion time from its normal time to its crash time equals the percentage increase in cost from its normal cost to its crash cost (7)

linear programming model a mathematical model that seeks to maximize or minimize a linear objective function subject to a set of linear constraints (3)

Little's formulas relationships that exist between the average number of customers in a system and the average customer waiting time in the system and between the average number of customers waiting for service and the average time a customer spends waiting for service (12)

lower control limit (LCL) the number on a control chart that equals the process mean minus three standard deviations (14)

M

management information systems (MIS) a quantitative approach used to evaluate and transform raw data into useful, relevant, and organized information (2)

management science the scientific approach to executive decision making, which consists of the art of mathematical modeling of complex situations; the science of the development of solution techniques used to solve these models; and the ability to communicate effectively the results of the analysis to the decision maker (1)

Mann-Whitney text a statistical procedure used to determine whether two data sets are drawn from the same population (13)

Markov processes (chain) a process consisting of a countable sequence of stages that can be judged at each stage to fall into a future state, independent of how the process arrived at the previous state (15)

master production schedule a forecast of the finished goods demand over a particular planning horizon (11)

matched pair test a statistical procedure that compares the data values of two policies by matching the observations and using the differences in the paired values to calculate the test statistic (13)

material requirements planning (MRP) a computer-based technique used for controlling inventory for a manufacturer that produces many different finished goods (11)

mathematical modeling a process that translates observed or desired phenomena into mathematical expressions (2)

mathematical programming a branch of management science that deals with solving optimization problems, in which the objective is to maximize or minimize a function, usually in a constrained environment (3)

matrix reduction the process of adding or subtracting a number from all numbers in a row or column of an assignment cost matrix (SCD5)

max flow/min cut theorem a network theorem that asserts that the value of the maximum flow equals the sum of the capacities of the minimum cut, and all arcs on the minimum cut are saturated by the maximum flow (6)

maximal flow algorithm an algorithm used to find the maximum volume of flow from a source node to a terminal

sink node in a capacitated network (SCD5)

maximal flow problem a network model used to find the maximum total flow possible from a source node to a sink node without violating arc capacities (6)

maximax criterion a decision-making criterion in which the optimal decision is determined by selecting the one that has the maximum payoff (8)

maximin criterion a decision-making criterion in which the optimal decision is determined by selecting the one that maximizes the minimum payoff (8)

M/D/1 queuing system a single-server queuing model in which customers arrive according to a Poisson process and are served at a constant (deterministic) rate (12)

mean absolute deviation (MAD) the average of the absolute values of the differences of the forecasted values from the actual values (9)

mean absolute percent error (MAPE) the average of the absolute values of the percentage differences of the forecasted values from the actual values (9)

mean recurrence time the average time required for a Markov process to return to a given state (15)

mean squared error (MSE) the average of the squared differences of the forecasted values from the actual values (9)

M/G/1 queuing system a single-server queuing model in which customers arrive according to a Poisson process and for which the mean and standard deviation of the service time distribution is known (12)

M/G/k/k queuing system a multiple-server queuing model in which customers arrive according to a Poisson process, the mean and standard deviation of the service time distribution is known, and no waiting line is permitted (12)

minimal spanning tree problem a network model used to find the minimum total distance that connects all nodes in a network (6)

minimax criterion a decision-making criterion in which the optimal decision is determined by selecting the one that minimizes the maximum costs (8)

minimax regret criterion a decision-making criterion in which the optimal decision is determined by selecting the one that minimizes the maximum "lost opportunity" as measured by the regret values for each payoff (8)

minimin criterion   a decision-making criterion in which the optimal decision is determined by selecting the one that has the minimum cost (8)

mixed integer linear programming (MILP)   a model in which some, but not all, of the decision variables are restricted to integers (5)

M/M/1 queuing system   a single-server queuing model in which customers arrive according to a Poisson process and service time follows an exponential distribution (12)

M/M/1/F queuing system   a single-server queuing model in which customers arrive according to a Poisson process, service time follows an exponential distribution, and a there is a limit to the number of customers who can be waiting for service (12)

M/M/1//m queuing system   a single-server queuing model in which there is a finite population and the interarrival time of customers as well as customer service times follows an exponential distribution (12)

M/M/k queuing system   a multiple-server queuing model in which customers arrive according to a Poisson process and service time follows an exponential distribution (12)

M/M/k/F queuing system   a multiple-server queuing model in which customers arrive according to a Poisson process, service time follows an exponential distribution, and a there is a limit to the number of customers who can be waiting for service (12)

M/M/k/k queuing system   a multiple-server queuing model in which customers arrive according to a Poisson process, service time follows an exponential distribution, and no waiting line is permitted to form (12)

modified distribution approach (MODI) a method used to determine the reduced costs of non-basic variables in a transportation model (SCD5)

Monte Carlo simulation   a simulator designed so that data values occur randomly and reflect the theoretical frequencies being modeled (13)

moving average method   a forecasting technique in which the forecast for any time period is the average of the values for the immediately preceding k periods (9)

multicriteria decision problem   a problem comprised of two or more conflicting objectives (2)

N

net marginal profit   the difference between the objective function coefficient and the total marginal cost of the value of the resources using the current values of the shadow prices (3)

network   a model that consists of a set of nodes, a set of arcs, and functions defined on the nodes and arcs (6)

newsboy problem   an inventory model that assumes demand occurs according to a specified probability distribution and deals with a stock-keeping unit with a limited shelf life of one period; also called a *single-period inventory model* (11)

next-event simulation   a simulation that updates simulated data when a particular event occurs (13)

node   a representation of entities in network models (6)

non-binding constraint   a functional constraint that is not satisfied with equality at the optimal point of a mathematical programming model (3)

non-linear term   any term other than one of the form A or AX, where A is a constant and X is a variable raised to the first power (16)

non-preemptive goal programming   an approach that involves determining the relative weights that act as a per unit penalty for failure to meet a stated goal, with the goal of minimizing the total weighted deviations from the goal (16)

O

objective function   an expression of the quantity the decision maker wishes to optimize (2)

100% rule   a linear programming property that states that if the total sum of the percent changes to objective function coefficients from their current values to their maximum or minimum limits is less than 100%, then the optimal solution will not change; or if the sum of the percent changes to the right-hand side coefficients from their current values to their maximum or minimum limits is less than 100%, then the shadow prices will not change (3)

opportunity costs   return possible from investments that could have been made with available capital had the firm not used the funds to finance its inventory (10)

optimal service level   the long-run percentage of periods in which inventory is sufficient to satisfy all customer demands (11)

optimization model   a mathematical model that seeks to maximize or minimize a quantity that may be restricted by a set of constraints (2)

order costs   costs incurred when a firm purchases goods from a supplier (10)

out-of-kilter algorithm   a streamlined form of the simplex method applied to a general network problem with sources, destinations, intermediate nodes, unit shipping costs, and maximum capacities between nodes (SCD5)

P

p chart   a process control chart used in attribute sampling to determine whether or not a process is in control (14)

parameter   a factor over which the decision maker has no direct influence; also called an *uncontrollable input* (2)

payoff table   the simplest way of presenting a decision problem in which the decision maker faces a finite set of discrete decision alternatives and states of nature and whose payoffs depend on the decision made and the state of nature that occurs (8)

periodic review system   an inventory system in which the inventory position is investigated on a regular basis and orders are placed only at these times (10)

periodicity   a phenomenon that occurs when a Markov process exhibits a regular pattern moving between states from one stage to the next (15)

PERT/COST   an accounting information system that aids management in determining whether a project is coming in on time and within budget (7)

PERT/CPM   an analysis used to determine the minimal possible completion time for a project and a range of start and finish times for each activity so that the project is completed within that time frame (7)

planned shortage model   an inventory model that assumes that there is a cost associated with an out-of-stock situation but that all customers will backorder (10)

Poisson distribution   a probability distribution used for describing customer arrival processes in which the conditions of orderliness, stationarity, and independence are satisfied (12)

postoptimality analysis   a quantitative analysis that provides information about the effects of changes to the solution of a problem as certain parameters change; also called *sensitivity analysis* (2,3)

precedence relations chart   a chart used to identify the separate activities of a project that details which ones must precede others (7)

prediction model   a mathematical model that describes or predicts events, given certain conditions (2)

preemptive goal programming   an approach that involves prioritizing goals into different priority levels (16)

principle of insufficient reason   decision criterion under which each state of nature is assumed to be equally likely (8)

probabilistic model   a mathematical model in which one or more of the input parameters' values are determined by probability distributions; also called a *stochastic model* (2)

process flow diagram   a flow chart diagram that details the chronology of the process used to produce a good or provide a service (14)

process-interaction approach   a simulation in which each iteration traces all relevant processes incurred by an item in the system under study (13)

procurement costs   the cost of obtaining items for inventory (10)

product mix problem   a linear programming model with a maximization objective function and "≤" functional constraints (3)

product tree   a pictorial representation of the bill of materials that make up a product (11)

production lot size model   a model that determines the optimal inventory policy for an item in which the demand for the item occurs at a constant rate, the production line for the enterprise is not continuously used to manufacture the same product, and the production facility operates at a rate greater than the demand rate for the item (10)

project   a collection of tasks a person or firm desires to complete in minimum time or at minimal cost (7)

project scheduling   a means of planning and controlling a project efficiently (7)

pull system   an inventory system in which a subcomponent is produced only on request from the work center that utilizes it in assembly (11)

push system   an inventory system in which decisions are made regarding the production schedule for the subcomponents based on the forecast demand for the finished good, "pushing" completed subcomponents up to the next level of assembly (11)

Q

quadratic loss function   a quadratic function based on the assumption that there is an ideal measurement for product conformance and that any deviation from this ideal results in a potential loss to society (14)

quadratic programming problem   a non-linear programming problem whose objective function is a concave quadratic function and whose constraints are linear (16)

quality   the ability of a product or service to conform to its design specifications (14)

quantity discount schedule   a list of the discounted cost per unit corresponding to different purchase volumes (10)

queuing theory   the study of waiting lines, or queues (12)

R

R chart   a planning control chart that records the range of each sample item to monitor the variability of the production process (14)

random number generator   a computer program that generates pseudo-random numbers by a mathematical formula (13)

random number mapping   a process for matching random numbers to simulated events (13)

range of feasibility   the set of right-hand side values of a resource over which the shadow prices do not change (3)

range of optimality   the range of values of the objective function coefficients within which the current optimal solution remains unchanged (3)

ranked position weight technique   a method of assigning tasks to work situations by ranking the jobs in descending order based on the sum of the job time and the time for all jobs for which that job is a predecessor (12)

reduced cost   the amount the profit coefficient of a variable will have to increase before the variable can be positive in the optimal solution (3)

redundant constraint   a constraint that can be eliminated from a linear programming model without affecting the feasible region (3)

relaxed problem   a linear model that ignores integer constraints (5)

reorder point   the inventory level at which an order is placed (10)

resource leveling   a method of controlling daily resource requirements and smoothing out their use over the course of a project (7)

resource scheduling   the process of assigning limited resources to minimize the total time to complete a project (7)

R_m control chart   a planning control chart that plots a moving range to estimate the common cause or uncontrollable variation in the production process (14)

S

safety stock   inventory that acts as a buffer to handle a firm's higher-than-average lead time demand or longer-than-expected lead time; also called *buffer stock* (10)

scenario writing   a decision-making technique that begins with a well-defined set of assumptions and builds several scenarios of the future based on these assumptions; the decision maker selects the scenario that corresponds to the set of assumptions believed most likely to occur (9)

sensitivity analysis   a quantitative analysis that provides information about the effects of changes to the solution of a problem as certain parameters change; also called *postoptimality analysis* (2,3)

set-up costs   the expense associated with beginning production of an item (10)

shadow price   the change to the optimal value of the objective function resulting from a one-unit increase in the right-hand side of a constraint; also expressed as a *dual price* (3)

shortest path problem   a network model used to find the path of minimum total distance that connects a starting point to a destination (6)

shrinkage   losses due to breakage of inventory and theft (10)

Silver-Meal heuristic   a procedure for determining a close-to-optimal inventory policy for situations in which orders are placed once per period and demand may vary greatly from period to period (11)

simplex   the figure created in n dimensions by an extreme point and the n other extreme points adjacent to it (3)

simplex algorithm (method)   the algebraic technique commonly used to solve linear programs which requires that all functional constraints be written as equalities so that elementary row operations can be performed without changing the set of feasible solutions to the problem (SCD3)

simplex tableau   a matrix used to keep track of the equations and other relevant information utilized in the simplex method (SCD3)

simulation   the development of a model to evaluate a system numerically over some time period of interest (13)

simulator   a computer program used to evaluate policy options in order to select the best action from a set of alternatives (13)

single-period inventory model   an inventory model that assumes that demand occurs according to a specified probability distribution and deals with a stock-keeping unit with a limited shelf life of one period; also called the *newsboy problem* (11)

slack   the amount of a resource that is left over when the value of the left-hand side of the constraint is subtracted from the constant on the right-hand side (3)

slack time   the amount of time an activity can be delayed from its earliest start time without delaying the project's estimated completion time (7)

smoothing constant   the weight given to the current period's actual value in the exponential smoothing method (9)

spanning tree   a tree that connects all the nodes in a network (6)

standard form   a linear program in which all the functional constraints are written as equations and all the variables are nonnegative (SCD3)

state of nature   a possible future event that may affect a decision (8)

state probability   the probability that a process is in state i at stage j (15)

state vector   the collection of state probabilities at a given stage (15)

stationary forecasting model   a time series forecasting model in which the mean value of the item being examined is assumed to be constant (9)

steady state   a condition in which the probabilities for the states of the process stabilize over time and assume their long-run values (12)

steady state probabilities   probabilities describing the long-run behavior of a Markov process (15)

stochastic model   a mathematical model in which one or more of the input parameters' values are determined by probability distributions; also called a *probabilistic model* (2)

stock-keeping units (SKU)   a collection of individual items in a firm's inventory (10)

sunk costs   the cost of the resources that is not included in the calculation of objective function coefficients of a mathematical programming model (3)

surplus   the amount by which some minimum restriction is exceeded at a given point when the constant on the right-hand side is subtracted from the value of the left-hand side (3)

T

tandem queuing system   a queuing model in which a customer must visit several different servers before service is completed (12)

time series   a past history of data values occurring at discrete time points used to prepare a forecast (9)

transient period   initial queuing system behavior not representative of long-run performance (12)

transition probability   the probability of the Markov process moving from state i at one stage to state j at the next stage (15)

transshipment problem   a network model in which goods may first be transported through one or more transshipment nodes before reaching their final destination (6)

transportation algorithm   a streamlined version of the simplex method used to find the minimum total shipping cost of a particular item from m sources, each with a different supply, to n destinations, each with a particular demand (SCD5)

transportation problem   a network model used to find the total minimum cost of shipping goods from supply points to destination points (6)

traveling salesman problem   a network model used to determine the minimum cost of visiting all nodes of a network and returning to a starting node without repeating any node (6)

tree   a series of connected arcs containing no cycles (6)

U

unbounded feasible region   a feasible region that extends "forever" in some particular direction (3)

unbounded solution   a condition in which feasible solutions exist for a linear program but there is no bound for the value of the objective function (3)

uncontrollable input   a factor over which the decision maker has no direct influence; also called a *parameter* (2)

undirected arc   a linkage that indicates that flow is not restricted to only one direction in a network model (6)

upper control limit (UCL)   the number on a control chart that equals the process mean plus three standard deviations

V

variable constraint   a constraint in a mathematical model that involves only one of the decision variables (2)

W

Wagner-Whitin algorithm   a dynamic programming technique to determine an optimal inventory policy, for situations in which orders are placed once per period and demand may vary greatly from period to period (11) weighted moving average technique a forecasting technique in which the sum of the weights used must equal one and the weights given to observation values are nonincreasing with their age (9)

work package   a set of related activities within a project that share common costs or are under the control of one contractor, department, or individual (7)

X

X control chart   a planning control chart that plots individual data values to determine if the production process is in control (14)

(X bar) chart   a planning control chart that records the mean value for each sample item in order to monitor the mean performance of the production process against a predetermined target value (14)

Chapter 2

2. A parameter is a quantity that cannot be controlled by the decision maker, whereas a decision variable is a controllable input whose values are determined by the decision maker.

5. In solving for the optimal policies at Ford, even small (a fraction of 1%) improvements can affect its bottom line by millions of dollars, which more than justifies the cost of the management science employees. At Villa Park Ford, such a percent savings probably would not justify the cost of a full-time management science employee.

8. a. $X1 + X2 = 1$

$X1 \geq 0$

$X1 \leq 1$

$X2 \geq 0$

$X2 \leq 1$

$X1, X2$ integers

b. MAX $-25000X1 + 35000X2$—Optimal: $X1 = 0, X2 = 1$, hold tournament indoors.

10. a. MAX $4X1 + 6X2 + 10X3$

b. $40X1 + 55X2 + 70X3 \leq 25000$

11. a. MAX $B - 30DX1 - 56EX2 - F$

s.t. $X1 \geq 2 + (T/1000)$

$X2 \geq N$

$X1, X2 \geq 0$ and integers

b. The negotiated price, B, and the fixed costs, F, are constants. Thus if we MIN $30DX1 + 56EX2$, this is equivalent to MAX $-30DX1 - 56EX2$.

c. MAX $10,000 - 450X1 - 672X2 - 1,000$

s.t. $X1 \geq 4$

$X2 \geq 2$

$X1, X2 \geq 0$ and integer

d. Change right side of first constraint to 4.4; 4.4 guards would make no sense, but if you *restricted the variables to be integers* this would be a correct formulation.

12. a. MAX $.1905X1 + .20X2 + .1719X3 + .05X4$

s.t. $X1 + X2 + X3 + X4 = 4000$

$X2 \geq 800$

$X4 \geq 1000$

$X1 \leq 2000$

$X3 \leq 2000$

All XJ's ≥ 0

b. MAX $8Y1 + 6Y2 + 11Y3 + .05X4$

s.t. $42Y1 + 30Y2 + 64Y3 + X4 = 4000$

$30Y2 \geq 800$

$X4 \geq 1000$

$42Y1 \leq 2000$

$64Y3 \leq 2000$

$Y1, Y2, Y3, X4 \geq 0$

c. Should get the same answer if shares were converted to dollars by $X1 = 42Y1, X2 = 30Y2$, and $X3 = 64Y3$ unless the shares (Y1, Y2, and Y3) are also restricted to be integers.

13. a. MAX $X1 + X2$

b. MAX $.02X1 + .01X2$

c. MAX $4X1 + 3X2$

15. a. $54X - 2X^2$

b. MAX $-2X^2 + 76X - 594$ s.t. $11 \leq X \leq 21$

c. Price = $19,000; # sold = 16; Monthly Profit = $128,000

Chapter 3

2. a. GE45 = 105, GE60 = 45

b. $8625

c. Yes both have 0 slack

3. a. $50–$150

b. $12.50/hr.

c. 150–450 hrs.

d. GE45 = 0, GE60 = 80; Profit = $24,000

e. −50; profit for GE45's would have to increase by $50 before they are profitable to produce

f. Yes

g. No

h. 100% rule is violated—optimal solution may change; optimal solution did not change; 100% rule only states the solution *may* change

4. a. Add constraint .5X1 + .75X2 ≤ 80; alternate optimal solutions exist giving a profit of $8000

b. GE45 = 130, GE60 = 20

c. GE45 = 80, GE60 = 53.33

d. GE45 = 106.67, GE60 = 35.56

e. (i) GE45 = 80, GE60 = 53.33, Profit = $7920; (ii) GE45 = 130, GE60 = 20, Profit = $8130

f. nonbinding (in fact, redundant)

5. a. $1.50/cow

b. Would cost $1.60/cow

c. Cow Chow = 50 oz./cow, Moo Town = 25 oz./cow

d. $25

10. a. MAX 30000X1 + 80000X2

    s.t.   X1   ≤   26

                        X2 ≤   5

         2000X1 + 8000X2 ≤ 40000

             X1   ≥   8

                        X2 ≥   2

b. Given the budget, there can only be a maximum of 20 daily or 5 Sunday ads.

c. Much of the same population is probably reading the daily and Sunday newspapers—may not truly get this increase in exposure on Sunday.

d. 12 daily ads, 2 Sunday ads, Exposure = 520,000

11. a. Daily 20,000 to ∞; Sunday −∞ to 120,000; within these ranges the solution found in problem 10 will still be optimal.

b. Shadow prices for Maximum daily ads, Maximum Sunday ads, and Minimum daily ads are 0 because they have slack; placing an extra Sunday ad will decrease exposure by 40,000, while extra advertising dollars will increase exposure by 15.

c. Place 20 daily ads only; −40,000

15. a. MIN 3000X1 + 1000X2

    s.t.   X2 ≤   5

        2000X1 + 800X2 ≥ 10000

           X1, X2 ≥ 0

b. Unbounded

c. Lease 3, Purchase 5, Monthly payments = $14,000

d. Solution is unbounded.

e. The number of machines leased or purchased must be integers.

16. 120 8-sq. ft. crates; 60 4-sq. ft. crates, Profit = $13,200; no slack on hours or space; 20 slack in the maximum number of 8-sq. ft. and 60 slack in the maximum number of 4-sq. ft. containers—these will not be shipped.

17. a. 8 sq. ft. $30 to $120; 4 sq. ft. $40 to $160

b. 720 to 1320; 36 to 60; 120 to ∞; 60 to ∞

c. Shadow price for extra sq. ft. $8.33; for loading time $66.67 per hour; for standard crates $0; for insulated crates $0; Square feet is an included cost—extra sq. ft. are worth $18.33, $8.33 above the current price of $10; loading time is a sunk cost and extra loading time hours are worth the shadow price of $66.67.

d. Crates must be integers, the optimal solution with one extra sq. ft. or hour of loading time may not be integer valued.

e. Sum of % change = 92% < 100%.

f. Reduces it to $6.33; extra hours are still worth $18.33.

19. MAX   .10X1 +   .12X2

s.t.   X1 +   X2 = 100,000

.000002X1 + .000004X2 ≥   .25

.000003X1 + .000008X2 ≤   .50

X1, X2 ≥ 0

Invest $60,000 in Tater, Inc. and $40,000 in Lakeside

20. a. MAX 15X1 + 25X2

s.t.   12X1 + 10X2 ≤ 150

50X1 + 40X2 ≤ 500

5X1 + 10X2 ≤ 90

15X2 ≤ 120

X1, X2 ≥ 0

b. 4 2/3 dz. (=56) custard, 6 2/3 dz. (=80) fruit

c. No; $30 is within its range of optimality

d. No

e. No change

f. Yes; $2.67 > $2.25

21. a. No

b. Yes

c. Marginal profit = −$1.50

d. $28.50

22. a. MIN 100X1 + 140X2

s.t.   20X1 + 40X2 ≥ 800

20X1 + 25X2 ≥ 600

20X1 + 10X2 ≥ 500

X1, X2 ≥ 0

Purchase 2000 lbs. of La Paz ore and 1000 lbs. of Sucre ore

b. La Paz $70 to $280; Sucre $50 to $200; within these limits the optimal solution remains unchanged.

c. Outside the range of optimality; reduced cost = $50

d. $3 for copper in the range 700 to 2000; $0 for zinc in the range −∞ to 650; $2 for iron in the range from 400 to 800; within these ranges the cost per extra lbs. of requirements will remain unchanged.

e. Infeasible

Chapter 4

1. 22.9358 standard Z345's, 22.9358 standard W250's, 45.8716 deluxe W250's; work in progress from one week to the next

2. a. 75%; if upper limit is increased from 75% profit would increase, if upper limit is decreased from 75% profit would decrease.

b. (i) Yes (ii) No (iii) Yes (iv) Yes (v) No

c. No, profit coefficient is very near one of the limits of its range of optimality, thus for small changes the coefficient would still be in its range of optimality and the solution would not change.

3. a. EAL = $7500, TAT = $2500, Long Bonds = $30,000, Tax-deferred annuity = $10,000; return = $5250

b. 10.5%; 11%; range of feasibility extends to $+\infty$

c. EAL, BRU, Long Bonds

d. $0.11 increase for each extra dollar invested, $0.15 decrease per dollar required in tax deferred annuities, $0.16 decrease for every extra dollar invested in TAT above 25%, $0.10 increase for each extra allowed to be invested in low-yield funds.

6. a. Multigrain Cheerios = .2 oz., Grape Nuts = 1.2245 oz., Product 19 = .3755 oz., Frosted Bran = .20 oz. OR Multigrain Cheerios = .2 oz., Grape Nuts = .8 oz., Product 19 = .8 oz., Frosted Bran = .2 oz. OR any weighted average of these two solutions; 19.8 grams of sugar.

b. 2 oz. of cereal, 1 cup of milk

c. Every extra percent (above 50) for vitamin D adds .39 grams; extra ounces of Multigrain Cheerios add 3 grams, and of Frosted Bran adds 6 grams.

d. Product 19 uses less sugar and gives percentages that are at least as good as those of Frosted Bran; Grape Nuts = 1.53 oz., Frosted Bran = .47 oz.

9. Turkey = 52, Beef = 100, Ham = 76, Club = 40, All Meat = 32; $67,200

10. Turkey $1.25 to $4.37, Beef $2.00 to $4.60, Ham $1.75 to $4.35, Club $3.60 to $4.75, All Meat $2.63 to $5.25

b. Each extra ounce of the following ingredients will increase daily profits by: Turkey $0.2292, Beef $0.4167, Ham $0.2708, Cheese $0.3333, Rolls (Space on Truck) $1.50

c. No

d. It may change

3. Roast beef

15. a. Alternate optimal solutions *in gallons*: (i) Pacific-Regular = 126,000, Gulf-Regular = 42,500, Middle East-Regular = 31,500, Gulf-Premium = 41,500, Middle East-Premium = 158,500 OR (ii) Pacific-Regular = 96,000, Middle East-Regular = 104,500, Pacific-Premium = 30,000, Gulf-Premium = 84,000, Middle East-Premium = 86,000 OR (iii) Pacific-Regular = 126,000, Middle East-Regular = 74,000, Gulf-Premium = 84,000, Middle East-Premium = 116,000 OR any weighted average of (i), (ii) and (iii); Profit = $61,620

b. Yes

c. $89,300; yes; no Gulf oil and very little Pacific purchased; domestic producers should decrease their price to be competitive

16. Wheat = 142.8571 ac., Corn = 142.8571 ac., Soybeans = 14.2857 ac., Profit = $197,200

17. a. $486.21; $3.92

b. Yes; $4400

c. Yes; $22,698.20 in net additional profit

21. Ketchup only = $550,000, Spaghetti sauce only = $450,000, Taco sauce only = $750,000, Joint = $250,000; $2,251,500; 12.575% return

22. a. $1.20

b. Taco sauce: $-\infty$ to $1.13; joint $1.02 to $1.12; since current estimates are close, these should be checked for accuracy.

c. None; none

d. $1500

23. Go = 7550, Power = 2500, Energy (2 oz.) = 5050, Energy (8 oz.) = 437.5, Profit = $7273.375

Chapter 5

1. a. Max $24000X1 + 30000X2$

$$
\begin{aligned}
\text{s.t.} \quad X1 \quad &\leq \quad 3 \\
X2 &\leq \quad 2 \\
50X1 + 60X2 &\leq 160 \\
X1, X2 \geq 0 \text{ and integer} &
\end{aligned}
$$

  b. (0, 0): $0, (1, 0): $24,000, (2, 0): $48,000, (3, 0): $72,000, (0, 1): $30,000, (1, 1): $54,000, (2, 1): $78,000, (0, 2): $60,000; 2 compactors, 1 drill press

  c. Rounding gives either (0, 2), which is not optimal, or (1, 2), which is not feasible.

  d. Fractional values would be work in progress.

2. a. MIN 3500X1 + 800X2

  s.t. 150X1 + 35X2 ≥ 750

  X1   ≥   1

  X2 ≤ 20

  X1, X2 ≥ 0 and integer

  b. 60-inch = 1, 27-inch = 18, cost = $17,900; 60-inch = 2, 27-inch = 13; no; $17,400

4. a. KCU = 900, KCP = 1000, Profit = $172,500; it is already an integer solution.

  b. $168.75 up to 1040 hours

  c. $1687.50; KCU = 887.5, KCP = 1025

  d. KCU = 888, KCP = 1025 is infeasible; KCU = 887, KCP = 1025 is feasible − profit = $174,150

  e. KCU = 886, KCP = 1026; no; no

  f. $30

6. Use 6 Nautilus machines and spend 21 minutes on treadmill; 81 points

10. Make 60,000 Jeeptrykes only—$160,000

11. Make 60,000 Herotrykes only—$117,500

13. b. Develop applications 1, 2, 3, 4—$12.6 million

14. b. Develop applications 1, 2, 6—$11.8 million

15. b. Part-time: 7AM–11AM = 7, 11AM–3PM = 13, 3PM–7PM = 12, 7PM–11PM = 14; Full-time: 7AM–3PM = 3, 11AM–7PM = 6, 3PM–11PM = 2; Total Cost = $1661

16. 3 patrols only—two possible solutions are: sectors 3, 7, 11 of 1, 4, 14

19. b. Springfield = 65,000, Westchester = 35,000, Total Cost = $25,335

22. Green - Baseball Stadium, Kalib - Street Lighting, SSS - High School Air conditioners, Burke - Courthouse Electrical Systems; Total Cost = $126,000

25. a. Project 2 - 95

  b. (i) Project 1 - 100; (ii) Projects 3 and 5 - 120; (iii) Projects 3 and 4 - 135

Chapter 6

1.

	Eureka	Cres. City	Coos Bay
Garberville	1600		
Grant's Pass	200	1400	
Willard	100		1500

Total Cost = $180,000

3. a. (In truckloads)

	I1	I2	I3		P1	P2	P3	P4
Cal	8	1		I1	3	5		
Mex		3	5	I2			4	
				I3				5

Total Cost $24,200

  b. (In truckloads)

	I1	I2	I3		P1	P2	P3	P4
Cal	3	3	3	I1	3	2		
Mex	2	3	3	I2		3	1	2
				I3			3	3

Total Cost = $28,900

  c. Inspection will eliminate some bad tomatoes.

5. Kansas City - St. Louis - Davenport - Wichita - Lincoln - Tulsa - Kansas City (or the other way around); Total Cost = $855

7. 14 North - Lakeview = 400, 14 North - Casual = 500, Lakeview - Lakeside = 100, Lakeview - Golf = 300, Golf - Lakeside = 200, Golf - Town Center = 100, Casual - Ocean Breeze = 300, Town Center - Ocean Breeze = 300, Lakeview - 14 South = 300, Ocean Breeze - 14 South = 600; Total Capacity = 900

9. a. Tony - News, Jim - Sports, Connie - Development, Linda - Features, Ann - Marketing; Total Years = 47

    b. Jim - Sports, Connie - Features/Development, Linda - News, Ann - Marketing; Total years = 46

11. a. Attach 3 to 2, 2 to 1, 1 to 5, 5 to 4, and 4 to 6; Total distance = 39 millimeters

    b. Same solution

12. a. Ann - Phoenix, Bill - Fresno, Ko - Austin, Dave - Miami; total cost = $10,350

    b. Ann's - Pheonix = 20, Ann's - Austin = 5, Bill's - Fresno = 7, Bill's - Miami = 11, Ko's - Fresno = 8, Ko's - Austin = 17, Dave's - Miami = 25; total cost = $250,110

15. a. Amy - Information Systems, Bob - Personal Tax, Sue - Financial Analysis, Maya - Corporate Tax, Koo - Auditing, Lyn - General Accounting; Total Test Score = 543

    b. Amy - Financial Analysis, Bob - General Accounting, Sue - Information Systems, Maya - Auditing, Koo - Corporate Tax, Lyn - Personal Tax; Total Test Score = 523

18. Budapest - Cieszyn - Lodz - Torun - Gdansk; 980 kilometers

22. To: Bradford   28   Route 1 - Main St.
        Northside   25   Route 1 - Route 3
        Barkley   47   Route 1 - Route 3 - Earl Road
        Downtown   8   Route 1
        Lincoln   40   Prince Street
        Valley   77   Prince Street - Kings Road - Route 7
        Riverbank   50   Prince Street - Kings Road

23. a. Home - Downtown - Northside - Barkley - Lincoln - Riverbank - Valley - Bradford - Home (or vice versa)

    b. 202 minutes

    c. 31.14 minutes

25. Produce 1250 in quarter 1 (regular time) for quarter 1; Produce 1875 in quarter 2 (1500 regular time, 375 overtime)—625 for quarter 2 and 1250 for quarter 3; produce 2500 in quarter 3 (1500 in regular time, 1000 in overtime) all for quarter 3, and 2500 in quarter 4 (1500 in regular time, 1000 in overtime) all for quarter 4; total cost = $520,500.

Chapter 7

2. 12 weeks; B-C-E-F; a delay in any of these activities will delay the expected project time beyond 12 weeks.

4. c. 8 weeks

6. b. One worker works only jobs on critical path at their earliest times; the other can work B (10:00–11:00), E (11:20–12:20), D (12:20–2:00), G (2:00–2:20), H (2:20–3:00), I (3:00–4:00), K (4:00–4:20).

7. a. 104 months

    b. (i) 5 months; (ii) 3 months

    c. (i) .000175; (ii) .012685; (iii) .185544; (iv) .622629

8. a. A-C-E-G; $\mu = 30$, $\sigma = 4.333$

    b. Delay of (i) 5 days; (ii) 0 days; (iii) 4 days; (iv) 4 days; (v) 4 days; (vi) 9 days

    c. 41 days = July 6

10. Yes; Expected cost if the $3000 is spent = $9612.70; Expected cost if the $3000 is not spent = $12,427.20.

11. b. Crash A by .5 weeks, B by .5 weeks, D by .5 weeks, E by 3 weeks, G by 3 weeks; total cost = $10,000,000

12. b. Crash E by 2 weeks; total time 21 weeks

15. b. B-I; 36 weeks

    c. Hire Colonial Landscaping; total cost = $14,000

20. a. 89 days; C-D-F-G-I-K

 b. .924143

 c. Yes

21. a. 117 days; A-B-C-D-E-J-L-N-R

 b. .295682

 c. Yes

 d. $1327.88

22. Under budget and ahead of schedule

Chapter 8

1. a. 400, b. 320, c. 360, d. 360

4. a. 2 commercials

 b. $130,000

6. a.

		Demand		
		10,000	50,000	100,000
	Do Nothing	0	0	0
Order	40,000	−130,000	130,000	80,000
Quantity	80,000	−250,000	110,000	360,000
	120,000	−370,000	−10,000	440,000

 b. Order 80,000

 c. Order 80,000

 d. $58,889

8. a. (i) custom, (ii) unfurnished, (iii) unfurnished

 b. $937.50 per lot, c. 57.69%, d. GNP is not a good indicator, other indicators that would specifically focus on the Atlanta housing market or economy (such as average per capita income) would be better.

11. a. If survey shows at least one customer likely to buy—order 2, otherwise order 1, b. $82.50, c. 14.04%, d. record number of survey customers who are likely to purchase.

13. a. $580

 b. .9952

 c. Approximately $1000

15. a. Payoff table in $1000's

		Demand				
		0	1	2	3	4
	1	−300	−75	−105	−135	−165
Number	2	−400	−175	50	20	10
Built	3	−300	−75	130	375	345
	4	−400	−175	5	275	500

 b. Build 3 computers and build 4 computers are undominated strategies.

 c. P(0) = .2401, P(1) = .4116, P(2) = .2646, P(3) = .0756, P(4) = .0081—build 3 computers.

17. Import scooters and advertise only if tariff is not imposed.

19. a.

		Number of Adoptions						
		0	1	2	3	4	5	6
	1	2000	2000	2000	2000	2000	2000	2000
Plan	2	1000	1300	1600	1900	2200	2500	2800
	3	0	700	1400	2100	2800	3500	4200

    b. Plan 2

    c. Plan 1

20. Midge should wait two months before buying her ticket.

24. a. Concave utility function—risk averse

    b. Buy land

Chapter 9

1. a. Yes

    b. $t = -.412$, $p = .689$

    c. January—19, for upcoming year—228

    d. 20.4

    e. 4 month moving average

3. b. $t = 37.1238$, $p = 0$

    c. 25 — 660, 26 — 671, 27 — 681, 28 — 692, 29 — 702, 30 — 712, 31 — 722, 32 — 732, 33 — 742, 34 — 753, 35 — 763, 36 — 773

5. Week 5: Su 318.89, M 371.72, Tu 353.72, W 397.54, Th 404.22, F 362.08, Sa 366.49; Week 6: Su 326.62, M 380.70, Tu 362.24, W 407.08, Th 413.89, F 370.71, Sa 375.20

7. 370,807 bottles of shampoo

9. b. No, $t = -.428$, $p = .674$

    c. $143.8*5 = 719$

    d. $147.2*5 = 736$

11. Year 6—134,189, year 7—139,288, year 8—144,387

13. Year 5: fall—850, spring—784, summer—193

15. b. Since $t = 1.916$ and $p = .071$, a stationary model is appropriate.

    c. $\$.45585*140,000 = \$63,819$

    d. Yes, futures are worthwhile.

17. a. 8.12

    b. −2.58, The model may be inappropriate since 2030 if too far into the future from the last observed time period. If the model is deemed appropriate, Kerf will have to do something different in the future if it wishes to remain solvent.

20. Jan 1569, Feb 1571, Mar 1574, Apr 1576, May 1578, Jun 1581, Jul 1583, Aug 1586, Sep 1588, Oct 1591, Nov 1593, Dec 1595

22. a. 16,509

    b. 16,515

    c. $\alpha = .10$, MSE = 964,750, $\alpha = .20$, MSE = 1,034,893

    d. $\alpha = .10$

    e. $\alpha = .10$

    f. $\alpha = .10$

24. b. Yes, $t = .402$, $p = .698$

    c. 4.9%

    d. $\alpha = .27$

Chapter 10

1. a. 894

    b. 50

    c. 128

    d. 2189.37

    e. $1617.58, assume demand occurs at a constant rate and will continue on at this rate forever.

4. a. 2400

    b. $1.26

6. 135

8. a. 400

b. 63

c. 117 days

d. 21,143.69, demand occurs at a constant rate and will continue on at this rate forever; safety stock was ordered at the discount price and the only cost associated with the safety stock is the holding cost.

10. a. 485,917

b. $38.895.54

c. 68.3 hours

d. 8.43

e. 532,295

12. a. 1000

b. 77

c. 100 days

d. $1,521,808.03

e. $506,160.77

14. a. 632

b. 62

16. Produce 1019 pounds of french roast, 501 pounds of amaretto cream.

18. a. 111

b. 39

c. 1.48

d. .4%

e. $304,937.15

20. a. $Q^* = 46$, R = 2, Profit = $22,332.16

b. $Q^* = 46$, R = 17, Profit = $22,484.20

c. Yes, allowing for backorders increases profit by approximately $150 per year.

22. a. $Q^* = 37,427.92$

b. $1,703,980.96

24. Recommend Machine I, annual profit is $160,750 versus $142,923 for Machine II.

Chapter 11

2. a. 1817 (note goodwill cost is −$40)

b. Profit = $96,361.03

c. Assume company pays royalty on plates produced even if they are destroyed.

5. a. 283

b. Initially order to satisfy demand for first five periods, then order in period 6 to satisfy demand for next two periods, and then order in period 8 to satisfy demand for periods 8 through 10—cost = $5560.

c. Initially order to satisfy demand for first five periods, then order in period 6 to satisfy demand for next two periods, then order in period 8 to satisfy demand for next two periods, and then order in period 10 to satisfy demand for that period—cost = $6460.

7. a. Order 640 in period 1, 540 in period 5, 260 in period 8—cost = $942.50

b. $155, $Q^* = 480$ and total cost = $1097.50.

8. Faucet Sets: order 800 in week 9, Drain Sets: order 500 in week 6, Levers: order 0, Stoppers: order 100 in week 3, Faucets: order 1100 in week 7, Handles: order 1000 in week 1, Valves: order 600 in week 4, Stems: order 0, Housings: order 300 in week 2, Trim: order 0, Spigots: order 200 in week 2.

10.

FAUCETS	LEAD TIME I WEEK	TIME PERIODS							
LOT SIZE Silver-Mail	SAFETY STOCK 200	11	12	13	14	15	16	17	18
GROSS REQUIREMENTS			800	600	400	200	600	400	500
SCHEDULED RECEIPTS									
BALANCE AVAILABLE		200	1400	800	400	200	1100	700	200
NET REQUIREMENTS			800				600		
PLANNED ORDER RECEIPTS			2000				1500		
PLANNED ORDER RELEASES		2000				1500			

13. 9591, assumes Clothesline will only get one order during the season.

15. a. Dressers: order 2200 on day 35, Shells: order 2150 on day 30, Frames: order 2050 on day 20, Gliders: order 15,600 on day 15, Drawers: order 8800 on day 25, Fronts: order 8600 on day 20, Faces: order 8000 on day 15, Handles: order 0, Bottoms: order 8000 on day 15, Slides: order 13,600 on day 15, Backs: order 5800 on day 20

b. 25 days

17.

FRONTS	LEAD TIME I WEEK	TIME PERIODS							
LOT SIZE 10000	SAFETY STOCK 100	3	4	5	6	7	8	9	10
GROSS REQUIREMENTS			7500	0	14500	0	0	13500	10000
SCHEDULED RECEIPTS									
BALANCE AVAILABLE	2500		5000	5000	500	500	500	7000	7000
NET REQUIREMENTS			5100		9600			13100	3100
PLANNED ORDER RECEIPTS			10000		10000			20000	10000
PLANNED ORDER RELEASES		10000		10000			20000	10000	

20. Order 4 mowers (note goodwill cost is −$170).

21. a. $Q^* = 13$, cost = $443

b. Period 1: order 17, period 3: order 74, cost = $332

c. Period 1: order 33, period 4: order 38, period 7: order 20, cost = $290.

23. Blenders: order 900 in week 9, Bases: order 700 in week 7, Housings: order 600 in week 3, Motors: order 400 in week 4, Containers: order 200 in week 8, do not order any other components.

25. $Q^* = 40$

Chapter 12

1. a. .224

b. .85

c. .49

d. 4.5 minutes

e. .49

f. 1.5

g. 60%

3. a. (i) 29.11, (ii) .15, (iii) 40%

   b. Yes, average customer service time is less and the store saves the space of the additional checkstand.

5. a. W = 6 minutes

   b. L = 3 in each line for a total of 9

   c. Existing system will cost $36 per hour, proposed system will cost $35.29 per hour—yes they should switch, proposed single line system is cheaper.

7. a. Front .528 minutes, rear .816 minutes

   b. Front 1.008, rear 3.651

   c. .06

   d. .99

   e. Front, average checkout time is less.

10. .375 minutes

12. a. .455819*.9712 = .4427

    b. .52

    c. 2.14 minutes

    d. .12

13. (i) Station 1 — Jobs B, A, G, C, D, I, E: time = 235 sec.
    Station 2 — Jobs H, F, J, K, L, M, N, P: time = 235 sec.
    Station 3 — Jobs R, O, S, Q, T, U: time = 190 sec.
    (ii) Station 1 — Jobs B, A, G, C, D: time = 175 sec.
    Station 2 — Jobs I, E, H, F, J, K: time = 155 sec.
    Station 3 — Jobs L, M, N, P, R: time = 175 sec.
    Station 4 — Jobs O, S, Q, T, U: time = 155 sec.

15. a. .1045

    b. 1.14 minues

    c. .456

    d. Service time is probably not truly a memorylessness process.

18. a. 6.25 minutes

    b. 2.92

20. 6.28 minutes

22. a. 99.7%

    b. 4.5

    c. 11.05 days

24. a. With 4 instructors profit/hr. = $10.77, daily profit = $107.70

    b. With 5 instructors profit/hr. = $8.46, hence it is not worthwhile to hire 5th instructor.

Chapter 13

Note: The answers in this chapter correspond to the approach illustrated in the Instructor's Solution Manual. Your answers may differ due to a different probability ordering or random number selection.

1. b. .0025, price in 30 days would be 32.075

   c. 31.125

   d. We would expect the simulation to be close to the expected value but not necessarily equal to the expected value.

3. a. (.6075, .7139)

   b. .6667 minutes

5. a. D-E, 15 weeks

   b. P(A) = .2, P(B) = .2, P(C) = .2, P(D) = .6, P(E) = .6, P(F) = .2, P(G) = .2

   c. (16.244, 19.756)

7. No, t = −1.797, p = .1059
9. Yes, F = 32.98, p = $5.65*10^{-8}$
11. It will take 8 days, there will be 4 backorders of ChannelMaster systems and 2 lost sales.
14. We cannot claim that there is a difference in mean weekly profit between the two policies, t = .7809.
16. W_q from simulation is .994 minutes, W_q from steady state is 2.4 minutes, one reason for the difference is the start up bias of the simulation.
20. L_q = .35
22. The average waiting time appears to be much greater for full serve than for self serve (15.4 minutes versus 3.7 minutes).
24. c. Based on the two simulations, Family should take the supplier's offer; total cost under stimulation for current policy is $401.33, for the supplier's offer the total cost is $155.
25. b. $5859.60

INDEX

Boldface page numbers indicate where term is defined.

PHOTO CREDITS